THE RELIGION AND PHILOSOPHY OF THE VEDA AND UPANISHADS

BY

ARTHUR BERRIEDALE KEITH

D.C.L., D.Litt.

Of the Inner Temple, Barrister-at-Law, and of the Scottish Bar; Regius Professor of Sanskrit and Comparative Philology at the University of Edinburgh; formerly of the Colonial Office

IN TWO VOLUMES
VOL. I

The first half, Chapters 1–19
Page 1 to page 312

GREENWOOD PRESS, PUBLISHERS
WESTPORT, CONNECTICUT

Keith, Arthur Berriedale, 1879–1944.
The religion and philosophy of the Veda and Upanishads. Westport, Conn., Greenwood Press [1971]

2 v. (xviii, 683 p.) 27 cm.

Reprint of the 1925 ed.
Includes bibliographical references.

1. Vedas. 2. Upanishads. 3. Philosophy, Hindu. 4. India—Religion. I. Title.

BL1150.K43 1971 294'.1 71-109969
ISBN 0-8371-4475-2 MARC

Library of Congress 71 [4]

Originally published in 1925 by Harvard University Press, Cambridge

Reprinted by Greenwood Press, Inc.

First Greenwood reprinting 1971
Second Greenwood reprinting 1977

Library of Congress catalog card number 71-109969

ISBN 0-8371-4475-2 (set)
ISBN 0-8371-4476-0 (Vol. I)

Printed in the United States of America

TO

MARY HINCKLEY LANMAN

WIFE AND HELPMATE

OF

CHARLES ROCKWELL LANMAN

PROFESSOR AT HARVARD UNIVERSITY

PREFACE

It is the object of this work to present to the student of religion, in objective form and with constant reference to the original sources and to modern discussions, a comprehensive but concise account of the whole of the religion and philosophy of the Vedic period in India. The difficulty of the task lies not merely in the abundance of the original sources, which I have had occasion to study in detail in making my translations of the Taittirīya Saṁhitā and the Brāhmaṇas and the Āraṇyakas of the Rigveda, but also in the extreme divergence of view among modern interpreters of Vedic literature. Doubtless it is owing to this cause that the extraordinary value of Vedic religion to the student of religious belief has been so completely overlooked by Sir James Frazer and Professor S. Reinach in their theories of religion, and that it has been so gravely misinterpreted by Professor Sir William Ridgeway in his essays on the origin of the drama. The account of Vedic religion given in this work will, I trust, do something to restore to that religion its just place in the study of theology.

The writer of such a work must at every turn derive much from his predecessors. An effort has been made to assign to their authors the most important of the theories mentioned, but I desire to acknowledge a more general obligation to certain scholars. In the treatment of the mythology I am deeply indebted to Professor A. A. Macdonell's *Vedic Mythology*, which is not merely an invaluable and exhaustive storehouse of facts, but is distinguished by unfailing sureness and clearness of judgement, and I have derived much help from Bergaigne's *Religion Védique*, Hillebrandt's *Vedische Mythologie*, and Oldenberg's *Religion des Veda*, though I have been unable to follow these authors in the more imaginative of their theories. For the ritual I owe many facts to Hillebrandt, Schwab, Caland, Henry, Weber, and last, but certainly not least, to my predecessor, Professor J. Eggeling. In its explanation I find myself often in agreement with Oldenberg, the brilliance and charm of whose work in this sphere can hardly be overestimated. I have made free use of the light cast on ritual by other religions, and I am conscious of having derived great profit from the works of Dr. L. R. Farnell;

but neither the totemism of Durkheim or S. Reinach nor the vegetation-spirits of Mannhardt and Sir J. Frazer have helped me in my study of the Veda. For the philosophy of the Brāhmaṇas and the Upaniṣads, Lévi, Oltramare, and Deussen have been of the greatest assistance through the completeness of the collections of material which they have made, and the fact that I have found it necessary to refuse to accept Deussen's main theories must not be taken to indicate any lack of appreciation of the great merits of his work. Nor should I conclude without an expression of indebtedness to Roth, Max Müller, Whitney, Hopkins, Bloomfield, and to the untiring labours and accomplished scholarship of Professor Charles R. Lanman, who has added to the many obligations which I owe to him by permitting these volumes to appear in the Harvard Oriental Series, that *monumentum aere perennius* of his unselfish devotion to the study of the life and literature of India.

A. BERRIEDALE KEITH.

EDINBURGH UNIVERSITY,
June 1, 1916.

Nonumque prematur in annum. When the Preface to this work was written neither author nor editor imagined that war conditions would compel obedience to the Horatian maxim in so literal a fashion. In revising the work for press I have taken note, so far as was compatible with the necessity of avoiding the expansion of the work beyond due bounds, of those contributions to our knowledge made since 1916, which appeared to me of most value in respect either of the results attained or of the methods adopted. Recent work on the origin of religion I have not discussed, as I have found nothing in it to throw light on Vedic beliefs, and a criticism on general grounds would involve transgression of the limits of these volumes.

I trust that nothing of first-class importance in the literature has escaped my attention ; if it has, some share of the blame must fall on the deplorably inadequate provision made for Sanskrit research in this University, as the result in part of public indifference, in part of the many insistent demands on strictly limited academic resources. It is deeply to be regretted that British opinion should be so heedless of the duty of contributing to the investigation of the ancient civilization of a land whence Britain has derived so much of her power and wealth. But a sense of this inexcusable neglect only increases my sincere gratitude to the founder and the editor of the Harvard Oriental Series, whose enlightened and impartial generosity alone have rendered possible the publication of my studies on the religion and philosophy of the Veda.

The delay in publication causes me one serious regret, that this work cannot now evoke the criticism of Hermann Oldenberg, that admirable scholar, to whose writings on Vedic religion and philosophy I desire once more—*inane munus*—to express my deep obligation.

To my wife I owe sincere thanks for much help and criticism. Mr. Frederick Hall and his staff have, as always, spared no trouble in the production and printing of the volumes, and I desire to express my high appreciation of their efforts.

THE UNIVERSITY OF EDINBURGH,
June 1, 1924.

CONTENTS

The twenty-nine chapters of this work are numbered, for practical convenience, in one single arithmetical sequence. But they are grouped in five main divisions, or PARTS, as follows:

CONTENTS OF PART I.—THE SOURCES

CONTENTS OF PART II.—THE GODS AND DEMONS OF THE VEDA

CONTENTS OF PART III.—VEDIC RITUAL

At this point occurs the break between Chapters 1–19 and Chapters 20–29
The latter group is bound up as volume 32

CONTENTS OF PART IV.—THE SPIRITS OF THE DEAD

CONTENTS OF PART V.—THE PHILOSOPHY OF THE VEDA

APPENDIX

TRANSLITERATION

The system of transliteration adopted by W. D. Whitney in his *Sanskrit Grammar* and C. R. Lanman in his *Sanskrit Reader* has been followed. For purposes of pronunciation the vowels may be treated as in Italian, but *a* is analogous to the sound in English 'but'. The consonants may be pronounced as in English, the diacritical marks being ignored, except in the following cases: *c* is similar to *ch* in church: *ç* and *ṣ* are approximately *sh* in shun: *s* is always surd as in sun: *ṁ* or *ṅ* is a nasalization of the preceding vowel: the aspirates like *th* are pronounced approximately like *th* in pothook. The letter *ṛ* may be taken as nearly *ri*. Similarly *ḷ* is *li* or *lri*.

The complete alphabet is as follows: vowels: a ā i ī u ū ṛ ṝ ḷ e ai o au;

gutturals:	k	kh	g	gh	ṅ;	palatals:	c	ch	j	jh	ñ;
domals:	ṭ	ṭh	ḍ	ḍh	ṇ;	dentals:	t	th	d	dh	n;
labials:	p	ph	b	bh	m;	semivowels:	y r l v;	further:	ṅ ṁ ḥ.		

ABBREVIATIONS

AA.	Aitareya Āraṇyaka.	Kauṣ.	Kauṣītaki Upaniṣad.
AB.	Aitareya Brāhmaṇa.	Kena.	Kena Upaniṣad (=JUB. 4. 18-21).
AGS.	Āçvalāyana Gṛhya Sūtra.	KhGS.	Khādira Gṛhya Sūtra.
AÇS.	Āçvalāyana Çrauta Sūtra.	LÇS.	Lāṭyāyana Çrauta Sūtra.
AU.	Aitareya Upaniṣad (=AA. 2. 4–6).	MB.	Mantra Brāhmaṇa.
AV.	Atharvaveda.	MGS.	Mānava Gṛhya Sūtra.
AV. Par.	Atharvaveda Pariçiṣṭa.	MP.	Mantrapāṭha.
ApDS.	Āpastamba Dharma Sūtra.	MÇS.	Mānava Çrauta Sūtra.
ApGS.	Āpastamba Gṛhya Sūtra.	MS.	Maitrāyaṇī Saṁhitā.
ApÇS.	Āpastamba Çrauta Sūtra.	Mahānār.	Mahānārāyaṇa Upaniṣad.
BAU.	Bṛhadāraṇyaka Upaniṣad.	Maitr.	Maitrāyaṇīya Upaniṣad.
BDS.	Baudhāyana Dharma Sūtra.	Muṇḍ.	Muṇḍaka Upaniṣad.
BGS.	Baudhāyana Gṛhya Sūtra.	Nir.	Nirukta.
BÇS.	Baudhāyana Çrauta Sūtra.	PB.	Pañcaviṅça Brāhmaṇa.
BhGS.	Bhāradvāja Gṛhya Sūtra.	PGS.	Pāraskara Gṛhya Sūtra.
CU.	Chāndogya Upaniṣad.	PU.	Praçna Upaniṣad.
GB.	Gopatha Brāhmaṇa.	RV.	Rigveda.
GDS.	Gautama Dharma Sūtra.	ÇA.	Çāṅkhāyana Āraṇyaka.
GGS.	Gobhila Gṛhya Sūtra.	ÇB.	Çatapatha Brāhmaṇa.
HGS.	Hiraṇyakeçi Gṛhya Sūtra.	ÇGS.	Çāṅkhāyana Gṛhya Sūtra.
HÇS.	Hiraṇyakeçi Çrauta Sūtra.	ÇÇS.	Çāṅkhāyana Çrauta Sūtra.
Īçā.	Īçā Upaniṣad (=VS. xl).	ÇU.	Çvetāçvatara Upaniṣad.
JB.	Jaiminīya Brāhmaṇa.	SVB.	Sāmavidhāna Brāhmaṇa.
JGS.	Jaiminīya Gṛhya Sūtra.	TA.	Taittirīya Āraṇyaka.
JUB.	Jaiminīya Upaniṣad Brāhmaṇa.	TB.	Taittirīya Brāhmaṇa.
KB.	Kauṣītaki Brāhmaṇa.	TS.	Taittirīya Saṁhitā.
KÇS.	Kātyāyana Çrauta Sūtra.	TU.	Taittirīya Upaniṣad.
KS.	Kāṭhaka Saṁhitā.	VS.	Vājasaneyi Saṁhitā.
KU.	Kaṭha Upaniṣad.	Vait.	Vaitāna Sūtra.
Kauç.	Kauçika Sūtra.	VārGS.	Vārāha Gṛhya Sūtra.

7

PART I. THE SOURCES

CHAPTER 1

THE RIGVEDA AND THE ARYANS

THE oldest and most important of the sources for Indian religion is the collection of 1,028 hymns known as the Rigveda Saṁhitā, which has been handed down to us in the Çākala recension. Preserved in its early stages by oral tradition and long regarded as too sacred to be reduced to writing, the text affords abundant internal proof of the general accuracy with which it was preserved. Moreover, an invaluable form of control exists in the texts of the other Vedas, the Yajurveda in its different recensions, the Sāmaveda, and the Atharvaveda, all of which contain much of the matter of the Rigveda. The older view, that in these texts might be found traces of earlier forms of the verses of the Rigveda, has not borne close examination and comparison in detail:[1] with a very few possible exceptions the variations which are found in these texts from the Rigveda can be unhesitatingly classed as products either of an inferior tradition on the one hand or of deliberate alteration on the other. Similarly the efforts which have been made by Hillebrandt[2] to prove that, in a stage earlier than that recorded, the Rigveda was a definitely practical collection of hymns, arranged according to their connexion with the sacrificial ritual, must be pronounced to have failed.[3] Whereas all the other Saṁhitās, except the Atharvaveda, which occupies a peculiar position, are definitely in their non-Brāhmaṇa portions manuals of the chants and formulae used by the priests in the ritual, the Rigveda is not a practical but a historical hand-book. It must represent a collection of hymns made by unknown hands at a time when for some unrecorded reason it was felt desirable to preserve the religious poetry current among the Vedic tribes.

The collection must have been made from a considerable area of country, for it contains hymns emanating from very varied families. Tradition ascribes to books ii to vii as authors the seers Gautama, Viçvāmitra, Vāmadeva, Atri, Bharadvāja, and Vasiṣṭha, but this view cannot be taken quite literally: the hymns themselves reveal abundant evidence that, for the most part at least, they were not composed by these personages, but by men claiming to be of the families bearing their names, and the family character of the hymns in these books is in the main clear. With these six books must be

[1] Oldenberg, *Prolegomena*, pp. 289 ff.; cf. Bloomfield, *Rig-Veda Repetitions*, p. 406; Brune, *Zur Textkritik der dem Sāmaveda mit dem VIII Maṇḍala des Ṛgveda gemeinsamen Stellen* (1909).

[2] ZDMG. xl. 708; GGA. 1889, pp. 418 ff.

[3] Oldenberg, GGA. 1907, pp. 211 ff.; Keith, JRAS. 1908, pp. 224–9.

classed the groups of hymns ascribed to different families or authors in book i, 51–191, and this may have been the extent of the oldest collection made, though it is perhaps more likely that i. 51–191 were collected later than ii–vii. The earlier portion of book i and the whole of book viii are ascribed to seers of the Kaṇva family; it would appear that these two separate collections were at some time added, the one in front of, and the other after, the existing Saṁhitā, but which addition was first made there is no clear ground to show.[1] When the collection had reached the compass of seven or eight books, another, now the ninth, was created by extracting from the other books all the hymns addressed to Soma Pavamāna, that is the Soma as it was poured through the filter, which were then united into one group: for this change no reason is obvious.[2] This did not, however, end the history of the collection: at a time when the nine books had already taken form, a tenth was added, consisting on the whole of more recent hymns.[3] The late character of this book can be established by a number of proofs. Its extent, 191 hymns, has obviously been brought up to that of book i; the language shows development in different aspects: hiatus becomes rarer, old words like the particle *sīm* disappear, new words and forms are found, and the metre shows affinities with the metre of the later Saṁhitās. The same result is indicated by the new features in religion which appear: the Dawn, the most poetic of Indian goddesses, all but disappears, Varuṇa, most moral and spiritual of Vedic deities, loses in position, while Indra, the Indian god *par excellence*, and Agni, the priestly god of fire, retain all their importance. The more or less abstract conception of the All-gods increases in importance, and real abstract deities appear in Faith and Wrath. The growth of religious thought is also shown by the occurrence of philosophical and cosmogonic hymns, and in imitation of the hymns to the gods the wedding and funeral services are now provided with elaborate hymnologies in place of the more simple formulae which were doubtless earlier in use.[4] The book shows also the employment of hymns for spells and incantations, and here again we must doubtless see the application to the lower side of life of the instrument devised primarily to placate the high gods. The advance in religion is paralleled by the advance in society: in this book we for the first time meet the fully developed system of the four castes or classes, Brahman, warrior, clansman, and Çūdra.

It is naturally tempting to seek to carry the process of dissection further, and to discover the different ages of the several portions of the Rigveda.

[1] That viii had no claim to age was indicated by Hopkins, JAOS. xvii. 23 ff., and is confirmed by the evidence of repetitions, Bloomfield, *Rig-Veda Repetitions*, pp. 640 ff.

[2] ix is usually superior to viii (Bloomfield, p. 644). As new books were added, the Soma Pavamāna hymns were added to what is now ix. Its position as ix, however, suggests that i–viii already existed.

[3] Oldenberg, *Prolegomena*, pp. 263 ff.

[4] Contrast Bloomfield, *op. cit.*, pp. 21, 649, who holds that x. 14. 14 and 15. 14 are later than i. 15. 9; 108. 12, but neither case is convincing. The wedding hymn is clearly late; x. 85. 18 echoes i. 108. 1, based on vii. 61. 1.

Within the groups it is often possible to prove introduction of later material by the violation of the rules of order adopted by the compilers of the collection,[1] but differences of age among the groups themselves and between individual hymns, which are not marked out as foreign to the groups in which they are found, cannot yet be established. The most elaborate attempt made of late to find strata in the Rigveda is that of Prof. Arnold,[2] who by the test of metre divides the collection into five layers which cut sharply across the traditional grouping; but his criteria are clearly unsound,[3] and depend on a purely hypothetical reconstruction of the metrical history of the hymns, to which objection can be taken on many grounds. Moreover, the results thus attained render any intelligible account of the development of Vedic religion impossible: the hymns to Dawn are certainly the most beautiful and least sacerdotal of all those of the Rigveda, and, for this reason and because in the later cult Dawn has but a small place, it is natural to assign them to the earliest period of Indian hymnology. The same conclusion is also indicated by the fact that this view alone harmonizes with the probable movements of the Vedic Indians. There can be little doubt that the bulk of the hymns cannot have been produced, as was formerly thought, in the Punjab, where the phenomena of the rains are poor and uninteresting and could not have given rise to the remarkable stress laid on these natural features by the Vedic poets in their conceptions of Indra and the Maruts. We must seek for the main home of the Vedic Indian in the country afterwards famous as Kurukṣetra, between the rivers Sarasvatī, now Sarsūti, and Dṛṣadvatī, probably the modern Chitang, and in the region of Ambāla, and the oldest hymns only, those to Dawn, can reasonably be supposed to have been composed while the invaders were still in the land of the five rivers.[4] But Prof. Arnold is forced by his metrical tests to ascribe the importance of the Dawn and of the deities, sky and earth, which, like the Dawn, seem among the oldest, to a secondary state of the Vedic religion, when Dawn and sky and earth were not revered for themselves, but because of their connexion with the fire ritual, dawn being the time of sacrifice and the fire serving as a pillar to join heaven and earth, but yet to keep them asunder, while in the earliest period he sets Indra, the warrior god.

If we cannot hope to reach any assured results as regards the different strata in the Rigveda itself, it remains to be seen what date can be ascribed to the Rigveda as a whole. The Saṁhitā is absolutely lacking in reference to any historical event which we can date. It had indeed been sought time after time to demonstrate the contrary, but no such attempt has yet approached plausibility. Ludwig[5] in an elaborate examination of the question decided

[1] Oldenberg, *Prolegomena* (1888) and *Ṛgveda-Noten* (1909–12).

[2] *Vedic Metre* (1905). Contrast Bloomfield, *Rig-Veda Repetitions*, pp. 535 ff., 640, 687, for the use of grammatical, lexical, metrical, ritual, sense, and other considerations as to repeated passages to decide relative dates.

[3] Keith, JRAS. 1906, pp. 486–90, 718–22; 1912, pp. 726–9.

[4] Hopkins, JAOS. xix. 19; cf. Keith, CHI. i. 80 ff.

[5] Proc. Bohem. Acad. 1885.

that from the mention of two eclipses in the Rigveda could be deduced a date of the eleventh century B.C. for the hymns in which these phenomena were mentioned, but this suggestion has been totally disproved by Whitney.[1] An alleged reference to the capture of Babylon by Aryan tribes which might be brought into connexion with the advent of the Kassite dynasty at Babylon in the eighteenth century B.C. is a wild guess of Brunnhofer,[2] which it is quite impossible seriously to consider. Much more substantial are the arguments adduced by Prof. Jacobi [3] who sees traces of evidence that the Rigveda goes back as far as the third millennium B.C. He thinks that the Rigveda shows that the winter solstice took place in the month Phālguna, and on the ground of the precession of the equinoxes this must mean that the observation thus recorded was made in the third millennium B.C. This view, which rests on the interpretation of a very doubtful passage in the Rigveda,[4] he supports [5] by the fact that in the Gṛhya Sūtras, or manuals of domestic ritual, of much later date, the ceremonial of the wedding includes an injunction to the wife to look at the star called Dhruva, 'fixed', and this can only have originated at the time when *α Draconis* was in the vicinity of the pole, there being no other star which could be called fixed at any period coincident with the probable age of the Rigveda: further he contends that the fact that Kṛttikās, the Pleiades, are placed at the head of the list of twenty-seven or twenty-eight Nakṣatras, 'lunar mansions,' in the Yajurveda and Atharvaveda Saṁhitās means that Kṛttikās marked the vernal equinox when the list was compiled, and this date fell in the third millennium B.C. The first of these arguments seems clearly to be based on a misunderstanding of the Rigvedic passage in question;[6] the argument from the pole star assumes an accuracy in the demands of the primitive Indian wedding ritual which is wholly unnatural; and the assumption that the Kṛttikās coincided with the vernal equinox is most improbable, if we are to regard the Nakṣatras as an Indian invention, since the equinoxes play otherwise no part in early Indian ideas, and if, as is far more probable, the Nakṣatras were borrowed from some other nation, then the period when Kṛttikās were chosen as the head is without relevance to the date of Indian literature.[7]

[1] JAOS. xiii. pp. lxi–lxvi.

[2] *Iran und Turan*, p. 221.

[3] *Festgruss an Roth*, pp. 68 ff.; GN. 1894, p. 110; ZDMG. xlix. 218 ff.; l. 69 ff.; JRAS. 1909, pp. 721–6; 1910, pp. 456–64.

[4] x. 85. 13; AV. xiv. 1. 13.

[5] A somewhat similar view is found in B. G. Tilak's *The Orion* (1893) and *The Arctic Home in the Vedas*. Cf. Bühler, IA. xxiii. 238 ff. Contrast A. C. Das, *Rig-Vedic India*, i. 356 ff.

[6] The argument involves (1) the deduction from RV. vii. 103. 9 that the year began with the summer solstice, and (2) from x. 85. 13 that the marriage of the sun in the Phalgunīs must fall at the beginning of the year, i. e. the summer solstice. Both views are most implausible; in vii. 103. 9 that *dvādaçásya* means 'year' is practically certain, and thus ruins the whole structure of conjecture.

[7] Oldenberg, ZDMG. xlviii. 629 ff.; xlix. 470 ff.; l. 450 ff.; JRAS. 1909, pp. 1090–5; GN. 1909, pp. 544 ff.; Thibaut, IA. xxiv. 85 ff.; Whitney, JAOS. xvi. pp. lxxxi ff.; Keith, JRAS. 1909,

We are compelled therefore to content ourselves in the main with internal evidence. There is, however, one point of interest arising from the discoveries at Boghaz-Köi,[1] where among gods invoked by the King of the Mitanni are found names suggestive of the gods Mitra, Varuṇa, Indra, and the Nāsatyas, i. e. the two Açvins, who often bear that name or epithet in the Rigveda. The existence of these gods seems, therefore, established for a period which may be placed about 1400 B.C., but unfortunately there is nothing in the record to show decisively whether these gods are to be regarded as the gods of an Aryan people, no clear separation of Iranian and Indian yet having taken place, or of the proto-Iranians, or of the proto-Indians. From the names of kings of the Mitanni preserved in the Tell-el-Amarna letters,[2] it has been deduced that there were proto-Iranian elements among the Mitanni, and this possibility is not to be denied, though it is at least certain that the people were not a pure Aryan race. But in view of its uncertain value no direct light can be thrown on the age of the Rigveda either in its earliest or its latest form. *A priori* it is clear that the gods must have existed before the hymns, and there is nothing special about the grouping of the gods as found at Boghaz-Köi which would justify us in holding that the pantheon had by that time assumed the definite form which it takes in the Rigveda, and that the Rigveda must then

pp. 1095–1100; 1910, pp. 465–8; Macdonell and Keith, *Vedic Index*, i. 420–31; Keith, *Taittirīya Saṁhitā*, i. pp. clix ff.; JRAS. 1917, pp. 135 ff.; Lehmann-Haupt, ZDMG. lxiii. 717.

[1] Winckler, MDOG. Dec. 1907; Jacobi JRAS. 1909, pp. 721–6; Meyer, SBA. 1908, pp. 14 ff.; KZ. xlii. 16 ff.; *Gesch. des Alt.*[3] II. i. p. 652; Keith, *Bhandarkar Comm. Volume*, pp. 81–92; Winternitz, *Gesch. der ind. Lit.* iii. 621 f.

[2] Bloomfield, AJP. xxv. 8; Hall, *Anc. Hist. of Near East*, pp. 201, 331. According to Winckler (OL. xiii. 291 ff.) the Aryan element bore the name Charri; the Susian version of Darius's inscriptions has Harriya for Aryan; their followers are named *marianni*, in which may be seen the Vedic *marya*, with suffix *āna*; cf. Leumann, *Zur nordarischen Sprache und Literatur*, pp. 5 ff. The theory is carefully criticized by W. E. Clark, *Am. Journ. Sem. Lang.* xxxiii. 261–82. Since then much evidence has been accumulated, without decisive result. Hrozný (*Keilschrifttexte aus Boghazköi* and *Völker und Sprachen des alten Chatti-Landes*), agreeing in considerable measure with E. Forrer, *Die acht Sprachen der Boghazköi-Inschriften* (1919), holds that the Chatti were non-Indo-Europeans ruled by persons of quasi-Indo-European origin, speaking a *centum* language, while the Charri were also non-European under rulers speaking a *satem* language of Indian, not Iranian type (Jensen, *Indische Zahlwörter in keilschrifthittitischen Texten*, Berlin, 1919). The efforts from the numerals and names to establish Indian rulers, as opposed to Iranian or Aryan, are not convincing, as we simply have no evidence of early Iranian, and the process of restoring the Avesta to its true form, undertaken by Andreas and Wackernagel, is still unfinished. The form Assara Mazāš of Assurbanipal's record, pointing to a much earlier borrowing, possibly during the Kassite dominion in Babylon, is clearly not Indian, and, while it may be Aryan, it is possible that it is proto-Iranian; cf. Hommel, PSBA. 1899, pp. 127, 138 f.; *Geographie und Geschichte des alten Orients*, p. 204; Moulton, *Early Zoroastrianism*, pp. 423 f.; Konow, JRAS. 1911, pp. 41 ff., argues that the Mitanni names are early Iranian. Cf. CAH. i. 311 f., 469, 553; Forrer, ZDMG. lxxvi. 250 ff.

have existed. Still less importance attaches to the occurrence of a name like Šuriaš (perhaps Sūrya, the sun) in Kassite records, which leads Meyer to the conclusion that the Kaššū were originally settled in Media and driven west by Aryan tribes.[1]

The internal evidence is more satisfactory, if less definite. It is practically certain that the Rigveda was to all intents and purposes complete before the other Saṁhitās came into being, and it is certainly anterior to the whole of the other literature of India, which presupposes it and takes it as given. With this fact accords its language, which is much more archaic than the language of the other early literature of India, and its metre, which has only emerged from the simplest form in which the number of syllables in each line was the sole mark of differentiation of verse from prose. For reasons which are given in the next chapter it is impossible to suppose that the later Saṁhitās date substantially if at all after 800 B. C., and this may probably be taken as the lowest possible date for the completion of the Rigveda. The real difficulty arises in deciding how much farther back the collection is to be carried, and in this regard it is probably necessary to beware of exaggeration.[2] There are many references in the Rigveda to former poets, and unquestionably, as we have seen, there was a distinct development of language and thought during the period of its production. But to allow too extended a time for the process of development and decline—for it is clear that the end of the period saw the passing from favour of original composition of hymns—is unnecessary, and there are two distinct grounds against adopting any such view. In the first place the poets never attain any very great command of their material, whether in language or metre, though in certain cases poetic results are attained by simple means.[3] To the end the structure of the sentences remains naïve and simple, and, when the poet seeks to compass more elaborate thought, his power of expression seriously fails him : it can hardly be supposed that in a period of many centuries the Vedic poet's control over his instruments of expression would not have risen superior to the difficulties which faced him. In the second place, if the Rigveda is put as far back as 1500 B. C., it becomes very difficult to explain the extremely close parallelism between the speech of the Avesta and that of the Rigveda, especially if the traditional date (660–583

[1] In CHI. i. 65 ff. the case for a western home of the Indo-Europeans is stated by Dr. P. Giles, who would clearly place the invasion of India after 1500 B.C. The eastern theory is defended by Feist, *Indogermanen und Germanen* (1919). Carnoy (*Les Indo-Européens*, pp. 55 ff.) decides for the Dnieper region. On Kassite names see Bloomfield, AJP. xxv. 1–14. The western home is supported by von Schroeder, *Arische Religion*, i. 214 ff. Hirt (*Die Indogermanen*, i. 22) places the migrations late. Cf. Ipsen, IF. xli. 174 ff.

[2] Bloomfield (*Religion of the Veda*, p. 20) prefers 2000 B.C. for the beginnings. But in *Rig-Veda Repetitions* (pp. 20, 21) he stresses the absence of archetype hymns and the epigonal character of the collection (cf. JAOS. xxix. 287), and in the earlier work he accepts 1600 B.C. in lieu of 1400 B.C. as the Mitanni date.

[3] Macdonell, *Hymns from the Rigveda* (1922), pp. 17 f.

B.C.) of Zoroaster is accepted.[1] It is possible to diminish the force of this objection by postulating an earlier epoch for Zoroaster ; [2] but, even so, it is very doubtful whether the prophet can be carried far enough back to make any earlier date than 1200 B.C. or 1300 B.C.[3] for the Rigveda reasonably probable. If we seek to ascribe a higher date than this, we must recognize that we are dealing with conjectures for which no very substantial evidence can be adduced.

A very serious difficulty, it must be added, presents itself in the way of the early dating of the Rigveda in the shape of the fact that it seems very dubious whether we can place at all early the period of the dispersal of the Indo-Europeans or of the Indo-Iranians. If the Rigveda belongs to even 2000 B.C. we must assume that the Indo-Iranians parted at some date decidedly before that epoch, and there certainly seems every reason, arguing from general probabilities, not to place the entrance of the Aryans into India substantially before 1600 B.C.,[4] and the process was probably one of long duration and slow accomplishment.

A proof of the long connexion of the Indians and the Iranians before the latter settled definitely in India is seen by Hillebrandt [5] in certain names in the Rigveda, which incidentally in this view aid us in assigning an earlier date to certain hymns at least of the sixth book, composed in Arachosia. This view involves the identification of the Paṇis not with mythological figures but with the Parnians, of the name Pārthava with the Parthians, the Dāsas with the Dahae, the river Sarasvatī with the Iranian Harahvaitī, the Hariyūpīyā with the Iryāb or Haliāb, a tributary of the Krumu, and the Ārjīkīya with a name connected with Arsakes, while Bṛbu Takṣan, the enemy of the Paṇis, is brought into connexion with the later city of Takṣaçilā, which may represent an eastern settlement of a tribe originally situated further to the west. Against this view, however, there are two serious objections. The identifications are all of the most dubious character,[6] and, even if they were genuine, it would be difficult to make out any chronological result from them, seeing that other possibly Iranian names occur in other books of the Rigveda, such as Sṛñjaya and Pārāvata in several books, Dṛbhīka in book ii, Sṛbinda in viii,[7] Parçu and Tirindira in viii.

[1] Jackson, *Zoroaster*, pp. 150 ff. ; Prášek, *Gesch. der Meder*, i. 204 ff. ; West, SBE. xlvii. p. xxviii ; cf. Hertel, IIQ. i. 7 ff.

[2] Moulton, *Early Zoroastrianism*, p. 18 ; Geldner, *Enc. Brit.* xxi. 246 ; xxviii. 1041 ; Bartholomae, *Altir. Wörterbuch*, p. 1675 ; Keith, JRAS. 1915, pp. 798, 799 ; Peters, JAOS. xxxi. 378 ; Jackson, CHI. i. 323.

[3] Macdonell, *Hymns from the Rigveda*, p. 7.

[4] Cf. Morgan, *Les premières civilisations*, pp. 264 ff., 314 ; J. L. Myres, *The Dawn of History*, pp. 189 ff. ; Kennedy, JRAS. 1909, p. 1119.

[5] *Ved. Myth.* i. 83 ff. ; iii. 268 ; (Kl. Ausg.), pp. 95, 114, 191 f. ; GGA. 1894, pp. 648 ff.

[6] See Macdonell and Keith, *Vedic Index*, i. 29, 349, 357, 450, 504 f., 518 f., 521 f. ; ii. 470 ; Keith, CHI. i. 86 f. The obvious possibilities of mere parallelism of name between India and Iran seem sometimes ignored (cf. Jackson, CHI. i. 322). Parçavas is certainly not a proper name in x. 33. 2.

[7] Brunnhofer, *Iran und Turan*, p. 122.

It is, however, an interesting question [1] how far there can be traced in the Rigveda evidence of closer connexions with Iran on the part of some of the families of poets, even if, as is doubtless proper, we reject the suggestions of Hillebrandt which would make certain of the hymns of the Rigveda (book vi) a product of the time when the seers dwelt beyond Indian limits proper. Here again, however, we must be contented in large measure with a negative result. Thus it has been suggested that we are to see special closeness of connexion in the case of book viii, on the strength of the occurrence of such names as the Gomatī, Suvāstu, Asiknī, Paruṣṇī, and the hostile aspect in which the Gandharva is viewed,[2] contrary to the usual honourable position occupied by that spirit. Ārjīka or Ārjīkīya is also cited as pointing to some Iranian locality. This, however, as has been said, is uncertain,[3] and the most certain indication of Iranian influence, the form *titaü* with an unparalleled hiatus,[4] is found in book x, other alleged instances of such influence being most dubious.

It may, however, be noted that from the Iranian side the suggestion has been made that the Tīr Yašt represents an Indian phenomenon, the breaking of the south-west monsoon, which has no Iranian parallel. Hope Moulton [5] connected this view with the appearance of gods, whom he regarded as Indian, among the Mitanni, thus arriving at the conjecture of a movement back out of India on the part of tribes which had become dissatisfied with conditions there, but carried traditions with them. Indo-Iranian relations might account for the phenomenon adequately, but the whole matter is too conjectural to yield any assured result.

The Rigveda is not, therefore, among the oldest literary monuments of the world viewed merely from the point of date, but its extent, which is comparable with that of the *Iliad* and the *Odyssey* put together, and the practically exclusively religious character of its contents, make it unique in its revelation of the religion of the Vedic tribes. Of the condition of life of these tribes comparatively little is made known to us, but there is enough to show that the people were divided up among small kingdoms, under hereditary princes, often engaged in war among themselves and still more often involved in conflicts with the ‘ dark skins ’, over whom they seem normally to have been victorious, perhaps as a result of the body armour which they wore, and the spears and battle-axes of metal—copper, or later iron—which, with the bow, formed their chief weapons in war. They were not merely a pastoral but also an agricultural people, but there is no clear trace of a town life : the forts, which both they and the aborigines owned, were doubtless nothing more than places of refuge, with ramparts of mud or wood, used both in time

[1] Cf. Hillebrandt, *Aus alten und Neuindien* (1922), pp. 8 ff. ; Hopkins, JAOS. xvii. 73 ff. See also below, Part II, Chap. 15, § 1 as to Asura.

[2] RV. viii. 1. 11. In Iran his parallel is a demon, but the suggestion is problematic.

[3] Macdonell and Keith, *Vedic Index*, i. 62 f. ; Stein, *Bhandarkar Comm. Vol.*, p. 27.

[4] Cf. Wackernagel, *Altind. Gramm.* i. § 37. 1 (*b*).

[5] *Early Zoroastrianism*, pp. 25 f., 436 f.

of war and in time of flood.[1] The richness in gold, which is characteristic of the age, may be compared with the wealth of the Aegean civilization of Crete, but there is no trace of the artistic spirit of the Aegean pre-Hellenic people. Nor is there any sign that large kingdoms had yet appeared : confederations of tribes, such as that of the famous five peoples, Anus, Pūrus, Druhyus, Turvaças, and Yadus, might exist, and we hear even of a battle of ten kings, but these were clearly not lasting federations, but loose unions for war. On the other hand a great homogeneity of culture and religion among the tribes seems to result from the evidence of the Rigveda and to attest the definite and distinctive character of the Vedic people as distinct from the tribes of aborigines.[2]

The language of the Veda is essentially akin to Iranian as seen in the Avesta, and more remotely to the other tongues which make up the Indo-European family. From this fact, and from the picture of strife against peoples of dark colour in the Rigveda,[3] has been deduced the theory that the Vedic Indians formed a body of invading tribes which broke into India from the north-west and carried with them a distinctive culture and religion, which they developed in a special manner under the influence of the new climatic conditions in which they found themselves in Northern India, and of intermixture of blood through marriage with the aboriginal population. Of the latter fact there are probably clear traces already in the language of the Rigveda, which contains in the cerebral letters a series in the main unknown to other cognate languages and most plausibly [4] to be ascribed to the deterioration of sounds in the mouths of generations of mixed blood. Moreover, all analogy is distinctly in favour of an early process of admixture. Complete destruction by invaders of pre-existing peoples is a comparatively rare phenomenon and connotes a bloodthirsty spirit among the invaders which is not suggested by anything in the Rigveda.

An alternative hypothesis has, however, been freely urged of late, which would see in the Aryan speech of the Rigveda no proof of real invasion of a people, and would, therefore, refer the religion of that Saṁhitā not to Aryans but to the aborigines, presumably the Dravidians, who are clearly the most important of the early inhabitants of India.[5] With this theory may be con-

[1] Cf. Feist, *Kultur der Indogermanen*, pp. 144–6 ; von Schroeder, *Arische Religion*, i. 247 ; Macdonell and Keith, *Vedic Index*, i. 539 f. ; Hopkins, *Trans. Conn. Acad.* xv. 32.

[2] Zimmer, *Altindisches Leben* (1879) ; Macdonell and Keith, *Vedic Index* (1912) ; Keith, CHI. i. 77 ff. ; Kennedy, JRAS. 1919, pp. 493 ff. ; 1920, pp. 31 ff.

[3] Reminiscences of an older non-Indian home (seen, e. g., by Weber, *Ind. Stud.* i. 161 ff., and B. G. Tilak, *The Arctic Home in the Vedas*) may be safely regarded as purely speculative.

[4] Cf. Wackernagel, *Altind. Gramm.* i. § 144 and p. xxii ; Macdonell, *Ved. Gramm.*, p. 33. Objections to the view of aboriginal influence are suggested but not proved by Michelson, JAOS. xxxiii. 145–9. Cf. Keith, CHI. i. 109 f. ; G. W. Brown, *Studies in honor of Bloomfield*, pp. 75 ff. ; Petersen, JAOS. xxxii. 414 ff.

[5] Srinivas Iyengar, *Life in Ancient India*, pp. 6 ff. ; G. Slater, *The Dravidian Element in Indian Culture* (1923).

nected the view suggested by Hall[1] that the Sumerians were originally Dravidians who developed their civilization in the valley of the Indus, and thence introduced it to the half nomadic Semites, teaching them the arts of writing, of town-dwelling, and of building in stone. The Aryans who invaded India were then civilized by the Dravidians, just as, according to the prevailing theory,[2] the Aryans of Greece owed their civilization to the Aegean race. The fatal difficulty from the point of view of proof presented by this theory is that there is not available any evidence by which it can even be made plausible. If the Sumerians were originally Dravidians, and attained a high civilization in the Indus valley, it is remarkable that no trace of this high civilization is to be found in India, which, as far as we know, first attained the art of writing from Semites not before 800 B.C., and which commenced building in stone and town-dwelling long after the age of the Rigveda. No traces of the stone buildings which presumably the Sumerians erected in the Indus valley have been discovered, and Dravidian civilization is first known to us as a historic fact many centuries after the latest date to which the Rigveda can be ascribed. The ascription to the Dravidians of the civilization of the Rigveda, therefore, remains a mere hypothesis, and one which is difficult to maintain in view of the clear opposition of the white and the dark races made in the Rigveda, where the white shows throughout its contempt for the black. Moreover, there is one very definite piece of evidence which suggests that the invaders were conscious, not merely of racial, but also of religious differences between themselves and the aborigines. In two passages[3] are mentioned phallus-worshippers and in both cases with abhorrence: it is certain that the Dravidians in historical times were addicted to this form of fetishism, and it is as probable as anything can be that the phallus-worshippers opposed by the singers were aborigines.[4] But it is of course obvious that, with the admixture of races which was inevitable, the admixture of religion was certain to follow, and traces

[1] *Anc. Hist. of Near East*, pp. 173, 174. The facial aspect of Gudea in his statues seems to me wholly un-Dravidian. Rapson (CHI. i. 43) accepting a connexion derives the Dravidians from Western Asia. A. C. Das (*Rig-Vedic India*, i. 208 ff.) believes in Aryo-Dravidian influence on the Sumerians, holding that the Punjab was the Aryan home even in the Miocene epoch, and peopling Egypt with Dravido-Aryans.

[2] E.g. Hall, *Aegean Archaeology* (1915); Evans, JHS. xxxiii. 277 ff. There is some exaggeration in this view; an Aryan infiltration may have preceded the Achaean, as suggested by Kretschmer, *Glotta*, i. 21 ff.; Keith, JRAS. 1912, pp. 473, 474.

[3] RV. vii. 21. 5 x. 99. 3; von Schroeder, VOJ. ix. 237. (These passages are erroneously cited by Dr. Farnell (*Cults of the Greek States*, v. 8) as applicable to Vedic religion.) That RV. x. 101 and ix. 112 imply ritual use of the phallus is certainly implausible. It is Çiva who is specially connected with the phallus from the epic onwards; Vaiçravaṇa (Kubera) and Īçāna (Rudra-Çiva) are worshipped for the bridegroom, a fact which Hopkins (CHI. i. 233) interprets as pointing to their phallic nature (PGS. i. 8. 2; ÇGS. i. 11. 7). RV. viii. 1. 34 has no reference to cult; cf. Hertel, VOJ. xxv. 172 ff. For a Greek parallel, cf. Keith, JHS. xxxvii. 238.

[4] Contrast A. C. Das, *Rig-Vedic India*, i. 267 f.; Güntert, *Weltkönig*, pp. 305 ff.

of such influence which are scanty in the Rigveda can be seen in greater abundance in the later texts.

It has been assumed that the Dravidians may be reckoned as the aboriginal population encountered by the Aryan invaders, and, though this cannot strictly be proved, it is rendered extremely probable by the existence of a people of Dravidian speech, the Brāhūis, in Baluchistan, whether we regard them in origin—now they are greatly mixed and un-Dravidian in type—as an advanced guard of a Dravidian movement from India, or as the remnant of an older population, left behind on the Dravidian advance from Western or Central Asia into India.[1] It is, however, possible that the aborigines met by the Aryans included members of the pre-Dravidians who are still found as jungle tribes, and who are by some authorities [2] brought into relation with the Veddahs of Ceylon and the Sakai and Semang of the Malay Peninsula; the term 'noseless' applied to their opponents by some Aryan invaders at least is held to accord better with the appearance of pre-Dravidian than with that of Dravidian tribes. The argument is not decisive, but there is no reason to doubt that both pre-Dravidians and Dravidians may have been encountered by the Aryans. Whether Muṇḍā-speaking tribes were among their enemies it is idle to enquire, for we know even less of Muṇḍā movements than of Dravidian; their physical appearance is now very much that of Dravidians, though their language proves to have affinity with the Mon-Khmer languages of Assam and Burma as well as with other forms of Austric speech scattered over the Pacific.

Physical evidence of the present day suggests that about the longitude of Sirhind there sets in a distinct change of type in Northern India, and the type to the west of the line has been characterized as Indo-Aryan, that to the east as Aryo-Dravidian, the first including the areas of Kashmir, the Punjab to the longitude of Ambāla, and Rājputāna, the latter the eastern border of the Punjab, the United Provinces, and Bihar. Taken in conjunction with the grouping of modern vernaculars, this distinction has been made the basis of a theory which asserts that the Aryan invasion of India took place in two distinct movements of very different character; the one was carried out by tribes which entered India through the passes of the Hindu Kush, passing through South Afghānistān, and the valleys of the Kābul, Kurram, and Gumal rivers, and settling in the N.W. Frontier Province and the Punjab. These tribes were accompanied by their wives and families, a fact which is held to explain the predominantly Indo-Aryan character of the population west of Sirhind. On the other hand the second invasion was by the difficult way of Gilgit and Chitral, and was carried out by men unaccompanied by women, who, therefore, had to form alliances on a wholesale scale with the

[1] *Imp. Gazetteer*, i. 292 ff.; Rapson, CHI. i. 40 ff.

[2] Thurston, *The Madras Presidency*, pp. 124 f. Cf. the Niṣādas of the Vedic texts; Chanda, *The Indo-Aryan Races*, i. 4 ff., who holds they originally were Muṇḍā speakers; Kennedy, JRAS. 1919, pp. 501 ff.; Thurston, *Castes and Tribes of Southern India*, i. pp. xx ff.; A. C. Das, *Rig-Vedic India*, i. 99 ff.; CAH. i. 27 f.

Dravidians, whence the changed type. The argument from ethnology is clearly unsatisfactory; in the first place it is impossible to ignore the fact that there is still doubt whether the Indo-Europeans were Nordic blonds [1] or Mediterranean brunettes or Alpine brachycephalics or a mixed race; that the north-west of India has been the scene of prolonged and repeated inroads; and that the present racial types are, therefore, very poor evidence for the racial types of 1200 B.C., not to mention 3000 B.C. Secondly, it is simple to explain the change as due merely to the fact that about the longitude of Sirhind the Dravidians were established in larger numbers and that the progress of the Aryans became seriously hampered; they had to convert rather than conquer, and the racial type is, therefore, naturally a compromise. The evidence from language [2] is clearly of even less value. The facts of the later dialectic differences can be wholly and satisfactorily explained [3] by the inevitable mode of propagation of linguistic influence; from the centre of that influence, the middle country of the Brāhmaṇa period, linguistic influence was exerted in a manner which necessarily became more and more feeble in proportion to the distance of the peoples affected from the centre; hence the phenomena of outer and inner languages are explained without recourse to the speculation which introduces invaders over an almost impossible route, and, what is far worse, demands that we should recognize a sharp break between the civilization of the Rigveda and that of the Brāhmaṇas, assigning the former to the Punjab, and the latter to the middle country. The literature of the Vedic period shows emphatically no break of any kind in culture; it displays instead evidence of the advance of the Vedic civilization from the Punjab to the middle country, in an orderly progress, which conforms precisely to what would *a priori* be expected.

The religion of the Rigveda is, therefore, the product of Aryans who must have been affected considerably by their new environment and whose blood must have been becoming more and more intermingled by intermarriage; but it is only proper to recognize that we really do not know, and have no means of ascertaining, how far the people at the period of the Rigveda can be styled Aryo-Dravidian, rather than Indo-Aryan.[4] For this reason it is hopeless to seek to estimate the relative contributions of Aryan and Dravidian to the intellectual product of the Brahmans, for we have insufficient knowledge of what was true Aryan, and we know facts regarding Dravidian thought only

[1] Von Schroeder, *Arische Religion*, i. 174 ff. The modern conditions are fully reviewed in Sir A. Baines's *Ethnography*.

[2] Grierson, *Imp. Gazetteer*, i. 357 ff.; Risley (*The Peoples of India*, p. 55) renders the theory untenable by placing the first invaders originally in Arachosia and Seistan.

[3] See Rapson, CHI. i. 50; cf. Keith, *ibid.* p. 119; Kennedy, JRAS. 1919, pp. 526 ff., who, however, errs in saying that the Bharatas found the speech of the Pūrus barbarous, for *mṛdhravāc* refers to hostile speech (*Vedic Index*, i. 471), nor is it at all clear that the Bharatas were late comers.

[4] Assertions of Dravidian predominance (Crooke, *North-Western Provinces of India*, p. 60) can neither be proved nor disproved, but the prevailing of Aryan speech must be remembered.

long after it had been affected by the Aryan invasion. Here as often confession of ignorance is preferable to the idle affectation of knowledge.

As the Rigveda is of so recent a period, it is natural to ask whether the religion which it contains has not traces of influence by the cultures of the great nations of the East and above all of Babylonia. The answer to this question cannot be given with any certainty as in the affirmative: the only cogent proof of the borrowing of deities by one people from another, in cases where the borrowing is not formally recorded, is afforded by the appropriation of the name and the similarity of character of the gods: mere similarity is wholly insufficient, unless the conception formed of the particular divinity is of so special a kind that parallelism is not a reasonable explanation. In the case of the Rigveda and of the later Vedic texts no such instance of borrowing is hinted at, and no case is known in which the similarity of name even suggests that a god has been taken over from another people, so that at most we are left to rely on the argument from similarity of character. Strength would doubtless be given to such arguments if the language of the Rigveda could be proved to contain loan-words from Semitic sources, but the only two which have with any probability been alleged, the word *manā*,[1] apparently meaning 'ornament' and described as golden, which is often equated with the Babylonian[2] Mina, and the word *paraçu*, axe, are too isolated to prove anything at all. Aššur cannot reasonably be connected with Asura[3] either as source or result and it is impossible to prove that the year of 360 days of the Rigveda is to be derived from the Babylonian year,[4] and still less that the sacred number seven is adopted under Babylonian influence for an Aryan nine.[5]

While the religion of the Rigveda seems to stand free of foreign elements, it cannot be assumed that the version presented to us in that collection is at all a complete record of the religion of the period of the composition of the hymns. It contains the poetry used by the priests in the sacrifices to the high gods, but not, with rare exceptions, the lower religious or magical beliefs. Even, however, of the hieratic views it gives no complete account: the collectors of the hymns in the main were interested in the Soma ritual, and the great majority of the hymns deal with some form or other of that rite: the animal sacrifice is hardly noticed, save in the case of the most important and rare sacrifice, that of the horse. Moreover it cannot be doubted that much of

[1] RV. viii. 78. 2; Macdonell and Keith, *Vedic Index*, ii. 128, 129. The alleged borrowing of the war chariot from Babylon is wholly dubious and in any case is probably pre-Aryan; von Schroeder, *Arische Religion*, i. 238. For guesses, see Brunnhofer, *Arische Urzeit*, pp. 89 f., 415; B. G. Tilak, *Bhandarkar Comm. Vol.*, pp. 29 ff.

[2] Wackernagel, *Altind. Gramm.* i. p. xxii; Kretschmer, *Gesch. d. griech. Sprache*, p. 106; Feist (*Kultur der Indogermanen*, p. 214) suggests possible borrowing from a third source by Babylon and India. But see Macdonell and Keith, *Vedic Index*, ii. 128 f.

[3] Cf. Thomas, JRAS. 1916, p. 364, with Chadwick in Moulton, *Early Zoroastrianism*, p. 31.

[4] Keith, JRAS. 1916, p. 355. Cf. Meyer, *Gesch. des Alt.*[3] I. ii. p. 913.

[5] Von Schroeder, *Arische Religion*, ii. 426 ff. Contrast Hopkins, *Origin of Religion*, pp. 291 f.

the poetry is highly artificial, the expression not of naïve faith but of refined speculation : there is much—usually empty—mysticism, and phrase making, the work of competing poets without religious inspiration. On the other hand there are numerous hymns which are perfectly simple in thought and even in diction, and part of the obscurity of the poetry is due merely to the fact that it is rich in references to myths, which are, as is inevitable in hymns, only alluded to and not set out in detail. Such references are of comparatively little importance in the consideration of Vedic religion, of which it is possible to obtain definite views irrespective of the exact force to be ascribed to obscure myths.

The accusation, however, which is often made against the Rigveda of being purely sacerdotal cannot be accepted, for it contains enough matter in its later portions to show that the compilers were perfectly familiar with the popular religion of the day. Thus we have hymns intended to act as spells against vermin,[1] or the disease Yakṣma,[2] to bring back the life of one apparently dead,[3] to destroy enemies,[4] to procure children,[5] to destroy the demon who kills offspring,[6] to induce sleep,[7] and even to oust a co-wife from a husband's affections.[8] Most of these hymns occur in book x, which preserves also the marriage hymn,[9] a piece of priestly ingenuity, and the funeral hymns.[10] These with four or five gnomic hymns,[11] some philosophic and cosmogonic speculations,[12] and some hymns, or portions of hymns, in praise of generous patrons of the priests relieve the monotony of the collection, and help to obviate the wholly erroneous view that the early religion of India consisted merely in the invocation of high gods.[13] But the real extent of the popular religion and much of the hieratic must be sought for in the later Saṁhitās, and above all in the Atharvaveda.

The limitations of the Rigveda have been ascribed by Hillebrandt[14] to the existence in the period of that text of a ritual distinction of fundamental importance, that between the Devayāna, the period when the gods are worshipped, and the Pitṛyāṇa, the period when the Fathers are revered. The former is the time when the sun is in the constellations in the north, and the moon in those to the south, while the reverse is the time of the Pitṛyāṇa, the distinction being marked in the mythology by the flight of the god Agni, possibly a reflection of the disappearance of the sun in the darkness of winter. The Rigveda, on this view, would represent the worship of the Devayāna; its exclusive character would be merely apparent. Unfortunately the sugges-

[1] i. 191.
[2] x. 163.
[3] x. 58 ; 60. 7–12.
[4] x. 166.
[5] x. 183.
[6] x. 162.
[7] v. 55.
[8] x. 145 ; cf. x. 159.
[9] x. 85.
[10] x. 14–18.
[11] ix. 112 ; x. 34, 71, 117.
[12] x. 81, 82, 90, 121, 129 ; i. 164, which, like viii. 29, is a riddle hymn.
[13] Macdonell, *Sansk. Lit.*, pp. 120 ff.
[14] *Ved. Myth.* iii. 67, 71, 204, 235, 299 ; (Kl. Ausg.), pp. 20, 50, 170, 177. Contrast Oldenberg, *Rel. des Veda*², p. 11, n. 1.

tion is open to two fatal objections. It is not in accord with tradition which does not thus connect the Rigveda with the ceremonies of the Devayāna or the Uttarāyaṇa,[1] with which Hillebrandt, without warrant, identifies that term, and, as a matter of fact, the Rigveda does contain, along with other matter not appropriate to its supposed purpose, a most important section of hymns dealing with the worship of the Fathers. We find, indeed, once more that only as a historical rather than a liturgical collection is the condition of the Rigveda logically explicable.

The form of the collection is entirely metrical, and it is matter of pure conjecture that in some cases the verses preserved represent merely one side of an ancient form of composition in which verses inserted in prose expressed the chief emotional points in conversation or narrative, or in the alternative that some hymns represent dramas *in nuce*. Neither hypothesis appears to have much plausibility, but for the purposes of the history of Vedic religion the question possesses no great importance.[2]

[1] For this term see Macdonell and Keith, *Vedic Index*, i. 529; ii. 467.

[2] See ref. in Keith, *Sanskrit Drama*, chap. i. For Hertel's theory of the origin of the Rigveda see Appendix A.

CHAPTER 2

THE LATER SAṀHITĀS AND THE BRĀHMAṆAS

Already in the Rigveda there are signs of considerable elaboration of ritual and of the employment of a number of priests at the sacrifice, and the later Saṁhitās and the Brāhmaṇas reveal to us a time when the functions of the priesthood have been definitely divided up and apportioned among sets of priests. The manual acts of the sacrifice are ascribed to the Adhvaryu priest and his assistants and are accompanied by muttered formulae, in prose or verse, styled Yajus: in addition at the greatest sacrifices, such as the Soma sacrifice, singers chant Sāmans, and reciters recite Çastras, while the Brahman priest supervises the whole performance, usually in silence. On this division of functions is based the division of the later Saṁhitās: the Sāmans are preserved in the song books of the Sāmaveda, the Yajuses in the Yajurveda, and the Atharvaveda is held to be connected with the Brahman priest, while the Çastras were composed of verses taken from the Rigveda. From the point of view of religion the Sāmaveda is mainly interesting for its form: the words which were sung were almost invariably taken from the Rigveda, but they were eked out as shown in the song-books, Gānas, with all kinds of interjections, doubtless for musical purposes, which must have converted their character in the most marked degree. The sense of the words cannot possibly have been understood in the mutilated form in which the chants were sung, and the conclusion is inevitable that their religious value lay not in the substance but in the form, so that the Sāmans have been compared, not altogether unaptly, to the revival hymns beloved by the African negro in the new world. In them doubtless the religious excitement of the priest found its fullest scope for expression.[1] That this form of chant was old need not be doubted: there are clear traces in the Rigveda itself in the strophic and metrical form of certain of the hymns,[2] that they were from the first intended for something more lively than mere recitation. With this fact accords the generally close relation of the Sāmaveda and the Rigveda, which renders it probable that that was of the first of the later Saṁhitās to take definite form.

The Yajurveda represents the literary fixing of the formulae used by the

[1] Bloomfield, VOJ. xvii. 156 ff.; JAOS. xxi. 50 ff. On the recensions see Caland's ed. of the *Jaiminīya Saṁhitā* (1907); VOJ. xxii. 436 ff.; Oldenberg, GGA. 1908, pp. 711 ff.; Simon, VOJ. xxvii. 305 ff. For the Pūrvārcika there are the Grāmageya and Āraṇya, for the Uttarārcika the Ūha and Ūhya Gānas.

[2] The chief metre of portions recited by the Hotṛ (as shown by internal evidence and ritual use) is Triṣṭubh, without strophic form; of those used by the Udgātṛ Gāyatrī and Pragātha in three and two verse sets; Oldenberg, ZDMG. xxxviii. 439 ff.

Adhvaryu and his assistants in their performance of the great sacrifices: clearly the actual use of such formulae must have been normal from the beginning of the sacrifice, but it was only after the collection of the Rigveda hymns that the idea of creating a similar Saṁhitā for the Adhvaryu became popular. This is shown unmistakably by the frequent application for the purposes of the Adhvaryu of verses from the Rigveda, in many cases without any real propriety and often with alterations deliberately planned to adapt them to their new use. Whereas the Rigveda has come down to us in but one collection, the Yajurveda [1] is preserved in two main recensions, which at comparatively early date received in India the names of the Black and the White Yajurveda. The origin of these appellations is uncertain, but later they were interpreted in such manner as to suggest that the White Yajurveda owed its name to the fact that in it the formulae of the Adhvaryu were collected separately from the explanatory remarks which accompany them in the texts of the Black Yajurveda. In making this distinction the compilers of the White Yajurveda, which has come down to us in the Saṁhitā called the Vājasaneyi, were merely restoring the primitive condition of the Yajurveda, which must at one time have consisted of a collection of the formulae, in prose and verse, only.[2] But already at a comparatively early period the formulae were accompanied by explanations, called Brāhmaṇas, texts pertaining to the Brahman or sacred lore, in which the different acts of the ritual were given symbolical interpretations, the words of the texts commented on, and stories told to illustrate the sacrificial performance. Hence in the Black Yajurveda we find three complete recensions, the Taittirīya, Kāṭhaka, and Maitrāyaṇī,[3] and one imperfect, the Kapiṣṭhala, in which formulae and Brāhmaṇa are closely allied, while in the case of the White Yajurveda the Brāhmaṇas are all collected in one great work, the most important of its type in Vedic literature, the Çatapatha Brāhmaṇa. Perhaps as a result of this separation, a mass of old material, partly formulae, partly Brāhmaṇa, which had not been incorporated in the Taittirīya Saṁhitā was collected together in the Taittirīya Brāhmaṇa, which in part contains matter more recent than the Saṁhitā, but in part has matter as old as, at any rate, the later portions of that text.

Explanations were not less required for the other Saṁhitās, and the Rigveda is dealt with in two Brāhmaṇas,[4] the Aitareya, and the Kauṣītaki, the latter of which is far more concise than the former, though it covers in some respects a wider sphere. The Sāmaveda formed the topic of the great

[1] See Keith, *The Veda of the Black Yajus School* (HOS. xviii and xix), 1914.

[2] Oldenberg, *Prolegomena*, pp. 290 ff.

[3] ii. 9 of this text is an obvious interpolation mentioning sub-Vedic deities such as Brahman, the four-faced, and lotus-seated; Karāṭa, elephant-faced and tusked; Gaurī, mountain born; Viṣṇu as Keçava Nārāyaṇa, &c. Similar interpolations are found in other Vedic texts, especially in the Khilas, or Apocrypha, of the Rigveda, and as a rule no mention of them is made in this work.

[4] Ed. and trans. Keith, HOS. xxv, 1920.

Pañcavinça Brāhmaṇa[1] and the Jaiminīya Brāhmaṇa,[2] the latter of which unhappily exists only in a very imperfect text and has only in part been published, beside a large number of minor and unimportant texts styled Brāhmaṇas, of which the Ṣaḍvinça, a sort of supplement to the Pañcavinça, and the Sāmavidhāna are of some value as dealing with magic practices of varied kinds.

Full as are the other Saṁhitās of magic rites, the Atharvaveda[3] differs from them in the fact that, whereas they are essentially connected with the sacrifice, its connexion with that operation is external and mechanical. In essence it is a collection of spells for every conceivable end of human life, spells to secure success of every kind, in the assembly, in public life, to restore an exiled king, to procure health and offspring, to defeat rivals in love, to drive away diseases in every form, to win wealth and so on. But at the same time the subject-matter has been thoroughly worked over by the priesthood, and it has even in its simplest spells throughout a priestly veneer. The priests have also added many spells directly bearing on portions of their sacrificial activities, and the wedding and burial hymns appear in more elaborate forms. Theosophy *qua* profit-bringing[4] is not absent, and a deliberate attempt was later made to bring the Atharvaveda into the circle of the three orthodox Vedas by the addition to the collection of book xx which contains the hymns to be used by the Brāhmaṇācchaṅsin priest in the ritual of the Soma sacrifice. It is, however, important to note that this Veda, despite the attempts made to raise it to an equal place with the others, never succeeded in achieving this position : useful as were its spells, and much as the priests of the school of the Atharvaveda thrust themselves forward as indispensable to princes through their magic powers, there were always not lacking voices to criticize its claim to be a fourth legitimate Veda.[5] In modern times this prejudice and recognition of the special character of the work are reflected in the suggestion that the text is actually the product of strata of society different from those of the Rigveda : Ridgeway[6] insists that the Atharvaveda is the record of aboriginal as opposed to Aryan religion. This view, however, cannot be pressed too far : the Atharvaveda reflects the practices of the lower side of religious life, and is closer to the common people than the highly hieratic atmosphere of much of the Rigveda : the common people, we cannot doubt, were largely influenced by aboriginal ideas through mixture with aboriginal races, but, as will be seen below, we have no criterion on which we can safely rely to decide that certain beliefs are non-Aryan and

[1] See Hopkins, *Trans. of the Connecticut Acad. of Arts*, xv. 20 ff.

[2] On the kindred, lost, Çāṭyāyana, see Oertel, JAOS. xviii. 15.

[3] Trans. in Çaunaka recension by Whitney and Lanman (HOS. vii and viii) ; on the Paippalāda, in course of ed. in JAOS., see L. C. Barret, *Studies in honor of Bloomfield*, pp. 1 ff.

[4] Edgerton, *Studies in honor of Bloomfield*, pp. 117 ff.

[5] Bloomfield, *Atharvaveda* (1899), and SBE. xlii.

[6] *Dramas and Dramatic Dances of non-European Races*, p. 122.

aboriginal. The same problem in effect presents itself as in the case of the Homeric poems. Are we to suppose that they represent Aryan religion, and that that religion was free from admixture with the lower side of religion, which is freely revealed in the later literature of Greece and foreshadowed by the evidence of Aegean cult objects ? The answer to that question given by Lang [1] in the affirmative seems most improbable, though not more so than the suggestion of Gilbert Murray [2] that the Homeric poems are the result of a process of conscious refining of older tradition. Like the Homeric poems the Rigveda does not cover the whole field of religious belief, and we have no sure ground on which to assign to the non-Aryan as opposed to the other elements in the population all the lower forms of religion.

The later Saṁhitās are doubtless of various date : the Sāmaveda must probably be reckoned as the earliest, and the Atharvaveda is certainly the youngest of all in its redaction, though it is doubtless in part old in material. Of the Yajurveda Saṁhitās the youngest is the Vājasaneyi, and the oldest perhaps the Taittirīya, but between it and the other two texts of the Black Yajurveda there is no clear distinction of time. The Brāhmaṇas are certainly later than the formulae of the Saṁhitās to which they relate, and they are distinguished sharply from them both by their prose form, which is quite different from the prose of the formulae, and by the characteristics of their language, which is much less archaic than the verse or prose formulae. The order in age amongst them, and the prose portions of the Saṁhitās, which are essentially akin to them is doubtful; it is, however, very probable that the Aitareya in its first five books is among the oldest, that the prose parts of the Yajurveda Saṁhitās, and, though later, the Pañcaviṅça are also old, and that the Kauṣītaki, Jaiminīya, and Çatapatha are the latest of the important works.[3] For the date of the Brāhmaṇas important evidence is furnished by the development of thought : the latest portions of the texts which are of the older Brāhmaṇa style are styled Āraṇyakas, books intended by reason of the dread holiness of their contents for study in the forests, and of these certain parts which bear a more definitely philosophical aspect are styled Upaniṣads, a word apparently derived from the session of the pupils round the teacher in the process of instruction. Thus there are attached to the Brāhmaṇas of the Rigveda the Aitareya and the Kauṣītaki or Çāñkhāyana Upaniṣads, to the Taittirīya Brāhmaṇa the Taittirīya Upaniṣad, to the Çatapatha Brāhmaṇa the Bṛhadāraṇyaka Upaniṣad : the Sāmaveda has the Chāndogya Upaniṣad which is the major portion of a Brāhmaṇa, and the Jaiminīya Upaniṣad Brāhmaṇa, which is one book of the Jaiminīya Brāhmaṇa, and contains in itself the Kena Upaniṣad. In the main it may be assumed that the doctrines of

[1] *The World of Homer* (1910).

[2] *Greek Epic* (2nd ed. 1911). Even Leaf (*Homer and History*, ch. viii) refuses to accept the theory of expurgation.

[3] Keith, *Aitareya Āraṇyaka*, pp. 21 ff. ; *Taittirīya Saṁhitā*, i. pp. clix-clxxiii ; *Rigveda Brāhmaṇas*, pp. 40 ff. On the Jaiminīya cf. Caland, *Over en uit het Jaiminīya-Brāhmaṇa* (1914), pp. 5 ff., whose conclusions are dubious ; see for the priority of the Kauṣītaki, Keith, BSOS. I. iv. 177.

these Upaniṣads are prior to the rise of Buddhism, which is derived logically from the system which they contain, and, as the date of the death of the Buddha may be placed with fair probability in or about the year 480 B.C., a lower terminus of 500 B.C. for the Upaniṣads is attained. The priority of the Brāhmaṇas proper to the Upaniṣads is quite undoubted, and thus a lower limit of about 600 B.C. for the latest Brāhmaṇas is obtained, from which may be deduced a date of about 800–700 B.C. for the Saṁhitās as a lower limit. The same conclusion is indicated by the facts of language : the grammarian Pāṇini, whose date can scarcely be later than 300 B.C.,[1] deals with a language which is decidedly more modern than that of the Brāhmaṇas to which, however, it is akin : prior to him was Yāska, whose expositions in his Nirukta of Vedic passages indicates clearly that the Rigveda was already far distant in time : earlier again than Yāska was Çākalya, by whom was produced the Pada Pāṭha of the Rigveda, that is the text in which each word is given in its primitive form unaffected by the Sandhi of the Saṁhitā, and earlier again than Çākalya was the making of the Saṁhitā Pāṭha, in which, to the utter detriment of the metre, the hiatuses which were allowed in the Rigvedic poetry are removed under the influence of the usage and grammatical theories of the day. But the Brāhmaṇas as a rule ignore the Saṁhitā text, and evidently knew only the primitive text without the latter rigid Sandhi rules, so that for them again we are forced to accept a date not later than 600 B.C.

Efforts to establish an earlier date for the Saṁhitās and the Brāhmaṇas have naturally been made, and of these two may be mentioned. Jacobi[2] has insisted that the post-Vedic period may be dated from *c.* 800 B.C. on the strength of the fact that the end of the Vedic period is marked by the simultaneous appearance of the Sāṁkhya-Yoga and Jaina philosophies, and the latter can be carried back to *c.* 740 B.C., seeing that the founder of the faith was probably Pārçva, whose Nirvāṇa falls 250 years before that of Mahāvīra, and the latter was contemporaneous with the Buddha, who died about 483 B.C. The argument is extremely unconvincing, apart altogether from our complete ignorance as to the historical character and the date of Pārçva. It assumes that the Jain doctrines as we know them go back before Mahāvīra, and that they presuppose the doctrines of the Upaniṣads as older. Neither proposition possesses the slightest plausibility, and neither need be seriously discussed in the absence of any effort of Jacobi to support his assertion in this matter by reasoned proof.

A second line of argument is based on the war which forms the main topic of the Mahābhārata ; by various modes of reckoning of dynasties recorded in the Purāṇas the date of 1000 or 1100 B.C.[3] is attained for the war,

[1] Efforts to place Pāṇini much earlier are frequent, but his reference to Yavanānī, Greek writing, is difficult to reconcile with a much earlier date than about the 4th century B.C. Cf. Keith, *Aitareya Āraṇyaka*, pp. 21 ff.; *Rigveda Brāhmaṇas*, p. x.

[2] *Die Entwicklung der Gottesidee bei den Indern* (1923), pp. 24 f.

[3] CHI. i. 275, 306 f. An excellent *reductio*

and, as the Pāṇḍus are unknown to the Saṁhitās and the Brāhmaṇas, it is contended that they must fall before the war of the Kurus and the Pāṇḍavas. It is difficult to appreciate the naïve credulity which accepts as having any value these late lists of kings, which are preserved to us in works dating at soonest fifteen hundred years after the alleged date of the war, and which, when they come into contact with known facts, immediately reveal themselves as without value. Thus into the dynastic list of Kosala we find that the eponymous founder of the Çākya line, the Buddha's father, he himself, and Rāhula have all been interpolated without the slightest historical justification, and it seems puerile, in the face of these facts, to insist on regarding these lists as the basis for chronological calculations of any kind. When the conflict between the Kurus and the Pāṇḍavas took place we do not know, and the assumption that it represented a vast struggle in which all the peoples of Northern India at any rate were engaged, because in the Mahābhārata in its final form it is so represented, argues a signal forgetfulness of the powers of poetic and popular imagination, and of the history of the Roland Romance among others or of the Odysseus or Aineias legend. Hence it appears wholly unwise to seek to derive a high date for the Saṁhitās and Brāhmaṇas from any argument based on the date of the epic war.

Nor probably is it safe to insist[1] that the period between the older Upaniṣads and Buddhism must be one of several centuries, and thus to increase the antiquity of these Upaniṣads, and consequently of the Brāhmaṇas and Saṁhitās. We have no means of estimating the rate of advance of thought in the period in question, and a further serious difficulty must be faced by those who wish to establish an early date for the Upaniṣads. The developed doctrines of Buddhism cannot be proved to be those of the Buddha, or to date from even the fifth century B. C.,[2] so that it is in all likelihood wiser to content ourselves with the belief, rather than the absolute assurance, that a date before 500 B. C. may reasonably be assumed for these Upaniṣads.[3] To assert a much greater antiquity is easy and it has the advantage of increasing the interest of the study of the Upaniṣads, but there seems little satisfaction in beliefs which cannot be supported by any serious evidence.

A decisive argument against any early dating of the Upaniṣads would be available if we accepted the view often held[4] that the Ajātaçatru who figures in the Kauṣītaki and the Bṛhadāraṇyaka Upaniṣads as king of Kāçī is

ad absurdum is found in A. C. Das, *Rig-Vedic India*, i. 279 ff.

1 Cf. Oldenberg, *Die Lehre der Upanishaden*, pp. 288, 357, n. 185.

2 See Keith, *Buddhist Philosophy*, chap. i. Cf. Oltramare, *La théosophie bouddhique* (1923), pp. 56, 64 ff., who recognizes that Açoka knew no canon. Max Walleser (*Sprache und Heimat des Pali-Kanons*, pp. 23 f.) still clings to the alleged Açokan date of the Kathāvatthu, a view as improbable as the theory of Pali as the language of the Sthaviras of Pāṭaliputra.

3 Cf. Hopkins, JAOS. xxii. 336; Rapson, *Ancient India*, p. 181; Keith, CHI. i. 112, 147.

4 See Keith, ZDMG. lxii. 134 f. Identity is assumed in Winternitz, *Gesch. d. ind. Lit.* i. 484.

identical with the Ajātasattu of the Buddhist texts,[1] who was contemporaneous with the Buddha. It appears to me, however, that any such identification wholly lacks justification, especially as the name is no more than an epithet and thus possesses singularly little probative value, while the king of the Buddhist texts is not king of Kāçī.

An effort has been made by Hopkins [2] to establish a more precise estimation of the period intervening between the Upaniṣad of the Jaiminīya and its Brāhmaṇa. The latter mentions Gauṣūkti, while the former has the same name as that of a teacher, giving after him ten recipients of the doctrine. This would give say three centuries, which he deems a not unreasonable time, in accord with the advance of the Upaniṣad in doctrine. The suggestion seems untenable; there is nothing whatever to prove that Gauṣūkti was a recent figure in the time of the Brāhmaṇa, nor does the fact that the Brāhmaṇa does not mention the other teachers referred to show that they existed after its composition, and, least of all, is there any evidence that we are to treat the list as representing generations. There is no evidence whatever that the record is one of teacher to youthful pupil.

The usual astronomical evidence has been adduced to establish the early date of the Brāhmaṇas, or at least of the statements recorded in them. As the lack of value of this evidence has been established,[3] it is sufficient to note one point which has been held to fix definitely the date of one passage in the Çatapatha Brāhmaṇa; there, in a discussion of the time for establishing the sacred fires, the Kṛttikās are recommended as a possibility, on the score[4] that they do not move from the eastern quarter, while the other Nakṣatras do move. It is really impossible to attach serious value to such an assertion, made in a passage which consists of foolish reasons for preferring one or other of the Nakṣatras; we are in the same region of popular belief as when in the Sūtra literature the existence of Dhruva, a fixed polar star, is alleged.[5]

There are clear traces in the later Saṁhitās and the Brāhmaṇas of social and religious changes in the people. The centre of Vedic culture is still, as probably in the period when the main part of the Rigveda was produced, the land of the Kurus lying between the Sutlej and the Jumna, but importance now attaches also to the kindred tribe of Pañcālas, whose name

[1] Vincent Smith's dating of this prince *c.* 554 B.C., putting the Buddha's death *c.* 546 B.C. (*Oxford History of India*, pp. 48, 58 n., 70), rests on a false interpretation of the inscription of Khāravela of Kaliṅga (see ref. in Keith, *Sanskrit Drama*, p. 89).

[2] *Trans. Conn. Acad.* xv. 30.

[3] See ref. above, p. 4, n. 7.

[4] ÇB. ii. 1. 2. 3. Kṛttikās must then (D. Mukhopadhyaya, *The Hindu Nakṣatras* (1923), pp. 41 ff.) have been on the equator, i.e. 3000 B.C. Cf. S. B. Dikshit, IA. xxiv. 245 f.; A. C. Das (*Rig-Vedic India*, i. (1921)) prefers even greater antiquity. For TB. iii. 1. 1. 5, adduced by him (p. 47) from Tilak (*Arctic Home*, p. 2), see Keith, JRAS. 1911, pp. 794 ff.

[5] In favour of a late date may be adduced the mention of iron if the introduction of that can be placed *c.* 1000 B.C. (CHI. i. 56, 615), but this also is merely conjectural. For the question of Ayas see *Vedic Index*, i. 31 f., 151; ii. 235, 398.

seems to signify that they were a union of five older tribes, but whose connexion in origin with the Kurus is attested by the record that they were once called Krivis.[1] The Pañcāla land stretched, eastward from Kurukṣetra, from the Merut district to Allahabad, and included the territory between the Jumna and the Ganges, called the Doab. But the Çatapatha Brāhmaṇa[2] records the advance of the Brahmanical system into Kosala and Videha, which roughly correspond with Oudh and Tirhut.[3] The Atharvaveda knows iron and silver as well as the copper and gold of the Rigveda. The comparative frequence of mention of the elephant and the appearance of the tiger and the panther in the later Saṁhitās, whereas lion and wolf are conspicuous in the Rigveda, as well as the mention of rice, are clear indications of the advance of the Vedic Indians further to the east and the south. The Açvattha (*ficus religiosa*) is rare in the Rigveda, but becomes common in the Atharvaveda, which also knows the Nyagrodha (*ficus indica*). At the same time it is clear that the system of classes became more and more complicated and the divisions were drawn more and more distinctly : the Yajurveda enumerates large numbers of special classes which in some degree at least seem to have been hereditary. The admixture of the people doubtless had proceeded very far : after the Rigveda it would be difficult to find any simple consciousness of the contrast of the colours of the Aryan and the Çūdra classes as opposed as white and black. The Rigveda, it is probable, already knew of the system by which normally the princely class, the priests, and the ordinary people were distinguished, and it knew also of the slaves made from the aborigines, but it was left to this later period to introduce a much more elaborate and fixed system of division. The Çūdras must on the one hand often have become rather serfs than slaves, when large bodies of them were reduced to subjection by the invaders, while among the ordinary people hereditary functions began to supersede the variety of choice of occupation which is evidenced by the Rigveda.[4] To these factors of differentiation must be added the result of mixture of races and rules of intermarriage : the doctrine familiar in later texts that many classes of the people were due to mixed marriages between men and women of different classes indicates that this factor must have been of considerable importance in assisting in the development of classes into castes, the process of which, however, we have to conjecture from most inadequate material. With the development of society there doubtless took place growth in prosperity and wealth, favouring the

[1] Hopkins's suggestion (CHI. i. 254) that the Pañcālas may represent five Nāga clans connected with the Kurus or Krivis (meaning 'serpent'), and that none of the families is of pure Aryan blood, seems decidedly speculative.

[2] i. 4. 1. 10 ff. ; Macdonell and Keith, *Vedic Index*, ii. 288 f.

[3] The reference to the Oḍras (Orissa) seen by CHI. i. 601, in TA. ii. 1. 11, is an error, due to a hasty reading of BR. i. 1120, which really refers to Trik. (i. e. Trikāṇḍaçeṣa) ii. 1. 11.

[4] Macdonell and Keith, *Vedic Index*, ii. 247–71. For Indo-European class distinctions cf. Feist, *Kultur der Indogermanen*, pp. 291 ff. ; Moulton, *Early Zoroastrianism*, pp. 117, 183 f.

constantly increasing elaboration of the sacrifice with its resulting exaltation of the importance of the trained priesthood, without which the offerings could not successfully be carried out. But while the tribes, in several cases at least, doubtless were more closely united, and while thus the royal power became greater, there is no proof of the growth of any large kingdoms or empires,[1] nor can we say that there was much development of city life.

As sources for knowledge of the Vedic deities the later Saṁhitās and the Brāhmaṇas cannot be ranked high : the essential aim of the Yajurveda is the correct performance of the sacrifice, and the deities are of little consequence in comparison with the mechanism of that operation, to which is ascribed the whole control of the universe, and in the performance of which the universe is ever renewed. In the case of the Atharvaveda the position of the deities is still less important : constantly as they are introduced, their connexion with the magic spells which are the most original and essential part of that text is external merely : the god, and still more his name, adds potency to the spell, and the more gods enumerated, however diverse their functions and spheres of influence, the better the result. Even where in that Saṁhitā a deity is celebrated, the spirit is quite different from the spirit of the Rigveda : the goddess earth has a whole long hymn in a late book of the Atharva,[2] but the careful catalogue of all that grows on the earth and the sights and sounds upon it is recounted in a spirit quite unparalleled in the Rigveda. Hence it is not surprising that many of the minor figures of the pantheon of the Rigveda disappear, or at best sink to mere names, while on the other hand the religion shows development in two different directions. On the one hand, theosophic speculation brings into existence new and in some degree abstract deities ; on the other, gods of the people receive a recognition which is not accorded to them in the Rigveda. Of the former tendency the most prominent example is the rise to high rank of Prajāpati, as the creator god and the father of the gods as of men, and the exaltation to the rank of deities of such abstractions as Kāla, ' time ', Kāma, ' desire ', Rohita, ' the ruddy one ', perhaps an aspect of the sun, the Vrātya, as the convert to the priestly faith was named, the Ucchiṣṭa, or ' remnant ' of the sacrificial offering, and so forth. Of the other tendency examples are to be seen in the increasing importance attached to Rudra and to Viṣṇu, who by the time of Megasthenes (*c.* 300 B.C.)[3] were two of the chief gods worshipped in Northern India, and in whom we must probably see contamination of aboriginal with Aryan deities, the direct worship of snakes, perhaps induced by the experience of their terrors in India, the stress laid on the popular figures of the Apsarases and the Gandharvas, who, whatever their origin, are clearly little more in this period than fairies and sprites, and perhaps the collective view of the Asuras as a horde of evil spirits opposed in eternal, if unsuccessful, struggles to the gods in which they

[1] Even AB. viii. 14, 23 shows how little real empire existed. Cf. *Vedic Index*, i. 19 f.; N. N. Law, *Ancient Indian Polity*, pp. 13 ff.

[2] xii. 1.

[3] i. 29–37; L.

defeat their adversaries, until by the discovery of some ritual device the gods outwit them, a conception the utility of which to the priesthood who devise the sacrifice is obvious.

On the other hand, the later Saṁhitās, if poor in their contribution to mythology and the higher aspects of religion, are rich in precise information regarding the ritual, and are veritable treasure houses of Indian magic. Their value in both these regards has often been under-estimated or misunderstood, doubtless through hasty preconceptions of the nature of Vedic religion based upon the theories of mythology which at one time found their chief sustenance in the Rigveda. We have here given to us for at least six, and often probably seven or eight centuries B.C., precise details of the actual carrying out of rites, accompanied in many cases by the interpretation placed by priests on the rites. In many instances these interpretations are obviously purely priestly speculation, but this is by no means always the case, and at any rate the genuineness of the practices recorded is in the majority of cases free from all doubt, as they were recorded not by students of anthropology under the influence of theories of religion, but by priests interested in the practical carrying out of the sacrifices.

It is, as in the preceding period, a question of the greatest interest to determine whether Indian religion in this period was subjected to any outside influence, and in this case the evidence for such influence, though it does not become of great importance, is nevertheless less impalpable than in the period of the Rigveda. The most important item of proof of Semitic influence is contained in the existence of the system of the Nakṣatras, 'lunar mansions', which appear in the Yajurveda Saṁhitās and the Atharvaveda as the stations in which the moon spends the successive nights of the periodic month. The foreign origin of the Nakṣatras [1] is suggested by the fact that they appear curiously isolated in Indian literature: the Rigveda [2] appears not to know them at all, nor to contain any hint that such a system was being developed, while they occur in China and in Arabia under conditions which render derivation from India or *vice versa* out of the question. That the system was derived from Babylon seems natural, but the requisite and conclusive proof of its existence there has not been brought despite the probability that it existed.[3] The same conclusion in favour of primitive Babylonian influence is suggested by the legend of the flood which is recounted for the first time in the Çatapatha Brāhmaṇa [4] in connexion with the sage Manu, who rescued a fish, in return was warned by it of the danger of the flood, and in due course

[1] Macdonell and Keith, *Vedic Index*, i. 409–31; Keith, CHI. i. 148 f.

[2] Save in the late hymn, x. 85.

[3] Oldenberg, GN. 1909, pp. 544 ff.; Whitney, *Oriental and Linguistic Essays*, ii. 341 ff.; Weber, *Naxatra*, agree in the Semitic theory of origin. Cf. Keith, CHI. i. 140. Suggestions of Semitic influence on Indian magic occur in Henry, *La magie dans l'Inde antique*, pp. 93, 184.

[4] i. 8. 1. 1 ff. The alleged reference in AV. xix. 39. 8 is denied by Whitney, p. 961. One is possible in JB. iii. 99 (Caland, *Das JB. in Auswahl*, p. 313). For Vend. ii, cf. Hertel, IIQ. ii. 35 ff.

was towed by the fish safely over the flood to a mountain peak on which his ship grounded. It is not inconceivable that the story is of independent Indian origin, but this appears to be rather unlikely,[1] and in that case Babylon seems the obvious source, though the story may have come from some other part of the Semitic area. Indeed it has been urged [2] that Indian writing was introduced *via* Mesopotamia about the eighth century B. C. and was based on the Phoenician script, having as its prototype writing of the character of that found on the Moabite stone,[3] but this conjecture is still too uncertain to be used as a conclusive support of Semitic influences at this time. The attempt [4] to find Sumerian influence in *loha* ' copper ' or ' bronze ' is clearly inconclusive,[5] though it has been suggested [6] that the use of both copper and, later, iron came to India from Mesopotamia.[7] It may be added that there is no trustworthy evidence of Egyptian influence on Indian thought in the Vedic period despite the contentions of Prof. G. Elliot Smith in his *Migrations of Early Culture, Influence of Ancient Egyptian Civilization in the East and in America*, and subsequent works, who would have us believe that this is the explanation of the development of Indian ideas in the sixth century B. C., ignoring the evidence of the slow emergence of the ideas of the Upaniṣads and Buddhism from Indian conceptions. Similarly it is unwise to demand Aryan influence on Egypt as an explanation of the rise for a brief period of the cult of Aten, however tempting it may be to connect this with the apparent worship of Šuriaš, the sun, among the Kassites, for the Egyptian phenomenon can be explained without any such hypothesis.

No specially close relation to Iran can be definitely traced in this period, though the fire cult may have been influenced by that of Iran, and Iranian influence has been seen in the development of the meaning of Asura and in the names of individual Asuras,[8] as in the reference to incestuous unions in the Aitareya Brāhmaṇa.[9]

[1] Lindner (*Festgruss an Roth*, pp. 213 ff.) defends its Aryan origin. See, however, Oldenberg, *Rel. des Veda*², p. 283, n. 4. Cf. also Gomperz, *Greek Thinkers*, i. 95 ; Keith, JRAS. 1909, p. 590, n. 1 ; Gerland, *Sintflut* (Bonn, 1912) ; Winternitz, *Gesch. der ind. Lit.* i. 182 f., 337 ; J. G. Frazer, *Ancient Stories of a Great Flood* (1916).

[2] Bühler, *Indian Studies*, III, and *Palaeographie* (1896) ; CHI. i. 62. Rhys Davids (*Buddhist India*, p. 114) prefers a pre-Semitic Euphratean origin *via* Dravidian traders. For the theory of ultimate Egyptian origin see K. Sethe, GN. Gesch. Mitth. 1916, pp. 88–161 ; Phil-Hist. 1917, pp. 437–7 ; Lehmann-Haupt, ZDMG. lxxiii. 51–79 ; Bauer, *Zur Entzifferung der neuent. Sinaischrift.*

[3] About 850 B. C. ; Hall, *Anc. Hist. of Near East*, p. 451.

[4] Feist, *Kultur der Indogermanen*, pp. 71, 199 ; von Schroeder, *Arische Religion*, i. 225, 233. For conjectures as to *taimāta* and *urugūlā* (AV. v. 13. 6, 8), see *Bhandarkar Comm. Vol.*, pp. 33 f.

[5] See Chap. 29 for a conjecture as to the Babylonian origin of the cosmic character of speech (Vāc, Logos).

[6] CHI. i. 615.

[7] On *hrūḍu* (AV.), see *Vedic Index*, ii. 509.

[8] See below, Chap. 15, § 1.

[9] vii. 13, but cf. JB. ii. 113 for an Indian rite.

CHAPTER 3

THE LATER LITERATURE

For the latest stages of the Vedic religion on its practical side the authorities are the Çrauta and the Gṛhya Sūtras,[1] which deal with different but complementary spheres, and which incidentally preserve for us a considerable amount of formulae, prose and verse, which by accident or other cause have not found a place in any of the Saṁhitās preserved to us. The necessity of some manuals for the actual practice of the great complicated rites of the sacrifice must have been felt from an early period, but we have not now extant any of these manuals. The Çrauta Sūtras which are now extant are all without exception later than the older Brāhmaṇas, and, while the ritual which they reveal is in general harmony with that supposed by the Brāhmaṇas, it would be idle to suppose that it actually represents it with perfect accuracy. This can be seen by one simple point: the Brāhmaṇas often show that on questions of the exact mode of the performance of certain rites there were considerable difference of opinions: in some cases the Brāhmaṇas reject definitely certain views, in others they allow varied views to stand as equally legitimate, but in the Sūtras in the great majority of such cases merely one view is laid down, the others having presumably come to be disapproved in the school in which the Sūtra arose. On the other hand, the Sūtras often give optional forms of procedure for which the Brāhmaṇas contain no hint, evidence of the development of practice in the schools. Moreover, there is clear proof that no Sūtra represents rigidly any one Saṁhitā: even when, as is normal, a Sūtra follows generally some Saṁhitā it is quite ready to accept portions of its material from another.[2] The Sūtras, therefore, while often giving valuable confirmation and explanation of the Brāhmaṇas, cannot be regarded as contemporary evidence of the practices of the Brāhmaṇas, and this conclusion based entirely on the ritual is confirmed by many lines of evidence. In addition to dealing with many rites which seem clearly elaborations and modifications of older rites, the Sūtras in language are markedly more modern than the Brāhmaṇas, approximating closely to the classical speech, from which they differ in the main in the use of forms of incorrect grammatical formation.[3] From this fact a conclusion may fairly be drawn with regard to their chronology: it

[1] The Dharma Sūtras, unquestionably later on the whole than the Gṛhya Sūtras, are valuable as confirming the latter, but the age of new matter in them is doubtfully Vedic.

[2] e.g. Āpastamba uses the other Saṁhitās as well as the Taittirīya. A direct descent from the Brāhmaṇas is asserted by Caland, *Das Śrautasūtra des Āpastamba*, pp. 1 ff., but this is not certain, nor very probable.

[3] Wackernagel, *Altind. Gramm.* i. pp. xxxii ff.

can scarcely be supposed that works, not popular in character, which so flatly disregard in some points the rules of Pāṇini, should have been produced after the general acceptance of the authority of that grammarian, which falls probably in the third century B. C. at latest, and thus the period of the Sūtras may be roughly set down at from 400 B.C. to 200 B.C., though neither date can be regarded as more than approximate.[1]

Of the two sets of Sūtras the Çrauta deal with the elaborate forms of the ritual in which the presence of a priest, and usually of several, was necessary, while the Gṛhya Sūtras deal with the household ritual, most of which could be performed by the householder for himself without extrinsic aid of any kind. In all probability the literary development of the household ritual was later than that of the Çrauta ritual. It is, of course, perfectly obvious that domestic rites must be as old as any form of religion, but there is a clear difference between this fact and the question of the date of the application to the simpler rites of literary forms, and the verses which are associated with the Gṛhya ritual show clear traces in language and metre of not belonging to the earliest stage of Vedic poetry. On the other hand, in the case of the existing Sūtras, they are compositions emanating from schools which were interested no less in the Gṛhya than in the Çrauta ritual, and the normal school manual seems to have embraced both topics. If the portions dealing with the two different topics were of different dates, the fact can hardly now be detected.[2]

Of the extant Sūtras of the Rigveda there are two complete collections, the Āçvalāyana and the Çāṅkhāyana Çrauta and Gṛhya Sūtras: the former is undoubtedly the older, and its reputed author may be assigned with reasonable probability to about 400 B.C.[3] The Sāmaveda has the Çrauta Sūtras of Maçaka, Lāṭyāyana and Drāhyāyaṇa, and Gṛhya Sūtras by Jaimini, Gobhila, and Khādira. In the case of the Black Yajurveda Sūtras are especially frequent, including the very important Mānava, the Baudhāyana, Bhāradvāja, Āpastamba and Hiraṇyakeçi, covering both the field of Çrauta and Gṛhya rites: the White Yajurveda is represented by the Kātyāyana Çrauta Sūtra and the Pāraskara Gṛhya Sūtra.[4] The Atharvaveda has the most important in some way of all the Sūtras, the Kauçika, which is invaluable as bearing a very close relation to the text of the Veda, and preserving in many cases what seem perfectly accurate accounts of the magic rites which were accom-

[1] Keith, JRAS. 1909, p. 591, n. 2; *Taittirīya Saṁhitā*, i. pp. xlv, xlvi; *Rigveda Brāhmaṇas*, p. 44; Hopkins (CHI. i. 249) places ApDS. in the second century B.C.

[2] Oldenberg, SBE. xxix and xxx. On the other hand, the Sūtras are often clearly interpolated, alluding to later customs, e. g. the lunar *tithi*, and the practice of marking the body with sectarian marks.

[3] Keith, JRAS. 1907, p. 411; 1909, p. 591, n. 1; *Taittirīya Saṁhitā*, i. pp. xlv f., clxxii ff. The author of the ÇÇS. and ÇGS. is Suyajña, and there is a parallel to the ÇGS. in the Çāmbavya Gṛhya Sūtra (Oldenberg, SBE. xxix. 4 ff.; IS. xv. 4 ff.); ÇGS. v and vi are late.

[4] Definitely late are the Vaikhānasa and Vārāha Sūtras. The Vādhūla may be earlier; for Kaṭha texts, cf. Caland, *Brāhmaṇa en Sūtra-Aanwinsten* (1920).

panied by the formulae in the text: when the Atharvavedins became desirous of assimilating their Veda in every possible manner to the three older Vedas, they invented an orthodox Çrauta Sūtra, the Vaitāna, to accompany it, and from the Vaitāna more directly and indirectly from the Kauçika is derived much of the matter of the curious work, the Gopatha Brāhmaṇa, which poses as the Brāhmaṇa of the Atharvaveda, and which, borrowing largely from the Aitareya and Çatapatha Brāhmaṇas with other texts, is in essence a pamphlet in exaltation of the Brahman priest and the Atharvaveda.[1] The date of this remarkable composition is unknown: it is of course more than possible that some of its material is old, even when it is not borrowed from existing texts, for an enormous amount of Vedic literature has been lost, some within quite recent times.

Beside the Çrauta and the Gṛhya Sūtras stand the Dharma Sūtras, which are more specially devoted to customary law, but which frequently contain references to religion: of these the oldest and most important are those of Gautama, Baudhāyana, Āpastamba, and Vasiṣṭha,[2] but with them and still more with the later law books we pass from the ideas of Vedic religion to those of Hinduism, though the change is of course gradual and without any sharp break. The Gṛhya and Dharma Sūtras, however, are of special value as preserving for us the more domestic side of the religion practised by the ordinary householder, as opposed to the great sacrifices which were confided to the hands of the priests.

The rest of the literature is of less importance. Some value attaches to the Buddhist texts, especially such works as the Petthavatthu, which gives a fullness of view on the question of the state of the dead according to the popular belief which has every sign of age and genuine tradition.[3] But, though these texts undoubtedly have in them much popular belief, the date of the Buddhist canon is now no longer to be placed so high as was once held, when it was believed that much of the canon really represented views prevalent in the time of the Buddha, and the use of Buddhist evidence for the Vedic period must therefore be subject to the most close scrutiny.[4] The same consideration applies to the great epics. The redaction of the Mahābhārata was not completed in all probability until the fourth century A.D. and possibly even later: its earliest form cannot now be restored,[5] and its evidential value for the period up to 500 B.C. is, therefore, of controversial character, and the

[1] Cf. Keith, *Taittirīya Saṁhitā*, i. pp. clxix f.; *Rigveda Brāhmaṇas*, pp. x, 45.

[2] For the late date of Vasiṣṭha see Hopkins, CHI. i. 249, against Bühler, SBE. xiv. p. xvii. The Arthaçāstra, alleged to be of *c.* 300 B.C., is much later; Keith, JRAS. 1916, pp. 130 ff.; 1920, p. 628; Jolly's ed. (Lahore, 1923).

[3] See B. C. Law, *The Buddhist Conception of Spirits* (1923).

[4] Franke, JPTS. 1908, pp. 1–80; VOJ. xx. 337; Keith, JRAS. 1909, p. 577; 1910, p. 216; *Buddhist Philosophy*, ch. i.

[5] Hopkins, *The Great Epic of India* (1899); *Epic Myth.*, pp. 1 f.; CHI. i. 258; Winternitz, *Gesch. der ind. Lit.* i. 396; iii. 627; Lévi, *Bhandarkar Comm. Vol.*, pp. 99 f.; JA. 1915, i. 122. Cf. Dumézil, *Le Festin d'Immortalité*, pp. x, 4 ff.

Rāmāyaṇa, which may in its origin belong to the fourth century B. C., has been subjected to much later recasting.[1]

From the nature of the sources it follows that for the period up to 500 B. C. there is a continuous stream of trustworthy literary evidence, and that after that date the sources are of less value. The care taken to compose and preserve Sūtras for centuries after that period shows the vitality of the Vedic religion : indeed in much later times the great sacrifices of antiquity, such as the horse sacrifice, were performed by kings desirous of asserting their high prowess, and in families of priests [2] many of the other rites prevailed down to at least the nineteenth century. But the old order of things was greatly affected by the rise of Buddhism, which was indeed but one of many conflicting sects, but which attained under the patronage of Açoka in the third century B. C. a leading place among religions in India. The inroads of foreigners from the north-west, which, commenced by Alexander, repelled for a time by Candragupta and his successors, became constant and effective from the second century B. C., aided in the disintegration of the religion, and materially promoted the development of that popular religion centred in the worship of Çiva and Viṣṇu respectively, which was noted by Megasthenes as the leading feature of Indian religion when he stayed at Pāṭaliputra as the Ambassador of Seleukos to Candragupta.[3] Moreover, it must be remembered that throughout this period the Hinduization of the people was proceeding : the process in question can still be observed at the present day in operation amongst the wild tribes, and in the period B. C. it may confidently be assumed that it was being carried on upon even a greater scale, nor is it wonderful that thus the Vedic religion should gradually lose its distinctive features and assume new forms.

The difficulties of applying information derived from the later texts is adequately illustrated by the case of the use of idols.[4] The epic [5] shows clearly and indubitably the use of idols of the gods, and both it and Manu mention Devalakas, persons who carry idols about, while the grammarian Pāṇini [6] recognizes the use of the name of a god to denote his idol. On the other hand, it is perfectly clear that save in the latest stratum of the Vedic literature [7] idols are not recognized in cult, and then only in the domestic ritual. What conclusion is to be drawn from such facts ? Are we to suppose that idols were

[1] Keith, JRAS. 1915, pp. 318–28 ; Winternitz, *op. cit.* i. 439 ; iii. 630 ; Lévi, JA. 1918, i. 5 ff.

[2] Cf. the modern Agnihotris ; Hillebrandt, *Ved. Myth.*, p. 54, n. 1.

[3] The representation of deities in human form is also probably to be ascribed to Greek influence ; cf. Bloch, ZDMG. lxii. 648 ff. ; A. Foucher, *The Beginnings of Buddhist Art*, pp. 1 ff. ; Thomas, CHI. i. 480.

[4] Arbman, *Rudra*, pp. 82 ff. Contrast Bloch, ZDMG. lxii. 651 ; Macdonell, *Journ. R. Soc. Arts*, 1909, p. 317.

[5] Hopkins, *Epic Myth.*, pp. 72 ff.

[6] v. 3. 99, with Patañjali ; Ludwig, *Festgruss an Roth*, pp. 57 ff. ; Kielhorn, VOJ. i. 8 ff. ; Konow, IA. xxxviii. 145 ff. ; Charpentier, JRAS. 1913, pp. 671 ff.

[7] Adbhutabrāhmaṇa (Weber, *Omina und Portenta*, pp. 335 ff.) ; PGS. iii. 4. 9 are clear ; cf. PGS. iii. 14. 8 ; Gautama, ix. 12 ; ApDS. i. 30. 22.

really in popular use among the Vedic tribes, but were not approved by the exclusive Brahmans, to whom we owe the texts ? It may be observed that when we take the ritual as a whole there is very little sign of the alleged exclusiveness of the Brahmans, whose character in this regard is assumed through the error of treating the Rigveda and the speculations of the Brāhmaṇas as completely representing their views. Other causes are equally possible and more plausible. The use of idols may have been influenced by the non-Aryan population, as it gradually became assimilated ; it may have used them and had fixed sanctuaries before the advent of the Aryaṇs, whose lack of idols or sanctuaries may either have been primitive or induced by their migrations, which uprooted their local connexions. Or the use may have been a natural innovation within the Vedic circle of tribes, or introduced through contact with non-Vedic Aryans. There is no proof that the Indo-Europeans practised the use of idols, and the evidence of German religion [1] suggests that the position there as certainly in Iran [2] was much as in Vedic India, and it is, therefore, perhaps more plausible to believe that their employment gradually developed in India itself, though under what influences we simply do not know. This is certainly more legitimate than to suppose an idolatrous people and an exclusive priesthood. What, however, is essential is to note that Vedic religion is normally aniconic, for the interest of any religious system largely depends on what is peculiar and distinctive and not on that vast mass of beliefs which it must possess in common with other religions.

[1] Cf. Helm, *Altgerm. Rel.* i. 216 ff., 287 f. On Greek religion see de Visser, *Die nichtmenschengestaltigen Götter der Griechen*, pp. 31 ff. Cf. Carnoy, *Les Indo-Européens*, p. 233.

[2] Moulton, *Early Zoroastrianism*, pp. 67 f., 391.

CHAPTER 4

THE AVESTA AND COMPARATIVE MYTHOLOGY

§ 1. *The Avesta*

WHILE the literary evidences for Vedic religion are of quite exceptional value and importance, it must be admitted that of other material for realizing the mode in which the gods were conceived there is none available :[1] we have not the statues and other forms of representation, such as paintings, coins, seals, statuettes, &c., which are of such value in the case of Greek religion. No Indian art products or coins of the early Vedic period have been discovered, and that any should so be discovered is most improbable. On the other hand, great value attaches to the Avesta as a source for the understanding of Vedic religion. The close similarity in form of the Avestan language and the Vedic is beyond all doubt : certain changes in sounds [2] make indeed an apparent external divergence, but the vocabulary, the formation of words, and the syntax correspond with much exactitude, and, what is even more important, the verses of the Avesta often breathe the same religious spirit as those of the Rigveda. The similarity of religious views in the pre-Zoroastrian period must have been of the most close and striking type : the prose formulae of the Veda no less than the verses show a profound likeness of form and content, and the practical identity of modes of thought between Iran and India is sufficiently indicated by the striking parallelism between the form of parts of the Buddhist canon and the Iranian literature. The extraordinary similarity of view as of speech, indeed, makes it hard to believe in any early separation of these two branches of the Indo-European family, and suggests that they must have continued to be in close touch with one another until a comparatively late period, when the advance of the Vedic section towards India interposed difficulties of communication between them and the Iranian tribes, and gave a decisive turn to divergences of view which were beginning to form themselves in the Aryan community. The divergence from the common religion of the still undivided Aryans is clearly far greater in the case of the Avesta : there is no good ground to doubt that its present form is the result of the definite individuality of Zoroaster at a comparatively late date,[3] though doubtless he merely brought to a head tendencies which had

[1] Jouveau-Dubreuil's *Vedic Antiquities* affords nothing of more than speculative value ; see also Marshall, CHI. i. 616 as to the alleged burial mounds of Lauriyā Nandangarh ; *Arch. Survey of India Rep.* 1904–5, pp. 38 ff.

[2] Exaggerated in the ordinary transcription of the Avestan sounds, which is now under revision by Wackernagel and others ; Andreas, GN. 1909, pp. 42 ff. ; 1911, pp. 1 ff. ; cf. Bartholomae, VOJ. xxiv. 129 ff.

[3] For a theory of Israelite influence, see Pettazzoni, *La Religione di Zarathustra*,

been developing before his time. Under that change much of the old Aryan mythology disappeared or was deeply altered, and it is, therefore, the more remarkable that so much similarity should remain.

The figure of Ahura Mazdāh cannot possibly [1] be dissociated from Varuṇa who bears the epithet Asura, the term applied to other Vedic gods, while in the later Saṁhitās the Asuras have become the foes of the gods. Like Ahura, Varuṇa is the lord of holy order, Ṛta, which corresponds to the Avestan Aša : he is closely united with Mitra, as Ahura with Mithra, the sun-god : he is the chief of the Ādityas as deities of light, as Ahura is connected with the Ameša Spentas,[2] who like the Ādityas are not at first fixed in number : Varuṇa guards the sun from falling and makes it a path wherein to wander along the heaven, as Ahura keeps the earth from falling and provides the sun with a pathway. But, apart from these coincidences, the mere moral grandeur of both deities can only be explained by a common origin : the history of Varuṇa in India is that of moral elevation which gradually disappears, and the god sinks to a mere god of the waters, of quite secondary importance. It is inconceivable that this fact should be explained in any other way than that as a god he was brought to India, when under less favourable circumstances his moral quality evaporated. This theory, moreover, renders it easy to understand the success of the Zoroastrian faith and its choice of Ahura as the great and only god in the proper sense of the term : it was not a creation, but a purification of a conception existing among the people of Iran. The loss of the name Varuṇa is natural enough, and it is now probable that we actually have a record of the period when Varuṇa and Mitra were Aryan or Iranian gods in the list of the gods of Mitanni, referred to above. The same list contains the name of Indra, and supports the view that this deity was Aryan, for the same conclusion is irresistibly suggested by the fact that the Avesta knows a demon Indra, and a genius of victory whose name Verethraghna is unmistakably equivalent to Vṛtrahan, the epithet *par excellence* of Indra, as slayer of Vṛtra his greatest foe.[3] We do not know the precise steps of the process by which Indra fell from honour among the Iranians : there was, however, an obvious incompatibility of temper between the moral and stately Varuṇa and the impetuous war god Indra, which comes out even in the Rigveda, but

pp. 82 ff., and a criticism by Keith, JHS. xli. 279 f. ; F. W. Thomas (JRAS. 1916, p. 364) suggests that Asura came from Assyria and that Zoroastrianism is a moralizing Assyrian creed ; the difficulty is to find its Assyrian parallel.

[1] Hillebrandt (*Ved. Myth.* iii. 11) denied this, but the argument is incredible ; cf. Oldenberg, ZDMG. l. 48 ; Meyer, *Gesch. des Alt.*[3] I. ii. pp. 913, 921.

[2] See B. Geiger, *Die Ameša Spentas* (Wien, 1916). The š really is a mere misrepresentation, Andreas and Wackernagel, GN. 1911, p. 3, n. 1 ; contrast Bartholomae, VOJ. xxiv. 173.

[3] Oldenberg, JRAS. 1909, pp. 1090–5 ; Moulton, *Early Zoroastrianism*, p. 69. The theory that the Iranian genius is the genuine old Sondergott of War, and Vṛtra an Indian creation, through a misunderstanding of the term 'assault repelling', is quite unacceptable. The old Armenian deity Vahagn defeats dragons ; Hillebrandt, *Ved. Myth.* iii. 188 f.

in India there was no religious reformation to regard Indra as the inferior deity and reduce him to the rank of a demon.

The identity of Ahura and Varuṇa lends great probability to the identification of the Ameša Spenta and the Ādityas. It is true that no great stress can be laid on the number seven, which is not certainly primitive and may be ethnic in significance, but it is a reasonable view that the highly etherialized and spiritualized conceptions of the Ameša Spenta are merely the reflex of the more substantial though still abstract deities, the Ādityas. It must be noted that in India also these gods are not in essence personifications of nature, but, as their names denote, represent activities of human life, and the Iranian development in their case is a natural parallel to the refinement of the character of Asura into something far above the average god; moreover Bhaga, the giver of good things, one of the Ādityas, bears a name which in Iranian as Bagha denotes a god in general. The identity of Mitra with Mithra is patent and undeniable, Iran seems to have known Dyaus,[1] and there are as clear identities in minor figures such as that of Apāṁ Napāt, and Apãm Napāṭ, Gandharva and Gandarewa, Kṛçānu and Keresāni, both of whom appear in connexion with the Soma, Vāyu and Vayu, a genius of air, Trita Āptya, and the two forms, Thrita and Āthwya. The Avesta and Rigveda agree in the terms Yātu and Druj (Druh) as applied to evil spirits. Still more interesting is the parallelism of Yama, son of Vivasvant, the first of men and ruler of paradise, with Yima, son of Vīvaṅhvant. The waters and plants as deities are invoked by both.

Quite as striking are the similarities in the cult. In both India and Iran a priest called Hotṛ or Zaotar must originally have been the chief performer, the name denoting the act of offering the libation. The fire cult produced the Atharvan priest of India, the Āthravan of Iran, though Agni seems a specifically Indian development,[2] a fact which explains perhaps why he does not appear with Mitra and Varuṇa, Indra and the Nāsatyas in the list of gods of the Mitanni. The sacrifice bears the same name Yajña and Yasna respectively, and many other words used in the ritual correspond. More important still is the fact that the Soma is celebrated by the singers in both lands as the plant that grows on the mountains, watered by the rain of heaven, and brought by the eagle. It was in both lands pressed, and the juice passed through a sieve and then mixed with milk. But the deposition of Indra, who in India is the Soma drinker *par excellence*, from that place of honour in Iran, has resulted in the alteration of the old ritual of the drinking of the Soma by the god and then by the priests.[3] Both peoples too at one time spread a strew, Barhis or

[1] Herodotos (i. 131) asserts that the Persians called the whole circle of the heaven Zeus, probably not an allusion to Ahura; Spiegel, *Eran. Alt.* ii. 15; von Schroeder, *Arische Religion*, ii. 338 ff.; Moulton, *Early Zoroastrianism*, pp. 391f. We need not seek to find the actual Iranian name in Herodotos, who naturally uses the Greek term.

[2] Moulton, *Early Zoroastrianism*, pp. 70, 71.

[3] Moulton (*op. cit.*, pp. 71–3) adopts the view that the opinion of Zoroaster was definitely hostile to Haoma, while in the West the original intoxicating

Baresman, for the god to sit upon when he came to receive their offerings, and the old term spread (*stereta*) was preserved by the Iranians even after they had ceased altogether to conceive of the idea of the god coming to seat himself at the sacrifice. In both countries the pious offerer is styled the man who has spread the strew; in both again the service of praise consisted in large measure of hymns, whose close similarity of language and thought has already been noted.

The similarity of the concept of moral order, Ṛta or Aša, has been also noted: the names of the Mitanni kings afford to us curiously enough the proof that the term Arta was known in the fourteenth century B.C. at the latest. The form Arta is of special interest as it does not show the sound change of the Avesta, if indeed that be real and not a mere mistranscription; it may of course have belonged to the Iranian of pre-Avestan date, or it may have been an Aryan dialectical form, but at any rate the vitality and age of the idea are thus early established. Moreover, the idea of Ṛta is one which, like the moral elevation of Varuṇa, has no future history in India, pointing irresistibly to the view that it was not an Indian creation, but an inheritance which did not long survive its new milieu.

Another conception, of minor importance, but of interest, which survived in the Avesta, is the conception of thirty-three gods. The origin of the idea is wholly unknown in the Rigveda, where neither for eleven nor for thirty-hree is any explanation available, and this points to its great antiquity. But beyond this we cannot go: the effort of Hopkins [1] to evolve the number eleven from a primitive ten, and to find a circle of ten gods known to India, Greece, and Teutonic mythology must be regarded as unsuccessful: the Greek number is not very early, and is twelve, and no legitimate means of reducing it to ten is known, and even twelve is not Homeric, while the Teutonic circle of twelve is so late as to be certainly no more than a mere borrowing.[2]

The curious phenomenon that in Iran the gods of India appear as demons, while in India the Asuras as demons are contrasted with the great Ahura Mazdāh, has naturally given rise to much discussion: the simplest view, that the divergence of terminology arose directly from a religious split among the tribes caused by the Zoroastrian reforms which led to the differentiation of the two as Indian and Iranian, is now usually admitted not to be tenable; but the terminology has been thought to reflect hostile conflicts between Iranians and Indians in times after the two nations had developed separate lives.[3] For this view we would have good authority if we could accept the identification [4] of a mysterious Gaotema who is found in the

plant was replaced by a harmless one, which was not drunk.

[1] *Oriental Studies*, pp. 153, 154.

[2] Golther, *German. Myth.*, p. 200; for Greece, see Farnell, *Cults of the Greek States*, i. 84, 85; cf. also Keith, JRAS. 1916, pp. 350–6.

[3] See below, Part II, Chap. 15, § 1.

[4] Moulton, *Early Zoroastrianism*, p. 28. His further suggestion that the demons Indra, Saurva (= Çarva), and Nāoṅhaithya are due to this later contact of Indra and Iran is quite untenable. On an alleged Zoroastrian period of Indian

Yašt,[1] and who was, it has been asserted, none other than Gautama Buddha. The identification, however, rests merely on the similarity of name, and this being the case, and the name being an old Indian one, it is perfectly clear that it should not be used for serious argument.[2] Still less seriously can we take the suggestion that the Buddhist religion was really suggested to the Buddha from an outside source, and that not Aryan. The effort [3] to show that Buddhism was Tibetan in origin, and the Buddha a Mongolian of Gūrkha type, by such evidence as that of the form of the Stūpa, and the alleged Tibetan affinities of the Vajjis or Licchavis, or the equation of Çākya with non-Aryan[4] Scyths, and the prevalence of Mongolian feature types on Barhut and Sanchī sculptures, is wholly fantastic, and certainly affords no reason to see any close intercourse with Iran in any early period. Of such intercourse the Vedic literature affords no clear evidence at all : the most that can be said is that the energy with which the fire cult was practised in the north according to the testimony of the Çatapatha Brāhmaṇa may be accounted for by the proximity of the north-west to Iran, and the difference between the two forms of fire cult is so great as to render even this conclusion uncertain and precarious.

§ 2. *Comparative Mythology and Religion*

While in the case of the Avesta clear aid is available for the study of Vedic religion, comparatively little can be gained from the comparison of other Indo-European systems of religion.[5] The reason for this fact is not any doubt that the Indo-Europeans before the separation of the race, in whatever way this took place, had a religious system : every probability points in this direction, but the question of the exact form of this system eludes scientific decision. The evidence as to the nature of Greek religion is large in quantity, and much of it is old, but it is perfectly certain that in Greece the Hellenes settled among men of another race and culture who had already developed a high or at least elaborate form of religion, and the Indo-European constituents of Greek religion are difficult to detect, and have been very variously estimated. Roman religion is partly obnoxious to the same defect and partly only known to us at a late date.[6] For Celtic, German, Lettish, Lithuanian,

history, see Keith, JRAS. 1916, pp. 138 ff., and cf. the articles in the *Modern Review* (1916), xix. 373 ff., 490 ff., 597 ff.

1 xiii. 16.

2 Keith, JRAS. 1915, p. 798.

3 Rawlinson, JBRAS. xxiii. 223, 224 ; Vincent Smith, IA. xxxii. 234 ; *Oxford Hist. of India*, pp. 47 ff. See B. C. Law, *Kṣatriya Tribes of Ancient India*, pp. 25 ff.

4 Even Minns (*Scythians and Greeks*, pp. 85 ff.) has been misled into taking as Mongolian practices which are Iranian and nomadic, this tendency reaching the absurdity of deriving Papaios = Zeus (Herodotos, iv. 59) from Uralo-Altaic *baba*, ignoring Phrygian Papas.

5 O. Schrader's account (ERE. ii. 11 ff.) is ingenious, but most of his conclusions are not proven. See also Carnoy, *Les Indo-Européens*, chaps. xix and xx ; L. von Schroeder, *Arische Religion*.

6 Warde Fowler, *Religious Experience of the Roman People*, p. viii.

and Slavonic religion we are practically [1] dependent on very late sources, and in all these cases again we cannot be sure of what are the Indo-European elements. As a rule, therefore, these religions can serve merely as other non-Indo-European religions serve, as sources of comparison with a view to explaining parallel customs and usages by the operation of the same ideas: they do not enable us to conclude that an Indian usage was actually brought by the Vedic Indians with them into India as part of their own religion. In many cases this was doubtless the case, but the lack of conclusive evidence renders it necessary to admit that certainty cannot be obtained.

There are a few cases where the parallelism existing among the words used by the different Indo-European peoples gives us the right to conclude the existence of a common worship. Thus we know that the conception of the gods as heavenly is Indo-European and that there existed the figure of Dyaus Pitṛ, the Greek Zeus Pater, the Latin Jupiter: [2] the similarity of this god as concerned with the thunder with the German Donar [3] and Norse Thorr is clear: moreover his connexion with the oak as at Dodona has a plausible parallel in Jupiter feretrius, in the Lithuanian Perkúnas,[4] the Slav Perunu,[5] perhaps the Phrygian Bagaios,[6] and also among the Celts [7] and the Germans, a fact which has recently been brilliantly explained by Warde Fowler, confirming the older views of Grimm, as directly due to the observation that the lightning strikes the oak far oftener than any other European forest tree. But this very case shows how little can be won for Indian religion: Dyaus is a faint and shadowy figure in Indian mythology, and it is impossible not to remember that in Aegean religion in Greece and in Asia Minor, whose connexion with Europe in religious matters was close before the rise of any of the Aryan religions in Europe, a thunder god is a conspicuous figure.

A still more striking case of the difficulty of using comparative mythology is afforded by the cult of fire. Among the Greeks Hestia, among the Romans Vesta, though her worship has been asserted to be merely derived from Greece, and among the Lithuanians Ugnis Szventà, seem to have been the object of deep veneration as the goddess of the family hearth. Of this worship we have a parallel in India, where the fire is among other names called the household fire, and where its sanctity is great in the extreme. But the difference of sex shows that there is a long way between the two conceptions, and suggests that

[1] There are important notices of Scythian religion in Herodotos (i. 216; iv. 59, &c.), of German in Caesar (BG. vi. 21) and Tacitus's *Germania*, and of the Slavs in Procopius (iii. 14. 22 ff.).

[2] The OHG. Ziu cannot be compared with certainty; it is parallel rather with *deva*; Kretschmer, *Gesch. d. Griech. Sprache*, p. 78; Moulton, *Early Zoroastrianism*, p. 393, n.; Feist, *Kultur der Indogermanen*, p. 344. But cf. Helm, *Altgerm. Rel.* i. 270 ff.

[3] According to Feist (*op. cit.*, p. 482) a loan word from Gallic Tanaros. Contrast Helm, *op. cit.* i. 278. Cf. Rhys, *Celtic Heathendom*, pp. 57 ff. for Celtic parallels.

[4] Cf. Gray, *Myth. of All Races*, iii. 358, n. 24.

[5] Cf. Machal, *ibid.* iii. 295; von Schroeder, *Arische Religion*, i. 545 f.

[6] Von Schroeder (*op. cit.* i. 288, n. 2, 553, n. 1) insists on connecting Bagaios with Bogu.

[7] Rhys, *Celtic Heathendom*, pp. 218 ff.

the worship of fire in Indo-European times was animatist rather than anthropomorphic. Similarly, while the worship of the earth is doubtless to be found in every Indo-European form of religion, there is nothing so characteristic of that worship to enable us to ascribe to it any special feature in Indo-European times, and the union of sky and earth is a world-wide myth, which we certainly need not suppose the Indo-Europeans had to borrow from any other source.[1] The worship of sun and moon may be assumed, and is probable enough, but it was perhaps of no very great moment. The waters also were objects of worship, and the wind god is found under the same name among the Lithuanians as in India, and that people has a celestial smith parallel to Tvaṣṭṛ. There are also cases in which identity of myth is of real importance: the Nāsatya of India occur among the Mitanni gods, they are undoubtedly parallel to the Dioskouroi and to the gods of a Lettish myth,[2] and they seem to have Germanic and Celtic parallels. Again, while the etymological equation of Erinys and the Vedic Saraṇyū is open to the gravest doubt, there can be little probability in denying any connexion between the legend of Saraṇyū's wedding and her taking the shape of a mare, and the legend of the Tilphossian Erinys.[3] Herakles or Hercules is not Indra, but the myth of the setting free of the cows from the control of the Paṇis has a clear parallel in the myths regarding Geryoneus and Cacus. If the verbal identification of Çabara and Kerberos is not above suspicion, still the mythical conception is parallel, and in a different case that of Kubera and the Kabeiroi Prof. Hopkins has sought, though probably without success,[4] to prove original identity of character as well as similarity of name. Other cases in which etymological identity of name is still claimed with a possibility of accuracy, though without any certainty, include the equation of Varuṇa and Ouranos, which could both arise from Indo-European Uoruenos, the Maruts and Mars, the Ṛbhus and the Norse Alfr, German Alb, elf, and the Bhṛgus and Phlegyai. Even Prometheus, though the connexion with the late *pramantha*, ' churning stick ', has long since been abandoned, has been identified by the high, though in this case not convincing, authority of Victor Henry [5] with the Māthava who, according to the Çatapatha Brāhmaṇa [6] played a prominent part in the advance of the Indian fire cult from the western to the eastern lands, and it is certain that the legend of the theft of fire has a claim to be Indo-European.[7] In the case of Uṣas the parallelism with Eos and Aurora is wholly beyond doubt, but the actual worship of the goddess is clearly in large measure an Indian development. Vedic Druh, Avestan Druj, have parallels in Norse Draug and Old English Dreág, ' malignant spirit '.

[1] Cf. Dieterich, *Mutter Erde*, pp. 92 ff.

[2] Mannhardt, *Die lettischen Sonnenmythen*. Wide's view (*Lak. Kulte*, p. 316) to the contrary is, I think, clearly wrong; cf. Gray, *Myth. of All Races*, iii. 320 ff.

[3] Lang, *Modern Mythology*, pp. 65–8; Max Müller, *Beitr. zu einer wiss. Myth.* ii. 107 ff.

[4] JAOS. xxxiii. 55 ff.

[5] *La magie dans l'Inde antique*, p. 21.

[6] i. 4. 1. 10, 17.

[7] It is also widely diffused; cf. von Schroeder, *Arische Religion*, ii. 224 ff., 566, 586 f.

One important fact regarding the early cult is practically certain: it is expressly recorded of the Persians, the Scyths, the Romans, and the Germans, and it is clear in the case of India, that no images or temples were used in the worship of their deities: the evidence of Greek religion in this case is plainly negligible, since we have the evidence of Aegean archaeology for the representation of deities long before the Greek invasion, and the fact that Homer in the main ignores images is an indication that the Indo-European religion was not in itself primarily iconic: the image and the temple alike are associated naturally with the city state which, it is certain, was not a primitive Indo-European form of society. On the other hand the gods were often revered in groves, a development of primitive tree worship which is recorded for India, Greece, Rome, Germany, Gaul, the Lithuanians and the Slavs, but we have no proof that the practice of treating first a dead tree, and then a shaped trunk, as the abode of the god, was Indo-European: it seems to have been a development in the separate peoples. The practice of paying worship on the mountain tops, which is recorded of Italians, Persians, and Bithynians, is also a usage which must have grown up severally among those parts of the Indo-European people who dwelt in lands of mountains.[1]

The question whether the Indo-European period knew a regular priesthood, or whether the householder was still his own priest, is impossible of decision, in the absence of any identity of name in the different speeches. The identity of the Indian Brahman with the Latin Flamen is not beyond reasonable doubt,[2] but the exact force of the terms is doubtful, and in any case the possibility of separate development is considerable in the case of so partial a similarity. The origin of the priesthood has been seen in the need of confederations of clans for those to care for the worship of the guardian deity of the federation, and in the Greek Selloi of Dodona, who with unwashed feet served Zeus, has been seen such a family; the name has also been compared with the Latin Salii, but without cogency. In Roman religion we find from a very early period groups of priests, and a strong priesthood—possibly not of Indo-European origin—existed among the Celts,[3] and also among the Prussians. It is probable that Caesar [4] is wrong in denying such a priesthood to the Germans: Tacitus,[5] who was possessed of better information, records it, and that it developed in the period between the two writers is at the least not probable. The existence of an Aryan priesthood is of course certain from the

[1] Hirt, *Die Indogermanen*, pp. 513 ff.; Feist, *Kultur der Indogermanen*, pp. 353 ff.

[2] Kretschmer, *Gesch. d. Griech. Sprache*, p. 128; Feist, *op. cit.*, pp. 348, 572; contrast Carnoy, *Les Indo-Européens*, p. 236, who prefers kinship to Scandinavian *brag*; cf. Osthoff, BB. xxiv. 113.

[3] See MacCulloch, *Religion of the Ancient Celts*, pp. 293 ff.; Moulton (*Early Zoroastrianism*, pp. 88, 116) denies the Iranians a sacerdotal class, but his theory of the non-Iranian Magi cannot be accepted; Keith, JRAS. 1915, pp. 790 ff.

[4] *Bell. Gall.* vi. 21. Among the Slavs only those of the Elbe developed a priesthood, Machal, *Myth. of All Races*, iii. 305.

[5] *Germania*, 7, 10, 11, 40, 43. Cf. Helm, *Altgerm. Rel.* i. 289–91.

close coincidence of Indian and Iranian names. But the evidence is clearly insufficient to decide anything for the state of the earliest Indo-European religion.

The question of the primitive sacrifice is clearly insoluble, since among certain similarities there are great differences of view. The facts that victims were usually chosen from among edible animals, that other offerings were normally motived by some special end, as in the case of the horse sacrifice, that in choosing the victims efforts were made to assimilate the animal in sex, colour, and other characteristics to the deity, are common to most of the Indo-European peoples, but they are shared with many other peoples as well. Human sacrifices are recorded all over the world, and in some form or other among nearly all Indo-European peoples, but many different elements may have entered into these sacrifices, and any ascription of this form of religion to the early period must be purely conjectural. Offerings of cereals were doubtless made, as they are made by most peoples, but prognostication though widely attested in Europe—partly with clear indications of derivation from Babylon [1]—is much less marked in Indian religion, and its separate development in the different nations is possible, although prognostication from the flight of birds has a strong claim to be considered Indo-European.

The same negative result is obtained when the question of the employment of magic and the more humble beliefs of the people are concerned. All the Indo-European races practised magic, and curiously enough the Lithuanian and Old Slavonic preserve words precisely equivalent to the use of *kṛtyā* in India for magic : the formulae of some of the spells used have been traced in almost identic form in more than one language,[2] but these things are widespread and close parallels for magic rites can be found in the most distant parts of the earth. Similarly stories of the swan maidens and their mortal lovers occur in one form or another in all the Indo-European mythologies, but there is nothing distinctive about such tales. It is not in the slightest degree doubtful that the lesser mythology was strongly represented among the earliest peoples. The same consideration applies to the demonology : these obscure and but slightly individualized figures naturally leave no proof of their primitive identity. Nor in any strict sense can identity be postulated in such cases. These mythological figures have no history like the greater gods : they are in a sense ever new creations, and in no real way are they traditional.

There is one further point of some interest. As we may have seen, the numbers of the gods as thirty-three are Indian and Iranian, but there is no similar grouping in any other of the religions, and the 12 of Greece which is not Homeric is only copied by Rome.[3] On the other hand, in connexion both with groups of gods and with attributes of deities and cult actions the number

[1] Meyer, *Gesch. des Alt.*[3] I. ii. pp. 587, 588.

[2] Kuhn, KZ. xiii. 49 ff., 113 ff. For the numbers 70 and 73 found in India see Mahomedan parallels in Steinschneider, ZDMG. lvii. 474 ff.

[3] Wissowa, *Rel. und Kultus der Römer*[2], pp. 61 ff.

3 with its multiple 9 are found not rarely in all the religions.[1] In those of Europe the number 7 is rarely of specially sacred character until after the influence of the Christian religion had begun to be felt, or at least until the Jewish week had become familiar in the western world. On the other hand the number 7 is very often found in the Rigveda, and must be considered as distinctly a typical sacred number. It has been often suggested that this fact points to Semitic and specifically Babylonian influence,[2] but it must be noted that the week of seven days is not clearly proved for Babylonia,[3] and there is therefore no obvious reason why the number should be denied as original in India.

In addition to the material presented by other religions of peoples of kindred speech and origin to the Indo-European element in the Indian people, there is available for consideration in dealing with the phenomena of Indian religion the vast mass of information as to religions of the different peoples, civilized and uncivilized, of the earth which has been brought to light by modern research. The use of this material, however, presents great difficulties, and opens the way to serious misunderstanding, unless it is remembered that the mere similarity of practice may often be due to very different causes, and that an explanation which may be perfectly reasonable, when viewed with regard to the other phenomena of a religion as a whole, may be wholly out of place when applied to a different religious system. It follows, therefore, that any explanation of a religious rite which is out of harmony with the general aspect of Vedic religion is *ipso facto* open to grave doubt, and that an explanation in itself less plausible may deserve preference, simply because it is consonant with the general tendency of Vedic religious thought. Moreover, it is precisely in the deepest beliefs of the people and in their original conceptions of religion that uniformity must be least expected: in the minor mythology there is much in all probability in common in every religion, but on the fundamental question of the nature of the great deities, their relations

[1] Warde Fowler, *Religious Experience of the Roman People*, pp. 98, 328, 441; A. Kaegi, *Die Neunzahl bei den Ostariern* (1891); Usener, RM. lviii. 1 ff., 161 ff., 321 ff.; Diels, *Sibyllinische Blätter*, pp. 40 ff.; G. Hüsing, *Die iranische Überlieferung und das arische System* (1909).

[2] There is there, but only in the first millennium B.C., a group of 7 gods corresponding to the 7 planets: below, Part II, Chap. 8, § 2.

[3] The nearest approach to it is the fact that in certain months the 7th, 14th, 21st, and 28th were days of penance and sacred duties, perhaps based on a fourfold division of a lunar month; Zimmer, *Die Keilinschriften und das alte Testament*[3], p. 592; Jastrow, AJT. ii. 312–52; E. Schürer, ZfNTW. 1905, pp. 1–71; Reinach, *Cultes*, ii. 443–6; Hehn, *Siebenzahl und Sabbat* (Leipziger Semit. Studien, ii), but see Meyer, *Gesch. des Alt.*[3] I. ii. pp. 587, 588, who much more plausibly holds that the sacredness of seven is due to its own character; von Schroeder (*Arische Religion*, i. 426–9), following F. v. Andrian (*Mitteil. der Anthropol. Gesellschaft in Wien*, xxxi. 225–74), holds that in the Aryan period a set of nine gods was, under Babylonian influence, reduced to seven. On the Celtic nine-night week, see Rhys, *Celtic Heathendom*, pp. 360 ff. See also Güntert, *Der arische Weltkönig*, pp. 178 ff.

to their worshippers, and the form of sacrifice, there are clearly great distances between peoples, which should be recognized, not removed by efforts to trace to a common source things which are in essence different. It is undoubtedly the greatest defect of modern theories of religion that they seek a greater unity than it is possible to find and ignore fundamental discrepancies of mental organization.

Moreover one serious charge must be brought against many of the theorists, and a charge which applies equally to Mannhardt, Sir J. Fraser, Ridgeway, Durkheim, and S. Reinach. These scholars assume that in the religious views of primitive savages are to be found the beginnings of religious belief, and that from their views must be reconstructed a scheme for the development of every form of religion. The fundamental absurdity of this view is the belief that savages of the nineteenth century are primitive man: it is logically wholly impossible to deny that the defects of the religions of these races may be precisely the cause why they have failed to develop and have remained in a savage state. Doubtless to prove this view is impossible, though many of the practices of savages are obviously open to serious disadvantages economic and social; but to disprove it is still more difficult, and, in view of this fact, to set up schemes of the development of religion based on the practices of the Australian aborigines is logically inexcusable, apart altogether from the fact that our knowledge of these customs is derived from students of ethnology, who observe peoples with whom they have no tie of blood or language and whose confidence they find as hard to win as their beliefs to understand. The mere controversy which has raged over the fact whether the Australian tribes or the Zulus have the conception of a supreme benevolent deity [1] is a striking proof of the almost hopeless difficulties attending the path of those who seek to attain real understanding of the aboriginal mind.

§ 3. *The Origin of Religion*

A further error engendered by the belief in the uniformity of religious development is the theory that it is possible on empirical grounds to determine the origin of religion. The mistake is again a logical one: the origin of religion is a question of philosophy,[2] and a fundamental one, the solution of which is far from probable. The hopelessness of any decision on empiric grounds may be seen from the diametrically opposite results which can be attained by arguing from the same facts. One theory, that of animism in one of its aspects,[3]

[1] Lang, *Magic and Religion*, pp. 8 ff., 224 ff.

[2] Cf. Dieterich, *Mutter Erde*, p. 4.

[3] Animism is often used merely as equivalent to the recognition of living powers in nature; for this sense some adopt animatism, reserving animism for specific connexion with the worship of the dead and beliefs therein derived; others distinguish naturalism from both animism and manism, perhaps better spiritism. On this view naturalism (animatism) denotes the recognition of external phenomena as identical with the powers revered, animism holds that objects are ensouled, and manism (spiritism) holds that they are ensouled by spirits of the dead. Animism in the second of these senses is accepted

as expounded by Herbert Spencer, which was perhaps most interestingly developed by Hugo Elard Meyer, and which in recent times has found a most determined supporter in Prof. Ridgeway and S. Eitrem,[1] holds that all religion originates in the honour and respect shown to the spirits of the dead : from this belief and respect for these spirits is easily derived the view that there are potent spirits in natural phenomena, whence develops nature worship. It is, on the other hand, asserted with equal insistence that, while no doubt honour is paid to the spirits of the dead and this source has been a fruitful one in the development of religion, none the less religion is more than that and springs from a direct recognition in nature of powers akin to but superior to those of men.[2] Such a view can arise prior to any clear discrimination of spirit and body : that view is later in development and more reflective : prior perhaps to animism, and in any case independent of it, there is in fact a stage preanimistic or animatistic or naturalistic, when man conceives of natural objects as living powers, not as objects filled with souls *ab extra*.[3] Logically [4] the second view appears in itself the more plausible, but it is obvious that the reconstruction is purely hypothetical, and admits of no proof. We do not know of any religion existing at any time of which we could certainly and convincingly affirm that an idea of the deity had been framed when a knowledge of the difference between body and spirit was not known,[5] and Dr. Marett's own treatment [6] of religion as including the whole field of the supernormal is so vague as to be of no positive value, a criticism equally applicable to Mr. Clodd's [7] conception of power, or rather many powers, as the basis of nature and spirit worship alike.

It is clearly erroneous to ascribe to primitive religion the conception of *mana* as something universal of which part is possessed by the objects of his worship. Rather matter is sentient and has mentality, the whole forming a unity, not a spirit abiding in something not spiritual, and each object has a specific power of its own. In this as in other cases progress must be from the concrete and individual to the formulation of the universal, from individual

for Egyptian religion by W. Max Müller, *Egypt. Mythology*, pp. 10, 15 ff. In the view adopted in this work animatism and spiritism are accepted as sources of religion, animism is regarded as a secondary development. The wider use of animism to denote indwelling power is defended by Alexander, *Myth. of All Races*, x. 269.

1 *Opferritus und Voropfer der Griechen und Römer* (1915); cf. Keith, JHS. xxxvi. 107 ff.

2 Cf. Lang, *Modern Mythology*, pp. xi ff.; *Anthropological Essays presented to E. B. Tylor*, p. 10; Helm, *Altgerm. Rel.* i. 13 ff.; Hopkins, *Origin of Religion*, chap. i.

3 Marett, *Threshold of Religion*, pp. 1–32; Ridgeway's criticism (*Dramas and Dramatic Dances*, pp. 47 ff.) is in part merely captious and irrelevant. Feist (*Kultur der Indogermanen*, pp. 322, 334, 344) still seems to hold Tylor's view that the process is from regarding a spirit as animating a tree to the worship of the tree (e. g.) *per se* and so with the sun. This is clearly open to grave objection.

4 Cf. Keith, JRAS. 1916, pp. 335, 336.

5 Cf. Marett, *Threshold of Religion*, p. x.

6 *Op. cit.*, pp. 138 ff.

7 *Trans. Third Int. Cong. Hist. Rel.* i. 33–5. Cf. the neo-vitalist theory of R. Dussaud, *Introduction à l'histoire des religions* (1914).

powers to the belief in one power, *mana, manitou, brahman,* or whatever other name it bears, through sharing in which the individual objects possess their force.[1]

From these sources, naturalism and spiritism, it is easy to imagine the development of the spirits or demons whom Wundt [2] classifies in five groups. Thus we have ghosts or spooks, which have no connexion with any special object, and which, therefore, have a close resemblance to the spirits of the dead; not unlike in character, though of quite different origin, are those which express the tricky or sometimes terrifying aspects of nature, abiding in the house, the air, the waters, the forest or the waste, elves or cobolds, dwarfs or giants. There are also vegetation spirits, the simplest being those animating the individual tree or plant, while in more complex cases we have spirits of the wood or the corn field or more vaguely of the life of vegetation as a whole; sometimes these spirits may be derived from souls of the dead, as the spirit which ensouls the plant growing from the grave of the dead, but more often they are nature spirits proper. Further there are spirits of heaven, of the air, the clouds, the waters, and the earth, the external vegetation demons of Wundt,[3] who emphasises by this name their relation to the growth of the crops. Akin to spirits of vegetation regarded as a whole, we have spirits entrusted with the care of whole fields of activity; spirits of the hunt, of seafaring, housebuilding, commerce and industry, war, marriage, government and law. Lastly there is the vast group of spirits of disease and madness, whose origin may be traced in part to spirits of nature and in part to the souls of the dead, and even more often to the creative imagination which extends indefinitely the number of such spirits.

With external vegetation demons in Wundt's sense and the spirits which preside over departments of activity, we attain something approaching gods, and, bearing in mind the fact that the souls of the dead are not fettered by connexion with any definite aspect of nature, it is possible to believe that the idea of a god not merely as superhuman but also as supermundane could develop itself easily. A definite theory of this process is evolved by Usener,[4] who postulates as the first stage momentary gods (Augensblickgötter), spirits which preside over any specific activity in the moment it takes place, and which, therefore, are real only for that moment and for him who then invokes their aid. The next stage is when, in lieu of these momentary deities, man

[1] Van Gennep (*L'état actuel du problème totémique*, pp. 47 f., 86 ff., 321) defends the universal aspect of *mana* as primitive, but, though his view is valid as against Ridgeway's effort (*Dramas and Dramatic Dances*, pp. 385 f.) to show that *mana* is later than spirit worship, it does not meet the obvious objection that so wide a conception cannot be treated as primitive. The conception is the basis of Indian philosophy, though it is primarily not philosophic, but popular, as among the North American Indians; Alexander, *Myth. of All Races*, x. 269.

[2] *Völkerpsychologie*, IV. i. 457 ff.; Helm, *Altgerm. Rel.* i. 30 ff.

[3] *Ibid.* 515 ff.

[4] *Griechische Götternamen*, pp. 75 ff., 279 ff. Cf. Carnoy, *Les Indo-Européens*, pp. 216–18.

advances to the conception of a single deity presiding over all similar activities, a Sondergott of sowing in general, for instance; deities of this kind are asserted to exist in Greek, Roman, and Lithuanian religion. The final step to give a god personality and permit him to be developed thus in myth, cult, poetry, and art is furnished by language; if the progress of phonetic change, or the disuse of a root in ordinary speech, leaves the proper appellation of the Sondergott isolated and no longer readily intelligible, then he can easily assume a wider character than can ever be his as long as his name betrays his real nature. So in India Dyaus never developed a real personality comparable to Zeus or Jupiter, because the word remained in living use to denote the sky in India, while it died out in Greek and Latin; hence also the reason why the names of gods are so often difficult to interpret etymologically.

Usener's views are not wholly convincing; his momentary gods [1] are not established by any historical evidence of value, and can only be regarded as a possible, but not necessary, stage of imagination. His Sondergötter are more real, and some gods of this type may be traced in Vedic religion.[2] But he certainly much exaggerated the value of his evidence which has been severely criticized for Greek, Roman, and Lithuanian religion by Farnell,[3] Wissowa,[4] and Warde Fowler [5] among others. It is in fact plain that the elaboration of the Sondergötter often represents the priestly working up of simpler ideas, and that they are later developments of naturalism under the influence of animism, and not really primitive. Nor can the argument from names be treated as of decisive importance; in fact the disuse of a word may often rather be because it had become a divine name and, therefore, was too sacred for indiscriminate ordinary use. Allowance in the development of personality must be made for several other factors, the cult certainly in high measure. Wundt [6] again insists on the importance of the hero as suggesting the development of the personal god, though he clearly exaggerates the importance of this factor. The practice of making images of the deity, which is in part an outcome of personification, at the same time must have aided in the development of that feature. Importance also must be attached to the influence of ethical considerations, though precisely how these operated is by no means easy to decide.

While many authorities are content to hold that in the interworking of these two forces, nature- and spirit-worship, there may be found the explanation of the origin of religion, others, conspicuous among whom is von Schroeder,[7] urge that a further source is essential, and that its existence is supported by an impartial examination of the account of observers of the

[1] Cf. Wundt, *op. cit.* IV. i. 560 f.

[2] Below, Part II, Chap. 11, § 3.

[3] *Anthropological Essays presented to E. B. Tylor*, pp. 81 ff.; *Greek Hero Cults*, pp. 78 ff.

[4] *Gesam. Abhand.*, pp. 306 ff.

[5] *Religious Experience of the Roman People*, pp. 158 ff. For an attempt, not specially successful, to resuscitate the view of Sondergötter, see Rose, JRS. iii. 233–41.

[6] *Op. cit.* II. iii. 420 ff.

[7] *Arische Religion*, i. 81 ff., 106 ff., 139 ff. See also below, p. 51.

religions of primitive tribes. This source is the belief in a highest being whose nature is goodness ; the Australian tribes, the Andaman islanders, the savages of the Tierra del Fuego, among others, are held to believe in such a being, whose commands are the moral principles which they obey. In other cases this belief has become faint and blurred, but it reveals itself in the ordeal which is an appeal to the decision of such a power. In some cases the belief in this deity pictures him as creator of the world and of men. Religion involves essentially the recognition of the existence of such a being, of man's dependence on him, and the desire to enter into relations with him. The conception is obviously not primitive ; it is due to reflection by man on the fact of the self-sacrificing instinct which is seen among animals in the love for offspring and which manifests itself in an increasing number of ways with the advance of man. The existence of this impulse can be explained by man only on the theory that there must be one whose will it is that men should so act, a view which easily is added to by the conception of that one as the creator. When, whether after a long period or possibly comparatively early through the effort of a specially gifted intellect, this idea came into being, it may be said that man was truly born as man, religion truly came into being and with it morality. Inevitably, of course, this conception blends with the other two sources of religion ; thus in India Rudra, in von Schroeder's view a spirit in origin, assumes both the features of a god of nature and of the high god ; similarly Viṣṇu, a god of nature, assumes the characteristics of the high god and of a spirit.

Von Schroeder strengthens his case by his care not to attempt to claim for his source of religion as great antiquity as for the others, and it is clear that he emphasizes an extremely important element in religion, its connexion with ethical principles. Apart from questions of origins, it is plain that by the Indo-Iranian period, and very probably even in the Indo-European period, this element had come effectively into operation as powerfully affecting the nature of the gods, so that it is a question of minor importance, for practical purposes, whether we assume this belief as a third source of religion or hold that ethical motives have been introduced *ab extra* into a religious scheme which came into life independent of ethics. What is clear is that many of the gods have no original ethical character, and fear often seems to have been more prominent than love or friendship as regards the spirits of the dead.

An instance of generalization on insufficient grounds is afforded by S. Reinach's [1] theory of totemism : he insists that the traces of the reverence paid to animals is always to be accounted for in one simple way : at one time the animal was the god : men revered animals by an excess of philan-

[1] *Cultes, Mythes et Religions*, i. 47 ff. On totemism see A. van Gennep, *L'état actuel du problème totémique* (1920) ; Hopkins, JAOS. xxxviii. 145–58 ; Frazer, *Totemism and Exogamy* (1910) ; Reuterskiöld, *Archiv für Rel.* xv. 1–23 ; Goldenweiser, *Journ. of Am. Folklore*, 1910, pp. 179 ff. ; Wundt, *op. cit.* IV. i. 327 ff.

thropy, by a hypertrophy of the same instinct which made human society a possibility : but at stated intervals the animal god was devoured in order to renew the tie of blood between the clan and the animal, which was then replaced by another specimen of the species, the god being the species, not the mere individual. To this feeling of man for the animal he attributes the domestication of wild animals and the greatest possible help to the progress of civilization. In later times, as the process of religious development proceeded, the animal gods faded away and appeared as animals in the train of anthropomorphic deities, or enemies of these deities. There is some obscurity in the conception of the mode of the introduction of anthropomorphism, which in Greece [1] at least Reinach seems to regard as a new element introduced from without the original religion, but the real objection to the theory is that it ignores many other possibilities explaining reverence paid to animals. The hunter who pays a semblance of reverence to the animal which he has killed does so often to avoid the anger of the spirit of the dead beast, and the revenge of the relatives of the slain, and no sacramental relation is involved. Again there is an essential distinction to be drawn between theriomorphism and actual worship of animals for themselves. The early religious imagination, it is clear, was not capable of the distinctions between human and animal which we draw so sharply : the innumerable legends of the transmutation of men into animals and *vice versa* show a certain instability of view, and a god like Indra or like Dionysos may be conceived as bull shaped, as well as in human or mixed form. Closely allied with this thought is the conception that the god may take actual embodiment in the form of the animal, more especially when the animal is led up to be offered to him in sacrifice : the classical example of the Bouphonia,[2] the flight of the priest, and the condemnation of the weapon with which the fatal blow is given to the ox can thus best be explained. For the time being, and in a certain sense, the victim may be said to become a fetish, and like a fetish it is an object filled with the holy power, but not abidingly, and, what is more important, not in and for itself sacred. There is at least as little difficulty in understanding this aspect of religious belief as in accepting the theory that totemism is a universal stage of religious faith.

A like one-sidedness mars the theories of Mannhardt and of Sir J. Frazer regarding the nature of sacrifice, which the latter in the most clear terms reduces to a magic device to prolong the life of the crops, men, and animals. From this position Sir J. Frazer [3] has advanced to the definite assertion that

[1] So for Egypt, Wiedemann, *Der Tierkult der alten Aegypter* (1912).

[2] Frazer, *Spirits of the Corn*, ii. 4–7 ; Farnell, *Cults of the Greek States*, i. 88 ff. ; cf., however, Stengel, *Opferbräuche der Griechen*, pp. 203–21 ; van Gennep, *op. cit.*, pp. 307 ff.

[3] *The Golden Bough*[3] (1911–15). See Keith, JHS. xxxv. 281–4. Warde Fowler, who insists on the distinction of religion and magic, nevertheless appears to believe that magic precedes religion in order of time (*Religious Experience of the Roman People*, pp. 47–9, 188, 223, 224). See also N. N. Law, *Ancient Indian Polity*, chap. ix. For a criticism of Wundt's belief in the original magic character of the sacrifice (*op. cit.* IV. i. 423 ff.) see R. M. Meyer, *Altgerm. Rel.*, p. 408.

all religion is derived from magic: that in the first instance the primitive savage conceives of himself as all powerful over the course of nature, and that he wields the means of magic to bring about the results he desires, but that in the long run, finding that his magic arts do not prevail to accomplish all his desires, he has instead recourse to the belief in unseen beings in whom abide the powers which he is denied, and of which he confesses himself barren, and seeks to win the favour of these beings by offerings and prayer, though continuing of course at the same time the practice of his old magic devices. Apart from objections to the attempt to reduce sacrifice to one primitive type alone, and to prove that the gift theory of sacrifice is late, the theory of the priority of magic rests upon the fundamental assumption that primitive man believes in his power to control by his arts the whole proceedings of the universe. It is difficult to conceive how such an idea can be deemed primitive, or how it could have developed in the mind of primitive man, whose experience from the first must have sternly checked any such high belief in the powers of mortal efforts. Magic and religion are to all appearance in essence distinct and irreconcilable things, as different in essence as science and religion as a philosophy, and the fact that they are inextricably conjoined in practically every religious system known to us does not in the slightest degree prove their identity, or render probable the derivation of one from the other.

Yet another view of the same false generalization is that of O. Gruppe,[1] which would make the whole of the theology of religion later than the cult and derive all myth from cult: thus in India the fire and Soma ritual would be the starting-point for the Vedic mythology, an idea which receives some support from the views of Bergaigne. The theory hardly admits of serious discussion when stated as a general rule. There are indeed, especially in Greek religion, not a few cases where the cult, for instance that of Dionysos, has begotten myths such as the death of Pentheus,[2] and the same principle may certainly be allowed to be applicable in India, but to go further than that is to leave all proof and probability behind.[3] The myths of the Rigveda in particular are usually simple and direct enough, and reflect too clearly the actual phenomena of nature to allow us to imagine that they have any other origin than the expression by man of the ideas which naturally occur to him from the observation of such things as the daily movement of the sun or the bursting of the monsoon with all that it means for Indian life.[4] To the worship of the gods the cult stands of course in the closest relation, but normally it takes in India the form of prayer or sacrifice in order to win the favour of the god: only when we leave worship proper and come to magic do we as a rule find a mimicry of the mythic action of the deity.

[1] *Griech. Myth.*, pp. 547 ff.

[2] Bather, JHS. xiv. 244 ff. Cf. Rohde, *Psyche*[3], i. 137 ff. on the Hyakinthos myth.

[3] Myths created by misunderstandings of pictorial representations which are not rare in Greece and Rome are excluded in Vedic religion by its aniconic character.

[4] Helm, *Altgerm. Rel.* i. 56 f. See also Lang, *Myth, Ritual, and Religion* (1906); Fox, *Greek and Roman Myth.*, pp. xliv ff.

Another aspect of the same view is to be seen in the theory of totemism presented by Durkheim,[1] who lays stress on the part played in religion by the tribal consciousness, and sees in the god the creation of that consciousness as a hypostasis of itself, the object chosen to render the conception present to the senses being often, but not necessarily always, an animal. He declares that animism or animatism cannot explain religion, but it is wholly impossible to concede to his arguments against either theory conclusive weight, while his own expression for the fundamental character of religion is obviously wholly incapable of proof, being purely a psychological theory, which has no strong support other than the postulate, which he never attempts to prove, that the mind of the Australian aborigine is the mind of a really primitive man.[2] He rejects the theories of totemism adduced by other scholars such as Tylor, Hill Tout, and Andrew Lang, but in no case are his own arguments convincing or even in the main plausible, nor can it be said that any real explanation of totemism is to be derived from them.

Yet another view of religion is that taken by Gilbert Murray,[3] who finds the first deity in the medicine man himself, a theory which obviously stands in very sharp contrast, though apparently its author does not recognize the fact, with the view of Durkheim. The medicine man with his control over the fertility of the earth and his other superhuman powers is held gradually to abandon his claims to deity, and to invent other gods whose agent and spokesman he is. But if the earliest deity is human there is an easy road for theriomorphic conceptions to creep in : men are prone to devour animals for the sake of securing their power or cunning or some other quality, and in some undefined way this passes into the belief in theriomorphic and even animal gods : the dance of the tribesmen wearing the skin of the animal slain developes the goat-formed deity and so on.[4] These speculations are acute and ingenious, but serious discussion they can hardly demand. The growth of a god from a magician, or from a rite, as the origin of religion, is a wholly superficial and unnatural conception : vegetation ritual cannot be said to create the conception of the dying and reviving god : the ritual rests on the conception of the death of the god and is inconceivable without the belief in a vegetation spirit, a conception for which Murray with Miss Harrison would substitute the monstrosity of an Eniautos Daimon, a view which yields the

[1] *Elementary Forms of Religious Life* (1915). Cf. J. E. Harrison, *Epilegomena to the Study of Greek Religion* (1921), chap. i.

[2] For a very different view of Australian beliefs as the result of race mixture see Rivers, *Essays and Studies presented to W. Ridgeway*, pp. 480 ff., and see van Gennep, *L'état actuel du problème totémique*, pp. 40 ff. Cf. Dixon, *Myth. of All Races*, ix. pp. xiii f.

[3] *Anthropology and the Classics*, pp. 74 ff. ; *Four Stages of Greek Religion*, pp. 39 ff. Contrast P. Ehrenreich, *Zeitschrift für Ethnologie*, xxxviii. 536 ff.

[4] The 'projection' theory of religion is carried to its logical conclusions in a most amusing, because serious, work by Miss J. Harrison, *Themis* (1912). The author has a personal animus against the Olympians as non-matriarchal, and now interprets religion in terms of sociological epistemology.

logical result that Here is found to be a old year spirit, her name being equated with the word ' year.' [1]

Certainly no more satisfactory is the belief that gods are sprung from kings or other famous and distinguished men, apart from any connexion with magic. This doctrine has always been a favourite one in connexion with Indian religion, a theory based on hasty generalizations from observation of modern instances, masquerading under the semblance of an unprejudiced study of Indian nature. The absurdity of interpreting Vedic religion of the period 1400 to 1000 B.C. by the light of investigation of the modern Hindu, separated by great differences in blood and tradition, would seem self-evident, and it is to be regretted that we have serious suggestions [2] made to prove the historical character of Indra as a great king, and even to localize his exploits, and not even the suggestion of primitive Euhemerists of India excuses the attempt [3] to discover two ancient kings in the Açvins, a view which is ludicrous in face of the widespread recognition of similar dual divinities, a fact which shows that their worship, whatever its exact cause, cannot be put down to the suppositious existence of two specially distinguished princes. The theory wholly omits to explain why these persons should be described in terms of solar or storm mythology, or why in many parts of the earth savages are found worshipping natural phenomena so frankly as to render belief in the phenomena being really dead men ludicrous. It is somewhat unfortunate that we should have escaped from the theory of Herbert Spencer which makes the Vedic Dawn-Goddess the ' ghost of a former Miss Dawn ' into one which makes a warrior king out of so naturalistic a god as Indra, and which, if it is consistent, ought to find in Uṣas a degeneration from the worship of some distinguished Vedic hetaira, seeing that her nature in the Rigveda suggests a distinct lack of Puritanism. On this issue the opinion of Hopkins [4] is clear and fundamentally correct : ' No one who reads the Rig-Veda impartially can question for a moment that Fire and Dawn and Wind were phenomenal gods from the beginning and a wider outlook only confirms this fact.'

An important practical result follows from the refusal to adopt as final and exclusive any of these theories of religion. It becomes impossible to adapt an order of exposition based on the different age of the religious phenomena presented, as for instance is done by Dr. Warde Fowler in his valuable exposition of Roman religion, in which he starts from survivals of the primitive magic, in which he sees the first expression of the relation of man to the mystery of the universe, and then proceeds to discuss the development of that attitude through the religion of the settled life of the agricultural family, and the faith of the city state, to its later development under Greek influence. Attractive as this method of procedure at first appears, it is perfectly clear

[1] Leaf, *Homer and History*, p. 266 *n.*

[2] Konow, *The Aryan Gods of the Mitani People* (1921).

[3] BSOS. III. i. 167 f.

[4] *Origin of Religion*, pp. 51 f. Cf. also N. N. Law, *Ancient Indian Polity*, pp. 112 ff.

that it cannot be justified as a scientific mode of exposition. The difficulty appears clearly when the figure of Jupiter comes under discussion. It is impossible for Dr. Warde Fowler to question the fact that he is a great god, a sky god, and a god who was not developed by the Roman people independently: indeed Dr. Fowler shows some disposition [1] to favour the view of Lang,[2] Jevons,[3] and others who accept the primitive belief of many peoples in one great god, which is anterior to polytheism, and which is often held to be the origin of Chinese religion.[4] But he never tries to connect this view with his other principle of the priority of magic to religion, nor to explain how the two ideas stand in relation to one another. It is, therefore, only possible in dealing with religion to indicate the diverse elements involved in it, and to trace the development of these several elements and their interaction and intermingling. To derive one element from the other is a task too difficult, too speculative, and ultimately too philosophical to be dealt with in the account of any individual faith, while to base on such theories the order of development of any individual religion is only misleading.

§ 4. *The Mingling of Races and Cultures*

Modern views of the religion of Indo-European peoples are strongly influenced by recognition of the fact that race mixture must be assumed to have been an important factor in the development of the religions of the historic peoples such as the Greeks and the Romans. The view that Greek religion is a real representative of a primitive Indo-European religion has been necessarily abandoned, when it is realized that the lands occupied by the Greeks were already the scene of a great and energetic civilization, which cannot be supposed to have left no trace in the beliefs of the invaders, apart altogether from the fact that the physical type of the invaders may have been seriously modified by the intermixture. Similarly, just as the religion of the Homeric poems has been treated as belonging to a small invading aristocracy, so the religion of Rome as revealed to us in the Calendar of Numa in its sanity and moderation has been held to be the work of invaders superimposing a higher faith on the lower form of belief which existed formerly, a view which Dr. Warde Fowler now inclines to favour,[5] urging in support the fact that we find a curious contrast between the orderly and decorous Parentalia as a festival of the dead in February and the Lemuria in May, which seems to have been a somewhat savage rite of the banning of ghosts. The latter he deems to

[1] *Op. cit.*, p. 142.

[2] *Making of Religion*, p. 206. Contrast C. H. Toy, JAOS. xxiii. 29–37.

[3] *Idea of God in Early Religions*, p. 30.

[4] Ross, *Original Religion of China*, pp. 128 ff.; cf. ERE. v. 395 (Japan); Petrie, *Religion of Egypt*, ch. i; Carnoy, *Les Indo-Européens*, pp. 163 ff.; L. von Schroeder, VOJ. xix. 1 ff.; P. W. Schmidt, *Der Ursprung der Gottesidee* (1912); above, p. 45. For North America see Alexander, *Myth. of All Races*, x. 271 f.

[5] *Religious Experience of the Roman People*, pp. viii, 393. For Greece, see Lang, *The World of Homer* (1910). Cf., for the Celts, Rhys, *Celtic Heathendom*, pp. 105 f.

have belonged to the primitive population, and to have been taken over by the framers of the Calendar of Numa in the desire to restrict the rite within due limits, and so to diminish the disorderly character of the more ancient belief which was too deeply rooted in the popular mind to be ignored entirely. Nor, of course, is there any doubt that mixture of religious beliefs has often taken place: recently a very ingenious theory[1] of the complication of early Australian religion has been put forward, based on the view that the religion of these people has been influenced by small bodies of invaders, who have visited the land from time to time but have failed to establish themselves or introduce in a lasting way a higher culture.

But, while in principle the theory of the effect of race mixture as producing religious phenomena is perfectly valid, it is of the utmost difficulty to make effective use of it in any examination of an actual religion. Prof. Ridgeway has laid stress on the failure of students of Vedic religion to emphasize the distinction between the faith of the invader as revealed in the Rigveda, and that of the aborigine as revealed in the Atharvaveda. A similar theory of the effect of the aboriginal population on the Aryan invaders has been in the development of the Sanskrit language: it has been urged that the development of Prākritic speeches is due entirely to the inability of the conquered population to reproduce precisely the speech of the invaders.[2] The theory in both cases is tempting, but the logical difficulties of applying it effectively are very great. In the first place we have no standard of comparison by which we can discriminate between the higher and lower elements in religion: what appears to us to be higher is and must be determined by our conceptions of religion, and as conceptions of religion vary as much to-day as ever, it is impossible for us confidently to hold that one form was higher than another. If, in the second place, we take the religion of Homer and set it up as a standard of true Indo-European religion, we are obviously making a completely unproved assumption, and one which can be rendered doubtful by reference to the poems themselves, which here and there contain hints of the lower side of religion, and more primitive beliefs, which can only purely arbitrarily be assigned to the subject population. Further difficulties manifest themselves, when it is sought to find out what was the racial character of this subject population: in the case of Rome, Prof. Ridgeway sees the Ligures,[3] but Dr. Binder a Latin people,[4] and the Latins cannot be denied the right to rank as Indo-Europeans. Similarly in the case of Greece: it is quite impossible to believe that the Achaeans were the first Indo-Europeans to enter Greece: the Ionians and many other tribes were doubtless there before them,[5] and there must therefore have been mixture of race and religion before the Achaeans.

Difficulties are also presented by the theory of Prof. Murray which admits

[1] Rivers, *Essays and Studies presented to W. Ridgeway*, p. 480. Cf. his *History of Melanesian Society* (1914), ii. 357 ff.

[2] Petersen, JAOS. xxxii. 414 ff. Cf. Keith, *Cambridge Hist. of India*, i. 109.

[3] *Who were the Romans?* (Proceedings of British Academy, 1908–9.)

[4] *Die Plebs.*

[5] Kretschmer, *Glotta*, i. 9 ff.; Farnell, *Cults of the Greek States*, iv. 155 ff.

that the Achaeans at one time were the possessors of an inferior form of religion, so that there is no question of the introduction of a high type of Indo-European religion, but that, in the course of their journeys from the north to Greece, they had laid aside much of this primitive barbarism. But, once we admit that they at one time were addicted to this lower religion, it becomes very difficult to distinguish between the remnants of this former state which they brought with them, and the results of contact with the same primitive religion in an unchanged condition. The problem is rendered more easy for Prof. Murray in that he accepts the view that the Homeric poems were made refined and freed from the primitive beliefs which they at one time evinced by deliberate remodelling in the sixth century B.C. and subsequently, but this wild theory can hardly be taken seriously.

Again, much reliance has been put on the mode of disposal of the dead as a sign of change of belief and of race. But, though it is often regarded as obvious that a change from burial to burning must accompany a new view of the dead, it is quite impossible to prove anything of the kind : neither the theory that changes of culture denote change of race, nor the view that change of culture has nothing to do with change of race, though both have distinguished exponents, has any real validity as a general proposition.[1] There is, however, much primitive evidence that burial and burning were means of disposing of the dead adopted by peoples without change of culture or recorded change of belief : thus the primitive neolithic tribes of Britain both buried and burned their dead, as did also the tribes of Tasmania, and the Romans in those periods of which we have records. Moreover it is probable that burial was always regarded as the normal and more primitive way : at least the fact that in the Rigveda burial seems to be contemplated as quite normal, and that in the later ritual, when burning was normal for all save sages and children under two years of age, it was considered proper to bury the bones left from the burning, stands in curious accord with the rule in Rome by which the burial of one bone was normal despite the burning of the body. The evidence in fact leaves the impression that it is quite impossible to treat burial and burning of the dead as marks of racial distinction : indeed it is not even possible to treat the two modes as indicating a different view of the position of the dead in every case : the Rigveda treats the two principles as one, and it has been argued that the same meaning must be seen even in Greek religion, where the distinction of burning and burial has been generally held to be fundamental as indicating change of race and religious belief alike.[2]

[1] Cf. Dieterich, *Mutter Erde*, p. 66. Helm (*Altgerm. Rel.* i. 153 ff.) insists that in Germany the change, manifesting an increasing fear of the proximity of the dead, is due to foreign influence ; he rejects Babylon as the ultimate source (with Ed. Meyer, *Zeitschrift für Ethnol.*, 1905, p. 296) against von Schroeder (*Arische Religion*, i. 260).

[2] Lawson, *Modern Greek Folklore and Ancient Greek Religion*, chaps. v and vi ; Fowler, *Religious Experience of the Roman People*, pp. 400, 401 ; Keith, JRAS. 1912, pp. 470–4 ; Meyer, *Gesch. des Alt.*[3] I. ii. pp. 827, 863, 864, 893 ; Hopkins, *Origin of Religion*, pp. 148 ff.

In the case of India we have further to face, as in that of Greece, but even more markedly, the absence of an early information as to the religion of the non-Aryan tribes. It is, of course, true that we may observe, and use observations earlier recorded of, the usages of the primitive tribes of India, but it would be absurd to claim that these represent the state attained by the non-Aryans [1] at the moment and the places where the Aryans came into contact with them. The material remains antedating the Hellenic invasions of Greece which shed a scanty light, pending the interpretation of the accompanying records, on pre-Hellenic religion are wanting in India, and the literary evidence of Dravidian religion comes far too late to enable us to state precisely what that religion was before the Aryans imprinted indelibly their influence on all higher religion in India. Whatever amount of Dravidian influence is to be traced on the religion of the Vedic texts,[2] it is certain that the epic already cannot be regarded as representing pure Aryan religion, and that indeed Dravidian influence may have been of great importance. By the epic period also we must make allowance, however, vaguely and uncertainly for the religious influences introduced by the hordes of invaders, Greek, Parthian, and Çaka from the north-west and still more perhaps for the contact of cultures, while in the Vedic period we are confronted with problems of Babylonian influence exercised either directly on India or on the Indo-Iranians, the possibilities of which have been largely increased by the discovery of Aryan deities in the records of the Mitanni.

The difficulty of decision as pre-Aryan or to foreign influences in any concrete case are admirably illustrated by the controversy as to the development of the Upaniṣad philosophy which has variously been claimed as the finest expression of the true Aryan spirit, and as fundamentally non-Aryan and in essence Dravidian.[3] The controversy cannot be decided by any form of argument, for the simple reason that we have no external evidence of the true Aryan spirit, on the one hand, nor of the Dravidian prior to the date of the early Upaniṣads. Similarly we do not and cannot know definitely whether the use of idols was gradually introduced into Indian religion by borrowing from the Dravidians, or whether the ideas of asceticism, of caste, of transmigration came from them, or in what degree, for instance, Rudra was a Dravidian god. On these subjects speculation is possible, but it is necessary to recognize that

[1] Presumably a Dravidian or Muṇḍā speech. If they were totemists, which is uncertain (it is denied for the Todas by W. H. R. Rivers (*The Todas*, pp. 140 ff.) and for the Nāgas by T. C. Hodson, *The Naga Tribes of Manipur*, pp. 70 ff.), then they certainly did not seriously effect the Indo-Aryans in this regard.

[2] Possibly the motive of fear as that of worship was made more prominent by this means: at any rate fear is apparently a dominant motive in modern India; Martin, *The Gods of India*, pp. 282 ff. Arbman (*Rudra*, p. 140) assumes, without proof, that we are to find very primitive ideas in Vedic religion, forgetting how far from primitive the Aryans were.

[3] Cf. G. W. Brown, *Studies in honor of Bloomfield*, pp. 75 ff.

beyond speculation in the great majority of cases we cannot possibly proceed, and the same remark applies to most of the efforts to trace Babylonian influences on Indian religion.

§ 5. *Popular and Hieratic Religion*

Nothing is more difficult than to determine in what measure the Vedic religion of the texts was really popular, and how far it merely represented the views of the priests. It would, of course, be folly to depreciate the value of knowledge of the latter, for it is to those only who deeply busy themselves with religion that, for good or bad, changes in popular views are ultimately due, and there is no valid reason to suppose that in the main the gulf between the religion of the Vedic priest and the Aryan people was greater than that between modern Churchmen and the ordinary citizen of the lower social orders.

It is doubtless tempting [1] to draw the lines between priests and populace as widely as possible, and to regard the Vedic priests as excogitating rituals with little regard for popular views, converting popular rites to suit themselves as far as practicable, and leaving others unnoticed or barely mentioned. For this view there is, of course, some justification ; in the details of the great Çrauta sacrifice and in the conception of the piling of the fire altar, as expressed at least in the Çatapatha Brāhmaṇa, we find priestly elaboration and priestly thought. But on the other hand investigation shows us essentially popular rites in much of the Vedic sacrifice, embellished by the priests but real and living ; the Rājasūya, the Vājapeya, the Mahāvrata, are no mystic rites but homely ceremonies, largely magical in character and easily comprehensible by the participators.[2]

The danger of seeking to minimize the connexion between priests and people is seen in the suggestion that the gods of the domestic ritual, who are in large measure those of the Çrauta sacrifices, are figures imposed by the priests on popular usage, for it leads to the doctrine that Brahman had not the slightest popular hold, a suggestion irreconcilable with the prominence given to that deity in the Buddhist scriptures. Similarly an artificial origin is attributed to the nature spirits and abstract hypostases which appear very freely in the domestic ritual. Yet comparative religion suggests at once that these are far from priestly inventions, that they belong rather to the type of Sondergötter,[3] who are genuinely popular figures, even if in the texts we have we can trace priestly elaboration. So again we cannot with any security assert that the fire as the means of sacrifice is a sign of priestly intervention, as opposed to the simpler Bali sacrifice in which the object offered is deposited on the ground or thrown into the air or hung on a tree. Fire, we must remember, is itself a deity, and the suggestion that it was so only to the priests is contrary to the ethnic fact of primitive fire worship. Thus offerings in the fire for it were

[1] Arbman, *Rudra*, pp. 64 ff.

[2] See below, Chap. 20, §§ 13, 14, 18, 20.

[3] See below, Chap. 5, § 1 (*c*) ; Chap. 12, § 5.

natural and primitive, and we can hardly assert that the giving to the gods of offerings in the fire was not a simple development even for the popular mind.

Other points of distinction between the priestly and the popular faith are equally difficult to determine. That the priests insisted on an aniconic worship while the people made offerings to idols is certainly unproved, and implausible. That the people rejoiced in bloody offerings while the priests objected to them contradicts the whole ritual of the animal offering, even if the blood of the victim is usually assigned to the Rakṣases to appease them, for this seems in Indian ritual the general use of the blood. The priests recognize the importance of women only in certain rites, namely those affecting marriage and agriculture ; but there is no distinction here between hieratic and popular views, for primitive peoples recognize in these fields the special importance of women, and we see that as often the priests were in full harmony with popular views.

More certain are other points of divergence. The priests do not like phallus worshippers,[1] but this is probably rather a distinction between Aryan and non-Aryan views than between hieratic and popular, and, while they recognize, they seem unenthusiastic regarding the mad Muni [2] who drinks poison—presumably some drug—from the same cup as Rudra. In this case, however, we have rather the opposition of one esoteric view to another, that of the sacrificial priests against the Yogin.

The priests, in fact, instead of standing apart from ordinary life and developing their own views in indifference to those of the people, appear to have aimed, as time went on, at absorbing *en masse* the popular rites and decking them out with their own poetry and their ritual elaboration.[3] If at one time they devoted themselves to certain cults only, they repaired this error in working up the whole field of domestic rites and magic, and it was by this fact that, preluding the process which has created Hinduism, they secured the firm hold on the people which enabled Brahmanism to defy the assaults of Buddhism and Jainism, neither of which ever succeeded in substituting anything effective for the ritual of the simple things of life, which was carried out by or under the directions of the priest. So far from the texts hinting at distaste for the popular ritual, they rather exhibit the priests determined to secure their participation in it to the fullest extent, at the expense of the field of action which at first lay open to the head of the family as his own domestic priest. If we are to understand aright the development of the Vedic priesthood we must think of the elaboration in certain families little by little of some outstanding sacrifices, especially that of Soma, and then the application of the new sacerdotalism to the religion of everyday life. Doubtless the application was not wholly complete ; it is quite possible that the popular religion made

[1] RV. vii. 21. 5 ; x. 99. 3.

[2] RV. x. 136 ; cf. below, Chap. 22, § 9.

[3] Cf. e. g. the working up of the Traiyambakahoma, where such details as the hanging of offerings on a tree are faithfully kept, and in it and the Bauḍhyavihāra the use of leaves in lieu of ladles is a relic of old usage.

more of tree worship than appears in our rituals, but it is by no means ignored. The truly popular nature of the ritual is seen in the case of agricultural offerings of which many are prescribed. Curiously enough a completely inaccurate view of these is taken by Arbman,[1] on the score of a failure to recognize the importance of the celestial deities in primitive religion. The ritual [2] provides an offering of the old Bali type to sky and earth at the eastern boundary of the field when the plough is being spanned. It is plainly absurd to assert that it is not to be assumed that this ancient divine pair had played any role in popular religion. No more natural deities can be imagined than the pair for a people which had advanced to the period of regular agriculture and separate fields, and it certainly did not require the priests to teach the peasant to what deities he should make offering. Similarly when it is desired to change the current of a stream an offering is made both in the fire and in the Bali form to Varuṇa; [3] no more obvious god can be imagined, and, however far back we might seek to trace a rite of this sort, we would expect to find that sacrifice would be made to the lord of waters. Even when against pests which would injure crops we find Bali offerings [4] to Āçā, 'hope,' Āçāpati, 'the lord of hope', Kṣetrapati and the Açvins, we should gravely err in setting the choice of deities down to the priests. The Açvins, as the legends show, were clearly the great popular helping gods, Kṣetrapati is the actual deity of the field to be protected, and, if Āçā and Āçāpati seem to us at first sight the work of the priests, we have only to remember that, apart from Greek and Roman religion, we have the Sondergötter of the Lithuanians, a people not dominated by priestly influence.[5] Even in the case where rites are evidently or probably performed to deities different from those who primarily received them, we must exercise caution in ascribing even the change of deity, and still more the rite itself to priestly invention. The priests, we may be assured, were not required always to intervene to induce the peasant to regard a great god such as Rudra-Çiva, Viṣṇu, or even Brahman, as the recipient of an offering originally made to some minor and less personalized spirit.[6]

[1] *Rudra*, p. 139, n. 1. Contrast Hillebrandt, *Ved. Myth.*, pp. 7 ff., who justly cites the evidence of Tylor (*Primitive Culture*, chap. viii), Brinton (*Religions of Primitive Peoples*, pp. 137 ff.), &c.

[2] ÇGS. iv. 13. 2.

[3] Kauç. xl. 7–9.

[4] Kauç. li. 21 f.

[5] Usener, *Griechische Götternamen*, pp. 279 ff.

[6] As in the funeral rite of the Vaikhānasa Sūtra (Caland, *Die altind. Todten- und Bestattungsgebräuche*, p. 26.)

PART II. THE GODS AND DEMONS OF THE VEDA

CHAPTER 5

THE NATURE OF THE GODS AND DEMONS

§ 1. *Nature Gods and Abstract Deities*

(*a*) Anthropomorphism

Already in the period of Indo-European unity there had in all probability arisen the conception of anthropomorphic deities of the sky, such as Dyaus, Mitra, or the Açvins, and it is therefore only natural that in the main the high gods of the Rigveda should be essentially conceived as human, as men of supernatural power, and free from death, but still as subject to birth and akin in their family relation to men. But, though it would be wrong to ignore the anthropomorphic [1] character of the gods, the Vedic pantheon has none of the clear cut figures of the Greek, and unlike the Greek deities it is seldom difficult to doubt that the anthropomorphic forms but faintly veil phenomena of nature. The difference is so striking that it is impossible to ascribe it to a mere difference between the records of the two religions, the secular and romantic poetry of Homer on the one hand, and the formal hymns used in the sacrifice of the Rigveda on the other. It is most probable that much of the vagueness of the physical nature of the Greek gods and goddesses is due to their origin either from direct borrowing from the Aegean people of Greece, or from contamination with Aegean deities.[2] In the process of amalgamation of beliefs it is scarcely surprising that the outlines of the characters of the gods should have been hopelessly blurred in comparison with the much clearer and more transparent figures of the Vedic hymns.

The degree of anthropomorphism exhibited by the Vedic deities is extremely variable. In some cases the active element is constantly present, and the view taken may be set down as almost animatistic : the waters are indeed goddesses, but they are also wholesome to drink ; the goddess Dawn

[1] Arbman's theory (*Rudra*, pp. 4 ff.) that the popular religion had far more fully personalized gods is clearly untenable, and contradicts all that we know of primitive religion. What is true is that the Vedic texts show both imperfect anthropomorphism and contamination of deities.

[2] Cf. Hall, PSBA. xxxi. 164 ff. ; Evans, JHS. xxi. 161 ff. See also Farnell, *Greece and Babylon*, pp. 72 ff. for Hellenic anthropomorphism. Cf. Cook, *Zeus*, i. 9 ff. ; Helm, *Altgerm. Rel.* i. 186 f., 194 ff. ; Fox, *Greek and Roman Mythology*, p. xlviii ; MacCulloch, *Celtic Mythology*, pp. 132 f.

bares her bosom like a beautiful maiden, but there is comparison here rather than identity, and, if in some cases the goddess seems to be considered as one who appears morn after morn to men, in others each separate dawn is a fresh divinity. Sūrya, the sun, by his rising is born as the child of the sky; the constant presence of the actual deity prevents any real development of anthropomorphism. The same consideration affects Agni, who never appears as a god disconnected from his element of fire: when he is hidden in the waters or in the clouds, it is as fire: as messenger of men he is the fire of the sacrifice flaming up to heaven to bring gods and men together. But the difficulties of this view were clearly felt in connexion with the question of the innumerable fires of earth and their relation to the god. Strictly speaking he must be present in each, and this view is often taken, but there appears also the conception that in some degree the god is free from the element and able to come to it, not merely to be manifested in it when it is produced. The evidence for this view is, however, it is important to note, late: in the Rigveda it is only suggested by the doubtful [1] phrase in a late hymn, in which Agni when enkindled at the sacrifice is said to sit down as priest coming to his own home, a conception based on the idea of the relation of the spirit of man to the spirit world to which he fares on death. In the ceremony of the piling of the fire altar, when the flame is lighted, Agni is invoked in the Yajurveda [2] to come from the furthest distance, and it is possible that in the ritual,[3] when at the kindling of the fire a horse is brought up to the place of kindling, it is due to the desire to induce Agni through his presence in his symbol to draw near to and enter the element which has been kindled. The contrast with the figure of Agni in later literature such as the epic is marked: in the epic the gods have long ceased to be nearly as closely connected with their natural bases as in the Rigveda, and Agni can figure as the main personage in tales which never had any relation to the fire as an element.

Indra, on the other hand, is a god who has in considerable measure [4] been emancipated from his connexion with the phenomena which produced the conception, primarily in all probability the thunderstorm, which brings down the rain to earth, one of the greatest of India's natural phenomena. It is possible enough that this freedom from strict connexion with nature is due to the difference of the elemental conception: the sun, the dawn, the waters, and fire are things ever seen, and the names bring back to the poet at once their essential character, but in the case of Indra the meaning of his appellation was as obscure to the Vedic poet as it is to us. Moreover, the fierce nature of Indra made him suited to be the war god of the conquering Aryans, and afforded thus a point of departure permitting of the development of other than nature myths. A similar contrast is seen in Germany between the character of

[1] RV. x. 12. 1; Oldenberg, *Rel. des Veda*[2], p. 44 (but see p. 529, n. 2).

[2] Weber, *Ind. Stud.* xiii. 227.

[3] ÇB. ii. 1. 4. 17.

[4] Cf., e. g., Rhys, *Celtic Heathendom*, p. 293, who thinks he might be deemed a deified man, a type of culture hero.

the sun and the storm god. The same consideration applies in even stronger degree to Mitra and Varuṇa: the identity of Mitra with the sun is strongly supported, but, whereas the personality of Sūrya remains, like that of the Greek Helios, of the most shadowy character, and Sūrya is always the material sun, Mitra even in the Avesta is far from chained to his natural basis: he comes into view over the mountain of sunrise, it is said, before the sun, and in the Rigveda his connexion with the sun can only be made certain by the parallelism of the Avesta, where he has distinct solar features: like Varuṇa he is a celestial god who watches over men and stirs them with his speech to activity, while he supports heaven and earth. Varuṇa is even more free from traces of nature, so that it remains yet doubtful whether that nature was really as is most probable the sky: his essential feature has nothing necessarily connected with his natural background: he is the lord of holy order, the watcher of men, whose vigilance nothing can escape. The Açvins also have lost any clear trace of their origin in nature: whatever that was, they are two radiant youths who travel in their chariot across the sky, and above all bring aid to men in trouble. The older school of mythology felt bound to seek for and find the natural background to all the myths of the Açvins:[1] the effort was doubtless futile, for, when once the gods attained, by whatever means and from whatever cause, the character of saviours of men, any cultural development and any feat of man in which he deemed himself preserved by divine guidance and assistance could be ascribed to the gods. Thus there could be developed myths which in no conceivable way were ever nature myths; there are also myths of origins, philosophical and allegorical myths, and myths of the hereafter, while again many nature myths are transformed by a poetic fancy, which has but little connexion with the original groundwork. The waters as we have seen are goddesses who do not free themselves from the element, but there exist figures which have been set free, the Apsarases: in the Rigveda[2] we find that they can be treated exactly like the waters and invoked to mix with the Soma, but their normal aspect is that of water maidens, who can freely leave their element and unite with mortal men, showing traits which render them the sisters of the Germanic swan maidens, and similar figures in many other religions. In these love adventures, it would surely be useless to find nature mythology. Soma again in the Rigveda and later is never fully anthropomorphic, though in the Avesta he appears to the priest in the form of a man of extreme beauty, but an interesting myth of the Rigveda[3] recounts the bringing down of Soma from the sky to Indra: the bird which bears down the drink is detected by the archer Kṛçānu who guards the Soma, and who shoots an arrow at it, failing to kill it but knocking off a feather: in this episode it is clearly an error to seek to explain mythically the item of the shot of the archer: we have, introduced from ordinary life, a natural and simple

[1] See, e. g., Max Müller (*Beitr. zu einer wiss. Myth.* ii. 150 ff.) on the legend of the quail (*vartikā*) saved from the wolf.

[2] ix. 78. 3.

[3] iv. 26 and 27.

motive.[1] Such intermixture of extraneous conceptions is specially frequent in connexion with sacrificial rites : when the god Rudra appears as a great dark man to Nābhānediṣṭha at the place of sacrifice, and demands as his share all that is left over from the offering to other gods, which has just been performed,[2] it is perfectly clear that we are dealing with a free invention of the priestly fancy.

One further function of the mythical faculty is of importance in regard to the nature gods. It was a natural conception which transferred to heaven the relations of men, and set beside each god a goddess to be his wife, even as on earth each Indian had one wife or more to share his home. The naïve simplicity [3] of the practice, which may have been helped by the prevailing conception of the sky as father, and earth as mother, reveals itself in the characteristic manner in which the names of the goddesses of this class are formed, being derived directly from their husbands' names by the use of a feminine termination. Indrāṇī, for example, the wife of Indra, has no myth of nature to explain her existence : she is quite different in this regard from the goddess Dawn, who is a natural phenomenon. The creation of such types led to further developments in myth, undermining natural mythology. One of the most obscure hymns of the Rigveda [4] tells us of a dispute between Indra and Indrāṇī over a being styled Vṛṣākapi, ' male ape ' ; to seek in it a naturalistic interpretation is rendered from the outset almost hopeless when we recognize that the chief figure in the dispute, the angry Indrāṇī, is clearly not a nature personification in any sense. It must, however, be admitted that this field of myth was little exploited in the literature left to us : it is also of interest to note that the pale figure of Dione, beside Zeus, suggests that the process which produced Indrāṇī and her fellows was already in working in the Indo-European period.[5]

(*b*) Theriomorphism and the Worship of Animals

While most of the Vedic nature deities are normally conceived as anthropomorphic, there did not prevail any rigid exclusion of theriomorphic conceptions of the deities. It is often asserted, even by Oldenberg,[6] that in earlier periods of religion theriomorphic conceptions were more frequent than anthropomorphic, but the proof for such a theory seems to be wholly lacking.

[1] Bloomfield, JAOS. xvi. 1–24.

[2] AB. v. 14.

[3] It is vastly more developed in the epic ; Hopkins, *Epic Myth.*, pp. 61 ff.

[4] RV. x. 86 ; von Bradke, ZDMG. xlvi. 465 ; Bloomfield, *ibid.* xlviii. 541 ff. ; Geldner, *Ved. Stud.* ii. 109 ; Winternitz, VOJ. xxiii. 137 ; Keith, JRAS. 1911, p. 1005 ; Hillebrandt, *Ved. Myth.* iii. 278, n. 2 ; Charpentier, *Die Suparṇasage*, pp. 100–2 ; Oldenberg, *Rel. des Veda*², pp. 166 ff.

[5] Kretschmer, *Gesch. der griech. Sprache*, p. 91. Cf. perhaps Freyr and Freyja, Fjörgynn and Fjörgyn.

[6] *Rel. des Veda*², pp. 39, 67. Cf. Helm, *Altgerm. Rel.* i. 202 ff., who also insists (p. 18) that the primitive apperception sees the soul in a beast form before a human form, following the views of Wundt (*Elemente der Völkerpsychologie*, pp. 173 ff.); for a good criticism, see van Gennep, *L'état actuel du problème totémique*, pp. 99 ff.

That the storm god should be conceived in human form appears to be as natural and as primitive as that he should be ascribed an animal form, unless indeed we are to be asked to believe that religious conceptions of animal gods were formed before the development of man as such. Apart, however, from theories such as these, there can be no question of the predominance of anthropomorphism in the Rigveda, while at the same time theriomorphism is not unknown, a condition which accords well with the observed fact that the distinction of man and beast is never drawn by early peoples with the definite precision of modern feeling. Two deities are recorded for us in animal form only, the one-footed goat, Aja Ekapād, and the serpent of the deep, Ahi Budhnya : it is not likely that either is in origin an animal deity : the one-footed goat may be the lightning flash that descends to earth in a single streak : the serpent has clear mythological meaning in its application to Vṛtra, the demon who is defeated by Indra, and who holds back the waters of the clouds which are desired. The mother of the Maruts, gods of the storm wind, is called the dappled cow, which deems to have been felt as a description of the clouds whence sprang the rain. The Ādityas themselves, sons of Aditi, herself either a personification of freedom, or an abstraction derived from their name, are also cow-born, reflecting perhaps—not probably—a conception of the birth of the luminaries from a celestial cow.[1] The sacrificial food is personified as early in the Rigveda as a lady with hands full of butter, but she is also styled a cow, and in the ritual [2] the cow is addressed with the words, ‘ Come, o Iḍā, o Aditi.’ Agni is often conceived of as a horse, and Indra as a bull. The clouds when the rain is brought down are normally and usually styled the cows. Saraṇyū according to an old tradition becomes a mare and in that condition brings forth the two Açvins.

Animals also figure in the entourage of the gods, and in this case it is only fair to allow for the natural tendency to assimilate gods to men and to give them animal followers. The goddess Saramā, who in dog shape finds for Indra the cows, and who has been explained as a wind-spirit, parallel to Hermes,[3] need not be assumed to be more than a copy of the ordinary facts of life on earth. The horses of the gods are likewise transferred from the human to the divine sphere. In other cases, however, it is quite possible to suspect that there lies beneath an animal as companion of the god a trace of the god himself. The eagle brings the Soma down to Indra, but already in the Rigveda there is a variant form of the myth which indicates that the Soma was obtained by Indra in the form of an eagle,[4] and, if we interpret the myth in the form of the bringing down to earth of the generous moisture by the action of the thunder

[1] Cf. AV. viii. 9. 1, where the two calves of Virāj may be sun and moon, children of dawn.

[2] Bergaigne, *Rel. Véd.* i. 325.

[3] Cf. Oertel, *Stud. zur vergl. Lit.* viii (1908), 124.

[4] RV. x. 99. 8 ; Bloomfield, JAOS. xvi. 8 ; Kuhn, *Herabkunft des Feuers*, p. 144. The view that the bird is Viṣṇu (Johannson, *Solfågeln i Indien*, p. 21 ; Charpentier, *Die Suparṇasage*, pp. 324 ff.) is less plausible. Sometimes the Soma is the eagle.

storm and the descent of the rain amid lightning, it becomes tempting to assume that the eagle was none other throughout than the god Indra. Pūṣan, again, has a team of goats, but we find that in the Rigveda he is a knower of paths, while at the horse sacrifice a goat is killed to precede the horse, as it seems, to the world of death:[1] a goat too is slaughtered at the ceremony of the burning of the dead:[2] hence it is a conjecture not without plausibility that the goat was a form of Pūṣan, as the sure-footed animal which could wander with safety over distant and difficult ways. The Açvins, again, are horsemen as their name denotes, and they are never described as actual horses: yet their mother according to an old, though not Rigvedic, tradition,[3] is a mare, and it is a legitimate hypothesis, though one wholly incapable of proof, that once they were conceived as in horse shape as well as in human shape; in yet other religions they may have been conceived as in the shape of birds. In the case of Indra and the eagle some confirmation is lent by the Bahram Yašt[4] of the Avesta in which we learn of Verethraghna flying to Zoroaster in the form of the bird Vāraghna, swiftest of all birds. But these cases of theriomorphism must be sharply distinguished from those of the birds of omen, which are styled messengers of the Fathers or of Yama:[5] the birds themselves were, we need not doubt, quasi-deities in their own right before they were reduced to the rank of messengers, and we need not suppose that their position as givers of omens is due to their being regarded as embodiments of souls of the dead.[6] The horse Açvins, if they ever existed, were not divine horses, but theriomorphic conceptions of nature powers.[7]

In comparison with the normal anthropomorphic conceptions of the deity and the less frequent theriomorphic, there are comparatively few instances in Vedic worship of the direct and wholly animatistic[8] veneration of natural objects. The most obvious is the cult of the snakes, which is not, however, Rigvedic, but probably borrowed from the aboriginal population, and occasional propitiation of ants, moles, &c.

(*c*) Animatism Sondergötter and Abstract Deities

Beside the concrete figures of the great nature gods with their extended spheres of action, there stand deities with definitely limited functions, though also nature powers. Of such deities we have good examples in the Kṣetrasya Pati and Vāstoṣpati, who appear in the Rigveda itself. These are, of course,

[1] RV. i. 162. 2–4.
[2] RV. x. 16. 4.
[3] RV. x. 17. 2 as rendered by Sāyaṇa with Yāska, Nir. xii. 10. Cf. Lanman, *Sanskrit Reader*, p. 381; Weber, *Ind. Stud.* xvii. 310; Oldenberg, *Ṛgveda-Noten*, ii. 217; Bloomfield, JAOS. xv. 185.
[4] Cf. Carnoy, *Iranian Mythology*, pp. 272 ff.
[5] RV. ii. 42. 2; x. 165; AV. vi. 27–9; xi. 2. 2, 11; TA. iv. 28; Kauç. cxxix; cf. the jackal, HGS. i. 16. 19.
[6] See Arbman, *Rudra*, pp. 255 ff.
[7] See Farnell's protest against prevalent errors as to animal forms (*Greece and Babylon*, pp. 55 ff., 70 ff.; *Greek Hero Cults*, pp. 177, 214, 215).
[8] Marett, *Threshold of Religion*, pp. 15, 16, 20; Goblet d'Alviella, *Croyances*, ii. 120.

no abstract deities; they are, the one, the spirit who dwells in the field, the other, the spirit who has his abode in the house, and neither conception can be asserted with any plausibility to be later than the period of the growth of belief in the great gods. More concrete still are such cases as Sītā, the furrow, and Urvarā, the field. It is significant of the great development of personification later that in the Rāmāyaṇa Sītā is predominantly a mortal woman, wife of Rāma, and daughter of Janaka. Traces, indeed, remain of her former divinity, for the legend tells that hers was no normal birth, but she sprang to life from the furrow when her father was ploughing, and, at the end, when she determines by a conclusive proof to show to Rāma and his court that her purity had suffered nothing at the hands of Rāvaṇa during her enforced abode in the palace of her captor, her prayer to the goddess Earth is answered by the appearance of the deity, who takes her into her bosom.[1] Not essentially different from these instances are the prayers addressed and the reverence paid by the warrior to his weapons, the chariot, the arrow, and the drum, by the ploughman to the ploughshare, and by the dicer to his dice. Plants and trees are sometimes conceived in this way, but, as all over the world, tree spirits, like water nymphs, tend to become less closely connected with their material embodiment and to pass over into anthropomorphic form.

We find also deities of very limited activity, who serve but one definite purpose. Thus in the Atharvaveda[2] the spirit Uttuda is invoked to stir up a damsel to love, while even in the Rigveda[3] it is possible that Nivartana is felt as a divine power which moves the cows when departed to return to their place. These instances correspond closely with the Sondergötter[4] of Usener evidenced by the Indigitamenta in Rome, and the Lithuanian spirits presiding over all sorts of departments of nature and human activity. It is argued by Usener that the great nature deities are derived from such special deities, and doubtless there is no difficulty on conceiving the growth of such divinities to a more important status. The claim, however, of general derivation is clearly untenable. There is much more force in the view which sees in these Sondergötter a distinct mental attitude from that involved in the case of the worship of the great gods. The latter impress themselves on the mind of the worshipper, commanding his respect and fear; the former correspond with the development of the animistic conception of everything in the world as animated by a spirit, but not necessarily a source of reverence, though from time to time an activity may be desired to operate to serve one's end, and for that purpose temporary reverence may be requisite.[5] The worship of the sun or the storm is *prima facie* likely to be older than respect paid to Vāstoṣpati or Kṣetrasya Pati, deities who imply settled life and agri-

[1] Cf. H. Jacobi, *Das Rāmāyaṇa*, p. 130; Hopkins, *Epic Myth.*, p. 12.

[2] iii. 25. 1.

[3] x. 19. 8.

[4] Cf. Servius, *Aen.* ii. 141: pontifices dicunt singulis actibus proprios deos praeesse; hos Varro certos deos appellat; Usener, *Götternamen*; Schrader, *Reallexicon der idg. Alt.* 679 f.

[5] See e.g. Carnoy, *Les Indo-Européens*, p. 207.

culture, and still less can Uttuda or Nivartana claim superior antiquity. It is, therefore, probably better to recognize that the worship of the sun and of these Sondergötter ultimately rests on the basis of animatism, regarded as that attitude [1] which 'endows [what we now consider] inanimate and material objects with quasi-human consciousness and emotions, and sometimes with a superhuman power and volition which suggest worship', and which passes over to animism. On that view it is natural to hold that worship was first given to the great phenomena, and only by a later process of more abstract thought was it accorded to such entities as Uttuda or Nivartana.

A further development of this attitude of mind gives us gods who have no immediate concrete background of any kind, comparable to such abstract deities as Fides, which form an important and interesting part of Roman religion and have recently received careful investigation from Axtell [2] among others. To call them abstract is perhaps misleading: it is not to be supposed that in the period of their creation they were felt to be other than real powers. It is possible that the creation of such figures goes back to Indo-Iranian times, for the goddess Puraṁdhi, 'plenteousness', is paralleled by Pārendi in the Avesta.[3] Such conceptions are found already in the Rigveda in such shapes as Wrath and Speech. Here too must be reckoned such figures as the gods Savitṛ, Dhātṛ, Trātṛ and Tvaṣṭṛ, whose names all denote them as agent gods, who impel, create, protect, and produce. The connexion of Savitṛ with the sun is fairly close, and is preserved from the earliest times in the repetition of the Sāvitrī verse,[4] when in the morning the orthodox Indian householder salutes the rising sun with the words: 'That desirable glory of the god Savitṛ we meditate, that he may inspire our thoughts.' It is at least possible, therefore, that in its origin Savitṛ was not an independent creation, but was an epithet of Sūrya, but that question is of little importance: the essential feature of the god is not his original basis, but his function as the inspirer or impeller to holy sacrifice: the ritual act is repeatedly said in the Yajurveda to be done 'on the instigation of the god Savitṛ'. To this stage of the creative imagination belongs also the conception of such gods as Prajāpati, the lord of all creatures, who is the great creator god, and who cannot be assigned to any natural basis. Perhaps too here must be reckoned the figure of Bṛhaspati [5] or Brahmaṇaspati, 'the lord of prayer'. The prayer with its magic potency or its effective appeal—the two ideas pass into each other in the later Rigveda —and the priest who wields this powerful instrument are blended in the

[1] See Farnell, *Greek Hero Cults*, p. 79.

[2] *The Deification of Abstract Ideas in Roman Literature and Inscriptions* (1907). See also Warde Fowler, *Religious Experience of the Roman People*, pp. 285, 291, 450, 451.

[3] Aramati and Ārmaiti are a parallel case, unless both originally had reference to earth; *contra*, Carnoy, JAOS. xxxvi. 309, where Aramati is only piety; cf. *Muséon* (n.s.), xiii. 133, n. 1, against Sāyaṇa, RV. vii. 36. 8; viii. 42. 3; Moulton, *Early Zoroastrianism*, p. 10.

[4] RV. iii. 62. 10. Cf. the epic goddess Sāvitrī; Hopkins, *Epic Myth.*, p. 86.

[5] *bṛh* is clearly an older form of *brahman*; see Oldenberg, *Die Lehre der Upanishaden*, p. 46, n. 1.

conception of the lord of prayer. Nor to this theory is it any conclusive objection that the god is credited in the Rigveda with abundant activity which seems to rest on nature myths, in particular the cleaving of the caves in the mountains and the setting free of the cows, a story which is usually deemed to be a myth of the setting free of the dawns from the darkness of the storm. It is possible that, as it is the prayer which is potent to induce Indra to perform his great feats of strength, so the prayer comes to be ranked with him in its hypostatized form as Bṛhaspati and even to take his place. The most likely alternative view is to conceive that the name is an epithet of Agni, and that the conception was then developed independently of Agni's natural basis by the priest : this is a perfectly conceivable idea, but in either case the essential feature is the fact that the natural basis, if any, is not the source of the mythology.

§ 2. *Fetishism*

The worship of natural objects, whether celestial, ethereal or terrestrial, is sharply to be distinguished from the reverence paid to earthly objects or animals, not as in themselves normally or continually divine, but because for a certain purpose and in certain conditions they are deemed to be filled with the divine spirit.[1] It is clear, however obvious the distinction is as a matter of theory, that in many cases it must be extremely difficult to distinguish the two phenomena. A simple example of the difficulty is afforded by the contrast which seems to exist between the reverence paid by the priest to his offering implements, such as the pressing stones and the offering post, and that paid by the warrior to his weapons. In both cases the reverence is that paid to the work of human hands, but it can hardly be held in the case of the warrior that his weapons are conceived as being filled by any external spirit for the time being : rather they have, though made by human hands, when made, a life and reality of their own, which renders it right on special occasions that they should receive due honour and veneration. For the whole time of their existence as such, before they are destroyed by the event of war or abandoned as outworn, they retain this character of their own. On the other hand, the reverence paid to the pressing stones and other implements of the sacrifice seems far more naturally to be attributed to the holy character of the sacrificial ground and of the surroundings through the presence of the god. The sacred strew on which the god is invited to take his seat and all the implements must surely be filled with the divine afflatus for the period of the offering. The offering post in the animal sacrifice is solemnly anointed, and surrounded with a girdle which acts in some measure as clothing. It has

[1] This is perhaps the most useful sense of the term fetishism, which sometimes is applied to what is here called animatism. See C. de Brosses, *Du culte des dieux fétiches* (Paris, 1760) ; Bastian, *Über Fetischismus* (1894); de Visser, *Die nichtmenschengestaltigen Götter der Griechen* (1903) ; Haddon, *Magic and Fetishism* (1906) ; R. M. Meyer, *Archiv für Rel.*, xi. 320 ff. ; Hopkins, *Hist. of Rel.*, pp. 35 f.

been suggested that in this action we are to see the bodily presence of the god, as in the case of the Semitic Ašera on one interpretation, and in the alternative Oldenberg [1] suggests that the treatment of the post is a relic of tree worship. Neither explanation is absolutely necessary; we need not suppose that the post was originally placed there for any other than its clear purpose to hold the sacrificial victim fast for sacrifice, but once there it was impossible that it should not be in some degree filled with the divine spirit, apart from its divine connexion with the tree spirit.

In other cases the purely temporary nature of the divine character of the fetish is quite obvious. Thus in the household ritual, during the nights after marriage in which the newly wedded pair are bidden to observe chastity, there is placed between them a staff clad in a garment and made fragrant, which is traditionally asserted to be the Gandharva Viçvāvasu, and the tradition is confirmed by the fact that the ritual prescribes for the taking away of the staff a formula addressed to that spirit.[2] Another fetish is the wheel which represents the sun: [3] in the Vājapeya sacrifice a wheel-shaped cake of grain is placed on the top of the post, to which the animal victim is tied: a ladder is brought: the sacrificer mounts upon it saying to his wife: 'Come, let us two mount to the sun.' He then mounts and seizes the wheel, saying, 'We have attained the sun, O gods.'[4] At the Mahāvrata festival of the winter solstice an Aryan and a Çūdra strove over a white round skin, which is stated to be a symbol of the sun: the Aryan conquers and strikes down the Çūdra with the skin.[5] There can be no doubt of the solar nature of the wheel, and the existence of this sun symbol among the Celts and the Germans suggests that possibly the symbolism may be Indo-European. A torch can also serve to represent the sun; if the offerer has forgotten to perform a libation before sunset, he can perform it to the light of a torch which brings back the light, or he can use gold in place of the sun.[6] This motive is of constant occurrence: in the piling of the fire altar a gold plate is set down to be an image of the sun.[7] Agni, as fire, is closely connected with gold: it is forbidden to study the Veda in a place where there is neither fire nor gold: gold is the seed of Agni, and in the piling of the fire altar [8] there is placed in the erection the gold figure of a man, who seems to be intended to represent Agni: while butter is poured over the figure, prayers are offered to Agni, and that fire is latent in the figure is shown by the warning to the priests not to pass before it, lest it consume them

[1] *Rel. des Veda*², pp. 87, 88. For fetishes in Greece and Babylon see Farnell, *Greece and Babylon*, pp. 225 ff. For religious vessels as fetishes in Rome in the worship of the Dea Dia, see Warde Fowler, *Religious Experience of the Roman People*, pp. 436, 489, 490. Helm (*Altgerm. Rel.* i. 20 ff.) insists on magic potencies as essential elements of fetishism.

[2] Winternitz, *Altind. Hochzeitsrituell*, p. 88.

[3] For Germany see Helm, *op. cit.* i. 173 ff.; for the Celts, Gaidoz, *Études sur la mythologie gauloise* (1886).

[4] Weber, *Ueber den Vājapeya*, pp. 20, 34.

[5] Keith, *Çāṅkhāyana Āraṇyaka*, pp. 80 ff.; von Schroeder, *Arische Religion*, ii. 17, 38, 66 f.

[6] ÇB. xii. 4. 4. 6.

[7] ÇB. vii. 4. 1. 10.

[8] Weber, *Ind. Stud.* xiii. 228 ff.

with fire. A similar rule forbids the priest to carry the Soma before the altars allotted to each priest, as they are the symbols of the guardians of the Soma, and would therefore be inclined to take the Soma away from the priests that were bearing it.[1] In the case of the Pravargya ceremony, milk is made hot for the Açvins in a great jar, the Mahāvīra, ' great hero ', pot : according to one authority the pot was given some semblance of a human face, and it is difficult to doubt that this pot was intended as a symbol of the sun.[2] Equally symbolic would be its use if we were to accept a suggestion made with all circumspection by Oldenberg [3] that we may have here a trace of the myth of the cutting off of the head of Makha, who is a demon of quite unknown nature, by Indra, and the drinking of milk from this ghastly relic, just as it seems from the body of Namuci, a demon with which Makha may have had associations, sweetness is said to have come.

Other examples of this fetishism can easily be cited, but in comparison with them a passage in the Rigveda [4] stands in a certain isolation of character. It is there said by a poet : 'Who will buy this my Indra for ten cows ? When he hath conquered his foe, let him return it to me ! ' This passage can have but one sense : some fetish of Indra must be meant, whether a rough anthropomorphic picture or merely something much ruder we cannot say : the latter view has, however, the greater probability, in that statues of deities are otherwise not hinted at until the end of the Vedic period,[5] when they may have been introduced under Western influences. It is characteristic that the god who is the hero of this episode is the warrior god, Indra : no other deity of first-rate importance in the Rigveda is treated habitually with such lightness of spirit [6] as he is, and the fact that he is dealt with in this commercial spirit reminds us that already in this age there were men who questioned the existence of the god Indra, perhaps because, unlike deities such as the Sun or Dawn, he was not to be discerned by the naked eye day by day.

Animals, too, later at least, served as living fetishes : of this, the instances, though not numerous, are singularly clear. At the Sākamedhas sacrifice, in an offering to Indra a bull was invoked : when it bellowed the offering was made ; [7] the meaning is made plain beyond doubt not only by the fact that Indra is elsewhere called a bull, that in the Atharvaveda [8] a bull is addressed with the words ' Men call thee Indra ', and that Verethraghna, the Avestan parallel to Indra, has a bull form, but by the express assertion of the Brāhmaṇa [9] that in the rite Indra is thus invoked to come to slay Vṛtra, and the bellowing of the bull establishes clearly the fact that the god has come with satisfaction

[1] Hillebrandt, *Ved. Myth.* i. 443 ff.

[2] Eggeling, SBE. xliv. pp. xlvi ff. ; Hillebrandt, *Ved. Myth.*, p. 11, n. 2.

[3] *Rel. des Veda*[1], p. 89.

[4] iv. 24. 10.

[5] The suggestion that the female figure on a gold leaf found in a Lauriyā Nandangarh tumulus is a presentation of Pṛthivī of the eighth century B. C. (CHI. i. 616) is wholly unproved and implausible.

[6] Cf. the list of his misdeeds, Oertel, JAOS. xix. 118 f.

[7] Weber, *Ind. Stud.* x. 341.

[8] ix. 4. 9.

[9] ÇB. ii. 5. 3. 18.

to receive the offering proffered to him by the sacrificer. Another sacrifice, recorded for us only in the Gṛhya ritual, the Çūlagava, shows us water and food offered to a bull, a cow, and a calf, the two former of which are each placed in a hut: when they have touched the offerings, the latter are offered to Rudra, his consort, and the victorious one.[1]

The horse plays a considerable part in this capacity, especially in connexion with the sun, which is compared to, and described as, a white horse, and fire. At the Ṣoḍaçin form of the Soma sacrifice when the chant at sunset is being performed, not only is gold held in the hands of the priest, but a horse, either white or black, is to be present,[2] clearly to represent the sun, and, in the case of the colour being black, to represent the setting of the sun. In the piling of the fire[3] the bricks of the fire altar are put in place in the presence of a horse, which is made to breathe over them; Agni thus in person superintending the making of the altar, which is specifically his own. Even more striking is the participation of the horse in the action of selecting the clay for the making of the fire-pan: to the place where the clay is to be found, the horse, with a goat and an ass, is taken: the place where the horse sets down its foot is chosen as the precise spot from which the clay is to be brought. The verses addressed to the horse before and after the process are addressed to Agni, and the goat is also treated in precisely the same way. Further some hairs are cut from the goat and mixed with the clay with the words, 'I mix thee herein, the well-born Jātavedas.' The verses are conclusive, but the Brāhmaṇa is equally decided: it is recognized that the essence of the action is to bring the nature of Agni into the closest connexion with the fire-pan. The ass is not so treated, but is used merely as a beast of burden in the rite, and we cannot fairly assume that it was felt to be or ever was a fetish: it may, however, have been present for a magic purpose, the giving of virility to the performance as a whole and thence to the performers, but this suggestion cannot be pressed.

The horse appears also as representative of Agni in the ceremony of kindling the fire from the firesticks,[4] a task of considerable trouble: during its performance, a horse, preferably white, but, if not, then red with black knees, looks on to encourage the advent of the flame: when the fire is kindled, a horse precedes it eastwards, and in its footsteps is the fire deposited. At a certain point in the rite the priest speaks in the horse's ear, asking it to bring forth that essence of Agni's nature, which is latent in cattle. In this case also the goat may play a part: the goat is often connected closely with Agni, and may be used to watch the production of the fire in the place of the horse. Or, if it is found impossible to produce the fire from the sticks, it is permissible to make an offering in the ear of a goat: then the offerer must refrain from goat

[1] HGS. ii. 8; Arbman (*Rudra*, pp. 110 ff.) wrongly accepts Haradatta's erroneous assumption of idols. See also BhGS. ii. 8. Cf. Keith, JRAS. 1907, p. 937; Hillebrandt, *Ved. Myth.*, p. 172.

[2] TS. vi. 6. 11. 6.

[3] Weber, *Ind. Stud.* xiii. 220 ff.

[4] ApÇS. v. 10. 10; 14. 17; KÇS. iv. 8. 25, 26; 9. 13 ff.

flesh : or he may offer on Darbha grass, and then must not sit down upon it. The sense is clear : the holy nature of the goat or the grass prevents its being treated in the normal way. The goat, however, is not merely connected with Agni. As we have seen above, it is at least probable that the goat was used in the horse sacrifice and in the burial rite as a fetish of Pūṣan, the lord of the ways. The cow also could serve as a fetish, and in the ritual be hailed as Iḍā and as Aditi : in the Yajurveda the cow which is given in payment for the Soma is addressed as Aditi.

These are scanty enough remains of fetishism, and we cannot assert that, even such as they are, they are proofs of a wider extension of the concept at an earlier period. The fire ritual, which is richest in them, is precisely that part of the religion of the Veda which is most completely sacerdotalized : the use of the horse and the goat may not in the slightest degree be original elements of the ritual, but may be deliberately introduced by the priests who were the most devoted admirers of symbolism, and who not only found symbolism in every conceivable rite, but were quite capable of inventing the rite to contain the symbol. The Çūlagava ritual, which, as belonging to the simpler household ritual, might be supposed to be earlier in conception, is only recorded at the very end of the Vedic period, and at a time when the priests had completely brought the household ritual under their own control : its symbolism is entirely in accord with their modes of thought. Nor *a priori* is there any ground, if we do not accept animism as the first step in religious life, to ascribe fetishism to the beginnings of religious thought, and still less to hold that animal fetishism is especially primitive. It is clearly derived from theriomorphism, which we find in the Rigveda : whether animal fetishes were known in the period of that Veda, as we know fetishes of lifeless objects were known, must remain undecided in the absence of conclusive positive evidence and the impossibility of satisfactory conclusions from reasoning *a priori*. It is, of course, often contended that in fetishism we must expect to find, and so far as records are available, do find, a chronological progression from the inanimate fetish through the animal form, to a half human, half animal form, and finally to the human form proper.[1] This view corresponds with the theory, already mentioned, under which it is held that the first conceptions of deities are animatistic, then theriomorphic, and only later anthropomorphic, so that, for instance, the sun is first represented by a wheel fetish, then by a horse and chariot, and only later by a man seated in a chariot or alone. The theory seems, however, to lack any definite foundation ; once the animatistic stage is passed, or even in this stage, whether man conceived his deities in animal or human forms appears to permit of no absolute reply ; there seems no ground for refusing to admit the contemporaneousness of both ideas ; we certainly cannot feel that Indra was pictured by primitive imagination as a bull more readily than as a man of superhuman prowess. As we have seen, in the Rigveda we have a definite suggestion of the existence of a primitive idol

[1] Helm, *Altgerm. Rel.* i. 172 ff.

of Indra, but no hint of animal fetishes, living or counterfeit. It is curious that even in the ritual we do not find the use of fetishes shaped in animal form ; we might have expected to discover the sun, for instance, represented not merely by something round, but by the semblance of a bird or a horse, but this is not recorded. Presumably the living animal was felt to be a more efficacious representative of the god.

§ 3. *Animism and the Spirits of the Dead*

The worship of natural objects and activities is by no means the whole basis of Vedic belief, even allowing in the fullest degree for the development of myth by the mythopoetic faculty, and for the growth of abstract gods not in any way connected with a natural basis. An independent [1] source of religious feeling lies in the regard paid to the spirits of the dead : it does not seem possible to deny as regards them that from the first two aspects were present in the feelings of those who remained alive : on the one hand, the dead was in need of aid and comfort from the living, but the dead was also a potential source of danger to the living and must be propitiated, even if the soul was that of a dear one, still more so if it were the soul of an enemy or some one whom the living had mishandled.[2] It is in no way inconceivable that from the reverence paid to a soul there might spring up the worship of a god analogous to the worship of nature gods : such an origin has been suggested for part at least of the character of Rudra,[3] of the Maruts [4] and of Yama, but in none of these cases have we attained anything like probability. On the other hand, it is probable enough that certain mythical priestly families, including perhaps the Bhṛgus, owe their position to the reverence paid to the dead. Nevertheless these families are not gods proper, nor treated as gods in the ordinary sense in the Veda : their human origin is distinctly remembered or believed in.

Still less than from souls of the pious dead can we trace in the Veda any sign of doctrine which is later prominent in India, the view that gods, like Kṛṣṇa, were originally men pure and simple, a doctrine to which Sir A. Lyall [5] has attributed much, if not all, of the religion of India. That a living man should by reason of his magic powers be deemed to be possessed by a divinity and to be divine so as to become an object of worship is a conception which is certainly not hinted at in any way in any part of the Vedic literature : the

[1] Usener, *Götternamen*, p. 254.

[2] Warde Fowler, *Roman Ideas of Deity*, pp. 23. 24 ; *Religious Experience of the Roman People*, p. 91; J. Harrison, *Themis*, p. 290. E. Meyer, *Gesch. des Alt.*[3] I. i. §§ 58 ff., lays great stress on the feeble character of the souls of the dead, but there is some exaggeration in this view, and he tends to ignore the persistent tendency of the illogical combination of beliefs as to the dead in the minds of the living. Cf. Helm, *Altgerm. Rel.* i. 17 ff.

[3] Oldenberg, *Rel. des Veda*[2], p. 60 ; von Schroeder, *Arische Religion*, i. 124.

[4] Von Schroeder, VOJ. ix. 248 ff. ; cf. Arbman, *Rudra*, p. 309.

[5] *Asiatic Studies*, 1st ser., pp. 25 ff. Cf. Sir W. Ridgeway, *The Dramas and Dramatic Dances of Non-European Races* (1915), with the incisive critique of van Gennep, *L'état actuel du problème totémique*, pp. 317 ff.

inspired Muni or medicine man is known as early as the Rigveda,[1] but it is not suggested that such a man was divine. In the later literature is found the idea of the divinity of kings: a king, even if but a child, is not to be despised, Manu tells us, since in him is incorporate a great divinity; but in the Veda if there are gods in earth they are normally the Brahmans, a view which may even be as old as the Rigveda, and which does not allow us to do more than believe that the priests felt themselves as in high degree sanctified by their close relations with the gods. The conception that the worship of gods at all was born from the worship paid on earth to the inspired medicine man[2] is not in itself a probable one, but at any rate it is wholly opposed to the Vedic religion as we have it.

When, however, we pass from the world of heaven to the world of demons the situation is changed. If the Indian believed in and worshipped gods of light and nature, he was doubtless in deep fear of countless demons who threatened men with every kind of evil, and who had to be combated even by the gods. In but few cases is it possible to reduce these demons to a certain natural foundation: the Gandharvas, who in the later Vedic tradition have a somewhat hostile appearance, are probable cases of derivation from a natural basis, and the greater enemies of the gods, such as Vṛtra, are doubtless naturalistic in origin. But this is not the case with many of the demons of the Veda, and it is a natural and probable conjecture[3] which sees in them conceptions based on the idea of hostile souls of the dead: it is easy to imagine that disease and troubles which fall to the share of man can be deemed to be produced by the souls of the hostile dead, and, once the concept of souls causing misfortune was arrived at, the same principle of creative activity, which has been seen at work in the making of new forms of gods, would generalize the conception of spirits which brought misfortune.

The idea that there are hostile spirits of the dead, which are the demons of disease and the bringers of ill fortune, is strongly supported by the very widespread belief in modern India that the most of the evil spirits are such souls of the dead, especially of men killed by tigers, or murdered, or who committed suicide through weariness of the misfortunes of life or other similar

[1] x. 136. 6. Cf. Chap. 22, § 9. For faint Vedic beginnings of royal divinity, see Ghoshal, *History of Hindu Political Theories*, pp. 27 f., and see N. N. Law, *Ancient Indian Polity*, pp. 116 f., 145 ff.

[2] Murray, *Greek Epic*[3], pp. 135 f.; *Anthropology and the Classics*, p. 76; Cornford, *Themis*, pp. 220 ff. See Warde Fowler, *Roman Ideas of Deity*, p. 39, and P. Ehrenreich, *Zeitschrift für Ethnologie*, xxxviii. 536–610, in criticism of K. Breysig, *Die Entstehung des Gottesgedankens und der Heilbringer* (1905); Hopkins, *Origin of Religion*, pp. 67–72; N. N. Law, *Ancient Indian Polity*, pp. 129 ff.

[3] Oldenberg, *Rel. des Veda*[2], pp. 57–9. Cf. for Babylonian belief, Farnell, *Greece and Babylon*, p. 206. See also Marett, *Threshold of Religion*, pp. 27, 28; Wundt, *Völkerpsychologie*[2], IV. i. 480; Helm, *Altgerm. Rel.* i. 33, 34. Both Wundt (pp. 462 ff.) and Helm (i. 30) recognize the existence of demons of the malignant aspects of nature, the mountains, the waste spaces, air, water, and even the house, a factor often underestimated. Another element is provided by personified diseases (Hopkins, *Origin of Religion*, pp. 74, 87).

cause.[1] The idea is proved to have existed for medieval India by the evidence of such tales as that narrated in the Siṅhāsanadvātriṅçikā [2] of a man who was betrayed by his wife and who died for grief at the betrayal, but after death used to come to vex her in punishment for her crime, in the guise of an evil spirit. Earlier evidence is that of the epic which makes out that the men who hate Brahmans in this life become Rākṣasas, perhaps in the Buddhist category of Yama-Rākṣasas, if their character is that they are evil men who become Rāksaṣas on death.[3] The Buddhist literature also knows Yakṣas and Bhūtas who dwell in cemeteries and Yakṣas who live in relic mounds. The Vedic evidence is not conclusive, but it is valuable : in addition to gods who were first men, and to gods by their deeds, who may be deemed to be the spirits of the friendly dead,[4] we find mention of Dasyus, who, assuming the appearance of ancestors, slip in amongst the ancestors at the funeral feast provided for the latter, and we are told of Asuras and Rakṣases who dwell among the Fathers.[5] In both cases the evil spirits must be deemed to be such as naturally consort with the spirits of the dead. In yet another passage of the Atharvaveda [6] some kind of demon which infests the cowstall and the house is addressed with the words 'whether ye be from the field or sent by men or be children of the Dasyus ', and the last of these conceptions suggests that the demons are conceived as being possibly the souls of the hostile Dasyu. Clearer evidence than this we really could not expect to find : for once the idea of hostile spirits generally was conceived it would be constantly and readily extended. There can be hardly any better example of this than the case of the Asuras : they are not in origin, as we have seen, enemies of the gods at all, but the Brāhmaṇa literature with monotonous regularity presents us with the picture of the gods and the Asuras being in conflict : the concept of the group of Asuras [7] is thus in the main due to the creative activity of the religious consciousness of the priests. Older than this group is that of the Rakṣases, who become, after the invention of the concept of the Asuras, more specifically the enemies of men, but who are also enemies of the gods themselves.

In regard to a third group of evil spirits, the Piçācas, it has been suggested by Sir G. Grierson [8] that they reflect human enemies, a race of cannibals, of whom traditions prevail throughout the medieval period of India, and whose language was the Paiçācī of the north-west. In principle it is perfectly possible that human enemies may be counted among demons, as well as the souls of human enemies, and it may be noted that the Brāhmaṇa [9] tradition which opposes the Asuras to the gods, and the Rakṣases to men, also opposes the Piçācas to the Fathers, from which it might be deduced that they were in

[1] Monier Williams, *Brahmanism*³, p. 239 ; Arbman, *Rudra*, pp. 156 ff.

[2] *Ind. Stud.* xv. 353.

[3] Feer, *Avadāna Çataka*, p. 491.

[4] ApDS. i. 3. 11. 3 ; ÇB. xiv. 7. 1. 34, 35.

[5] AV. xviii. 2. 28 ; Kauç. lxxxvii. 16.

[6] ii. 14. 5 : the sense of Kṣetriya is obscure.

[7] As enemies of men they occur in AV. viii. 6. 5 ; Kauç. lxxxvii, 16 ; lxxxviii. 1.

[8] ZDMG. lvi. 68 ff. Cf. for the Rakṣases, Hillebrandt, *Ved. Myth.* iii. 426 ; for both, *Ved. Myth.*, p. 185. Cf. Macdonell and Keith, *Vedic Index*, i. 533.

[9] TS. ii. 4. 1. 1.

large measure deemed to be souls of the hostile dead. Nor need we doubt that some of the demons who are defeated by the gods were mere mortal men, the enemies of the singers, for there is no such difficulty in accepting the view that a living man can be deemed an evil spirit as in believing that he can be deemed a god. The rarity of the word Piçâca in the earliest literature is also to be noted, but on the whole it is more probable that the term was in origin applied to demons as spirits, not to an actual tribe of men, whence it came to have its demoniac sense, which is certain in the only instance of its use in the Rigveda.[1]

It is clear that the relations between the two species of divinities, the gods of nature, especially the lesser deities, and the spirits of animistic belief, must have been close in the extreme, and that there may have been a tendency for the latter sphere to intrude on the former, especially with the development of the belief in the transmigration of the soul, the origin of which we will have cause to consider later. Thus in the Petavatthu [2] the spirit resident in a tree declares that it is not a god nor a Gandharva nor Indra, breaker of cities, but a dead man from Beruva, and the same text [3] places on the same basis the souls of the dead and the deity of a spot, clearly suggesting that the two are closely akin. These passages cannot safely be used with Oldenberg [4] in support of the derivation of spirits from the souls of the dead : the spirit in the tree in more primitive thought must surely have been, as the Vedic evidence proves, a tree spirit, and the *genius loci* was not, we may be sure, primitively merely the soul of a dead man.

The demoniac spirits are naturally conceived in human form, a fact which is in harmony with their origin from the souls of the dead, but which would not in itself establish that origin. But they are also figured as with animal shapes,[5] and, unlike the great gods whose forms are normal, they are regarded often as not merely animal, but of utter and hideous deformity. Or again in some cases they are conceived as a mixture of the human and the animal forms.

In a wide sense the term animism, which here has been employed to cover only the beliefs which are founded on the regard had for the souls of the dead, is employed to cover all cases of belief in spirits : thus the anthropomorphic gods are styled a product of animism, and abstract deities are derived from the same conception. The question is in the main one of terminology : by Herbert Spencer the term animism covers cases which we have classed as animatism, where personality is assumed without any definite theory of spirit. But it is by no means certain that we are to consider animism as the normal procedure by which we pass from animatism to anthropomorphism,

[1] i. 133. 5.

[2] ii. 9. 13.

[3] i. 4. 1.

[4] *Rel. des Veda*², pp. 59, 60.

[5] Cf. for Babylon Farnell, *Greece and Babylon*, pp. 53–5. He (p. 74) points out that e totemism and theriolatry found by Cook (JHS. xiv. 81 ff.) in Minoan religion is in fact due to a grave error in taking fantastic representations for serious figures (Evans, *Ann. Brit. School*, 1900–1, p. 30 ; JHS. xxi. 169 ; Hogarth, JHS. xxii. 92).

if we are to consider animism as essentially connected with the souls of the dead. We cannot say that belief in the existence and nature of the soul was produced by the observation of the phenomena of death only: the dream on which Tylor laid stress, or the trance, to which Lang [1] attached importance in connexion with the power of foresight, are sources from which the view of the existence of the spirit could be derived, apart altogether from the phenomena of death, and Dr. Marett [2] holds that in the conception of the souls of the dead an additional element of the supernatural was added by the feeling of horror and surprise felt by the savage in the presence of a dead body. It is, therefore, perfectly legitimate and natural to hold that the transition from animatism to anthropomorphism was due to the development of the conception of spirit as connected with the living and not as connected with the dead. Hence the use of the term animism in this connexion is scarcely desirable, though almost inevitable.[3]

§ 4. *The term Deva*

The word Deva undoubtedly denotes a being connected with the heaven, and there can be doubt only regarding the precise sense which had been developed during the Aryan period when the word was common to the Indians and the Iranians to be. Such evidence as there is suggests that the term had already come to be applied generically as a term for the gods of all kinds, though this must remain doubtful. What is clear is that in the use of the Rigveda the word has essentially this sense; the Devas stand out against the demons whether Dāsas, Dasyus, or Rakṣases, while the Brāhmaṇas show the term Asura degraded from its old higher sense and opposed to Deva.[4] The generic sense of Deva is revealed in the negative Adeva which is opposed to Deva and is used of the demon Vṛtra.[5] So also we have the terms *mūradeva* used of those who had roots as their gods, and *çiçnadeva* of those who were phallus worshippers.[6] It is, therefore, clear that the connexion with the heaven had long been lost. That the term Devas when used in the Rigveda and other Vedic literature normally denotes the narrow circle of the sky gods, and that the term Viçve Devās applies to the gods as a whole, in opposition to this narrower group, is a hypothesis [7] wholly without plausibility or support. It is absurd to suggest that when gods are opposed to demons the sky gods alone are meant, still more absurd to find them alone designated when gods,

[1] *Making of Religion* (1898).

[2] *Threshold of Religion*, pp. 25, 26.

[3] Helm (*Altgerm. Rel.* i. 13, 14) adopts the term as denoting the recognition of natural forces as alive and ensouled as opposed to manism, which derives worship of these forces from the worship of the dead, naturalism indicating the view that the appearances in nature are identic with the powers man recognizes. Reville (*Hist. des Rel.* ii. 237) distinguishes naturism and animism; cf. Lang, *Making of Religion*, pp. 291 f. See above, p. 42, n. 3.

[4] Cf. Macdonell, *Ved. Myth.*, pp. 156 ff.; Oldenberg, *Rel. des Veda*², pp. 160 ff.

[5] RV. vi. 22. 11; iii. 32. 6.

[6] RV. vii. 21. 5; x. 99. 3.

[7] Arbman, *Rudra*, p. 154.

fathers, and men are discriminated, and in the Gṛhya ritual when a sacrifice to the gods and one to Bhūtas is found, the two classes, as the enumerations of the Sūtras prove, do not correspond in the slightest degree to a distinction between heavenly gods and others.[1]

Did Deva ever include demons in Vedic usage ? It has been suggested [2] that the popular religion of the time used the word widely to cover demons as well as gods, while the priests developed the special use as heavenly gods, or—as it should rather be put—restored to the term its primitive denotation. The answer cannot be given in the affirmative with any certainty ; that gods may be hostile on occasion is recognized, and thus gods that disturb the sacrifice [3] may be real gods, and, if the Atharvaveda [4] gives a conjuration against Devas, we cannot assume that these were demons, and not possibly hostile gods, Gandharvas or serpents. Still less possible is it to regard as a demon a god who sends disease,[5] and the Yajurveda [6] certainly does not refer to a class of demons as being gods, but explains that Beings is a generic term applying to deities. The term Devajana is used of the serpents [7] who are certainly divine, and it has no demoniac sense, but naturally enough we come across cases where the term is extended beyond the strict limit of deities, so that the Rakṣases may figure as Devajana.[8] But there is no hint that this is a normal usage, or that Deva applied to anything demoniac save incidentally. The Devajanas who are invoked with Yama and Çarva [9] are divine, not demon hosts, like the Rakṣases, and, when in the epic [10] we hear of the Rākṣasī who became the the house deity (*gṛhadevī*) of the king, we are not to imagine that the term house deity really means house demon ; the Rākṣasī, as the tale shows, took the place of a beneficent house spirit.

Naturally enough, we find the term Deva expanding in use with the development of religion and the spread of the doctrine of transmigration which ultimately allows of no vital difference between gods and demons, so that the epic [11] can talk of the gods beginning with Brahman and ending with Piçācas ; but here again it is idle to antedate and to read into Vedic times an obscuration of sense which was a natural later development. To attribute to the Vedic period all that is in the epic is at least as rash as to deny to it everything not explicitly found in Vedic texts.

1 Cf. Chap. 21, § 2.
2 Arbman, *Rudra*, pp. 149 ff.
3 TS. iii. 5. 4. 1.
4 AV. iii. 26, 27 ; TS. iv. 5. 10.
5 MGS. ii. 14.
6 TS. vi. 2. 8. 3.
7 CU. vii. 1. 2, 4 ; 7. 1 ; AGS. ii. 1. 9, 14 ; AV. vi. 56 ; xi. 9.
8 KB. ii. 2 ; in MGS. *l. c.* the Devas *may* include demons, but are not all demons. Devajana, opposed to Itarajana in GGS. iv. 8. 1, of course, cannot mean demons or Yakṣas as Arbman (p. 99) holds.
9 AV. vi. 93. 1.
10 MBh. ii. 17 f.
11 MBh. xiii. 14. 4. This is abnormal ; Hopkins, *Epic Myth.*, p. 3, n. 1.

CHAPTER 6

VEDIC COSMOLOGY AND COSMOGONY

THE cosmology of the Veda is simple and natural, and it shows little of the spirit of the cosmology which is characteristically Indian and which is first revealed to us in post-Vedic texts, though the source whence it is derived is unknown.[1] The simplest conception is that of sky and earth, which gives to mythology the idea of the dual deity Dyāvāpṛthivī, at first united, then parted; but this division is often supplanted by another which distinguishes earth on the one hand, the atmosphere or the air on the other, and places the heaven above the air. In that case the boundary of the visible sphere is the vault (*nāka*) of the sky. The triple division is the favourite one in the Rigveda, which loves triads, and, when it is accepted, the solar phenomena are assigned to the heaven, and those of lightning, rain, and wind to the atmosphere, while in the simpler twofold division all are ascribed to the sky. The triple division is, however, crossed by yet another; apparently from the use of the term the 'skies' or 'earth' to mean the three divisions—as in the case of *pitarau*, 'fathers', used for parents, there grew up the idea that there were three divisions of each of the main divisions. If the simpler dichotomy were kept, then the number of six divisions was arrived at. A further complication is introduced by the addition of the vault of the sky, not as the boundary between heaven and air, but as a separate entity; but this view is isolated and unimportant.

The heaven is essentially the abode of the gods, the Fathers, who are also especially connected with the moon [2] where Yama, first of mortals, lives in hare shape, and the Soma, and when three divisions of heaven are conceived they are said to abide in the third and highest of them all. The constant endeavour to refine is reflected in phrases such as the ridge of the vault, or the summit of the vault, in place of the simple phrase, the vault, and even the third ridge in the luminous space of heaven is mentioned. When the sky and earth are conceived as including the whole universe, they are compared to two bowls turned towards each other: a different but allied conception is that they are the two wheels at the end of the axle of a chariot. From the heaven to the earth is a distance which no bird can fly, the Rigveda[3] declares; but the

[1] See W. Kirfel, *Die Kosmographie der Inder* (Bonn, 1920); Lukas, *Die Grundbegriffe in den Kosmogonien der alten Völker*, pp. 65 ff.; Geldner, *Zur Kosmogonie des Rigveda* (1908); ERE. iv. 155–61.

[2] JB. i. 28; cf. below, Chap. 23, § 2.

[3] i. 155. 5.

Atharvaveda [1] states that the two wings of the sun bird flying to heaven are a thousand days' journey apart, and the number is repeated by the Aitareya Brāhmaṇa,[2] which fixes the distance as a thousand days' journey of a horse, while the affection of the priest for cows results in the truly remarkable view of the Pañcaviṅça Brāhmaṇa [3] that the true measure of distance is that afforded by placing 1,000 cows on the top of one another.

The atmosphere is described sometimes as watery or dark: it is most often conceived of as divided into the upper or heavenly and the lower or earthly region, but the threefold division is also found. In that case, however, there is confusion with the heavenly region: the third of the spaces is declared to be the place where are the waters, the Soma, and the birthplace of the celestial Agni, and again Viṣṇu is placed there: a similar confusion of the upper one of the regions, when but two are reckoned, with the heaven which is properly above it, can be noted. The presence of the waters of the sky in the air leads to its being conceived as an ocean, while from a different point of view the clouds are regarded as mountains, and the conception of seven rivers is transferred bodily from its original home on earth to the upper regions.

The position of the different sub-divisions of the air appears to lie above the earth, though it has been suggested that the view was held that there was air above and below the earth,[4] thus explaining the appearance and disappearance of the sun. No passage of the Rigveda proves this suggestion: if the sun, as Savitṛ, is said to go round night on both sides,[5] this expression need mean, and probably does mean, nothing more than that night is enclosed between the two bounds of sunrise and sunset. On the other hand, there is one passage at least where the presence of the whole of the air above the earth is clearly asserted.[6] Moreover, a passage in the Aitareya Brāhmaṇa [7] suggests that the view taken of the motion of the sun was that, after it had travelled across the sky with light blazing upon the earth, during the period of the night it returned back by the same way as it had come, but with its light turned away from the earth. With this it is in perfect harmony if the Rigveda [8] declares once that the light which the steeds of the sun bear is sometimes bright and sometimes dark, or the other statement [9] that the *rajas*, which accompanies the sun to the east, is different from the light which rises with the sun. Elsewhere [10] the question is raised, but not answered, Where in the daytime are the stars?

The earth is described as the great, the extended, even the boundless: no trace appears of the theory that the earth is bounded by an ocean, but in

[1] x. 8. 18.
[2] ii. 17. 8.
[3] xvi. 8. 6; cf. xxi. 1. 9; Hopkins, *Trans. Conn. Acad.* xv. 31, n. 2.
[4] Zimmer, *Altind. Leben*, pp. 357–9. Contrast A. C. Das, *Rig-Vedic India*, i. 509 f.
[5] v. 81. 4.
[6] i. 81. 5.
[7] iii. 44. 4; Speyer, JRAS. 1906, pp. 723 ff.
[8] i. 115. 5.
[9] x. 37. 3.
[10] i. 24. 18.

the Rigveda [1] its shape is compared to that of a wheel, and the Çatapatha Brāhmaṇa [2] directly calls it circular, a conception which, however, is varied in another view taken by the Rigveda of the heaven and the earth as bowls turned towards each other. The Rigveda reckons four points of the compass, or occasionally five, where the centre, the place of the speaker, is the fifth : the Atharvaveda adds the zenith as the sixth and sometimes also a seventh,[3] an idea which may be found in the seven regions and seven places of earth mentioned in the Rigveda. The predilection of the Rigveda for the number seven is already marked, and there is no ground for the view that it is borrowed from Babylon.

It is of importance for Vedic mythology that the knowledge of the heavenly bodies displayed is the most meagre possible. The sun and the moon are of course known, but there is no proof of the worship of any other constellation in the Rigveda, and the rudimentary knowledge of even the divisions of time is seen in the fact that a year of 360 days and 12 months is, apart from the occasional mention of a 10-month year of gestation, the only year clearly known to the whole of the Vedic literature prior to the later Sūtras. That the year of 12 months, which seems to have been a rough adaptation to the solar year of the synodic month of between 29 and 30 days, was not a perfect year seems, however, to have been recognized, for the Rigveda already contains the mention of a thirteenth supplementary month which must, we may assume, have been intercalated periodically, but there is no evidence worth serious consideration for the view that the Vedic period knew a period of five years as a unit for intercalation.[4] The planets are not known to the Rigveda, nor apparently to any Vedic text which can claim to be early : the identification of Bṛhaspati with the planet Jupiter which has been accepted for the Rigveda by so high an authority as Thibaut [5] is clearly untenable, and in the absence of the slightest evidence that the planets were known, it is wholly inadmissible to seek to interpret the number 34 which occurs in a Rigvedic riddle [6] as denoting the sun and moon, the five planets, and the twenty-seven Nakṣatras. The Nakṣatras themselves are recognized in the Yajurveda Saṁhitās and in a late passage of the Atharvaveda as 27 or 28, but, as we have seen, they seem wholly unknown at any rate in the main body of the Rigveda, the only clear references occurring in a very late hymn.[7] They mark the nightly stations of the periodic month, and reference has already been made to the uncertainty of their origin and the possibility that they are borrowed from some Semitic

[1] x. 89. 4.

[2] Weber, *Ind. Stud.* ix. 358 ff.

[3] Bloomfield, AJP. xii. 432.

[4] Macdonell and Keith, *Vedic Index*, ii. 162, 412, 413.

[5] *Astronomie*, p. 6. See Keith, JRAS. 1911, pp. 794–800.

[6] i. 164. See also Oldenberg's notes on RV. i. 105. 16 ; x. 55. 3 ; *Weltanschauung der Brāhmaṇatexte*, p. 36, n. 1, where he sees in Soma's thirty-three wives (TS. ii. 3. 5. 1) the Nakṣatras, planets, and sun, but implausibly. If they were so well known as to be understood in such references, why are they never mentioned distinctly ? The pole star, Dhruva, appears in the Gṛhya Sūtras only. Cf. below, Chap. 11, § 10.

[7] x. 85.

source. A similar hypothesis is, of course, as has already been pointed out, possible as regards the Vedic year, which is of the same length as that of Babylon, but for this suggestion there seems no solid ground whatever: traces of a sexagesimal form of reckoning which have been seen in Gothic and more faintly in Latin and Greek and assigned to a Babylonian origin cannot be found in India.[1] Moreover, if Babylon has been able to influence early India in any effective degree, it would have been natural that some trace of astral mythology should have been discoverable in India, and this is certainly not the case.

No simple or consistent view is expressed as to the origin of the world. In one view the world is a thing which has been measured out and established by the gods: Indra measures out the six regions, makes the wide earth and the high heaven, but the feat is attributed to other gods such as Tvaṣṭṛ, or Varuṇa, or Viṣṇu, while the sun is made out to be the instrument used in the measuring. The stretching out of the earth is similarly attributed to Indra, Agni, the Maruts, and other gods, and, by another metaphor, the wood whence the house of the world was built is mentioned. Heaven and earth are supported by posts, but the air is rafterless and its steadfast condition raises wonder: again the air is placed in the doorway of heaven. Foundations are mentioned, Savitṛ makes fast the earth with bonds, Viṣṇu with pegs, and Bṛhaspati supports the ends. In the myth of the one-footed goat Oldenberg[2] has seen the conception of a goat which holds apart sky and earth, but this view is hardly likely, and there is no trace of any other similitude in Vedic religion to the legend of Atlas or Tantalos.

In other passages the relation of parentage[3] is prominent, and this idea has the most varied forms. What is prior in time is the parent of the subsequent phenomenon: thus the Dawn is born of night, though she is also her greater sister, and yet generates the sun, and again the sacrifices of the Fathers are said to produce the Dawns, since they take place before the appearance of dawn. Spatial relations are similarly enough to explain paternity: the quiver is the father of the arrows, the steeds of the sun are the daughters of the car: the parent *par excellence* is Dyaus, and earth also is the mother of the many things she bears. Sky and earth too are universal parents: the sky fertilizes the earth, and again both produce life in the world, the one by the gift of rain, the other through providing food. But the parenthood of sky and earth leads to one of the contrasts in which the Vedic poet delights: the gods, as we have seen, constantly are represented by the seers as measuring out the sky and the earth, and thus the paradox arises that they

[1] Hirt, *Die Indogermanen*, pp. 535, 536; Feist, *Kultur der Indogermanen*, pp. 490 ff.; J. Schmidt, *Die Urheimat der Indo-Germanen* (*Abh. Berl. Akad.* 1890); von Schroeder, *Arische Religion*, i. 225, 428; Carnoy, JAOS. xxxvi. 300 ff.

[2] *Rel. des Veda*², p. 70. See below, Chap. 9, § 5.

[3] This is earlier than the idea of letting go (*sṛj*), which is prominent in the Upaniṣads (Oldenberg, *Die Lehre der Upanishaden*, pp. 82 ff.).

produce their own parents, and it can be said of Indra that from his own body he produced his father and his mother. Agni, again, is the child of the waters, which contain the fire of lightning, and the rain cloud is the mother of the lightning and of the waters. In another application the chief of a group is its father, Vāyu of the storm gods, Rudra of the Rudras or Maruts, Sarasvatī of rivers, Soma of plants. Or again the quality in which a deity is pre-eminent is made to be his father: the gods are sons of immortality as well as of skill, Agni is son of strength or force, Indra son of truth, and also of might (*çavas*), whence his mother bears the name Çavasī, mighty. Pūṣan is son of setting free, Mitra and Varuṇa sons of great might. It is possible [1] that the goddess Aditi is no more than an example of a figure born of a misunderstanding of this usage, and it is certain that in the later religion, from the Jaiminīya Brāhmaṇa at least, the wife of Indra, Çacī, is merely a misunderstanding of the epithet *çacīpati*, 'lord of strength', applied to that god.

In the late parts of the Rigveda and in the subsequent literature more serious attempts are made to solve the riddle of the production of the world, and Prajāpati appears as the creator god, though beside him there usually is to be found a primordial matter upon which he works. These ideas, however, belong not to the religion so much as to the philosophy of the Veda, and will more appropriately be treated later. One hymn,[2] the famous Puruṣa-sūkta, 'hymn of man', may contain in its very elaborate sacerdotal form traces of an early idea. It is there told how the world was produced by the gods from the sacrifice of a primeval giant: his head became the sky, his navel the air, and his feet the earth. The moon sprang from his mind, the sun from his eyes, Indra and Agni from his mouth, the wind from his breath, the four castes from his mouth, arms, thighs, and feet in order of dignity. The hymn itself is frankly pantheistic, declaring that Puruṣa is all that is, that has been, and that shall be, and the mere precision by which the four castes are equated with the appropriate parts of the giant is clear proof that the idea as found in the hymn has been completely worked over in the interest of the priests. But the recurrence of the exception in Norse mythology is an indication, though not a proof, that the idea may be also popular and old. In the Brāhmaṇas Puruṣa takes naturally upon himself the character of Prajāpati.[3]

[1] Below, Part II, Chap. 12, § 5.

[2] RV. x. 90. For a quasi parallel in Babylon (Marduk and Tiāmat), cf. Farnell, *Greece and Babylon*, p. 181. Carnoy (JAOS. xxxvi. 320) suggests Babylonian influence, and Tilak (*Bhandarkar Comm. Vol.*, pp. 32 ff.) argues that in AV. v. 13. 6 *taimāta* is Tiāmat, Indra *apsujit* (RV. viii. 13. 2; 36. 1; ix. 106. 3) is a parallel to Marduk's victory over Apsu, chaos (originally borrowed by Babylon), &c.; cf. A. C. Das, *Rig-Vedic India*, i. 226 ff. for further guesses. Rhys (*Celtic Heathendom*, pp. 111 ff., 561 ff.) tries to reconstruct an Indo-European myth (Ouranos's mutilation).

[3] In RV. x. 72 we may have the idea of creation by a primitive Yogin, Uttānapad; Oldenberg, *Rel. des Veda*², p. 279; Hamer, *Die Anfänge der Yogapraxis im alten Indien*, pp. 28 ff. Possibly old is the idea of the throwing up of the earth by a primeval boar; ÇB. xiv. 1. 2. 11, and a cosmic tortoise is conceived

Neither in the philosophical hymns nor in the mythology are the gods treated as existing from all eternity to all eternity. The philosophy of the Veda makes them born after the creation of the world, or derives their being from the non-existent or the element of water, while the mythology finds in them most often the children of sky and earth. In one late hymn [1] the gods are born from Aditi, from the waters, and from the earth, doubtless in accordance with the threefold division of the Universe. Aditi is the parent of the Ādityas, the Dawn is mother of all, and the function of paternity is assigned to Soma and Brahmaṇaspati. Hence there are recognized different generations of the gods, the older and the younger, and the Atharvaveda [2] speaks of ten gods as being before the rest, but the passage is not mythological and cannot support a theory [3] that originally the Vedic Indians had ten great gods, whence, by inclusive reckoning and multiplication by the favourite number 3, the 33 of the normal reckoning are attained. Nor in origin were the gods immortal: they are said in the Rigveda to have been given this gift by Savitṛ [4] or by Agni,[5] or to have attained it by drinking the Soma.[6] Indra is said to have attained it by austerity.[7] The later literature agrees: the gods are expressly asserted to have been originally mortal, and this fact is asserted individually of such deities as Indra, Agni, and even Prajāpati. The Atharvaveda [8] ascribes their attaining immortality to Rohita, or to their continence and austerity, while the prevailing view in the Brāhmaṇas ascribes their success to some performance of a ritual act in an accurate manner. That the immortality thus won was not, as in post-Vedic literature, merely for the space of a cosmic age may be regarded as certain, since the conception of the four ages of the world (Kṛta, Tretā, Dvāpara, and Kali) is wholly unknown [9] to the Vedic literature and first makes its appearance in the epic and in the law-book of Manu.

Like the gods, men came into being by creation: seemingly they must be considered as included among the offspring of the universal parents, sky and earth. But there are other versions of their parentage: one account makes them the offspring of Manu, son of Vivasvant, the first of sacrificers and the first of men.[10] Another and famous version makes them sprung from Yama,

as finding the earth in the ocean, JB. iii. 272 (Akūpāra Kaçyapa; cf. PB. xv. 5. 30; ÇB. vii. 5. 1. 5).

[1] RV. x. 63. 2.

[2] xi. 8. 10.

[3] Hopkins, *Oriental Studies*, pp. 153, 154; see Keith, JRAS. 1916, pp. 353, 354.

[4] RV. iv. 54. 2.

[5] RV. vi. 7. 4.

[6] RV. ix. 106. 8.

[7] RV. x. 167. 1.

[8] xi. 5. 19; iv. 11. 6. So AB. iii. 4 (of Agni); viii. 14. 4 (Indra); ÇB. x. 1. 3. 1 (of Prajāpati); 4. 3. 3 (all the gods).

[9] Jacobi (GGA. 1895, p. 210) and Garbe (*Sāṃkhya und Yoga*, p. 16) see the germ of the cosmic ages in AV. x. 8. 39, 40, but this is clearly wrong; cf. Garbe, *Sâṃkhya-Philosophie*², pp. 285 f. For the alleged occurrence of the four ages in the AB., see Macdonell and Keith, *Vedic Index*, ii. 193. Cf. ERE. i. 200 ff.; Keith, *Rigveda Brāhmaṇas*, p. 302. Certain mysterious Kalis occur as Gandharvas in JB. i. 154, and as friends of the (cosmic) tortoise, Akūpāra, in JB. iii. 272.

[10] RV. x. 63. 7.

Vivasvant's son, and his sister Yamī, a legend of which the Avesta preserves a record also.[1] Yet in another passage[2] the Gandharva and the heavenly maiden are described as the parents of the twins, in place, we must assume, of Vivasvant. Agni is father of men and in particular the Añgirases claim descent from him, and other families likewise boast of origin from individual gods : Vasiṣṭha claims birth from Mitra and Varuṇa jointly through their love for the nymph Urvaçī.[3] In the Puruṣasūkta, again, quite a different account is found in the derivation of the four castes as wholes from the offering of Puruṣa by the gods. Like the gods too, man was not originally immortal, but, when the gods learned by sacrifice the path to immortality, men would have followed it, had not it been ordained to please the lord of death that men should be forbidden immortality save through laying aside their own bodies.[4] To this differentiation of gods from men corresponds the fact also recorded by a Brāhmaṇa that the gods at one time used to come in their bodily presence among men, but had ceased to do so.[5]

In the physical world there rules a regular order, Ṛta, which is observed repeatedly, and which is clearly an inheritance from the Indo-Iranian period, since the term Aša (Urta) is found in the Avesta, and has there the same triple sense as in Vedic India, the physical order of the universe, the due order of the sacrifice, and the moral law in the world. We are doubtless justified in seeing in the word Arta as it appears in the names recorded in the Tell-el-Amarna correspondence the same word, and in inferring that the sense was somewhat the same at that early period about 1400 B. C.[6] The identity of the Vedic and Avestan expressions is proved beyond possibility of doubt by the expression 'spring of Ṛta', which is verbally identical in the Avesta[7] and the Rigveda.[8] The Dawns arise in the morning according to the Ṛta, the Fathers have placed the sun in the heaven according to the Ṛta ; the sun is the bright countenance of the Ṛta, and the darkness of the eclipse is contrary to law, Vrata. The year is the wheel of Ṛta with twelve spokes. The red raw milk, the product of the white uncooked cow, is the Ṛta of the cow under the guidance of the Ṛta. Agni, the fire, which, hidden in the waters and the plants, is produced for man from out the kindling sticks, becomes the shoot of Ṛta, born in the Ṛta. The streams flow in obedience to the law of Ṛta. From the physical it is an easy step to the conception of the Ṛta not merely in the moral world, of which we shall have cause to speak later,[9] but also in the sphere of the sacrifice : the

[1] RV. x. 10 ; JAOS. xxxvi. 315.

[2] RV. x. 10. 4.

[3] RV. vii. 33. 11.

[4] ÇB. x. 4. 3. 9.

[5] Cf. TS. iii. 5. 2 ; KS. xxxvii. 17 ; PB. xv. 5. 24.

[6] Bloomfield, *Religion of the Veda*, p. 12, who places the evidence about 1600 B. C., which is too early ; Hall, *Anc. Hist. of Near East*, pp. 260 ff. Cf. Darmesteter, *Ormazd et Ahriman*, pp. 7 ff. ; Oldenberg, GN. 1915, pp. 167 ff. ; von Schroeder, *Arische Religion*, i. 348 ff., who insists that Ṛta is essentially Varuṇa's possession. Carnoy (JAOS. xxxvi. 307) suggests Babylonian influence.

[7] Yasna, x. 4 ; RV. ii. 28. 5.

[8] Derivation from *ar-*, 'fit' (*áram*, *ἀραρίσκω*, *ars*), or *er-*, 'move', is possible. Cf. Güntert, *Der arische Weltkönig*, pp. 141 ff.

[9] See below, Chap. 16.

conception of Agni as performing his functions of carrying the offerings to the gods, or bringing the gods to the offerings, under the control and guidance of the holy power of order is at once natural and obvious. The stress laid on the conception of the Ṛta in the sphere of the sacrifice which furthers it and which it pervades [1] seems certainly to be no more than a reflex of its importance at once in the physical and the moral sphere.

As a deity, however, the Ṛta does not obtain an established rank. The occurrence of such phrases as the idea of the Dawns coming forth from the place of the Ṛta, or of the place of sacrifice as the seat of the Ṛta, or of the charioteer or the wheel or the steeds or the vehicle or the ship of the Ṛta,[2] shows nothing more than the natural concreteness of expression of the Vedic age: there is no prayer to it, and in all the mass of deities invoked in the cult the Ṛta is not included. The deities, with whom the working of law in nature and in moral life was connected, were above all Varuṇa and Mitra, less often Agni and Savitṛ; the Dawns obey not only the Ṛta, but also the law of Varuṇa: the stars in the sky disappear by day by the rule of Varuṇa. In the moral sphere the gods naturally are more prominent than the paler figure of the Ṛta; but in the famous hymn [3] in which Yamī, the sister of the first man, urges him to commit incest with her in order to produce the race of men, Yama, in rejecting her plea, appeals not merely to the principle of the Ṛta, but to the ordinances of Mitra and Varuṇa. Hence we have not merely cases in which the Ṛta appears as an independent authority,[4] but also instances where it is treated as the possession of some god. The streams go on their way according to the Ṛta of Varuṇa; heaven and earth further the Ṛta of Mitra, and the two gods appear as the lords of the Ṛta, the right. Yet on the other hand they are reduced to a lesser grade in that they appear also as the charioteers of the Ṛta, the furtherers of the Ṛta, the guardians of the Ṛta, something which therefore exists apart from them. But the connexion of the gods and of Varuṇa with the Ṛta is always close and marked: so it is said of Agni who has some connexions also, as the god of the sacrificial order *par excellence*,[5] 'Thou dost become Varuṇa, when thou strivest for the Ṛta.' No other god has any really constant connexion with it save the pair, Mitra and Varuṇa,

1 For prayer and the Ṛta, see RV. ii. 32. 1; viii. 76. 12; 13. 26; x. 138. 2; the Sadas of Ṛta, iii. 7. 2; x. 111. 2; the Vedi, TS. i. 1. 9. 3; cf. RV. vi. 15. 14; vii. 39. 1.

2 RV. i. 164. 11; iii. 6. 6; v. 7. 3; viii. 6. 2; ix. 89. 2; x. 5. 4.

3 RV. x. 10. With this idea may be compared the suggestion of Hertel (VOJ. xxv. 135 ff.) that in Purūravas, son of Iḍa or Iḍā, we have the relic of tracing the origin of man to a bi-sexual being, a view which he supports by the use of passages where in the Brāhmaṇas Prajāpati appears as of bi-sexual nature—later Çiva is of course sometimes androgynous. But the evidence is wholly unable to bear out this hypothesis; see Keith, JRAS. 1913, pp. 412–17; below, Appendix B.

4 So Ṛta is said to have ordinances (*vrata*) followed by the gods (RV. i. 65. 3); Soma flows under the law (*dharman*) of Ṛta (RV. ix. 7. 1); Mitra and Varuṇa rule by law and Ṛta (RV. v. 63. 7). Cf. RV. i. 105. 6; viii. 100. 4; ix. 86. 32.

5 RV. x. 8. 5.

and in the case of some gods like Indra, whose greatness makes them necessarily come into some degree of contact with the Ṛta, the superficiality of the connexion is obvious.[1]

It is characteristic of the nature of the Vedic gods that the various ideas regarding the relation of the Ṛta and the gods remain side by side without feeling of contradiction or possible collision. The fascinating relation of Moira and the gods, especially Zeus, of the world of Homer is not to be expected, as it certainly is not found in the religion of the Veda.[2]

[1] Bergaigne, *Rel. Véd.* iii. 220 ff.

[2] For Hertel's views as to the Indo-Iranian conception of the heaven, see Appendix C.

CHAPTER 7

THE INTERRELATION OF THE GODS

THE Rigveda recognizes the number of the gods as 33, a figure given also in the Iranian tradition, and these it further divides into three groups of 11, connected with the heaven, the earth, and the waters of the air: more often the connexion of the gods with these three regions is mentioned without any precise statement of number. Of this 33 no explanation in detail can be gathered from the Rigveda: it is certain that it is not exhaustive, for other gods are mentioned in addition to the 33. The absence of any established tradition is shown by the Brāhmaṇas which recognize the 33 gods, and agree in making them out to include 8 Vasus, 11 Rudras, and 12 Ādityas, but differ as to the remaining two: the Çatapatha[1] gives either Dyaus and Pṛthivī, with a thirty-fourth in Prajāpati, or Indra and Prajāpati, while the Aitareya[2] adds Prajāpati and the Vaṣaṭ call, a technical introduction from the sacrifice which is manifestly not primitive.[3] It is not unnatural, therefore, that Hopkins should have sought to find the origin of the number in an older 10, but there is, as we have seen, no tolerable evidence in tradition of an older set of ten gods either in India or in any other Indo-European religion.

The triple division is adopted by Yāska in his Nirukta,[4] where he divides the gods into those whose place is the earth, those whose place is the atmosphere, and those whose place is the heaven, and he records that in the opinion of the school of Nairuktas the whole of the deities could be reduced to three, Agni on earth, Vāyu in the air, or, in place of Vāyu, Indra, and Sūrya in the heaven. The doctrine may have owed its origin to such passages as the Rigveda[5] verse 'May Sūrya protect us from heaven, Vāta from air, Agni from the earthly regions', or the declaration of the Maitrāyaṇī Saṁhitā[6] that Agni, Vāyu, and Sūrya are the children of Prajāpati, while the presence of Indra as a variant for Vāyu may be due to his affinity in one aspect to Vāyu, and still more to the fact that, if a god were to be chosen to represent the atmosphere, it was hardly possible without absurdity to omit Indra. It

[1] iv. 5. 7. 2; xi. 6. 3. 5.

[2] ii. 18. 8. Cf. PB. vi. 2. 5; TS. iii. 4. 9. 7.

[3] Von Schroeder (*Arische Religion*, i. 429) suggests an original group of nine superior gods of Indo-Iranian unity, Dyaus Pitṛ, Asura, Varuṇa, Mitra, Aryaman, Aṅça, Bhaga, Dakṣa (Dhātṛ or Dātṛ), Parjanya; but this is quite unproved, and rests on the false views as to the number nine; cf. G. Hüsing, *Die iranische Überlieferung und das arische System* (1909); W. Schultz, *Mitteil. der Anthropol. Ges. in Wien*, xl. 101–50; A. Kaegi, *Die Neunzahl bei den Ostariern* (1891).

[4] vii. 5.

[5] x. 158. 1.

[6] iv. 2. 12.

should, however, be noted that Yāska does not himself accept the theory of the reduction of all the gods of the several spheres to forms of one god only, and in the Naighaṇṭuka, the text on which his Nirukta comments, the lists of gods given are not based on the principle of identity adopted by the Nairuktas. Nor can the list be regarded as having any special value or authority, though in the main the assignment of the gods to the three spheres is in accordance with the indications of the Rigveda itself. Where a god has different activities, his name is repeated in more than one sphere: thus Tvaṣṭṛ and Pṛthivī appear in all three divisions, Agni and Uṣas in the terrestrial and the aerial, and Varuṇa, Yama, and Savitṛ in the aerial and the celestial.

The identifications made by the Nairuktas were not unnatural and point to a marked similarity prevailing among the great Vedic gods. They are all, as we have seen,[1] conceived as anthropomorphic, mention is made in connexion with many of them of the head, face, mouth, hair, arms, hands, feet, and other members. They wear garments, that of Dawn being marked out by its brilliance, and the gods often are represented as wearing coats of mail, and bearing weapons such as the bow, the spear, the battle-axe: it is a rare thing when one is so specially marked out as is Indra by his constant association with the thunderbolt. All the gods too have luminous chariots, and only in one or two cases have we mention of any but normal steeds to draw them. Pūṣan is associated with the goat, the Açvins with birds, the Maruts with spotted deer as well as with horses, and Uṣas has cows as well as horses. They live together in the highest heaven, and together they come when invoked to the offering strew in their chariots, or, remaining in the heaven, they receive the oblations which are brought to them by the god Agni, the messenger between men and the gods. Their food is the same, milk, butter, barley, oxen, goats, and sheep, though some gods have special predilections for food; so Indra prefers bulls, which are therefore offered to him in hecatombs, and Pūṣan eats mush and has no teeth. They enjoy together the Soma drink, by which they won immortality. Their relations are those of peace and friendship: Indra alone breaks the harmony of heaven: he shattered the chariot of the Dawn, he even slew his own father, he warred against the gods, and an interesting hymn shows to us a dispute between Indra and the faithful followers, the Maruts, whom he threatens to slay, until his anger is appeased. But, generally speaking, the gods share the same attributes of might, light, goodness, and wisdom.

Further considerations help to diminish the differences which might be expected to exist between deities whose natural basis is different. On the analogy of the pair of gods, Mitra and Varuṇa, whose union is in all probability Indo-Iranian, were formed other pairs,[2] in which Indra usually formed one member. The attribution to the pair of gods of the feats of either

[1] Part II, Chap. 5, § 1 (*a*).

[2] In the Mitanni list Indra and Našatia appear together, and the Rigveda (viii. 26. 8) has actually the compound word Indra-Nāsatyā, but the case is isolated.

naturally and inevitably led to the association of one god with feats which were not his in the beginning. Again the gods were assimilated in consequence of their possessing the same power though exercising it in different forms. Thus Agni by the fire repels demons, but Indra performs the same feat with the thunderbolt, and the two gods, agreeing in part, come to agree in whole. Agni, therefore, is given the thunderbolt of Indra: he is styled slayer of Vṛtra, he wins the cows and the waters, the sun and the dawns. The task of extending the earth and of propping the air and the sky is one which is attributed to very varied gods: it can as easily be performed by Varuṇa as by Indra or by Viṣṇu, by the first as the upholder of the physical order of the universe, by the second as the great active god, and by Viṣṇu as the strider through the worlds. The tendency to syncretism is also increased by the close connexion of the elements in nature: thus the water is on the one hand divine in itself, but from the waters of the clouds springs forth the fire of the lightning, and that fire in its descent to earth enters into the water: the water contains, therefore, always an element of fire, and Agni himself is accordingly the son of the waters, thus commingling in his nature two very diverse elements. But Agni is not merely the fire on earth or the lightning in the air, he is also the sun in the sky, and thus Agni is closely and intimately related to Sūrya. But the sun is placed in the sky or produced or given a path to go in by about a dozen different gods. Other gods, again, are essentially akin by the reason of their being aspects merely of the same natural phenomenon.

The result was that the tendency was certainly steadily growing throughout the period of the Rigveda to regard the gods as closely related, rather than as in Greece to devise from time to time individual characteristics. Thus a poet[1] can say: 'Thou, at birth, O Agni, art Varuṇa: when kindled thou dost become Mitra; in thee, O son of strength, all gods are centred; to the worshipper thou dost become Indra.' From this view a further step is taken in the express assertion,[2] which carries us from Vedic religion to the beginnings of philosophy, 'In many ways the priests speak of that which is but one; they call it Agni, Yama, Mātariçvan', or 'The bird that is one priest and poets with words make into many'.[3] The reduction to unity of the divine nature carries with it as a consequence the further conception of the unity of the whole universe: thus Aditi is declared to be identical with all the gods, with men, with all that has been and is to be,[4] and Prajāpati is given the same position.[5] But this is characteristic of the latest stage of the poetry of the Rigveda.

It is a question of some interest to ascertain exactly what was the view of the poets in their exaggerated invocations of the minor deities with declarations of their power which would make them the greatest of gods. Are we to suppose that the poet actually for the time being dismissed from his mind

[1] RV. v. 3. 1.
[2] RV. i. 164. 46.
[3] RV. x. 114. 5.
[4] RV. i. 89. 10.
[5] RV. x. 121.

the other gods, and as a psychological fact felt his heart go out to the god, to whom his hymn was directed, in an outpouring of admiration and belief in him as really the supreme deity ? This is the theory which has been called Henotheism or Kathenotheism,[1] and which, invented by Max Müller, has in this form hardly survived criticism. The key to the view of the poets is perhaps more surely provided by the fact that in the Atharvaveda [2] a late poet, celebrating the mystic virtues of Darbha grass for magical purposes, attributes to it the properties of having extended the earth and supported the sky and the heaven. The idea that a Vedic poet could for a moment even shut from his mind the other figures of the pantheon seems incredible : apart from the hymns to the All-gods which were frequently used at the sacrifice, and in which the various gods find mention in close conjunction, the majority of the hymns even of the Rigveda were composed, without doubt, for definite use at the Soma ritual, in which a large number of gods found their definite allotted places, so that the poet knew precisely for what point in the ritual his poem was composed. Moreover, the practice of the invocation of pairs of gods or groups of gods was constant, and naïve statements [3] like ‘ Agni alone, like Varuṇa, is lord of wealth ’ show clearly enough the real value to be put upon assertions of unique authority or power. If, therefore, we add to the natural tendency of the poet to magnify the god to whom for the moment his worship was addressed—just as the panegyrist magnified the king whose bounty he was celebrating above all other kings—the indefiniteness of the outlines of the Vedic gods, and the constant tendency to confuse the characteristic nature of the deities, there is provided a satisfactory explanation of the facts of the Rigveda. For this stage of view the term Henotheism may survive, though it cannot be accepted in the precise interpretation given to it by its author.[4]

In the Rigveda this tendency to assimilation, which may be called in some degree monotheistic, but with a pronounced tendency to pantheism, practically excludes the growth of any real hierarchy among the gods. The Rigveda,[5] indeed, expressly says of the gods that some are great, some small, some young, some old, and there is no reason to doubt that this was a view widely held : the mere fact that another poet [6] assures the gods that they are none of them small or young, but all great, is rather proof of the prevalence of the contrary view than an indication that the assurance which he gives was generally accepted as correct. Moreover, there is the patent fact that, when all allowances are made for the nature of the subject-matter, two Vedic deities do appear as being of much greater importance than the others, Indra as the great ruler, and Varuṇa as the lord of physical and moral order. In the Avesta, on the other hand, Indra is only to be discerned dimly as a demon, and Varuṇa

[1] Max Müller, *Phys. Rel.*, pp. 180 ff.
[2] xix. 32. 9.
[3] Macdonell, *Ved. Myth.*, p. 17.
[4] Whitney, PAOS. Oct. 1881 ; Hopkins, *Class. Stud. in honour of Drisler*, pp. 75 ff.
[5] i. 27. 13.
[6] RV. viii. 30. 1.

has his counterpart in the glorious and righteous Ahura Mazdāh. It is therefore natural enough to imagine that the original great god of the Aryans was Varuṇa and that it was in India that Indra was made up to the stature of Varuṇa, and even overthrew his prominence. In the alternative it has even been maintained, as by Jacobi,[1] that the Avesta did not know Indra at all as a god, and that he is really of Indian origin.

The discovery among the gods of the Mitanni of the names of Indra as well as of Mitra and Varuṇa is on the whole decidedly in favour of the view that the Iranians knew of Indra as a god equally with Varuṇa. If so, then the history of the two gods in Iran has been determined by a long development culminating in the state of religion preserved in the reforms of Zoroaster, and we cannot draw any conclusion from Iran as to the earlier history of the gods. In India there is no evidence to show that even in the earliest times known to us there was any priority of Varuṇa over Indra, and the greatness of Indra and his close association with the ideals of the Vedic Indian suggest that he was from the earliest times of which we have knowledge a great Indian god. The same remark, however, applies to Varuṇa for the whole of the early period of the Rigveda, and the practical equality of the two gods for this period seems to be established by the very hymn [2] which has often been adduced as showing the supersession of the older by the younger god. In it Varuṇa claims for himself the kingship, on the ground that all the immortals obey him, that he rules over the highest heaven, that he has established the earth, the air, and the sky, and has made the waters to flow. Indra replies that he is the irresistible one, on whom men call in time of conflict, and that the worlds tremble when the praise of men and the draughts of Soma have evoked his great powers. In the mere argument Indra would seem to have the worse rather than the better part, but the end of the hymn asserts that the wife of Purukutsa honoured both the gods, and received from them in reward the son Trasadasyu, who is one of the most famous of the kings of the Rigveda. But at the same time it must be admitted that in the later period of the Rigveda Varuṇa's popularity seems to be declining : the argument from the fact that in the tenth book he has no hymn addressed to himself alone, while Indra has forty-five, is not conclusive, because the number of hymns addressed to Indra even in books ii and iii amounts to forty-five and Varuṇa has no hymn in iii and but one in ii; but it is true that Varuṇa is comparatively seldom mentioned in book x, and, what is far more important, by the time of the Atharvaveda he is already reduced to a very inferior position, while Indra is deliberately placed above all the gods, including Mitra and Varuṇa.[3]

[1] JRAS. 1910, pp. 457, 458.

[2] RV. iv. 42. The meaning of x. 124, which is taken by some as showing the decline of Varuṇa, is obscure; Oldenberg, *Rel. des Veda*², pp. 95 ff.; Hillebrandt, *Ved. Myth.* iii. 67–71, who distinguishes Varuṇa from the father Asura here mentioned, but see Güntert, *Der arische Weltkönig*, p. 207.

[3] xx. 106. Hillebrandt (*Ved. Myth.*, pp. 82, 131), while accepting Hoernle and Grierson's views of two strata of immigration, wisely does not connect the two with Indra and Varuṇa.

This shows clearly that the nature of Varuṇa failed to satisfy the needs of the specifically Indian character which must have been developing during the period, which divides the earlier parts of the Rigveda from the later, and the practical equality of the gods in the middle period of the Rigveda was to be decisively upset in favour of Indra.

The case of Indra and Varuṇa indicates faintly the existence of different standpoints among the tribes which shared in greater or less degree the Vedic civilization. That there was uniformity of belief among the tribes it would be absurd to expect; we hear of their struggles, especially of the great battle of the ten kings, and we need not assume that accusations of being without gods, without sacrifice, without Indra, necessarily always apply to non-Aryan foes. It is reasonable also to believe that families of priests had special affections for certain deities. What, however, is the fact is that in the Rigveda as we have it, it is hard to discover any certain evidence of preferences, tribal or otherwise. Hillebrandt's failure to elicit any secure results of much importance illustrates this proposition. The view [1] that book vi of the Rigveda places the Bharadvāja family in Arachosia, while iii and vii show the Viçvāmitras and the Vasiṣṭhas in the Punjab, under Sudās, a descendant of the Divodāsa celebrated by the Bharadvājas, cannot successfully be maintained, and much of his evidence for preferences is founded on equally inadequate foundations. It is, however, interesting to note [2] that Tvaṣṭṛ, in whose service the Neṣṭṛ priest stands, has but a slight hold in the Rigveda, while the ceremonial rituals in connexion with fertility magic in which this priest engages and his connexion with the Surā, not the Soma, suggest that the god was derived from a different *milieu*, not necessarily un-Aryan, from the bulk of the text. Again, the Gandharva, normally a friendly creature, is in two hymns of the eighth book treated as hostile, while in the Atharvaveda we find a distinctly different conception of the Gandharvas.[3] The connexion of Indra with the Maruts [4] as his aiders is distinctly conspicuous in book iii, of the Viçvāmitra family; in book v the Atris seem rather to treat the Maruts in the guise of priestly adorers of the god, while they are on Hillebrandt's view marked out also by preferring to regard Çuṣṇa as the chief foe of Indra in lieu of Vṛtra. Save for one hymn (66) the Bharadvājas of book vi take little note of the Maruts or Rudra, the Vasiṣṭhas of book vii make little of the Indra legend or the Maruts, Vṛtra appears normally merely as a generic term for a foe, and Indra is united with the Vasus in one place instead of with the Rudras. The Ṛbhus are most prominent in book iv.[5] The Bharadvājas are markedly less interested in Varuṇa than the Vasiṣṭhas, as is natural since Vasiṣṭha claims descent from Mitra and Varuṇa.[6] The pale figure of Aryaman is hardly recognized in the Family books, especially iii and viii.[7] The Viçvāmitras are marked by offering

[1] *Ved. Myth.* i. 85 ff.
[2] *Ibid.* i. 262, 514; ii. 16.
[3] RV. viii. 1. 11; 77. 5; *Ved. Myth.* i. 438 ff. Cf. Chap. 11, § 2.
[4] *Ved. Myth.* iii. 312 ff.
[5] *Ibid.* iii. 135 f.
[6] *Ibid.* iii. 63.
[7] *Ibid.* iii. 87.

food to Indra's bays,[1] the Bharadvājas lay stress on the worship of Pūṣan,[2] the Vasiṣṭhas take more note of Viṣṇu than normally.[3] The Gṛtsamadas of book ii and the Bharadvājas seem comparatively indifferent to the Açvins, who on the other hand are favoured by the Atris and the Vasiṣṭhas.[4] The latter family seems to have been less addicted to the Soma cult than the others, possibly under the influence of devotees of the Surā [5] from the eastern lands, who favoured the cult of the Surā-drinking Açvins. The Çatapatha Brāhmaṇa [6] assures us that Rudra was styled Çarva among the eastern folk, Bhava among the Bāhīkas of the west, and in the Pāli [7] texts we have adequate evidence of the contrast between east and west which is already attested in the Vedic tradition by the dislike of the man from Magadha.

We must doubtless also see signs of tribal and family differences in the multiplication of forms of the same deity; the sun, for instance, might be revered in one place as Sūrya, in another Pūṣan might be held in special honour, in yet another Savitṛ; Vāyu and Vāta represent in diverse ways the wind, while the Maruts are especially the storm winds; Viṣṇu we may suspect of having been the aspect of the sun especially adored by one clan. Unfortunately it is difficult to proceed beyond such general speculations in view of the available material, in which local and tribal distinctions have been largely removed by syncretism. The process has clearly gone far even in the Rigveda; if we reckon in the Atharvaveda and the other Saṁhitās, we can discern clearly further syncretisms in progress, which give us such forms as those of Rudra and Viṣṇu in the rank of great gods, and show us new aspects of the natures of such deities as Yama, the Maruts, and the Gandharvas. In cases such as these we need not see efforts of the priests of the Rigveda to elevate crude conceptions or transform deities of the underworld to celestial rank,[8] for it is easier and more plausible to accept the view that we have contamination, sometimes of divergent Aryan views, sometimes of Aryan and un-Aryan conceptions.

Syncretism is shown not merely in the complex form of the combination of different aspects into one deity, but in the union in the ritual of deities between whom there is no natural connexion. Thus we have the rather forced union of Indra and Varuṇa; [9] the royal consecration appears in our sources either as a Varuṇa rite or the great consecration of Indra, for both gods are kings and claim the devotion of the ruling power. Kātyāyana bids the Kṣatriya perform the establishment of the sacred fire according to the rule of Varuṇa, the Rājanya according to that of Indra. The treatment of the

1 *Ved. Myth.* iii. 214 ff.
2 *Ibid.* iii. 367.
3 *Ibid.* iii. 347.
4 *Ibid.* iii. 394 ff.
5 On the contrast of Surā and Soma cf. *Ved. Myth.* i. 250, 253, but against exaggerated views, see Oldenberg, *Rel. des Veda*², pp. 91 ff.; GN. 1915, pp. 373 ff.
6 i. 7. 3. 8.
7 Oldenberg, *Buddha*¹, Excursus I.
8 e.g. Arbman, *Rudra*, p. 307.
9 Hillebrandt, *Ved. Myth.*, pp. 82 f.

Ṛbhus is possibly significant in this regard ;[1] whatever their origin, they had come in considerable degree to be associated with the seasons, Ṛtus. In the ritual we find that the Ṛbhus are given a share in the Vaiçvadeva litany at the third pressing of the Soma sacrifice, while in the Gṛhya ritual[2] the Ṛtus appear in connexion with the Aṣṭakā offering, and along with the All-gods and the Fathers rank as deities of the Aṣṭakās. In the Çrauta ritual[3] we find that there is care taken to avoid connexion between the Ṛtus and the Ṛbhus ; where one set appears, the other is omitted, and the Ṛtus are not given full rank as sharers in the oblations ; on the contrary, the gods are merely asked to drink with them the so-called Ṛtu cups. It is natural also to see syncretism in the arrangement which turns Indra and Agni[4] into the deities of the new moon offerings, for to find in Agni here a designation of the moon while Indra denotes the sun, the two being united at 'new moon', i. e. when the moon disappears wholly, is a decided *tour de force*. Viṣṇu and Varuṇa again are by no means a natural pair. Similarly we find Pūṣan brought into connexion with Indra, while Viṣṇu is made to share in the defeat of Vṛtra. Pūṣan is also introduced into the legends connecting the Açvins and Sūryā, and Indra is made the guardian of the ordinances of Mitra and Varuṇa.

There is throughout the Rigveda no trace of any consistent subordination of one god to another. The lack of system in this regard is clearly shown by such assertions as those made by both Indra and Varuṇa that they are obeyed by all the gods, and other passages tell us that Varuṇa and Sūrya are subject to Indra, that Varuṇa and the Açvins submit to the power of Viṣṇu, who otherwise is of comparatively little moment among the Vedic gods, and that Indra, Mitra and Varuṇa, Aryaman and Rudra cannot resist the ordinances of Savitṛ, who is not, after all, a very important deity. Nor are we in a position to estimate more precisely even the comparative importance of the great majority of the gods mentioned in the Rigveda, for the collection, being in large measure immediately connected with the Soma sacrifice, gives less than normal room to those deities who do not for whatever reason come into special contact with that sacrifice. Thus, on the numerical figures[5] of frequency of mention of their names, the gods of the Rigveda can be arranged in five groups as (1) Indra, Agni, Soma ; (2) Açvins, Maruts, Varuṇa ; (3) Uṣas, Savitṛ, Bṛhaspati, Sūrya, Pūṣan ; (4) Vāyu, Dyāvāpṛthivī, Viṣṇu, Rudra ; (5) Yama, Parjanya. There can be no doubt of the importance of Agni and Soma to the priests, but we may doubt their popularity in equal degree with the people. The Açvins again were doubtless popular deities, but their prominence numerically is due to their connexion with the morning light and the offering of the sacrifice, while the Maruts are brought into a high place by their association with Indra. It follows, therefore, that any classification of the gods by their relative frequency of mention in the Rigveda

[1] Hillebrandt, *Ved. Myth.* iii. 146–50.
[2] GGS. iii. 10 ; AGS. ii. 4. 12.
[3] ApÇS. xii. 26. 8 ff.; ÇÇS. vii. 8 ; ÇB. iv. 3. 1. 3 ff.
[4] Hillebrandt, *Ved. Myth.* iii. 294–300.
[5] Macdonell, *Ved. Myth.*, p. 20.

would be futile, and the alternative of following the order of the origin of the mythological conception is open to the fatal objection that to determine this order no means are available.

Any division of the subject-matter must therefore in the main be based on considerations of convenience. These considerations lead to the view that the most satisfactory order is to treat first of the greater gods as celestial (Chap. 8), aerial (Chap. 9), and terrestrial (Chap. 10), of the minor nature deities (Chap. 11), of the abstract deities (Chap. 12), and of the groups of divinities (Chap. 13). Then will follow the priests and heroes of old times, including some figures who may be suspected of being faded gods (Chap. 14). The demons will be treated together in the next chapter (15). In origin they are clearly in part derived from natural phenomena, as is the case with the chief enemies of the gods as opposed to the demons which afflict men: of the latter some may doubtless be derived from the conception of the spirits of the hostile dead, others are more vaguely animistic in origin, while yet others seem developed from a naturalistic or animatistic basis in the noxious or tricky forms of nature. The relations between the gods and their worshippers, apart from the sacrifice and the ritual, will be dealt with in Chap. 16, while the question of the spirits of the dead and the cult of ancestors, the Fathers, will be reserved for connected treatment in Part IV.

CHAPTER 8

THE GREAT GODS—CELESTIAL

§ 1. *Dyaus the Father*

DYAUS has the honour of being the only Indo-European god who is certainly to be recognized as having existed in the earliest period, and he has been claimed for that time as a real sovereign of the gods, much as Zeus among the Greeks.[1] For this view there is clearly no cogent evidence available, though equally there is no cogent evidence to the contrary, for the fact that Dyaus is not a great god in India may be due to decline in greatness, not to the absence of such greatness originally. In the Rigveda he has not a single hymn of his own, and his appearance is nearly always in one or other of two capacities : either he is the parent, who has as children Uṣas, the Açvins, Agni, Parjanya, Sūrya, the Ādityas, the Maruts, and the Aṅgirases, or he is coupled with the earth, Pṛthivī, or at least mentioned with other deities of whom Pṛthivī is normally one[2]; the legend of the union and separation of the two is often referred to, but without detail. Where he stands alone, he is mentioned as father of Indra, of Agni, as a father, as rich in seed, as a red bull which bellows downward, or, by another theriomorphic idea, as a black steed decked with pearls, an obvious allusion to the midnight sky. He smiles through the clouds, a trait which can only refer to the lightening sky, and an incipient anthropomorphism appears in the statement that he holds the bolt. With Pṛthivī he shares six hymns, but they have little force or significance ; of more interest is the fact that sky and earth are called the two mothers, and that not rarely the word *dyaus* is feminine, a fact which shows that much weight cannot be laid on the contrast between male and female, stress upon which as a principle of Vedic religion has been laid by Bergaigne.[3] With the higher life of the community Dyaus has little to do ; he bears the usual title of the great gods, Asura, and with earth he is asked to avert sin committed against the gods or a friend or the head of the clan, but this is merely an application to the god of a commonplace prayer.[4] The Vedic evidence

[1] von Bradke, *Dyaus Asura* ; von Schroeder, *Arische Religion*, i. 299 ff. Moulton (*Early Zoroastrianism*, pp. 391–3) finds this god expressly recorded by his South Indo-European name in Herodotos, i. 131, but not very plausibly. Contrast Helm, *Altgerm. Rel.* i. 272 ; Rhys, *Celtic Heathendom*, pp. 109 f.

[2] The two receive a good deal of attention in the ritual ; Hillebrandt, *Ved. Myth.* iii. 397.

[3] Hopkins, *Rel. of India*, pp. 43, 59. The idea has been revived in K. J. Johansson, *Ueber die altind. Göttin Dhiṣaṇā* (1919), but see Oldenberg, GGA. 1919, pp. 357 ff.

[4] The theory of the ghost origin of Dyaus (Feist, *Kultur der Indogermanen*, pp. 339 ff.) is wholly improbable and quite contrary to the Veda.

is, it should be noted, clearly opposed to the view of Warde Fowler,[1] which does not recognize physical paternity as the primitive sense of *pater* in religion.[2]

§ 2. *Varuṇa, Mitra, and the Ādityas*

The slight prominence of Dyaus in the Indian period is doubtless in part at least due to the prominence of Mitra and Varuṇa, of which pair the greatest by far is Varuṇa. Mitra, indeed, by his close association with Varuṇa has lost any real independence of character. Though Varuṇa is anthropomorphic and has arms, hands, feet, walks, drives, sits, eats, and drinks, the cosmic character of his eye is brought very clearly: the eye of Mitra and Varuṇa is repeatedly declared to be the sun, and it figures conspicuously in all the hymns regarding Varuṇa. Varuṇa is also far-sighted and thousand-eyed: he wears a golden mantle and a shining robe. He and Mitra drive with the rays of the sun as with arms, and like Savitṛ and Tvaṣṭṛ they are beautiful handed. In striking contrast with this picture of a fair god is that suggested by a passage in the Çatapatha Brāhmaṇa,[3] where Varuṇa is described as a bald yellow-eyed old man; but this passage must be read in its context, from which it appears clearly that we have to deal not with a primitive, but with a mystical, view of the nature of Varuṇa.

Like other gods, Mitra and Varuṇa have a chariot which they mount in the highest heaven, and in heaven is their golden abode, which is lofty with a thousand columns and a thousand doors. To that palace resorts the all-seeing sun to report to Varuṇa the deeds of men: in it the Fathers behold him, and the Çatapatha Brāhmaṇa[4] represents Varuṇa as seated in the midst of heaven, gazing upon the places of punishment around him.

With Mitra, or alone, Varuṇa is often styled a king; he is king of both gods and men, of all that exists, of the whole world. He bears also the title of independent ruler (*svarāj*) which is more specially Indra's, and, much oftener than Indra, he is called universal monarch (*samrāj*), a title found a few times also of Agni. With Mitra and twice also with Aryaman, he is accorded the attribute of sovereignty (*kṣatra*) which is elsewhere given but once each to Agni, Bṛhaspati, and the Açvins; similarly the term ruler is given to him in four of its five occurrences, and but once to the gods in general.[5] He and Mitra are the noble lords of the gods, and the epithet Asura[6] is given to him in proportion far oftener than to Indra and Agni.

[1] *Religious Experience of the Roman People*, pp. 155 ff. Contrast von Schroeder, *Arische Religion*, i. 309 ff., 569 f.

[2] In the case of Dyaus the regular use of the word as a common noun doubtless told against his personality; see Usener, *Götternamen*, pp. 315 ff.

[3] xiii. 3. 6. 5.

[4] xi. 6. 1. 1.

[5] A relic of this is seen in the Brāhmaṇa legend that the gods made him their king, despite the fact that he was merely their brother, because he had the form (*rūpa*) of Prajāpati, their father, JB. iii. 152; cf. PB. xiii. 9. 22 ff.

[6] An effort to find in the epic Asura Maya a trace of Mazdāh in India may be rejected (Keith, JRAS. 1916, p. 138).

Characteristic of the two gods is their mystic power, Māyā.[1] With it Varuṇa measures out the earth with the sun as with a measure ; Varuṇa and Mitra make the sun to cross the sky, the rain to fall, and send the dawns. All physical order is subject to the control of Varuṇa with or without Mitra : the law of Varuṇa holds earth and sky apart ; the three heavens and the three earths are deposited within him ; heaven, earth, and air are supported by the two gods ; the wind is the breath of Varuṇa. By his ordinances the moon moves at night and the stars shine. He embraces the nights and establishes the mornings. He regulates the seasons : the kings, Mitra, Varuṇa, and Aryaman, dispose the autumn, the month, day and night. From another point of view Mitra and Varuṇa are essentially connected with rain, and among the gods they are most frequently invoked to bestow the gift of rain. Occasionally even in the Rigveda Varuṇa appears connected with the waters of the ocean, to which flow the seven rivers, but the ocean [2] is little known in the Rigveda, and his real connexion with water is that with the waters of the air, whence comes it that in the Naighaṇṭuka he is ranked as an aerial no less than a celestial god.

But more important than these physical attributes of the god are his moral qualities, his control of the order of the world in its ethical aspect no less than in its physical, his connexion with the worshipper as the saviour in time of peril and distress, the freer from sin, the merciful god, as well as the punisher of the sinner to whom he sends the disease, dropsy, which accords with his nature as lord of the waters. This characteristic of Varuṇa is one which will most conveniently be considered below (Chap. 16), but it is essential to note that this side of Varuna's nature is one which steadily disappears in the later texts, though it does not absolutely vanish.[3]

In the later literature there are other marked changes in the character of the god. In the first place Mitra and Varuṇa come to be placed into relation with the sun and the moon respectively : Mitra is said to have produced the day, Varuṇa the night : the night is Varuṇa's, the day Mitra's. In the Atharvaveda [4] it is said ' At evening he is Varuṇa, Agni ; Mitra he becometh arising in the morning ' and ' That which Varuṇa hath drawn together, shall Mitra asunder part in the morning.' Even more significant is the fact that in the ritual to Mitra and Varuṇa respectively white and black victims are sometimes ascribed : there can be no doubt of the significance of this distinction in treatment of the two gods. In the second place there is a marked

[1] Von Bradke, ZDMG. xlviii. 499–501 ; Hillebrandt, VOJ. xiii. 316 ff.

[2] It is invoked, RV. vi. 50. 14 ; vii. 35. 13 ; viii. 12. 2 ; x. 66. 11 ; TS. iv. 6. 2 ; MS. iv. 9. 8 ; AGS. ii. 4. 14 ; MGS. i. 13. 15 ; Kauç. lxxiv. 6, &c.

[3] It is hardly fair to speak of his demoniac power (Hopkins, *Trans. Conn. Acad.*, xv. 44) on the strength of PB. xviii. 9. 7, 17 (offerings *nirvaruṇatvāya*, i. e. to deprecate punishment for error). But his curse is feeble (PB. xii. 18. 2), and his chief use is to dispose of errors in the offering, PB. xiii. 2. 4. ; xv. 1. 3 ; 2. 4 ; 7. 7 ; he guards what is well offered, Viṣṇu repairs errors, AB. iii. 38.

[4] xiii. 3. 13 ; ix. 3. 18 ; cf. TS. ii. 1. 7. 4 ; vi. 4. 8. 3.

tendency to reduce Varuṇa to the control of the waters. In the Atharvaveda [1] he is connected with the waters as is Soma with the mountains ; his golden house is in the waters ; he sheds rain waters, and he and Mitra are the lords of waters. In the Yajurveda [2] similarly the waters are his wives, and he is the child of the waters, in which he establishes his abode, and Mitra and Varuṇa are the leaders of the waters. It is true that for these conceptions close parallels exist in the Rigveda, but the essential feature is that, in the new matter supplied by these Vedas, nothing which is not specifically connected with the waters is of much account. It is quite possible that the connexion with the moon aided the connexion with the waters, but this cannot be proved; in the Brāhmaṇas we find not merely the recognition of the connexion of the moon with rain, but equally the view that rain comes from the sun. Some force may be assigned to the view that with the growing knowledge of the ocean the tendency to restrict Varuṇa to that element increased parallel with the steady decline in the importance attached to the moral aspect of Varuṇa as a universal ruler.

Apart from his connexion with Varuṇa we know little of Mitra : one hymn alone is given to him in the whole of the Rigveda,[3] whence we learn that he brings men together by the utterance of his voice, and watches the tillers with unwinking eye. In one passage Savitṛ is identified with him, and Viṣṇu is said to take his three steps by the laws of Mitra, whence it may be assumed that he is supposed to regulate the course of the sun. The name is normally supposed to have been derived from the use of the word as friend, with which accords the fact that Mitra is essentially a kindly god, and in the Taittirīya Saṁhitā [4] appears as promoting concord : Oldenberg [5] has suggested that the use of the word arises rather from the name of the god whom he believes to have been invoked in compacts, perhaps with the use of a fetish of the god as part of the rite and the seven steps, which are mentioned in the Rigveda [6] as a bond of friendship, and which in the marriage ritual are an essential part of the rite. The Iranian Mithra is obviously the same god, and, as his sun nature is almost absolutely certain, it is reasonable and natural to ascribe to the Vedic Mitra the same character. It is no objection to this view that the sun is described as the eye of Mitra : apart from the fact that the separation of the god from the natural substratum is perfectly natural, and can be seen in progress even in the Avesta where Mithra comes forth over the mountain of sunrise before the sun, it must be remembered that, in association with Varuṇa, Mitra can easily have obtained a description which strictly applied only to Varuṇa.

The Ādityas form a somewhat indefinite group of gods : in the Rigveda they are accorded six whole hymns and portions of two others. The original number is slightly uncertain ; once [7] only in the Rigveda is it given as seven,

[1] iii. 3. 3 ; iv. 15. 12 ; vii. 83. 1 ; v. 24. 1–5.
[2] TS. v. 5. 4. 1 ; vi. 4. 3. 2 ; VS. x. 7.
[3] iii. 59.
[4] ii. 1. 8. 4.
[5] *Rel. des Veda*², p. 188, n. 3.
[6] iv. 8. 1.
[7] ix. 114. 3.

and once [1] also as eight, but in that passage the priority of seven is clearly shown by the fact that it is stated that Aditi, their mother, at first presented only seven to the gods, and the eighth, Mārtāṇḍa, 'sprung of a dead egg,' came afterwards. The number seven is also found observed in the ritual of the Yajurveda [2] at a time when unquestionably the number twelve was normally accepted for the Ādityas. But the Rigveda at no time enumerates more than six and that once only, when the list is Mitra, Aryaman, Bhaga, Varuṇa, Dakṣa, and Aṅça. Sūrya, however, is an Āditya in the Rigveda, and he may be taken to make up the seven, with Mārtāṇḍa as the setting sun as the eighth. The Atharvaveda [3] gives Aditi eight sons and the Taittirīya Brāhmaṇa [4] gives their names as Mitra, Varuṇa, Aryaman, Aṅça, Bhaga, Dhātṛ, Indra and Vivasvant. The term Āditya is, however, applied to Indra, once in connexion with Varuṇa and once as the fourth Āditya. The Āditya *par excellence*, however, is Varuṇa, next comes Mitra, and next Aryaman. In the Brāhmaṇas the number of the Ādityas is normally fixed at twelve, and they are identified with the twelve months. This explanation of their number is much more natural and plausible than the view of Oldenberg [5] that the number is borrowed from the Jagatī metre which is associated with the Ādityas. In the Maitrāyaṇī Saṁhitā [6] we find Indra distinguished expressly from the group of twelve. More generally, however, all the gods seem not rarely to be styled Ādityas, as is natural enough since the only real characteristic the group can be said to possess is that they are the gods of the light of the heaven.

The Ādityas, sons of Aditi, as their name denotes, are bright, golden, unwinking, sinless, pure, and holy. They hate falsehood and punish sin ; they fetter their enemies, but protect as with armour their votaries, and forgive their wickedness ; sickness and distress they repel, and grant the usual boons of long life and offspring.

Of the individual deities Aryaman, who is Indo-Iranian in character, and may even be akin to the Irish ancestor Airem, has practically no distinctive feature save his friendly nature which makes him a parallel with Mitra : the word also denotes groomsman, and this idea is, it seems, associated with the god, who is thus brought into connexion with human life and marriage. His path is alluded to, whence Indian tradition regards him as the sun, but Weber as the milky way.[7] Bhaga, as his name denotes, is the bountiful, or perhaps rather the god of good fortune, the disposition which produces in a woman luck in marriage, for a man success in the assembly, in the hunt, in dicing, or in winning pupils, and plays on the name of the god are not unnatural in a religion so full of the spirit of greed for the bounty of the patrons

[1] x. 72. 8.

[2] TS. ii. 3. 1. 5. This fact is of consequence and Hillebrandt (*Ved. Myth.* iii. 103, 104) does not answer it. Cf. von Schroeder, *Arische Religion*, i. 427 ff., who thinks Parjanya was the seventh Āditya.

[3] viii. 9. 21.

[4] i. 1. 9. 1.

[5] *Rel. des Veda*[1], p. 186, n. 2.

[6] ii. 1. 12.

[7] Sāyaṇa on ÇB. v. 3. 1. 2 ; Weber, *Festgruss an Roth*, p. 138 ; *Rājasūya*, p. 84, n. 2.

of the priests ; Dawn is his sister, and Yāska describes him as presiding over the forenoon. His name is the equivalent of the Avestan *bagha*, 'god,' which is an epithet of Ahura himself, of Bagaios in Phrygia, and of the Old Church Slavonic *bogŭ*, 'god'.[1] Aṅça is mentioned but three times in all : his name denotes the apportioner and nothing but his bounty is recorded. Dakṣa occurs about twice as often, and is a more interesting figure : in one hymn of the late tenth book [2] he is said to be the father of Aditi and also the son of Aditi, and the gods are made later in origin : in another passage the existent and non-existent are said to have been in the womb of Aditi, the birthplace of Dakṣa. The word means no more than 'clever', and there can be no doubt that he is the product of priestly ingenuity. The Ādityas and also Mitra and Varuṇa are called sons of skill, just as they are called sons of strength : from this epithet the element skill has been elevated into the name of a god, and in the Çatapatha Brāhmaṇa [3] Dakṣa is exalted to the rank of Prajāpati : at no time can he have been anything but a mere abstraction of a type especially dear to the later priestly intelligence, which delighted in the conception of the god, who was at one and the same time the father and the son of his mother.

The natural conception which lies at the root of Varuṇa and the Ādityas, is, it is clear, far from obvious. Both Varuṇa and the group of Ādityas have lost or never had immediate connexion with nature, and have developed their individuality in such a way as to make their original identity uncertain. Contrast with Indra shows that Varuṇa's original nature must have been something which afforded little chance of the growth of mythology : practically no myth is connected with Varuṇa at all, while the strong god Indra is the subject of by far the greater number of Vedic myths. The name of Varuṇa gives little assistance : it has been connected with the Greek Ouranos, but the phonetic correspondence [4] is not yet clearly made out, and the identity must remain doubtful : it seems naturally to be derived from the root *vṛ*, cover, so that the first meaning would be the coverer or encompasser, and native tradition explains it in this sense as the god who envelops like darkness or covers with his bonds. If so, the parallel and contrast with Vṛtra are interesting. It is possible that it originally was an epithet of sky, as the all-encompassing, but it would be too dangerous to lay any stress on the apparent etymological sense as denoting the character of the god.

In the view of Oldenberg,[5] Varuṇa was originally the moon, as Mitra was

[1] This may be a loan word. There is no decisive evidence ; cf. Oldenberg, *Rel. des Veda*², p. 190, n. 2 ; von Schroeder, *Arische Religion*, i. 288 ff., 562–7, who distinguishes the Greeks, Romans, Germans, and Celts as of *centum* speech, and adorers of a warlike god, and one who patronizes political activity, from the *satem* speakers with their milder deity, but unconvincingly (Oldenberg, GN. 1915, pp. 361–72).

[2] x. 72. 4, 5 ; 5. 7.

[3] ii. 4. 4. 2.

[4] Macdonell, *Ved. Myth.*, p. 177 ; Meillet, JA. 1907, ii. 156 f.

[5] *Rel. des Veda*², pp. 187 ff. ; ZDMG. l. 43–68 ; cf. F. W. Thomas, JRAS. 1916, pp. 363 f. ; T. Segerstedt (RHR. lvii. 195 ff.) finds in Varuṇa an aboriginal deity. Carnoy (JAOS. xxxvi. 307 f.) inclines to suggest comparison with Sin for Varuṇa, and Šamaš for Mitra,

the sun, and he with the Ādityas, of whom he is one, were not originally Indo-European gods, but were borrowed by the united Indo-Iranian people from some Semitic race, which had a more advanced knowledge of astronomy than the Vedic Indians, and which knew the five planets, which with the sun and moon made up the seven Ādityas. But he does not consider that, when the gods were taken over, they were really fully understood in their original nature by the Indo-Iranians, and in particular he believes that the strongly ethical aspect of Varuṇa had already been developed, since this fact alone can explain how a moon god took precedence of the sun god Mitra. He rejects of course connexion with Ouranos, and he lays stress on the fact that these two gods seem a distinct innovation as compared with the ordinary Indo-European gods. The conception of Varuṇa as moon god is also shared by Hillebrandt[1] and by Hardy.

The arguments of Oldenberg are of importance and weight: it is perfectly true that the moral quality of Varuṇa and of the Ādityas is of a different species from that of Indra and most of the other members of the Vedic pantheon, to whom morality is rather an outward accretion than an internal principle. It is true also that the history of Indian religion is one of the decadence of Varuṇa before the claims on the one hand of the warrior god Indra, the god *par excellence* of the Indian warrior, and on the other hand of Agni, the god of the sacrifice and of the sacrificial priest, and of Prajāpati, in whom the cosmological and pantheistic views of the more reflective section of the priesthood found their expression. Prajāpati is from the philosophic point of view a much greater personage than Varuṇa, but he has no real connexion with morality, just as the philosophy of India has no place in which to ascribe to morality any real value. But to hold that this ethical quality must have been introduced from without not only into Indian, but also into Iranian religion, seems to go far beyond what can be made even probable. What ground have we, it must be asked, for denying to the people of Iran the capacity of developing such deities for themselves? The reform of Zoroaster is a proof that Iran was capable of moral fervour and energy, and that Iran was subjected to effective Semitic influence has been rendered most improbable.[2] The decline of Varuṇa in India is not a proof that the Vedic Indians were incapable of having such a deity as Varuṇa brought with them from earlier Iranian homes, but that the effect of the admixture of race in India itself was fatal to the

whence Mitra's nature as this sun (*Les Indo-Européens*, pp. 172 ff.). He sees a triad in India, Varuṇa, Mitra, Aryaman, parallel to Ahura Mazdāh, Mithra, Anāhita, and thinks the number seven connected with the seven spirits of good and evil, Igigi and Anunnaki.

[1] *Ved. Myth.* iii. 1–51. He denies the identity of Asura and Ahura Mazdāh, but this is a hopeless idea; above, Part I, Chap. 4, § 1. For the seven gods of Babylon and the seven planets see also Jeremias in Roscher's *Lexicon*, iii. 67. The Ameša Spenta are discussed by Moulton, *Early Zoroastrianism*, pp. 73 ff., 96 ff., 296 ff.; L. Gray, *Archiv f. Relig.* vii. 345–72; B. Geiger, *Die Ameša Spentas* (1916); L. von Schroeder, *Arische Religion*, i. 430 ff.

[2] Moulton, *Early Zoroastrianism*, pp. 67, 98, 237–43; von Schroeder, *Arische Religion*, i. 439 f.

conception of Varuṇa. Moreover, borrowing of deities can only be made plausible when the precise deity borrowed can be specified and identity of character indicated if not proved, and when the name in addition can be traced. In the case of Varuṇa and the Ādityas the effort to show the group of deities which has been borrowed cannot even be made, and the suggestion of borrowing is therefore methodologically unsound.

Nor is there really any insuperable difficulty in finding another naturalistic basis for Varuṇa and an explanation of his moral authority. The old view that Varuṇa is the all encompassing sky is not open to any serious objection. It explains perfectly well all that he does in the physical world : his place, in the highest heaven, his sending of rain, the fact that the sun is his eye, his epithet of far-seeing, his thousand eyes which doubtless point to the stars of night—possibly his spies, though that conception may be otherwise explained as belonging to the conception of him as king [1] it is no objection that Varuṇa is represented as mounting a car in the highest heaven with Mitra : the god is clearly to some degree detached from his material substratum, and therefore is treated in this point as any other deity. The conception of an almighty ruler is most easily developed from the vast expanse of the sky, on which the sun moves in its regular course, and which seems to gaze upon the deeds of men. It is of course impossible to prove that Zeus has attained his position in the Hellenic pantheon entirely in this way, but the parallel is certainly striking enough to render the view that Varuṇa thus became a great moral ruler reasonable enough.

On the other hand the comparison of the Ādityas and the Ameša Spenta seems certainly right and the objections which have been raised to it are not of a serious kind.[2] It is true that neither in India nor in Iran is the number seven absolutely fixed, but as early as the Rigveda the number seven is evidently becoming the normal one, and similarly in the Avesta the number seven is springing up, in the close connexion between Zoroaster and six other spirits. The fact that these six spirits do not correspond in name or function precisely with the Indian deities is of no consequence, if we adopt the view that the deities were not in the Indo-Iranian period very closely connected with any sphere of nature.[3] This is certainly supported by the obvious fact that in India the figures of Bhaga, Aṅça, Dakṣa, and Aryaman are abstract, while the whole six in Iran are of this type. To presume an independent

[1] Foy, *Die königliche Gewalt*, pp. 80–6 ; Moulton (*op. cit.*, p. 61) inclines to deny any celestial character in the god ; von Schroeder (*Arische Religion*, i. 343) finds two roots of Varuṇa's character, the observation of the glories of the sky and the consciousness of the moral law, in harmony with his belief in the latter consideration as one of the three essential roots of religion, beside nature worship and belief in souls.

[2] See Macdonell, *Ved. Myth.*, p. 44 ; Hillebrandt's objections are in *Ved. Myth.* iii. 122 ff. ; Moulton's *Early Zoroastrianism*, p. 98 ; cf. Oldenberg, ZDMG. l. 43 ff.

[3] L. H. Gray (*Archiv für Religionswissenschaft*, vii. 345–72) sees in them pre-Iranian nature powers, but without cogent grounds ; cf. von Schroeder, *Arische Religion*, i. 282, n. 1 ; Güntert, *Der arische Weltkönig*, pp. 170 ff.

development of the ideas in both countries is really to assume something much more improbable than a common origin. Oldenberg's theory that the five other than Mitra and Varuṇa represented the planets is wholly without support either in Iran or India, where the knowledge of the planets cannot be attributed at all to the age of the Rigveda or even much later.

Apart from the question of Semitic origin the identification of Varuṇa with the moon is absolutely without support. It can only be justified by the later Saṁhitās, which, however, are far more readily explained by the obvious fact that Varuṇa was being superseded in his position of greatness by Indra, Agni, and Prajāpati, and that accordingly it was natural for the priest to seek to find some position for him, which would naturally explain his connexion with Mitra, whose nature as a sun god was never forgotten in Iran or India. With the hypothesis of Varuṇa as a moon god might, of course, be brought into connexion the fact that the Ādityas are seven, which has also been cited for their Semitic origin. But there is no real proof of the existence of any knowledge in Vedic India of a seven-day week,[1] and it may be added that, save for the Jewish seven-day week, no such period is proved [2] for any Semitic civilization at an early date.

Yet another view of the position of Varuṇa and Mitra is that presented by E. Meyer.[3] He sees in them later productions of the religious conception : while Indra, if not in name, at least in essence, is an Indo-European god, being really one aspect of the sky god, Varuṇa and Mitra are essentially products of the Indo-Iranian period of religious thought, and the Asuras never are on the same level with the Devas : in India for a time, that is in the period of the Rigveda, they seem to have been to some extent recognized as at least equal with the Devas, and Varuṇa actually in some circles ranked above Indra, but this condition did not last, and, while in the case of Iran the Zoroastrian reform developed the essential character of the Asuras and made the Daēvas demons, in India the Asuras sank to demons, and Varuṇa was relegated to the position of lord of the sea, while Mitra was little but a name. The origin of the deities he traces in moral, not natural concepts, the nature connexion of the gods being due to the inability of primitive thought to remain at the high pitch of moral conception. Mitra is primarily[4] the lord of the contract, that between individual men no less than that between clans and states, while Varuṇa is the god of the oath.[5] Hence perhaps Varuṇa is to be deemed to

[1] Hopkins (*Oriental Studies*, p. 159) assumes it for the AV. but without proof.

[2] Above, Part I, Chap. 4, § 2.

[3] *Gesch. des Alt.*[3] I. ii. pp. 922–4.

[4] Meillet, JA. 1907, ii. 143; Carnoy, *Les Indo-Européens*, pp. 172 ff. Moulton (*Early Zoroastrianism*, pp. 62–7) tries to make out that Mitra is a combination of a god of contract and a Semitic Rain god (Assyrian Meṭru), but this is clearly wrong. Cf. Hillebrandt, *Ved. Myth.*, p. 123.

[5] Lüders, SBA. 1910, p. 931. The occurence of both in the Mitanni treaty is assumed to support this view by Cuny, *Rev. ét. anc.* 1909, pp. 279 f. Speculations as to Mitra in Egypt and his influence on the Aten worship are interesting but of no importance for Indian religion. Cf. Max Müller, OLZ. 1912, pp. 252 ff.

have been connected with the ocean surrounding the world, by which, as in the case of the Styx in Greek religion, oaths might be taken, and from this connexion with water developed his connexion with the waters of the heaven, the earth, and the ocean alike. But from their moral position the two gods are both essentially celestial, Mitra being especially connected in thought with the sun, while Varuṇa was less definitely restricted in his physical range. The possibility of connexion between Varuṇa and Ouranos Meyer naturally denies.[1]

The evidence adduced to the views of Meyer is inadequate ; it is quite clear that Varuṇa and Mitra came into special connexion with the agreement and the oath respectively, but neither fact is enough to show that the deity was developed from either conception alone, and we cannot prove that it is more plausible to assume such a derivation than to accept the view that to these great gods of the sky the conception of the control of moral order and contract was naturally assigned. The importance of the sun as a deity is sufficiently shown for Iranian religion by the fact that he became the chief god of the Massagetae,[2] and the importance of Mithra as a sun-god in later Iran is notorious. It is on the other hand more easy to understand how concrete gods attained moral aspects [3] than to believe that moral gods became so remarkably concrete in nature.

§ 3. *Sūrya, Savitṛ, and Pūṣan*

In Sūrya we have the sun-god [4] in his simplest and most direct form, and ten hymns of the Rigveda are devoted to him. His natural character is very obvious in all that is told of him : he is the eye of the sky or of Varuṇa and Mitra : he is far-seeing, the spy of the whole world who looks on the deeds of men and rouses them to action. He is an Āditya, but is also distinguished from the Ādityas. Like other gods he is a son of Dyaus. In the Puruṣasūkta he is made to be born from the eye of Puruṣa, and by an inversion of this idea the eye of the dead man is said to go to the sun. A late and absurd legend of the Atharvaveda makes the sun as Divākara born from the demon Vṛtra.

Many gods stand in close connexion with Sūrya : from the lap of the dawns he shines forth, and he is also the husband of Dawn : Pūṣan is his messenger, Varuṇa, Mitra, Aryaman make his path ; Indra, Viṣṇu, Soma, Dhātṛ, and the Aṅgirases all are said to create him or produce him.

The chief feat of Sūrya is his shining for the world, for gods, and men :

1 Feist (*Kultur der Indogermanen*, p. 343, n. 1) admits the similarity of the two ideas and names, and therefore ascribes them to a non-Indo-Germanic common source ; he treats Saraṇyū-Erinys, Gandharva-Kentauros, similarly.

2 Herodotos, i. 216. There is no reason to deny the Iranian character of this people, even if it were in part of mixed blood ; the similarity of Mongolian and Aryan religion is doubtless due to similar conditions of development on the steppes (cf. Minns, *Scythians and Greeks*, pp. 85 ff. ; Meyer, *Gesch. des Alt.*[3] I. ii. pp. 887–95).

3 For Mithra's guardianship of truth see Yašt, x. 2. Güntert (pp. 146 ff.) holds him and Varuṇa (*ver*, bind) abstract.

4 For the Indo-European sun-god see L. von Schroeder, *Arische Religion*, ii. 3 ff.

he smites away the darkness and triumphs over the powers of darkness and witches; he prolongs the lives of men and drives away sickness, disease, and evil dreams. He is also the divine priest of the gods, and is entreated on his rising to declare men sinless before Mitra and Varuṇa. When invoked with Indra he becomes a slayer of Vṛtra. But another myth tells that Indra defeated him and stole his wheel, a fairly obvious allusion to the obscuration of the sun by the thunderstorm.

The chariot of the sun is drawn by a single horse, Etaça, or by seven horses, or seven mares, or by an indefinite number of either. But the more primitive view that the sun himself is a steed is found in one passage,[1] where he is said to be the white and brilliant steed brought by Uṣas. But he is also a flying bird,[2] or an eagle, and a mottled bull.[3] He is also, however, a gem of the sky,[4] the variegated stone set in the midst of heaven, a brilliant weapon obscured by Mitra and Varuṇa with cloud and rain, the felly of Mitra and Varuṇa, a brilliant car, or a wheel. In the ritual the horse and the wheel appear as sun fetishes.

While Sūrya represents the concrete aspect of the sun, Savitṛ, the stimulator or instigator, seems to denote the sun as the motive power which drives men to action. In some passages the two gods are apparently used as identical, but in others the two gods appear in connexion with each other and as different: Savitṛ is said to impel Sūrya, to declare men sinless to the sun, to combine with the rays of the sun, or to shine with the rays of the sun. Savitṛ is also implored to strengthen the worshipper when the sun is risen.

Savitṛ is pre-eminently a golden god: his eyes, hands, tongue, and arms are of gold: his hair is yellow: he wears a tawny garment and fares in a golden car. But, unlike Sūrya, he has two, not seven, steeds. The type of his action is the raising of his arms to rouse men: the action of Agni, Bṛhaspati, and the dawns is compared to it. He travels through the air on dustless paths, and is implored to convey the departed souls to the place where the righteous dwell. He grants the gods and men immortality, and makes the Ṛbhus immortal. Like Sūrya, he drives away the evil spirits and the wizards. His power is sometimes extolled in striking terms, as when Indra, Varuṇa, Mitra, Aryaman, and Rudra are said not to be able to resist him, and like other gods he supports the sky and extends the earth.

From Agni he borrows the epithet of son of the waters, and probably also that of domestic: from this connexion also perhaps comes his assignment by the Naighaṇṭuka to the aerial as well as to the celestial world. His power of stimulation leads to his identification with Prajāpati in the Brāhmaṇas. With Pūṣan he is equated or closely connected: the Sāvitrī verse,[5] which is used in the daily ritual of the orthodox Hindu, occurs immediately after an invocation of the god Pūṣan. Bhaga again is identified with Savitṛ, or Savitṛ with

[1] RV. vii. 77. 3.
[2] RV. i. 191. 9.
[3] RV. v. 47. 3.
[4] RV. vii. 63. 4.
[5] RV. iii. 62. 10.

Bhaga, in the single conception of Savitṛ Bhaga ; [1] it is natural that elsewhere he should be distinguished.

The later tradition of Yāska [2] suggests that the distinction was drawn between Sūrya and Savitṛ in that the latter was the sun before his rising and after the dawn ; but this conception is artificial, and is not supported by the Rigveda, where rather Savitṛ seems especially invoked at the beginning of the day and at its close, and his sound (*çloka*) may be compared to the Germanic belief in the noise emitted by the sun in his rising.[3]

In nearly half its occurrences the name Savitṛ is coupled with Deva, a fact which strongly suggest that the word still was felt in large measure as an epithet : indeed in two passages the name seems to be given as an epithet to Tvaṣṭṛ. It is, of course, possible that, as Oldenberg [4] holds, the god is an abstract deity pure and simple, and that he is merely assimilated to the sun, but the simpler and more natural view is to assume that Savitṛ is one aspect of Sūrya, the most important aspect of the power which wakens man to his work and the priest to his sacrifice.

Pūṣan is a curious and enigmatic figure : he is the subject of eight hymns only, five of them in book vi. He has, like Rudra, braided hair, and a beard. He carries not only a spear, but an awl, and a goad. He differs from other deities in that his chariot is drawn by goats, and that he eats mush, either because he is toothless as the Çatapatha Brāhmaṇa [5] declares him to be, or, as is much more likely, for some cause unknown to us, in which case the ascription of lack of teeth to the god is due no doubt to transfer from the habits of men.

Pūṣan shares with the gods in general the usual attributes of strength, glory, wisdom, generosity, and like the Açvins he is termed wonder worker, while with Agni alone he bears the epithet of Narāçaṅsa, probably felt as 'extolled by men'. He is most frequently invoked with Bhaga and Viṣṇu of the other gods : in joint laudations he is found with Soma and Indra, while his food is expressly distinguished from the Soma of Indra, nevertheless in one passage it is attributed to Indra, and in two passages the libation to Indra is said to be mixed with it. The characteristic epithets of Pūṣan's activity are those which denote him as the bringer of prosperity, who loses neither goods nor cattle. Pūṣan is essentially concerned with safefaring on paths : he is born himself on the far path of paths, the far path of heaven and earth, and between the two beloved abodes he goes and returns. Hence it follows that he is a guardian of roads, he makes the paths safe by removing the wolf and the waylayer : his epithet *vimuco napāt* may be rendered either 'son of unyoking' after safe arrival, or 'son of deliverance', and in the Atharvaveda [6] he is definitely called upon to deliver from sin. As he is lord

[1] Bergaigne, *Rel. Véd.* iii. 39.

[2] Nir. xii. 12.

[3] RV. v. 82. 9 ; Tacitus, *Germania*, 45 ; Grimm, *Deutsche Myth.*[4], pp. 606, 621.

[4] *Rel. des Veda*[2], pp. 63, 64 ; ZDMG. li. 473 ff. ; lix. 253 f. ; GN. 1915, p. 193. But the detachment of epithets is not uncommon ; cf. Farnell, *Greek Hero Cults*, pp. 80 ff. ; Güntert, pp. 157 ff.

[5] i. 7. 4. 7.

[6] vi. 112. 3.

of the roads and a guide, he is invoked by the man who proposes to make a journey and by the man who on his way is lost.[1] In the morning and evening of the Gṛhya ritual, the offering made to Pūṣan is performed on the threshold of the house.[2] It is Pūṣan who preserves cattle, who keeps them from falling into pits and finds them when lost and brings them again home.[3] He guides straight also the furrow, guards horses, and weaves the coats of sheep. Cattle are sacred to him and he is called the producer of cattle.

Pūṣan has also other than agricultural connexions. He is exclusively called the glowing (*āghṛṇi*), and once bears the epithet, ' not to be concealed,' which is almost peculiar to Savitṛ. With golden ships he moves in the aerial ocean, acting as Sūrya's messenger under the influence of love. As best of charioteers, he is said to have driven downwards the wheel of the sun. Like Sūrya too he is the wooer of his mother and lover of his sister :[4] the gods gave him [5] to Sūryā, the sun-maiden, for a husband. In the marriage hymn he is bidden to take the hand of the bride, to lead her away, and to bless her in her marriage.

Pūṣan again plays a part of the ritual of death : he is entreated to conduct the dead to the fathers, as Agni and Savitṛ lead them to the place of the righteous, and he conveys them in safety to their destined place. The goat of Pūṣan leads the horse when sacrificed to its place.

The similarity of Pūṣan to Hermes is undoubted :[6] both have in common the duty of conducting men or the souls of the dead on the roads : they are closely connected with the herds, confer wealth, act as convoys, are connected with the goat, and even the braided hair of Pūṣan has been compared with the Krobalos of Hermes.[7] But it is impossible to lay much stress on the parallelism in view of the lack of similarity of name, and the difficulty of determining the original character of Hermes is much greater than that of determining that of Pūṣan. His name denotes the prosperor, and Yāska [8] distinctly declares him to be the sun. This traditional interpretation is not inconsistent with any of his characteristics : it certainly accounts for his character as glowing, for his connexion with the sun-maiden, and his wealth : again it accounts for his power to show paths, from which it is not difficult to deduce his duty of conducting the souls or his going on errands. As the increase-giving sun, his close connexion with cattle is natural : Mithra in Iran, an almost undoubted sun-god, has the power to increase cattle, and bring lost animals home. The goat would be a natural animal to be associated with the god whose duty it was to

[1] AGS. iii. 7. 9 ; ÇÇS. iii. 4. 9.

[2] ÇGS. ii. 14. 9.

[3] RV. vi. 54. 7, 10. In verse 1 there is referred to the prototype of the Khojis of the Punjab, skilled trackers of stolen cattle (Hillebrandt, *Ved. Myth.* iii. 365). Cf. the Homeric Hymn.

[4] RV. vi. 55. 5.

[5] RV. vi. 58. 4.

[6] Von Schroeder's objection (*Arische Religion*, ii. 11) is without substance. Etymological connexion with Pan (W. Schulze, KZ. xlii. 81, 374) is unproved.

[7] Siecke (*Hermes der Mondgott* and *Pūṣan*) sees in both moon gods, but this is unattractive. Güntert (pp. 41 ff.) treats him as the patron god of herdsmen.

[8] Nir. vii. 9.

go on difficult pathways. As against this natural explanation it is difficult to take very seriously the theory that he is not the representative of any natural phenomenon, but a god of the ways.[1] Much of his nature can thus be explained, but not the close connexion with the prospering of cattle and of men which is clearly his, but which cannot without difficulty be deduced from his nature as a god of ways, though attempts to do so may have been known in the oldest times. The only explanation which is possible as an alternative is to regard Pūṣan as in origin an animal god, embodied in the goat, or a vegetation spirit which might be conceived in goat shape.[2] But in that case much of the mythology would remain wholly unexplained.[3]

§ 4. *Viṣṇu*

In the Rigveda Viṣṇu can claim but five whole hymns, and his name occurs not more than a hundred times in all. He is said to be young, but vast in body, not a child, and his one action is the taking of three strides: hence he is called the wide strider. Of these strides two are visible, the third is beyond the ken even of the birds, or, as it is also put, his third name is in the bright region of the heaven. But again it is said that the liberal see the highest place of Viṣṇu like an eye in the sky. The highest place is Viṣṇu's favourite dwelling, there also are the gods and pious men, there is Indra and the many-horned swiftly moving cows, doubtless the clouds. There can be little doubt as to what the three steps are: the later Saṁhitās, the Brāhmaṇas, and Çākapūṇi,[4] a predecessor of Yāska, agree in equating them with the three divisions of the universe, and the alternative view of Aurṇavābha that they correspond with the rising sun, the zenith, and the setting is in flat contradiction with the references of the Vedas to the nature of the highest place. The motive for the strides is variously given as for men in distress, to bestow the earth upon man as a dwelling, to obtain wide-stepping existence or the existence of men. Again Viṣṇu is essentially the swift of motion and

[1] *Rel. des Veda*², pp. 234–7.

[2] e. g. the goat in the Dionysiac ritual: Farnell, *Cults of the Greek States*, v. 161–72; *Greece and Babylon*, p. 240.

[3] Hillebrandt (*Ved. Myth.* iii. 362 ff.) also agrees that Pūṣan was a sun-god, the special deity of a pastoral clan, the Bhāradvājas; Perry, *Drisler Memorial*, pp. 241 ff. For various views of the nature of Hermes, see Murray, *Four Stages of Greek Religion*, pp. 74 ff. (primitive phallic stone); Farnell, *Cults of the Greek States*, v. 1 ff. (pre-Hellenic in character); Carnoy, *Les Indo-Européens*, p. 212 (in part a wind-god); Fox, *Greek and Roman Myth.*, pp. 191 ff.

[4] Nir. xii. 19. Rarely they are on earth, RV. i. 155. 4; vii. 100. 3; hence Hopkins (JAOS. xvi. p. cxlviii) makes them from horizon to horizon. Veneration of the footstep appears in i. 22 and 154; there is use in cult of the hoof of the horse in the piling of the fire, and of the footprint of the Soma cow; Hillebrandt, *Ved. Myth.* ii. 80; i. 73; iii. 353. Localization of Viṣṇu's step in Nir. xii. 19 (IA. xlvii. 84) is speculative. BDS. ii. 5. 9. 10, where an extended list of Viṣṇu's names is given, is an obvious late interpolation as are the planets preceding. Cf. A. C. Das, *Rig-Vedic India*, i. 544 ff., against Tilak, *Arctic Home in the Vedas*, p. 328, who both drag Çipiviṣṭa into the connexion.

an ordainer: he measures out the earthly spaces. He sets in motion his ninety steeds with the four names, an allusion clearly to the 360 days of the year, divided into four seasons. He is a dweller on the mountains, and in the Yajurveda [1] he is called the lord of mountains.

Viṣṇu is closely associated with Indra: one hymn is devoted to the pair of gods, and, when Viṣṇu is celebrated by himself, Indra is the only other god who is given a place; when about to perform his supreme feat of slaying Vṛtra, Indra implores Viṣṇu to step out more widely. Through his association with Indra, Viṣṇu becomes a drinker of Soma, and he cooks for Indra 100 buffaloes and a brew of milk. Through his connexion with Indra Viṣṇu also is associated with the Maruts, with whom he shares honour in one hymn.

Another side of Viṣṇu appears in the statement that he is a protector of embryos, and in his invocation with other deities to promote conception.[2] Moreover, in one obscure allusion, reference is made to the fact that in battle he assumed a strange form.[3]

There can really be little doubt as to the nature of the god. The name can be diversely explained as 'the active one' from the root *viṣ*, or as 'crossing the back of the world or the earthly regions' from *vi* and *snu* (akin to *sānu*), but the solar nature of the deity is reasonably plain. In the Atharvaveda [4] he is asked to bestow heat: in the Brāhmaṇas [5] his head cut off becomes the sun; in post-Vedic literature his weapon is a rolling-wheel, his vehicle Garuḍa, the sun-bird, and the breast jewel which he wears is clearly the sun. His dwelling in the mountains may be either derived from the conception of the sun on the cloud mountains, or, more simply, from the idea that he who dwells in the farthest distance must be on a mountain peak. The only alternative theory which requires mention is that of Oldenberg [6] that he is merely the wide-stepping god, and this has no such probability as to displace the obvious meaning put upon his nature by Vedic India.

It would be impossible to deny to Viṣṇu the position of a great god in the period of the Rigveda, for that would be to forget that the comparative prominence of the gods is not necessarily brought out fully in that collection, which is mainly concerned with the Soma sacrifice, and which does not, therefore, take great account of those deities who are not of much consequence in that sacrifice. Of course, that the god is not a great god of that sacrifice is to a certain extent a proof that he is not a god regarded with the highest impor-

[1] TS. iii. 4. 5. 1.

[2] RV. vii. 36. 9; x. 184.

[3] RV. vii. 100. 6. The epithet Çipiviṣṭa, there found and then in TS. ii. 4. 5; iv. 4. 9; vii. 3. 15; MS. ii. 2. 13, is very uncertain in sense; Hillebrandt, *Ved. Myth.* iii. 356, n. 2; Keith, *Taittirīya Saṁhitā*, ii. 622; Hopkins, *Epic Myth.* pp. 211, 274. On the etymology, cf. Bloomfield, AJP. xvii. 427; Oldenberg, GN. 1915, p. 374. Bloch (*Wörter und Sachen*, i. 80) sees *vi* with suffix *snu*, the name designating the sun-bird directly.

[4] v. 26. 7.

[5] ÇB. xiv. 1. 1. 1 ff.

[6] *Rel. des Veda*², pp. 229–34. He is clearly right in negativing the idea of Viṣṇu as connected with the souls of the dead (K. F. Johansson, *Solfågeln i Indien* (1916), pp. 8 ff.). Güntert (pp. 305 ff.) makes him an ithyphallic (*çipi-viṣṭa*) sun-god.

tance by many of the priests.[1] But his interest in human life as a protector of embryos is a sign of his importance in ordinary life, which should not be overlooked. It is quite impossible to make such a detail the ground of the attribution to the god of any other than a solar character, for, as we have seen in the case of Pūṣan, the connexion of the sun with the increase of the animal world is too obvious an idea not to be found in religion.

In the later Saṁhitās and the Brāhmaṇas we find that Viṣṇu is assuming an importance and prominence in the minds of the priests which give him, along with Rudra, undoubtedly the leading place in the living faith of the Brāhmaṇas. His three strides are now definitely located in the earth, air, and heaven, and in imitation of them the sacrificer strides in the ritual the steps of Viṣṇu,[2] which result in placing him in the world of heaven : by this simple act he thus puts himself in the closest connexion with the deity, for in the imitation he doubtless in some measure and degree assimilated himself to the deity. It is of interest that in the Avesta the three steps of the Ameša Spenta from the earth to the sun are similarly imitated, but there is no reason to assume that the two acts are historically derived from an earlier Indo-Iranian usage : such parallels may as easily rise independently. Moreover the three strides become a matter of great importance in the preservation of the world from the Asuras, who, in the imagination of the Brāhmaṇas, are no longer individual enemies of the gods, but a strong band before whose onslaught the gods are often compelled to yield. The Indian imagination, however, never contemplates the idea of any final victory of the Asuras, but the gods are bound to repel them often by guile and still more often by knowledge of some special rite. Thus in the Aitareya Brāhmaṇa [3] it is agreed by the Asuras with Indra and Viṣṇu that so much of the earth should be assigned to the latter as Viṣṇu could step over with three strides : Viṣṇu then proceeds to appropriate by his strides the worlds, the Vedas, and speech. The Çatapatha Brāhmaṇa [4] declares that Viṣṇu by his strides acquired for the gods the all-prevading power which they possess, and the Taittirīya Saṁhitā [5] states that by taking the form of a dwarf, whom he had seen, Viṣṇu conquered the three worlds. The dwarf form, which is the germ of the post-Vedic story of the dwarf incarnation of Viṣṇu, is found, though not with express mention of the three steps, in the Çatapatha.[6] It is there recorded that the Asuras overcame the gods and began to divide the earth : the gods with Viṣṇu, the sacrifice, at their head demanded a share, and the Asuras seeing that Viṣṇu was but a dwarf consented to grant them so much as Viṣṇu could lie on. The gods then sacrificed with Viṣṇu, and won the whole earth to themselves. In this account is to be seen the most important factor in the elevation of Viṣṇu to

[1] RV. i. 22. 16 ff. ; 154–6 ; vii. 100 show that to some he ranked higher.

[2] Keith, *Taittirīya Saṁhitā*, i. p. cxxvii.

[3] vi. 15.

[4] i. 9. 39.

[5] TS. ii. 1. 3. 1. The PB. makes in Hopkins' view (*Trans. Conn. Acad.* xv. 41) little of Viṣṇu.

[6] i. 2. 5. 1 ff. For the later views, see Keith, *Ind. Mythology*, pp. 121 ff. ; Macdonell, JRAS. 1895, pp. 168 ff.

his rank of a most high god, his constant identification with the sacrifice. The precise train of thought by which this identification was reached cannot be reconstructed with certainty : it is not to be supposed that Viṣṇu's importance is accidental, or due merely to this identification : he must have been a great god both for the people and the priests before he was given the similitude to the sacrifice, the greatest of all things in the estimation of the priesthood, but his identification undoubtedly aided in the increase of that greatness, and made it permanent and abiding.

In the dwarf form [1] thus assumed by Viṣṇu there is no reason to see more than the natural adoption of a cunning device to deceive the Asuras, an idea perhaps prompted not only by the appropriateness of the form in question for the purpose aimed at, but by the common view of men that the misshapen form of the dwarf is accompanied by inhuman cleverness or power, an idea so widespread in the world that there need be no hesitation in believing it to have existed in Vedic India, despite the fact that, naturally enough in view of the scanty knowledge we have of many sides of Indian thought, we have no direct proof of the existence of such a view in Vedic times regarding dwarfs.

The germ of a further incarnation of Viṣṇu is found in the Brāhmaṇas in the transformation of a myth, which is found in the Rigveda itself. In that text [2] it is recounted that, having drunk the Soma, Viṣṇu carried off a hundred buffaloes and a brew of milk, which belonged to the boar, and Vṛtra, shooting across the mountain, slew the boar. There can be no doubt that this is merely a version of the slaying of Vṛtra, the great work of Indra in the world, and the mountain must be the cloud mountain. In the Taittirīya Saṁhitā [3] the boar keeps the wealth of the Asuras concealed on the far side of seven hills : Indra picks up a bunch of Kuça grass and pierces the hills and slays the boar. Viṣṇu, the sacrifice, then carried off the boar as a sacrifice for the gods, and thus the gods attained the goods of the Asuras. Now this boar, which is called Emūṣa from its epithet *emuṣa*, fierce, in the Rigveda, is stated in the Çatapatha Brāhmaṇa [4] to have raised up the earth from the waters, and the Taittirīya Saṁhitā [5] further identifies the cosmogonic boar which raises up the earth with a form of Prajāpati. From this new aspect of the tale it is an easy step to the making of the boar an incarnation of Viṣṇu himself, and this step is actually taken in the Rāmāyaṇa and the Purāṇas. The transfer of myths from Prajāpati to Viṣṇu is illustrated in an interesting way in the case of two other of his incarnations in post-Vedic literature. The fish, which according to the Çatapatha Brāhmaṇa [6] in the flood legend saved Manu, is identified in the

[1] The victim or sacrificial fee is often a dwarf animal ; TS. i. 8. 8 ; ii. 1. 3. 1 ; MS. ii. 5. 3, &c. The thumb at an offering to the Manes is pushed into the food with verses to Viṣṇu in certain cases (Caland, *Altind. Ahnenkult*, p. 188), possibly to drive away the Rakṣases ; any real connexion with Viṣṇu is implausible ; Oldenberg, *Rel. des Veda*², p. 232.

[2] RV. i. 61. 7 ; viii. 77. 10.

[3] vi. 2. 4. 2, 3.

[4] xiv. 1. 2. 11.

[5] vii. 1. 5. 1.

[6] i. 8. 1. 1.

Mahābhārata with Prajāpati, but in the Purāṇas becomes Viṣṇu, and, while in the Brāhmaṇas [1] Prajāpati is stated to have become a tortoise, moving in the primeval waters, when about to create offspring, the Purāṇas turn the tortoise into an incarnation of Viṣṇu, devised in order to recover various objects which were lost in the deluge.

As the sacrifice Viṣṇu is the subject of a strange myth : [2] through comprehending the issue of the sacrifice, Viṣṇu became the highest of the gods : but this result caused Viṣṇu to be unduly puffed up with glory, and yet his greatness was such that no god dared attack him. He was apart from them all with his bow and three arrows, leaning his head on the end of his bow. The ants then undertook, on the promise of the reward of being able to find water even in the desert, to bring him to ruin, and this they accomplished by gnawing the bow string, so that the bow sprang asunder with great vehemence, and the head of Viṣṇu was cut off, becoming the sun. The Taittirīya Āraṇyaka adds that the Açvins as physicians replaced the head of the sacrifice, and, as the gods were now able to sacrifice with it in its complete form, they conquered heaven. The myth is an odd and curious one, but to ascribe to it any symbolic sense would doubtless be a mistake.

In the Aitareya Brāhmaṇa [3] Viṣṇu is declared to be the highest of the gods and Agni the lowest, but the declaration has no possible reference to the place of the two gods in the hierarchy, but is rather due to the physical situation of the gods, the terrestrial fire, and the sun. It accords also, somewhat artificially, with the fact of the arrangement of the litanies of the two gods in the Soma sacrifice, but it is not probable that originally that was its sense. The Aitareya also declares that Viṣṇu is the doorkeeper of the gods, an idea which it supports very ineffectively by the Rigvedic verse,[4] Viṣṇu with his friend opened the stall.

§ 5. *Vivasvant*

Vivasvant is not the subject of any complete hymn in the Rigveda, where, however, he is mentioned about thirty times. The most important thing about him is his relation to Manu, the ancestor of the human race, who thence bears the name Vaivasvata or Vivasvant, taking simply his father's name as a sign of paternity. Men are also in the Brāhmaṇas styled directly his offspring, and the Rigveda ascribes to him as to other gods the fathership of the gods. His wife is Saraṇyū, the daughter of Tvaṣṭṛ, and he is the father of the Açvins. To him and to Mātariçvan Agni was first manifested, and he has Mātariçvan or Agni as his messenger. Soma again dwells with Vivasvant and is cleansed by his daughters, doubtless, in the ordinary mythical style of the

[1] ÇB. vii. 5. 1. 5 ; JB. iii. 272 (Akūpāra Kaçyapa).

[2] ÇB. xiv. 1. 1. 1 ff. ; TA. v. 1. 1 ff. Cf. the same tale of Makha (=sacrifice), PB. vii. 5. 6–16. Agni, Indra, and Rudra are slayers of Makha.

[3] i. 1. Viṣṇu's connexion with Varuṇa is slight and artificial ; TS. ii. 1. 4. 4 ; AB. iii. 38. 3 ; PB. viii. 8. 6 ; AV. vii. 25.

[4] i. 156. 4.

Soma hymns, his fingers. In the prayer of Vivasvant Indra rejoices, and places his treasure beside him. Varuṇa also is mentioned along with him. In one passage the worshippers of the Ādityas pray that the well-wrought arrow of the god may not slay them before old age.[1] In the Atharvaveda [2] he is said to protect from Yama.

The seat of Vivasvant is a special feature of the god: it is mentioned five times: in it the singers praise the greatness of Indra or of the waters; the gods and Indra delight in it, nor can it be doubted that it is meant, when it is said that a new hymn is placed in Vivasvant as a centre (*nābhi*).

The word *vivasvant* is used occasionally as an epithet of Agni and Uṣas in the etymological sense of shining forth, which is specially appropriate in the goddess Dawn. The Çatapatha Brāhmaṇa [3] explains the god Vivasvant's name by the doctrine that he illumines night and day, which are connected with him in the Rigveda: it calls him Āditya, and this name is elsewhere found in the Yajurveda,[4] and in post-Vedic literature Vivasvant is a name of the sun.

In the Yasna of the Avesta we find Vīvaṅhvant, father of Yima, who is the first man to prepare the Haoma, the second being Āthwya, and the third Thrita. The parallelism is perfect, for not only is Vivasvant the father of Yama, but it is said in one passage of the Rigveda [5] that Indra drank Soma beside Manu Vivasvant and Trita. From the parallelism it is possible to support the theory of Oldenberg,[6] which sees in Vivasvant nothing more or less than a deification of the first sacrificer, the ancestor of the human race. But the theory is, on the whole, somewhat inadequate to account for all that is said of Vivasvant. His connexion with the Açvins, with Agni, and with Soma can be explained, as well as the importance laid upon his seat, by the theory that he is the sun, especially the rising sun. This also suits best the obvious etymological sense of his name. Further refinement of his essence, such as making him, with Ludwig,[7] the god of the bright sky, or, with Barth,[8] the heaven of the sun, is hardly necessary. The god in any case bears the appearance of having lost much of his original colour and life.

§ 6. *The Açvins*

The Açvins are, next to Indra, Agni, and Soma, the gods most frequently mentioned in the Rigveda, where they claim more than fifty hymns and are mentioned over 400 times. The most constant feature is their duplicate nature: they are compared to eyes, hands, feet, wings, and animals which

[1] RV. viii. 67. 20.
[2] xviii. 3. 62.
[3] x. 5. 2. 4; RV. x. 39. 2.
[4] MS. i. 6. 12.
[5] viii. 52. 1.
[6] *Rel. des Veda*², p. 122.
[7] *Rigveda*, iii. 333; v. 392.
[8] *Rel. of India*, pp. 9, 10. Hillebrandt (*Ved. Myth.*, pp. 150 f.) holds that sometimes his name is applied to the sacrificer himself, e. g. RV. ix. 14. 5.

go in pairs. They are bright, young, yet ancient, many-formed, beautiful, agile, strong, red, and they possess profound wisdom and power. Alone of gods are they described as having ruddy paths or golden paths. The epithet *dasra*, wondrous, is almost exclusively theirs, and they are called the Nāsatyas, and once the encompassing Nāsatya is mentioned alone. The sense of the epithet, which in the singular Nāoṅhaithya is the name of a demon in the Avesta, is unknown : its great age is proved by its occurrence among the names of the gods of the Mitanni ; naturally the Indian mind explained it as not untrue (*na-asatya*), but the value of such an etymology is obviously nil.[1]

The Açvins are peculiarly connected with honey : they have a skin of honey, the birds of their cars are full of honey ; they bestrew the sacrifice and the worshipper with a honey whip, their car is honey hued and honey bearing. They are honey-handed and give the bee its honey. In comparison they are less vitally connected with Soma, though they are said to drink it at each pressing, and in some circles they were probably not at first reckoned among the Soma-drinking gods, though for this [2] the proof is rather inadequate.

The chariot of the Açvins has curious qualities : it is not merely golden in all its parts, but it is three-wheeled, has three fellies, and all its parts triple. One of its wheels is said to have come off when the Açvins went to the wedding of the maiden Sūryā, and it is possible that the three wheels are connected with the fact that, unlike other gods, the Açvins in their chariot bear with them Sūryā, for whom, therefore, there must be provided a third seat. Possibly too the triplication, of which much appears in the myths of the Açvins, owes its being to this simple cause, though it has been traced to the three seasons of the year. The steeds which draw their car are sometimes horses—there is no trace of the Açvins as horsemen—but more often birds, swans or eagles, occasionally buffaloes, and even a single ass : in the Aitareya Brāhmaṇa [3] they are said to have won a race at the wedding of Soma and Sūryā with a car drawn by asses. Their chariot in a single day traverses heaven and earth, a power attributed also to the chariots of the Dawn and the sun : it goes round the sun, and the epithet going round (*parijman*) is often given to their car or them, as also to Vāta, Agni, and Sūrya.

The presence of the Açvins is ubiquitous : they are declared to be in the heaven, the air, in plants, houses, the mountain top, above and below. The

[1] Cuny (*Rev. ét. anc.* 1909, p. 280) argues that the etymology is strengthened by the mention of the gods in the treaty, but at most this would only prove the early existence of this conception. Brunnhofer (*Vom Aral bis zur Gaṅgā*, p. 99) suggests *nas*, ‘ save ’, as in Gothic *nasyan*. Connexion with *nāsa*, ‘ nose ’, is implausible, though epic (Hopkins, *Epic Myth.*, p. 169).

[2] Hillebrandt, *Ved. Myth.* i. 241 ff. ; iii. 393, n. 5. They are more prominent in RV. v and vii than in vi.

[3] iv. 7–9 ; cf. KB. xviii. 1 ; JB. i. 213 (where Uṣas herself shares in the race, like Atalanta) ; Oertel, *Trans. Conn. Acad.* xv. 174 ; possibly an echo of a marriage competition custom ; see below.

time of their appearance, however, is *par excellence* the early dawn, when they waken Uṣas, or in their car follow after Uṣas, who is born at the yoking of their car. The appearing of the Açvins, the kindling of the fire of the sacrifice, the break of dawn, and the sunrise are even treated as simultaneous, but the normal place of the Açvins is clearly after the dawn and before the sunrise. In the Aitareya Brāhmaṇa [1] the Açvins, Uṣas, and Agni are stated to be the gods of dawn : they also receive in the ritual red-white animals in accordance with their own colour. On the other hand, they have both in the Rigveda and elsewhere offerings at midday and evening as well as at dawn, which, however, is their place *par excellence*, as they are the recipients of the morning litany, Prātaranuvāka, for which the appropriate time is the period when the dawn has arisen. Their special connexion with the light is shown by the fact that they drive away the darkness and put to flight the evil spirits.

The Açvins have many parents : they are children of Dyaus, but also the ocean is their mother ; they are the sons of Vivasvant and Saraṇyū, daughter of Tvaṣṭṛ, and they are the parents of Pūṣan and have the Dawn, as it seems, for their sister. But their more important relationship is with the maiden called Sūryā or the daughter of Sūrya. She is their wife and mounts their car, and she bears the name Açvinī as the outcome of this relationship. But Sūryā is also the wife of Soma, in which case the Açvins appear as groomsmen who seek the bride for the husband.[2] In this connexion they are at the marriage of mortals invoked to conduct the bride home to her husband on their chariot. Their connexion with marriage appears also in their being invoked with other deities to make the union fruitful. With this their feats agree : they make the barren cow to give milk, and they bestow a child on the wife of the eunuch. They bring lovers together and they give an old maid a husband.

The power of the Açvins as the helpers in time of trouble is extraordinarily often extolled : no other gods are so steadfastly helpful as they are. They differ in essential features from Indra, who is also a present aid to his devotees. Indra is the warrior god who helps his followers in battle and who brings them in safety across the streams as they advance to attack their enemy. The Açvins appear not to do combat, but to save those who are in distress of any kind. They are the gods who are connected with the ocean, and they rescue from it in ship or ships. Bhujyu, son of Tugra, was alone in the midst of the ocean in the darkness, or was clinging to a plank in the midst of the waves : the Açvins heard his supplications and rescued him in a ship of a hundred oars, with four ships, with a winged boat, with three flying cars with a hundred feet and six horses, with their headlong flying steeds, or with their chariot swift as thought. They are the physicians of the gods, and guardians and granters of immortality and freedom from disease. The old and decrepit Cyavāna they released from his decrepitude and made him young again, and desirable to his wife. In the

[1] ii. 15. [2] RV. x. 85. 9, 26.

Çatapatha and Jaiminīya Brāhmaṇas [1] the tale is told at full length, and the centre of it is the magic water, in which Cyavana bathes and so recovers youth and beauty, a motive of world-wide fame. The same story seems to have been told of a certain Kali referred to in the Rigveda. To the young Vimada they brought as a wife Kamadyū, who seems to have been the wife of Purumitra: apparently in so doing they imitated the action of Aphrodite to Helen. Viṣṇāpū, like a lost animal, they found and restored to his father Viçvaka, their worshipper. They revived and saved Rebha who had been stabbed, bound, and cast into the waters, and abandoned as dead for ten nights and nine days.[2] They brought Vandana out of a pit in which he lay as dead. From a burning pit they rescued Atri Saptavadhri, and placed him in a cool place, a feat once attributed to Agni, who may have been deemed to have acted through the Açvins. A quail was saved by them from the jaws of a wolf. At the prayer of a she-wolf they restored the sight of Ṛjrāçva who had slain for her to eat a hundred and one sheep. They cured Parāvṛj of his blindness and his lameness. To Viçpalā—mare or maiden—whose limb was cut off in battle like the wing of a bird, they give an iron limb. Pedu received from them a strong steed dragon-slaying, and Kakṣīvant abundant blessings including the making to flow for him of a hundred jars of honey or wine from a strong horse's head. Akin to this story is the legend that they placed on Dadhyañc, son of Atharvan, a horse's head, which then told them of the place of the mead of Tvaṣṭṛ.

This is a formidable list of achievements and many more are given by name of the recipients in the Rigveda. For one and all explanations based on natural phenomena have been found: [3] thus the blind man is healed when the sun is released from the darkness—whether of winter, as Max Müller holds, or the arctic, as Tilak, or the rains, as A. C. Das, and it may be that, in many of the incidents, there is more than the mere record of remarkable rescues of real men from misfortunes. There is not the slightest doubt that such rescues might give rise to traditions of the sort recorded in the hymns, but the explanation is one which cannot be given with certainty in all cases: the giving of an iron limb to a horse is a feat which no modern could accomplish, and, while it might be ascribed to the Açvins in recognition of their great powers, still it is rather doubtful if this is enough to explain the incident, though the

[1] ÇB. iv. 1. 5; Hopkins, JAOS. xxvi. 45 ff.; JB. iii. 120–8; V. Henry (*Mythes naturalistes*, p. 12) sees in him the setting sun and compares Sisyphos. The RV. has Cyavāna. Cf. Macdonell and Keith, *Vedic Index*, i. 244 f.

[2] On this mode of reckoning cf. Rhys, *Celtic Heathendom*, pp. 360 ff. Conceivably there is here a relic of a nine-day week, but the notion is isolated. Cf. von Schroeder, *Arische Religion*, ii. 666. Max Müller (*Beitr. zu einer wiss. Myth.* ii. 160) prefers the twelve nights of the winter solstice, and suggests a Lettish parallel.

[3] Various views are suggested by Myriantheus, *Die Açvins* (Munich, 1876), and since him many more have been put forward. Cf. Tilak, *Orion*, pp. 363 ff.; Max Müller, *Beitr. zu einer wiss. Myth.* ii. 150 ff.; Baunack, ZDMG. l. 263 ff.; von Schroeder, *Arische Religion*, ii. 441 ff.; A. C. Das, *Rig-Vedic India*, i. 530 ff.

suggestion that Viçpalā is the first quarter of the new moon is no more plausible. The rescue of the quail from the mouth of a wolf and the slaying of 101 sheep by Ṛjrāçva are episodes also which seem mythical. But to recognize that there may be a mythical foundation to a story and to discover that foundation, when the episode is given in the form of a mere reference in a few words in the Rigveda, are totally different things, and it would be contrary to sound method to seek to penetrate the exact force of these legends: it is not difficult to interpret them, but the fatal objection to such attempts is that several ways of interpretation are always open, and that we have no standard of criticism by which to judge of the comparative merits of the different views.

It is a different matter with the question of the essential nature of the two gods: while that is obscure, some effort to elucidate it is made requisite by the abundance of the material. In the first place, however, it is important to note that in part at least the Indo-European character of the deities is beyond all reasonable doubt:[1] there is a very famous Lettish myth which shows us the two sons—or one son—of a god who are helpers in time of need and who come riding on their steeds to woo the daughter of the sun for themselves or for the moon, just as in the Rigveda the Açvins are both wooers of the sun-maiden for themselves and also for Soma, the moon. Here the god or gods are also described as the morning star. In the Greek myth of the Dioskouroi and their relation to Helene we have a clear variant of the legend, and the Dioskouroi are of course *par excellence* the saviours of men, especially at sea.[2] Moreover, the evidence of Boghaz-Köi, as we have seen, proves the early existence of the Nāsatyas,[3] and makes it most probable that the Avesta knew them; before the reform of Zoroaster the Nāoṅhaithya must have been great gods. This fact explains in great measure the obscurity of the mythic conception of the gods; they have in the course of transmission attained greater personality, and therefore the natural substratum of the gods is hard to recognize.

The difficulty was fully known in the earliest period of Vedic interpretation: Yāska[4] gives as alternative views sky and earth, which is the view of the Çatapatha Brāhmaṇa,[5] or day and night, or sun and moon, or two kings, performers of holy deeds. The last view is naturally that of Geldner,[6] who denies their connexion with the Dioskouroi and asserts that they are merely Indian saints who save in time of trouble, a view which is clearly based on a false effort to dissociate Indian from Indo-European mythology. The view

[1] Cf. the prayer of Alkaios in eleven-syllable metre as in Vedic, E. Leumann, *Buddha und Mahāvīra*, pp. 8 f.; Mannhardt, *Zeitschrift für Ethnologie*, vii. 312 ff. *Contra*, Farnell, *Greek Hero Cults*, pp. 175 ff.

[2] Cf. J. Rendel Harris, *Essays and Studies presented to W. Ridgeway*, pp. 549–57.

[3] Germanic and Celtic parallels are alleged in Tacitus, *Germ.* 43; Timaios in Diod. iv. 56. Cf. Helm, *Altgerm. Rel.* i. 321 ff. More distantly von Schroeder (*Arische Religion*, ii. 404 ff.) compares the sacred marriage of Zeus and Here, Jupiter and Juno, &c.

[4] Nir. xii. 1.

[5] iv. 1. 5. 16.

[6] *Ved. Stud.* ii. 31.

that the gods are sun and moon has the support of Ludwig,[1] Hillebrandt,[2] and Hardy,[3] but nothing else whatever can be said for it. The explanations as day and night and sky and earth have equally feeble support, and more plausibility attaches to the suggestion, perhaps made by Yāska and adopted by Goldstücker, that the twilights are meant, the half-dark, half-light period before dawn, and this would account for the fact that one only is said to be a son of Dyaus. The more probable alternative to this view is that of Mannhardt[4] and Oldenberg,[5] who, on the strength in part of the mention of the morning star and the evening star in the acçount of the Lettish god or gods, take the two gods to be the morning and the evening star respectively. The difficulty of this conception is, of course, the fact that the gods are so essentially twin, and the view, if adopted, necessitates the supposition that this fact had gradually been obscured. There are indeed some traces of their separate character in the Rigveda[6] itself: thus they are called 'separately born' and 'born here and there', and Yāska preserves a verse[7] of which he says: 'One is called the son of night, the other the son of dawn.' This is, it must be admitted, far from convincing evidence of a real recollection of the twin character of the stars, but the suggestion of Weber,[8] that they are to be taken as the twin stars of Gemini, is open to the quite fatal objection that there is nothing but the twin nature to commend it. Nor is the loss of the primitive connexion at all impossible, with the growing importance of the morning as the time of sacrifice.[9]

A very different conception of the nature of the twins is suggested by Harris,[10] whose collections of ethnic materials reveals the idea that of pairs of twins one is often held to have a divine origin, without there being any myth of nature involved. Whatever the value of the theory for other cases, it seems to have no special plausibility for Indian religion,[11] in which the natural background is clear, as it is in the Lettish myths, whose importance seems unduly to be depreciated by failure to realize the remarkable character of the parallels with the Indian legends.

Other questions are suggested by the nature of the steeds of the Açvins. The conjecture that they were once not merely regarded as borne on chariots with horses, but were conceived as horses, can be supported by analogy: thus the sun is certainly called a horse, and the mother of the Açvins is, according

[1] *Rigveda*, iii. 34.
[2] *Ved. Myth.* iii. 379–96.
[3] *Ved.-brahm. Periode*, pp. 47–9.
[4] *Loc. cit.*
[5] *Rel. des Veda*², pp. 209–15.
[6] v. 73. 4; i. 181. 4.
[7] Nir. xii. 2.
[8] *Rājasūya*, p. 100.
[9] Wide (*Lak. Kulte*, p. 316) denies the star character of the Dioskouroi, and Farnell (*Greece and Babylon*, pp. 112, 113) follows him. But see von Schroeder, *Arische Religion*, ii. 445 ff.; Fox, *Greek and Roman Myth.*, pp. 246 f.; Cook, *Zeus*, i. 760 ff.; Güntert, pp. 253 ff.
[10] *The Cult of the Heavenly Twins* (1906) and *Boanerges* (1913).
[11] Oldenberg, *Rel. des Veda*², p. 211, n. 1, suggests that the native legend may have borrowed aspects from the magic powers ascribed by many peoples to twins as uncanny.

to an old, if not Rigvedic, tradition, called a mare. Beyond this we cannot go. The fact that the chariots are also borne by birds is of some interest: are we to see in this fact, as suggested in another connexion of the Dioskouroi by S. Reinach,[1] a relic of a time when the Açvins were regarded themselves as birds, and in special swans? It is clearly impossible to determine this with any security: there is no trace of such a view in the Vedic literature, and to conjecture it into that literature is, therefore, illegitimate, since it is not necessary thus to explain the fact that the chariot of the gods is borne by birds.

The connexion of the gods with Sūryā presents difficulties in that it is not at all clear what Sūryā represents: Mannhardt [2] suggests for her the Dawn, E. H. Meyer [3] the goddess of the clouds, while Oldenberg [4] thinks that Sūryā means literally the sun-maiden as the feminine form of the sun, the alternative expression 'daughter of the sun' being invented to remove the apparent inconsistency of the usage. It is difficult to feel any certainty as to this identification: the fact that Soma is said to marry the maiden does increase the probability that she is the sun, but the further fact that Pūṣan also marries her makes the idea less likely. Ingenuity might also connect the legend of the victory of the Açvins in a chariot race at the wedding of Sūryā to Soma as a trace of an older version, in which the Açvins were able to win her hand by showing their superior swiftness to the other wooers in a chariot race, and this idea would carry us into the sphere of conceptions which are seen in the Indian Svayaṁvara, but common sense forbids us to combine priestly speculations in this manner.[5]

§ 7. *The Goddess Dawn*

Uṣas the goddess is no small figure in the Rigveda: she is the subject of twenty hymns and is mentioned not less than 300 times in all, and the hymns addressed to her are among the most brilliant in the whole of the Saṁhitā. The personification of the dawn is of the slightest description, and takes the form of picturing her as a maiden decked by her mother in gay attire, who reveals her bosom to mortal eyes. She is young, being born again and again,

[1] *Cultes, Mythes et Religions*, ii. 42–57. Cf. the bird form assumed by the Hotṛ when reciting the morning litany at the Atirātra, AÇS. vi. 5. 4.

[2] *Op. cit.*, p. 295; so AB. iv. 7 f.

[3] *Indog. Myth.* ii. 673.

[4] *Rel. des Veda*², p. 213; von Schroeder (*op. cit.* ii. 414, n. 3) regards her as the young sun, who is renewed yearly and celebrates a fresh marriage.

[5] The legend of Pelops has, it is well known, of late led to the most remarkable speculations of annual victims, determined as the result of races, by the Cambridge school of religion; see *Themis*, pp. 220 ff. Usener (*Götternamen*, pp. 228, 229) compares the wedding of Soma and Sūryā to that of Zeus and Here; see also von Schroeder, *op. cit.* ii. 392 ff. Hillebrandt (*Ved. Myth.* ii. 41 f.) strongly supports Sūryā as Uṣas. The apparent polyandry of Sūryā in myth, *not* the wedding hymn, is clearly not to be taken as a reflex of human usage despite von Schroeder (*op. cit.* ii. 402); cf. the connexion of the morning and evening stars with the twilights, Gray, *Myth. of All Races*, iii. 325. Different ideas may easily lie at the bottom of the myths.

and yet is ancient: she wastes away the life of mortals. She shines now, and shall shine in the future as in former days; she shines forth, shortening the days of men, the last of the days that have dawned, the first of those that have to come. Uṣas on her coming awakes to life men and animals: the birds fly up from their nest, and men seek their work. She illumines the ways, and drives away the spirits of darkness and evil: bad dreams she sends to Trita Āptya. She opens the gates of darkness as the cattle their stall, and she is called the mother of cattle. She is borne on a shining swift car drawn by steeds, or ruddy kine or bulls, perhaps the red rays of the light of morning rather than the red clouds of the morning: in a day she traverses thirty Yojanas.

The Dawn stands in the closest relation to the sun, who follows her as a lover. She is the wife as well as the beloved of Sūrya, but, as she precedes him as well as is followed by him, by another train of thought she appears as the mother of Sūrya or yet again as created by him. She is also the sister of the Āditya Bhaga, the kinswoman of Varuṇa, and the sister, the greater sister, of night, from whom, however, she is also born, and who appears invoked jointly with her; both are mothers or wives of Sūrya or Agni.[1] Beyond all she is the daughter of Dyaus, and even once she appears as the beloved of heaven. With Agni she is closely connected, appearing before or with or after him as the fire lit for the morning sacrifice. She is the friend of the Açvins and is born at the yoking of their car: moreover, if she is Sūryā, she is also their wife. Once too, like Sūryā, she is associated with the moon, which precedes the dawns as the harbinger of day. Indra is said to have lighted up the dawn as is natural in the great finder of light, but once he appears as hostile and as shattering her car:[2] the myth is obscure, and has been variously interpreted of the thunderstorm overwhelming the light of dawn, and as a victory of Indra bringing the sun over the dawn, which seeks to delay his advent. With the latter view may be compared the prayer that is once offered to her not to delay her coming, that the sun may not scorch her as a thief or an enemy.[3] Normally, however, the Dawn never infringes the law of order: she goes straight along her path and never misses her way. She awakes the devout man to sacrifice, and is besought to let the niggard sleep on. But, by the usual inversion of ideas, she is sometimes represented as being awakened by the worshippers. To her worshipper she brings wealth, long life, renown, and glory, to her and to the sun the dead man is said to go,[4] and the Fathers are seated in the lap of the ruddy dawns.[5]

[1] Perhaps wives of Vivasvant; RV. x. 17. 1 f.; Hillebrandt, *Ved. Myth.* ii. 44–7.

[2] RV. ii. 15. 6; iv. 30. 8–11; x. 138. 5; 73. 6. An Australian parallel is given by Lang, *Custom and Myth*, p. 210. The Brāhmaṇas have a tale of the incest of Prajāpati and Uṣas, apparently a myth of nature; RV. i. 71. 5, 8; iii. 31. 1; v. 42. 13; x. 10. 1; 61. 5 ff.; ÇB. vi. 1. 3. 7 f.; i. 7. 4. 1 f.; MS. iv. 2, 12; PB. viii. 2. 10.

[3] RV. v. 79. 9.

[4] RV. x. 15. 9.

[5] RV. x. 15. 7.

Throughout the conception of dawn there runs the multiplicity of the actual dawns on the one hand and the unity of the goddess on the other hand; the poet here and there inclines to treat each dawn as a separate being, but this tendency is over-crossed by the unity of the substance of the deity. She is, of course, the Aurora of Rome and the Eos of Greece, but the parallelism is no proof of an Indo-European cult, and the Teutonic Ostara and the Lettish Uhsing represent rather a worship of the young sun in the spring.[1]

It would, of course, be an error to suppose that these hymns to Dawn are generically different from the other Vedic hymns: they are not in the slightest degree inconsistent with the position which in the ritual the goddess has assigned her: she in the morning before the birds begin to sing is invoked with other deities, but receives no share in the Soma drink. On the other hand, while in much of the poetry there is, as a result in part of this fact, a freedom from connexion with the details of the offering, the priests were well aware of the value of the Dawn to them as bringing the activity of the sacrifice, and ensuring them the largesse which they desired: hence it is not impossible that the epithet Dakṣiṇā attributed in one passage to the goddess does directly identify her with the sacrificial fee, and reduce the dawn to the aspect of a valuable commercial asset.[2] It would be wrong, therefore, to accept the view[3] that the worship of Dawn died out as the Vedic Indians wandered further south-east, as was long ago suggested by Weber. On the other hand, it is clear that this worship must have had a commencement, and that too in some place where the phenomena of nature are such as to evoke the real poetry of the Vedic descriptions of dawn; that this must have been in the Punjab is all but certain. This fact alone would suggest the early date of the Uṣas hymns, for the heart of the Rigveda was not, we may be certain, composed there, but rather in the later Kurukṣetra country south of Ambāla, where alone the phenomena, which are seen in the myth of Indra, appear in their full form.[4] In these later seats of Vedic civilization the goddess continued to receive her meed of praise, and hymns based on the old were composed for her, but the worship of the goddess was never of importance in the ritual. Hillebrandt's[5] theory that the Dawn celebrated in the Rigveda is the first dawn of the new year, is wholly unsupported by any evidence, and depends on a theory of the Rigvedic view of the year which is arbitrary. He identifies dawn with the

[1] Uṣas's dance (RV. x. 29. 2) may be compared with the dance of the sun on Easter day in German and Slav mythology; von Schroeder, *Arische Religion*, ii. 51 ff. For Celtic parallels, see Rhys, *Celtic Heathendom*, pp. 299 f., 384 f., 456.

[2] Bloomfield, *Rel. of Veda*, p. 71.

[3] Weber, *Omina et Portenta*, p. 351. Hillebrandt (*Ved. Myth.* ii. 38 f.) thinks that the dawn cult is to be traced to a place where winter conditions cause the cattle to be stalled in security from the cold, as in Vend. ii. 23; Vergil, *Georg.* iii. 352.

[4] Hopkins, JAOS. xix. 28 ff.; above, Part I, Chap. 1.

[5] *Ved. Myth.* ii. 25 ff., followed by von Schroeder, *Arische Religion*, ii. 58 f. For the fact that night in the Vedic conception preceded day see Keith, JRAS. 1916, pp. 143–6, 555–60. Virāj in AV. viii. 9. 1 may be dawn. For the dawns and Indra's contest with Vala see Chap. 9, § 1.

Ekāṣṭakā, which falls in the dark half of the month Māgha, and is connected with the Manes, but this is purely arbitrary. Nor is there any force in Brāhmaṇa assertions of Uṣas as wife of the year and wife of the seasons.[1]

§ 8. *The Moon*

Apart from his connexion with Soma,[2] the moon is not prominent in the Vedic literature, unless with Hillebrandt we recognize him under such guises as that of Bṛhaspati, Apāṁ Napāt, Varuṇa, Yama, Narāçaṅsa, or Tvaṣṭṛ, or Viçvarūpa. He appears rarely in conjunction with Sūrya in the compounds Sūryāmāsā and Sūryācandramasā, but little is said of the pair beyond noting their alternate appearance, which is once attributed to Bṛhaspati, their creation by the creator, and the fact that they are the two bright eyes of Varuṇa.[3] The birth of the moon from the sun is recognized, as well as its regular death.[4] The connexion of the moon with the mind is early recorded,[5] and may stand in relation to its connexion with the Fathers.[6] In addition to the influence of the moon on vegetation, its connexion with the tides is recognized.[7] The moon phases also receive some degree of worship,[8] and the darkness in the face of the moon is accounted for in various ways.[9] The Jaiminīya Brāhmaṇa[10] already records the existence in the moon of a hare, identified with Yama, whence the later name of Çaçin, a view corresponding to the occidental belief in the man in the moon. Among other identifications Prajāpati appears once equated with Candramas, but the more normal view is found in the idea of the Kauṣītaki Brāhmaṇa that from the asceticism of Prajāpati there sprang up five beings, Agni, Vāyu, Āditya, Candramas, and Uṣas. Another passage tells that the first four of these deities made good the members of Prajāpati when the work of creation exhausted him and he fell to pieces.[11]

Much stress has of late[12] been laid on the moon as the source of many myths which appear in our texts in connexion with the sun; thus the ritual

[1] ÇB. vi. 1. 3. 8; MS. ii. 13. 10. For Tilak's theory of a polar dawn see *Arctic Home in the Vedas*, pp. 82 ff., and a refutation in A. C. Das, *Rig-Vedic India*, i. 390 ff.

[2] See below, Chap. 10, § 3. For Iran, see Herodotos, i. 131, and for other religions, von Schroeder, *Arische Religion*, ii. 459 ff.

[3] RV. i. 102. 2; x. 68. 10; 190. 3; viii. 41. 9; i. 72. 10.

[4] AV. xi. 5 (Hillebrandt, *Ved. Myth.* i. 471 f.); RV. x. 55. 5 (where Soma is clearly the moon); TB. ii. 5. 7. 3.

[5] RV. x. 90. 13 (moon born from mind); AA. ii. 4. 1; BAU. i. 3. 16; iii. 2. 13.

[6] Stereotyped in BAU. vi. 2; CU. v. 10; see below, Chap. 28, § 10. For this connexion cf. Plutarch, *de facie in orbe lunae*, 28, pp. 943 A, 943 C; Iamblichos, *V. P.* 82. The moon is the place, eye, light of the Fathers, KB. i. 2; MS. iv. 2. 1; ÇB. ii. 4. 2. 2.

[7] AB. vii. 11. For the origin of rain from the moon, see AB. viii. 28. 15; Darmesteter, ZA. ii. 308; Pliny, *N. H.* xx. 1.

[8] See below, Chap. 11, § 9.

[9] The offering-place on the earth is placed in the moon, VS. i. 28; ÇB. i. 2. 5. 8 f.

[10] i. 2. 8.

[11] ÇB. vi. 1. 3. 16; KB. vi. 1; TB. ii. 3. 6. 1.

[12] Von Schroeder, *Arische Religion*, ii. 559 ff.; F. Schultze, *Psychologie der Naturvölker*, pp. 318 ff.

use of swinging has plausibly been regarded as unnatural as a sun rite, but easily explicable as one derived from the moon; the conception of the sun as a boat or a vessel stands in a similar relation, while in German mythology such Indian beliefs as the hare in the moon, and the ceremonial striking of the calves with a fresh twig to produce milk in connexion with the new and full moon offerings, appear transferred to the sun. The importance of the moon in early times as giving the means of measuring time is insisted upon, and even the connexion of the fish with fertility is traced to the apparent connexion of shape between the fish and the sickle of the moon. These conjectures, fortunately, need not be seriously considered in regard to Vedic mythology; if they have any validity, they refer to a period distinctly earlier than the religion of the Veda.

It is probable in any case that the question is not one of the supersession of a moon mythology by a sun mythology, but of simple contamination. If we hear that in the highest step of Viṣṇu there is the well of the mead,[1] it is not necessary to bring into connexion with this the Lettish legend of the footprint of the horse in which Uhsing, god of the spring sun, brews beer, and to suggest that there was an Indo-European myth which saw in the marks on the moon the footprint of a steed, the conclusion ultimately being drawn that behind both Viṣṇu and Uhsing we have a moon deity. The mead is from the heaven, Viṣṇu's highest step is in the heaven; the combination of ideas is thoroughly in the spirit of the Vedic imagination. Or again Agni's flight into the waters,[2] and assumption of animal forms therein, are easily enough explained from his character as the lightning from the clouds, and we are not really helped by the suggestion that the myth goes back to the loss of light when the moon disappears, the theriomorphic conception being due to the sickle shape of the moon which suggests a fish,[3] naturally equated with the salmon form in which Loki evaded his pursuers, or even the Dolphin shape of Apollo. Agni, after all, is not conceived as a fish, and the imaginative efforts required to introduce the moon suggest that the whole suggestion of the importance of the moon is greatly exaggerated. The moon by its waxing and waning doubtless was of great importance in fixing times of offering, but in India at least it is difficult to see how fundamental importance could be attached to this figure in comparison with the vital energy of the sun. The ethnic evidence for the importance of the moon is valuable,[4] but it is idle to suppose that every religion has developed on parallel lines and we may believe that Indo-European religion, owing perhaps to the place of its development, was less than some others inclined to make much of the moon.

[1] RV. i. 154. 5.

[2] See below, Chap. 10, § 1.

[3] Von Schroeder naturally finds here an explanation of the Christian fish symbol, discussed by Scheftelowitz, *Archiv für Rel.* xiv. 1–53, 321–92; Cumont, *Die orientalischen Religionen im römischen Heidentum*, pp. 137 ff., 283 ff.

[4] See Hillebrandt, *Ved. Myth.*, pp. 13 ff.; Rhys, *Celtic Heathendom*, pp. 672 f. For Germany see Caesar, *B. G.* i. 50; Helm, *Altgerm. Rel.* i. 257 f.; for Rome, Wissowa, *Rel. der Römer*², p. 315; Fox, *Greek and Roman Myth.*, pp. 244 f.

CHAPTER 9

THE GREAT GODS—AERIAL

§ 1. *Indra*

INDRA is the greatest god of the Rigveda, with the solitary exception of Varuṇa, who may be deemed to equal him in might.[1] His connexion with the Soma offering is, however, far closer than that of Varuṇa ; he is the subject of 250 hymns, or almost a quarter of the whole of the collection, and he shares with other deities at least fifty more. He is, however, like Varuṇa in one thing : he is not a god whose physical nature overwhelms the anthropomorphism of the poets : he has, therefore, become the subject of many myths, which it would be idle to seek to bring into any connexion whatever with the normal basis of his nature.

Of the personal appearance of Indra a much more vivid picture is given than of any other of the gods : he has head, arms, hands, and a great belly which he fills full with the Soma, so that it comes to be likened to a lake. His lips are often mentioned : his beard is agitated when he moves, and, like his hair, it is tawny ; his arms are long and strong, as becomes the wielder of the bolt, and he can assume any form at will. His favourite weapon is the thunderbolt,[2] of metal or of gold, with four or a hundred angles, with a hundred or a thousand points. His is *par excellence* the epithet *vajrin*, 'bearer of the bolt', which is else given but once each to Rudra, the Maruts, and Manyu. When he bears a bow, his arrows are hundred-pointed and winged with a thousand feathers. He has also a hook with which he gives wealth or fights, and the Atharvaveda [3] gives him a net wherewith to overcome his foes. His chariot is drawn by horses, normally two, but sometimes a thousand or eleven hundred : their hair is like peacock's feathers. His favourite food is the Soma, which he drinks on the very day of his birth, and of which he consumed three lakes when seeking to slay Vṛtra : on yet another occasion he drank thirty lakes. The epithet Soma-drinker is so essentially his that it is given only to Vāyu apart from him, and a few times to Bṛhaspati and Agni, when associated with him. His connexion with Vāyu in this regard is close : he is said to have Indra for his charioteer. Indra, however, also drinks milk mixed with honey, and is partial to buffaloes, eating as many as

[1] For his parallelism with Thorr, see Mannhardt, *Germ. Myth.*, pp. 1 ff. ; von Schroeder, *Arische Religion*, ii. 625 ff. ; Rhys, *Celtic Heathendom*, pp. 291 ff. ; with Herakles, von Schroeder, *Herakles und Indra* (1914). See also B. Schweitzer, *Herakles* (1922).

[2] In the epic Indra has the boomerang (MBh. iii. 309. 24), as also Thorr.

[3] viii. 8. 5–8.

100 or even 300. He also eats cakes and grain, of which his horses likewise partake.

The birth of Indra is mysterious, like that of other heroes ; he declines to be born save through his mother's side :[1] this may be interpreted[2] as the lightning bursting through the cloud, or it may be merely treated as one of the many cases of miraculous births, which may be ascribed to nothing more than popular fancy, and of which the birth of Athene is on one view a famous case. His mother is called once a cow, and he is styled a calf : once[3] she is called Niṣṭigrī, identified by Sāyaṇa with Aditi. Twice she is styled Çavasī, as he is the son of strength (*çavas*). The Atharvaveda[4] makes her Ekāṣṭakā, daughter of Prajāpati, which is of course merely speculation. His father is Tvaṣṭṛ or Dyaus, and a legend[5] clearly indicates that, in order to obtain the Soma, he seized his father by the foot and slew him : perhaps for this reason we find one clear record of the hostility of the gods to Indra. Only late speculation[6] makes him the oldest, or the favourite, son of Prajāpati, while with Agni he springs from the mouth of the giant in the Puruṣasūkta. Agni and Pūṣan are made his brothers, and his sons once occur, but without indication who they are ; he has, however, a son Kutsa, produced from his thigh and precisely like him, in the Jaiminīya.[7] His wife is Indrāṇī, but the Aitareya Brāhmaṇa[8] gives him two wives, Senā and Prāsahā, who are clearly legendary ; the regular post-Vedic wife, Çacī, daughter of Puloman, is clearly derived from his epithet *çacīpati*, ' lord of strength ', understood as husband of Çacī, a meaning which Pischel[9] vainly reads into the Rigveda. She definitely appears in the Jaiminīya Brāhmaṇa in a curious legend in which Kutsa Aurava, born of Indra's thigh and his double, lies with her and is marked by Indra to distinguish him. But another tale alluded to in the Atharvaveda[10] tells how in love of an Asura woman, the Dānavī Vilisteñgā,[11] he went to live among the Asuras, assuming a female form among women, a male among men. Here perhaps should be reckoned his invocation as Menā, ' wife ' or ' daughter ' of Vṛṣaṇaçva in the Subrahmaṇyā.[12] A vulgar tale[13] records how, as Sumitra, he had

[1] RV. iv. 18. 1–2.

[2] Macdonell, *Ved. Myth.*, p. 56 ; cf. Carnoy, *Les Indo-Européens*, p. 196 ; *contra*, Hartland, *Legend of Perseus*, i. 71 ff. ; Oldenberg, *Rel. des Veda*², p. 132, n. 3 ; Hillebrandt, *Ved. Myth.* iii. 409 ; Fox, *Greek and Roman Mythology*, p. 170.

[3] RV. x. 101. 12. For Çavasī, see RV. viii. 45. 5 ; 77. 2.

[4] iii. 10. 12, 13.

[5] RV. iv. 18. 12 ; iii. 48. 4.

[6] TB. ii. 2. 10. 1 ; ÇB. xi. 1. 6. 14 ; PB. xvi. 4 ff.

[7] iii. 199 ; this legend is aetiological and curious ; Kutsa is spared by Indra despite his act in posing as him to Çacī, but refuses him sacrifice and kills the son of Suçravas, his Purohita, who does sacrifice to him ; at Suçravas' entreaty Indra revives him. That RV. iv. 16. 10 knows this legend (Caland, *Over en uit het Jaiminīya-brāhmaṇa*, p. 74) is dubious.

[8] iii. 22. 7.

[9] *Ved. Stud.* ii. 52. Cf. Bloomfield, ZDMG. xlviii. 548 ; JB. iii. 199–202.

[10] vii. 38. 2.

[11] Weber, *Ind. Stud.* iii. 479 ; Oertel, JAOS. xix. 120.

[12] Cf. Hillebrandt, *Ved. Myth.* ii. 209 ; JB. ii. 79 ; ÇB. iii. 3. 4. 18.

[13] JB. i. 162 f. ; PB. xiii. 6. 9 ff. ; Oertel, *Actes du Onzième Congrès Int. des Orient.* i. 225 ff., who cites RV. ix. 101. 1. He appears as an aged dancer, with

intercourse with Dīrghajihvī, an Asura woman, who licked the Soma and had unlimited organs of sex.

Of the other gods Indra is closely connected with his troop, the Maruts, with Agni whom he generates or finds in the waters, and to whom he is akin in nature, with Varuṇa, Vāyu, Soma, Bṛhaspati, Pūṣan, and Viṣṇu, whose relation to him becomes in some passages a close one. With Sūrya he is actually here and there identified, he receives the epithet Savitṛ, and the Çatapatha Brāhmaṇa[1] declares him to be the sun and Vṛtra the moon. But he differs from all the gods in his physical magnitude which makes the two worlds but half of him, heaven and earth insufficient for his girdle, and ten earths not equal to him. No language is too strong for the Vedic poets in expressing his greatness: Sūrya and Varuṇa are made inferior to him, he is invoked to destroy the foes of Varuṇa, Mitra, Aryaman, he makes broad space for the gods in battle: he is an independent ruler *par excellence*, and occasionally, like Varuṇa, a universal ruler. He is the mighty (*çakra*), an epithet rarely used of any other god. He practically alone is styled 'of a hundred powers' (*çatakratu*); he is strong, young, immortal, and ancient.

There is nothing here to show clearly the nature of Indra, save in so far as his connexion with the sun and the fire suggests his fiery character, and that with Vāyu his fierce onset. But the myth of the slaying of Vṛtra, which is the great deed of the god, is not doubtful in sense. It takes the form of the slaying by the god with the aid of the Maruts and of Viṣṇu, or without their aid, of a serpent which was lying on the mountains keeping in with its coils the waters of the streams. The flood of the waters flows then swiftly to the sea, and at the same time the light shines forth. The god strikes Vṛtra on the back, or smites his face, or pierces his vital parts. But the action is not done once, but ever and again, and Indra is implored to perform it in the future as in the past. The waters set free are likened often to lowing cows, and such is the fury of the onset that the heaven and earth tremble with fear. It is important to note that the terms used of the myth are essentially restricted with very rare exceptions to the words, bolt, mountain, waters, or rivers, in place of lightning, clouds, and air. The cows which occur here and there are open to two interpretations; they may be simply the waters, for in a few cases the waters are clearly so designated, as when it is said that the cows roared at the birth of Indra. But they may also be the rays of light, set free when the waters are loosened.

In the view of Oldenberg[2] the use of the terms mountain and streams is proof that in the Vedic period the poets conceived the deed of Indra as the setting forth from mountains on earth of streams terrestrial, the invaluable

a yoke on his shoulders, supporting a basket of cakes and a pot of curds and butter, to Upamā, wife of Kṣatra, a presage of victory in battle; JB. iii. 244 ff.

[1] Cf. Hillebrandt, *op. cit.* iii. 44. For Vṛtra's distinction in the Brāhmaṇas cf. Hopkins, *Trans. Conn. Acad.* xv. 43 f.

[2] *Rel. des Veda*², pp. 137 ff.

waters of the Punjab: he grants that in the oldest period the myth was one of the thunderstorm, the fall of rain, and the coming of the light.[1] But, while he admits that this view of the myth was perfectly well known to Yāska and to the later literature, he denies that it was appreciated by the Vedic poets. This is, however, difficult to accept: the arguments adduced for it are not by any means conclusive. The absence of direct mention normally—occasionally there is such mention as Oldenberg admits—is due to the fact that the story is a myth; it has passed the stage when it is merely a description of phenomenon, and it is not only a myth but a very popular myth. Moreover, it is impossible to accept the view that Vajra, the name of the bolt, is not the thunderbolt, which it is throughout the Vedic literature, often in quite clear fashion. The comparison of mountains with clouds is natural and easy: the mountains are the clouds, which before the storm hang in heavy darkness refusing to yield the rain: the storm comes, the lightning bursts forth, the rain falls, and the sun shines out. A different view is suggested by the theory of Hillebrandt[2] which sees in the story of the contest with Vṛtra, not the storm-god bringing down the rain to earth, but the defeating of a serpent demon, the glacier which with the winter cold holds fast the waters in ice.[3] The suggestion is brilliant and attractive, and, if such a glacial myth existed, it would clearly be natural to find its remnants in the tale of Vṛtra, but the evidence which can be adduced from the language of the Rigveda is of the most inadequate nature to prove the thesis desired.

The slaying of Vṛtra is not merely attributed to Indra: by the syncretism of the Veda, it is also attributed to Agni and Soma. The gods as a whole are supposed to aid Indra in the contest, but at the roaring or hissing of the serpent they fled, leaving the Maruts only to aid him, and once at least even they fled, and left him alone. Viṣṇu is also an aider in the struggle and even earthly priests lend aid.

Another myth tells of the slaying of the three-headed Viçvarūpa by Indra:[4] it is, however, clear that this is a more modern form of a myth in which Viçvarūpa was slain by Trita, for this form of the myth appears in the Rigveda, and in the Avesta Thraētaona is said to slay a three-headed serpent with six eyes, freeing thus two fair ladies. In the classical myths of Herakles and Geryoneus, and of Hercules and Cacus, the monsters have likewise three heads, and, when slain, the hero wins the cattle which they have taken and

[1] Cf. the Avestan demon Apaoša, really allied verbally to Vṛtra; Wackernagel, *Festschrift Kuhn*, pp. 158 f.; and Helm, *Altgerm. Rel.* i. 192 ff.

[2] *Ved. Myth.* iii. 174–201; (Kl. Ausg.), pp. 85 ff. Cf. Barth, *Rev. de l'histoire des rel.* xxxix. 69; Bloomfield, *Rel. of Veda*, pp. 178 ff. Hopkins (JAOS. xxxvi. 242 ff.) finds in Indra a deity of fertility, originally of the Kuçikas and Gotamas who won acceptance by the Bharadvājas as war-god, and became generally revered as a great god. Güntert (pp. 11 ff.) makes him a war-god and demon-slayer.

[3] Von Schroeder (*op. cit.* ii. 613) compares Thorr's relation to ice and glaciers.

[4] Hillebrandt (*Ved. Myth.* i. 531–5) holds that Viçvarūpa is the moon in its hostile aspect.

hidden away. The motive of winning cows is found also in the Viçvarūpa myth, and it is perfectly clear that these four myths are one and the same in nature: in the case of the Avesta the part of restoring lost cattle has past over to Ahura himself, who is *par excellence* the discoverer of lost things.

With this myth may be compared the legend [1] of Saramā and the Paṇis. The Paṇis stole and hid away cows in a cave among the rocks, and Indra's dog, Saramā, pursues them and finds the place where are the cows: them she demands back from the Paṇis in a dialogue which is preserved to us in an interesting, if not very old, hymn of the Rigveda. The Paṇis refuse to give them back and the later tradition makes Saramā unfaithful to her mission. This, however, is not recorded in the Rigveda, and from other accounts it seems that Indra advances against the Paṇis and recovers the cows. Moreover, we find Bṛhaspati engaged in the same feat: the priestly god with his prayers cleaves the barriers behind which the cows are hidden, and brings them forth. Agni too takes a share in the struggle: the priestly god of fire is naturally active in this important undertaking. The Aṅgirases also take a great part, or, in their place, the seven seers, the eponymous fathers of the priestly clans. They pray and they offer sacrifice, and thus attain the same end. A further element in the picture of Vala: Indra cleaves his ridge in attaining the cows. The meaning of the myth can hardly be doubtful when it is noted how often Indra is brought into prominence as the maker of the dawn and the finder of the sun. The cows must be, not rain-clouds, as sometimes in the myth of Vṛtra, but the morning beams of light, or perhaps the red clouds of dawn; there is little difference between the two conceptions. The nature of Vala, 'the Keeper', is clearer still: he is merely the personification of the place in which the cows are kept. But the Paṇis are not quite so easy to explain: Hillebrandt [2] has found in them an historical people, and has argued that the mention of the Paṇis is a piece of history turned into myth. It is perfectly possible that this could be the case, but in the case of the Paṇis, who are assimilated to Parnians, the references are not satisfactorily taken as historical in ultimate essence: the theory too involves speculations regarding the places in which the Rigveda was composed which will not stand very close investigation.[3] The natural and satisfactory view is that the Paṇis were the misers, who refuse to give the priests gifts, and who are overthrown, a conception which is interwoven with the mythical winning of the clouds.

A further question, however, arises as to the exact circumstances in which

[1] RV. x. 108. Oldenberg (*Rel. des Veda*², p. 147) treats the legend as an aetiological myth to explain men's ownership of cows. A similar view of the waters myth is also unlikely. Rhys (*Celtic Heathendom*, pp. 299 ff.) holds him a culture hero, but admits contamination with Trita or Dyaus.

[2] *Ved. Myth.* i. 83–116; he finds the dawn in Saramā, and sun and moon in the Sārameyas, and so with Saraṇyū (ii. 48–50).

[3] Macdonell and Keith, *Vedic Index*, i. 471–3. Meyer (*Gesch. des Alt.*³ I. ii. p. 905) also rejects Hillebrandt's view, which is repeated in *Ved. Myth.*, pp. 95 f. See Oldenberg on RV. vi. 61. 1; GGA. 1914, p. 447.

the clouds are won. Is it to be supposed that the legend is only another side of the winning of the light in the Vṛtra legend, which means, no doubt, the appearance of light after the thunderstorm ? The answer to this question is usually given in the affirmative, but it seems much more likely that the myth is an independent one, the winning of the sun and the dawn from the dark mountains of the night, as is the view of Oldenberg. To suppose that this is a secondary development from the other myth is not necessary, nor very probable. But it is impossible to follow Oldenberg in the view that the winning of the light and the sun, which is connected with the Vṛtra myth, is not an expression of the recovery of the light after the storm, but a poetical embellishment of the theme.

While it is in these mythical forms that the feats of Indra as bringing down the rain and finding the light are mainly celebrated, there are passages in which he is credited with creating the lightnings and turning the waters of heaven downwards, and very much more freely is his feat of winning the dawn and the sun celebrated. Such a god was clearly essentially suited to be the god of the warrior, and Indra is the great aider of the Vedic Indian, the Aryan, in his fights, whether with other Aryan foes, or more often in the tradition with the Dāsas or Dasyus, in whom we must often see the aborigines. It would be wholly impossible to believe that in every case the Dāsas are human enemies, and they include doubtless evil spirits who are none other than the gods of the hated races : twice in the Rigveda [1] we find phallus worshippers regarded as hostile, and everything points to the probability of such deities being among the enemies overthrown by Indra in the Rigveda. But, equally obviously, historical men may be reckoned as among the foes of the gods, and invested with traits of demons. Or again they may simply be mentioned as defeated by Indra, as princes whom we have no reason to doubt as Aryan are represented as being defeated for another prince by the aid of the god, as when for Tūrvayāṇa, Āyu, Atithigva, and Kutsa are overthrown.

The hostile Dāsas or Dasyus are regarded as black skinned [2] and noseless, doubtless a reference to flat noses, but their chief characteristic, and the one which makes them no real men, is their refusal to worship the Aryan gods, and to give gifts to the priest, the two essential duties of the true Vedic warrior. Of the princes favoured by Indra the greatest, or one of the greatest, is Atithigva or Divodāsa, ' the servant of the heaven ', whose name has wrongly induced Hillebrandt [3] to treat him as a Dāsa and to find the Dāsas among the Dahae, instead of among the aborigines of India itself. Among his foes are men with names like Karañja and Parṇaya,[4] whose appellations seem very possibly aboriginal, and above all Çambara. That foe has forts, ninety or ninety-nine,

[1] vii. 21. 5 ; x. 99. 3 ; above, p. 10, n. 3.

[2] Macdonell and Keith, *Vedic Index*, i. 356 ff.

[3] *Ved. Myth.* i. 96, 106 ff. ; iii. 269 ff. See Macdonell and Keith, *Vedic Index*, i. 347 ff.

[4] Mysterious is Rahasyu, who slays the seers, the Vaikhānasas, whom Indra revives, PB. xiv. 4. 7 ; JB. iii. 190. The dolphin (Çarkara Çiñçumāra) alone refused Indra, praise but was forced to yield by Parjanya drying up his ocean, JB. iii. 193 f.

or a hundred, and with the aid of Indra he destroys them and defeats him in his home in the mountains. Mythical these references may of course be, and clouds be meant, but it is quite as easy to see in them the real palisades of the aborigines stormed by Aryan princes, and their pursuing their enemy to the hills in which as always the defeated forces from the plains take refuge. Çambara is also defeated by Indra for the sake of Ṛjiçvan, son of Vidathin. He also lulls to slumber and to ruin Cumuri and Dhuni for the sake of Dabhīti, and this reference may not inaptly be applied to an attack on the enemy made by night when the camp was wrapped in slumber.[1] Another foe overcome by Indra is Ilībiça: his name like that of Pipru and of other of Indra's foes seems un-Aryan.

In other cases there may be a more mythic basis. The demon Urāṇa is described as having ninety-nine arms which is rather inhuman:[2] Arbuda is so little specified as to be of doubtful origin. Çuṣṇa seems from his name to be the hisser,[3] in which case he would have analogies with Vṛtra, whose snorting (*çvasatha*) so frightens the gods that they run away, leaving Indra to fight alone with the monster. He is also called a wild beast[4] and he seems to be horned, which may of course merely refer to the head-dress of a chief of the aborigines. His chief rival is Kutsa, who appears as battling against him, and as victor by the aid of Indra, who for his sake tore from the sun a wheel, prolonging the daylight and thus enabling, it may be assumed, Kutsa to turn the issue of battle. The feat of Indra is several times mentioned, and the fact that Kutsa is a real hero is suggested, though not proved, by the fact that elsewhere he appears in hostile relation to Indra,[5] just as Atithigva, who is normally the protégé of Indra, in one or two places appears in the reverse relation. It is true that it is not to be expected that a god, or a hero of divine dimensions, would be thus placed in opposition to the god, though, as the god is the uncertain Indra, the argument is by no means conclusive. Kutsa in the case of his real personality must be a king, and this is not inconsistent with his being called a seer: royal seers are not unknown. The Jaiminīya Brāhmaṇa makes him born from Indra's thigh and disloyal to him. No other god has anything like the same place as Indra in the overcoming of the Dāsas for the sake of the Aryans: the feat is ascribed elsewhere only to Agni, the Açvins, and the gods generally.

Other Dāsas are certainly not real men; such are Vyaṅça, whose jaws Indra struck off, and Namuci, who is the hero of a strange tale;[6] Indra, it

[1] RV. ii. 15. 9.

[2] RV. ii. 14. 4.

[3] Macdonell (*Ved. Myth.*, pp. 160, 161) refers the name to the scorching of the earth by drought. Hillebrandt (*Ved. Myth.* iii. 290) thinks the demon who eclipses the sun may be meant.

[4] Hillebrandt (VOJ. xiii. 316) compares the later legend of the gazelle form of Mārīca.

[5] Macdonell and Keith, *Vedic Index*, i. 228; Oertel, JAOS. xviii. 31. See Oldenberg, *Rel. des Veda*², pp. 154 ff.; Hillebrandt, *Ved. Myth.* iii. 292; JB. iii. 199–202.

[6] Bloomfield, JAOS. xv. 143 ff. Oldenberg, GN. 1893, pp. 342 ff.; Frazer, *Golden Bough*,³ xi. 280; Hillebrandt, *Ved. Myth.* iii. 255 ff.; Weber, *Rājasūya*,

seems, made a compact with him not to slay him by any weapon, by wet or dry, by day or night, and, true to this compact, when he did slay him it was with the foam of the sea at the twilight on the margin of the sea, and the head, struck off, follows him, reproaching him with treachery. The story is especially interesting because of its clear reference to the idea of the external soul: doubtless that of Namuci was deemed to be placed in the sea foam. Noteworthy also is Indra's consciousness of guilt in slaying.[1] A further curious tale tells how Indra as the result of over-indulgence in his favourite Soma became ill, and how he was cured by drinking with Namuci, or by extracting in some way from his body, a curious mixture of Soma and Surā. The Sautrāmaṇī rite of the Brāhmaṇas is clearly a case of a rite founded on the strange and unedifying myth. In the Rigveda [2] Indra twists off the head of Namuci, which suggests the natural phenomenon of a waterspout amidst a storm.

The Asuras also are more probably to be taken as the powers of darkness than as men, though individual Asuras may be quite well nothing but men: thus Pipru is called a Dāsa, and also an Asura, and the Asura Varcin, whose hundred and thousand men are slain by Indra and Viṣṇu when they overthrow Çambara, may fall in the same category. As we have seen, the Asuras appear but seldom as foes in the Rigveda; in one hymn, however, we learn that Agni abandons the Asuras, and joins the gods, that Indra slays Vṛtra, and that the wiles of the Asuras depart from them.[3] In the Brāhmaṇa literature Indra of course, like the other gods, fights against the Asuras, and after the usual period of defeat succeeds in defeating them in turn by the adoption of some ritual device or the repetition of some formula.[4]

In some cases we have full evidence of historical happenings. Turvaça and Yadu, that is the kings of the two tribes of that time, in whose historical character we have no ground to doubt,[5] are declared to have been brought safely over the stream by Indra's aid, doubtless procured by the help of the priest, and he is the great god who assists Sudās at the instance of Vasiṣṭha [6] in the battle with the ten kings, and makes him overthrow his rivals, bringing them to death in the stream of the Paruṣṇī, and then assisting the king to overthrow Bheda. Similar is the statement that he aided Suçravas and slew 60,099 of his enemies, though the number is fabulous. It is he on whom men

p. 102, n. 4 (morning mist). See MS. iv. 3. 4; 4. 4; TS. i. 8. 14; TB. i. 7. 1. 6; 8. 2; ÇB. v. 4. 1. 9; xii. 7. 3. 1; PB. xii. 6. 8.

1 So with Vṛtra, TS. ii. 5. 3. 6; PB. xxii. 14. 2; Tvaṣṭṛ's son, TS. ii. 5. 1. 2; PB. xvii. 5. 1, &c.

2 v. 30. 7, 8; vi. 20. 6; viii. 14. 13; Lanman, JASB. lviii. 28–30.

3 Magic powers are used both against (RV. vii. 98. 5; PB. xix. 19. 1) and by Indra (RV. viii. 14. 14; PB. xiii. 6. 9). For his wars, cf. Hopkins, *Trans. Conn. Acad.* xv. 44.

4 In the Subrahmaṇyā formula (ÇB. iii. 3. 4. 18; JB. ii. 79; iii. 233) Indra is invoked as ram of Medhātithi, an episode brought by some scholars into connexion with the Ganymede legend; Weber, *Ind. Stud.* ix. 48; Oertel, JAOS. xvi. p. ccxl; xviii. 38; RV. viii. 2. 40; *Vedic Index*, ii. 178.

5 RV. i. 174. 9.

6 RV. vii. 18 and 33. Indra appears to him face to face (PB. xv. 5. 24; TS. iii. 5. 2), and he gains his love (PB. xii. 12. 9 f.).

call in battle, and, little as the Vedic poetry is inspired with warlike spirit, here and there it is clear that the poet has caught some of the tone of war poetry.[1] Doubtless part of the lavishing of wealth which is a merit of Indra's was manifested in the giving of victory in the strife for cows, which, as the chief form of property of primitive Indian society, made up the main object to be won in a mere foray. Indra too appears in close relations with his worshippers, as a friend, a brother, a father or father and mother in one. The epithet Kauçika denotes him as the family god of the Kuçikas. He is the generous god *par excellence*, whence the title Maghavan, bountiful, is almost exclusively his in the Vedic ritual literature, and is his common name in post-Vedic texts. His bounty includes wives and also children.

In other cases myths are attached to Indra, in which we need not seek any direct connexion with his nature : as a great god he can stretch out heaven and earth, and in particular he settles the quaking mountains, while in the later Vedic texts he is said to have cut off the wings of the mountains and to have reduced them to a stationary condition.[2] The wings then became the thunder clouds. The separation of heaven and earth is sometimes attributed to his victory over a demon,[3] who held them together : the faint parallelism with the Hesiodic myth [4] is hardly worth note. If anything more than imagination is to be seen in the idea, it may be that the light appearing seems to separate the heaven and earth joined by the darkness. Probably, too, we must not see any reference to the myth of Vṛtra is the oft repeated wonder of the poet that Indra places in the red or raw cow the cooked milk. The problem seems to have been a favourite one in India. A less satisfactory side of his character is revealed in his addition to the drinking of Soma : a curious, if late, hymn [5] is represented as the monologue of the drunken Indra, who sees himself able to do anything he likes in the intoxication produced by his deep draughts. His over-indulgence in the drink has been noted, and it was his desire for it which drove him to slay his father. He is also the hero of more than one amour ; an old litany, the Subrahmaṇyā, addresses him as the lover of Ahalyā, a Brahman, calling himself Gautama, from which the Brāhmaṇas derive the natural explanation that he approached Ahalyā, wife of Gautama, under her husband's name and form.[6] To Weber the episode denotes that the dawn of morning ascends the bright sky, but their loving commerce is broken by the cloud coming up, but it would be unwise to press the accuracy of such an explanation. It may be rather ranked with the many aetiological myths of

[1] Hence in the Mahāvrata armed warriors represent his power, PB. v. 5. 21.

[2] RV. ii. 12. 2 ; x. 44. 8 ; iv. 54. 5 ; MS. i. 10. 13 ; Pischel, *Ved. Stud.* i. 174.

[3] RV. v. 29. 4 ; viii. 6. 17.

[4] *Theog.* 166 ff. ; Lang, *Custom and Myth*, pp. 44 ff. For heaven and earth as united and severed, see Hopkins, *Trans. Conn. Acad.* xv. 33, n. 1.

[5] RV. x. 119 ; Deussen (*Gesch. der Phil.* I. i. 99 ff.) sees in it a satire, but dubiously, see below, Part V, Chap. 26.

[6] Weber, SBA. 1887, p. 903. This view is criticized by Oldenberg, *Rel. des Veda*², p. 166. Hopkins (JAOS. xxxvi. 264) compares Ahalyā with the unploughed land. Cf. Hillebrandt, *Ved. Myth.* iii. 209, n. 4 ; JB. ii. 79, in JAOS. xviii. 34 ff. ; xxvi. 186.

different countries in which a family claims divine descent through the intercourse of a god with an ancestress, whose honour is saved by the representation that the god approached her in the guise of her lawful spouse. A still more obscure story [1] tells how a maiden, Apālā, found Soma beside a river, and having pressed it dedicated it to Indra, from whom she received the fulfilment of certain desires. Yet more obscure if possible is the famous Vṛṣākapi hymn,[2] which narrates a dispute which arose between Indra and Indrāṇī over an ape, Vṛṣākapi, which was the dear friend of Indra, but which had aroused the anger of Indrāṇī by destroying some of her property. Vṛṣākapi is induced, despite his caution, to be caught by Indrāṇī and is beaten by Indra, and banished from the house. Indra, however, misses his companion, and in some way not intelligible a reconciliation is effected. It would be idle to seek mythological conceptions in this strange confusion of ideas, and von Bradke [3] has ingeniously suggested that the hymn is none other than a satire on a contemporary prince and his consort under the titles of the god and goddess. The problem is plainly insoluble. Another odd tale is that of his stealing Aiṣakṛta Çitibāhu's Soma in monkey form, this power of change of shape adhering to him in later tradition,[4] where he appears as a leech, parrot, or cat.

Nothing is more interesting in Indra's nature than the contrast between the strongly moral character of his rival Varuṇa and his own lack of moral quality. He is occasionally given moral attributes, and faith in him is enjoined, but the very fact that the existence of sceptics who denied his divinity is recorded shows that the nature of Indra was not in all quarters considered to be worthy of the conception of divinity, doubtless as compared with the figure of Varuṇa. A list of his sins includes the killing of Viçvarūpa, Vṛtra, the Arurmaghas, and the Yatis, and quarrelling with Bṛhaspati, to whom priestly partiality is shown.[5]

The existence of Indra in the period of Indo-Iranian unity, which was rendered probable by the existence of a demon Indra, and of the god of victory Verethraghna,[6] who is clearly equivalent to Vṛtrahan, is made practically certain by the discovery of the name of Indra along with those of Mitra and Varuṇa and the Nāsatya among the gods of the Mitanni. While the name is of quite uncertain origin,[7] the parallelism of the myth of the finding of the cows proves that part of the conception of the god is Indo-European.

[1] RV. viii. 91; von Schroeder, VOJ. xxii. 223–44; xxiii. 270 ff. (Apālā as earth); Frazer, *Golden Bough*³, xi. 192.

[2] RV. x. 86.

[3] ZDMG. xlvi. 465. Other views in Bloomfield, xlviii. 541 ff.; Geldner, *Ved. Stud.* ii. 22 ff.; Hillebrandt, *Ved. Myth.* iii. 278 (a constellation); von Schroeder, *Mysterium und Mimus im Rigveda*, pp. 304 ff.; Tilak, *Orion*, pp. 170 ff.; Ludwig, *Ueber d. neuesten Arb.*, pp. 126 ff.; Winternitz, VOJ. xxiii. 112.

[4] JB. i. 363; Oertel, JAOS. xxvi. 192, 195, 314.

[5] AB. vii. 28 (Keith, trs., p. 314); KU. iii. 1; TS. ii. 5. 1.

[6] His bird form Vāraghna is parallel to the eagle form of Indra when he brings down the Soma; Oldenberg, *Rel. des Veda*², p. 72. The name denotes 'assault-repelling', but the idea of an abstract deity (Carnoy, *Iran. Myth.*, p. 271) is implausible, despite Moulton, *Early Zoroastrianism*, p. 69.

[7] Bergaigne (*Rel. Véd.* ii. 166) suggests

§ 2. *Trita Āptya*

Trita Āptya is a deity, whose importance in the Rigveda is much less great than the account of the feats attributed to him would at first sight seem to warrant. He is not the subject of any hymn, and his name is mentioned no more than forty times in all. His associations are predominantly with Indra, but also with the Maruts, Agni, and Soma. The name Āptya belongs to him seven times in four hymns.

The deeds of Trita have often the closest resemblance to those of Indra, and still more to those of Thrita in the Avesta. Thus, exhilarated by the Soma, he slays Vṛtra, he overthrows Vala, he destroys the three-headed Viçvarūpa, or again he assists Indra to overthrow Arbuda, while Indra is said to overthrow Viçvarūpa for him. He brings the Maruts on his car, and he sharpens Agni and makes his flames to rise. Agni also he finds. He has a secret and remote abode, whither the Ādityas and the Dawn are besought to remove ill deeds and evil dreams. This home seems to be in the regions of the sun or the heaven. He is also a preparer of Soma, with powers of healing, and all wisdom centres in him. More characteristic is the legend that, being in a well, he prays to the gods for help: Bṛhaspati hears him and sets him free. Another version has it that, being in a pit, he prays to his father and goes forth claiming his father's weapons to fight with Viçvarūpa. His shadowy figure becomes yet more obscure in the later Saṁhitās; the Yajurveda [1] ascribes to him the giving of long life, doubtless merely because he is the presser of Soma, and the Atharvaveda [2] knows him only as some far off deity to whom guilt or dreams may be banished. In the Brāhmaṇas we come across a tale of three brothers, Ekata, Dvita, and Trita, the first two of whom throw Trita in a well. Dvita actually occurs in the Rigveda,[3] once with Trita and once in an Agni hymn apparently as identical with Agni.

The Avestan parallel of Trita is Thrita, the third preparer of the Haoma, who received from Ahura 10,000 healing plants, which grew round the healing Haoma. Cognate with Thrita is Thraētaona, son of Āthwya, who slays the serpent of three heads and six eyes, Aži Dahāka; in his expedition for this purpose he is accompanied by two brothers who seek to slay him. The name Trita of course is third, while Āptya seems to refer to water and to be equivalent to Apāṁ Napāt.

The original nature of so obscure a god is not easy to decide. The connexion of Trita with Triton led Roth [4] to the view that he was a wind and water god: Hardy [5] finds in him a moon god, for which view there is no evidence at all;

indh; Jacobi (KZ. xxxi. 316 ff.) 'manly'; Bezzenberger (BB. i. 342) compares AS. ent, 'giant,' OHD. entioc; Güntert (*Weltkönig*, p. 14), οἰδέω.

1 TS. i. 8. 10. 2.

2 i. 113. 1, 3; xix. 56. 4.

3 viii. 47. 16; v. 18. 2.

4 ZDMG. ii. 224. The divergence of quantity can be explained by folk etymology; Güntert (p. 31) makes him the 'friendly' third of a divine triad.

5 *Ved.-brahm. Periode*, pp. 35–8.

Hillebrandt[1] holds that he is god of the bright sky revered in the Āptya family, or a deified ancestor, which is certainly inadequate as an account of his nature, and Pischel's[2] suggestion that he was originally a human healer, who was later deified, can hardly be taken seriously. Perry[3] is unquestionably right in seeing in him an older god than Indra, who seems to have largely usurped his position as an important deity. His connexion with the Soma, which is peculiarly close and which shows him as more active in the details of its preparation than Indra, who is rather the drinker of Soma than the preparer of the plant, suggests the conclusion, which is also made plausible by his name as Third, that he is a form of fire, the lightning in which the Soma descends to earth. This would agree with his nature as watery, Āptya, and does not contradict any of his known features.[4] But it is possible to hold that he was really a water deity, a parallel to the Greek Triton and the German Mimi.[5]

§ 3. *Apāṁ Napāt*

The deity Apāṁ Napāt, 'child of the waters,' is more distinguished than Trita Āptya by being the subject of one whole hymn in the Rigveda, where his name occurs some thirty times in all. He is essentially connected with the waters, his relation being envisaged in diverse ways: three divine females desire to give him food, he sucks the milk of the first mothers, but he also engenders the embryo within them, as a bull. On the other hand he shines without fuel in the waters; clothed in the lightning he mounts upright the lap of the shining waters; around him the swift golden-coloured waters go. He is golden in form, he comes from a golden womb. His food is ghee, he has in his home a cow which gives him milk. He dwells in the highest place, and grows in secret, and in the hymn addressed to him he is directly identified with the god Agni, but elsewhere, though associated with Agni, he is distinguished from him. In the ritual he is connected with the waters; when the priests go for the waters required for the sacrifice, it is to Apāṁ Napāt that they address their prayer, and to him they offer butter in order to procure suitable waters; offerings are likewise made to him in the case when the sacrificial victim perishes in water, or when the Kārīrīṣṭi, a rain spell, is performed.

In the Avesta there is found a spirit Apãm Napāṭ, who lives in the depths of the waters, surrounded by females; he is said to have recovered the glory when in the flight between Ātar and the dragon it fell in the ocean Vourukaša. In this trait there is clearly a connexion with fire, and the igneous nature of the spirit is asserted by Spiegel[6] and Darmesteter,[7] the latter of whom considers

[1] *Varuṇa und Mitra*, p. 94. Cf. *Ved. Myth.* iii. 39, 343 f.

[2] GGA. 1894, p. 428.

[3] JAOS. xi. 142–5.

[4] Macdonell, JRAS. xxv. 419–96.

[5] Carnoy, JAOS. xxxviii. 294 ff.; *Les Indo-Européens*, pp. 199 f. Wackernagel (GN. 1909, p. 61) holds that Trita is a short form of Tritavana 'the thrice strong', Thraētaona corresponding to Traitavana (RV. once Traitana), and Āptya being a popular etymology for Ātpya. This is not plausible.

[6] *Ar. Per.*, pp. 192, 193.

[7] SBE. iv². p. lxiii; cf. von Schroeder, *Arische Religion*, ii. 490 f.

him to be the fire-god born from the cloud in the lightning. The natural conclusion is that the traditional view is correct, and the Apāṁ Napāt is the same god as Agni, who is conceived as the lightning in the clouds. Of the moon character as connected with the waters which Hillebrandt [1] ascribes to this deity, a view accepted by Hardy,[2] it is difficult to see any clear trace, and of resemblance to the sun as suggested by Max Müller [3] there is small evidence. Oldenberg's [4] view that Agni and Apāṁ Napāt were originally distinct and that the identification, which he does not deny, is later, is of course possible, but it is not supported at all conclusively by the ritual, which naturally emphasizes the water side of the god, but which by no means proves that he was a water deity. The fact that the only hymn [5] addressed to him already identifies the deities precludes us from certain knowledge of an earlier period in the history of the deity. The other deities beside Agni with whom the god is found mentioned, such as Ahi Budhnya and Aja Ekapād, are probably also akin in part to Agni, and this is clear of Savitṛ, with whom the god seems to be identified once.[6]

§ 4. *Ahi Budhnya*

Ahi Budhnya, 'the serpent of the deep', is closely associated in the few cases, twelve in all, in which his name is found in the Rigveda with the gods Aja Ekapād, Apāṁ Napāt, the ocean, and Savitṛ. His name never occurs save in the hymns to the All-gods, and there it is regularly found among the spirits of the atmosphere, and in the Naighaṇṭuka [7] he is definitely assigned to the middle or aerial region. The only definite traits ascribed to him are that he is born of the waters, sitting at the bottom of the streams in the spaces, language which the normal spirit of the Rigveda no less than the express assertion of Yāska [8] induces us to refer to the ocean of the air, and not to the earthly waters. His dangerous character is hinted at by the fact that he is implored not to give over his worshippers to evil.[9]

The explanation of the nature of this spirit is by no means obvious. The serpent *par excellence* of the Vedic poets is Vṛtra, who encloses the waters, but also is described as lying upon them, or in the depth of the waters. Agni, however, is also described as a raging serpent and is said to have been produced in the depth (*budhna*) of the great space. To Hardy [10] the god is another form of the moon, to Oldenberg [11] a water snake, and Macdonell [12] suggests that he is really a form of Ahi-Vṛtra regarded as divine, and not as merely an enemy

[1] *Ved. Myth.* i. 365 ff.; ii. 133; iii. 338.
[2] *Ved.-brahm. Periode*, pp. 38, 39.
[3] *Chips*, iv². 410; Magoun, JAOS. xix. ii. 137 ff.; AJP. xxi. 274 ff. Cf. Gray, *Archiv für Rel.* iii. 18 ff.
[4] *Rel. des Veda*², pp. 117–19.
[5] RV. ii. 35; cf. x. 30. 3, 4.
[6] Macdonell, *Ved. Myth.*, p.
[7] v. 4.
[8] Nir. x. 44.
[9] RV. vii. 34. 17; v. 41. 16.
[10] *Ved.-brahm. Periode*, p. 41.
[11] *Rel. des Veda*², p. 70. Cf. the German dragons; Helm, *Altgerm. Rel.* i. 206 ff.; Hillebrandt, *Ved. Myth.* iii. 340 (ein Rest vom Quellenkult).
[12] *Ved. Myth.*, p. 73.

of Indra. More vaguely it may be thought that the god is nothing more than a personification of the writhing cloud, whose serpentine form is a simple enough conception ; the difference between this conception and that of Vṛtra would lie in the fact that the latter conception applies to the thunder clouds rather than to the mere clouds of the sky. The prayer for safety from harm would be natural enough addressed to a deity conceived in serpent form. It is, however, also possible that the god is merely another form of Agni ; in the later Vedic texts the god is connected with Agni Gārhapatya,[1] and with Aja Ekapād he receives a formal share in the offering at a Gṛhya ceremony, from which, however, it would doubtless be wrong to deduce that he was then a living deity.[2] Such a deity he cannot have been for even the earliest period of the Rigveda, and the occasional mention of these gods even in the latest texts is testimony not to the life of the god but to the commanding influence of the Rigveda. In the post-Vedic literature the name survives as an epithet of Çiva and the name of a Rudra.

§ 5. *Aja Ekapād*

Aja Ekapād, 'the one-footed goat', is mentioned five times with Ahi Budhnya, and but once alone. The deities with whom he is mentioned are the ocean, the stream, the aerial space, the thundering flood, and all the gods, and his aerial connexion seems clear despite the preference for the celestial region evinced by the Naighaṇṭuka.[3] In the later literature he appears as making firm the two worlds, according to the Atharvaveda,[4] and as born in the east according to the Taittirīya Brāhmaṇa,[5] and in the domestic ritual he is once joined with Ahi Budhnya. Native tradition, but only at a very late date, makes him out to be a form of Agni or the sun.[6]

It is difficult from these scanty facts to make anything out as to the nature of the god : Roth [7] taking Aja, not as 'goat' which is its proper sense, but literally as 'driver', saw in him the storm ; Bergaigne [8], rendering Aja as 'unborn', thinks he is a mysterious deity of the isolated world ; Hardy [9] finds in him as usual the moon ; Victor Henry [10] and Bloomfield [11] the sun, while Macdonell [12] suggests the interesting, and, so far as the evidence allows, satisfactory, hypothesis that the lightning form of Agni is meant, the goat denoting his swift coming, and the one foot the solitary streak which smites the earth. This view is clearly preferable to that of Oldenberg,[13] which sees in the figure the myth of a goat which holds apart the worlds, an idea which has no adequate support in the reference in the Atharvaveda.

[1] VS. v. 33 ; AB. iii. 36 ; TB. i. 1. 10. 3.
[2] PGS. ii. 15. 2.
[3] v. 6.
[4] xiii. 1. 6.
[5] iii. 1. 2. 8.
[6] Durga on Nir. xii. 29.
[7] *Nir.*, pp. 165, 166 ; cf. Weber, *Rājasūya*, p. 53, n. 4, who suggests the whirlwind.
[8] *Rel. Véd.* iii. 23.
[9] *Ved.-brahm. Periode*, pp. 41, 42.
[10] *Les Hymnes Rohita*, p. 24.
[11] SBE. xlii. 664.
[12] *Ved. Myth.*, p. 74.
[13] *Rel. des Veda*², p. 71.

§ 6. *Mātariçvan*

The god Mātariçvan, unlike the one-footed goat and the dragon of the deep, is not an ancient god : his name occurs but twenty-seven times in the whole of the Rigveda, and of these instances twenty-one are found in the latest parts of the Rigveda : he occurs five times in book iii, so that he seems to have been a favourite of the Viçvāmitra family, and once in book vi. His connexion with Agni is of the closest : his name is thrice applied to Agni, and it is said of Agni[1] 'As germ of the heaven he is named Tanūnapāt ; when born he becometh Narāçaṅsa ; when in his mother he was fashioned as Mātariçvan, he became the wind's swift flight.' He is also identified with Bṛhaspati, and the poets who divide the one into many are said[2] to call it Agni, Yama, Mātariçvan. On the other hand Agni appears as distinct from Mātariçvan : Agni appears to him and to Vivasvant, Mātariçvan brings Agni to Bhṛgu : he brings Agni from the sky, from afar for men, or from the gods. He is also said to produce him by friction and to set him up in human abodes. He is occasionally mentioned in connexion with Indra, and he serves as the messenger of Vivasvant between the heaven and the earth. In the wedding hymn he is asked with other deities to join the hearts of the husband and wife.

The meaning of the word as 'he who grows in his mother' is clearly authentic :[3] the root is *çu*, and the formation of the word is not open to serious exception ; the accent, which is on the third syllable, is due to the analogy of such words as *prātarítvan*. The nature of the god can hardly be doubted in view of his relation to Agni : he must be the Agni who descends to earth in the form of lightning, and who like Agni himself grows in his mother. The only alternative view which has any plausibility is that of Oldenberg[4] who sees in him a Prometheus only, without any divine nature other than the bringing down of fire. This view is, however, open to the fatal objection that it is only reasonable to interpret the Prometheus legend in itself in the sense of the descent of fire ; the god originally himself descends : it is later speculation which makes an independent personage the cause of his descent.

Mātariçvan, however, in the Yajurveda and in the Brāhmaṇas is overwhelmingly the god of wind, not of fire, and this nature of his is already hinted at in the Rigveda where the epithets boundless and wandering are applied to him. In the view of Hillebrandt[5] the conception of the wind lies at the bottom of the nature of the Vedic god, and he points to the fact of the important part played by the wind in the production of forest fires,[6] and the striking character of dust storms in India in support of his thesis. He suggests, however, that there may have been a tendency in the Rigveda to identify the

[1] RV. iii. 29. 11.
[2] RV. i. 164. 46.
[3] Fay (KZ. xlv. 134) suggests 'in materia turgens', but unconvincingly ; cf. JAOS. xxxii. 392.
[4] *Rel. des Veda*[2], p. 122 ; SBE. xlvi. 123. Contrast von Schroeder, *Arische Religion*, ii. 485, 526, 530, 567, 587. For Loki, see Much, *Der germ. Himmelsgott*, p. 54.
[5] *Ved. Myth.* ii. 149 ff. Cf. RV. ix. 67. 31.
[6] AV. xii. 1. 51 ; Hopkins, JAOS. xx. 218.

wind and the fire which would account for the relation of Mātariçvan to Agni. To this theory the main objection is simple: it ignores the essential and not accidental connexion of Mātariçvan with Agni which is the most real part of his nature, and it is easy to point out that the transition from the fire god to a wind god is natural enough, and already hinted at in the Rigveda, where of Agni himself it is said that he is like the rushing wind.

Like the serpent of the deep and the one-footed goat, Mātariçvan is not a popular deity, and plays but little part in the cult. Mātali, Indra's charioteer in the post-Vedic literature, may be a faint reminiscence of his nature.

§ 7. *Vāyu and Vāta*

The real wind gods of the Rigveda are Vāyu and Vāta, who differ however quite distinctly in character and in importance. Vāyu has one whole hymn [1] addressed to him, and shares half a dozen with Indra, while Vāta has only two short hymns in the tenth book.[2] The former is the more anthropomorphized of the two gods; hence he is joined with Indra, while Vāta is associated with Parjanya, who in comparison with Indra is an elemental deity. The close connexion of Indra and Vāyu is seen in the fact that Yāska [3] gives Vāyu, or Indra, as the second member of the triad of gods, into which the Nairuktas reduced the Vedic pantheon.

Vāyu is beautiful, touching the sky, thousand-eyed: he travels on his impetuous course in a car with 99, 100, or 1,000 steeds yoked by his will. Indra rides with him in his car. He is said to have been generated by the two worlds for wealth, and to be the son-in-law of Tvaṣṭṛ, but the name of his wife is not given. He is also said to have generated the Maruts, and is once accompanied by them, but he has otherwise little connexion with them. In the Puruṣasūkta he is born of the giant's breath. Like his friend Indra, he is fond of the Soma, which he drinks in its pure form and which he protects. He is entitled to the first draught of the Soma as the swiftest of the gods: when the gods race, the Aitareya Brāhmaṇa [4] makes him come first, then Indra second. Like the other gods he is asked to grant fame, children and riches, and to protect the weak, but these are quite secondary traits.

Vāta is merely the wind in its power, sweeping along great clouds of dust, shattering and thundering: his form cannot be seen by the mortal eye, though his roaring is heard, nor is the place of his birth known. He is the breath of the gods and the recipient of oblations. Stress is laid on his whiteness, and, as the wind heralds lightning and the appearance of the sun, Vāta is said to produce ruddy lights and to make the dawns to shine. His roaring is often alluded to,

[1] RV. iv. 46. For the Indo-European gods of wind, cf. Carnoy, *Les Indo-Européens*, pp. 208 ff.

[2] RV. x. 168 and 186. In the Avesta Vāto appears only as a demon, like Indra and Saurva; von Schroeder, *Arische Religion*, i. 285.

[3] Nir. vii. 5.

[4] ii. 25.

and he is credited with healing power, doubtless from the purifying effect of his blasts.

In the ritual the offerings especially of animal victims are made mainly to Vāyu : Vāta has a few offerings only made to him. The latter literature adds nothing of importance to the characterization of either god : stress is laid on the power of the god, Vāyu, to diminish the heat of the sun, and in the Taittirīya Āraṇyaka [1] 11 male and 11 female powers are given to him as attendants.[2]

The identification of the name Vāta with Wodan is open to the most grave objection on the score of form, nor is the parallelism in character of decisive importance.[3]

§ 8. *Parjanya*

Parjanya, like Vāta, is a god whose natural character is obvious and undeniable. He has three hymns in the Rigveda and his name occurs some thirty times, but in other passages it has beyond doubt the simple sense of rain cloud. More often, however, the rain cloud is made into a real person, often in theriomorphic shape : thus he is a bull who roars and impregnates the plants, and his roaring waters delight the earth. But, as the waters are normally conceived as feminine, he becomes in other cases a barren cow, or even a productive cow. He is the rain giver, and is besought to bestow rain, but in his actions he is subject to the control of Mitra and Varuṇa. He also thunders and smites trees and evildoers in anger, and, when he quickens the earth with his seed, the winds blow, and the lightning flashes. He is often associated with Vāta, as Vāyu with Indra. As a rain god plants spring up through him, and he is also credited with the increase of cattle, of mares, and of women. He is even exalted as an independent monarch, the ruler of all the world, in whom are established the three worlds and all beings. From another point of view he is essentially the father, and even the divine father. [4]

In one place Dyaus is stated to be his father, and in his character, especially in the stress laid on his paternity, and his bull shape he is like to his father. His wife is the earth, though once [5] she is called Vaçā. He has a son [6] who may be Soma, for that god is called son of Parjanya,[7] but the lightning may also be meant. He is not rarely connected with Indra, rarely with Agni, and

[1] i. 9. 2.

[2] Hillebrandt, *Ved. Myth.* iii. 329–31.

[3] Cf. Feist, *Kultur der Indogermanen*, p. 343, who accepts connexion of Wodan with *vates* and Irish *faith* and treats him as a god of spirits, in accordance with his belief that the gods are sprung from spirits. Helm (*Altgerm. Rel.* i. 260 f.) regards Wodan as a wind and spirit god. Cf. von Schroeder, *Arische Religion*, i. 127 f., 488 ; Rhys, *Celtic Heathendom*, pp. 278, 280 ff.

[4] Von Schroeder (*Arische Religion*, ii. 602 f.) argues that Parjanya is a hypostasis of the heaven god, as Perun among the Slavs, Perkúnas among the Lithuanians, Pehrkon among the Letts ; cf. i. 417 ff.

[5] AV. x. 10. 6.

[6] RV. vii. 101. 1.

[7] RV. ix. 82. 3.

occasionally with the Maruts. In an interesting hymn [1] the frogs are spoken of as raising their voices when aroused by Parjanya, though it is uncertain if the god or the cloud is meant.

The nature of Parjanya as the thunder cloud is preserved throughout the Vedic literature and is recognized in the later period, where his name is also applied to Indra with whom in much he is identical, though his character has clear similarities also to that of Dyaus. The identification of him with the Lithuanian god Perkúnas, the Slav Perun, and the Norse Fjörgynn, which would make him to be in origin a god of the oak, or of the thunder which smites the oak, is open to the gravest difficulties of phonology,[2] and must be considered as too doubtful to be worth more than serious consideration.[3] No other attempt to explain his name is yet made plausible, though it has been attempted to show that he is a rain god pure and simple.

§ 9. *The Waters*

Four hymns of the Rigveda and many verses praise the waters as goddesses,[4] but they have little personality and the element is nearly always plainly to be recognized. Their anthropomorphic form is the Apsaras, who will be treated below. They are mothers, or young wives : they flow in channels to the sea, but they are also celestial : they abide in the seat of the gods and of Mitra and Varuṇa : Varuṇa moves in the midst of them, looking down on the good and base deeds of men. In them Agni dwells and they are his mothers. They cleanse and purify the worshipper, even from moral sins such as lying, cursing, and violence.[5] They bestow long life and wealth and immortality.

The waters are also associated with honey : their waves are rich in honey, their milk is mixed with honey, and from tasting it Indra grows strong. For Soma they come with ghee, milk, and honey, and Soma takes them as his brides.

In the Naighaṇṭuka the waters are reckoned as terrestrial only, but in some of these cases at any rate it is clear that the celestial waters are meant ; and that like all deities the waters are thought of as having a home in the heaven, even when also present on earth. The connexion with honey is of interest : it confirms the view that the essential conception is that the waters in their refreshing drink are the honey as they also are the Soma : thus the

[1] RV. vii. 103.

[2] Kretschmer, *Gesch. der griech. Sprache*, p. 81. See Hillebrandt, *Ved. Myth.*, iii. 331, n. 5 ; Macdonell, *Ved. Myth.*, pp. 85, 177 ; E. Meyer, *Gesch. des Alt.*[3] I. ii. p. 870 ; Carnoy, *Les Indo-Européens*, pp. 164–6 ; von Schroeder, *Arische Religion*, ii. 422, n. 2, 519, n. 1, 531–4, 544 ff. ; O. Schrader, ERE. ii. 33 ; Helm, *Altgerm. Rel.* i. 278, n. 1. Cf. Gray, *Myth. of All Races*, iii. 320, 322 ff. ; Rhys, *Celtic Heathendom*, p. 220 ; Brückner, KZ. l. 195.

[3] Grassmann and von Schroeder prefer derivation from *pṛc*, 'fill' ; Bloomfield (*Rel. of Veda*, p. 111) suggests modulation to suggest *pari-jana*, one who surrounds the folk. Perun's name seems clearly to be from *per*, 'strike'.

[4] For their Indo-European character, cf. Carnoy, *Les Indo-Européens*, pp. 197–201.

[5] RV. i. 23. 22 ; x. 9. 8.

myth of the descent of Soma is no more than the tale of the descent to earth of the refreshing rain when the storm breaks forth.

With the growth of the ritual the distinction is made and developed between the various sources of the waters; thus standing water becomes unfit for use since it is Varuṇa's and Varuṇa would seize the sacrifice; in the Rājasūya, the consecration of the king, seventeen different kinds of water are used to confer each some special power on the king at the consecration:[1] the horse sacrifice sees also a similar use of the different powers of the waters to which under many aspects offerings are made. The purifying and protecting power of the waters is seen further in the domestic ritual, in which water is placed near a woman in child-bed.[2]

With the waters are connected not only gods like Agni, but various plants[3] and animals, of whom the most prominent are the snakes, the ants, and the frogs. The connexion with the water of the snakes appears to be a case of theriomorphism, as seen in the deity Ahi Budhnya, and in the snake form of Agni as well as in the case of the demon Vṛtra. The ants[4] are evidently brought into connexion with water, because of their ability to find for themselves water in apparently dry places as the Brāhmaṇa legends show, and the frogs[5] are invoked to send water, because of their close connexion with the waters in which they move and have their being. The ritual emphasizes this connexion by the use of a frog in rites where cooling is needed, and several plants are employed in the same way. The most important of the terrestrial waters are the streams and these will be treated in the next chapter. Among the minor figures who have some connexion with water must be included the Gandharvas and Apsarases.

§ 10. *Rudra*

Still less than Viṣṇu has Rudra the greatness which in the later literature attends him. He is the subject of but three hymns in the Rigveda, shares one with Soma, and is mentioned in all only about seventy-five times. In the Rigveda he has braided hair, like Pūṣan, beautiful lips, firm limbs; his colour is brown, and he is multiform. He is essentially radiant (*çuci*), bright as the sun or gold, resplendent, the Asura of heaven; he wears golden ornaments and sits on a chariot seat. The Yajurveda and the Atharvaveda have much more to tell of his appearance: the latter[6] calls his belly blue, his back red, his neck blue, and mentions his mouth and his teeth. The Yajurveda[7] calls him copper coloured and red, and his neck is blue-black (*nīlagrīva*), though his

[1] Weber, *Rājasūya*, pp. 33, 34; TS. i. 8. 11. 1; KÇS. xv. 4. 22 ff. Cf. RV. vii. 49. 2; TB. iii. 1. 2. 3; ii. 7. 15. 3 ff.

[2] HGS. ii. 4. 5.

[3] Karīra, Kharjūra, Vetasa, Avakā, Maṇḍūkaparṇī, Dūrvā, Darbha (TA. v. 10. 6), &c.

[4] TB. i. 1. 3. 4; TA. v. 1. 4; 2. 9. Cf. E. H. Meyer, *Gandharven-Kentauren*, pp. 156 f.

[5] RV. vii. 103; MS. iii. 14. 2; cf. the modern frog worship in October, IA. xxii. 293.

[6] AV. xv. 1. 7, 8; xi. 2. 6.

[7] VS. xvi. 7, 51, 2–4.

throat is white (*çitikaṇṭha*);[1] it mentions that he is clothed in a skin and dwells in the mountains.

The character of Rudra in the Rigveda is distinctly formidable: he wields the lightning and the thunderbolt and is an archer, but his fierce character is not manifested as that of Indra in his onslaughts on demons, for that is no part of his nature. He is as destructive as a terrible beast, the ruddy boar of heaven. He is unassailable, rapid, young, unaging, ruler of the world, and its father. From this side of his nature may be derived his aspect as wise, beneficent, bountiful, easily invoked and auspicious (*çiva*), but the last epithet,[2] which furnishes the late Vedic name of the god, is not appropriated to him even in the Atharvaveda. He is also a god of healing; he has healing remedies, the chief being Jalāṣa,[3] which is explained variously as the Soma or as the rain, whose property as healing is recognized freely in the Rigveda. Nor is this element in his nature a minor one: it is given as one of his characteristic in a hymn, where the gods are named only by their epithets, and both the Rudras and the Maruts are mentioned with him in this connexion.

On the other hand the majority of the passages of the hymns, which deal with him, are concerned with deprecating his wrath, and praying that his shaft may not fall upon his worshippers, their parents, children, men, cattle, or horses; he is besought to avert his great malevolence and his bolt from his worshippers, to avert from them his cow- and man-slaying weapon. He is even once directly called manslaying.[4]

Rudra is in the Rigveda closely associated with the Maruts, whose father he is and who are often spoken of as the Rudras or the Rudriyas. He bears also once the epithet Tryambaka, which appears to mean 'having three sisters' or 'mothers'; the interpretation of the reference as an allusion to the three divisions of the universe is possible enough, as the allusion is not made in an early hymn. In one passage of the Rigveda he is identified, among other gods, with Agni.[5]

In the later Saṁhitās and in the Brāhmaṇas Rudra has become, like Viṣṇu, and with him, one of the two great gods of the Brahmans. Some of his aspect as a god of healing is still remembered: the Sūtras [6] prescribe offerings to him for the sake of the cattle, and he is lord of cattle; doubtless in part this

[1] TS. iv. 5. 5; cf. iv. 5. 1; Arbman (*Rudra*, pp. 274 ff.) insists that red and blue-black are connected with the dead and thus prove this as a primitive feature of Rudra's character, but it is clear that primarily he is merely bright (RV. viii. 29. 5) and brown rather than red, and the epithets are best explained as referring to fire, Jacobi, ERE. ii. 803 f.

[2] Connexion with Tamil *çivan*, 'red-man', is neither proved nor plausible, despite BSOS. II. iv. 810.

[3] Bloomfield, AJP. xii. 425–9 (rain = *mūtra*); Bergaigne, *Rel. Véd.* iii. 32 (= Soma). His rain is denoted by *mīḍhvāṅs*, and is referred to RV. i. 64. 6; 85. 5. Arbman's (*Rudra*, pp. 19 f.) objections are clearly invalid.

[4] RV. iv. 3. 6.

[5] RV. ii. 1. 6.

[6] AGS. iv. 8. 40; Kauç. li. 7. Cf. PB. vii. 9. 18; xxi. 14. 13; Mahādeva slays cattle, PB. vi. 9. 7–9.

attribution of cattle to his care may be due to the anxiety of their owners to induce him to spare them from his wrath, but the other side of his figure may also be a factor in producing the result. On the other hand his malevolence is very prominent: his wrath is continually deprecated, he is invoked not to assail his worshippers with celestial fire, and to make his lightning fall elsewhere. He is said in the Atharvaveda [1] to attack with fever, cough, and poison, and that Veda [2] also conjures up the image of his wide-mouthed howling dogs, who swallow unchewed their prey. In the Çatarudriya litany [3] he bears the most remarkable epithets, which designate him as the patron of robbers, highwaymen, cheats, swindlers, and other similar people.

The express and complete identification of Rudra with Agni, which is first found only incidentally in the Rigveda, is now a received feature of his nature and the principle is widely extended. In the Yajurveda [4] the names of Çarva and Bhava are ascribed to him, while in the Atharvaveda [5] these two seem still to be separate gods, who, however, have destructive arrows and lightnings. In a later passage [6] they are called his sons, as Mahādeva, and compared with wolves. A late part of the Vājasaneyi Saṁhitā [7] enumerates as forms of the one god Agni, Açani, Paçupati, Bhava, Çarva, Mahādeva, Īçāna, and Ugradeva with others. In the Brāhmaṇas [8] is found a list of names of Agni as Rudra, Çarva, Paçupati, Ugra, Açani, Bhava, and Mahān Deva, while Çarva, Bhava, Paçupati and Rudra are said to be names of Agni.[9] Açani obviously means lightning, and is so explained by the Çatapatha Brāhmaṇa, but according to the Kauṣītaki Brāhmaṇa it is equivalent to Indra. The Vājasaneyi Saṁhitā [10] also gives Ambikā as the sister of Rudra: she seems to be derived from the epithet Tryambaka: later on she appears as his mother; his wife, Umā Haimavatī or Pārvatī, appears first in the Taittirīya Āraṇyaka [11] and the Kena Upaniṣad.[12]

In the Brāhmaṇas we find the power of Rudra at its height. The gods even are afraid lest they be killed by the god. Under the name of Mahādeva he is essentially the slayer of cattle, and he is said to be prone to slay men.[13] His

[1] xi. 2. 22, 26; vi. 90.

[2] x. 1. 30. Cf. Wodan's corpse-eating wolves; Helm, *Altgerm. Rel.* i. 208, n. 92.

[3] VS. xvi; TS. iv. 4.

[4] VS. xvi. 18, 28, from *çarāva* in a legend in JB. iii. 261. Here he appears as Akhala (cf. Çiva); as Īçāna akhala, ii. 254 (Agni in PB. xxi. 2. 9); cf. JUB. i. 5; Īçāna alone in JB. ii. 222.

[5] AV. ii. 27. 6; v. 93. 1; x. 1. 23; xi. 2. 1. 12.

[6] ÇÇS. iv. 20. 1. Arbman (*Rudra*, p. 29) most arbitrarily asserts that these gods were originally identical with Rudra, worshipped outside Vedic circles.

[7] xxxix. 8. For the identity of Agni and Rudra, cf. Hopkins, *Trans. Conn. Acad.* xv. 36 f.; JB. iii. 261.

[8] ÇB. vi. 1. 3. 7; KB. vi. 1 ff.; AGS. iv. 8. 19 has Hara, Mṛḍa, Çarva, Çiva, Bhava, Mahādeva, Ugra, Bhīma, Paçupati, Rudra, Çaṅkara, and Īçāna. Cf. PGS. iii. 8. 6; HGS. ii. 3. 8. 6 ff.

[9] ÇB. i. 7. 3. 8.

[10] iii. 5; MS. i. 10. 20; TB. i. 6. 10.

[11] Cf. Weber, *Ind. Stud.* i. 78; ii. 186 ff.; Arbman, *Rudra*, p. 305.

[12] iii. 15.

[13] AGS. iv. 8. 32. In PB. xiv. 9. 12 he appears as *mṛgayu*; Vāyu (PB. xxiii. 13. 2) is overlord of forest cattle.

origin is traced in the Aitareya Brāhmaṇa,[1] to the evil deed of Prajāpati in consorting with his own daughter ; the gods in their anger make up the most appalling of beings, who pierces the father god and thus asserts outraged morality. Another story in the same Brāhmaṇa [2] reveals him as a great black [3] being who appears on the place of sacrifice, and claims all that is over as his own, a claim which Nābhānediṣṭha is told by his father must be recognized as being valid. In the ritual we find that he is marked out emphatically from the other gods : at the end of the sacrifice a handful of the strew is offered to him to propitiate him,[4] at the end of a meal any food left over is placed in a spot to the north for him to take ; [5] his abode is in the north, while the other gods abide in the east, the place of the rising of the sun. The bloody entrails of the victim are made over to his hosts, which attack men and beast with disease and death, in order to avert their anger ; [6] the red colour of the god is the colour of fire and of blood. Moreover, the snakes [7] are clearly conceived as being among his servants. When the gods reached heaven, it is said, Rudra was left behind.[8] Still more important is the tendency seen to generalize the operations of Rudra : in the Çatarudriya litany of the Yajurveda he is credited with activity in almost every aspect of nature, in the mountains, the woods, the paths, and the streams. So in the ritual it is prescribed that offerings should be made to Rudra in the most manifold places and on varied occasions.[9] In a place infested by snakes one should offer to Rudra who lives among the snakes, at a mound of manure to Rudra who is lord of cattle, in a river to Rudra who lives in the waters, at a cross way to Rudra of the roads, at sacred trees, at the place of sacrifice and so on.[10] A verse in the Yajurveda reveals to us Rudra as a god haunting the lonely woods ; the cowherds, and the maidens, who are drawing water, catch a glimpse of him.[11] He haunts the hills and is closely related to the trees, on which he deposits his weapons when he lays them aside.[12] It is clear that this wide extension of his power, which applies to the waters and to the fish in them and to the whole animal and vegetable kingdom, is due to a deliberate tendency to see in him a god with a comprehensive control over all nature.

Another sign of the greatness of Rudra is found in the Aitareya Brāhmaṇa :[13] it is prescribed that a formula must be altered from the form in which it occurs in the Rigveda in order to avoid the direct mention of the name of the god : this is clear proof of advance in the conception of him since the Rigveda. In another passage of the same text he is never named, but is referred to as

[1] iii. 33. 1 ; a later variant in JB. iii. 221–3 ; cf. ÇB. i. 7. 4.
[2] v. 14.
[3] Cf. AV. ii. 27. 6 (black hair) ; xi. 2. 18.
[4] GGS. i. 8. 28.
[5] ApDS. ii. 24. 23.
[6] ÇÇS. iv. 19. 8 ; cf. AB. ii. 7. 1.
[7] AGS. iv. 8. 28. Cf. Arbman, *Rudra*, p. 252.
[8] ÇB. i. 7. 3. 1.
[9] If he is the *akhalā devatā* in JUB. i. 5 (Caland, *Over en uit het Jaiminīya-brāhmaṇa*, p. 47, n. 69), then he is credited with repelling (from heaven) the man who does evil.
[10] HGS. i. 16. 8 ff. ; PGS. iii. 15. 7 ff.
[11] TS. iv. 5. 1. 3.
[12] TS. iv. 5. 10. 4.
[13] iii. 34. 7.

'the god here', and the same avoidance of direct use of the name is to be seen elsewhere.[1]

In the late Sūtra literature we find ascribed to him the names of Hara, Mṛḍa, Çiva and Çaṅkara;[2] the last three at least are evidently intended to be euphemistic: the great and dread god must be treated as auspicious in order to make him so in point of fact. The specific account of him as the lord, or the great god, shows a development of his character even within the period of the later Saṁhitās, for these epithets are not found in the earlier books of the Vājasaneyi Saṁhitā, but only in the later portion of that text.[3]

The original nature of Rudra is far from clear. The name itself is clearly derived from the word *rud*, which India tradition takes as having the normal meaning of cry: the suggestion of Pischel[4] that *rud* means to be ruddy or, as Grassmann suggests, to shine, must be regarded as too hypothetical to found any theory upon. From the etymology Weber[5] derives the view that the deity was originally the howling of the storm, the plural therefore denoting the Maruts, but that the deity as known to the Yajurveda is essentially a compound of the two gods of fire and storm, both being alike in their sound. The view of Hillebrandt[6] insists that Rudra is the deity of the hot season in India from the advent of summer to the autumn, and he points out that it is possible that this idea was associated with some constellation as in the conception *saevus Orion*. He also points out that Rudra appears in conjunction with the archer Kṛçānu and with Tiṣya, who is generally regarded as a constellation, and that the Aitareya Brāhmaṇa[7] makes the myth of the slaying of Prajāpati to have an astronomical signification, Prajāpati in his form as a deer becoming the Mṛga, which the commentary explains as the constellation Mṛgaçiras, Rudra the Mṛgavyādha, Prajāpati's daughter in antelope form the constellation Rohiṇī, and the arrow with which Prajāpati was pierced the Iṣu Trikāṇḍā in the sky. But he recognizes that any precise identification is not to be obtained by the material available. L. v. Schroeder,[8] on the other hand, insists that Rudra is nothing more than the elevation to the rank of a high god of the chief of the souls of the dead: it is an idea, for which almost an indefinite amount of evidence is forthcoming, that the souls of the dead rush along in the storm winds and that besides being terrible they bring with them blessings to cattle. Oldenberg,[9] while noting this as a possible source of the character of the god, prefers to point out the similarity of the nature of Rudra

[1] iii. 33. Cf. Hirzel, *Der Name*, pp. 15 ff.

[2] AGS. iv. 8. 19.

[3] xxxix. 8.

[4] ZDMG. xl. 120. Other suggestions make Rudra or Çiva, or both, Dravidian words. Cf. Segerstedt, RHR. lvii. 298, who emphasizes his connexion with the un-Aryan Niṣādas.

[5] *Ind. Stud.* ii. 19–22.

[6] *Ved. Myth.* ii. 179–208; (Kl. Ausg.), pp. 164–5.

[7] iii. 33. For an implausible guess at the sense, cf. Arbman, *Rudra*, pp. 30 ff.

[8] VOJ. ix. 233–52; *Mysterium und Mimus*, pp. 19, 21 ff.; Charpentier, VOJ. xxiii. 151 ff.; Johansson, *Ueber die altind. Göttin Dhiṣaṇā*, pp. 88, 92. The views of Tilak in his *Orion* are unacceptable; see Whitney, JAOS. xvi. pp. lxxxii ff.

[9] *Rel. des Veda*², pp. 215–24; Winternitz, IF. Anz. viii. 38; Pischel, GGA. 1895, pp. 150 f.

in its essence to such figures as the mountain and wood gods or demons, like Mars Silvanus, the Fauni,[1] and so on, and he also points out that it is a common idea that disease comes from the mountains. Moreover, this view suits the connexion of Rudra with the north, since in India the mountains of importance to the Vedic Indians were in the north.[2] Umā, who is given in late texts to Rudra as wife, is styled Haimavatī, from the Himavant.

The chief defect of these views is that they are based too exclusively upon the later accounts of the nature of the god, which really represent a time when he is ceasing to be connected with the original natural basis, on which the conception rests. There is nothing in the conception of the god as he is found in the Rigveda, which cannot be explained by the idea of a storm god considered mainly in the form of lightning, the tempest being viewed on its destructive rather than its healing aspect.[3] From this could be derived easily the god's character as father of the Maruts, while from the beneficent rains loosened by the storm comes the aspect of him as a healing god, which is an essential feature of his character in the Rigveda and without which indeed he could hardly have been accepted as a god by the religion of the Rigveda. This theory explains in a satisfactory manner his connexion with Agni, which is close and obvious. Moreover, the theory of the original relation of Rudra with the dead is contradicted by the fact that he never appears in any close connexion with the dead: he is not their king, nor does he lead them to, or receive them in, his realm; his is the Svāhā not Svadhā call in the offering; his place is the north, not the south, which is essentially that of the dead, and, though in certain aspects the ritual of the dead has analogies with that for Rudra, that point is adequately and naturally explained by the fact that both the dead and Rudra have terrible characteristics. The clear connexion of Rudra with the sky is fatal to Oldenberg's theory, for the period of the Rigveda at any rate.

The Çatapatha Brāhmaṇa [4] tells us that Çarva was a name of Agni among the eastern people and that Bhava was used among the Bāhīkas, which suggests that in Rudra there have combined the forms of different but kindred gods. A reference to the cult of Rudra by the Vrātyas has been seen as the explanation of the curious Vrātya hymn of the Atharvaveda [5] and of the ceremonies which are used for the introduction into the Vedic religious life of the non-Brahmanical Aryans. The evidence for this view, however, must be

[1] Warde Fowler, *Roman Festivals*, pp. 258 ff.; *Roman Ideas of Deity*, pp. 93, 94.

[2] Hillebrandt (*Ved. Myth.* ii. 207) finds the connexion with the north in the fact that the sun is to the north during the period of the most dangerous season of the year.

[3] Hopkins, JAOS. xvi. pp. cl. ff.; Bloomfield, AJP. xii. 429; Macdonell, *Ved. Myth.*, pp. 76 ff.; JRAS. 1895, p. 956; 1900, pp. 383 ff.; Hardy, *Ved.-brahm. Periode*, p. 83. Ludwig (*Rigveda*, iii. 320 ff.) holds that Dyaus develops on the moral side into Varuṇa and on the physical to Rudra. Bergaigne (*Rel. Véd.* iii. 31 ff.) treats him as 'le père céleste'; Siecke (*Archiv für Rel.* i. 113 ff., 209 ff.) as the moon.

[4] i. 7. 3. 8.

[5] xv. 1; Charpentier, VOJ. xxiii. 151 ff.; xxv. 355 ff.

regarded as quite insufficient to make it even plausible.[1] The question, however, does arise whether in the late Rudra we have not the syncretism of more than one deity, and possibly the influence of the aboriginal worship on the Aryan. It is certainly possible that a forest and mountain deity or some kindred god, such as a vegetation spirit, and even a god of the dead may be united with the Vedic lightning god to form the composite figure of the Yajurveda : the view preferred by Oldenberg, that the god is really the same throughout the whole period, and that it is the nature of the tradition which obscures the fact, cannot be accepted in face of the obvious probability of development of religion, and the admitted ease with which deities absorb foreign elements into their character. In the later Çiva there are many traces of conceptions commonly associated with vegetation spirits, and his phallic cult is one which is condemned by the Rigveda, but which doubtless remained as popular among the aborigines as it now is among Çiva worshippers throughout India.

A very elaborate effort to show that the Rigveda presents a later and priestly conception of Rudra as a celestial deity, a priestly refinement from an ancient cannibalistic death demon, is made by Arbman.[2] He contends that the nature of the post-Vedic Rudra is already indicated very clearly in the later Vedic texts, suggesting that the popular god of the Rigvedic period was very much the same as the post-Vedic deity, and that it is more probable that the priests of the Rigveda transmuted a popular god than that a god such as that of the Rigveda developed by any means into the later Rudra-Çiva. It appears unnatural and unreasonable to accept this suggestion, as opposed to the simple and plausible hypothesis that the later Çiva represents the fusion of more than one deity. We have for such fusion the increasing number of distinct names, which are allotted by the texts to Çiva, as seen both in the Çatapatha Brāhmaṇa and the Kauṣītaki Brāhmaṇa, and syncretism of deities is so common and notorious that it seems strange to find so much reluctance to accept what is notoriously a trait of the post-Vedic Çiva, whose cosmopolitan character enables him to absorb local god after god. Moreover, in order to bolster up the view of the primitive chthonic character of Rudra, it is necessary to make the Maruts chthonic also, which is a decidedly implausible view. Further, it is difficult not to recognize the strong differences between Yama, a real death god, and Rudra, which indicate an original difference of origin ; they belong to different regions, Yama to the south, Rudra to the north. Everything in the ritual goes to support the view of Rudra as a complex figure at the time when it was recorded ; he combines clear traits of

[1] Keith, JRAS. 1913, pp. 155–60. A different but implausible view of the Vrātyas as Kṣatriya Yogins is developed by Hauer, *Die Anfänge der Yogapraxis im alten Indien*, pp. 172 ff. The epic does not encourage these vagaries (Hopkins, *Epic Myth.*, p. 231, n. 2), nor need we see in them Indo-Europeans of uncertain connexion.

[2] *Rudra. Untersuchungen zum altindischen Glauben und Kultus* (1922).

divine and chthonic character, as is natural in a god formed by the syncretism of different beliefs.

Stress is laid by Arbman on the term Tryambaka which is accorded to Rudra in the Rigveda, and which he interprets as referring to the god as having three mothers, a fact which connects him in Arbman's view with the cult of mothers, i. e. demonesses as patron goddesses in medieval and modern India.[1] If the connexion were real, we might then see in the Rudra of the Rigveda a figure already complicated by contamination with an aboriginal deity, for there is little evidence or probability of mother worship as Aryan or Indo-European,[2] and every sign that it was dear to the Dravidian or other aboriginal population. But the suggested interpretation is wholly dubious; we do not hear later of Çiva as having three mothers, though Skanda has seven, and our only early tradition asserts that Ambikā is the sister of Rudra, not his wife, and that she is the autumn.[3] It is, therefore, much more probable that the epithet refers to the god either as connected with three seasons, or as connected with the three worlds, heaven, air, and earth, as is the case with the Maruts and is natural in a god of igneous connexions. It is admitted that with Agni Rudra is most intimately connected, and of Agni nothing is more assured than his triple nature. Nor is it possible to find any support for the view of Tryambaka suggested by Arbman in the Traiyambaka offering of the Çrauta ritual,[4] in which nothing whatever appears to explain the name in this sense, apart altogether from the fact that we have no evidence whatever that the rite in question was known to the Rigveda, and later rites frequently stand in no vital connexion with the original nature of the deities to whom they are addressed or who are invoked in them.[5]

Arbman's theory leads to a curious and unnatural result in the case of the intimate connexion with Agni which the texts admittedly reveal, and which is shown by the interchange of Rudra's names with Agni. The obvious explanation afforded by the Rigveda is that Rudra is in a sense fire, for he is a lightning god; to Arbman it is necessary to hold that Rudra's dangerous nature was expressed in the minds of his votaries by the term fire, a conception bizarre and implausible. Moreover we have on every hand evidence of the syncretism of gods in Rudra; Arbman seems to feel doubt over his desperate

[1] Arbman, *Rudra*, pp. 296 f.; Hopkins, *Epic Myth.*, p. 226; Monier Williams, *Brāhmanism and Hindūism*, pp. 222 ff.

[2] In Germanic mythology they seem to be Celtic borrowings, and Celtic deities are rather European than Indo-European; cf. Helm, *Altgerm. Rel.* i. 391 ff. (guardian deities of the family, later of places); Carnoy, *Les Indo-Européens*, p. 68. Triads are, of course, ethnic, thus denoting completeness; Hopkins, *Origin of Religion*, pp. 291 ff.

[3] TB. i. 6. 10. ÇB. ii. 6. 2. 9 explains as *strī-ambakā*. Hillebrandt (*Ved. Myth.* ii. 188, n. 2) suggests that *tri* is equal to *stṛ*, 'star'.

[4] *Rudra*, pp. 48 ff.

[5] The suspension on trees of the offerings at the Tryambaka offering and the Bauḍhyavihāra (below, Chap. 20, § 5) suggests a vegetation or tree ritual, but by no means necessarily. It may be merely a natural mode of offering to the god whose lightning strikes the tree, or to a spirit of the air (Helm, *op. cit.* i. 245).

suggestion that in the Çatarudriya the term Rudra means 'the demon', and not Rudra at all, and gives it up for Rudra Vāstoṣpati. What is obvious is that the great god absorbs, as other great gods have done, a mass of Sondergötter, though in the Çatarudriya form we have priestly ingenuity extending and amplifying Sondergötter in the best manner of the Roman Indigitamenta. It is probably to syncretism again that we owe the connexion of Rudra [1] with thieves, robbers, and highwaymen, whose patron he seems to have been, and from whom, therefore, he is expected to protect his votaries, and we need not press the suggestion that he was regarded himself as tricky,[2] or connect this aspect with the uncertain character of the lightning. Nor in the Vedic texts does he ever become a snake god; his connexion with snakes is only incipient,[3] and it becomes much more marked in the epic, showing us clearly the process of identification in its advance. On the other hand, it is probable that some of his characteristics in the later Vedic period come from a god of death; this may primarily be due to identification with Çarva and Bhava, and it is suggested in his connexion with birds of evil omen [4] and howling dogs,[5] for such birds and dogs are closely connected with Yama as a god of the dead.

Nor is any useful light shed on Rudra's nature by the endeavour to deduce from the account of the mad Muni in the Rigveda [6] the picture of Rudra as the god of an orgiastic cult, whose epithet of *vyuptakeça*, 'with disordered hair', in the Yajurveda [7] hints at his exploits as a lord of the orgiastic dance. The fact is that the Rigveda tells us merely that the Muni drinks poison from a cup with Rudra, and the rest of the hypothesis is as baseless as the suggestion that the cup was really a skull. The orgiastic traits of Çiva in the later mythology are doubtless due to the amalgamation with Rudra of a vegetation deity, an Indian Dionysos.

§ 11. *The Maruts or Rudras*

The Maruts share in the greatness of Indra, and, therefore, they have a prominent place in the Rigveda, thirty three-hymns being exclusively theirs, while they share seven with Indra, and one each with Pūṣan and Agni. They are essentially a troupe, thrice seven [8] or thrice sixty [9] in number, the children

[1] Cf. Durgā's later patronage of Thugs (Garbe, *Beiträge zur ind. Kulturgeschichte*, pp. 185 ff.), Hermes, patron of thieves, and Laverna in Rome (Roscher, *Lex.* I. ii. 2372; II. i. 1917).

[2] Dhūrta is an epithet in MS. i. 8. 5; KS. vi. 7; ĀpÇS. vi. 11. 3; HÇS. iii. 18, but more usually of Skanda, AV. Par. xx; BG. Par. iv. 2.

[3] Cf. AGS. iv. 8. 22 ff. The Anukramaṇī treatment of AV. iii. 26, 27; vi. 56. 2, 3; xii. 1. 46 as connected with Rudra (cf. Vait. xxix. 10) is very late evidence.

[4] Cf. AV. xi. 2. 2, 11; iv. 28. 4; TA. iv. 28. Cf. the euphemistic Çiva as name of the jackal, the omen of death; HGS. i. 16. 19.

[5] AV. xi. 2. 30; cf. VS. xvi. 28.

[6] x. 136; Arbman, *Rudra*, pp. 297 ff. Cf. below, Chap. 22, § 9.

[7] TS. iv. 5. 5. That the Çūla was a Vedic weapon of Rudra is certainly not proved by AV. vi. 90; Kauç. xxxi. 7 (Arbman, p. 113, n.).

[8] RV. i. 133. 6.

[9] RV. viii. 96. 8.

of Rudra, whence they are called Rudras or Rudriyas : their mother is Pṛçni, or a cow, and they come with cows with distended udders : the cows can scarcely be anything other than the swollen rain clouds. Agni is also said to have produced them, and they are born of the laughter of the lightning. Vāyu also is said to have produced them from the womb of heaven, and they are also sons of heaven, they have the ocean for their mother or are self-born. They are brothers of equal age, of equal birth, of one mind and one abode. They have as their bride the goddess Rodasī, and are connected with the goddesses Indrāṇī and Sarasvatī.

The home of the Maruts is in the three heavens or in the three worlds. Their brightness is one of their leading features : hence they are directly called fires. They are also intimately connected with the lightning, which serves as their spears. On their feet they wear anklets, golden ornaments on their breasts, golden helmets on their heads, they carry the lightning in their hands, and spears on their shoulders. They have also axes of gold, while from Rudra they borrow the bow and arrow, and once even from Indra the thunderbolt. They ride in golden cars drawn by tawny steeds, which are often described as spotted, and called *pṛṣatīs*. But they are also said to have yoked the winds as steeds to the poles of their cars.

The Maruts are great, young, unageing, terrible like wild beasts, but playful like children or calves : they are lions or iron-tusked boars or black swans. The noise of their onset is the roaring of the wind or thunder : they rend the mountains, crush the forests, and whirl up the dust with their steeds, which are the winds. They bring rain with them in their train : a river, the Marudvṛdhā, bears trace of their power, but the rain they send is as usual sometimes called honey or milk or ghee. The rain which they send comes with the thunder and the lightning. Though they avert heat, nevertheless they are also said to bring the light, to dispel the darkness, and like many other gods they hold apart the two worlds. They sing a song, or blow a pipe, and their singing strengthens Indra for the slaying of Vṛtra. Sometimes they appear as drinkers of Soma, and even as pious sacrificers, since they are singers.

The main deed of the Maruts is the rendering of aid to Indra in the slaying of Vṛtra, though they are mentioned also as aiding Indra's predecessor, Trita, in this feat. Occasionally in place of aiding Indra only, the overthrow of Vṛtra and the winning of the cows are attributed to them. They are styled sometimes sons or brothers of Indra.[1] But two or three times they appear as having left him at the critical moment, and Indra seems to have sought in revenge to slay them, and to have been appeased with difficulty by Agastya,[2] in connexion with a sacrifice which that seer was anxious to offer to them.

[1] In the Brāhmaṇas as rain-gods they rank, on the analogy of agriculturists, as the common folk of the gods (e. g. PB. xviii. 1. 14.; xix. 14. 1; xxi. 14. 3), whom Indra, as a sovereign, shamelessly plunders (PB. xxi. 1. 1 ff.).

[2] RV. i. 165, 170 ; Pischel, *Ved. Stud.* i. 59 ; Hertel, VOJ. xviii. 153 ; v. Schroeder, *Mysterium und Mimus*, pp. 91 ff. ; Oldenberg, *Ṛgveda-Noten*, i. 170 ; Keith, *Sanskrit Drama*, pp. 15, 19 f.

Their connexion with Rudra is also distinctly marked in the deprecation of their wrath, which is several times expressed, and their cow- and man-slaying bolt is referred to, as is that of Rudra.[1] They are said to send evil and to have the wrath of the serpent. From Rudra again comes the fact that they are entreated to bear from the Sindhu, the seas, the mountains, the Asiknī, healing remedies, and by rain they are said to bestow medicine, which is no doubt rain like the Jalāṣa of Rudra. From the waters comes no doubt their purifying power.

In the ritual they differ from Vāyu in their relation to the Soma sacrifice, as they have a place at the midday and the evening pressings, while the morning pressing alone is the place for Vāyu, and they play a considerable part in the four-month offerings. It has been sought to show that their cult is specially connected with the Viçvāmitra family and is not a subject of much interest to the Bharadvājas and other priestly families, the Vasiṣṭhas for instance being mainly concerned with the relations of Indra and Vāyu; but this theory is not supported by the references in the various books which seem to show throughout a recognition of Indra's relations to the Maruts.[2]

For the nature of the Maruts two explanations alone are really plausible : the most natural [3] is that they are the deities of the winds in their aspect as bearing the storm clouds : the mere winds are inadequate to explain the constant association of the gods with fire and lightning. The native tradition is that they are the winds,[4] and the word in post-Vedic literature simply means wind. The name itself throws no light on the conception, as, though the root may be set down as *mar*, it is wholly doubtful what that root is to mean : with the normal view of the nature of the gods, it is taken either as to shine or as to crush, according as it is believed to denote the Maruts as radiant gods, or as the winds which crush the woods. The alternative view is sometimes based on the etymology of *mar* as to die,[5] and the Maruts are claimed as the spirits of the dead, conceived as storming along in the winds, and then merely as the winds. The view has the support of Kuhn, Benfey,[6] E. H. Meyer,[7] v. Schroeder,[8] and Hillebrandt,[9] but the last alone has made any serious attempt to prove his thesis. He calls attention to the fact that the Maruts are sometimes treated in a manner analogous to Rudra or the Manes. Thus, after an offering to Indra on one occasion, a quite separate offering is made to them,[10] and the reason alleged is that they are not eaters of the oblation as gods proper are ; [11] they also receive an offering of an embryo, which is

[1] RV. vii. 56. 9, 17 ; 57. 4 ; i. 171. 1 ; 172. 2 ; 64. 8, 9.

[2] Hillebrandt, *Ved. Myth.* iii. 325, 326.

[3] Macdonell, *Ved. Myth.*, p. 81.

[4] Yāska, Nir. xi. 13.

[5] Leumann (*Buddha und Mahāvīra*, p. 11) gives *mās-mṛt*, man-slayer, by dissimilation *māvṛt*, Latin *mavort*, *mart*.

[6] On RV. i. 6. 4.

[7] *Indog. Myth.* i. 218.

[8] VOJ. ix. 248, 249.

[9] *Ved. Myth.* iii. 317 ; (Kl. Ausg.), pp. 102 ff. ; Arbman, *Rudra*, pp. 309 ff.

[10] PGS. ii. 15.

[11] ÇB. iv. 5. 2. 16, 17. The face, according to Hillebrandt, is to be averted at an offering given in KÇS. xviii. 4. 23 ff., but see Oldenberg, GN. 1915, p. 388,

normally not fit for sacrifice, they appear as destroying offspring,[1] as seeking to injure the sacrifice,[2] as barring men from advancing through their realm of the air.[3] Moreover, they are often regarded as like birds, and birds are often the souls of the dead.[4] Hillebrandt lays no stress on the etymology of the word, and even seems to think that the derivation may be from the Dravidian word *marutta*, a medicine man,[5] but, in view of the late date at which the Dravidian word is known, this is quite an impossible and unscientific suggestion. But the main ground of this thesis cannot obviously be taken seriously. The connexion with Rudra explains the special treatment of the Maruts at certain sacrifices, while, for the most part, as connected with Indra, they have an honourable share in offerings. The connexion with birds is most natural of the winds, and needs no reference to the souls of the dead, and often they have connexion with the Ādityas.[6]

Arbman,[7] developing and improving upon a suggestion of Hillebrandt's [8] regarding the double sense of the Maruts as the storm winds and also the hosts of Rudra, representing various aspects of his nature, holds that in the Rigveda the Maruts are the Rudras, while after that the Rudras become a host of demons, quite different from the Maruts, late Vedic times forgetting the connexion of Rudras and Maruts. This is no doubt an exaggerated view. The process is not one of sudden or vehement change; the extension of Rudra's nature carries with it the development of the character of his troupes; the Rudras are wider in character than the Maruts *per se* would have been. But it is a complete error to treat the Rudras as demons, because they are destructive and sometimes act in an evil way as demons might do; [9] equally on this theory most Vedic gods might be made out to be demons. The contention that the Rudras are demons, because Rudra is lord of beings, Bhūtapati,[10] is wholly untenable; Bhūta does not, as suggested, in the Vedic literature, until possibly a very late period, bear the sense 'demons', but it denotes 'beings' pure and simple.

n. 3. No Svāhā call at the offering, ÇB. iv. 5. 2. 17.

[1] TB. i. 6. 2, 2.

[2] TB. i. 3. 4. 4.

[3] AB. i. 10. 2; TS. vii. 1. 5. 4.

[4] BDS. ii. 14. 10. Arbman (*op. cit.*, p. 309) actually denies that gods have bird forms, forgetting the sungod as a bird, Indra's bird form, &c.

[5] ZDMG. xxiii. 518.

[6] RV. x. 77. 8; i. 106. 2; TS. ii. 3. 1. 5; TA. v. 4. 8; their names are Çukrajyotis, Citrajyotis, Satyajyotis, Jyotiṣmant, &c., VS. xxvii. 80; ÇB. ix. 3. 1. 26; as rays and months, PB. xiv. 12. 9.

[7] *Rudra*, pp. 18, n. 1, 162 ff.

[8] *Ved. Myth.* iii. 301.

[9] TS. vii. 1. 5. 4; MS. i. 8. 4 (Asuras in ÇB. ii. 4. 3. 2 ff.). In TS. vi. 1. 1. 1; TA. v. 8. 4 ff. the Rudras are clearly not demons.

[10] AV. xi. 2. 1; cf. AB. iii. 33; see Chap. 12, § 5; 21, § 2.

CHAPTER 10

THE GREAT GODS—TERRESTRIAL

§ 1. *Agni*

AGNI is clearly in the eyes of the priest only second to Indra in importance: in the Rigveda he has some 200 hymns for himself alone.[1] From Indra, however, he is essentially distinguished by his nature; he is intimately connected with the element of which he is the deity, and his nature is therefore far less anthropomorphic; moreover, what there is of human in him is derived, not from the conception of the warrior god, but from that of the ideal priest: if both gods are expected to send fortune and happiness to their votaries, Indra gives rather victory in battle and power, Agni the prosperity and happiness of the home. Moreover, while Agni is assimilated in much to Indra and as usual is accorded several of his feats and his powers, Indra remains comparatively unaffected by the qualities of Agni. Indra also is not, like Agni, the messenger between gods and men, an office, which, if it makes Agni in some ways a god of the closest intimacy with the life of men, still does tend to reduce his status, and renders him in some sense inferior to the other gods. Nor is Soma the normal drink of Agni: he is indeed a Soma-drinker, but only in a minimal degree for a great god, and often because of his connexion with Indra.

The appearance of Agni is clearly merely a description of the fire, and in one passage he is truly called headless and footless: elsewhere he is called butter-faced, butter-backed, butter-haired, flame-haired or tawny-haired. He has three or seven tongues, which receive in the later literature names of their own; his steeds are similarly given seven tongues. He has butter for his eye, four or a thousand eyes, and a thousand horns. He is also an archer. He is likened to, or identified with, a bull or horse or bird, an eagle or Haṅsa: even once he is called a raging serpent. Again he [2] is a hatchet or a car.

His food is ghee, but he also devours the woods, and eats thrice a day. Or he is the mouth by which the gods eat the sacrifice. He is invoked to come to sit on the strew to receive the offerings for himself, or the gods.

Agni's brightness is often mentioned; he is like the sun, dispels darkness, and bears the epithet 'waking at dawn'. But, when he drives through the forest, shaving the earth like a barber a beard, his path is black. His flames roar terribly, and his light reaches the sky. But he has also a car drawn by two or more horses, with which he brings the gods to receive the offerings of men.

[1] For Indo-European fire gods, see von Schroeder, *Arische Religion*, i. 466 ff.
[2] RV. i. 79. 1.

Agni's mythic parents are Dyaus and Pṛthivī, or Tvaṣṭṛ and the Waters. But he is also produced by the gods whose father, however, he is; he is brought into existence by Indra or Indra and Viṣṇu, or by the Dawn, and is the son of Iḍā, the personification of the sacrificial food. All these accounts are open to obvious explanations and are of no consequence. More important is the birth from the two fire sticks, the upper being deemed the male, the lower the female, and in mythical form being described as Purūravas and Urvaçī, from that famous pair of lovers. They are also called two mothers, and many plays on the curious infant and his mothers occur.[1] As friction is engendered by the action of the hands in turning the one stick in the other, he is credited with ten mothers, the ten fingers. As force is needed for his production, Agni is the son of strength. He is born ever new and is called the youngest, but still is old as being born for ever. Here and there occurs, in the Brāhmaṇa literature, the idea that the fire at the end of a year is outworn, but the idea that the fire is at the beginning of each year to be formally renewed in a special rite is not to be recognized. For the sacrifices such as the Agniṣṭoma, the four-monthly rites, and the animal offering, the fire is solemnly produced anew by friction, but there is no evidence that the winter solstice was felt to be a time when the fire as such was in need of any special renewal. If such an idea existed,[2] it has not left any clear trace in Vedic ritual.

As Agni springs from the wood, it is regularly stated that he dwells in plants. On earth too he has a place in the navel (*nābhi*) of the earth, a reference doubtless to the hole in the high place of offering in which the fire is deposited: hence Agni is the navel of immortality.

Agni is also born from the waters: he is the embryo of the waters, kindled in the waters, a bull who has waxed great in the waters, and he descends from the clouds. In these cases it is probable that the waters of the clouds are meant: in this aspect he is Apāṁ Napāt, who has become practically a separate deity. On the other hand, there is a widely prevalent view that the waters are terrestrial: several late hymns of the Rigveda tell of the flight of Agni because of unwillingness to perform the sacrifice, and his being found among the waters and the plants, and this legend is a common-place of the Brāhmaṇa period. In the Atharvaveda the Agni in the waters is clearly distinguished from the lightning, and is made terrestrial. The Rigveda itself recognizes the existence of Agni in the streams. In the ritual there are many traces of the same view of Agni as in waters other than those of the clouds.

[1] The long period of gestation (RV. v. 2) is probably an allusion to the long latency of fire in the wood, ere evoked by friction. The old mode of lighting the fire was preserved in the rite of rekindling on March 1 the fire of Vesta in Rome and in the occasional use of this method in kindling the 'need fire' in Germany (von Schroeder, *Arische Religion*, ii. 596 f.).

[2] Hillebrandt, *Ved. Myth.* ii. 77 ff. Cf. his theory of Dawn as the Goddess of a New Year (above, Part II, Chap. 8, § 7). Cf. von Schroeder (*Arische Religion*, ii. 485), who regards Agni as reborn at the opening of spring, comparing the return of Apollo in spring (p. 523).

At the dedication of tanks of water and similar rites, offerings are made to Agni in the waters;[1] the Brahman student, when he performs the bath marking the end of his period of pupilship, takes water from a vessel, appropriating to himself the bright form of Agni and repelling the other forms of Agni, which have entered into the water.[2] The waters used at the royal consecration are regarded as being full of Agni.[3] In the ceremony of the piling of the fire altar, when it is desired to diminish the heat of Agni, cooling plants and a frog are placed on the altar, and Agni is asked to enter the waters of which he is the gall.[4] It is clear, therefore, that the view that Agni is connected with the waters of the earth is an old one, but it must be noted that at no period is his connexion with the waters of the air forgotten: we find it expressly asserted in a Sūtra[5] text which shows that it was perfectly well understood. It is impossible, therefore, to accept the view of Oldenberg that the connexion of Agni in the terrestrial waters is the normal one, as opposed to the Agni of the aerial waters: both conceptions are clearly found equally authenticated. The explanation of the belief in the presence of Agni in the terrestrial waters may be a transfer from the belief in his presence in the aerial waters, but it can also be accounted for in other ways. Thus the phenomenon of the lightning coming down to and entering the waters may well have played a more important part than the more elaborate idea, clearly valid for the Brāhmaṇa period, which sees in the plants the closest connexion with the waters, and which pictures a cycle from the water to the plants, from the plants to the flame, from the flame to the smoke, from the smoke to the cloud, and thence to the water again.

In the third place Agni has a birth in the heaven; he is born there and was brought down by Mātariçvan, who is doubtless his lightning form. The Aitareya Brāhmaṇa[6] calls him at once heavenly and in the waters. Agni, however, is often as the god contrasted with the lightning. Agni as heavenly is the sun, born in the morning. The Aitareya[7] says that on setting the sun enters into Agni, and in the Rigveda[8] Agni unites himself with the rays of the sun. But this side of the nature of Agni is little referred to: the sun was too great and prominent a deity to be treated merely as a form of Agni.

The three births of Agni are constantly referred to: he is made threefold, has three heads, tongues, stations. The order of his abodes is variously stated, as heaven, earth, the waters; or earth, heaven, the waters; or sky, air, and earth. Hence we must doubtless trace the view of the Nairuktas preserved for us by Yāska,[9] which makes the whole Vedic pantheon reducible to the three gods, Agni, Indra or Vāyu, and Sūrya. The second member of the triad must be taken to have replaced the lightning, which would be more easy, since the lightning has no mythic name to give it substance, and, therefore, the god

[1] ÇGS. v. 2. 5.
[2] PGS. ii. 6. 10.
[3] AB. viii. 6.
[4] TS. iv. 6. 1. 2; VS. xvii. 6.
[5] ApÇS. v. 16. 4.
[6] vii. 7. 2.
[7] viii. 28.
[8] v. 37. 1; vii. 2. 1.
[9] Nir. xii. 19.

of the middle space is better represented by a deity of more concrete nature. On the other hand, it would be an error to underestimate the importance of lightning in Vedic mythology, on the ground that it is too transient in character to serve as the basis of mythology.[1]

Still more important is the fact that the three forms of Agni explain the practice that in the ritual Agni is worshipped on three altars, the Gārhapatya, the Āhavanīya, and the Dakṣiṇa,[2] which are kept quite distinct from the ordinary household fire. The alternative view that these fires are to be regarded as the source of the myth of the three forms of Agni can hardly be taken seriously. More plausible is connexion with fire as the sun, as domestic, and as driving away evil spirits, as von Schroeder suggests.[3]

Though the birth of Agni is most often triple, yet in many passages he is given but two births, the one on earth, the other in the sky, or, less often, the one in heaven and the other in the waters. The idea is already found in the Rigveda that Agni descends into the waters, and that from the plants he arises again, and, from the distinction of the aspects of fire, we arrive at the frequent Vedic idea that the god is to sacrifice to himself, or bring himself to the sacrifice, or descend with the gods to the sacrifice. Moreover, by another view Agni is kindled not only by men or earth, but by the gods in heaven:[4] this doubtless points at once to the necessity of some kindler for the Agni of the heaven as for him of earth, and to the tendency to see in the gods the precise analogues of pious sacrificers among men. But from yet another point of view Agni is manifold, since there are many fires on earth: the unity of the conception, however, as in the case of Dawn triumphs: the other fires are likened to the branches of the tree, Agni. This manifold nature of his origin is sometimes developed in detail, as when he is said to be born from the heavens, the waters, stones, woods, and plants.[5] The rock whence it is born may be the stone from which he is struck out or the cloud: he dwells also in man as animal heat, in beast and birds, in biped and quadruped.[6] He is the germ therefore of all that is.

The three births of Agni give rise to the legend of his three brothers, or his brothers generically, who again with him make up the four Hotṛs, of whom three die according to the Kāṭhaka Saṁhitā.[7] The legend of death seems purely imaginative. Of the gods Varuṇa is once his brother, and Indra is his twin brother. From Indra Agni borrows, as we have seen, some of his feats, such as vanquishing the Paṇis. In one hymn Agni is mentioned with Soma. He lends himself also to identifications with other gods: thus in the evening he is Varuṇa, rising in the morning Mitra, as Savitṛ he traverses the air, as

[1] Oldenberg, *Rel. des Veda*², pp. 112 f.; Hardy, *Ved.-brahm. Periode*, p. 64; Hillebrandt, *Ved. Myth.* i. 368; ii. 129 ff.

[2] It is connected with the dead, and they with the winds and the air. Hence it corresponds to the aerial, as the Āhavanīya to the celestial Agni.

[3] *Arische Religion*, ii. 487 f.

[4] RV. vi. 2. 3; cf. AB. ii. 34.

[5] RV. ii. 1. 1.

[6] RV. x. 5. 1; AV. iii. 21. 2; xii. 1. 19; 2. 33; TS. iv. 6. 1. 3.

[7] xxv. 7. Cf. TS. ii. 6. 6; Bṛhaddevatā, vii. 61 with Macdonell's note.

Indra he illumines the sky; so the Atharvaveda [1] tells us. He has various forms and many names, he embraces all the gods, and once even in the Rigveda [2] he is successively identified with twelve gods and five goddesses.

Agni is not without martial traits, but his activity is quite different from that of Indra, who wars on the Asuras and on the Dāsas. Agni is in place of that the destroyer of the demons; with iron teeth he consumes the sorcerers, he drives away the goblins, he is the slayer of Rakṣases *par excellence*. Indra borrows this feature of his character from him, and it is also attributed to the Açvins, Bṛhaspati, and Soma, but the primary claim of fire to destroy the wizards and the demons is an obvious one, and recorded by anthropology [3] over all the earth. It is also most strongly attested in the ritual.

The domestic side of the fire worship is revealed mainly by the constant reference to Agni as the friend in the homes of men, whence comes his description as father, or brother, or son, or even mother. He has the epithet domestic, and is styled lord of the house. He is the immortal who abides among mortal in human habitations. He is further the protector of settlers, the man who makes mortals to settle down, and he is the lord of the clan (*viçpati*). The close relation of men to him is attested by the fact that we hear expressly of the Agni of Bharata, of Devavāta, of Divodāsa, of Trasadasyu, and of Vadhryaçva. His relation to the Aṅgirases and the Bhṛgus may have been mythical, but were not so conceived in all probability in Vedic times, and he certainly stood in close relation to families like the Vasiṣṭhas. His connexion with Aryan settlement is told clearly in the legend of the advance of the Aryans to the east under the guidance of Gotama Rāhūgaṇa and Videgha Māthava,[4] the latter of whom has been compared rashly with Prometheus; the story preserves in the clearest way possible the record of the essential connexion between the introduction of the fire cult, and the advance of Aryan settlement and of Aryan culture.

The ritual hardly gives a clear picture of these aspects of the character of Agni as the domestic friend and father, and as the protector and leader of the people. In it stress is laid in the main on the ritual of the three fires of the more elaborate sacrifices performed for an individual, and this elaboration is old, since in the Rigveda, while the name of only one of the later fires expressly occurs, that of the Gārhapatya, there are references to the later practice of transporting the fire from one altar to another: thus Agni is said to be led round, to go round the sacrifice three times, to be led east and then west. But the importance of the domestic fire, which can be assumed for the earliest period, and which is preserved in some degree in the domestic ritual, is also attested by the fact that in the later ritual, and perhaps also in the earlier, the fire was first placed on the Gārhapatya altar, a name which indicates that the

[1] xiii. 3. 13.
[2] ii. 1. 3–7.
[3] Frazer, *Balder the Beautiful*, i. 325 ff.
[4] ÇB. 1. 4. 1. 10; von Negelein (VOJ. xviii. 97–9) lays stress on the function of fire as burning the wild and preparing the way for agriculture, the value of which in India is almost unlimited.

real domestic fire was the starting-point of the late development. There are fainter traces of the worship of fire not merely by an individual, but as the fire of the clan or community. In the later ritual [1] we hear of the fire of the Sabhā and the Āvasatha, which were respectively the council-house and a place of reception for those who came to the Sabhā, as it seems, and it may be conjectured from the fact that the word Sabhya as an epithet of fire is found in the Atharvaveda,[2] though not in the Rigveda, that we are entitled to conceive of the fire as being lighted in the Sabhā for the cult of the clan or community on the solemn occasions of the meeting of the people in council. There are parallels among other peoples of the Indo-European stock, and among the Iranians where such fires as those of the head of the clan and of the canton were known,[3] but in the case of the Rigveda, the traces are scanty, unless stress can be laid on the term 'lord of the clan' applied to the god, and the title of king of the clans of men. It is, however, notorious that the Sabhā, which appears as a real institution in the Rigveda, in the later period disappears, and is reduced at most to a small council, first of warriors and priests and then of priests only,[4] so that it is possible that an earlier public cult disappeared in the course of time. Analogy suggests this conclusion, which is merely rendered doubtful by the imperfection of the evidence which can be adduced to prove the positive existence of the cult.

On the other hand we have abundant references to the activities of Agni as a sacrificer, and he serves as the model for sacrificers. He is an essential element in the transmission of the sacrifice to the gods who cannot enjoy it without him. On the one hand he brings the gods down to the sacrifice and seats them on the strew that they may enjoy the food and drink offered. On the other hand he bears the oblation to the gods in the heaven. In either case he is constantly serving as an envoy between the gods and men, and is especially often called the messenger of men, though also that of Vivasvant. The Yajurveda [5] elevates him into the messenger of the gods, and places over against him Kāvya Uçanas as the messenger of the Asuras. A Brāhmaṇa [6] deals with him, not as the messenger of, but as the path leading to the gods. He is called the Hotṛ, the Adhvaryu, the Brahman, and Purohita of the gods, thus combining in himself all the activities of the human priest. He is thus the one most fitted to worship the gods, he makes the oblations fragrant. But there is also a tradition that he wearied of his office, and required to be induced by promise of rich reward to be the bearer of the oblation.[7] It seems that he had to be found in the waters and the plants, and that he was

[1] ApÇS. v. 19. 2 ff.; KÇS. iv. 9. 20 ff.; Hillebrandt, *Ved. Myth.* ii. 118, 126; *contra*, Caland, VOJ. xxiii. 59 as to Āvasathya.

[2] xix. 55. 6; cf. viii. 10. 7 (Gārhapatya, Āhavanīya, Dakṣiṇāgni, Sabhā, Āmantraṇa) with KS. vi. 8 (Odanapacana, Gārhapatya, Āhavanīya, Madhyādhidevana, Āmantraṇa).

[3] Geiger, *Ostir. Kult.*, p. 472.

[4] Macdonell and Keith, *Vedic Index*, ii. 426, 427; Foy, *Die königliche Gewalt*, p. 10.

[5] TS. ii. 5. 8. 5.

[6] TB. ii. 4. 1. 6.

[7] RV. x. 51–3; Oldenberg, ZDMG. xxxix. 71 ff.

reluctant to undertake the duties. Hillebrandt,[1] who thinks that the reluctance was connected with the death of his brothers, which is not, however, quite clearly referred to in the Rigveda and which may be only a later myth, and of independent origin, deduces from the story the view that it refers to the contrast between the two periods of the year, the northern and the southern course of the sun, Uttarāyaṇa and Dakṣiṇāyana, Devayāna and Pitṛyāṇa, and that the legend explains the winning back of Agni at the end of the southern course of the sun, at the period of the winter solstice. He interprets the waters into which Agni retires as the fate of the sun at the winter solstice, an idea which, however, in India he considers to have been absorbed in that of the rainy season. The conjecture unhappily lacks any verisimilitude: the picture of the bringing of Agni to work seems no more than the conception of an individual poet of the constant theme of the mode, in which Agni comes to be employed as the sacrificer on earth.

In connexion with the sacrifice three forms of Agni are distinguished in the Yajurveda,[2] the eater of raw flesh, the eater of corpses, and the sacrificial, and this distinction is perfectly well known in the Rigveda [3] so far as concerns the Agni which bears the offering, and the Agni which devours the bodies of the dead. The term *kravyād* alternates in the Rigveda with *kravyavāhana*, later *kavyavāhana*, and a fire named *kavyavāhana*, appears as invoked with Yama at an offering to the Manes, which is performed on the afternoon of the new moon sacrifice at the last of the four-monthly offerings. From these facts Hillebrandt deduces the theory that from the fire, with which the dead was burned, there was taken a brand to rekindle the fire for the Manes, which he believes to have existed in the time of the Rigveda under the title of the Narāçaṅsa.[4] The procedure is clearly wholly contrary to the spirit of the ritual, which regards death as requiring the extinction of all fires which are made thereby impure, and the evidence adduced for the theory is obviously inadequate to make it even plausible.

Another division of the forms of Agni is given by the Taittirīya Saṁhitā,[5] where the Agni which bears the oblation is distinguished from that which bears the funeral offering, called *kavyavāhana*, and that associated with the goblins (*saharakṣas*).

As a sacrificer Agni has this advantage over the human sacrificer that he does not make mistakes, and if he errs in any way he can put all right. Hence he is all knowing, the sage, possessed of all wisdom, and exclusively bears the epithet Jātavedas,[6] used about 120 times of him in the Rigveda and explained there as he who knows all generations, though some modern scholars prefer the sense 'having innate wisdom'. The priest prays, therefore, to him to accord him power of memory and wisdom. He produces wisdom, and is himself eloquent,

[1] Hillebrandt, *Ved. Myth.* ii. 137 ff. Von Schroeder (*Arische Religion*, ii. 523) compares Apollonine legend, but without plausibility.

[2] VS. i. 17.

[3] x. 16. 9.

[4] *Op. cit.* ii. 98–107, 107–10. Cf. Oldenberg, RV. ii. 215 f.

[5] ii. 5. 8. 6.

[6] SBE. xxvi. pp. xxxi f.

and a cause of eloquence in others. In all other matters too he befriends his worshippers, he gives food, wealth, long life, he defeats enemies, and demons : even in battle he leads the van, which may be a reference to the carrying of fire before the host in its onslaught. He is also occasionally given the power to remit sin, to make guiltless before Aditi, to avert the anger of Varuṇa,[1] and in the later texts he is said to free from the crimes committed by man's father and mother.[2]

Agni is also as a great god magnified by being declared to be above all the gods : Varuṇa, Mitra, the Maruts, and all the gods worship him. He delivers the gods in battle, he defeats the Dasyus for the Aryan, he vanquished the Paṇis and is even called breaker of forts and Vṛtra-slayer, but these aspects of his are really derived from Indra. He measures out the air and supports the vault of heaven like all the greater deities, but he has a special function of his own, the strengthening of the sun when at the Agnihotra in the morning he is produced.[3] This is recognized occasionally in the Rigveda and quite frankly in the Brāhmaṇa literature. But in many cases the two acts are regarded merely as simultaneous, and the later texts [4] discuss the question whether the Agnihotra is to be offered just before or just after the sun rise.

Agni is said to have produced men as also are other gods, but this relationship is neither often mentioned nor prominent. It is not probable that it stood in any special relation to the act of producing Agni from the fire sticks, though that act was naturally enough compared to the production of life : it lies rather in his close association with the worship of the family, which brings him into close contact with men.

The derivation of Agni's name, Latin *ignis*, Lithuanian *ugnis*, is uncertain, though connexion with *aj*, ' drive ', is not impossible. In the Avesta the name is unknown as such and it does not appear among the Mitanni gods, which speaks in favour of the view that it is a specific development of the Indian priest.[5] But the worship of fire itself, apart from the special conception of it as Agni, is undoubtedly strongly marked in the period of the unity of the Indo-Iranians. The fire in the Avesta is the centre of a strong and developed ritual : the fire priests Āthravans are clearly the same in origin as the Vedic Atharvans, and Ātar must have been conceived as a great and powerful god, giver of food, of fame, of offspring, the friend of the house, the repeller of foes, probably known as in the lightning and the plant-born forms. Oldenberg [6] holds that, as in Greece and in Rome Hestia [7] and Vesta are

[1] RV. iv. 12. 4 ; vii. 93. 7 ; iv. 1. 4.

[2] AV. v. 30. 4 ; TB. iii. 7. 12. 3, 4.

[3] Oldenberg, *Rel. des Veda*², pp. 109, 110.

[4] AB. v. 30 ff.

[5] Oldenberg, JRAS. 1909, p. 1096.

[6] *Rel. des Veda*², p. 102. Kretschmer (*Gesch. der griech. Sprache*, pp. 162 ff.) argues that Vesta is a mere borrowing from Greece ; Warde Fowler (*Religious Experience of the Roman People*, pp. 73–79) treats her as essentially Roman. So also Farnell, *Cults of the Greek States*, v. 364 ; *Greece and Babylon*, p. 133. Cf. von Schroeder, *Arische Religion*, ii. 584. For the Ugnis szventà of the Lithuanians see *ibid*. ii. 579 f.

[7] Feist, *Kultur der Indogermanen*, p. 526.

feminine, there cannot have been an early Indo-European worship of fire of any distinct character. This is true so far as the personification of the fire is concerned, but the close connexion of the fire with the home which is emphasized by these two faiths, and which is also in harmony with the indications of Vedic religion, suggests that the cult of fire must have been a very real one in the Indo-European period, a conclusion the more natural if, as is probable, the original home of the Indo-European is to be placed in a comparatively cold climate.[1] The stress laid on the fire in India would, therefore, be changed in emphasis, as not the domestic, but the sacrificial fire became the more important in a land where the sun provided for many things which elsewhere fire was required to accomplish.

§ 2. *Bṛhaspati and other forms of Agni*

Bṛhaspati is a god of much importance in the eyes of the Rigveda, since it devotes to him eleven hymns and mentions him, under that name or as Brahmaṇaspati, about 170 times. He forms with Indra a pair in two hymns. But his character appears very clearly as a compound of the activities of other gods. Thus his appearance is like that of Agni : he has seven mouths, seven rays, a beautiful tongue, he is bright, pure, ruddy, and clear-voiced. He has sharp horns and a hundred wings ; he carries an iron axe, wrought by Tvaṣṭṛ, or a golden hatchet, and rides on a car with ruddy steeds. But he is marked out by having a bow whose string is Ṛta, which here doubtless refers to the holy rite, the sacrifice, showing that his weapons are also priestly. He is said to have been born from great light in the highest heaven, and with thunder to have dispelled the darkness, but also to be the half of the two worlds or of Tvaṣṭṛ, and he is the producer of the gods.

Bṛhaspati is especially the divine priest ; he is the Purohita, but also the Brahman, and the Brāhmaṇas constantly play on his position as the Brahman priest or the Brahman, ' the holy power ', of the gods. In the later texts as Brahman he is probably denoted as the technical priest of that name, who oversees the sacrifice and, like Agni, is able by his invention to make good any defects which he may observe in the sacrifice. In the Rigveda the technical sense is doubtful : the Brāhmaṇācchaṅsin priest may, however, be meant in one or two cases.[2] He sings hymns, metre is his, he has singing hosts and thence is called Gaṇapati, a term once given to Indra. He is, as his name denotes, the lord of prayer, the generator of prayer which he communicated to

[1] Cf. Wissowa, *Religion und Kultus der Römer*², p. 142 ; E. Meyer, *Gesch. des Alt.*³ I. ii. p. 872. Von Schroeder's views as to Apollo and the Charites (cf. Agni's flames as maidens) are interesting (*Arische Religion*, ii. 497 ff.), but not conclusive. The legend of the theft of fire (Prometheus, Loki) is only faintly seen in the figure of Mātariçvan (Chap. 9, § 6) and possibly that of Bhṛgu (Chap. 19, § 1).

[2] Oldenberg, *Rel. des Veda*², pp. 38 ff., correcting Geldner, *Ved. Stud.* ii. 143 ff. ; GN. 1916, pp. 731 ff.

men : hence in the later texts he is lord of speech, Vācaspati, a name which is specially his in post-Vedic literature.

Bṛhaspati is often named beside Agni, but he is not rarely identified with him : [1] he is given three abodes, is called son of strength, associated with Narāçaṅsa, Mātariçvan and the Aṅgirases. He is lord of the dwelling, while Agni for his part is called lord of prayer. Like Agni, however, he is associated with Indra, and becomes specially connected with the myth of the overthrow of Vala and the release of the cows, in which he acts with his singing host. He splits the mountains, drives out and distributes the cows, and the Atharvaveda [2] makes his conquest of Vala proverbial. In winning the cows he finds the light, the Dawn, and Agni. He is also said to roar like a bull, to shatter forts, to overthrow Vṛtras and conquer foes. He is even given the epithet of bolt-bearer and is made a friend of the Maruts. He has also the more general traits of being a bestower of wealth and long life, a remover of disease, and a father. He stimulates also the life of the plants, through him the sun and moon rise alternately, and in the Yajurveda [3] he is made the regent of the constellation Tiṣya, while in post-Vedic literature he is the ruler of Jupiter.

It is clear that the name was held by the Rigvedic poets to be derived from a word *bṛh* in the sense of Brahman, prayer, as it is parallel with Brahmaṇaspati, and the meaning of the name is, therefore, lord of prayer or devotion. The great similarity to Agni, which makes Bṛhaspati in much merely his double, can best be explained on the theory that Bṛhaspati is Agni in his priestly form, but that the connexion was one early developed.[4] The most plausible of alternative views is undoubtedly that of Roth,[5] which takes the god as a direct personification of the power of devotion, and Oldenberg [6] develops a similar idea in insisting that Bṛhaspati is the typical priest who assists in the feats of the gods by his songs and his prayers. In that case it is necessary to suppose that he has won to himself the attributes of the gods by his close association with them in their activities, a view to which there is no good ground of objection in itself, but which is on the other hand not in any way more probable than the idea that the name was at first an epithet of the god. On the other hand Weber [7] and Hopkins [8] start from the marked similarity to Indra in the warlike deeds of Bṛhaspati, and make him out to be derived from the character of Indra modified under the views of the priesthood : [9] this view is also legitimate, but is subject to the objection that on the whole it is easier to explain the development, if the Agni side be taken as the standing

[1] RV. i. 38. 13 ; iii. 26. 2 ; v. 43. 12.
[2] ix. 3. 2.
[3] TS. iv. 4. 10. 1 ; TB. iii. 1. 1. 5 ; cf. Keith, JRAS. 1911, pp. 794 ff.
[4] Macdonell, *Ved. Myth.*, p. 103. Hillebrandt (*Ved. Myth.* i. 408) took *bṛhas*— as growth, but (Kl. Ausg., p. 60) accepts ' das magische Fluidum ritueller Zauberkraft.' Cf. Chap. 27, § 2.
[5] ZDMG. i. 73.
[6] *Op. cit.*, pp. 66–8 ; SBE. xlvi. 94 ; GN. 1915, pp. 196 ff.
[7] *Vājapeya*, p. 15.
[8] *Rel. of India*, p. 136.
[9] Their preference is visible in AB. vii. 38 (cf. KU. iii. 1 ; TS. ii. 5. 1), where insult to him is censured in Indra ; cf. Weber, *Rājasūya*, pp. 109 f.

point in the discussion of the nature of the god. It is, however, impossible to accept the efforts of Hillebrandt [1] to prove that Bṛhaspati is the moon, especially as a god of magic and the magic southern fire ; the long list of parallels with Soma which he adduces will on investigation be found merely to refer either to points which are commonplaces of many Vedic gods, or to points in which Agni and Soma agree. The fact that Bṛhaspati produces effects on the plants is wholly inadequate to make out that he is a moon god, for there is no very clear trace in the Rigveda of the doctrine that all growth or even that most growth is due to the action of the moon : the heat and the water which are characteristic of Agni are essentially connected with plant life.

The chief importance of Bṛhaspati lies in the fact that he is in the earlier Vedic period the root from which sprung the god Brahman, who appears first in the later stratum of the Brāhmaṇa texts.[2]

While the identity of Bṛhaspati with Agni has been obscured by the development of the character of the deity, the identity of Vaiçvānara is made absolutely certain by the constant mention of Agni under that epithet in the Rigveda. It denotes 'pertaining to all men', and is normally believed to refer to Agni in all his aspects, celestial as well as terrestrial. In point of fact, however, the mention of Vaiçvānara is mainly in certain definite contexts. He appears in connexion with the descent of celestial fire and the agency of the Bhṛgus and Mātariçvan, and once [3] Agni Vaiçvānara is styled Mātariçvan. In the Brāhmaṇas Vaiçvānara has a direct reference to the sun in the fact that it is said that Agni Vaiçvānara is the year, and that cakes offered on twelve potsherds are frequently presented to him. Vaiçvānara appears also in comparison with the Maruts as connected with the princely rank : the Dhruva cup which is offered to Vaiçvānara is guarded by a prince,[4] and is employed in a variety of rites for the preservation or restoration of lordly power.[5] It is clear also that in these texts the fire specially related to Vaiçvānara is the Āhavanīya, so that we have a good warrant for seeing in the god a form of the sun, which on earth has a counterpart in the Āhavanīya fire. This explains well the controversy which existed even in early days regarding the nature of the god : it was maintained by the Yājñikas that Vaiçvānara was the sun, while Çākapūṇi, with whom in effect Yāska [6] agrees, held that he was the terrestrial Agni. Vaiçvānara would then be a suitable epithet of the sun, who is common to all men and seen of all.

The name Narāçaṅsa is also used of the god, and with it is connected one of the great ritual distinctions of the Vedic ritual : some families took in the Āprī hymns, used at fore-offerings in the ritual of the animal sacrifice, a verse

[1] *Ved. Myth.* i. 606 ff. ; ii. 102 ff. ; (Kl. Ausg.), pp. 60 ff. ; *contra*, C. Strauss, *Bṛhaspati im Veda* (1905) ; Oldenberg, GN. 1915, pp. 200 ff.

[2] Keith, *Aitareya Āraṇyaka*, p. 350.

[3] RV. iii. 26. 2.

[4] ApÇS. xii. 16.

[5] Hillebrandt, *Ved. Myth.* ii. 112 ff. He sees in Vaiçvānara's connexion with the Pūrus and the Bharatas, and in RV. i. 59. 1 ; iii. 23. 4 ; v. 1. 10, traces of a *κοινὴ ἑστία* of the Vedic tribes, but this is implausible.

[6] Nir. vii. 23 and 31.

addressed to Narāçaṅsa, others took in place Tanūnapāt, while only a few families, such as that of Medhātithi Kāṇva and Dīrghatamas Aucathya, solved the dispute by including invocations of both in the hymns.[1] In the long run the tradition of the Jamadagni[2] family prevailed and their invocation of Tanūnapāt was accepted, the Vasiṣṭha family, however, remaining faithful to their invocation of Narāçaṅsa. The god has little that is characteristic about him in the Rigveda : he thrice a day sprinkles the sacrifice with honey ; he anoints the three heavens and the gods. Soma is said to go between Narāçaṅsa and the celestial one, which may refer to the contrast of terrestrial and celestial fires. In the Brāhmaṇas there is more distinct information : five cups are styled Nārāçaṅsa, two at each of the first two pressings and one at the third : after being tasted by the priests they are placed on the south oblation-holder.[3] The epithet 'drunk by Narāçaṅsa' is used of Soma in connexion with an offering to the Fathers, and the connexion of Narāçaṅsa and the Fathers appears in one passage in the Rigveda,[4] which may conceivably point to the later ritual having been in this respect known to the Rigveda. Moreover in two hymns Narāçaṅsa seems to be identified with Bṛhaspati.[5] On this ground Hillebrandt[6] concludes that Narāçaṅsa is a designation of a moon god of the dead, equivalent to Bṛhaspati, and of the Dakṣiṇa fire for the Fathers. He strengthens this view by pointing out that in a Brāhmaṇa text[7] the term three-headed and six-eyed is applied to Narāçaṅsa, which would seem to identify him with Viçvarūpa, son of Tvaṣṭṛ, who, like Bṛhaspati, is in his opinion the moon as the home of the Fathers. The conjecture, however, is too bold, and rests upon the mistaken identification of Bṛhaspati and the moon, and the still less plausible version of Viçvarūpa as the moon. It necessitates also the making of the word to mean 'he who praises men', applicable to a judge of the Fathers, instead of 'praise of men' in the sense 'praised by men', which is the more natural sense.[8] The comparison of the Avestan Nairyosaṅha leads to no further conclusion : traces of connexion with the Fathers are seen by Hillebrandt, but they are very faint, and his chief certain characteristic is that of messenger, which makes him merely a normal form of

[1] Narāçaṅsa occurs in RV. ii. 3 ; v. 5 ; vii. 2 ; x. 70 ; Tanūnapāt, i. 188 ; iii. 4 ; ix. 5 ; x. 110 ; both, i. 13 and 142.

[2] RV. x. 110.

[3] AB. ii. 24. 3 ; ApÇS. xii. 25. 25–27.

[4] x. 57. 3.

[5] RV. i. 18 ; x. 182.

[6] *Ved. Myth.* ii. 98 ff. ; iii. 445–50 ; (Kl. Ausg.), pp. 58 ff. He quotes RV. i. 95. 1 ; 96. 5 ; x. 88. 6 as proofs of Agni as the moon, also Indrāgnī as deity of the new moon (sun and moon), but implausibly. For spirit connexion with the moon he cites RV. x. 90. 13 ; AA. ii. 4. 1 ; BAU. i. 3. 17 ; iii. 2. 13.

[7] MS. iv. 13. 8 ; TB. iii. 6. 13. Oldenberg (GN. 1915, p. 222) suggests a possible reference to Narāçaṅsa's partaking of the three Savanas daily, duplicated by the twin offices of Hotṛ and Udgātṛ (i. 185. 9).

[8] Macdonell, *Ved. Myth.*, p. 100. The alternative is to regard the praise as deified. Cf. Oldenberg, GN. 1915, pp. 210–24. RV. x. 57. 3 on this view alludes to the Fathers as authors of praises. But his denial of connexion with fire is implausible, in view of RV. iii. 29. 11 ; VS. xxvii. 13, &c., and the parallel of Nairyosaṅha (cf. Gray, *Archiv für Rel.* iii. 48 ; Güntert, *Weltkönig*, p. 287).

Agni. It is impossible, therefore, to say more than that Narāçansa is a form of Agni: Bergaigne [1] thinks that he is specifically a god of prayer like Bṛhaspati, and this accords with the identification of the two gods which seems certainly intended by the Vedic poets.

Tanūnapāt is even more obscure than Narāçansa. His name means either 'son of his self', a reference to the fact that Agni generates Agni, fire being *sui generis*, or 'own son', i. e. of the divine father as suggested by Bergaigne.[2] He is contrasted with Narāçansa and Mātariçvan as the divine embryo. The dawns kiss Agni, the Tanūnapāt of the ruddy one. He takes the sacrifice to the gods: Varuṇa, Mitra, Agni honour him thrice a day. Who is meant is impossible to say: Hillebrandt,[3] who once identified him with Agni as a guardian of the Soma and as lunar fire, has abandoned [4] the suggestion: in the Brāhmaṇas he is variously identified with summer and Indra, while in the ritual he plays a part only in the Tānūnaptra ceremony in which the patron and the celebrants of the rite engage not to injure one another: in this rite he serves, it seems, as the god who watches over the fulfilment of the mutual oaths of fidelity.

Closely connected with Agni are other figures: the gods Mātariçvan, Ahi Budhnya, Aja Ekapād are in some degree associated with him, and the priestly families of the Atharvans, Bhṛgus, and Angirases are closely related to him: they will be considered later together with the other families of priests, to whom they are perhaps more closely related in origin than to the god himself.

§ 3. *The God Soma*

The poetry of the Rigveda is mainly connected with the Soma sacrifice, and this fact must be borne in mind in estimating the importance of the god Soma. In its present form the whole of the ninth book of the Saṁhitā is devoted to him and he has six hymns in other books: moreover he is invoked in parts of four or five others, and also as a joint deity with Indra, Agni, Pūṣan and Rudra. The number of times his name occurs is incapable of accurate calculation, as the name is constantly mentioned without it being possible to say whether the god is really referred to.

Soma resembles Agni in the fact that the anthropomorphism of the god is constantly coming into collision with the actual form of the plant and thus is prevented from attaining any clear development. Hence myths of a concrete character cannot spring up around the name, and the deeds which are given to Soma are simply borrowed by him from the other gods, especially Indra and Agni, with whom he is very nearly associated, since the former is the great Soma drinker and the latter for his part is a god of ritual like Soma. But on

[1] *Rel. Véd.* i. 305–8.

[2] *Op. cit.* ii. 99. An implausible suggestion to assimilate Tanūnapāt to Narāçansa as praise, as incorporating the ancestral poetry, is made by Oldenberg, GN. 1915, p. 214, n. 4.

[3] *Ved. Myth.* i. 339.

[4] *Op. cit.* ii. 110–12.

the other hand the Soma is the great object of priestly interest, and the most elaborate imagery seems to have formed round the simple operations of pressing and straining the juice: the monotony of the ninth book is only equalled by its obscurity in detail, and, it must be admitted, much of the obscurity hides no real depth of thought but merely puerile fancies.

For the juice pressed from the Soma plant the Rigveda offers various names, such as *andhas*, applied also to the whole plant, *pitu*, and often *mada*, the intoxicating beverage; it is even called food, and very often honey, a term which is applied also to milk and to ghee.

Frequently it is Amṛta, 'ambrosia' the drink of immortality, or milk, or the wave from the stalk, or the juice of honey. A common name of the plant and the drink is Indu, the bright drop. The plant is brown, ruddy or most often tawny, and, in accord with this, it is the rule that the cow, with which in the rite the Soma is purchased, must be brown or ruddy, and that any substitutes used for Soma must be similar to it in colour. The plant is made to yield its juice by being pounded with a stone or pressed with stones, which lie on a skin and seem in contravention to the ritual usage to be placed on the altar.[1] The stones are called *adri* or *grāvan*, the latter usually employed with verbs meaning to speak and therefore more mythical than the word *adri*. It is almost, if not quite certain, that the extraction of the juice by pounding with a pestle in a mortar was known to the Rigveda [2] as well as the normal pounding with stones which is repeatedly mentioned: the Avestan ritual knows the use of mortar and pestle in connexion with the Haoma. When pounded the juice is strained through a sieve, which is called a skin, hair, wool, filter, or metaphorically perhaps ridge. In this state Soma wins the title Pavamāna, under which, as becoming clear, it is celebrated in the ninth book of the Rigveda. In the purified form it is called Çukra or Çuci, 'the bright,' and is offered in this shape to Indra and Vāyu, who is the drinker of the pure Soma *par excellence*, a fact which is confirmed by the ritual where the unmixed Soma is reserved for Indra and Vāyu, while it is mixed with milk for Mitra and Varuṇa and with honey for the Açvins. It is clear that after the purifying process Soma was often mixed with water: so in the ritual the pressing is followed by the mixing of water (*ādhavana*). Water however does not bear the technical name of *āçir*, which is reserved for the milk, fresh or curdled, and the barley with which Soma clothes himself as with a garment. The refreshing of the stalks of the plants with water, which is known in the later ritual as the Āpyāyana, is possibly but not certainly, referred to in the Rigveda. The three offerings of the Rigveda [3] correspond in some measure at least to those of later times: Indra is present at both the morning pressing

[1] Cf. RV. v. 31. 12; Hillebrandt, *Ved. Myth.* i. 179 ff.; Oldenberg, *Ṛgveda-Noten*, i. 328.

[2] RV. i. 28; Hillebrandt, *op. cit.* i. 158 ff. Oliphant (*Studies in honor of Bloomfield*, pp. 225–50) holds that mortar and pestle were normally used, but does not prove this theory.

[3] Bergaigne (*Rel. Véd.* i. 179) thinks the three tubs mythical, but cf. TS. iii. 2. 1. 2.

and at the midday pressing which is his alone, whence it later has a Çastra called Niṣkevalya, and the Ṛbhus have a place in the third offering. The term ' of three abodes ' given to the god may allude to three tubs of the ritual, but this is uncertain, and the same doubt attends the three Soma lakes, of which mention is made, as drunk by Indra. The three backs of the god are probably the three admixtures.

So much of the mythology of Soma is clear enough : the actual plant lies immediately behind the god, and explains his characteristics. But there are other traits which show that the plant is a very powerful one. The waters which are mixed with the Soma give rise to many metaphors, and Soma is said to be the producer of the waters, and to be born of the waters : he streams rain from the sky, and he flows clearly with a stream of honey like the cloud full of rain. He is the father of the waters as well as their son, and the Soma seems in some cases to be deemed to be rain. The Çatapatha Brāhmaṇa [1] directly identifies the ambrosia with the water. The sound of the pouring of the Soma is likened to thunder, and lightning is associated with the process. Again, as a thunderer and a loud-sounding god, Soma is a bull and the waters are his cows : he fertilizes the waters. He is a sharp-horned bull. But he is also for his swift flow a steed or bird, and again he is identified for his bright colour with the sun, and made to dispel the darkness and defeat it. In all this there is clearly evident the fact that Soma is no mere plant on earth, but is in addition a great celestial deity.

The same double side of Soma appears in the legends which make him drunk by the gods as well as by men. He is for both the drink of immortality, which makes them live for ever. In less exalted phrase he is of high value in healing, he makes the blind to see, and the lame to walk. He even destroys sin and promotes truth : *in vino veritas*. He inspires speech and so Soma is lord of speech : he has all wisdom and knowledge. He surveys all things with his thousand eyes. A votary declares [2] ' We have drunk the Soma, we have become immortal, we have attained the light, we have known the gods.' The Fathers too love the Soma with whom they sometimes go, and who in their life excited them to their great deeds.

The god who is most closely united with Soma is Indra, who needs the drink to strengthen him to perform the slaying of Vṛtra : hence the drink is called the bolt, and Soma even takes the title of Vṛtra-slayer. Again Indra makes the sun to rise when he has drunk Soma, so that Soma is credited with this feat also. From this it is a short step to becoming a great cosmic power, who generates the two worlds and wields universal sway. He rides in a chariot with Indra, and is connected with the Maruts. He becomes a great and terrible warrior with a bow and shaft : he (alone of Vedic gods [3]) is described as killing the wicked and he also kills the demons. The Yajurveda [4] says that Brahmans who drink the Soma can slay their foes by their mere look. Through

[1] xi. 5. 4. 5.
[2] RV. viii. 48. 3.
[3] RV. ix. 28. 6.
[4] MS. iv. 8. 2.

Indra he is associated with Vāyu, and, more superficially, he is connected with Pūṣan and Rudra.

The dualism in the character of Soma appears in the two quite different accounts of his birth, in heaven and on the mountains. The mountain birth of Soma is made more precise by the epithet Maujavata, which seems to point to mount Muñjavant, and the Avesta declares that Haoma grows in the mountains. But it is by no means certain that the rock, from which the eagle brought Soma, is to be so taken; it seems rather to refer to the clouds and to point to his celestial form. Of the celestial abode of Soma there is abundant evidence of all kinds: he is the bird in the heaven, his home is in the highest heaven, but the contact with the terrestrial is clear in the fact that Soma going over the filter is also Soma on the summit (*sānu*) of the sky.

The bringing of Soma from the mountains was no doubt a physical act, performed regularly by the priests or on their behalf: the ritual shows that the tradition of using Soma was kept up, when the priests had long left the place where the Soma grew, and when it had to be brought from afar off. The sacred character of the plant, however, vindicated itself in a curious manner. It had come to be necessary to purchase the drink, or rather the plants whence the juice could be extracted, but the ritual shows the Soma seller [1] regarded as a disgraceful creature from whom is taken away, with blows, the price, a cow, paid to him for the stalks. On the celestial side there stands the Rigvedic myth of the descent of Soma which is brought down by an eagle to the earth. The myth is told at some length in two hymns of the Rigveda [2] and referred to in others. The eagle was restrained by a hundred iron castles, but it none the less secured the Soma and fled with it from the sky: the archer Kṛçānu, however, who saw the bird as it fled away shot at it and severed one feather: the Brāhmaṇas [3] add that the feather or claw or the leaf of the shoot became a tree, the Parṇa or Palāça, or a porcupine. The eagle is in the legend represented as bringing down the Soma for Indra, and Indra is once [4] directly called an eagle, when seated at the Soma offering, but not in immediate connexion with the myth. On the other hand Agni is called the eagle of heaven once [5] and often a bird; the term eagle is applied in a Brāhmaṇa [6] to Agni as lightning, and from these data Bloomfield [7] derives the conclusion that the whole origin of the myth of the descent of Soma is the lightning flash, which comes forth from the cloud, the castle of iron, and which brings down to the earth the refreshing rain. With this accords the fact that in one passage of the Rigveda [8] the descents of the lightning and of Soma are combined. It is not, it should however be noted, of much importance whether the eagle be treated as Agni or as Indra, since an essential feature of Indra is the lightning which breaks

[1] Hillebrandt, *Ved. Myth.* i. 69–82.
[2] iv. 26 and 27.
[3] Kuhn, *Herabkunft des Feuers*, pp. 195 ff. Cf. Charpentier, *Die Suparṇasage*, chap. v.
[4] RV. x. 99. 8.
[5] RV. vii. 15. 4.
[6] TB. iii. 10. 5. 1.
[7] JAOS. xvi. 1–24.
[8] i. 93. 6.

forth while the rain falls, and it is probable that, when he is hailed as an eagle at the Soma sacrifice, he is regarded as the bringer of the Soma.

Soma is a plant, and the most lordly of all the plants, and therefore he is king of the plants: he is also the king of the gods, of the whole earth and of men, but the Yajurveda [1] shows that the Brahmans had asserted that he was the only king of the Brahmans: at the royal consecration the other men might recognize the king, but to the Brahmans he was not announced as their king, who was Soma alone. Doubtless at this most sacred and trying moment of their inauguration kings had to accept theoretical claims of immunity from their control, which they knew how to value at their true worth for practical affairs.

The connexion of Soma with the plants was, however, of high importance for his future as a god: the connexion of the moon with plant life seems to have been often noted by early peoples, and was very probably recognized by the Aryans in India; moreover the growth of the moon and its decline was significant of the same progress as the swelling up of the Soma shoots: the fiery clear drops of the Soma, as it fell from the plant, were likened to the rays of the moon reflected upon the water: the Soma had come to be held to be a bright deity. Hence it may be there rose the idea that the Soma was really at the same time the moon: it is asserted in the Chāndogya Upaniṣad [2] in so many words that the Soma is the moon and is the food of the gods and is drunk by them. The Brāhmaṇas regularly identify Soma and the moon; thus the Nakṣatras are said to have been the wives of king Soma, who, however, preferred to stay with Rohiṇī only, wherefore the other ladies went to their father, and, as a result, disease seized the king, who was fain to agree to live loyally with all his wives each in turn.[3] The phases of the moon are explained by the fact that the gods and the Fathers eat the substance of the Soma which is ambrosia. In the Atharvaveda [4] we find that Soma is several times certainly the moon. In the Rigveda itself by far the most certain case is the wedding hymn,[5] which is, however, by its confused character not an early hymn. There Soma is the husband of Sūryā, who is far more often connected with the Açvins, or occasionally with Pūṣan, and both these two gods and Pūṣan also are introduced into the hymn, as if in recognition of their claim to have share in the wedding. Here Soma is said to be in the lap of the stars, and a distinction is drawn between the Soma which the priests know and that which they crush. That the identification was priestly and late is here asserted as clearly as anything of the sort can be expected to be asserted. It is possible that there are some other references to the moon character of the Soma in the Rigveda, as when it is spoken of as a drop going to the ocean, looking with the eye of a vulture,[6] but the effort of deciding what are these passages is quite out of all proportion to the value of the results

[1] Weber, *Rājasūya*, p. 31.
[2] v. 10. 1; cf. ÇB. ii. 4. 2. 7; BAU. vi. 2. 16.
[3] Weber, *Naxatra*, ii. 274 ff.
[4] vii. 91. 3, 4; xi. 6. 7.
[5] RV. x. 85.
[6] RV. x. 123. 8.

which can be obtained. In the chaos of the ideas of the ninth book of the Rigveda there are passages which may be referred to Soma as the moon, or at least to comparison of Soma and the moon, but it is a very significant fact that the commentators on the Rigveda, despite their familiarity with the moon theory of Soma, never identify the Soma there with the moon.

In opposition to this theory Hillebrandt [1] insists that the moon nature of Soma exists throughout: that the deity is the moon *sans phrase*, but that in the moon there is an ambrosia which is eaten by the gods in heaven and in the form of the Soma plant is eaten by the men on earth, who in eating it thus, like the gods, partake of the substance of the moon. This god, he argues, was the greatest and most popular of all Vedic gods, and ranked even above Indra and far above the sun gods. He therefore treats, among others, Bṛhaspati as a moon god. The most serious objection to this view is the fact that, while in the later literature [2] the nature of Soma as the moon is apparent on every hand, in the Rigveda it can only be restored by conjecture, and there is a definite assertion in one hymn that the conception of Soma as the moon is mythic and known to the Brahmans only. Again, in the vast majority of passages, it is perfectly plain that the Soma plant and its qualities are referred to. If we could show *ab extra* that the plant is also the moon, this would not be a fatal objection to the theory of Hillebrandt, but, as this cannot be done, and as the ordinary view that the plant is deified and made into a great god is adequate to account for the facts, it is an offence against sound principles of method to adopt any other theory.

That the Soma cult goes back to the Avesta [3] is notorious: it is there said to grow on a mountain watered by the rains of heaven: as Varuṇa is said to place it on rock, so a god places it on Mount Haraiti: it is brought by an eagle in the Rigveda from the sky: in the Avesta it is taken from its mountain by skilled birds. It is in both India and Iran the king of plants, it gives long life and removes death: it grows in the waters. It was pressed twice a day according to the Avesta: its yellow juice was mixed with milk. But the plant had also a celestial character, and that character distinguished it from the mere terrestrial plant. It is brought down from heaven and is a mighty king. Even the epithet 'slayer of Verethra' has been found applied to the Haoma. Beside minor similarities, which attach to any divine natures, there are found the most striking similarities in the legend of the preparers of the Soma: they are in the Avesta Vīvaṅhvant, Āthwya, and Thrita, while those of the Rigveda are Vivasvant and Trita Āptya.

Soma is derived from the root *su*, and means merely the pressed drink, and there is no parallel word in the other Indo-European languages, so that it must be recognized that the Soma cult was a special Indo-Iranian innovation,

[1] *Ved. Myth.* i. 274, 309, 326, 340, 450; ii. 209–45; (Kl. Ausg.), pp. 76 ff. Cf. von Schroeder, *Arische Religion*, ii. 462, 656; Henry, *Sôma et Haoma* (1907); Gray, *Spiegel Memorial Vol.*, pp. 160 ff.

[2] E.g. KB. iv. 4; xii. 5; TB. i. 4. 10. 7; Hillebrandt, *Ved. Myth.* iii. 38, n. 2.

[3] W. W. Wilson (AJP. xxx. 184 ff.) sees a Soma offering in a fragment of Alkman, but this is fanciful.

presumably produced by the discovery of some plant which when pressed produced a juice pleasant to drink or at least intoxicating. It is also most probable that the plant grew only in some area which was far from the homes of the Vedic Indians : substitutes came freely to be used for it, and all efforts to decide precisely what the plant was have failed to achieve more than probable results.[1] But the word *madhu*, 'honey,' is cognate with the Greek *methu* and the Anglo-Saxon *medu*, and the parallelism of the legends of the eagle and Soma, the nectar-bringing eagle of Zeus, and the eagle, which fetched the mead and which was really Odin, is obvious and undeniable. The question, therefore, arises what was the mead which is thus conceived to have been brought down, and it seems difficult to deny that it was originally simply the water of the rain or the dew. This is certainly the natural way of interpreting the myth of Soma and the eagle, and the change made in the conception in the Indo-Iranian period would be merely that this rain would have been identified with the Soma drink, thus transforming the old myth into something very important and real. If, as has been suggested, the old myth made the home of the mead in the moon,[2] the identification of Soma and the moon would be at once explained, but this is not at all clearly made out.

Oldenberg, however, does not accept the view that the legend of the descent of Soma can be explained in this simple and satisfactory way, and he does not, therefore, adopt the same view as is here taken of the process by which the Soma came to be sacred. He would seem to hold that the rise of the Soma cult was independent at first of the older belief in the mead, and it is true that the Avesta does not actually apply the term mead to Haoma; it seems, however, much simpler to adopt the view that the mead was an Indo-European view, and that the identification of Soma with it, and, therefore the application to it of the Soma legend, were the immediate outcome of the discovery of the intoxicating drink.

§ 4. *The Rivers*

It is perhaps doubtful whether the rivers can claim to be regarded as among the great gods of the Rigveda, but their importance in the mind of the Vedic Indians was perhaps sufficient to justify their treatment in this place. One whole long hymn[3] is accorded to the Sarasvatī, and in two verses of it are enumerated her tributaries and other affluents, while the Vipāç and Çutudrī claim another hymn[4] of some poetical beauty. By far the greatest of rivers

[1] Hillebrandt, *Ved. Myth.* i. 3 ff.; Macdonell and Keith, *Vedic Index*, ii. 475; Havell (JRAS. 1920, pp. 349 ff.) suggests the millet of the eastern Himālayas; B. L. Mukherjee (*ibid.* 1921, pp. 239 ff.) bhāng, but without proof.

[2] Roscher, *Nektar und Ambrosia*, pp. 79 ff.; Oldenberg, *Rel. des Veda*², pp. 170 ff.; Henry, *L'Agniṣṭoma*, pp. 470 ff. The fig-tree that drops Soma has a possible parallel in the Germanic ash, Yggdrasill; E. H. Meyer, *Germ. Myth.*, p. 81. For further speculations see G. Dumézil, *Le Festin d'Immortalité* (AMG. xxxiv), esp. Pt. II, chap. i; below, App. D.

[3] RV. x. 75; cf. Stein, *Bhandarkar Comm. Vol.*, pp. 21 ff.

[4] RV. iii. 33.

is the Sarasvatī, which has in all three hymns devoted to it : she flows from the mountains, tearing them down ; she has seven sisters and is mother of streams : she is daughter of the lightning (*pāvīravī*) and has a spouse, who later is called Sarasvant. She is divine, she comes with the Fathers to the sacrifice, and is stated to be descended from the sky, an early anticipation of the common Indian belief of the divine birth of the Ganges. She has other and more intimate connexions with human life : she bestows progeny, wealth, and immortality, she gave Vadhryaçva a son ; she is terrible and a Vṛtra-slayer, but to her worshippers a protector.

Sarasvatī is connected with Indra and with Pūṣan, but in the main with the Açvins : she takes part in the rite by which they heal Indra, and she is spoken of in the Yajurveda [1] as the wife of the Açvins. She forms also one of the triad of goddesses Bhāratī, Iḍā, and Sarasvatī, or Mahī, Hotrā, and Sarasvatī, who are invoked in the Āprī hymns of the animal sacrifice : Iḍā is a mere abstraction of the idea of the sacrificial offering, and Mahī and Hotrā are clearly deities of the same kind : Bhāratī, however, must refer to the lady of the Bharatas, and the identification is of first-rate importance as it enables us to decide which Sarasvatī is meant in these cases. The Bharatas, we know, dwelt on the Sarasvatī and the Dṛṣadvatī, and sacrifices on the Sarasvatī are prescribed in the Brāhmaṇas and the Sūtras : the combination of the goddesses must have grown up when Sarasvatī meant the stream which is connected with the Dṛṣadvatī.[2] Nor is it at all improbable that the same river is meant in every or nearly every case : the older view [3] that Sarasvatī meant the Indus, or the view [4] that in any case it refers still as originally to the Harahvaitī cannot be supported by any conclusive proof : it is true that the present river Sarasvatī is small, and loses itself in the sand, but it may well have been more important than this in the time of the Rigveda, and in any case there is no doubt of its holiness in the Brāhmaṇa period, a fact which really disposes of the argument against it, based on its size.

In the Rigveda in Sarasvatī we need not see anything more than a river goddess somewhat strongly anthropomorphized in certain details who inspires prayers of devotion. But in the Brāhmaṇas she is connected with speech, perhaps because Vedic culture and poetry flourished specially there, and in the post-Vedic literature she is the goddess of eloquence and the wife of Brahman. The nearest approach to this is the statement of the Yajurveda [5] that, when Indra was ill, Sarasvatī by speech communicated vigour to him, where speech

[1] VS. xix. 12, 94.

[2] Max Müller, SBE. xxxii. 60 ff.

[3] Zimmer, *Altind. Leben*, p. 10.

[4] Hillebrandt, *Ved. Myth.* i. 99 ; iii. 374 ff. He takes the celestial Sarasvatī as the milky way (i. 382, 383). Carnoy (*Les Indo-Européens*, p. 199) compares Anāhita in Iran and suggests borrowing from the Babylonian Nīn Ella, mother of waters.

[5] ÇB. iii. 9. 1. 7 ; AB. iii. 1. 10 ; TS. vii. 2. 7. 4 ; MS. iii. 6. 4 ; TB. i. 8. 1 ; 4. 2 ; AV. v. 7. 4 ; 10. 8 ; PB. vi. 7. 7. That Sarasvatī in RV. x. 17 is the river severing quick and dead, the later Vaitaraṇī, is most implausible.

is merely her instrument, not her nature, and her healing power must rather be deemed to be due to her nature as the purifying water.

Beside Sarasvatī in one hymn [1] we have an invocation of Sarasvant to give offspring, protection, and plenty: his fertilizing waters and breast are referred to. Agni as Sarasvant once appears as a giver of rain. It is hardly necessary to see in him more than a male counterpart of Sarasvatī: there is nothing to support the more important character of guardian of the celestial waters which is accorded to him by Roth or the identification with Apāṁ Napāt proposed by Hillebrandt [2] and Hardy.[3]

Other streams are addressed as great, such as Sarayū and Sindhu, and the conception of seven streams is particularly often found, doubtless because of the Vedic predilection for the number seven. It is probably needless to press the number for an exact identification, especially as it is quite probable the idea came with the Indians from Iran.[4]

§ 5. *The Earth*

The goddess Pṛthivī plays a singularly restricted part in the Rigveda except in so far as she is invoked along with Dyaus. She has but one short hymn of her own,[5] and a long and interesting hymn ascribed to her in the Atharvaveda [6] is conspicuous rather for its accuracy of enumeration of the sights of the earth than for religious fervour. She is rich in heights, bears the burden of the mountains, and supports in the ground the forest trees. She is great, shining, and firm, and quickens the earth, by scattering rain from the cloud, a fact which shows that she is not rigidly confined to her element. doubtless because she has borrowed an attribute of Dyaus himself. The Brāhmaṇas [7] follow the Rigveda in referring her name as broad to the fact of her having been extended. In the funeral hymn [8] she is appealed to be tender to the dead as to a child, and she is called kindly mother earth. In the domestic ritual offerings to her as Bhūmi are not rare.[9]

§ 6. *The Sea*

All the available evidence points to the fact that the Vedic Indians had little accurate knowledge of the sea, and that none of the tribes were actually settled by the banks of the ocean, but at the same time the legend of the Açvins and their ships and of the saving of Bhujyu must be allowed, when taken in connexion with a few passages where the sea seems clearly a real sea,

1 RV. vii. 96.
2 *Op. cit.* i. 380–2.
3 *Ved.-brahm. Periode*, pp. 42, 43. Usener (*Götternamen*, p. 31) wrongly suggests that he is prior to Sarasvatī.
4 See Macdonell and Keith, *Vedic Index*, ii. 242. Cf. Tilak, *Arctic Home*, pp. 288 ff.; N. G. Sardesai, *Bhandarkar Comm. Vol.*, pp. 93 ff. (Russian Turkestan).
5 RV. v. 84. Cf. L. Sütterlin, *Archiv für Rel.* ix. 553; Dieterich, *Mutter Erde* (1905).
6 xii. 1.
7 TS. vii. 1. 5; TB. i. 1. 3. 5.
8 RV. x. 18. 10.
9 Cf. above, Chap. 8, § 1.

and not the sea of the sky, to prove that the Indians had heard of the sea, and knew by hearsay, if not by experience, of undertakings directed towards obtaining wealth by sea commerce. But the conception of the sea as a deity, Samudra, is most rudimentary, whether we are to apply it to the ocean proper or merely to the lower course of the Indus, where it assumes a breadth which prevents the other bank being seen.[1] He is invoked with Aja Ekapād, Ahi Budhnya, and Pṛthivī, and occurs once or twice in other enumerations, once with Sindhu: a personification of Arṇava, who in one case occurs beside him, is still more feeble. The ritual agrees with the Rigveda: occasionally offerings are made as at the horse sacrifice to the god,[2] and even in the Gṛhya ritual [3] he is not unknown, as, for instance, at the Baliharaṇa he is given an offering along with beings like Dhanvantari and Oṣadhi, 'the plant', but in the main these offerings occur in enumerations of many deities, and emphasize the unreal character of the god. The same rule applies in the later literature: the ocean is often poetically described,[4] but a real god of the ocean seems not to have been created in India except under Mahommedan influences. In the Rigveda there is no hint that the realm of Varuṇa lies in any special connexion with the ocean, and it is not until the Brāhmaṇas begin their speculations that the identity of the ocean and Varuṇa is asserted, but still at a time when Varuṇa is lord of all waters, and not those of the ocean merely. The same point is made clear by the ritual, for the only specifically sea offering which is made to Varuṇa is that of a *nakra*,[5] which may have been a crocodile, and which is given in the lists of victims at the Açvamedha, and it must be remembered that the aim of the compilers of the lists of victims was evidently not to trouble regarding real offerings, but to multiply as much as possible the number of victims to be offered, in theory not in fact.

[1] Macdonell and Keith, *Vedic Index*, ii. 431, 432; Weber, *Skizzen*, p. 135; Hillebrandt, *Ved. Myth.* iii. 15 ff. Contrast A. C. Das, *Rig-Vedic India*, pp. 32 ff., 44–6.

[2] TS. iv. 6. 2; v. 7. 16; MS. iv. 9. 8; TA. iv. 9. 1.

[3] Kauç. lxxiv. 6.

[4] Hopkins, AJP. xxi. 378 ff.

[5] TS. v. 5. 13. 1; MS. iii. 14. 2; VS. xxiv. 21.

CHAPTER 11

THE MINOR GODS OF NATURE

§ 1. *The Ṛbhus and the Ṛtus*

THE minor figures of the Vedic mythology are distinguished as a rule by the obscurity of their outlines : even when they are freely mentioned, as in the case of the Ṛbhus, it is a matter of the utmost difficulty to decide their precise character : it is probable indeed that in many cases the nature of the gods was little better understood by their worshippers than it is by us. Of this there is an excellent example in the Ṛbhus : they occur in eleven hymns in the Rigveda, being special favourites of the Bharadvāja family, and they are mentioned over a hundred times, but their mythical nature is very doubtful, and the Atharvaveda mentions them but eight times in seven hymns, and adds nothing to their character, indicating that in the popular side of the Vedic religion they had little hold.

It appears that there are strictly three Ṛbhus, named Ṛbhukṣan, ' lord ' or ' chief of the Ṛbhus ', which is also an epithet of Indra, Vāja, and Vibhvan. It was, however, natural that the number should be increased, and we hear of all the Ṛbhus, or Ṛbhu with the Ṛbhus, or Vibhvan with the Vibhus, and, it may be added, the Praiṣa for the god Indra at the evening pressing in one version adds Prabhus. They are called Saudhanvanas, offspring of Sudhanvan, ' the good archer ', or sons of Indra, and by a play on Indra's epithet, ' son of strength ', they appear as ' descendants of strength '. On the other hand they are also sons of Manu, and claim Agni as brother. They are bright deities, who ride on a car drawn by fat steeds ; they have metal helmets and fair necklaces.

The essential features of the Ṛbhus is their connexion with Indra, through whom they are also connected with the Maruts and obtain a share of the Soma drink, which, however, in the ritual is whittled down to a share in an invocation to Indra. With other gods they have but slight connexion such as the Mountains, Rivers, the Ādityas, Savitṛ, and Tvaṣṭṛ. Their chief distinction is their skill, which wins them the favour of Indra and immortality, for they are distinctly regarded as men of the air, who earned for themselves immortality by their deeds, not as from the beginning divine. The Aitareya Brāhmaṇa [1] states they obtained their position by means of austerities, a view which of course entirely agrees with the priestly estimate of the due means of securing divine rank, but which ignores the older and simpler conception of their skill as the adequate cause. Having attained that position, they are addressed as

[1] iii. 30. 2.

gods, and are besought to bestow boons on their worshippers, including the dexterity which is theirs specially : they also aid in battle.

Five great feats of skill are enumerated as performed by the Ṛbhus, the making of a car which, horseless, reinless, with three wheels, travels space, for the Açvins ; the fashioning for Indra of two bay steeds ; the making out of a hide of a cow, seemingly for Bṛhaspati, to milk nectar, of which a variant seems to be the uniting of the mother with her calf ; the rejuvenating of their ancient and frail parents, doubtless heaven and earth ; and, last but not least, the making of Tvaṣṭṛ's one cup into four. This they did on the bidding of the gods through Agni, and the promise of immortality was the bait : Tvaṣṭṛ seems to have approved the proposal,[1] but in one place [2] he is said to have been fain to slay them for this desecration of the cup of the gods, while they deny the desecration. Other feats are more commonplace : they fashion the sacrifice or the two worlds.

In a curious myth they are connected with Savitṛ. It seems that they went round the sky in swift flight, and came to the house of Savitṛ, who bestowed immortality upon them, when they came to Agohya. When after twelve days of slumber they had enjoyed Agohya's hospitality, they made the fields to flourish and the streams to flow over the earth. They after a year looked around : they asked Agohya who had wakened them. When they slumbered in his house, they made grass on the heights and water in the depths.[3]

An elaborate theory of their nature has been proposed by Hillebrandt.[4] He lays stress on the fact that, when they pleased the gods by their work, they became the artificers of the gods, Ṛbhukṣan of Indra, Vibhvan of Varuṇa, and Vāja of the gods generally.[5] Now the four-month offerings are the Vaiçvadeva, the Varuṇapraghāsas, and the Sākamedhas, and he puts the three Ṛbhus in contact with the three sets of offerings, and sees, therefore, in them the three seasons. Further, he holds that the twelve days' slumber must refer to the period of twelve nights at the winter solstice known in German folklore and mythology : [6] in this still period of the year when the sun is at a standstill, the geniuses of the seasons exert their creative power. In the ritual this is the Dvādaçāha, 'the twelve day rite', which is of the utmost importance for the ritual as it serves as a model for all Sattras, and it is in this rite that most of the Ṛbhu hymns are used. Moreover, he adds that at the end of the year the Ṛtus,[7] 'the seasons', are offered to in the Gṛhya ritual of the Aṣṭakās, and also occur in the Çrauta ritual. But all this is mere conjecture, as is the suggestion which has been made that the cup of Tvaṣṭṛ is the moon,

[1] RV. iv. 33. 5, 6.

[2] RV. i. 161. 4, 5.

[3] RV. iv. 33. 1, 7 ; i. 140. 2 ; i. 161. 11, 13.

[4] *Ved. Myth.* iii. 135–54 ; (Kl. Ausg.), pp. 144–8 ; cf. Ludwig, *Rigveda*, iv. 160 ; v. 510. But see Oldenberg, *Rel. des Veda*,[2] pp. 239 ff. ; ZDMG. lix. 262 ff., who refutes Hillebrandt's view that in RV. i. 110. 3 Agohya appears as Savitṛ; Thibaut, *Indian Thought*, i. 107.

[5] RV. iv. 33. 9.

[6] This view is accepted by J. H. Moulton, *Essays and Studies presented to W. Ridgeway*, p. 259, n. 1.

[7] RV. i. 15 ; ii. 37 ; ÇÇS. vii. 8 ; ApÇS. xii. 268 ff. ; GGS. iii. 10 ; AÇS. ii. 4. 12.

the four parts being either replicas of the four months of each of the seasons, or four moon phases.[1] The attempt to bring the four-month offerings into conjunction with the Ṛbhus is a very forced one and is not supported by anything save the vague connexion of names, by which almost anything could be established ; the belief that the Indians and the Germans preserve a tradition of twelve days' rest of nature at the winter solstice is a most improbable idea,[2] and the Dvādaçāha obviously connects with the number of the months. Nor is it in the slightest degree intelligible how, if that were the case, the three seasons by sleeping then would procure grass and water in abundance. Nor is the assertion that the Ṛbhus are really the Ṛtus in the slightest degree plausible : the seasonal cups of the Soma sacrifice have no real relation to Ṛbhus at all. Finally he makes the ingenious suggestion that the contemned position of the Ṛbhus is due to the fact that these are the gods of a particular clan, who took to the work of chariot making, were not admitted for a long time to the Brahmanical circle, but eventually found admission through their skill in this useful art, a fact which may stand in relation to the name Ṛbhu, which he equates not with the German ' Elbe ', but with the root *arb* seen in ' Arbeit '.[3] The evidence for this theory consists simply in the fact that at the laying of the fire a Rathakṛt according to some Sūtras [4] should mention as his forefathers the Ṛbhus, and the name Saudhanvana is stated in late texts to denote a caste. The case is an interesting one, not because it makes the theory of Hillebrandt at all tenable, but because it shows how the Rathakṛt, being a skilled chariot maker, was advised to claim as his forefathers the Ṛbhus, the chariot makers *par excellence*.

Other theories are even less plausible : Weber [5] sees in them the geniuses of the past, present, and future, and in Agohya the sun who may not be concealed, i. e. driven from his course even by the winter solstice ; Bergaigne [6] takes them as three ancient skilful sacrificers who attained immortality, and whose number three stands in connexion with the three fires. The evidence forbids any certainty or even probability : it is, however, most probable that they are identical with the German ' Elbe ', and that they are elves of the air or the earth who have won their way to a divine greatness.[7] By an extraordinary freak we find them in the Mahābhārata elevated to the stature of the greatest of gods imaginable.[8]

[1] Macdonell, *Ved. Myth.*, p. 133 ; Henry, *Journal des Savants*, 1903, p. 496.

[2] Keith, JRAS. 1915, pp. 131–3.

[3] On the etymology cf. Kluge, *Etym. Wörterbuch der deutschen Sprache*, *s.v.* Alp.

[4] ApÇS. v. 11. 7 ; KÇS. iv. 9. 5. ; Weber, *Ind. Stud.* xvii. 196.

[5] *Ved. Beitr.* 1894, p. 37.

[6] *Rel. Véd.* ii. 412.

[7] Macdonell, *op. cit.*, p. 134 ; Carnoy, *Les Indo-Européens*, p. 219.

[8] iii. 261. 19 ff.

§ 2. *The Gandharvas and the Apsarases*

In the Rigveda the word Gandharva occurs twenty times, but only thrice in the plural, from which it is fair to deduce that the nature of the spirit was originally conceived as one. What is still more important is that it occurs but once in book ii–vii, and is found twice in the eighth book as a being hostile to Indra. The epithet *viçvāvasu*, ‘ possessing all good things ’, which accompanies it, appears once in the Rigveda [1] itself, and often later, to denote a definite individual. The Gandharva of that text is a high being of the air of the sky, a measurer of space who stands erect on the vault of heaven. He is brought into relation with the sun, the sun-bird, the sun-steed, and Soma likened to the sun. He is also connected with the rainbow in a late hymn.[2] He is, however, especially connected with Soma, whose place he guards, standing on the vault of heaven. Kṛçānu, the archer, who shoots at the eagle which steals the Soma, is expressly said in a later text [3] to be a Gandharva. But the Gandharva is also connected with the waters : Soma in the waters is said to be the Gandharva of the waters : the parents of Yama and Yamī are the Gandharva and the maiden of the waters : the Gandharva is the lover of the Apsaras. The Gandharva is further found in the marriage ceremony : the bride is claimed by him, and he is in the beginning of the marriage a rival of the husband.[4] Further the Gandharva has a fragrant garment,[5] and is wind-haired.[6]

In the later Saṁhitās the account of the Gandharvas is fuller, but not essentially different : there is now a class which can be mentioned beside the gods, Fathers, and Asuras ; they have a definite world of their own like the gods or the Fathers, to which a man may attain ; [7] the number is sometimes twenty-seven, which is the number of the Nakṣatras, or even 6333.[8] Celestial traits are still numerous : [9] his abode is in heaven, Rohiṇī and the stars of the moon's orbit are brought into connexion with the Gandharva ; he is mentioned with such deities as Agni, sun, moon, and wind, and in the post-Vedic literature the Fata Morgana are connected with the Gandharva.[10] But the Soma myth is especially developed. We learn that the Gandharvas kept Soma for the gods, but, allowing it to be stolen, were punished by exclusion from drinking it.[11] Viçvāvasu has to be eluded by Soma in eagle form, a fact which no doubt explains the hostility of Indra to the Gandharva in the eighth book

[1] x. 85. 21, 22.

[2] RV. x. 123, a hymn however very differently interpreted ; Oldenberg, *Rigveda-Noten*, ii. 342.

[3] TA. i. 9. 3 ; RV. iv. 27. 3.

[4] RV. x. 85. 22.

[5] RV. x. 123. 7 ; cf. AV. xii. 1. 23.

[6] RV. iii. 38. 6.

[7] JB. i. 166 ; cf. 259 (yonder world, Gandharva-, Deva-, Svarga-loka) ; ÇB. xi. 5. 1. 17. Hence perhaps the Kali Gandharvas in JB. i. 154 f.

[8] AV. xi. 5. 2.

[9] BAU. iii. 6 places the Gandharva world between the atmosphere and the sun, but cf. ÇB. xiv. 6. 6. 1. See also AV. ii. 2. 1, 2 ; xiv. 2. 36 ; VS. ix. 7 ; xviii. 38 ff.

[10] *Epic Myth.*, p. 157. The alleged Iranian parallel is dubious ; E. H. Meyer, *Indog. Myth.* i. 99 f.

[11] MS. iii. 8. 10.

of the Rigveda.[1] Soma is stated to have been stolen by Viçvāvasu or at least to have lived among the Gandharvas, but the gods by the bribe of Vāc, 'speech', were able to induce them to give him up,[2] the Gandharvas being fond of women, while Vāc agreed to come back when her former owners called her, a fact which is an interesting parallel to the legend which makes the Soma seller lose the price paid to him for the Soma. The connexion with the waters appears in the mention of his abode with the Apsarases in the waters in the Atharvaveda.[3] That text also states that the Gandharva knows plants, doubtless the Soma, and that the odour of the earth arises to him, probably an idea due to folk etymology with *gandha*, odour.

In the Brāhmaṇa texts and in the ritual the connexion between the Apsarases and the Gandharvas is especially close: the Gandharva Ūrṇāyu sits among the Apsarases, who swing themselves, and is beloved by them:[4] in a rite the priest can point to the young men and the young maidens present, when he means to indicate the Gandharvas and Apsarases.[5] They are besought to bestow progeny,[6] and in the Buddhist texts the being, which by the law of transmigration enters the womb at the time of conception, is called a Gandhabba.[7] For the nights immediately after the marriage, when the newly wedded couple are not allowed to consummate the marriage, a staff which represents the Gandharva Viçvāvasu is placed between them, and not until it is formally dismissed to the highest region is the marriage completed.[8] A different and lower view of the Gandharvas is also found in the Atharvaveda[9] where the plant goat's horn is used to drive off the Gandharvas, who are regarded as shaggy with half animal forms, and are said to seek to ruin women in the guise of an ape, a dog, a hairy child, or a friend.

In the Avesta there is a being, a Gandarewa, who dwells in the sea Vourukaša and is defeated by the heroic Keresāspa. He is also a lord of the bays, who dwells in the waters, and his identity with the Gandharva is clearly undeniable. The further comparison of Kentauros[10] is certainly untenable phonetically, unless it be assumed that both are loan words, and is open to the gravest objections on the grounds of the nature of the two conceptions: the few points of similarity cannot be traced in the Rigvedic conception at all.

The nature of the Gandharva cannot well be expressly defined: there can be no doubt whatever that he is in his origin a creature of the heaven: the light side of his nature is obvious and persistent despite other traits. The

1 viii. 77. 5; I. 11. Carnoy (JAOS. xxxvi. 312) suggests contamination of an Indo-European storm myth and a Semitic monster of the abyss.

2 TS. vi. 1. 6. 5; MS. iii. 7. 3; AB. i. 27; ÇB. iii. 2. 4. 3–6.

3 ii. 2. 3; iv. 37. 12.

4 PB. xii. 11. 10.

5 ÇB. xiii. 4. 3. 7, 8.

6 PB. xix. 3. 2; cf. ÇGS. i. 19, 2.

7 Oldenberg, *Rel. des Veda*², p. 253, n. 1; *contra*, Hillebrandt, *Ved. Myth.* i. 427; *Zur Bedeutung von Gandharva* (1906); cf. Garbe, *Sâṃkhya-Philosophie*², p. 306.

8 RV. x. 85. 22.

9 AV. iv. 37; cf. viii. 6. 19. Their assimilation to Piçācas is seen in iv. 37. 8–10, and we find in Saṁyutta Nikāya, i. 33, Piçācas beside Apsarases as infesting a wood.

10 Feist, *Kultur der Indogermanen*, p. 343, n. 1.

connexion with water can be traced to various sources : either the waters of the sky are the basis on which his activity has been transferred to the waters of earth, or his association with the Apsarases has led to his connexion with the waters, or as is quite possible the obscuration of his original nature has rendered it possible to associate him with elements not originally his own. It is more difficult to see how the demons of the Atharvaveda who are no better than Piçācas—indeed in a Buddhist text [1] Piçācas replace Gandharvas in conjunction with the Apsarases—can be developed from the Gandharva of the Rigveda. It is most probable that this is simply a case where demons have been allowed to obtain a name which is not theirs by right, the point of contact being found in the connexion of the Gandharva with marriage, which leads to the doubtless secondary connexion of the Gandharva with the embryo. The Gandharva, therefore, is not in the secondary period of the Vedic religion any longer a single concept : he is compounded of different and in essence disparate ideas.

What the original nature of the Rigvedic Gandharva was, cannot, as has been said, be precisely elucidated : to Kuhn [2] he is a cloud spirit, to Wallis [3] the rising sun, to Bergaigne [4] Soma, to Hopkins [5] a genius of the moon, and to Roth [6] the rainbow. To a different idea belongs the view taken by Mannhardt,[7] E. H. Meyer,[8] and von Schroeder,[9] which sees in him a wind spirit developed out of the conception of the spirits of the dead as riding in the wind and passing therefore into wind spirits. Hillebrandt [10] thinks that the real meaning of the name Gandharva is giant, and that the name is applied to different potencies, now and then to wind spirits, in other cases to the sun, since he finds that it is mentioned of Viçvāvasu that he kept Soma hidden for three nights : as Soma is the moon in the view of Hillebrandt, this can refer only to the obscuration of the moon for three nights by the sun, and therefore of course the Gandharva must be the sun. This form of argument is by no means convincing, and, as against the theory of wind gods, it must be pointed out that only once in the Rigveda is there any possible mention of wind in connexion with the Gandharva, and from such an incidental idea no conclusion can ever be drawn to the nature of a Vedic deity.

Of the Apsaras in the Rigveda is mentioned her connexion with the Gandharva upon whom she smiles in the highest heaven. Vasiṣṭha also claims birth from an Apsaras, and the Vasiṣṭhas are said to have sat close to the Apsarases.[11] The long-haired Muni, or ascetic with magic powers, moves

[1] Saṁyutta Nikāya, i. 33.
[2] *Herabkunft des Feuers*, p. 153.
[3] *Cosmology*, pp. 34, 36.
[4] *Rel. Véd.* iii. 64–7.
[5] *Rel. of India*, p. 157.
[6] *Nirukta*, p. 142, and cf. *St. Petersburg Dict.*, *s. v.*
[7] *Wald- und Feldkulte*, i. 201.
[8] *Indog. Myth.* i. 219 ff.
[9] *Griech. Götter*, i. 71. Cf. *Mysterium und Mimus*, pp. 57 ff. ; Arbman (*Rudra*, p. 309) argues that the Rigvedic conception is a priestly refinement, ignoring the much more plausible view of 'contamination' of deities.
[10] *Ved. Myth.* i. 426–49 ; (Kl. Ausg.), pp. 72 101.
[11] RV. vii. 33. 9.

on the path of the Gandharvas and the Apsarases.[1] The water nymph who is the spouse of the Gandharva is clearly the Apsaras. The connexion with water is brought out still more clearly in its most primitive form when the Apsarases of the sea are described as flowing to the Soma, a mythic description of the mixing of water with the Soma. The description of the Apsarases, therefore, agrees entirely and completely with the meaning of their name : [2] they are ' the goers in the water ', water nymphs, and already in the Rigveda they are not confined to the waters of the earth, though they were perhaps there first located.

In the Atharvaveda and the Yajurveda the connexion of the Apsarases with the waters is frequently expressed : they abide in the waters, they are often asked to depart from men to the river and the bank of the waters, possibly a hint at the dangerous quality of the nymphs.[3] The Apsarases who accompany the Gandharva Viçvāvasu are connected with clouds, lightning, and stars, and all the later Saṁhitās agree in calling them the wives of the Gandharvas. In the Çatapatha Brāhmaṇa [4] they appear as swimming about in a lake in the form of birds (*ātī*), and the later literature often treats them as water spirits, in forest lakes, in rivers, even in Varuṇa's palace in the ocean. But they have also a further field of activity ; they dwell in the banyan and the fig-tree, according to the Atharvaveda,[5] where their cymbals and their lutes resound. The Gandharvas and Apsarases in these trees are begged to be propitious to a passing wedding party.[6] They are also said to be engaged in dance and song and play, but the Atharvaveda [7] mentions some sinister characteristics : if they are fond of dice, and bestow good luck in gambling, they are also liable to cause madness, and magic has to be employed against them in this regard. The post-Vedic literature also finds them with the Gandharvas in trees, and adds mountains [8] to their places of habitation. It is perhaps from them that the Gandharva attains his power of causing derangement or at least mental excitement, which is attested for the Brāhmaṇa period by the phrase ' seized by a Gandharva ', used of a lady who is inspired or demented.[9]

One Apsaras only is named in the Rigveda, the famous Urvaçī. She was the mother of Vasiṣṭha,[10] who claimed also descent from Mitra and Varuṇa, and she is invoked with the streams. But the chief reference to her is in a

[1] RV. x. 136. 6.

[2] Not as Wackernagel (*Festschrift Kuhn*, pp. 159 f.), ' shameless ', or ' formless ' ; see Oldenberg, GGA. 1915, p. 131.

[3] Cf. Mannhardt, *Wald- und Feldkulte*, ii. 36 ff.

[4] xi. 5. 1. 4.

[5] iv. 37. 4 ; Mannhardt, *Wald- und Feldkulte*, i. 99 f.

[6] AV. xiv. 2. 9 ; Kauç. lxxvii. 7 ; TS. iii. 4. 8. 4.

[7] ii. 2. 3 ; 3. 3.

[8] Holtzmann, ZDMG. xxxiii. 640 f. ; Hopkins, *Epic Myth.*, pp. 156, 160.

[9] A Gandharva, in conjunction with an Apsaras (appearing identical with a mortal woman), brings about the madness and death of the Brahman Yavakrī ; see JB. ii. 269–72.

[10] RV. vii. 33. 11, 12. Possibly an idea due to mystic visions at the Dīkṣā ; cf. Hauer, *Die Anfänge der Yogapraxis im alten Indien*, pp. 72 f.

hymn [1] of considerable interest and obscurity, in which she is loved by Purūravas. She is there connected with water, filling the atmosphere and traversing space. It is said that she spends four autumns among mortals, and she is invoked to return, but that request she refuses, promising, however, Purūravas that his offspring will worship the gods, and he himself will enjoy happiness in heaven. The hymn clearly refers to one of those alliances of nymphs and men, which are common in all literatures as in the stories of Thetis and of the German swan maidens, who often for as long as seven years are allowed to stay with mortal men. In the Çatapatha Brāhmaṇa [2] several interesting details are given, which, however, cannot be read into the Rigvedic account, and, therefore, may rest on later alteration and embellishment of the narative. Purūravas is united to Urvaçī, but only on condition that she shall never see him naked: the Gandharvas envying their union, which subtracts her from their midst, devise a plan by which the sheep which Urvaçī keeps with her is stolen away: Purūravas leaps from his couch to prevent the theft: he forgets to put on his garment, 'for he thought it long that he should do so,' and he is revealed in a flash of light to the nymph who departs forthwith. Purūravas seeks desperately for her over the earth, until he comes upon her swimming in a lotus lake along with other Apsarases in the shape of aquatic birds. Urvaçī reveals herself to him and consents to receive him on a night a year later, when the Gandharvas enable him to become one of themselves by producing the sacrificial fire in a certain way. The tale has, of course, in any case been remodelled to suit the purpose of advocating the special mode proposed of producing the fire, but the episode of the taboo of seeing the hero naked is of interest and primitive in nature. It may be, as von Schroeder [3] suggests, an inversion of the same rule applied to the maiden, since the German legends of swan maidens lay always stress on the absolute necessity of the maiden not being seen in her true nature, but the transfer need not be certainly assumed. Purūravas is only once elsewhere mentioned in the Rigveda, [4] where it is said that Agni caused the sky to thunder for the righteous Purūravas, though, as the name means 'he who calls aloud', it is possible that in that passage the word is merely an epithet. In any case the view of Weber [5] and Max Müller [6] that Purūravas is the sun and Urvaçī the dawn is quite unnecessary, while Siecke's [7] attempt to show that Urvaçī is the moon is based on the same curious reasoning as all his efforts to fill the Rigveda with moon deities. Purūravas is simply a hero, not necessarily ever a real man, but conceived as one: later tradition derives the lunar race of kings from him.

Other names of Apsarases are given in the later Saṁhitās: the Atharva-

[1] RV. x. 95. 10, 17.

[2] xi. 5. 1; Geldner, *Ved. Stud.* i. 243–95; Oldenberg's notes. For a revised version, Çāntanu and Gaṅgā, see MBh. i. 3888 ff.; cf. Mannhardt, *Wald- und Feldkulte*, i. 69, 103 f., 152.

[3] *Griech. Götter*, i. 53 ff.

[4] i. 31. 4.

[5] *Ind. Stud.* i. 196.

[6] *Chips*, iv.[2] 109.

[7] *Die Liebesgeschichte des Himmels.*

veda [1] mentions Ugrajit, Ugraṁpaçyā, and Rāṣṭrabhṛt, and the Yajurveda [2] names among many others Menakā and Urvaçī. The Çatapatha Brāhmaṇa [3] mentions also a nymph, who is famous in later story, Çakuntalā, as the mother of the king Bharata.

§ 3. *Spirits of the Forest, the Trees, and the Plants*

The references to the worship of the tree and the plants are very scanty in the Vedic ritual and mythology alike, but they are quite adequate to show that as among all other peoples these objects were not without their share of reverence.[4] A long hymn in the last book of the Rigveda [5] is devoted to the deification of the plants with special reference to their healing properties, and plants also appear in the Atharvaveda,[6] where they are used in spells for healing, and for driving away demons of all kinds : the plant is even besought to bestow a horse, a sheep, a garment, and the life of the patient, who doubtless was to be the instrument by which the prayer of the medicine man was to be made good if the spell succeeded in attaining its purpose. In the Rigveda [7] Soma is already the king of the plants, and they are called mothers and goddesses : the Atharvaveda [8] poetically describes a plant as a goddess born of the goddess earth. On the other hand plants have power to hinder child-birth, and in that case the offering of an animal victim to them is prescribed by the Taittirīya Saṁhitā [9] in order to procure their favour.

The cult of trees, and above all of forest trees, Vanaspati, is recognized by the Rigveda,[10] which in a few passages invokes either one or many along with the Waters and the Mountains. In the later Saṁhitās, as we have seen, trees are the favourite homes of the Apsarases and also of the Gandharvas. The Taittirīya Saṁhitā [11] assigns to them as their homes the trees Açvattha, Nyagrodha, Udumbara, and Plakṣa. When the wedding procession passes by large trees, these deities are to be besought to afford their favour. More directly, in the same ceremony, in some accounts the tree is solemnly honoured on the fifth day after marriage with gifts of flowers, of food and clothing, and the part of trees in the marriage ritual is one of the commonest features of Indian marriage among the less advanced tribes.[12] There is, however, no trace in the Vedic literature of the marriage to a tree, which in modern India often precedes certain classes of marriages. Again, if a man is driving out on

[1] vi. 118. 1, 2.

[2] VS. xv. 15 ff.

[3] xiii. 5. 4. 13 ; cf. Holtzmann, ZDMG. xxxiii. 635 ff. ; Leumann, xl. 80–82 ; v. Bradke, *ibid.* 498 ff.

[4] Meyer (*Gesch. des Alt.*[3] I. ii. p. 915) lays stress on the fact that Aryan religion pictures the deities as only faintly localized, and so, unlike other faiths, could not develop any strong belief in tree worship. This may be explained by migrations.

[5] x. 97 ; Roth, ZDMG. xxv. 645–8.

[6] Bloomfield, *Atharvaveda*, p. 67.

[7] x. 97. 18.

[8] vi. 136. 1.

[9] ii. 1. 5. 3.

[10] vii. 34. 23 ; x. 64. 8.

[11] TS. iii. 4. 8. 4.

[12] Winternitz, *Altind. Hochzeitsrituell*, pp. 101, 102 ; BhGS. i. 13. Viçvāvasu can hardly be a relic of tree marriage.

a new car, and he comes across a good tree, he should go round it from left to right, the way of the sun, and take from it branches with fruit.[1]

The belief in the life of the tree is very clearly seen in the treatment of the tree from which the sacrificial post is to be taken.[2] The necessary cutting is performed after a blade of grass has been put over the place where the blow is to be inflicted, and the blade is hidden to protect the tree, while the axe is expressly ordered to harm not the tree : the prescription is precisely the same as that adopted in the domestic ritual when the hair is cut, and in the ordinary cult when the victim is slain : the aim is clearly to avoid injury to the life in the tree by pretending that it is not being injured. The tree is also, when made into the form of a post, adorned with a band placed round it and is anointed, and this doubtless proves its living character, while it is possible that the verse in the Āprī litany of the animal sacrifice, addressed to the forest tree, is really an adjuration to the sacrificial post. The evidence must not be unduly pressed, as in this case, owing to the presence of the god at the place of sacrifice, it is beyond doubt that the surroundings of the sacrifice are filled with his presence, and that, therefore, they may attain a sanctity not their own; but the conception of the life of the tree is clear, even if its divinity is not so certain in this special instance.

The belief in the presence of spirits in trees is, of course, ethnic and the Buddhist literature has many traces of it, showing the different sets of conceptions which are easily formed ; the tree is primarily the spirit, then the spirit with or without its children lives in the tree, and, if it perishes, has to go away to seek a new abode, while at a further stage the tree becomes more and more remotely connected with the deity. This literature is also instructive in the fact that it mentions other than tree spirits, spirits of terrible form and uncanny and hostile nature, who may well be of double origin, arising from a direct or animatistic conception of the darkness and hostility of the woods,[3] and also from the conception of unfriendly spirits which develops from the belief in the hostile spirits of the dead.[4] The Rigveda [5] preserves one hymn in its last book, describing the forest goddess, Araṇyānī, in a poetical and graphic manner which brings out clearly the uncanny sounds heard in the solitudes, the many beasts which abound, and the food which is raised without tillage. It is easy from this hymn alone to realize how spirits of dangerous character could, independently of any connexion with spirits of the dead, be deemed to abound in the forest.

[1] AGS. ii. 6. 9.

[2] The ritual seems implied in RV. iii. 8.

[3] Cf. Wundt, *Völkerpsychologie*, IV. i. 462 ff.; cf. the evil spirits of the woods, Hopkins, *Epic Myth.*, pp. 40, 57.

[4] Oldenberg, *Rel. des Veda*², pp. 264 ff.

[5] x. 146.

§ 4. *Spirits of Agriculture, Pasture, and the Mountains*

The deity of the field as Kṣetrasya Pati, 'lord of the field', in the Rigveda [1] is invoked to grant cattle and horses, and with sweetness to fill heaven and earth, the plants, and the waters. In another hymn [2] he is asked, along with Savitṛ, the Dawns, and Parjanya to bestow prosperity, and elsewhere it is said that worshippers are fain to have him as a neighbour. The full nature of the deity is made clear in the Gṛhya ritual,[3] which prescribes offerings to him when the field is ploughed, and he is, it is clear, no more than the deity believed to be in the ploughed land.[4] Similarly the Rigveda contains an invocation of Sītā, the furrow, to grant rich blessings and crops.[5] The figure of this goddess naturally has more life in the Sūtras,[6] which deal with the operations of agriculture: she appears as the wife of Indra, which may be due to the fact that in the Rigveda [7] the god is once called Urvarāpati, 'lord of the plough field,' and her existence is manifested in the four Sondergötter, the deities Sītā, Āçā, Araḍā, and Anaghā, who are to be worshipped at the furrow sacrifice, the threshing-floor sacrifice, the sowing of the crop, and the reaping and the putting the crop into the barn.[8] In another Sūtra [9] we have, beside the offering to Sītā and to three other deities, Yajā, Çamā, and Bhūti, who are less concrete than is she, offerings to the guardians of the furrow on the four sides; these guardians are called various names which are hardly more than epithets, 'having good bows and quivers', on the east, 'not winking the eyes' and 'wearing armour', on the south, 'prosperity', 'earth', Pārṣṇi, Çunaṁkuri, on the west, and 'those that are terrible' and 'like Vāyu in swiftness', on the north.[10] These figures are interesting: they cannot properly in any sense be classified with abstract deities, even if that class of deities can properly be set up: they are not personifications of human activities or feelings, but they are the deities involved in the operations of nature, Sondergötter, who live in the growth of the crop and may best perhaps be called animatistic spirits of vegetation, whose precise differentiation of character may plausibly be ascribed as in the case of the Roman Indigitamenta to the work of the priests. On the other hand Sītā has always a more elevated character than the rest of such spirits: she is called Sāvitrī in the Taittirīya Brāhmaṇa,[11] and she becomes the heroine of the Rāmāyaṇa, and the model of wifely truth and chastity, preserving none the less here and there traces

[1] iv. 57.
[2] RV. vii. 35. 10.
[3] AGS. ii. 10. 4; ÇGS. iv. 13. 5; BhGS. ii. 10.
[4] Cf. Warde Fowler's view (*Religious Experience of the Roman People*, pp. 77, 78) of the primitive nature of the *Lar familiaris* in Roman religion.
[5] RV. iv. 57. 6.
[6] PGS. ii. 17. 9.
[7] viii. 21. 3.
[8] GGS. iv. 4. 27.
[9] PGS. ii. 17. 13 ff.
[10] Hillebrandt, *Ved. Myth.* iii. 407.
[11] ii. 3. 10. 1. For the Rāmāyaṇa see Jacobi, *Das Rāmāyaṇa*, p. 130; Hopkins, *Epic Myth.*, pp. 78 f.

of her connexion with the furrow and the fruitful earth. Urvarā, the plough field, is also a goddess in the Sūtra literature, and is described as having a garland of threshing floors.[1] It would of course be absurd to suppose that these scanty remnants of worship represent the whole of the agricultural side of Vedic religion, and as a matter of fact in the ritual there are abundant traces of other ceremonies having to do with agriculture, but the deities of the field were evidently as such not of great importance in Vedic religion, the care of the prosperity of men in these respects having been taken over by the great gods. When agricultural and vegetation spirits as such have great honour among and importance in the ideas of a people, then their figures are elevated to the rank of the great deities, as is the case with Attis, Adonis, or perhaps even Osiris in the lands of Asia Minor and of Egypt,[2] and the fact that other deities are the great gods of Vedic religion cannot be explained on any other hypothesis than that the specific religious instinct of the Vedic people chose these forms as the favourite objects of its devotions. Curiously enough, the later religion of India gives a picture of the differences of religious predilection : the young Kṛṣṇa is represented as opposed to the worship of Indra by the pastoral world : [3] he prefers instead that they should worship the mountains, their cattle, and the woods, just as ploughmen worship the furrow. In cases like these it is impossible not to observe a definite cleavage of religious sentiment, which it is perfectly legitimate to apply as a principle to Vedic religion. The theory which seems sometimes to be held that the Vedic literature does not really give us the popular religion of the time cannot be supported, when it is applied to the literature as a whole, including the Sūtras of the domestic ritual, which are packed with popular ideas and magic practices of every kind.

The mountains are according to the young Kṛṣṇa essentially the deities of pastoral folk : the Ṛigveda,[4] which shows no trace of the old belief of mountains as the home of the gods generally,[5] also invokes here and there the mountains, nearly twenty times in the plural, and four times in the singular. They never, however, occur alone, but only with other deities such as Indra or Savitṛ, or with the waters, trees, plants, heaven and earth. They are described as rejoicing in the sacrificial offering and abiding securely. Parvata, ‘ the mountain ’, is once found invoked as a companion of Indra in the dual compound Indrāparvatā, and asked to come to the offering. In the ritual the mountains make but little appearance, but we hear in the Brāhmaṇas [6] a good deal of a salve from the mountain Trikakubh which has wonderful powers,

[1] PGS. ii. 17. 9.

[2] Cf. Meyer, *Gesch. des Alt.*[3] I. ii. pp. 76, 728 ff. ; Frazer, *Adonis, Attis, Osiris* ; Max Müller, *Egypt. Myth.*, pp. 92 ff.

[3] Harivaṅça, ii. 16. 2 ff. ; Viṣṇu Purāṇa, v. 10. 29 ff.

[4] vi. 49. 14 ; vii. 34. 23, &c. For seven mountains, as doors of heaven, see TS. iii. 12. 2. 9 ; vi. 2. 4. 3 ; Viṣṇu is lord of mountains, TS. iii. 4. 5. 1 ; Kauç. li. 8.

[5] Cf. Arbman, *Rudra*, pp. 40 ff., who seeks to find Rudra on Mūjavant (cf. TS. i. 8. 6).

[6] Macdonell and Keith, *Vedic Index*, i. 329 ; ii. 62. For the mountains in the epic see Hopkins, *Epic Mythology*, pp. 6 ff.

and in the late Hiraṇyakeçi Gṛhya Sūtra [1] there occurs an obscure phrase, which suggests that it was thought in applying the salve to the eyes that the spirit of the mountain entered into the performer of the rite. The idea is of course perfectly in harmony with primitive ideas.

§ 5. *Deities of the House*

The deity of the house and the home is Vāstoṣpati, 'lord of the dwelling', who is invoked in one short hymn of the Rigveda [2] to bless man and beast, to remove diseases, to make cattle and horses prosper, to afford protection, and to grant a favourable entry. He is elsewhere described as destroyer of diseases, is identified with Soma, brought into close connexion with Tvaṣṭṛ as an artificer, or again he is likened to Indra as a cuirass of Soma pressers. In the late tenth book [3] he appears as an observer of ordinances, who was fashioned by the gods along with prayer. His character is made more clear by the fact that the Gṛhya Sūtras [4] prescribe that offerings are to be made to him when a new house is entered. There is no possible ground for supposing that either Pūṣan,[5] or Rudra,[6] or Agni,[7] or any other god is designated by the title, though Rudra actually bears the style in one passage.[8] The god is clearly the god of the house, who when a new house is built comes and abides in it. In the Sūtras [9] we hear more generally of deities of the house.

§ 6. *Divine Implements*

There is no very essential distinction between the worship of natural objects conceived as living and the worship of objects made by human hands, but it is obvious that the worship of such objects tends to be restricted in effect and importance. This is borne out by the evidence of Vedic religion where such religion is of very minor importance, despite the fact that it receives further attention in the Rigveda than might *a priori* have been expected. Thus we find there [10] that two implements of the ploughman, Çuna and Sīra, which may be the ploughshare and the plough, are invoked, and that in the Çatapatha Brāhmana a cake is assigned to them in the sacrifice. The warrior invokes his arrow as divine,[11] and begs it to protect him and assail his foes: his armour, his bow and quiver, are also celebrated, and the drum is invoked to drive away the demons and the danger: in the Atharvaveda [12] a whole hymn is devoted to its praises. But the priest naturally is more

[1] i. 11. 5; Oldenberg, *Rel. des Veda*[1], p. 255, n. 3.
[2] vii. 54. 1–3.
[3] RV. x. 61. 7.
[4] AGS. ii. 9. 9; ÇGS. iii. 4; PGS. iii. 4. 7.
[5] Perry, *Drisler Memorial*, p. 241.
[6] *Festgruss an Weber*, p. 21.
[7] Wallis, *Cosmology*, p. 22.
[8] TS. iii. 4. 10. 3.
[9] AGS. i. 2. 4; MGS. ii. 12. 6; PGS. ii. 9. 2; Kauç. lxxiv. 10; so in the epic, Hopkins, *Epic Myth.*, pp. 41, 57.
[10] RV. iv. 57. 5–8: ÇB. ii. 6. 3. 5; they are taken as constellations by Hillebrandt, *Ved. Myth.* iii. 221–4.
[11] RV. vi. 75. 11, 15, 16; 47. 26 ff.
[12] v. 20.

prominent in the Rigveda, where not only the sacrificial post is deified, perhaps as a remnant of tree worship, is called divine, and is asked to allow the sacrifice to go to the gods, but the sacrificial grass [1] and the divine doors [2] are celebrated. The pressing stones have three hymns [3] given up to them : they are unaging, immortal, more powerful than the heaven itself. They are compared to steeds or bulls, their sound in the pressing reaches the sky. They bestow wealth and offspring, driving away the demons. The mortar and pestle [4] were deified also, and the Atharvaveda [5] adds to the category various ladles and invents a great deity in the remnant of the sacrifice, the Ucchiṣṭa.

It is possible to draw a distinction between the cases of the deities of the plougher and the warrior, and those of the priest. In his case the presence of the deity at the sacrifice may be held to be the cause why the instruments of the sacrifice are treated with so much reverence, while in the former cases the reverence is not due to anything save the essentially valuable character of the objects, and the mystic powers which are deemed by man to lie within them. It is particularly easy to understand how the arrow or even the plough can be regarded as animate : the worship of the priestly implements would thus be rather more fetishistic in origin than real and direct worship of the implements for themselves, and this is perhaps the more accurate manner of considering the question.[6]

§ 7. *Divine Animals*

The place of animals in the Veda is restricted and of comparatively little importance so far as it concerns direct worship of animals, whether individuals or species, as distinct from the theriomorphism of gods who are not animal gods, and the use of animal fetishes. But the existence of these different ways, in which an animal may seem to be divine, renders it difficult in each case to say whether or not direct worship of animal is to be detected.

Dadhikrā or Dadhikrāvan is the most famous of horses in the Rigveda where he is praised in four rather late hymns.[7] He was, it is clear, especially famous among the Pūrus : his speed is extolled, he is compared to, and even directly identified with, the eagle. He is even described with epithets appropriate to Agni as the swan dwelling in light, the Vasu in the air, the priest at the altar, the guest in the home.[8] He is a hero who wins booty, and who pervades the five tribes with his might, as Sūrya the waters with his light. He is a gift to the Pūrus of Mitra and Varuṇa, and is invoked with Agni, with the Dawn, with the Açvins, Sūrya, and other gods, but in such invocations he has the first place.

[1] RV. ii. 3. 4 ; x. 70. 4.
[2] RV. i. 142. 6.
[3] RV. x. 76, 94, 175.
[4] RV. i. 28. 5, 6 ; so the 2 carts, RV. x. 13.
[5] xi. 7.
[6] See Part II, Chap. 5, § 2. That the millstone on which offerings are deposited in the Bhūtayajña and which figures in the marriage ritual was the recipient of direct worship is conceivable (Arbman, *Rudra*, p. 203, n. 1), but not proved.
[7] iv. 38–40 ; vii. 44.
[8] iv. 40. 5.

The name appears to mean ' he who scatters the curd ', and from the name and his general divine appearance Roth [1] holds that he is none other than the sun in the form of a swift steed. With this agrees the fact that the sun is constantly associated with Uṣas, that it is compared to or identified with a steed, and that it is said to be a bird. Bergaigne's [2] view that lightning is specially referred to may be supported by the swiftness ascribed to the steed, but it is not clear that the conception could possibly be explained, unless the sun were taken as meant. The alternative view of Ludwig,[3] Pischel,[4] and Oldenberg [5] sees in the steed a real horse, a famous race-horse, which won its fame by its swift pace, but this is to exaggerate beyond all possible measure the value attached by the Vedic Indians to the sport of horse-racing.

Hillebrandt,[6] therefore, suggests, with much more plausibility, that the steed is divine as being the horse which was to be sacrificed at the end of the period of a year, during which the sacrificial horse for the horse sacrifice of the king was allowed to wander at pleasure, guarded by the king's sons and warriors, as a sign that his sovereignty was acknowledged on all sides. The suggestion is interesting and is correct, in so far as it is clear that the horse at the horse sacrifice was addressed in terms appropriate to divinity : it cannot seriously be doubted that for the time being the horse was considered as being in a sense divine, nor that in the offering the horse represented the embodiment of the sun. It is, therefore, probable that we have in the horse of the sacrifice a sun fetish,[7] and this being so we have support for the theory that Dadhikrāvan is the sun in horse shape, but we need not suppose that Dadhikrāvan in the hymns in question was actually the horse of the horse sacrifice : he is instead the theriomorphic form of the sun, which in the horse sacrifice is represented by a real horse.

The nature of Tārkṣya seems to be similar to that of Dadhikrāvan : he is described in part in the same terms, as pervading the five tribes with his power, and his character as a steed is shown by his bearing the name Ariṣṭanemi, ' whose fellies are uninjured.' From this epithet in the Yajurveda [8] a new entity Ariṣṭanemi is created and invoked along with Tārkṣya. He is in later Vedic texts once or twice called a bird, and this may be compared with the bird character of Garuḍa, who is beyond question the sun bird. It is difficult, therefore, to doubt that Tārkṣya is merely a form of the sun, conceived as a bird or horse: his name is possibly derived from the prince Tṛkṣi Trāsadasyava

1 *St. Petersburg Dict.*, *s.v.*
2 *Rel. Véd.* ii. 456, 457.
3 *Rigveda*, iv. 79.
4 *Ved. Stud.* i. 124 ; cf. von Bradke, ZDMG. xlvi. 447.
5 *Rel. des Veda*², p. 69 ; SBE. xlvi. 282.
6 *Ved. Myth.* iii. 401, 402 ; (Kl. Ausg.), pp. 170 f.
7 Totemistic suggestions (J. v. Negelein, *Zeitschrift für Ethnologie*, 1901, p. 78 ; E. Monseur, RHR. li. 16) are refuted by van Gennep, *L'état actuel du problème totémique*, pp. 291 f. The ceremonial lying of the queen beside the dead horse is doubtless intended to secure her fertility through contact with the divine.
8 VS. xv. 19. Garuḍa appears in TA. x. 1. 6, and in the Suparṇādhyāya ; see Charpentier, *Die Suparṇasage*, chap. v.

who is mentioned in the Rigveda,[1] and naturally it has been suggested that he is a real horse deified.[2]

Another horse is Paidva, who was given by the Açvins to Pedu, is white, praiseworthy, and is compared to Indra and Bhaga, and called slayer of the dragon, conqueror invincible.[3] All this will pass as a description of the sun horse. Even more certain is the sun nature of Etaça : in the plural the word denotes often the horses of the sun, and in the singular it denotes the sun horse who draws the sun : in a curious legend Indra is said to have aided Etaça in contest with the sun, perhaps by causing a wheel of the sun car to fall off : Etaça picks it up and gives it to the sun, but now is able to take the lead of the sun, who finally, moved by the nobility of Etaça, concedes to him the front place in his chariot.[4] It would probably be idle to see in this more than a mythological fancy, but the nature of Etaça is quite certain.

In these cases, and in those which have been noted above, there is no trace of direct worship of the horse as such, whether as an individual of special qualities or as a species. Nor is any such worship of the bull to be found : as the sun and Agni are represented in the ritual by horse fetishes, so also in the ritual Indra and Rudra are represented rarely by bulls, and a bull plays an obscure part in the legend of Mudgala and his wife,[5] which has been interpreted in the most diverse ways and which is clearly without value for mythology : the bull is the theriomorphic form of Indra, Dyaus, and more rarely of other gods. The cow is often the theriomorphic form of the rain cloud or the beams of dawn : hence the many-coloured cows which yield all desires in heaven mentioned in the Atharvaveda,[6] and the post-Vedic Kāmaduh, a wish-milking cow who dwells in the heaven of Indra. Iḍā and Aditi are also addressed as cows, and the gods are born of cows. But the actual worship of the cow as such is not found in the Rigveda : the most that can be said is that perhaps from her connexion with the Iḍā and Aditi the cow was becoming invested with sacred character : the term *aghnyā*, which is addressed to her, or used of her, sixteen times, denotes that she should not be killed, an idea which was not, however, the early idea. One great Vedic hero, Atithigva, has his name from his hospitable habit of slaying oxen or cows for guests ; the tradition that beef was the proper food for guests prevailed throughout the Vedic age, and the eating of meat was never a general taboo, seeing that the great Vedic ritual authority Yājñavalkya was credited with the dictum that he ate meat if it was in a certain condition, variously interpreted as coming

1 viii. 22. 7.

2 Foy, KZ. xxxiv. 366, 367.

3 Bergaigne, *Rel. Véd.* ii. 51, 52. For a possible Daurgaha, cf. Hillebrandt, GGA. 1903, pp. 243 f.

4 Bergaigne, *Rel. Véd.* ii. 330–3 ; Oldenberg, *Rel. des Veda*², p. 155 ; Geldner, *Ved. Stud.* ii. 161 f. Hillebrandt (*Ved. Myth.* iii. 278–84) takes the myth as Indra aiding the charioteer (= Aruṇa) of the sun at the critical moment of the winter solstice : this is fanciful.

5 RV. x. 102 ; cf. Bloomfield, ZDMG. xlviii. 541 ff. ; Keith, JRAS. 1911, p. 1005.

6 AV. iv. 34. 8. Cf. the Çabalī offering of the domestic ritual ; PB. xxi. 1. 5 ; Hopkins, *Trans. Conn. Acad.* xv. 27, n. 2 ; Güntert, *Weltkönig*, p. 368.

from the shoulder, or firm.[1] The opposite doctrine of Ahiṅsā which forbade the taking of life, even animal, is however reflected in many passages such as the declaration that he who eats beef is born again in earth as a man of evil fame,[2] and the warnings of retribution in the next world which are offered to eaters of meat [3] in this. Moreover, in the Atharvaveda [4] we find the express assertion of the sacred character of the cow, which points to that animal having become in itself an object of worship.

The goat is the animal which draws the car of Pūṣan, and it may be that in some cases Pūṣan was conceived in goat shape : it is also the name of the 'one-footed goat', Aja Ekapād, which seems to be the lightning : here and there it is conceived as Agni. The ass draws the car of the Açvins. The boar is the theriomorphic form of the Maruts, Rudra, and Vṛtra : in the Brāhmaṇas it also occurs as the form assumed by Prajāpati when he raises the earth from the waters,[5] which is the beginning of the boar incarnation of Viṣṇu of the post-Vedic literature. The dog occurs in the two brindled dogs, Çabala, reminiscent of Kerberos, and Çyāma of Yama, the god of the dead, who are called Sārameya, a name denoting descent from Saramā.[6] This indicates, though it does not conclusively prove, that Saramā, who figures as the messenger of Indra in the myth of the Paṇis, was treated as a dog, and this tradition, which is not expressly set out in the Rigveda, is the account of the later texts and of Yāska, who calls her the bitch of the gods. In all these cases there is clearly either theriomorphism, or the natural association of animals with the gods on the model of the relation of man and the animals. This last fact explains in all probability the figure of the male ape Vṛṣākapi who causes trouble between Indra and Indrāṇī : [7] the effort to find some deity behind the ape is of doubtful validity, though it has naturally been thought possible to connect him with the monkey god Hanumant, who has been explained plausibly as a god of the monsoon, rather than as a case of direct zoolatry.

The case of the tortoise is by no means so simple as that of most of the animals. In the piling of the fire altar in the ritual a tortoise is built into the altar, where it is left as lord of the waters to continue its existence ; [8] it is possible that here we have a trace of the reverence paid to the beast for itself, though it may be merely so treated as representing the waters. In the Çatapatha Brāhmaṇa,[9] however, the tortoise is treated as the form assumed by Prajāpati for creating all creatures, and this view is embodied by the later mythology in the tortoise incarnation of Viṣṇu. The tortoise as Kaçyapa

[1] Macdonell and Keith, *Vedic Index*, ii. 145–7.

[2] ÇB. iii. 1. 2. 21.

[3] KB. xii. 3.

[4] xii. 4, 5. Cf. RV. viii. 101. 15, 16.

[5] Macdonell, JRAS. xxvii. 178–89.

[6] RV. x. 14. 11 ; Yāska, Nir. xi. 25. Bloomfield (JAOS. xv. 163–72) makes them sun and moon. Carnoy (*Les Indo-Européens*, pp. 194, 226) treats them as kindly guardians of the dead ; Arbman (*Rudra*, p. 260) as destroyers of the dead.

[7] RV. x. 86. Hillebrandt (*Ved. Myth.* iii. 278, n. 2) sees in him a constellation marking the beginning of the pressing of the Soma each year; Güntert (*Weltkönig*, p. 310), a vegetation spirit.

[8] Weber, *Ind. Stud.* xiii. 250.

[9] vii. 4. 3. 5 ; 5. 1. 1.

appears also beside Prajāpati in the Atharvaveda,[1] and in the Aitareya Brāhmaṇa [2] it is said that Viçvakarman promised the earth to Kaçyapa. In these cases there is merely theriomorphism. Theriomorphism is also found in the case of demons, who are not seldom called *mṛga*, 'wild beast', and specific enemies are called Aurṇavābha, 'spider brood', and Uraṇa, 'ram'. By far the most frequent case, however, is that of Vṛtra, who is called the serpent repeatedly: we find also Ahi, 'serpent', not merely identified with Vṛtra, but occasionally alone, when he is described exactly as Vṛtra is described, as encompassing or swallowing the waters, and defeated by Indra. From this conception arises that of several Ahis of whom he is the chief.[3] The term is also applied to Agni, and one god, Ahi Budhnya, has no other name.

Among the birds also theriomorphism is the normal explanation of their mention. The sun is essentially a bird, and is twice in the Rigveda [4] called Garutmant, whence arises the sun bird Garuḍa of the latest Vedic period. The eagle is connected with Indra, and Indra seems, like Verethraghna in the Avesta and Odin in Germanic mythology, to have assumed an eagle shape: Agni is also an eagle, and Soma is often called a bird.

There are, however, some traces of real reverence of animals, more certain than that of the tortoise, and more direct in origin than that of the cow whose divinity is really on the growth in the Vedic period. Thus in the case of birds the Rigveda [5] twice invokes a bird of omen to give auspicious signs: it relegates, however, the owl and the pigeon to the rank of the messengers of Yama, but it is reasonable in this case to suggest more direct reverence of a sort at an early period. It must, however, be admitted that this cannot be proved: even in the later literature [6] the owl is styled the messenger of the evil spirits, and the beast of prey, covered with blood, and the vulture, which preys on the dead, are called the messengers of Yama, or of Yama and Bhava. A bird king is Tārkṣya Vaipaçyata according to the Çatapatha Brāhmaṇa.[7]

Direct worship is clear in the homage paid to the snakes at the beginning and the end of the rains when they are specially dangerous.[8] Of this there is no trace whatever in the Rigveda: the only deity, as opposed to demon, is Ahi Budhnya and that his snake character was real, and not mere theriomorphism, is not suggested by anything we know of that deity. The demon Vṛtra was not a snake, but a natural phenomenon in origin, and the Rigveda does not propitiate him. But in the later Saṁhitās we do find the apotropaeic worship of the snakes set on a level with that of such beings as the Gandharvas. They are stated to be in earth, air, and heaven, and in one hymn of the Atharvaveda,[9] which knows snake deities well, some individual snakes may

[1] xix. 53. 10.
[2] viii. 21. 10.
[3] RV. ix. 88. 4; x. 139. 6; cf. i. 32. 14.
[4] Hopkins, *Rel. of India*, p. 45. For parallels cf. von Schroeder, *Arische Religion*, ii. 77.
[5] ii. 42, 43.
[6] HGS. i. 16. 19 ff.; Kauç. 129; TA. iv. 28.
[7] xiii. 4. 3. 9.
[8] Winternitz, *Der Sarpabali* (Vienna, 1888). Cf. Arbman, *Rudra*, pp. 77 ff.; Hopkins, *Trans. Conn. Acad.* xv. 30, n. 1.
[9] xi. 9; Bloomfield, SBE. xlii. 631–4. Such worship in Greece is often only theriomorphic; Farnell, *Greece and*

be referred to. In the Sūtras offerings are prescribed for the snakes of the three regions,[1] they are washed, combed, presented with collyrium, ointment and garlands, and duly fed ;[2] they receive offerings along with gods, plants, and demons, and blood is poured out for them,[3] a fact which brings them into conjunction with Rudra. It is only reasonable to recognize in this direct worship of the terrible snake, which is thus propitiated and honoured in the hope that it will stay away from the houses of those who show it respect. The feeling is common in modern India, and is a good case of a propitiation due to terror and awe rather than to loving admiration. It is possible that the mention of snakes of the air and the sky may have been aided by the conception of the snake Vṛtra, but it may be due merely to the formalism of the ritual, and the constant tendency to spread every power over the three parts of the universe. Several names of great snakes are known to us, e. g. Takṣaka, and Arbuda Kādraveya is at once a snake-priest and a snake-king.

While the snakes are the most lasting and prominent instance of a worship intended in the main to avert danger, it is of course possible that the common ideas that the earth spirit takes the form of a snake, and that the soul of an ancestor lives on in a snake which is about the house, had something to do with the sacred character and kindly treatment of the snakes. There are other instances of a temporary propitiation of animals, which might else be harmful : thus the Kauçika Sūtra [4] tells of the making of offerings to ants, the white in the east, the black in the south, and so on : the ants [5] are regarded, as we have seen, as important beasts in that they can find water everywhere, and in the myth they play the part of the means of depriving Viṣṇu as the sacrifice of his head. If there are worms in a cow, an offering is made to worms,[6] and similarly an offering may in a case of need be made to the king of the moles.[7] These acts indeed are not precisely of the greatest importance : they merely amount to the recognition of the power of the animals to injure, and the desirability of making them a present to appease their will to work injury : the precise parallel is the practice in Greece [8] of offering something to the flies to deter them from infesting the sacrifice. The case of the frogs, who seem in one hymn of the Rigveda [9] to be treated as having power to send prosperity through the rain which marks their awakening from their slumber in the mud, is obscure. The frog often serves in the ritual as a representative of the cooling water, and therefore this case might be reduced to theriomorphism, but that is less likely.

Babylon, pp. 78, 79. See also PB. iv. 9. 6 ; xxv. 15. 1 ff. ; ÇB. ii. 5. 2. 47 ; iv. 6. 9. 17 ; xiii. 4. 3. 9 ; AB. vi. 1.

1 AGS. ii. 1. 9 ; PGS. ii. 14. 9 ; BhGS. ii. 1.

2 AGS. iii. 4. 1 ; ÇGS. iv. 9. 3 ; 15. 4.

3 AGS. iv. 8. 27.

4 116 ; Weber, *Omina und Portenta*, p. 382.

5 Hillebrandt, *Ved. Myth.* iii. 277, 337.

6 TA. iv. 36.

7 GGS. iv. 4. 31. The mole is itself offered to earth, VS. xxiv. 26 ; it is Rudra's beast, ApÇS. viii. 17. 1 ; Hillebrandt, *Ved. Myth.* ii. 187, n. 1, 200, n. 1.

8 Farnell, *Greece and Babylon*, p. 78.

9 RV. vii. 103 ; Bloomfield, JAOS. xvi. 173–9 ; Oldenberg, *Rel. des Veda*², p. 68. *Contra*, Max Müller, *Sansk. Lit.* pp. 494, 495 ; Deussen, *Gesch. der Phil.* I. i. 101, 102.

It should be added that in the list of sacrifices given in the Yajurveda [1] we find some animal offerings to such entities as the bull-king and the tiger-king : these would be worth consideration onlyif it were possible to take seriously all the lists of offerings prescribed in these cases : considerations of common sense enable us to relegate many of them to the realms of priestly fancy.

§ 8. *Totemism*

The nature and meaning of totemism are so uncertain and ill defined that it would be necessary to examine the concept in detail, if it were not for the fact that, on any theory of totemism which does not reduce it to the worship of animals, there is no support for the view that that phenomenon is to be found in Vedic religion. The essential feature of a totemist community as conceived by S. Reinach,[2] who is now its most consistent supporter, assumes that the men and women of that community conceive themselves severally to be related to some animal or plant or other thing,[3] and that they normally treat that plant or animal with great care and respect, only on special occasions in the case of an animal or plant destroying it in the course of a formal meal, in which they enter into communion among themselves and with the god, through devouring the representative of the god : the species and not the mere animal being sacred, as soon as one animal is killed, another takes its place. To this conception of totemism the most value is attributed by Reinach because of his view that the domestication of animals and plants came about through this belief, which he traces to a hypertrophy of the same social instinct which allowed of the growth of human society by forbidding killing within the family and the clan. He does not regard it as primitive in totemism that the members of the totem group should regard the totem as an ancestor : this is in his view the sort of wrong explanation which is inevitably given by savages when asked to explain uses of which they do not know the real origin.

This theory of totemism in itself is open to the gravest doubts,[4] but it is unnecessary to discuss it or the alternative views that totemism is derived from ancestor worship and metempsychosis,[5] or is economic *au fond*,[6] or

[1] TS. v. 5. 11.

[2] *Cultes, Mythes et Religions*, i. 9–29 ; 41 ff. ; ii. 112, 113 ; iv. p. iii (review of E. Durkheim, *Les formes élémentaires de la vie religieuse*, Paris, 1912). The suggestion of Frazer (*Golden Bough*³, iv. 104 ff.) that the form of Vṛtra may conceal totemism as well as a nature myth may be passed over without comment. Cf. his *Totemism*, iv. 13 ; Warde Fowler, *Religious Experience of the Roman People*, pp. 25–7 ; A. van Gennep, *L'état actuel du problème totémique* ; Hopkins, JAOS. xxxviii. 154–69. For Germany cf. R. M. Meyer, *Altgerm. Rel.*, p. 486 ; Helm, *Altgerm. Rel.* i. 157–63 ; for the Celts, S. Czarnowski, *Le culte des héros et ses conditions sociales* (1919), pp. 331 ff.

[3] Van Gennep (*op. cit.*, p. 343) accepts this fact as vital, but not the rest.

[4] Cf. Keith, JRAS. 1916, pp. 542 ff.

[5] Wundt, *Elemente der Völkerpsychologie*, pp. 173 ff. Cf. Wilken, *De verspreide Geschriften*, iii. 85 ff. ; iv. 109 ff. ; E. B. Tylor, JAI. xxviii. 138 ff.

[6] Hopkins, *loc. cit.* Cf. Frazer's second theory and that of Haddon. Van Gennep (*op. cit.*, pp. 339 ff.) argues for a classificatory theory, ' parentiste et territorialiste.'

originates from the desire of the savage, at the time of puberty in connexion with the new birth which he then undergoes, to provide himself with a safe resting place [1] for the external soul, or from his ignorance of the true nature of conception, which is Sir J. Frazer's latest opinion on this subject. In the Vedic religion there is not a single case in which we can trace any totem clan which eats sacramentally the totem animal or plant, and, therefore, the most essential feature of totemism on Reinach's theory does not even begin to appear in the Veda. The only point on which there is anything to be gleaned from the Vedic literature is the question of descent from animals, or plants. The evidence is the following: the Rigveda [2] mentions among the tribes the names of the Matsyas, 'fishes', Ajas, 'goats', Çigrus, 'horse radishes', and the names of Vedic families include Gotamas, which includes the base *go*, 'cow', Vatsas, 'calves', Çunakas, 'dogs', Kauçikas, 'owls', and Māṇḍūkeyas, 'descendants of Maṇḍūka (frog)'. The family of Kaçyapas bear the name tortoise, which as we have seen is occasionally a name of Prajāpati, or even an independent semi-divine animal. In a passage of the Çatapatha Brāhmaṇa [3] where Prajāpati appears as a tortoise, the remark is made that people say that all beings are the children of the tortoise. The last statement is so obviously due to the fact that Prajāpati is the father of all beings, and that if he is also a tortoise, the tortoise is obviously the father of all beings too, that it cannot be considered seriously at all. Of the other cases, it is sufficient to remark that in not a single one of them have we even the hint of a tradition that the families claimed their origin from the animals mentioned: it is most probable that some of them may be nicknames given by their too candid friends, other again for causes which we cannot know, such as the prevalence of the thing mentioned (e.g. fish or horse radishes in the land) and so on.[4]

Oldenberg [5] adduces some later evidence which is in itself irrelevant for the Vedic age, since he admits that in the case of the best instance of all, the rinces of Chota Nagpur who claim descent from a snake, the belief is probably aboriginal. But what is adduced from the epic is of no value: the name Ikṣvāku, which is known in the Veda, of the line of princes is in sense sugar cane; Ṛkṣa, father of Saṁvaraṇa, a name found in the Rigveda,[6] means bear, and Sagara's wife brought forth a cucumber in which were 60,000 sons. The value of such evidence is obviously minimal.[7] Moreover, it must be remembered that such legends need have nothing whatever to do with totemism at all, but may simply belong to the very old idea which draws no

[1] Frazer, *Totemism and Exogamy*, iv. 52 ff.; *Belief in Immortality*, i. 95.

[2] vii. 18. 6, 19.

[3] vii. 5. 1. 5. As a seer Kaçyapa is found in RV. ix. 114. 2; cf. AB. vii. 27.

[4] Hopkins, JAOS. 1894, p. cliv. The fish people of King Matsya Sāmmada in ÇB. xiii. 4. 3. 12, are of course merely fictitious as the context shows.

[5] *Rel. des Veda*², pp. 82 ff. (modified from ed. 1 in view of Keith, JRAS. 1907, pp. 929 ff.; *Taittirīya Saṁhitā*, p. cxxi).

[6] v. 53. 10.

[7] The same remark applies to Hopkins' suggestions (*Epic Myth.*, p. 24) that the Pañcālas may mean 'five snake clans (*āla*, cf. eel)' and the Kurus and Krivis are Nāga names.

persistent or accurate distinction between men on the one hand, and animals on the other. Of such ideas there are remains not merely in the theriomorphism of the gods, which is undeniable and clear, but also in such fictions as that of the genus man-tiger which is found from the Yajurveda [1] onwards, and which in post-epic religion has its classical example in the man-lion incarnation of Viṣṇu, but also in the Nāgas, who are first so called in the Sūtras,[2] and who according to the later tradition were human beings in appearance but really serpents. This view is widely spread in later India and results in the solemn question being put to initiates into the Buddhist community whether they were men or Nāgas, the latter kind of being being excluded from the privilege of becoming a member of the Saṅgha.

Oldenberg [3] has suggested that the existence of taboos in some cases may be due to totemism, and has instanced the wearing of an antelope skin by the Brahman pupil as sign of possibly the wearing of the skin of the divine animal. It is proper to note these cases, but in none recorded in the Vedic ritual is there any trace of the conditions necessary to lend even a possibility of totemism, namely the existence of the totem community which observes the taboo, or the connexion of the animals whose skin is worn with the wearer. That the skin may have been worn in certain cases for magic purposes is perfectly possible without any element of totemism being visible or existing.

Nor again is it possible to lay any stress on the argument that the occasional offering of food to animals in place of the sacrifice of animals points to totemism : the best known instances are the offerings made at the spit-ox ceremony to a bull, a cow, and a calf in place of Rudra, his consort, and Jayanta respectively instead of slaughtering an ox, and the similar rite at the Aṣṭakās.[4] With these usages may be compared the legends, which seem to show that in the worship of the wolf-god Apollo at Sikyon an offering was made to wolves, regarded as in some degree the temporary incarnations of the god.[5] But not much stress can be laid on the Indian cases, as they are recorded merely in Sūtras, which show the influence of the desire to avoid animal offerings, partly no doubt for economy, partly perhaps on humanitarian grounds.[6]

§ 9. *The Lesser Nature Goddesses*

Not one of the goddesses of the Rigveda, with the doubtful exception of the Dawn, can be said to be of any real importance. Sarasvatī and Pṛthivī have already been mentioned : in the Sūtras Bhūmi also appears, but with little character of any kind, doubtless as a direct expression for the earth

[1] VS. xxx. 8 ; ÇB. xiii. 2. 4. 2. Such ideas are common in Babylonian religion. Cf. werwolves, Carnoy, *Les Indo-Européens*, p. 226. These have been seen in the Sālāvṛkas of RV. x. 95. 15 ; Brunnhofer, *Arische Urzeit*, p. 284.

[2] AGS. iii. 4. 1 ; Hopkins, *Epic Myth.*, pp. 23 ff.

[3] *Rel. des Veda*², p. 83.

[4] Below, Part III, Chap. 21, § 2.

[5] Farnell, *Cults of the Greek States*, iv. 115.

[6] Cf. Keith, JRAS. 1907, pp. 933, 934. The cases may be instances of a vegetation spirit in animal form, but the evidence is wholly inadequate for any theory to be established.

goddess. The Rigveda [1] also celebrates Rātri, 'night', as the sister of the Dawn, and the daughter of heaven. But night is here conceived as the bright starlit night, which fills the valleys and the hills and drives away the darkness, keeping away the wolf and the thief. Night is also a few times invoked together with the dawn as joint goddesses, and their importance such as it is seems derived from her connexion with that goddess.

Another goddess who is clearly connected with nature is Pṛçni, the mother of the Maruts, who is doubtless the storm cloud: [2] the word is properly an adjective 'speckled', used of the bull, or the cow, and in the plural of the cows, which milk Soma for Indra. More interesting is the figure of Saraṇyū [3] who occurs in a curious legend in the Rigveda, in which it is narrated that Tvaṣṭṛ made a wedding for his daughter, that at the news all the world came together, that during the wedding Saraṇyū disappeared, but not it seems until she had been married to Vivasvant, that the gods hid the immortal from mortals, and making one of like form they gave her to Vivasvant: it is added that Saraṇyū bore the two Açvins when this happened and left two pairs behind her. Yāska tells us that she first bore the pair Yama and Yamī, and then changed her form to that of a mare and ran away: Vivasvant in the form of a horse pursued, and then were born the Açvins, while on the female of like form was born Manu Sāvarṇi. The tale is a strange one, and may be compared with the legend of the Tilphossian Erinys,[4] who bore in horse form the steed Areion; the two myths probably belong to the same order of ideas, but it is difficult to say what the origin of the conception should be taken to have been. The horse form of Saraṇyū does not occur in the Rigveda: it can only be inferred and we do not know from what source Yāska obtained the details of the legend: it may have been an old tradition or merely a speculation: moreover the idea may have been caused by nothing more than the conception of the Açvins who may have been thought to have been in horse form, and not merely lords of horses, in which case the comparison with the Erinys must probably be given up. On the other hand, especially if the comparison is held to be valid, the figure of Saraṇyū may be brought into connexion with the Dawn, or the sun-maiden, whose swift nature her name would then be a good expression, since it is essentially derived from the root, *sṛ*, 'run'. The verbal correspondence with Erinys cannot however be accepted as proved, as it is clearly contrary to the phonology. Such a view, which is defended by Bloomfield, is more plausible than the suggestion which connects Saraṇyū with the storm, and which, accepting the identity with Erinys, seeks to trace the character of the Erinyes to this conception. S. Reinach [5] again has traced

[1] RV. x. 127.

[2] Roth, *Nir.*, p. 145.

[3] x. 17. 2; Bloomfield, JAOS. xv. 172–88; Hillebrandt, *Ved. Myth.* i. 503 (Yama's mother = night, Saraṇyū = dawn).

[4] Lang, *Modern Mythology*, pp. 65 ff. Feist (*Kultur der Indogermanen*, p. 343, n. 1) suggests connexion between Saraṇyū and Erinys as loan words from another tongue. The conjecture is possible that the term Erinys did not originally belong to the horse goddess at all, but that she bore a name really corresponding to Saraṇyū, but later confused with Erinys.

[5] *Cultes, Mythes et Religions*, iv. 54–68.

in Europe an old horse goddess (originally totemistic), found in Arcadia, in the legend of Cloelia, and as Epona in Gaul.

There is another group of goddesses of whom it can safely be said that in the later Saṁhitās they are the deities of natural objects, though the Rigveda leaves their character wholly uncertain and unexplained. These are Rākā, who twice appears in the Rigveda [1] as a rich and bountiful goddess, with which her name, probably containing the root *rā*, 'give', accords; and Sinīvālī, described as a sister of the gods, with broad hips, fair arms and fingers, who is begged to give children. She is invoked with Rākā, Sarasvatī, and with Guñgū, who only occurs in this place.[2] These later Saṁhitās, however, have a scheme under which Rākā is the full moon day, Anumati the day before full moon, Kuhū new moon, and Sinīvālī the day before new moon. Sinīvālī is also said by the Atharvaveda [3] to be the wife of Viṣṇu. While it is true that the explanations are not given in the Rigveda and that, in the case of Anumati, the position given seems to be secondary, it is difficult to be certain as to the others, with whom may be connected the otherwise unknown Guñgū.[4]

Possibly another deity who plays some part in the development of Vedic thought may be traced to a natural origin, namely Vāc, 'speech'. In the Rigveda [5] she has a hymn in which she describes herself as accompanying all the gods, and supporting Mitra and Varuṇa, Indra and Agni, and the Açvins, and as bending the bow of Rudra against the unbeliever: she claims to have a place in the waters, in the sea, and to encompass all beings, while in another hymn she is styled the queen of the gods. In the Brāhmaṇas [6] she is specially famed in the legend of the purchase of the Soma from the Gandharvas by means of a woman, Vāc taking that form to tempt the Gandharvas, as lovers of the sex, to surrender the Soma which they guard: she agrees,[7] however, with the gods, before the transaction takes place, to return to them and does so when called upon. The goddess seems to have too much life and reality in the Rigveda to be a mere abstraction, and it is important perhaps that in the Naighaṇṭuka [8] she is ranked among the gods of the atmosphere. Therefore it is possible that thunder, which in the Nirukta appears as the Vāc of the middle region, may be the starting-point of the goddess who naturally develops in connexion with human speech.

It is also possible that in Umā, who appears at the very end of the Vedic period proper [9] as the wife of Rudra, we have a goddess of the mountain, as she

See also Farnell, *Cults of the Greek States*, iii. 50 ff. Cf. E. Monseur, RHR. li. 16 f.

1 ii. 32. 7; v. 42. 12.

2 ii. 32; x. 184.

3 viii. 46. 3; ZDMG. ix. p. lviii.

4 Cf. Weber, *Ind. Stud.* v. 228 ff.; Hopkins, *Epic Myth.*, p. 70.

5 x. 125; cf. x. 71.

6 TS. vi. 1. 6. 5; MS. iii. 7. 3; ÇB. iii. 2. 4. 3–6.

7 AB. 27. She also figures in the strife of Ādityas and Añgirases, assuming the shape of a mare or lioness, JB. iii. 187 f.; AB. vi. 34 f., &c.

8 v. 5; Nir. xi. 27. From a very different root has sprung the Babylonian doctrine of the word; Farnell, *Greece and Babylon*, pp. 176–9. Cf. below, Chap. 29.

9 Kena Up. iii. 12. Cf. Oppert, *Orig. Inhab. of India*, p. 421 (Umā = Ammā); Hopkins, *Epic Myth.*, pp. 224 ff.

is given the epithet Haimavatī, and is recognized in the later mythology as the daughter of the mountain Himavant. On the other hand it must be remembered that, as Rudra is essentially a god of the mountains in the Vedic texts, it was only natural that his wife should be made out to be from the mountains, and that, therefore, we may have to do here simply with the same principle of setting a female beside the god which gives us Indrāṇī, and the other wives of the gods, though it is tempting to see in Umā a form of the mother goddess of the Dravidians.

A goddess who owes her nature to the actual sacrificial food is Iḍā,[1] the offering of milk and butter which occurs several times in the Rigveda, and more often later. Like Aditi and more naturally, she is brought into connexion with the cow, and a cow is used in the ritual to represent her and Aditi, and addressed with her name. She bears the names butter-handed and butter-footed, which express clearly her nature, and she normally appears with the goddesses Sarasvatī and Bhāratī. Agni is said to be her son, because of his birth from the place of the Iḍā, and a mortal man Purūravas is called Aiḷa,[2] which seems to denote him as an offshoot from Iḍā. She is also connected in the Rigveda with Urvaçī,[3] with Dadhikrāvan, and with the Açvins. She figures in the legend of Manu, who after the flood through her generated the human race, Iḍā being called his daughter.[4] She is styled also the daughter of Mitra and Varuṇa.[5] Bhāratī, who occurs with Iḍā, is clearly the offering (*hotrā*) of the Bharatas, a fact which accords with the importance of the Bharatas in cult.[6] Iḍā, Sarasvatī, and Bhāratī are called in the Yajurveda the wives of Indra,[7] and in the Rigveda a goddess Bṛhaddivā, ‘of the broad sky’, is mentioned with Iḍā, Sarasvatī, and Rākā, but of her nature nothing more is known.[8]

§ 10. *Constellations and Time Periods*

There is a certain curious paucity of evidence of worship of constellations other than the sun and the moon, especially in its connexion with Soma,[9] and the planets seem to have attracted little notice. Whether we believe or not that they were known to the Vedic Indians, at any rate it is obvious that they received no direct worship in the period of the Rigveda, and it is not until the close of the Vedic ritual that we have enumerations of them such as that of the Baudhāyana Dharma Sūtra,[10] which gives in a late passage sun, moon, Aṅgāraka, Budha, Bṛhaspati, Çukra, Çanaiçcara, Rāhu and Ketu. Planetary

[1] RV. vii. 16. 8; x. 70. 8 and often in the Āprī hymns.
[2] RV. x. 95. 18; see Keith, JRAS. 1913, pp. 412–17.
[3] RV. v. 41. 19.
[4] ÇB. i. 8. 1. 8; xi. 5. 3. 5.
[5] ÇB. i. 8. 1. 27; xiv. 9. 4. 27; AÇS. i. 7. 7.
[6] Hillebrandt, *Ved. Myth.* iii. 377, n. 6.
[7] VS. xxviii. 8.
[8] ii. 31. 4; v. 41. 19; 42. 1; x. 64. 10.
[9] See above, Chap. 8, §§ 2–5, 8; Chap. 9, § 3.
[10] ii. 5. 9. 9. A Kāṭhaka frag. (Caland, *Brāhmaṇa- en Sūtra-Aanwinsten*, pp. 8, 29) has sun, Çukra, Bṛhaspati, Budha, Arka, Saura, Rāhu, and Ketu.

influences, signified in the term Grahas, ' seizers ', applied to the planets, seem not to have troubled the imagination of the early Indians.[1]

The Nakṣatras figure early in the myths of Soma and his marriage with them which is recorded in the later Saṁhitās and Brāhmaṇas, and in the ritual they receive occasional offerings, but appear to be of little religious consequence.[2] The same consideration applies to the seasons, months and half months, the days and nights, and the year,[3] or even the night of new moon, that is when the moon is invisible, or the night of full moon, or the period when the moon first appears (*amāvāsyā, paurṇamāsī, darça*), though the latter three entities are honoured by Atharvan hymns.[4] More personality is accorded to the moon phases, Anumati, Sinīvālī, Rākā, and Kuhū, which have already been denoted,[5] and still more to Ekāṣṭakā, a lunar day near the beginning of the year, which is celebrated as being the daughter of Prajāpati, and the mother of Indra.[6] Such importance, however, as this or any other of the Aṣṭakās,[7] lunar days in the middle of the fortnight of declining moonlight, may possess, is doubtless really due to connexion with the offerings then made to the Fathers, whose connexion with the moon was doubtless strongly felt, since it is accepted as a dogma in the Upaniṣads.

In the domestic ritual we find the pole star,[8] Dhruva, accorded a measure of respect, and similar honour is paid to the Seven Seers,[9] that is the Great Bear, and Arundhatī. The Seven Seers already receive in the Rigveda the credit of having in a time of trouble secured for Purukutsa's wife a son, Trasadasyu, but in their case we have unquestionably to do with the conception of the souls of the dead entering into the stars. They are said to have settled in heaven to practice asceticism, and with the five Adhvaryus to guard the hidden footprint of the bird, and their relation with the seven Hotṛs on earth is obvious, whether it be that of prototypes or derivatives. The suggestion [10] that the five Adhvaryus denote the planets, because of the similarity of their movements to and fro may be deemed most implausible. Mysterious are the five Bulls who stand in the middle of the sky;[11] it is certain

[1] Possibly they are meant in HGS. i. 3. 10. 4, where Çāka may be connected with the mysterious Çakadhūma of the Atharvaveda (vi. 128; SBE. xlii. 160, 532 ff.).

[2] See above, Chap. 10, § 3. For the domestic ritual, see ÇGS. i. 25. 5 f.; ii. 14. 8; PGS. iii. 2. 3; GGS. ii. 8. 12. Images of the Nakṣatras are alleged to be referred to in ÇGS. iv. 18. 5, but dubiously. Cf. AV. xix. 7, 8, and Nakṣatrakalpa.

[3] Offerings for the lunar day (*tithi*) of birth, ÇGS. i. 25. 5 f.; GGS. ii. 8. 12.

[4] AV. vii. 79–81. [5] AV. vii. 20, 46, 48, 47.

[6] AV. iii. 10; Weber, IS. xvii. 218 ff.; TS. iv. 3. 11; HGS. ii. 5. 14. 1 ff. Cf. Āgrahāyaṇī, as new year day, PGS. iii. 2; HGS. ii. 7. 17. 1 ff.

[7] Cf. ÇGS. iii. 12 ff.; AGS. ii. 4; GGS. iii. 10; PGS. iii. 3.

[8] HGS. i. 7. 22. 14 f.; cf. AGS. i. 7. 22; BLGS. i. 19.

[9] Seven Ṛkṣas ' bears ', RV. i. 24. 10; identified with Seven Ṛṣis, ÇB. ii. 1. 2. 4. For the Seers, ÇB. xiii. 8. 1. 9; JUB. iv. 26. 12 (middle of the sky); RV. iv. 42. 8; x. 109. 4; iii. 7. 7 (seven Vipras); vi. 22. 2; x. 35. 10 (Hotṛs); TA. i. 11. 2; HGS. i. 7. 22. 14; BhGS. i. 19. Cf. A. C. Das, *Rig-Vedic India*, i. 375 ff.

[10] Hillebrandt, *Ved. Myth.* iii. 423.

[11] RV. i. 105. 10. The constellation Çarkara, Dolphin (*çiṅçumāra*), appears in JB. iii. 194; cf. TA. ii. 19. 3. For the

from the terminology that they are not the planets, and we may best suppose that they are the stars of some asterism, seen there by the Indian mind.

Hillebrandt [1] suggests that the pole star is to be found not merely in the Dhruva of the domestic ritual, but in the Aghnya to whose head the Açvins are said to fasten one wheel of their chariot, while the other encircles the heaven, comparing the view of later times that the sun, moon, and stars are fastened to the pole star. An alternative view makes the inviolable one the sun, and it is clear that to assume the pole star in the absence of any other hint of its existence in the Rigveda is unwise. He treats Etaça,[2] who is usually regarded merely as the steed of the sun, as the morning and evening star, comparing him to the later Aruṇa, who does not certainly appear in the Vedic literature. Other efforts have been made to discover the Pleiades [3] and the Milky Way [4] as well as other stars in various mythological figures, but without marked plausibility.

constellations in AB. iii. 33, see above, Chap. 9, § 10.

[1] *Ved. Myth.* iii. 384; RV. i. 30. 19.

[2] *Ved. Myth.* (Kl. Ausg.), p. 183; contrast p. 98; *Ved. Myth.* iii. 281–4. It has been suggested that Aruṇa, not Varuṇa, is mentioned among the Mitanni gods, but implausibly.

[3] The Maruts, Hillebrandt, *Ved. Myth.* iii. 321, n. 1.

[4] Sarasvatī as the Milky Way, Hillebrandt, *Ved. Myth.* i. 382 f., but see iii. 377 f.

CHAPTER 12

ABSTRACT DEITIES AND SONDERGÖTTER

§ 1. *The Nature of Abstract Deities*

It is unfortunate that no term has yet been found which can be used to describe the gods, who do not rest on the basis of some natural phenomenon or some activity which is taking place in external nature, without conveying the false impression which is created by the adoption of the current term 'abstract'.[1] The idea of the deification of an abstraction inevitably suggest that the god was the production of priestly speculation; that he, therefore, could never be a really popular god; and that it could not be felt that the god was active and powerful to help in the same way as a god based on some phenomenon of nature. This is clearly far from being the case: whatever the origin of the gods which are called abstract, many of them attained in India to genuine and real popular belief, and were every whit as much living to the popular mind as gods for whom we can see a basis in nature.

The nature of some of the abstract gods is perfectly plain; they are human faculties made divine, such as wrath or faith. There seems no distinction of principle between the act of mind which makes these passions divine, and that which makes external things or rather activities into gods: that the latter process comes before the former is only in keeping with the development of the self-consciousness of man, which appears to be at first directed on the external world, and then to be reflected upon the internal world in the normal sense of these terms. But deification of this sort seems to have been practised into the Indo-Iranian period, and, therefore, is not a new feature of the Vedic religion.

A second class of gods who may be called abstract is afforded by the agent gods, such as Dhātṛ, whose name expresses a function which they perform, so that they can be called functional gods. In all the cases which are to be found in the Vedic literature we are able to say with a fair degree of plausibility that the conception formed itself from the use of the epithet in question in the first place of some concrete god, and then, after denoting that deity in the special field of action, it was gradually made into a separate deity concerned merely with the sphere of action in question. This, however, cannot be proved beyond doubt: it will for instance always be open to question whether Savitṛ is really an aspect of the sun, or whether he is god of stimulation who by reason

[1] Cf. Hillebrandt, *Ved. Myth.* iii. 403, 404. 'Special deities' or 'Sondergötter' expresses a different side of development; 'symbolic' also is inadequate.

of similarity of nature has been made like to the sun. In other cases there can be less doubt: the god Viṣṇu cannot really be explained as a god of wide stepping: he is a sun god, who happens to have a special sphere of activity.

A third class of deities is closely allied to the preceding as far as the Vedic religion is concerned. While the agent gods are concerned each with some special aspect of activity, these gods take upon themselves the whole of activity and are therefore creator gods, and universal gods. In the Veda all of them seem to be traceable to epithets of other gods regarded as creators and universal lords, which have been chosen to be the designation of the supreme lord, to the conception of whom the religious and philosophic impulses of the Vedic poets inclined.

As a fourth class we may reckon those deities who express a state, activity, or condition such as wealth, or destruction and misfortune, good fortune, greatness, fame, strength, or almost any other idea. It is often difficult in the extreme to decide what deities must be placed among the abstract deities as opposed to those which may be held to be concrete: the two classes flow into one another, and no absolute bases of distinction exist or can exist. Nor again in many cases can we know to what extent in personifications we have to do with real recognition of divine powers, nor what conceptions exactly attached to the personifications. It is clear that these ideas grew up in a period when the conception of evil spirits which threatened injury was well known, and this conception may have been matched with one which recognized good spirits which would afford help,[1] and these spirits could be conceived in the most varied and unsystematic forms. The enumerations of divine personages who are asked to aid in many cases seem simply devices to secure the utmost degree of protection for the suppliant: the Sūtras in particular seem often determined to invoke as many and as curiously varied deities as possible, reviving for the purpose gods [2] who would otherwise be held to be of no possible consequence, as well as providing us with deities elsewhere unknown and unheard of.[3]

§ 2. *Tvaṣṭṛ and other Agent Gods*

By far the most important of the agent gods is Tvaṣṭṛ, who is mentioned some sixty-five times in the Rigveda, most often in the late first and tenth books, but also in the family books, though rarely in the seventh of the Vasiṣṭha family, and in the eighth. Like the other gods of the Rigveda he goes to the heaven, and bestows blessings,[4] but his characteristic feature is the

[1] This phase of belief is that currently termed Animism or Polydaemonism. To trace to it the origin of all religion is unscientific: it naturally connects with other forms as in early Babylonian religion (Farnell, *Greece and Babylon*, pp. 42, 43); it is not earlier than the animatistic worship of natural powers, and it has a different psychological aspect; cf. Carnoy, *Les Indo-Européens*, p. 217. See above, pp. 71 ff.

[2] Such as Ahi Budhnya or Apāṁ Napāt.

[3] e.g. Ākāça, 'ether'; PGS. i. 12. 2; KhGS. i. 5. 31; GGS. i. 4. 9.

[4] RV. x. 10. 5; AV. vi. 78. 3.

iron axe, which he bears in his hand, and which marks him out as the skilled artificer. He forges the bolt of Indra, and the axe of Brahmaṇaspati, and especially the cup out of which the gods drink. He is, further, the power which shapes the germ in the womb for men and animals alike: he fashions husband and wife for each other from the womb, and presides over generation: so in the later Vedic texts [1] he is constantly mentioned in connexion with the making of forms, and the pairing of men and animals. These texts also ascribe to him the production of the horse.

Tvaṣṭṛ stands in special relation to the human race in that his daughter Saraṇyū, wife of Vivasvant, produced the twins, Yama and Yamī, whence came the human race. He is also father of Bṛhaspati, of Agni, and even of Indra, who, however, seems to have slain him for withholding from him the Soma. Indra also was hostile to Viçvarūpa, the three-headed son of Tvaṣṭṛ, from whom he sought to win the cows: he slew Viçvarūpa, and, when Tvaṣṭṛ in anger refused to allow him to take part in his Soma sacrifice, Indra came and drank the Soma by force.[2] As Tvaṣṭṛ is himself called more often than any other god Viçvarūpa, it is difficult not to suspect that the connexion of Tvaṣṭṛ with Viçvarūpa of the three heads is due to the similarity of name, and it is perhaps hence that there arises the hostility between Tvaṣṭṛ and Indra: the old character of the Viçvarūpa myth is vouched for by its Indo-European parallels. As son in law of Tvaṣṭṛ Vāyu once is mentioned.

In the Rigveda Tvaṣṭṛ is normally mentioned along with gods of similar character, such as Savitṛ, Dhātṛ, Prajāpati, and, less naturally, Pūṣan. With Savitṛ he is twice [3] indeed, it seems, identified in the phrase 'god Tvaṣṭṛ, the stimulator, omniform,' and the identification with Savitṛ and Prajāpati is asserted in the Kauçika Sūtra.[4] In the ritual [5] his most prominent feature is his combination with the divine ladies, who seem to be the wives of the gods, presumably because of his connexion with generation. We hear also of his daughters who cure Indra's ophthalmic sleeplessness, and evoke him from a cow in which he takes refuge from Vṛtra, thus becoming his mothers.[6]

It results also from the special position of Tvaṣṭṛ with regard to generation that, when in the Soma ritual at a certain point in the rite the wife of the sacrificer comes up to perform an act intended to be symbolic, and productive of the process of generation, she is brought up by the Neṣṭṛ, the priest who stands in the closest relations to the god.[7]

The etymological sense of Tvaṣṭṛ seems clear: it is formed from a root *tvakṣ*, which has a parallel in the Avesta, and which has the sense of fashion, like the normal *takṣ*. Oldenberg [8] considers that the god is no more than the personification of creative activity, and so far as the Rigveda goes it

[1] TB. i. 4. 7. 1; ÇB. xi. 4. 3. 3.
[2] TS. ii. 4. 12. 1; ÇB. i. 6. 3. 6.
[3] RV. iii. 55. 19; x. 10. 5.
[4] Weber, *Omina und Portenta*, pp. 391, 392.
[5] As in RV. i. 22. 9, &c.
[6] PB. xii. 5. 19 ff. For the eye motif Hopkins (*Trans. Conn. Acad.* xv. 49) compares the legend in TS. vi. 1. 1. 5; ÇB. iii. 1. 3. 13.
[7] TS. vi. 5. 8. 6; ÇB. iv. 4. 2. 18.
[8] *Rel. des Veda*², p. 237. Cf. the German Wieland, E. H. Meyer, *Germ. Myth.*, pp. 300 f.

seems difficult to deny that this theory is adequate. On the other hand Hillebrandt,[1] who, for no adequate reason, suggests that the etymology may be really from some aboriginal word, is strongly of opinion that the mythical conception is the concrete one of the sun, his son Viçvarūpa being the moon. The theory is open as regards Viçvarūpa to fatal difficulty, but there is no objection, having regard to the case of Savitṛ, to see in Tvaṣṭṛ another case of an agent god, who has come into separate existence from being at first merely an epithet of a more concrete divinity. The post-Vedic mythology indeed regards him as an Āditya, but this fact is of very little consequence. Ludwig [2] takes him to be a god of the year, but this is obviously much less likely than the suggestion of the sun as a great creative power.

Tvaṣṭṛ figures also in the myth of the Ṛbhus making his cup into four; even if the cup be the moon, as is possible, it does not shed any light either on the original nature of Tvaṣṭṛ or on his connexion with the moon.

The other agent gods are of very minor importance. Dhātṛ, the creator, is a development, only found about a dozen times, and only once outside the tenth book, of the epithet creator, applied to Indra or Viçvakarman, and often used of the priests as establishers of the sacrifice. He is the creator of the heaven, air, earth, sun and moon, is besought to grant offspring, a clear eye, and length of days, and in the post-Vedic period is a synonym of Brahman or Prajāpati as the all-god. Vidhātṛ, 'disposer', is used with Dhātṛ as an epithet of Indra and Viçvakarman once each: it in two enumerations [3] attains a slight existence. With Dhātṛ in its solitary occurrence in book vii is found Dhartṛ,[4] 'supporter', elsewhere an epithet of Indra and other gods. The god Trātṛ, 'protector', is found five times [5] with other deities, referring perhaps to Savitṛ and Bhaga: the word is usually an epithet of Indra, Agni or the Ādityas. A leader god, Netṛ, is invoked in one hymn only, and asked to lead to prosperity in life.[6] Of goddesses we have Deṣṭrī, who is invoked with Dhātṛ and Mātariçvan in the marriage hymn, and the class of protectors, Varūtrī, known from the Rigveda onwards.

§ 3. *The Creator Gods*

Two hymns [7] of the Rigveda are devoted to the honour of Viçvakarman, who is described as all-seeing, with eyes, face, arms, feet, on every side, a trait which is preserved in the post-Vedic representations of the god Brahman. But he is also said to have wings, and stress is laid on his being lord of speech, and the source of all prosperity. He is styled Dhātṛ, and Vidhātṛ, the establisher of earth and the disposer of the sky, and also the highest apparition.

[1] *Ved. Myth.* i. 517; Hardy, *Ved.-brahm. Periode*, pp. 30, 31. Hillebrandt holds that Agni (RV. i. 95. 2; x. 2. 7) as son of Tvaṣṭṛ is the moon.

[2] *Rigveda*, iii. 333–5.

[3] RV. vi. 50. 12; ix. 81. 5.

[4] vii. 35. 3.

[5] RV. i. 106. 7; iv. 45. 5, 7; viii. 18. 20; x. 128. 7.

[6] RV. v. 50.

[7] RV. x. 81, 82; 87. 2; x. 170. 4.

The name is applied as an epithet to Indra, and to the sun as all-creating, and probably it was from the latter god that it developed into a name for the creator active god : in the Brāhmaṇas [1] Viçvakarman is identic with Prajāpati, and in post-Vedic literature he sinks to the humble level of the artificer of the gods. A class of Viçvasṛj gods, all-creators, is just alluded to in the Brāhmaṇas.[2]

Prajāpati is even a slighter figure than Viçvakarman in the Rigveda, and his name as a distinct deity occurs only four times, one late hymn being given to him.[3] In that hymn, however, as it now stands, in an appended verse his supremacy is clearly asserted, and in more effective manner than in the older hymns, when they assert the greatness of one of the popular gods. He is there said to have created and established the heaven and the earth, to be the lord of all that is, the king of all that breathes and moves about, god above the gods, whose ordinances the gods and all beings obey, and who embraces all creatures. The deliberate intention to set out the nature of a creator god is expressed in the fact that the hymn is put in interrogative form, and the answer is given in the last verse. The form of the hymn is of importance as it gave rise to the most weird of the gods created by the Indian imagination in the Vedic age, the god Ka, ' Who ? ' He is in the Brāhmaṇa literature expressly identified with Prajāpati,[4] but he is also in the ritual and in the Mantras distinguished from that god, separate offerings to this abstraction from a pronoun being duly provided for.

The name, Prajāpati, means lord of offspring, and is applied once in the Rigveda [5] to Savitṛ, who is described as the Prajāpati of the world, and the supporter of heaven, and also to Soma as compared with Tvaṣṭṛ and Indra. As a distinct deity Prajāpati is naturally invoked to bestow offspring, in one case along with Viṣṇu, Tvaṣṭṛ, and Dhātṛ ; he is said to make cows prolific, and in the Atharvaveda and the other texts of the later literature his connexion with offspring is regularly referred to. But Prajāpati is essentially in the later Saṁhitās and the Brāhmaṇas regarded as the chief of the gods, and in special the father god, who produces everything, who is the father of the gods [6] on the one hand, but also of the Asuras,[7] and who is of course the first sacrificer.[8] Prajāpati is the hero of the cosmogonic myths of the whole of the Brāhmaṇa period ; he creates the worlds and the Vedas,[9] and the castes.[10] In the Sūtras he is specifically identified with Brahman,[11] the god, the masculine of the idea of Brahman, ' holy prayer,' or the ' holy power'. The predominance of

[1] ÇB. viii. 2. 1. 10 ; 3. 13 ; AB. iv. 22.
[2] PB. xxv. 18. 2 ; verse in TB. iii. 12. 9. 7.
[3] RV. x. 121 ; 85. 43 ; 169. 4 ; 184. 1. For his later history see below, Part V.
[4] TS. i. 7. 6. 6.
[5] iv. 53. 2.
[6] TB. iii. 1. 3. 4 ; ÇB. xi. 1. 6. 14.
[7] TB. ii. 2. 2. 3.
[8] ÇB. ii. 4. 4. 1 ; vi. 2. 3. 1.
[9] AB. v. 32 f. ; JB. i. 357 f. ; ÇB. xi. 5. 8 ; JUB. iii. 15. 4–17. 10 ; CU. iv. 17 ; ṢB. i. 5. 6–8. Cf. Geldner, *Ved. Stud.* ii. 139 (RV. vii. 33. 7) ; Oertel, *Trans. Conn. Acad.* xv. 155 ff.
[10] TS. vii. 1. 1. 4–6 ; PB. vi. 1. 6–13 ; JB. i. 68 f. ; Oertel, *Trans. Conn. Acad.* xv. 196 ff.
[11] AGS. iii. 4.

Prajāpati, however, is not in the slightest affected by the development of this god in the Brāhmaṇas.

Of the myths in which Prajāpati figures, the most interesting by far is that of his incest with his daughter Uṣas,[1] who changed herself into a gazelle, whereupon he assumed the form of the male animal corresponding to it. In the version of the Maitrāyaṇī Saṁhitā [2] Rudra aimed an arrow at him, but was induced to lay it aside by a promise of Prajāpati to make him the lord of beasts, if he did not shoot him. In the Aitareya Brāhmaṇa [3] the gods in anger at the incest of Prajāpati make from the most terrible substances the form of Rudra, who shoots Prajāpati in the form of a deer, the myth being transferred to the sky, where the deer, Mṛga, the archer Mṛgavyādha, and the three-pointed arrow, Iṣu Trikāṇḍā, are pointed out. It is apparently a transfer to the god Prajāpati as creator god of a legend which seems in the Rigveda [4] to be told, though in the most obscure terms of a father, who is probably to be taken as Dyaus with his daughter, presumably meant to be the earth, for an archer is alluded to in that legend. Elsewhere Prajāpati is recorded to have given Uṣas in marriage to Bṛhaspati or Soma,[5] or to have married all his daughters, the Nakṣatras, to Soma.[6]

Prajāpati also appears in other animal forms, which is in keeping with his position as the great generator: his eye swells, and, because it did so (*açvayat*), the horse came into being; he assumes the form of a boar in order to raise the earth out of the waters, a legend which is recounted in the Taittirīya Saṁhitā [7] and which is the starting-point of the boar incarnation of Viṣṇu, and he also assumed the form of a tortoise to produce all creatures according to the Çatapatha Brāhmaṇa,[8] whence arises the view that all men are the children of the tortoise. He is also identified with the primeval Puruṣa or giant from whom by the sacrifice the gods created the whole of the world, and also men and the gods.

In the hymn [9] addressed to him Prajāpati bears the title of Hiraṇyagarbha, the golden germ, and this mention of him is itself elevated by the Atharvaveda[10] and by the later literature [11] to the rank of a supreme deity. In the Atharvaveda he appears as the embryo, which is produced in the waters on the process of creation. His position is definitely identified with that of Prajāpati in the Taittirīya Saṁhitā, and in the post-Vedic literature he becomes the expression of the nature of the personal god, Brahman, as opposed to the impersonal Brahman.

The Atharvaveda,[12] which combines theosophy with magic in the most

[1] Oldenberg, SBE. xlvi. 78 ff.

[2] iv. 2. 12.

[3] iii. 33. Cf. ÇB. i. 7. 4. 1 (Dyaus or Uṣas); PB. viii. 2. 10.

[4] i. 71. 5; x. 61. 5–7; Hillebrandt, *Ved. Myth.* ii. 52 f.

[5] JB. i. 213; AB. iv. 7; KB. xviii. 1; Oertel, *Trans. Conn. Acad.* xv. 174; Bloomfield, JAOS. xv. 181.

[6] TS. ii. 2. 5. 1; KS. xi. 3; MS. ii. 2. 7.

[7] Macdonell, JRAS. xxvii. 178 ff.

[8] vii. 5. 1. 5.

[9] RV. x. 121. 1.

[10] iv. 2. 8.

[11] TS. v. 5. 1. 2.

[12] Deussen, *Gesch. der Phil.* I. i. 209 ff., 264 ff.; Edgerton, *Studies in honor of Bloomfield*, pp. 117 ff.

curious way, is fond of inventing new expressions for the supreme deity. Thus it looks upon Kāla,[1] 'time', as the one existing thing in the universe, and again it invents Skambha,[2] 'support', as the necessary substratum on which the structure of the universe must rest, and exalts it to the position of a supreme god. Prāṇa,[3] 'the breath', is also deified and identified with Prajāpati. Another god, Rohita,[4] is doubtless really an epithet of the sun as 'ruddy', but it becomes identified by the Atharvaveda with Prajāpati : the alternative theory presented by Bloomfield [5] that it is the development of the abstraction of red as advantageous for all those suffering from jaundice is not indeed inconceivable, but it is not necessary and, therefore, should not be preferred to the more obvious explanation which presents itself.[6] Even in that text the Vrātya,[7] who is the un-brahmanical Aryan when induced to enter the Brahmanical fold by a performance of some complication, the Vrātya Stomas, is celebrated as a universal god, a fact which has erroneously been interpreted as an allusion to the worship of the god Çiva by a special section of the population. The remains of the sacrificial offering [8] are also celebrated as being the supreme god, and naturally so also the Brahmacārin or Brahman student,[9] as well as other figures. To these aberrations of the Atharvaveda no attention is paid subsequently.

On the other hand the god Brahman is not found even in the Atharvaveda and still less in the other Saṁhitās. He may be traced merely in such later texts [10] as the Taittirīya [11] and the Kauṣītaki Brāhmaṇas.[12] The earlier conception in this case is unquestionably the neuter, Brahman, which denotes the prayer, the spell, and also more widely the holy power, whether embodied in the prayer or spell or manifested in the universe. The transition to the personal god is to be seen in the phrase, the world of Brahman : in its earliest occurrences that phrase may mean no more than the place of the Brahman, but it was inevitable, even if this is the case, that the idea of a personal god, whose world was meant, should have superseded the older idea. But it must be recognized that in the Vedic period there is no trace whatever of Brahman becoming a god of such importance as to supersede Prajāpati. The importance of the god Brahman can be shown only for a period during the development of Buddhism, since in the Buddhist texts we find many references to Brahman as apparently a very great and popular god among the Brahmans. He bears there an epithet Sahampati, which cannot be explained by anything known in the Brāhmaṇa literature, and this suggests that he may

1 AV. xix. 53, 54.
2 AV. x. 8.
3 AV. xi. 4.
4 AV. xiii. 1–3 ; TB. ii. 5. 2. 1–8.
5 *The Symbolic Gods*, pp. 42 ff.
6 Hillebrandt, *Ved. Myth.* iii. 407.
7 AV. xv. 1 ; above, Part II, Chap. 9, § 10.
8 AV. xi. 7.
9 AV. x. 2 ; xi. 8.
10 Keith, *Aitareya Āraṇyaka*, pp. 304, n. 23 ; 367 ; JRAS. 1910, p. 216 ; Windisch, *Buddha's Geburt*, p. 33 ; Deussen, *Phil. of Up.*, p. 199, who wrongly sees the god in AU. iii. 3. He occurs in BAU. iv. 4. 4 ; CU. iii. 11. 4 ; KU. i. 7, often in the Sūtras.
11 ii. 7. 17. 1.
12 xxv. 1.

have been specially in honour among the eastern tribes of the Indians, and have received among them an epithet which is not recorded in our texts, which are essentially of the middle country lying further to the west than the home of the earliest Buddhism. It is of importance to note that in the Upaniṣads, where, if anywhere, the mention of Brahman as the creator god would be expected to be frequently found, it is comparatively rare, and Prajāpati is the normal name of the creator, and so in the Sūtra texts also.

§ 4. *Subjective Deities*

The clearest example of what may be called physical or subjective deities in the Rigveda is Manyu, 'wrath', who is invoked in two hymns.[1] He is described as self-existent, irresistible. He slays Vṛtra, bestows wealth, grants victory like Indra, and is accompanied by the Maruts : doubtless the conception is deduced from that of the wrath of Indra as a destructive force. Tapas, mentioned along with him, denotes ardour : the conception plays a part of the utmost importance in Vedic cosmogony, as a refined form of physical heat, but it is hardly directly deified. The Rigveda [2] also deifies Çraddhā, 'faith,' through which the fire of sacrifice is kindled, ghee offered, and wealth obtained, and which is invoked at morning, midday, and night. The Brāhmaṇas [3] make her out to be the daughter of the sun, or of Prajāpati. The conception clearly means belief in the existence and the generosity of the gods in its first appearance : its decay in the process of the religion will be dealt with later.

In the Atharvaveda [4] is found the conception of Kāma, 'desire' or 'love'. He is described as the first to be born, and he has arrows [5] which pierce all hearts. He is not, however, as far as appears from the scanty notices we have of him a god primarily of human love, though that side of his character may have existed from the first or have been soon attributed to him. In his cosmic aspect, which is in accordance with the theosophic tone of the Atharvaveda the one in which he is described in it, he is probably derived from the mention of Kāma in one of the most important cosmogonic hymns of the Rigveda [6] as the first seed of mind, regarded also as cosmic. It is not until the later literature in the last strata of the epic that we meet with the Indian Cupid with his arrows, who is described as the disturber of the hearts of men whom he vexes with the pangs of love.[7]

[1] x. 83, 84. So in the Sūtras Balis are offered, KhGS. i. 5. 31 ; GGS. i. 4. 10 ; ApDS. i. 9. 26. 13.

[2] x. 151 ; Oldenberg, ZDMG. l. 450 ff. ; Bloomfield, *Rel. of Veda*, pp. 186 ff.

[3] TB. ii. 3. 10. 1 ; ÇB. xii. 7. 3. 11.

[4] ix. 2 ; xix. 52. For Balis in the Sūtras, see KhGS. i. 5. 31 ; GGS. i. 4. 10 ; other offerings, ApDS. i. 9. 26. 13 ; PGS. iii. 12. 9 ; GDS. xxv. 4 ; BDS. ii. 1. 34 ; iv. 2. 10.

[5] AV. iii. 25. 1. Eros in Boeotia is a probable parallel ; Farnell, *Greece and Babylon*, p. 181.

[6] RV. x. 129. 4.

[7] Hopkins, *Rel. of India*, p. 416, n. 3.

§ 5. *Deified States or Conditions*

Of these divine figures special interest attaches to Aramati, ' devotion ', who is also described as the great one : in the Avesta Aramaiti is a genius of the earth and also of wisdom, and there seems no real reason for objection to the view that the personification goes back to the Indo-Iranian period,[1] though it is doubtful whether we can see in the Rigvedic epithet ' great ' a suggestion that the earth which often bears this epithet was placed under the care of this spirit, and still more whether we can believe Sāyaṇa's assertion that Aramati is the earth. Another spirit who may with propriety be referred to the Indo-Iranian period is Puraṁdhi,[2] whose name occurs some nine times in the Rigveda : she is usually mentioned along with Bhaga, who himself is a representative of this class of gods, but who has become an Āditya, twice or thrice with Pūṣan and Savitṛ, and once with Agni and Viṣṇu. She clearly corresponds to the Avestan Pārendi, who is normally ranked as goddess of plenty and abundance : the view of Hillebrandt [3] sees in her and in the Vedic Puraṁdhi a goddess of activity : the scanty evidence leaves us with no conclusive means of testing either version, especially as the two ideas can be made by a little ingenuity almost synonymous. A goddess Dhiṣaṇā [4] who is mentioned about a dozen times in the Rigveda [5] may also be a goddess of abundance or of impulsion. Anumati, ' favour of the gods ', is twice personified in the Rigveda,[6] and is besought to be propitious and to grant long life. In the Yajurveda and in the Atharvaveda she appears as a goddess who presides over propagation and favours love, and in the Sūtras she is clearly understood as connected with the moon, denoting the day before full moon.[7] It is difficult to suppose that this view of the deity is anything but a later conception, for there is nothing to support it in the early mention of the deity. Sūnṛtā,[8] ' bounty ', is here and there personified in the Rigveda, while on the contrary the spirit of niggardliness, Arāti,[9] ' avarice ', is represented as a demon in the Atharvaveda. Asunīti,[10] ' spirit leading ', is besought in the Rigveda in one hymn to grant long life.

Most of these abstractions are clearly rather thin and feeble, and some at least seem more poetic than living realities. This is not, however, the case with the goddess Nirṛti, dissolution, or misfortune, who is found in the Rigveda [11] as a personification presiding over death. In the ritual the reality of Nirṛti

[1] Hopkins, *op. cit.*, p. 136 ; Hillebrandt, *Ved. Myth.* iii. 405 ; Moulton, *Early Zoroastrianism*, p. 98 ; Carnoy, *Muséon*, xiii. 127 ff. ; Sāyaṇa, RV. vii. 36. 8 ; viii. 42. 3. That Ara is connected with ἔραζε is improbable.

[2] Pischel, *Ved. Stud.* ii. 202–16 ; Bloomfield, JAOS. xvi. 19.

[3] VOJ. iii. 188–94, 259–73.

[4] Johannson (*Über die altindische Göttin Dhiṣaṇā und Verwandtes*) has based on this deity speculations on sexual elements in Vedic conceptions of deity, which to me as to Oldenberg carry no conviction (GGA. 1919, pp. 357–9).

[5] Pischel, *Ved. Stud.* ii. 82 ff. ; Oldenberg, SBE. xlvi. 120 ff.

[6] x. 59. 6 ; 167. 3.

[7] Weber, *Ind. Stud.* v. 229 ; see above, p. 199.

[8] RV. i. 40. 3 ; x. 140. 2.

[9] AV. v. 7.

[10] x. 59. 5, 6.

[11] Macdonell, *Ved. Myth.*, p. 120.

appears in the many rites, which are mentioned in connexion with her, and which display certain marked peculiarities. The Maitrāyaṇī Saṁhitā [1] connects with her specifically dice, women, and sleep as the three most evil things. Her ceremonies are performed with black grain or with nail parings. The sacrificial fee in such cases is a black cow with imperfect horns. In the piling of the fire altar, black bricks are built in for her. In the consecration of the king the wife of the king who has failed to give him a child is brought into connexion with Nirṛti, and the oblations to that deity are offered in her house.[2] Other points in the ritual affecting her will be noted later on.

Another deity which is of importance in the popular thought, but which is very late in appearing in the literature, is the goddess Çrī, first definitely recorded in literature in the Çatapatha Brāhmaṇa.[3] She was, however, as we know from representations of her which are found among the early records of Buddhist art,[4] really a concrete goddess in the eyes of her votaries, though there is no reason to doubt her abstract origin. It is very possible, however, that she was assimilated to the goddess of the earth, which as Bhūmi is not rarely mentioned in the Sūtra literature. Çrī appears in the Sūtra literature, where we find at the offering to the All-gods that it is prescribed to make offerings at the end of the bed to Çrī, at the foot to Bhadrakālī, and in the privy to Sarvānnabhūti.[5] Bhadrakālī suggests of course the name of Çiva's fierce wife Kālī, and carries us to the very end of Vedic ideas, since Kālī does not occur in any Vedic text: the other two though localized cannot be regarded as in origin other than abstract deities, Sondergötter,[6] having regard to the somewhat unimportant and artificial character of the place allotted to Çrī, and to the consideration that the names occur only in a list of oblations to the All-gods, and not in a separate list. In post-Vedic mythology Çrī or Lakṣmī is the wife of Viṣṇu, but of these conceptions the Veda save at the close is ignorant.[7]

Other examples of these abstract deities of the Sondergötter type are to be found in the Sūtras. Thus in the worship of the furrow, Sītā, which is itself concrete, we find that in addition to her there should be invoked the goddess Yajā, who is nothing else than the action of sacrificing, Çamā, which is exertion, and Bhūti which is prosperity: the guardians of the furrow there invoked are probably to be taken as personifications of nature, but conceivably may be treated as mere abstractions. But this constant mention

[1] iii. 6. 3.

[2] Hillebrandt, *Ved. Myth.* iii. 406. Following Speyer, Henry (*La magie dans l'Inde antique*, pp. 160 ff.) sees in her a goddess of earth; see TS. iv. 2. 5; KS. xvi. 12; VS. xii. 64. Cf. Arbman, *Rudra*, p. 261. Connexion with Nerthus is most dubious.

[3] xi. 4. 3. 1; Saṁhitā references seen by Scheftelowitz (ZDMG. lxxv. 37–50) for both Çrī and Lakṣmī are dubious; VS. xxxi. 22; xxxix. 4; TS. ii. 1. 5. 2; TB. ii. 4. 6. 6; ÇB. xiv. 3. 2. 19 f.; BDS. ii. 5. 9. 10; Mahānār. Up. xxxv. 2; HGS. i. 11. 1.

[4] E. g. Rhys Davids, *Buddhist India*, p. 217.

[5] ÇGS. ii. 14. 10 ff.

[6] PGS. ii. 17. 13 ff.; GGS. iv. 2. 27.

[7] Thus such a Sūtra as the Bhāradvāja ignores both.

of these kinds of deities with the most concrete is proof that they were not felt to be any different in essence by the people, for whom the Sūtras were composed. Thus in the ceremony of handing over the pupil [1] by the teacher to the charge of various powers the list includes besides Sarasvatī and the Açvins, Kaṣaka elsewhere unknown, perhaps Kṛçana or Karçana is meant, Antaka, Aghora, diseases, Yama, Makha, the sacrifice personified as often, Vāçinī, 'the ruling lady,' earth with Vaiçvānara, waters, herbs, trees, heaven and earth, welfare, holy lustre, the All-gods, all beings, and all deities, where the distinction between the older group of the All-gods [2] and the later conception of all the gods is noteworthy. A very remarkable list is given in the formula of the Tarpaṇa recorded in the Gṛhya ritual as accompanying the close of Vedic study. The deities honoured, all in the same manner, are Agni, Vāyu, Sūrya, Viṣṇu, Prajāpati, Virūpākṣa, Sahasrākṣa, Soma, Brahman, the Vedas, the gods, the seers, the metres, the Om, Vaṣaṭ and Mahāvyāhṛti calls, the Sāvitrī, which is treated with great respect in the Jaiminīya Upaniṣad, the sacrifice, heaven and earth, the Nakṣatras, the atmosphere, day and night, the numbers, the twilights, the oceans, the rivers, the mountains, fields, herbs, trees, Gandharvas and Apsarases, serpents, birds, Siddhas, Sādhyas, Vipras, Yakṣas, Rakṣases—all classed as Bhūtas, beings—Çruti, Smṛti, firmness, delight, success, thought, belief, insight, memory, cows, Brahmans, movable and immovable things, and all beings, as well as various teachers and ancestors, paternal and maternal.[3] In the list of offerings of the human sacrifice, a pure piece as we have it of priestly imagination, there is ample room for abstractions; a Brahman is offered to the Brahman class, a warrior to the royal power, a Çūdra to asceticism, a thief to night, a murderer to hell.[4] More real are offerings at the Pravargya to glory, fame, strength, and prosperity, and at the Vājapeya to rivalry and desire to succeed.[5] It is impossible to discern any distinction between such offerings and those prescribed for such more apparently concrete deities as the asterisms, Çravaṇa, Mṛgaçiras or Açvayuj, the full moon in the months Çrāvaṇa, Mārgaçīrṣa, or Āçvayuja, the autumn, the winter, the quarters, &c.[6] At the opening of Vedic study Pāraskara [7] lays down offerings to the earth and Agni for a student of the Rigveda, the atmosphere and Vāyu for one of the Yajurveda, the heaven and the sun in the case of the Sāmaveda, and the quarters and the moon in the case of the Atharvaveda. In all cases offering is also to be made to Brahman, the metres, Prajāpati, the gods, the seers, faith, insight, Sadasaspati, and Anumati. Āçvalāyana's list [8] for this occasion includes besides faith and insight, knowledge, memory, and the Sāvitrī. In the Bali offerings [9] of the householder we find the curious admixture of concrete and abstract deities; thus Pāraskara gives as recipients Brahman, Prajāpati, the deities of

[1] HGS. i. 6. 5.
[2] *Viçve* and *Sarve devāḥ*. Cf. AV. xi. 6. 19 f.; Kauç. lvi. 13.
[3] ÇGS. iv. 9; AGS. iii. 4; PGS. ii. 12.
[4] VS. xxx; TB. iii. 4. 1 ff.
[5] Hillebrandt, *Rituallitteratur*, pp. 135, 141.
[6] *Ibid.* pp. 77 f.
[7] ii. 10. 3 ff.
[8] iii. 5. 4.
[9] PGS. ii. 9; ÇGS. ii. 14. 5 ff.; GGS. i. 4. 5 ff.

the house, Kaçyapa, Anumati, these offerings being made in the fire; in the water-pot offerings are made to Parjanya, the waters, and earth; to Dhātṛ and Vidhātṛ at the doorposts, and further offerings are prescribed for the deities of the quarters, Vāyu, Brahman, the atmosphere, the sun, the Viçve Devās and all beings, Uṣas, and the lord of beings. At the harnessing of the plough we find offerings made to Indra, Parjanya, the Açvins, the Maruts, Udalā-kaçyapa, Svātikāri—perhaps Sphātiṁkārī, 'she who gives abundance'—Sītā, and Anumati. The Yava, barley, is invoked to ward off enemies, possibly an idea evoked by the apparent connexion of the word with the root *yu*.[1]

We hear also in the Kauçika Sūtra [2] of an enumeration such as Agni, Brahman, Udañkya, Çūlvāṇa, Çatruṁjaya, Kṣātrāṇa, Mārtyuṁjaya, Mārtyava, Aghora, Takṣaka, Vaiçāleya, Hāhāhūhū, &c. Of these some have obviously reality of some kind or another: Takṣaka is a famous snake, and Hāhāhūhū seem to be two Gandharvas. We learn also [3] of goddesses who weave, spin, spread out, and draw the threads of a garment, of night walkers and day walkers,[4] of divine hosts and hosts not divine; [5] in the funeral ritual [6] Khyātṛ, Apākhyātṛ, Abhilālapant, and Apalālapant are addressed; [7] and the list of some more or less abstract figures which are addressed as in some degree sacred might be considerably lengthened both from Vedic times and later on, such as the Ghoṣiṇī, who guards the cattle at pasture,[8] or Dhanvantari, who in the epic becomes the physician of the gods,[9] and who is possibly [10] an old cloud deity, 'whose boat is the cloud island'.

One collective class is found early, the Bhūtas, beings, whence Rudra derives his style of Bhūtapati, lord of beings. The generality of the term is certain for the Vedic literature; the Bhūtayajña, offering to beings, is generic in character,[11] and there is not the slightest reason to doubt that this was its early sense. The theory [12] that there was originally a Bhūtayajña confined to certain inferior divine figures, which, owing to the ambiguity of the term, and the tendency of the priests to idealize the popular religion, came to be made into a sacrifice for all beings, is wholly unsupported and most implausible. The term Bhūt in modern usage has come to denote a malevolent spirit of the dead, one who has existed, and has ceased to exist, but this is palpably not its early meaning; indeed even in modern usage it is applied to nature spirits as well as to ghosts,[13] and it is impossible to show that in the

[1] Hillebrandt, *Ved. Myth.* iii. 407.
[2] Kauç. lvi. 13.
[3] PGS. i. 4. 13. Cf. AV. xiv. 1. 45.
[4] AGS. i. 2. 7, 8.
[5] GGS. iv. 8. 4.
[6] Hillebrandt, *Ved. Myth.* iii. 407.
[7] Caland, *Todten- und Bestattungsgebräuche*, p. 62.
[8] ÇGS. iii. 9. 1.
[9] Kauç. lxxiv. 6; AGS. i. 2. 2; 3. 6; 12. 7; ÇGS. ii. 14. 2 (Bharadvāja Dhanvantari).
[10] Louis H. Gray, JAOS. xlii. 323 ff.
[11] ÇGS. ii. 14; AGS. i. 2. 3; PGS. ii. 9; GGS. i. 4; KhGS. i. 5. 20 ff.; also decisively ÇGS. iv. 9; AÇS. iii. 4. 1.
[12] Arbman, *Rudra*, pp. 193 ff. His rendering of TS. vi. 2. 8. 3; MS. iii. 8. 5; KS. xxv. 6 (p. 213) is impossible.
[13] Arbman, pp. 168 ff.

Vedic period it had any specific sense [1] referring to inferior or hostile demons. The wide sense of beings is natural enough for a religion which saw divinity readily on every side, and is probably merely a recognition of popular belief. It is a striking fact that in the medical literature [2] the Bhūtavidyā is by no means confined to evils brought about by evil spirits, but includes those caused by the gods. The tendency of the term to become narrowed down to hostile beings in later literature [3] is interesting, but not surprising in view of the much more remarkable history of Asura. The origin of the limitation can be traced to the domestic ritual, in which the Bhūtayajña was artifically differentiated so as to create a distinct Devayajña, with the result that there seemed to be some opposition between Bhūtas and Devas, though the original Bhūtayajña covered all those beings to whom it was deemed wise to make offering when man partook of food.

We have traces of classes of Sondergötter in the long enumerations in the Çatarudriya, whether we assume that these classes are assimilated to Rudra or treated as independent objects of devotion.[4] In either case we have, as in the Roman Indigitamenta, priestly ingenuity working on primitive conceptions. A similar spirit is seen in the elaborate discrimination of aspects of gods, as when the Maruts are separately invoked as Svatavas, Sāṁtapana, Gṛhamedhin and Krīḍin, differences which are obviously rather hieratic than popular.[5]

§ 6. *Aditi and Diti*

The place of Aditi in the Vedic pantheon is very remarkable, if, as is on the whole most probable, she is to be regarded as an abstract deity. She has, indeed, no entire hymn in the Rigveda, but she is mentioned not less than eighty times, and in the great majority of these with her sons, the Ādityas. Of her personality little is said beyond the fact that she is intact, extended, bright, and luminous, a supporter of creatures, an epithet enjoyed by Mitra and Varuṇa, and belonging to all men. She is invoked at morning, noon, and evening. While the Ādityas are normally her sons, she is once said to be their sister, and to be the daughter of the Vasus.[6] She appears in the Yajurveda [7] once as the wife of Viṣṇu : in the post-Vedic mythology she is especially the daughter of Dakṣa and the mother of Vivasvant, and of Viṣṇu, but also of all the gods.

Aditi is constantly invoked to release from sin : in this respect she stands in the closest connexion with Varuṇa, who fetters the sinners. Varuṇa, Agni, Savitṛ, and other gods are besought to release from sin before her. But in some cases the goddess cannot be distinguished from the primitive

[1] Arbman, p. 180, suggests Gespenster.
[2] Suçruta, i. 3. 10.
[3] Possibly in CU. vii. 1. 2, 4 ; 7. 1, but this is quite unproved. The wide sense occurs later, e.g. Manu, iii. 93.
[4] Arbman, pp. 230 ff.
[5] Hillebrandt, *Ved. Myth.* iii. 325 f.
[6] RV. viii. 101. 15 ; cf. AV. vi. 4. 1.
[7] TS. vii. 5. 4 ; VS. xxix. 60.

sense of the name, which denotes unbinding, or freedom from bonds. The Ādityas are besought to place the offering in sinlessness and freedom from bonds,[1] and a worshipper seeks to be given back to great Aditi to seek his father and mother again.[2] Aditi thus is asked to release her worshippers like bound thieves.

Aditi, however, appears in other connexions than the freeing from sin. Not only the Ādityas, but all the gods are said to be born from her: as the sky she supplies them with honied milk. But the Taittirīya Saṁhitā [3] and other texts expressly assert her identity with the earth, and by the time of the Naighaṇṭuka this is so much the accepted version that the word is placed as a synonym for earth. But she often in the Rigveda [4] is clearly differentiated from both. Again she is identified pantheistically with sky, air, mother, father, son, the five tribes, what has been or shall be.[5] Dakṣa, who is her son, is also her father,[6] and she appears as celebrating Savitṛ and producing a hymn for Indra.

More important is the fact that Aditi is sometimes at least conceived as theriomorphic, a fact which is clearly shown by the fact that in the ritual [7] a cow is addressed by her name. It is also to be seen, however, in the Rigveda itself: where not only is she occasionally spoken of as a cow,[8] but Soma is compared to her milk, and milk must be meant in the daughter of Aditi, who yields to Soma as he flows to the vat.

Though rarely, Aditi is credited with the usual powers of the gods, and is prayed to for wealth and other boons: the special gift of light which she bestows may be due to her connexion with the Ādityas.

The explanations of Aditi differ widely, according as she is treated as an abstract or a concrete deity. Pischel [9] holds that she is the earth, but this is not borne out by anything save the view of the later Vedic texts, and does not suit at all the picture of the goddess presented in the Rigveda. Hillebrandt,[10] in fairly close agreement with one view of Roth's,[11] that she is the eternal principle underlying the celestial light, urges that she is essentially connected with light and the highest heaven, and explains her as the light of day in its imperishable aspect, a view which agrees in substance with that of Colinet [12] that she is the light of the sky, thus in essence a sort of feminine form of Dyaus. This in some measure agrees with the theory of Bergaigne [13] that the goddess is a development from the phrase Dyaus Aditi, supplying the gods with milk as the boundless sky, but in his view stress is laid on the imperishable nature of the light, not on the boundless space of the sky. Max Müller [14]

[1] RV. vii. 51. 1.
[2] RV. i. 24. 1; cf. i. 185. 3.
[3] Apparently also in RV. i. 72. 9; AV. xiii. 1. 38.
[4] x. 63. 10.
[5] RV. i. 89. 10.
[6] RV. x. 72. 4, 5.
[7] Bergaigne, *Rel. Véd.* i. 325.
[8] i. 153. 3; viii. 101. 15; x. 11. 1; ix. 96. 15; 69. 3.
[9] *Ved. Stud.* ii. 86.
[10] *Ved. Myth.* iii. 408 ff. Cf. RV. i. 115. 5.
[11] ZDMG. vi. 68 ff.
[12] *Trans. 9th Or. Congress,* i. 396–410; *Muséon,* xii. 81–90.
[13] SBE. xxxii. 241.
[14] *Rel. Véd.* iii. 88–98.

takes the view that the boundless sky as the expression of visible infinity is the phenomenon meant. Wallis [1] and Oldenberg,[2] on the other hand, acquiesce in the view that Aditi denotes simply freedom from bondage. Oldenberg, however, lays stress also on the fact that Aditi is regarded as a cow, and that the gods appear as cow-born and suggest that there may have been a tradition according to which the celestial gods are the offspring of a celestial cow,[3] or cow fetish. It is difficult to understand exactly how he considers this concept related to that of Aditi, and in point of fact it is very doubtful whether the stress laid upon the idea of the cow is to be justified by the appearance of the cow in the mythology. It seems rather that the cow is not a primitive conception, but a secondary view.

An interesting suggestion of the origin of Aditi is due to Macdonell,[4] and on the whole it has more to say for it than any other explanation of the deity. The Ādityas are here and there called sons of Aditi, and he suggests that, just as Çavasī is found in the Rigveda itself as the name of Indra's mother, arising from the phrase ' son of strength (*çavas*) ', applied to Indra as the most strong one, so Aditi was conjured up from a phrase meaning sons of freedom or rather perhaps guiltlessness. The personification would then by a most natural and simple process be invested with the leading characteristics of her sons, as the mother of the Ādityas she would be brought into conjunction with heaven and earth, the universal parents, while she would retain her special connexion with the idea of freedom. In that case Āditya would be a term produced and applied to Mitra, Varuṇa, and the other gods after Aditi had been created, and the original gods, who were called sons of freedom or guiltlessness, would probably be Mitra and Varuṇa, and perhaps some others. It must be assumed that these others had already been formed into a close group before the separation of the Indo-Iranian stems as the connexion of the group of Ādityas with the Ameša Spentas is obviously probable if it cannot be proved, but there is no objection to this view to be raised on the ground of the theory of Aditi here accepted, since it is clear in any case that the name Āditya is an invention of India.

Compared with Aditi the goddess Diti is merely a name. She occurs thrice in the Rigveda,[5] twice with Aditi, who with Diti is said to be seen by Mitra and Varuṇa from their car. Agni is also begged to grant Diti, and preserve from Aditi. Finally Diti is said to give what is desirable. In the later Saṁhitās [6] she appears as a colourless deity beside Aditi, except that in the

[1] *Cosmology*, pp. 45 ff. Cf. von Schroeder, *Arische Religion*, ii. 400.

[2] *Rel. des Veda*², pp. 202 ff. ; SBE. xlvi. 329. Geldner (*Zur Kosmogonie des RV.*, p. 5) holds that Aditi is ' undividedness ', ' completeness '.

[3] RV. vi. 50. 10 ; vii. 35. 14. In Greece we have a cow-headed figure in Arcadia (BCH. 1899, p. 635) and Here's epithet Boōpis (Farnell, *Greece and Babylon*, pp. 76–80).

[4] *Ved. Myth.*, p. 122. Bloomfield's suggestion (*The Symbolic Gods*, p. 45) that Āditya means ' from of old ' is opposed to the usage of the language, and in *Rel. of India*, p. 131, it is not pressed.

[5] v. 62. 8 ; iv. 2. 11 (both with Aditi) ; vii. 15. 12.

[6] AV. xv. 18. 4 ; xvi. 6. 7 ; VS. xviii. 22.

Atharvaveda [1] we find already mentioned the Daityas as her sons: in the post-Vedic mythology the gods and the Daityas are the sons of Aditi and Diti respectively, the common father being Dakṣa Prajāpati. It is obvious that, even assuming that the second of these passages is not to be explained as having no connexion with deities at all, and as merely referring to giving and not-giving, regarded perhaps as powers, just as Arāti in the Atharvaveda is deified, the existence of Diti is merely derived from Aditi, and that it is idle to give any real meaning to such a personality.[2]

§ 7. *The Wives of the Gods*

In some cases the wives of the gods are obviously based on natural phenomena, the relation of two such phenomena presenting for some reason or other traits which suggest their close connexion: the primeval pair is that of heaven and earth, and on this doubtless the other accounts of the marriages of the gods are in part based. Other examples are also obviously suggested by natural events: thus the wedding of Soma the king as the moon to the twenty-seven or twenty-eight Nakṣatras is a mythical account of the obvious relation of the moon to the constellations in question. Again, the wedding of Soma as the moon with the sun-maiden may conceivably be due to some primitive astronomical views. The making of the Dawn the wife of the Açvins is also explicable on mythological grounds. The wedding of the same goddess to Pūṣan, the sun-god, is also not unnatural.

On the other hand, there are clearly cases in which the wife of the god is to be classed as an abstraction in the sense that she owes her existence not to any natural phenomenon at all, but merely to the application to the gods of the rule of human life which, in Vedic India, gave the man normally one wife, though it also allowed polygamy,[3] a fact which is reflected perhaps in the relation of the Gandharva with the Apsarases as well as in Soma's many brides. Thus, Vedic religion sets beside the god Indra the goddess Indrāṇī, who is merely his wife: the legend which makes them quarrel over an ape, Vṛṣākapi, has been alluded to. Varuṇānī also occurs in the Rigveda, and the wife of Agni, Agnāyī, the names of the deities being fashioned from those of their husbands precisely in the same way as feminine nouns are occasionally made from masculine stems. Rudrāṇī,[4] on the other hand, is not found until the Sūtras, and, though she plays in the ritual a much more real part than that played by any of these other abstractions, still it is perfectly obvious that she is only a mere copy of her husband. Indrāṇī occasionally receives offerings, and she has borrowed a trait or two from Uṣas, as for instance she is credited

[1] vii. 7. 1.

[2] Bergaigne, *Rel. Véd.* iii. 97; Max Müller, SBE. xxxii. 256.

[3] Macdonell and Keith, *Vedic Index*, i. 478, 479.

[4] Oldenberg, *Rel. des Veda*², p. 218. Çrī and Lakṣmī as wives of Viṣṇu, and Umā as wife of Çiva, have already been mentioned as of more independent origin.

with the thirty leagues which that goddess traverses in the day.[1] The Aitareya Brāhmaṇa mentions Senā and Prāsahā as Indra's wives, obvious abstractions of his nature, and the later mythology gives him Çacī from his epithet, 'lord of strength'.[2] As a body the wives of the gods are given a certain place in the ritual in connexion with Tvaṣṭṛ, receiving offerings especially at the new and full moon offerings. Mention is also made of protecting deities who are the feminine counterpart of the agent gods, but who are rarely mentioned.[3]

[1] MS. iii. 8. 4; she receives a libation, e.g. TS. ii. 2. 8. 1.

[2] Bloomfield, ZDMG. xlviii. 548 ff.

[3] TS. iv. 1. 6; VS. xi. 61.

CHAPTER 13

GROUPS OF DEITIES

§ 1. *The Dual Deities*

THE type of the dual deities, who form quite a marked feature of the Rigveda in which some sixty hymns are addressed to such gods, is given by the pair Dyāvāpṛthivī, heaven and earth, the primeval parents. The two individual gods are comparatively little mentioned in comparison with the pair: Dyaus has no hymn, Pṛthivī one only, and the pair have six. Other names are Dyāvākṣāmā, Dyāvābhūmī or Rodasī, in which the male character of Dyaus, never perfectly established, has yielded to the prevailing femininity of Pṛthivī. The pair are two fathers, two mothers. They are the makers of all creatures, but also they are made by many individual gods, Indra, Viçvakarman, Tvaṣṭṛ, or even produced from the sacrifice of the giant Puruṣa. One is a bull, the other a cow: they are unaging, they grant wealth, and are also wise and promote righteousness. They are also conceived as coming to the sacrifice or taking the sacrifice to the gods, but they are not of much importance in the ritual.[1] They have, however, a hymn addressed to them in the Vaiçvadeva Çastra of the Agniṣṭoma, and an offering is made to them by the plougher, with the result that Parjanya sends him rain. The priests liken the two to the oblation holders or the earth to the altar, and the sky to the sacrificial fee.[2]

Mitra and Varuṇa have twenty-three hymns addressed to them as dual deities: the mythology is practically all borrowed from that of Varuṇa, and the chief point of interest is that the same phenomenon of double invocation can be seen in this case already in the Avesta. The priority of Mitra in the compound name has been argued [3] to indicate the superior importance at one time of that god, but the order accords also with the preference of the language for the placing of the shorter word in such a compound in the first place.[4]

With Indra Varuṇa shares nine hymns: the characteristics of both gods are ascribed to the pair, but also they are found with the warlike deeds given to Indra, and Varuṇa's wisdom is celebrated. Indra appears with Agni in eleven hymns,[5] as sharing in the Soma, as slayers of Vṛtra and the Dāsas, and also as skilled priests and offerers: once they are called—presumably because of their close connexion with each other—the Açvins. Indra and Vāyu are seven times invoked in hymns together, and practically always in connexion

1 TS. iii. 4. 3. 3.

2 AB. i. 29. 4; AV. xiii. 1. 46, 52.

3 Oldenberg, *Rel. des Veda*¹, p. 193.

4 Wackernagel, *Altind. Gramm.* II. i. 168.

5 They are the gods of the new moon offerings, a curious connexion; Hillebrandt, *Ved. Myth.* iii. 294–300.

with the drinking of the Soma; the same feature is to be found in the two hymns given to Indra and Bṛhaspati. Indra and Soma have two hymns: the deeds attributed are those of Indra. Indra and Pūṣan in their one hymn are described as the one drinking Soma, the other eating gruel or mush: elsewhere mention is made of their abode, to which the goat convoys the steed at the horse sacrifice. With Viṣṇu, Indra in one hymn divides Soma-drinking and wide-stepping.

Soma shares one hymn each with Pūṣan, Rudra, and Agni. For Soma and Pūṣan, Agni is invoked to put the ripe milk in the raw cows: Soma and Rudra are asked to set free from the fetter of Varuṇa. Agni and Soma are said to have released the stream, obtained the light: one is brought from heaven by Mātariçvan, the other by the eagle from the rock. Except in this one hymn they appear only twice as a pair in the whole of the Rigveda, showing that the close connexion which existed in the ritual and in the later Saṁhitās was not primitive.[1] They appear several times in the Atharvaveda, and still oftener in the Yajurveda, where they are called the two eyes, or brothers, the sun being ascribed to Agni, the moon to Soma. In the ritual the victim which is offered before the main portion of the rite, or in the rite itself, is offered to Agni and Soma, and they also receive cakes, but not a share in the Soma, which certainly suggests that the Soma ritual had been fairly definitely settled before they were united as a joint deity.

In isolated verses a few more pairs occur, Agni and Parjanya as producing the oblation and offspring respectively, and apparently as connected with Dyaus, Parjanya, and Vāta. Dawn and Night appear as sisters, daughters of Dyaus, mothers of order, weaving the web of sacrifice, and the sun and moon appear as Sūryāmāsā or Sūryācandramasā, who are little personified, but who are doubtless meant by the two bright eyes of Varuṇa or the two eyes of heaven.

§ 2. *Groups of Gods*

It is a characteristic trait of the Rigveda that some forty hymns are devoted to the group of gods called All-gods, Viçve Devās, and the impression given by the Rigveda is borne out by the ritual in which the All-gods receive frequent attention.[2] The fact must be carefully borne in mind in framing any theory as to the feeling of the poets as to the rank of the several gods: they must have known of these joint invocations, in which as many gods as possible are propitiated, and the same tendency to be catholic in the reverence

[1] Oldenberg, *Rel. des Veda*², p. 95, n. 3, correcting Hillebrandt, *Ved. Myth.* i. 461; that they denote sun and moon is as improbable as that Indra and Agni are sun and moon. The connexion may be due to a Gautama (cf. RV. i. 93). The two gods were naturally enough connected as sacrificial, and hence the animal victim preceding the Soma offering is given to them.

[2] Arbman (*Rudra*, p. 154, n. 3) suggests that the term includes all the gods as opposed to the heavenly gods of the Vedic sacrifice; but this clearly is wrong, the term denoting the whole of the gods of the sacrifice taken collectively.

paid to the gods is to be noted in the Sūtras where offerings are prescribed to all the gods, including even unknown gods. The Rigveda already shows the tendency to set up individual gods as outside the number of All-gods : in the Sūtras there is perfectly obvious the distinction between all the gods and the older All-gods.[1] The religious conception which lies at the back of it is one which can be paralleled from many religions. By inventing a comprehensive group no deity at any rate could justly complain that it had been passed over altogether.

Of the other groups of gods the Maruts are the most important : they also in the Rigveda bear the name of Rudras. This group is, however, distinguished from the Maruts in the later texts, and its number is placed at 11, though 33, which is the traditional number of all the gods, is given in the Taittirīya Saṁhitā.[2] The Ādityas, who are seven or eight in the Rigveda, become 12 in the Brāhmaṇas, and are often mentioned especially in contrast with the Añgirases, who are rather a priestly family than actual deities.[3] With the Ādityas and Rudras the Vasus are invoked in the Rigveda :[4] it is clear that there they are connected with Indra. But in the later texts they are connected with Agni, not Indra, and their number, not defined in the Rigveda, is fixed at 8, though the Taittirīya Saṁhitā,[5] by a freak gives 333. In the Chāndogya Upaniṣad[6] we find five groups, Indra with the Rudras, Agni with the Vasus, Varuṇa with the Ādityas, Soma with the Maruts, and Brahman with the Sādhyas. The last group is a set of gods of whom practically nothing can be said : they are mentioned occasionally from the Rigveda[7] onwards, occurring in the usual way even in the Sūtras, but except that they are ancient, nothing more is to be learned of their nature.[8]

1 Kauç. lvi. 6.
2 i. 4. 11. 1.
3 Levi, *La doctrine du sacrifice*, pp. 65, 66.
4 vii. 10. 4 ; 35. 6.
5 v. 5. 2. 5.
6 iii. 6–10.
7 x. 90. 7 (with gods and seers) ; i. 164. 50 ; TS. vi. 3. 4. 8 ; 5. 1 ; 5. 6. 1 ; PB. viii. 3. 5 ; xxv. 8. 2 (before the gods) ; AB. viii. 12. 4 (with Āptyas) ; 14. 3 ; HGS. ii. 19. 1 ; ÇGS. iv. 9. 3 ; BhGS. iii. 9.
8 A triad of gods associated in worship or by connexion of descent is not known in Vedic religion, nor practically in Greek or Babylonian belief; Farnell, *Greece and Babylon*, pp. 180 ff. The current view which finds triads in the Greek mysteries is given in Legge, *Forerunners and Rivals of Christianity*, i. ch. ii. We have only the three forms of Agni, and his three names and casual triads like Varuṇa, Mitra, Aryaman, for which we need not seek any prototype in the Semitic Anu, Enlil, Ea, or Sin, Ramman, Šamaš ; the later Brahman, Rudra, Viṣṇu appear only in Maitr. iv. 5 ; v. 1, preluded by Mahānār. Up. xi. 12. See Hopkins, *Origin of Religion*, pp. 294 ff. Cf., on Trita, Güntert, *Der arische Weltkönig*, pp. 30 ff.

CHAPTER 14

PRIESTS AND HEROES

§ 1. *The Priests of the Fire Cult*

With the cult of fire are connected three great families of priests, the Aṅgirases, the Atharvans, and Bhṛgus, in all of whose cases it is at first sight impossible, and in any case difficult, to decide whether we have to do with real traditions of priestly families of the past, or with deities who have fallen in rank and become confounded with men. The case of the Aṅgirases is of special interest. Agni is not rarely called an Aṅgiras, but he is also called the chief or the most inspired Aṅgiras, and the name Aṅgiras is used in one passage of the god on the one hand, and on the other of the ancestor of the invoker of the god. On the other hand, Indra also is described as veriest Aṅgiras, and in his feat of the overthrow of Vala the Aṅgirases play a great part by their singing and their prayers. In point of fact the myth is sometimes attributed to them and not to Indra at all, or he is given a secondary role in it. They appear in the myth of the Paṇis as obtaining the cows: this is, it is probable, simply another side of the overthrow of Vala and the release of the cows, and Bṛhaspati who is credited with the same feat is once called Āṅgirasa, and once even Aṅgiras. They are repeatedly called fathers by the poets, they are associated with Manu and are once with the Atharvans and the Bhṛgus connected with Yama:[1] but they appear also with the Ādityas, Rudras, and Vasus, Soma is offered to them, they are invoked,[2] and they are praised as sacrificers who attained Agni and won by the sacrifice immortality.

A very important feature of the mythology is the quarrel of the Ādityas and the Aṅgirases, of which the Brāhmaṇas give full accounts: the Aṅgirases proposed to win their way to heaven by sacrificing, and to make the Ādityas act for them: they sent Agni to bid the Ādityas perform that function, but the Ādityas cleverly forestalled the Aṅgirases by undertaking the offering at once, so that the Aṅgirases had to officiate for them to their indignation. They received, however, from the Ādityas for their work the fee of a white horse, which is clearly the sun.[3]

On the other hand, there is abundant proof that the Aṅgirases were treated by the poets as a real clan, and that many Vedic personages claimed to be descended from them: we cannot really doubt that there was such a family: in the Atharvaveda[4] we have clear enough evidence that the Atharvans and

[1] RV. x. 14. 3–6.

[2] RV. ix. 62. 9; iii. 53. 7; x. 62.

[3] ÇB. iii. 5. 1. 13 ff.; AB. vi. 34; KB. xxx. 6; PB. xvi. 12. 1; GB. ii. 6. 14; Hillebrandt, *Ved. Myth.* ii. 166 ff. See also JB. iii. 187 f.; BÇS. xviii. 22 f.

[4] Bloomfield, SBE. xlii. pp. xvii ff.

the Aṅgirases were two sets of priests who contributed the former the auspicious, the latter the black magic side of that Veda. We find many points in the ritual such as the Aṅgirasām Ayana, the Aṅgirasāṁ Dvirātra, and many individual inventors of ceremonies who claimed to be Aṅgirases.

The view of Hillebrandt [1] is that the Aṅgirases were originally a family which was rather outside the main Vedic tradition, as shown by their lack of prominence in the books ii–ix, and which practised the cult of its ancestors, so that, when the Aṅgirases came into the Vedic tradition at all, they carried with them their ancestors as semi-divine. With this view may be compared that of Weber [2] that we have in them Indo-Iranian priests. The alternative view [3] is that they were originally regarded as a race of beings higher than men, and intermediate between them and the gods, as attendants of Agni who as Aṅgiras is the messenger [4] between the sky and the earth, the name being identic with the Greek ἄγγελος. The evidence is too slight to allow of any certain conclusion, except that the conception of Aṅgiras in the historical period clearly generated a family, if there was not originally a family involved.

The Virūpas who occur in close connexion with the Aṅgirases are clearly merely a subdivision of that family : the eponymous Virūpa also occurs.

Other priests mentioned in conjunction with each other and usually allied either with the Aṅgirases or in the performance of the winning of the cows, which is the special deed of the Aṅgirases, are the Daçagvas and the Navagvas. The latter are the more often mentioned, and their name contains as first element the sacred number nine, so that the Daçagvas are probably a later invention. They seem to be a group of nine and ten priestly ancestors : possibly the second element in their name suggests, however, according to Bloomfield,[5] the idea that they are persons who win nine or ten cows apiece : usually, however, the latter part of the word is interpreted as from the root denoting to go, and the compound then means going in sets of nine or ten respectively, unless indeed Navagva is *nuntius*.[6]

The Atharvans are mentioned in the Rigveda thrice only in the plural, and eleven times in the singular. The essential feature of Atharvan is that he produces Agni, to become the messenger of Vivasvant. He practised devotion along with Manu and Dadhyañc, and was helped by Indra. According to the Atharvaveda,[7] Atharvan brought to Indra a cup of Soma, received from Varuṇa a mystic cow, and dwells in heaven. The Atharvans as a family appear with the Aṅgirases, Navagvas, and Bhṛgus and live in heaven, destroying goblins. In some passages the word certainly simply means priest as

[1] *Ved. Myth.* ii. 159 ff.

[2] *Ind. Stud.* i. 291 ff.

[3] Macdonell, *Ved. Myth.*, p. 143.

[4] Louis H. Gray (JAOS. xlii. 332–4) treats them as intermediaries or shamanists. He sees in the late Bharadvāja Dhanvantari a priest in whom the cloud deity is embodied, but this is to go far beyond the evidence.

[5] JAOS. xvi. p. cxxv ; AJP. xvii. 426.

[6] Macdonell, *Ved. Myth.*, p. 144. For astronomical theories, see Tilak, *Arctic Home in the Vedas*, pp. 160 ff. ; A. C. Das, *Rig-Vedic India*, i. 451 ff. Cf. Güntert, *Der arische Weltkönig*, pp. 282 f.

[7] xviii. 3. 54 ; v. 11 ; vii. 104 ; xi. 6. 13.

when Atharvans receive cows from Açvatha as gifts,[1] and a Bṛhaddiva Atharvan [2] seems to have been a real poet. In the ritual they appear to have used honey as real priests. Plants are described as connected with them in the Atharvaveda, as they are connected with the Añgirases, but the Atharvans seem clearly not to be connected with witchcraft and similar practices. The alternation of the compounds Atharvāñgiras and Bhṛgvañgiras points to their being closely related to the Bhṛgus, but there is no adequate evidence for the theory of Hillebrandt [3] that the Bhṛgus are the clan and Atharvan its priest.

The word is probably, not certainly, to be identified with the Āthravan of the Avesta, which must mean fire priest, the Avestan Ātar being akin to *atharyu*, flaming, used as an epithet of Agni. There is therefore every reason to see in the Atharvans the elevation to divine rank of fire priests of old time.[4]

A special figure is that of Dadhyañc Ātharvaṇa, who is mentioned once in book vi, which is specially fond of the Atharvans, and elsewhere only in books i, ix, and x. The essential legend of him is that with the head of a horse he declared to the Açvins the mead.[5] Further, Indra is said to have found in Çaryaṇāvant the head of the horse hidden in the mountains, and to have slain ninety-nine Vṛtras with the bones of Dadhyañc. He is the son of Atharvan and the kindler of fire, and he obtains cows from Indra, and opens cowstalls by Soma's power. It is clearly difficult to make much of this figure ; the telling of the mead which is made into the delivery of philosophic doctrine by the theologians is interpreted more prosaically by Hillebrandt [6] as referring to the use of honey in the ritual by the Atharvans, which seems clearly attested. But the horse-head suggests connexion with the steed Dadhikrāvan, and the name may either mean 'united with curd' or 'turning towards curd in pleasure'. Bergaigne [7] considers that he is to be taken as the Soma, but this is hardly enough to account for his curious form and myth. It has been suggested that he is the lightning, the horse's head indicating speed, the voice the thunder, and the bones the thunderbolts ; the connexion of lightning with Soma would explain the reference to Soma, to Indra, and to Agni. The suggestion is ingenious, but the mixed form of the deity suggests that there is at work some conception of demoniac kind : the demons of the Vedic religion often have the confusion of human and animal form, but not the deities.

The Bhṛgus occur but twenty-three times in all in the Rigveda, and despite the fact that they are marked with the Atharvans and Añgirases as Fathers, they show certain clear distinctions of character from the Añgirases. While the latter are essentially active in the business of the finding of the cows, or aid Indra at least by their songs in it, the task of the Bhṛgus is confined to the discovery of the fire, its lighting up, and its care. Moreover, in the Brāhmaṇa

1 RV. vi. 47. 24.
2 RV. x. 120. 9.
3 *Ved. Myth.* ii. 173 ff.
4 Bloomfield, SBE. xlii. p. xxiii, n. 2; Macdonell, *Ved. Myth.*, p. 141. Cf. also JB. iii. 269.
5 RV. i. 84. 13, 14; 116. 12; 117. 22; 119. 9.
6 *Ved. Myth.* ii. 174.
7 *Rel. Véd.* ii. 456–60; Macdonell, *Ved. Myth.*, pp. 142, 143. Cf. also JB. iii. 64; JAOS. xviii. 17.

literature the father of Bhṛgu is Varuṇa,[1] while Añgiras is connected with Agni. They appear side by side with the Druhyus as apparently an historical people,[2] and possibly, when Bhṛgu appears with the Yatis in a friendly relation to Indra, real facts may be alluded to.[3] On the other hand, they drive away a personage named Makha, of whom little or nothing else is known.[4] From Mātariçvan, who shares with them the credit of establishing the fire, they differ, in that they do not fetch it down from the sky but diffuse the use on the earth.

In the ritual there are clear references to real Bhārgavas and to their practices as at the fire-piling and the mode of dividing the offerings: the Aitaçāyana Ājāneyas in a curious story appeared as cursed by their father, and as therefore becoming the worst of the Bhṛgus.

The word Bhṛgu clearly means shining, from the root *bhrāj*: it is therefore natural enough that there should be a considerable body of opinion in favour of the view that Bhṛgu is originally the designation of the fire,[5] or more especially the lightning, and the Greek Phlegyai have been compared as fire priests.[6] The comparison is not certain; it is, however, clear that the Bhṛgus are mythical fire-priests, possibly, but not probably, the historic reminiscence of an actual family.[7]

§ 2. *Other Ancient Priests*

Of other ancient seers the most famous are the Seven Seers, who are four times mentioned in the Rigveda.[8] They are called divine fathers and secure Trasadasyu for Purukutsa's wife in her dire need; possibly the number is merely the frequent mystic number seven, or again it may be derived from the seven priests of the ritual [9]—who again, however, may be due to the desire to make up the sacred number. Their names are not given before the Brāhmaṇas. In the Çatapatha [10] they are regarded as the seven stars in the constellation of the Great Bear, and are declared to have been in origin bears, a theory explained by the similarity of the words Ṛṣi, seer, and Ṛkṣa, which means both star [11] and bear.[12] It is probably the same number who are the seven Hotṛs with whom Manu made his first offering.[13] A couple of divine Hotṛs, who are mentioned about twelve times in the Rigveda,[14] seem to be based on some pair of sacrificers in the ritual.

1 AB. iii. 34. 1; PB. xviii. 9. 1; JB. i. 42; ii. 202.

2 RV. vii. 18. 6.

3 RV. viii. 3. 9; 6. 18; cf. AV. v. 19. 1; AB. ii. 20. 7.

4 RV. ix. 101. 13. He is identified with the sacrifice in the Brāhmaṇas; Hopkins, *Trans. Conn. Acad.* xv. 41 f.

5 Von Schroeder (*Arische Religion*, ii. 486) sees in the story of Bhṛgu's hauteur and his visit to hell a faint echo of the Prometheus legend.

6 Kuhn, *Herabkunft des Feuers*, pp. 21, 22; Weber, ZDMG. ix. 240 ff.; Carnoy, *Les Indo-Européens*, p. 207.

7 Macdonell, *Ved. Myth.*, pp. 100, 141.

8 iv. 42. 8; x. 109. 4; 130. 7.

9 RV. ii. 1. 2. Cf. iii. 7. 7; iv. 1. 12; vi. 22. 2; x. 35. 10.

10 ii. 1. 2. 4; xiii. 8. 1. 10; JUB. iv. 26. 12; names in BAU. ii. 2. 6; HGS. ii. 19. 1.

11 RV. i. 24. 10.

12 RV. v. 56. 3.

13 RV. x. 63. 7.

14 Oldenberg, SBE. xlvi. 11.

Of individual seers Atri is the most famous, mainly through the myth of his being saved by Agni and by the Açvins, who took him from a burning chasm, and refreshed him : once too they are said to have made him young again. The other legend attaching to him, or to the Atris, is the finding of the sun, when it was hidden by the demon Svarbhānu, and placing it again in the sky.[1] This legend is often mentioned in the Brāhmaṇas and the Çatapatha [2] adds the detail that Atri originated from and is even identical with Vāc. The Atris, besides claiming a share in their father's exploit, are an historical reality, and the fifth book of the Rigveda is assigned by tradition to them, a tradition to a large extent borne out by the references in the work. With Atri, Saptavadhri seems to be identical : he is only named in immediate juxtaposition with Atri,[3] and the same rescue seems to be performed for him as for Atri.

Atri probably denotes the devourer, from *ad*, 'eat', and indeed once occurs as an epithet of Agni,[4] whence Bergaigne [5] has suggested that Atri is really in origin Agni himself.

Kaṇva, whose descendants, the Kaṇvas, are the reputed authors of the poems of the eighth book of the Rigveda, is celebrated as an ancient seer, often in connexion with persons in whose existence we have no reason to disbelieve. He is, however, said to have had his sight restored by the Açvins, and this, taken in conjunction with his connexion with the fire worship, has suggested the theory of Bergaigne [6] that he is really the sun during the night, or more generally the hidden Agni, a suggestion for which there is nothing to be said. On the other hand, it is probable that Kaṇva was merely an eponymous hero : nothing said of him seems to prove contemporaneity with any Rigvedic poet.[7] Medhyātithi and Priyamedha, who are among the descendants of Kaṇva, seem to have been real personages. Of the other seers, to whom the various books of the Rigveda are assigned, Gotama, Viçvāmitra, Vāmadeva, Bharadvāja, and Vasiṣṭha, there is still less reason to disbelieve the historic existence, or at least the existence of the families bearing the names from which the ancestors may have been reconstructed.[8]

A more mysterious appearance belongs to Kāvya Uçanā, whose main characteristic is wisdom : Soma is compared with and identified with him on this ground. He appears as a protégé of Indra and associated with him when with Kutsa he vanquished Çuṣṇa : he also forged his bolt for Indra, and is said to have established Agni as Hotṛ priest. He appears, however, in the Pañcaviṅça Brāhmaṇa as the Purohita of the Asuras, and has been compared with the famous Iranian figure of saga, Kai Kāōs.[9]

[1] RV. v. 40. 6, 8 ; AV. viii. 2. 4, 12, 36.
[2] iv. 3. 4. 21 ; i. 4. 5. 13 ; xiv. 5. 2. 5.
[3] RV. x. 39. 9 ; v. 78. 5, 6 ; viii. 73. 8, 9 ; Bergaigne, *Rel. Véd.* ii. 467.
[4] RV. ii. 8. 5.
[5] *Op. cit.* ii. 467–72. Cf. Max Müller, *Beitr. zu einer wiss. Myth.* ii. 155, 162.
[6] *Op. cit.* ii. 465.
[7] Oldenberg, ZDMG. xlii. 216, 217.
[8] ÇGS. ii. 14. 2 invents a Bharadvāja Dhanvantari, but AGS. i. 2. 2 ; 3. 6 ; 12. 7 has Dhanvantari alone.
[9] PB. vii. 5. 20 ; Hillebrandt, *Ved. Myth.* iii. 442.

§ 3. *Warriors*

Of the warriors who are mentioned as having been engaged in battles and aided by the gods, we have absolutely no reason to assign the majority to any but the world of past reality. Historic reminiscence and poetic imagination are sufficient to account for what is said about them, just as the same factors together with aetiological myths explain adequately the legends of the priest of old days. To seek in any of them gods is erroneous :[1] treated as history, it is perfectly possible to make good sense out of the history of Sudās, and even of the older and more mystic Divodāsa Atithigva.[2] With Sudās Viçvāmitra and Vasiṣṭha stand in the closest relation : we have a poem which tradition places in the mouth of Viçvāmitra extolling the rivers Vipāç and Çutudrī for giving an easy crossing to his master's hosts,[3] and another hymn recounts with jeers at the expense of Viçvāmitra[4] the failure of the great coalition which he had brought against his former master, and the success of the army of Sudās through the help of Vasiṣṭha.

The other heroes are of less consequence except Kutsa,[5] who is important for the part played by him in connexion with Indra. In order to assist Kutsa to overthrow Çuṣṇa, Indra tore off one wheel of the sun, and gave the other to him to drive on with. The mythic element seems merely to be the introduction of this deed of Indra ; as Indra defeated for him Smadibha, Tugra, and the Vetasus, and on the other hand defeats for Tūrvayāṇa Kutsa, Āyu, and Atithigva, it seems most probable that Kutsa is a real enough prince. Bergaigne[6] sees in him, as too often, a figure of Agni, and the Naighaṇṭuka[7] includes his name among the synonyms of the thunderbolt.

§ 4. *The First of Men*

In the Rigveda there can be no doubt as to who is the real first man : it is Manu or Manus, whose name, cognate perhaps with the Gothic *manna*, and the root *man*, ' think ', appears as a definite forefather of men nearly forty times in the Rigveda. He is essentially the first of sacrificers, and the establisher of sacrifice, though he appears with other old sacrificers also, Aṅgiras, Bhṛgu, Atharvan, Dadhyañc, Atri, and Kaṇva. The gods, Mātariçvan, or Kāvya Uçanā, are said to have given Agni to Manu.[8] Again it is the three lakes of the Soma of Manus that Indra drinks to strengthen himself for the fight with Vṛtra. A bird brings Soma to Manu. In the Brāhmaṇas he con-

[1] Gruppe, *Griech. Culte*, i. 298 ff. ; Oldenberg, *Rel. des Veda*², pp. 287, 288 ; cf. Leaf, *Homer and History*, chap. i. ; Farnell, *Greek Hero Cults*.

[2] For all the following see Macdonell and Keith, *Vedic Index*, *s.vv.*

[3] RV. iii. 33 ; cf. 53 ; Hillebrandt, *Festgruss an Boehtlingk*, p. 403 ; Geldner, *Ved. Stud.* ii. 158 f.

[4] RV. vii. 18 ; Oldenberg, ZDMG. xlii. 203 ff. ; Oertel, JAOS. xviii. 47, 48 ; Hopkins, JAOS. xv. 260 ff.

[5] Bergaigne, *Rel. Véd.* ii. 333–8 ; Oldenberg, ZDMG. xlii. 211 ; Hillebrandt, *Ved. Myth.* iii. 284–93.

[6] *Loc. cit.*

[7] ii. 20.

[8] RV. i. 36. 10 ; 128. 2 ; viii. 23. 17.

stantly appears as connected with the sacrifice, and the dictum is laid down that, whatever Manu said, was medicine, a fact which accounts in part for the tradition which makes him the great legal authority of India.

Of the legends of Manu [1] the most important is that of the deluge, of which he is warned by a fish, and which he escapes through the agency of the fish, which carries his ship about until it rests on a mountain peak, in post-Vedic mythology called Naubandhana.[2] The fish in the epic becomes Brahman, and in the Purāṇas the full legend of the Avatar of Viṣṇu is recounted. Thereafter Manu with his daughter Iḍā, the personification of the sacrificial food, produces the human race. The legend may be alluded to in a very late book of the Atharvaveda,[3] but its late appearance, at a time when the Nakṣatras had probably been borrowed from a Semitic source, renders the theory of its independent Indian and even Indo-European origin, defended by Lindner,[4] rather dubious, though not impossible.

Another story connects him with the law of the division of property. Nābhānediṣṭha was deprived by his brothers of a fair share in the patrimonial heritage, which they divided up, when he was keeping his period of studentship. Manu, however, enables the young man to console himself by obtaining, in place of his share in the heritage, a boon from the Ādityas, after he has appeased Rudra who appears on the place of sacrifice to claim all the cattle which had been left by the sacrificers as a fee for Nābhānediṣṭha.[5]

It seems that Manu was already in the Rigveda considered to be the son of Vivasvant, whose name he actually bears in one case.[6] In the later texts he is quite regularly called son of Vivasvant.[7] He is accordingly a brother of Yama, or a duplication of that personage, but Manu unlike Yama is concerned with the living, and Yama with the dead: hence in the Çatapatha Brāhmaṇa [8] the difficulty is reconciled by making Manu the ruler of men, Yama of the dead. Yāska,[9] relying on an obscure passage of the Rigveda, finds in him the son of Vivasvant, and the *savarṇā* who was substituted for Saraṇyū, when that lady left her husband,[10] and in the Rigveda [11] we actually hear of Manu Sāṁvaraṇi, whose epithet may be either a mistake for Sāvarṇi which would point to a very early date for the legend, or may have been misunderstood and have created the legend.

The alternative connexion of the origin of man is from the union of the pair

[1] Rhys (*Celtic Heathendom*, pp. 377, 659 ff.) believes in Manu's identity with Tacitus's Mannus, ancestor of the Germans, the Celtic Manann, and Greek Minos, and holds the theory of an Aryan deluge.

[2] ÇB. i. 8. 1. 1–10.

[3] xix. 39. 8.

[4] *Festgruss an Roth*, pp. 213–16; Max Müller, *India*, pp. 133–8; Hopkins, *Rel. of India*, p. 160; above, Part I, Chap. 2. For a rational explanation, see A. C. Das, *Rig-Vedic India*, i. 221 f.

[5] AB. v. 14.

[6] RV. viii. 52. 1.

[7] AV. viii. 10. 24; ÇB. xiii. 4. 3. 3.

[8] xiii. 4. 3. 3–5.

[9] Nir. xii. 10.

[10] RV. x. 17. 2.

[11] RV. viii. 51. 1; cf. Scheftelowitz, *Die Apokryphen des Ṛgveda*, p. 38, with Oldenberg, GGA. 1907, p. 237.

Yama and Yamī, an idea which is found also in the Avesta ; [1] in an interesting dialogue of the tenth book of the Rigveda, Yamī is represented as having to persuade Yama that their wedlock is desirable and right against his doubts. Yama, however, is so intimately connected with the dead that further treatment of him can best be deferred to the discussion of Vedic eschatology. By a quite different order of ideas the four castes are elsewhere deemed to be derived from the body of the giant offered in sacrifice by the gods.[2]

[1] RV. x. 10 ; see below, Part V, Chap. 26.

[2] RV. x. 90 ; AV. xix. 6 ; TS. vii. 1. 1. 4–6 ; PB. vi. 1. 6–13 ; JB. i. 68 f., &c. See below, Appendix B.

CHAPTER 15

THE DEMONS

§ 1. *The Enemies of the Gods*

THE enemies of the gods *par excellence* throughout the Yajurveda, the Atharvaveda, and all the subsequent Vedic literature are beings called Asuras, but this connexion can be traced only in the latest parts of the Rigveda and even there but occasionally. In the singular the meaning is found but three times certainly, used of Varcin,[1] Pipru,[2] and the wolfish Asura ; [3] a fourth case is very doubtful, and may instead refer to Varuṇa.[4] In the plural there are at most eight cases, predominantly in the tenth book : in them the gods as a body appear opposed to the Asuras as in the later texts, or Indra scatters them.[5] The term Āsura is applied also to Namuci, and to Svarbhānu, while Indra, Agni, and the sun are called slayers of Asuras. In the Atharvaveda,[6] on the other hand, the singular is used in the hostile sense three times, the plural thirty times, and the application of the term to the gods, which is found very occasionally in the later literature,[7] is confronted with a regular application to the enemies of the gods. In the Rigveda, on the contrary, it is the normal attribute of Varuṇa and, more rarely, of other high gods.

The theory of Haug [8] that the change of meaning of Asura as between Asura in India and Ahura Mazdāh in Iran was due to a divergence in religion in the Indo-Iranian people, which ended in the schism of the two nations, is hopelessly opposed to the fact that the change of meaning takes place in India itself, and, since Darmesteter,[9] the theory has prevailed that the change by which Asura became the name of demons in India, while in Iran the Devas became demons, is an internal change of meaning in the two languages, brought about by causes which can be made more or less clear. In the case of India the development of Asura into a hostile sense is traced to its use in connexion with the word Māyā, ' wile ' [10] or ' occult power ', assisted by the

[1] RV. vii. 99. 5.
[2] RV. x. 138. 3.
[3] RV. ii. 30. 4.
[4] RV. x. 124.
[5] RV. viii. 96. 9 ; 97. 1 ; x. 157. 4; 53. 4 ; 82. 5 ; 124. 5 (dubious) ; 151. 3 ; *Āsura*, v. 40. 5, 9 ; x. 131. 4 ; *Asurahan*, vi. 22. 4 ; vii. 13. 1; x. 180. 2. Cf. Macdonell, JRAS. xxvii. 168–77.
[6] Von Bradke, *Dyāus Asura*, pp. 101 ff.
[7] Ludwig, *Rigveda*, iv. p. xvii ; TS. i. 6. 6.
[8] Criticized by Justi, GGA. 1866, pp. 1466 ff. ; Ludwig, *Rigveda*, iv. pp. xvii f.
[9] *Ormazd et Ahriman*, pp. 266 ff. ; Geldner, *Ved. Stud.* i. 142.
[10] Hillebrandt, VOJ. xiii. 320. The derivation from *mī*, ' injure ' (Geldner, *Glossar zum RV.*, p. 135), is clearly wrong ; it is from *mā*, ' fashion ', RV. v. 85. 5 ; i. 159. 4 ; iii. 38. 7 ; ix. 83. 3 ; cf. Neisser, *Festschrift Hillebrandt*, pp. 144 ff. ; Schayer, *Mahāyān. Erlösungslehre*, pp. 22 f.

popular derivation which saw a negative in the first letter of the word, and vaguely conceived the meaning as 'not heavenly', this view leading to the creation of the term *sura* for god in the Upaniṣads, and perhaps also by the absence of any collective name for the enemies of the gods proper. The change of Deva was by Darmesteter attributed to the misunderstanding under the régime of Zoroaster of the old phrases 'wrath of gods and men', and 'trouble made by gods or men', but this argument is of very problematic value indeed.

Hillebrandt [1] has recently opposed the prevalent doctrine, and asserted the opinion that the difference of view is due to religious relations with the early Iranians before the reform of Zoroaster, but after the period of the Rigveda in its main portions. He points out that the real cleavage in view is considerable: that the fall of the Nāsatya, Indra, Vāta, and Çarva to be demons as Nāoṅhaithya, Indra, Vāto, and Çauru (Saurva) is significant; that the Vedic Kavis and the Uçij family of priests fell in rank; and that there is no trace of the gradual change of sense, which would be expected, if the prevailing view were correct. He also points to the fact that among the names of Asuras, who appear in the accounts of the Brāhmaṇas, there are some with an Iranian aspect: namely Çaṇḍa and Marka, the latter being Avestan Mahrka,[2] Kāvya Uçanā, who is comparable with Kai Kāōs, Prahrāda Kāyādhava,[3] perhaps Avestan Kayadha, and Sṛma,[4] Iranian Salm, son of Thraētaona. The evidence is, however, clearly inadequate to prove the thesis, and the efforts of Hillebrandt to show that in the Rigveda occur names of Persian princes who patronized the singers, a fact which would indicate the possibility of close intercourse during the late Rigveda period natural, must be definitely taken to have failed to produce conviction.[5]

Another suggestion is made by von Schroeder,[6] based on von Bradke's view [7] of the term Asura, as applied to the gods, as meaning not 'spirit' as usually held, but 'master' or 'lord', and cognate with Latin *erus*. The name would thus normally have applied specifically to Dyaus, as the great sky god, or rather the god created by the moral sense of men, and also regarded as a nature deity, but as usual with the Vedic poets would have been extended

[1] *Ved. Myth.* iii. 430 ff.; cf. Moulton, *Early Zoroastrianism*, pp. 115, 140; von Bradke, *Dyāus Asura*, pp. 108 f. Greek influence for Vedic times (V. Smith, JASB. 1889, p. 133; 1892, p. 60) is implausible.

[2] TS. iv. 4. 10. 1; MS. iv. 6. 3; ÇB. iv. 2. 1. 16. Hillebrandt treats him as Death; these demons receive the Çukra and Manthin cups at the Agniṣṭoma, invented by the gods to rid themselves of them, and the Manthin cup brings disease. Çaṇḍikas in RV. ii. 30. 8 are foes of Indra. The Avestan Karapans who are in evil odour he connects with the *kalpa* of the Vedic priests.

[3] TB. i. 5. 9. 1.

[4] MS. iv. 2. 9.

[5] Macdonell and Keith, *Vedic Index*, i. 29, 349, 450, 509, 518; ii. 63. Jackson (CHI. i. 319 ff.) adds nothing new to Hillebrandt's conjectures. It is noteworthy that Bloomfield's evidence (*Rig-Veda Repetitions*, p. 645) shows book vi as by no means early as it should be if it deals with events in Iran before the invasion of India.

[6] *Arische Religion*, i. 317 ff.

[7] *Dyāus Asura*, pp. 29 ff.

by henotheism to other gods, such as Varuṇa, Parjanya, Indra, Agni, and Savitṛ. The degradation of such a term seems unlikely, and accordingly von Schroeder believes that there originally existed two distinct words, *asura*, 'lord', and *asura*, 'spirit'. In India the latter use prevailed, and the older or contemporaneous *asura*, 'lord', was given up, because perhaps of risk of confusion with the other term, while the Iranians retained the use of Ahura as 'master'. This suggestion is ingenious, but purely hypothetical, and hardly necessary to explain the facts. Moreover, the idea that *asura* as 'spirit' is naturally applied to evil beings is decidedly fantastic. The precise sense which *asura* had in the minds of those who used it is unknown to us, but there is nothing to show that it had any connexion with the worship of the spirits of the dead, as frequently suggested.[1] On the contrary, even from its possible connexion with *asu*, 'breath', the word may rather have meant that which is essentially alive and possessed of power and strength.[2]

The view of these personages taken by the Brāhmaṇas is that they are equally sons of Prajāpati, though born of a less worthy part of the god, from the descending breath, not the mouth, and that they are in constant conflict with the gods, and have to be defeated by some ritual performances. They are associated with the darkness, untruth, and error, as opposed to the gods. The term 'pertaining to the Asuras' is freely given to any ritual performance which the priests do not approve. Thus the Asuras are said to have only a morning and afternoon pressing,[3] not three as the Vedic Indians, a point which has some affinity to the Avesta, and the mode of making the grave differs.[4] We have one fairly clear proof that Aryan enemies are included, for the Çatapatha Brāhmaṇa[5] has preserved to us two barbarous (*mleccha*) words used by the Asuras, *he 'lavo*, which, despite various efforts to interpret them as Assyrian or something equally implausible, seem merely a Prākritic version of the Vedic *he 'rayaḥ*, 'O enemies', pointing to an eastern dialect as in Māgadhī.

Among names of Asuras we learn of Kirāta and Ākuli,[6] Araru (with which may be compared the Arurmaghas or Aruṅmaghas, foes of Indra), Aru, Kustā,[7] in opposition to Aditi, Etadu, from the use of *etad u* in a formula, Daivya as their messenger as opposed to Agni, Dābhi as the address of the Gāyatrī

[1] Thus Moulton (*Early Zoroastrianism*, p. 150; *Early Rel. Poetry of Persia*, pp. 34 ff.) argues that the high Ahura worship comes from ancestor worship as contrasted with the inferior worship of Daēvas, nature deities. But he himself (*Early Zoroastrianism*, pp. ix, 344, &c.) renders Ahura by 'lord', which disposes of any connexion with ancestor worship. Varuṇa sufficiently refutes for India and Ahura for Iran Schroeder's doctrine that morality and ancestor worship are more closely related than the worship of the gods and conduct.

[2] Cf. Oldenberg, *Rel. des Veda*², p. 160, n. 2. On the whole, the sense 'lord' seems adequate for Veda and Avesta alike. On the Gaulish Esus, see Rhys, *Celtic Heathendom*, pp. 60 ff.

[3] TS. vi. 2. 5. 3.

[4] ÇB. xiii. 8. 2. 1.

[5] iii. 2. 1. 23, 24; Macdonell and Keith, *op. cit.* ii. 181, 279, 517.

[6] PB. xiii. 12. 5; ÇB. i. 1. 4. 16; JB. iii. 168 ff.

[7] MS. iv. 2. 3.

metre,[1] in place of Viçvakarman, Asita Dhānva, their king,[2] Pūru, the name of a Vedic prince, Vibhinduka and Viṣād. More important are the Kālakañjas,[3] who figure in a story similar to that of Otos and Ephialtes, the bricks of the altar taking the place of mountains.

In comparison with the Asuras the Paṇis are unimportant demons, who play no great part in the literature after the Rigveda. They are the demons who withhold the cows, or, as it is differently put, the ghee in the cow, from Indra or his allies, Agni, Bṛhaspati, the Añgirases or Soma, and are overthrown by him. The word is normally plural, but a single Paṇi four times represents the group. The most probable explanation [4] is undoubtedly that which sees in the Paṇis the personification of the enemy, who will not sacrifice to the gods or bestow gifts on the priests, and who is therefore an enemy of the gods and men alike, and has been brought into the old myth of the winning of the light in cow shape. Hillebrandt [5] seeks to show that the Paṇis are an historical tribe, comparing the name Parnians, but the suggestion is most improbable.

The Dāsas or Dasyus are also made into enemies of the gods, though, like the Paṇis, their primitive function was doubtless different; in their case it probably was that of aborigines, who opposed the Aryan advance, though Hillebrandt [6] changes them into Dahae. That in many cases historic men may be meant when Dāsas are overthrown, is true; but gods of the defeated aborigines may also be denoted, and more generally powers of the air opposed to the gods: Dasyus seek to scale heaven,[7] Indra vanquishes them from birth,[8] he wins the sun and waters after defeating them,[9] a Dāsa is husband of the waters,[10] and the Dāsas have seven autumnal forts, doubtless in the air, not on the steppes.

Of the individual names of the enemies of the gods Vṛtra ranks first; he is a serpent with power over the lightning, mist, hail, and thunder, when he wars with Indra; his mother is Dānu, apparently the stream or the waters of heaven, but he bears that name himself as well as Dānava, offspring of Dānu. His abode is hidden in the waters, but is also on a summit or on lofty heights, which suggest the waters of the air. He is by name the encompasser of the waters, rather than the holder back by congealing them: the cloud mountain is, therefore, said to be within his belly. He has ninety-nine forts which Indra shatters as he slays him. From the single Vṛtra the Vedic conception, as often, produces many Vṛtras, and we find also the plural used of foes who must be clearly human, perhaps, however, never without a sub-reference to Vṛtra, though, as the neuter is used in this way, it may be that the use is not simply a direct generalization of Vṛtra as a demon. The Brāhmaṇas, which tell many

[1] TS. ii. 4. 3; MS. ii. 1. 11.
[2] ÇB. xiii. 4. 3. 11.
[3] TB. i. 1. 2. 4–6; Eggeling, SBE. xii. 286.
[4] Oldenberg, *Rel. des Veda*², p. 143; Macdonell, *Ved. Myth.*, p. 157.
[5] *Ved. Myth.* i. 83 ff.; ZDMG. lxx. 512 ff.
[6] *Op. cit.* i. 95; (Kl. Ausg.), pp. 96 f.
[7] RV. viii. 14. 14; i. 33. 7.
[8] RV. i. 51. 6; viii. 77. 1–3.
[9] RV. i. 100. 18; x. 73. 5.
[10] RV. i. 32. 11.

tales about Vṛtra,[1] make him out to be the moon, swallowed at new moon by Indra as the sun.

Vala is a pale figure compared to Vṛtra : he is mentioned in the myth of the Paṇis: Bṛhaspati or Indra takes from him the cows which he had in his forts, his fences are burst by Indra, or his hole is opened. The word means literally covering, and is found often in this sense or in some cognate meaning. The fold of Vala is also mentioned, and he is clearly simply the personification of the pen in which the cows are supposed to be kept, as is indicated by the fact that he is not said to be slain, but to be pierced, broken, or cloven. In the post-Vedic mythology he appears in the epithet of Indra, ' piercer of Vala ', and is deemed brother of Vṛtra, with whose myth, however, he had, it is clear, little originally to do.[2]

Arbuda appears seven times as a beast whose head Indra struck off : he seems to be cognate to Vṛtra with whom or Ahi he is mentioned.[3] Svarbhānu,[4] the Asura, is more interesting : he is clearly the demon who eclipses the sun, and who has to be overthrown by Atri or the Atris, and by Indra. Though he is several times mentioned in the Brāhmaṇas, his place is in post-Vedic mythology regularly taken by Rāhu. The Atharvaveda [5] also knows of Grahas who affect the moon. Of Uraṇa who had ninety-nine arms we know no more.[6] But we hear a good deal of Viçvarūpa, the three-headed son of Tvaṣṭṛ, slain by Trita and by Indra for the sake of his cows, and who in the Brāhmaṇas [7] appears as the Purohita of the gods, though akin to the Asuras. Tvaṣṭṛ, it is said, sought to punish Indra for the death of his son, but his effort to exclude him from the Soma sacrifice was defeated by Indra, who insisted on taking a share in it. The legend tells also of the origin of three birds from the three heads of the demon, as they were struck off by Indra, and explains the use of each of the three heads for drinking respectively the Soma, the Surā, and taking other forms of nourishment.[8] To Hillebrandt [9] the moon seems to be meant by this form, and he lays just stress on the fact that the Brāhmaṇas are aware of the hostile character of the moon, which they often equate with Vṛtra, and which seems once regarded in a hostile light in the Rigveda ; but this view cannot be regarded as probable as that which insists on the identity of the legend with those of Herakles and Geryoneus and Hercules and Cacus.[10]

[1] Hillebrandt, *Ved. Myth.* iii. 239 ff. Usener (*Götternamen*, p. 206) finds the Danaoi in the Dānava as demons, despite the change of quantity. Implausible is the view that Vṛtra is a creation of the imagination, *vṛtrahan*, as in the Avesta Verethraghna, denoting ' assault repelling ' (Bartholomae, *Air.Wb.* 1420).

[2] Hillebrandt, *Ved. Myth.* iii. 260–6.

[3] RV. ii. 11. 20 ; 14. 4 ; i. 51. 6 ; viii. 3. 19 ; 32. 2 ; x. 67. 12. Cf. the snake priest Arbuda Kādraveya, ÇB. xiii. 4. 3. 9.

[4] RV. v. 60 ; Rāhu occurs in AV. xix. 9. 10, a late passage.

[5] *Loc. cit.*

[6] RV. ii. 14. 4.

[7] TS. ii. 5. 1. 1. For the three heads, cf. Hopkins, *Origin of Religion*, pp. 297 ff.

[8] ÇB. i. 6. 3. 1 ff. ; v. 5. 4. 2 ; TS. ii. 4. 12. 1.

[9] *Ved. Myth.* iii. 531 ff.

[10] Oldenberg, *Rel. des Veda*², p. 142, n. 6.

Of the Dāsa enemies of Indra the chief is Çambara, the son of Kulitara,[1] who had 90, 99, or 100 forts and was the great foe of Divodāsa Atithigva. His historical reality seems reasonably assumed.[2] Pipru is styled a wild beast, an Asura, and a Dāsa, and is defeated for the sake of Ṛjiçvan: it seems unnecessary to see in him a spirit of the air.[3] Dhuni, the roarer, and Cumuri, whose name is not connected with any known root, are apparently chiefs defeated for Dabhīti. Varcin is both Asura and Dāsa, but his 1,100 or 100,000[4] warriors do not seem wholly mythical, and the names Anarçani, Ilībiça, Dṛbhīka, Rudhikrā, and Sṛbinda, which are those of other foes, seem human enough. On the other hand, Namuci, as we have seen, seems to be a demon, and Çuṣṇa has been explained not as a human enemy of Kutsa, but as a demon of drought from his name interpreted as scorcher.[5] But this seems unlikely: he is child of the mist and moves in the water and a Dānava; if, therefore, he is a demon, he is rather the hisser, for Vṛtra's hissing drove Indra away in fear, and this applies to other enemies than drought demons.

§ 2. *The Enemies of Man*

It is impossible, when we deal with the lesser demons of the Vedic religion, to ascertain with any reasonable certainty the origin of the different conceptions exhibited, for the lack of clearness of the notices given in our sources is in accordance with the fact that the demons are objects of aversion, and that therefore they are not minutely described, but only indicated in vague terms. It is probably true that in many cases the idea of such spirits is born of the idea of the hostile dead,[6] or again the demons are the product of independent creative thought, corresponding to the 'abstract' deities, but they may also often be more naturalistic in their origin. It must be remembered that there are poisonous plants, that waters are often regarded as cruel and dangerous as well as kindly, as in the widespread belief that a river must be propitiated by the life of man at least once a year, that the savage character of the forest creates the view that it is inhabited by a dread spirit, that the hail is regarded as evil, and that trees are awe-inspiring[7] and sometimes deadly in their fruits. The animatistic growth of such ideas as that of hostile spirits is as natural as the animistic, or the spiritist, but in the case of the demons the distinctions cannot be made with certainty in the confused figures which we find in the literature. Nor in the case of the demons can we overlook the fact that actual men may be included as well as spirits of the dead, and actual animals also be considered a very natural fact.

1 In this name Brunnhofer (*Arische Urzeit*, pp. 71, 72) finds as usual an ethnic reference without any conceivable ground.

2 He considered himself a godling, RV. vii. 18. 20.

3 Macdonell, *Ved. Myth.*, p. 161.

4 RV. ii. 14. 6; iv. 30. 15.

5 Macdonell, *op. cit.*, p. 160.

6 As in Babylonian religion, Farnell, *Greece and Babylon*, p. 206. Cf. Arbman, *Rudra*, p. 169.

7 Cf. Hopkins, *Epic Myth.*, p. 7, n. 3.

The forms of the demons are conceived either anthropomorphically or theriomorphically, or, and this is a distinction between them and the gods, as compounded of both forms. They are enumerated in groups, but the distinctions between the groups are not carefully drawn, and in addition we have many names of individuals, derived from their activity or appearance, or fancy names, or names perhaps of real enemies.

The Rakṣases are the most famous of the classes of demons, and occur in the Rigveda upwards of fifty times, nearly always in connexion with the mention of a god who is desired to deal with them. In two hymns [1] the Rakṣases seem to be more precisely defined as Yātus or Yātudhānas, words which denote wizard or sorcerers, and the latter may be regarded as a subdivision of the Rakṣasas, a fact of the utmost importance as showing how important even in the Rigveda was the belief in such beings, many of them probably real men. The Rakṣases are often, as is natural, theriomorphic; they appear as dogs, vultures, owls, and other birds flying about at night; [2] they can assume the form of husband, brother, or lover,[3] and they are a constant peril to the woman in child. In dog or ape form they are ready to attack her; [4] at the wedding service they prowl around, and small staves are flung in the air to pierce the eyes of the demons.[5] When they have human forms, they are often hideously deformed, with two mouths, three heads, four eyes, five feet, with feet turned backwards, without fingers, or with horns on their hands, and bear-necked.[6] Blue, yellow, and green are their colours, and they are not without social organization, having both families and kings: [7] unlike the gods, they are mortal, and have not won immortality.[8] They are essentially blood-suckers who seek to enter men, especially by the mouth in the process of eating and drinking, but also by other inferior passages which the gods are therefore besought to protect.[9] When within they eat the man's or beast's flesh and cause disease; [10] they bring about madness and destroy the power of speech; [11] they invade human dwellings [12] and dance around houses in the evening; they make a noise in the forest, pray aloud, or laugh and drink out of skulls as cups,[13] a point which shows that the ghouls of the places of burial must have contributed an element to the conceptions: in such spirits the idea of the spirits of the dead, especially the dead not duly buried or burnt, and the spirits, which are, like Vāstoṣpati in the house, resident in the place of the dead, must inevitably inextricably combine.

Like most evil spirits, the Rakṣases love the night,[14] especially the night when there is no moon, for in the east the sun disperses them, and in this

[1] RV. vii. 104; x. 87. In JB. iii. 266 Ṛkṣa appears in the sense of Rakṣas.
[2] RV. vii. 104. 18, 22.
[3] RV. x. 162. 5.
[4] AV. iv. 37. 11.
[5] MGS. i. 4. 10.
[6] AV. viii. 6; HGS. ii. 3. 7.
[7] AV. v. 22. 12; HGS. ii. 3. 7.
[8] AV. vi. 32. 2.
[9] AV. v. 29. 6–8; viii. 6. 3.
[10] RV. x. 87. 16, 17; viii. 60. 20; AV. vii. 76. 4.
[11] AV. vi. 11. 1, 3; HGS. i. 15. 5.
[12] Kauç. cxxxv. 9.
[13] AV. viii. 6. 10, 11, 14; HGS. ii. 3. 7.
[14] RV. vii. 104. 18.

connexion with night they are akin to the souls of the dead. Hence, it seems, a falling meteor [1] is considered to be the embodiment of a Rakṣas.

As is natural in a priestly collection, we hear much of the attacks of the Rakṣases on the sacrifice: with the Yātus they taint it and throw it into confusion.[2] On the other hand, the sorcerer can use a spell, and by the Rakṣases and the Yātudhānas ruin the sacrifice of his enemy.[3] In order to obtain the advantage of sacrifices, the evil spirits often assume the form of souls of ancestors and come to the offerings for the dead.[4] But the demons can be yoked by a skilled man to his own ends; in the Atharvaveda we find that demons are invited to attack the man who sends them, and the later texts recognize the need of providing against the attacks of sorcerers.[5] In these cases and for the protection of the offering the essential aider is Agni, the burner, who therefore represents the primitive and universal belief in the power of fire to repel hostile demons. An isolated mention is made of Kubera Vaiçravaṇa as their king.

The meaning of the term is doubtful: the root 'protect' is the obvious one, in which case the word must apparently mean that which is to be guarded against, unless we suppose that they are given a good-sounding name, in order to make them good. In the sense 'injure', there is little authority for *rakṣ*. Bergaigne [6] thinks that they are named as guardians of celestial treasure, who being greedy are hated, for which view the parallel of the Gandharvas and the Soma may be cited, as well as the fact that Kubera is their king. Bartholomae connects Rakṣas with the root seen in Greek ἐρεχθεῖν.

The Piçācas are only once mentioned in the Rigveda,[7] where Indra is invoked to crush the yellow-peaked, watery, Piçācī and every Rakṣas. In the later Saṁhitās they figure, however, in the plural, and they are opposed to the Fathers, as the Asuras to the gods, and the Rakṣases to men, but not consistently.[8] They may, however, have been supposed to be specially of the ethnic type of theriomorphic ghouls of the dead, as they have the name *kravyād*, 'eaters of raw flesh'.[9] But they also are treated as eating away the flesh of a sick man, while again they appear as infesting human dwellings and villages, and even as will-o'-the-wisps.[10] The view that these Piçācas are really, or originally, a special tribe who were addicted to cannibalism, and who were the speakers of the Prākrit known to the grammarians as Paiçācī, has been put forward of late, but has no probability, the reverse process being much more likely.[11] Similarly, the idea that the Rakṣases are originally conceived as hostile aborigines cannot be accepted as explaining the class

1 Kauç. cxxvi. 9.
2 RV. vii. 104. 18, 21; x. 182. 3.
3 AV. vii. 70. 2.
4 AV. xviii. 2. 28; Caland, *Altind. Ahnenkult*, pp. 3 ff.
5 RV. vi. 62. 9; vii. 104. 23; viii. 82. 20; AV. ii. 24; TS. ii. 2. 3. 2.
6 *Rel. Véd.* ii. 218.
7 i. 133. 5.
8 TS. ii. 4. 1. 1.
9 AV. v. 29. 9.
10 AV. iv. 36. 8; 20. 9; 37. 10.
11 Grierson, ZDMG. lxvi. 68.

generally, but merely as one element in the conception.[1] Charpentier [2] finds in the Piçācas the souls of the dead conceived as glow-worms. The Brāhmaṇas[3] tell a curious tale of a Piçācī who married the Ikṣvāku King, Tryaruṇa, and dulled his fire, until the priest Vṛça by a rite had her burned up.

The Arātis, who occur about a dozen times in the Rigveda and frequently later, are clearly abstract deities of illiberality, but clothed with quite a real life in the imagination of the indignant Vedic poet, who asks the gods to overthrow them. The Druhs are found about as often in the Rigveda,[4] but they are Indo-Iranian, the Avestan being *druj*, and, like all the older conceptions, are not living features of the religion, being merely vaguely conceived as injurious spirits. The Kimīdins as a pair of demons occur already in the Rigveda,[5] contrary to the more normal practice of grouping the demons in sets, perhaps owing to the influence of the dual deities. The names which we have of such Kimīdins, Mroka and Anumroka, Sarpa and Anusarpa, show, however, their entire distinction from the dual deities which have distinct personalities and quite different appellations.[6]

Among the homes of these spirits, especially probably those of the dead, one is especially noteworthy, the cross way, which is the scene of various magic rites. It is there that evil spirits and disease are banished by the sorcerer; there is performed the spell to find what has been lost, there Rudra is said to dwell, after a death the fire which becomes thus impure is deposited there.[7] It is doubtful what motive in each case can be seen for the superstition which is world-wide: unquestionably the spirits of the dead are thought to live there, especially perhaps evil spirits, as evil dead are often so buried, but it is possible to find other motives: the cross-roads is the place whence all ways deviate, so that it is the proper centre for a spell to seek for what is lost: or again by depositing there what is impure, the idea may be that the impurity is induced to go one way, the former owner of it another, or the evil which is laid aside may enter into and be taken away by one of the many wayfarers who pass that way.

One set of demons seems still to show its essential connexion with a natural object, those which are conceived as embodied in plants. Agni and Indra are implored to destroy the demons together with the root,[8] and the point, or three points, of demons is alluded to: it is natural to assume that the root is the incorporation of the deity, and this view is strengthened by the reference [9] to those 'whose god is the root', an expression which surely denotes that the

[1] Macdonell and Keith, *Vedic Index*, ii. 516.

[2] *Kleine Beiträge zur indoiranischen Mythologie* (1911). But see Winternitz, VOJ. xxvii. 229–32.

[3] PB. xiii. 3. 11–13; JB. iii. 94–6; Sieg, *Die Sagenstoffe des RV.*, p. 64; Oertel, JAOS. xviii. 21 ff.; Oldenberg on RV. v. 2. 1.

[4] Macdonell, *Ved. Myth.*, p. 8.

[5] RV. vii. 104. 23; x. 87. 24; Weber, *Ind. Stud.* xiii. 183 ff.

[6] AV. ii. 24.

[7] Kauç. xxvi. 30; xxvii. 7; xxx. 18; lii. 14; ÇB. ii. 6. 2. 7; HGS. i. 16. 8; AGS. iv. 6. 3; Oldenberg, *Rel. des Veda*², pp. 269 f.

[8] RV. iii. 30. 17; x. 87. 19.

[9] RV. vii. 104. 24; x. 87. 2, 14.

root was the actual demon, rather than merely that the demon was supposed to have taken up his abode [1] in the root, though the former conception might easily be passing into the latter.

In the case of the disease demons it is not easy precisely to determine what conception was formed of them. The idea formed of them certainly hovers between the conception of a spirit like Takman, 'fever', who brings the disease, and a more materialistic, or scientific, conception of some substance which carries the disease itself. The constant efforts to drive out diseases by means of spells and sympathetic magic may, according to Oldenberg, fairly be held to contain a more advanced conception of the nature of disease than the more simple concept of a demon disease. But this is not at all clear, unless we accept Oldenberg's animistic views. The real question is whether the demon disease was conceived in the first place abstractly, the disease being caused by a demon, and the demon identified with the disease it caused, or whether the disease was conceived as something real and material, with a life of its own. The latter view seems to accord most with primitive thought, and with the material, if less personal, character of the disease as attacked by the means of the sorcerer in the Atharvaveda, in which, however, constant hints of the personal character are still to be found. The actual signs of the disease, the symptoms visible to the eye, are in the primitive mind the disease itself, which is, as the symptoms come and go, clearly a living entity.

The demons are not, however, merely repelled by the use of fire, and by many spells; they are actually occasionally propitiated with offerings, as in the case of the Rakṣases and Yātudhānas who are thus treated in the Taittirīya Brāhmaṇa,[2] a fact which may stand in relation with the use which sorcerers were able to make of these spirits. Tricks are also tried to deceive them: thus in the period [3] of continence immediately after marriage, there has been seen by Oldenberg [4] an ingenious device to prevent any hostile action on the part of the demons, whether by attacking the bride or seeking to enjoy her,[5] and in any case the sympathetic magic of the device is obvious. The practice in the acts of driving away fiends of enumerating as many names as possible is parallel to that of enumerating as many gods in the offerings of the Vaiçvadeva rite in the domestic ritual, and it has preserved to us several lists. To protect the woman in child-birth a fire is lighted,[6] and the spirits are banned under the names of Çaṇḍa and Marka, Upavīra, Çauṇḍikeya, Ulūkhala, Malimluca, Droṇāsa, Cyavana, Ālikhant, Animiṣa, Kiṁvadanta, Upaçruti, Haryakṣa, Kumbhin, Çatru, Pātrapāṇi, Nṛmaṇi, Hantrīmukha, Sarṣapāruṇa, Cyavana.

[1] Oldenberg, *op. cit.*, p. 268, n. 4; the natural origin of such spirits is seen in Celtic religion; MacCulloch, *Rel. of Anc. Celts*, pp. 173, 185; cf. Farnell, *Greece and Babylon*, pp. 110, 111, 43.

[2] iii. 4. 1. 5.

[3] Winternitz, *Altind. Hochzeitsrituell*, p. 87; J. J. Meyer, *Das Weib im altindischen Epos*, pp. 235 f.

[4] *Rel. des Veda*², p. 273.

[5] AV. iv. 37. 11; ÇB. iii. 2. 1. 10.

[6] PGS. i. 16. 23; ApGS. xviii. 1; MP. ii. 16. 1 ff. A longer list in HGS. ii. 3. 7; Pramṛçant, Kūṭadanta, Vikleça, Lambastana, Uraspeça, &c.

Still more interesting is the treatment of a child which has a barking cough ; [1] the demon within him is exorcized to let loose the child, being addressed as Kūrkura, good Kūrkura, and doggy ; he is assured that Saramā is his mother, Sīsara his father, and the brindled dogs of Yama his brothers : the idea of the demon cough in dog form is perfectly clear : its name is also given as Kumāra. When the man performs the Vaiçvadeva offerings of the domestic ritual, his wife outside the house offers food [2] to the man, to the woman, to every age, to the white one with black teeth, the lord of bad women, to those who allure her children, whether in the wood or the forest. On the day of the final bath the pupil banishes from him all the evil forms of Agni, ten in number, which he enumerates.[3] Demons figure among those to whom he is given in charge by the teacher on his reception.[4] In the ritual we find in the Taittirīya Āraṇyaka [5] a list of hideous forms to be driven away from the offering, Viçīrṣṇī, Gṛdhraçīrṣṇī, and so on. The sacrifice is full of all sorts of magic devices to repel the evil spirits, who, on the one hand, are allowed to have offerings of the blood, though only with inaudible words of offering lest the speech of the speaker should become the voice of a Rakṣas,[6] but on the other hand are kept off by the use of the enclosing sticks, by the free employment of fire, by the drawing of magic circles, and by the sound of the pressing stones.[7]

The great gods of the Vedic period are not reduced to demons, nor do they approximate to them : it is true that their names are invoked in very trivial occasions such as that of Indra in an idiotic spell to induce a slave not to run away from his master,[8] or to secure connexion,[9] but that merely denotes that the gods were familiar enough to their votaries not to despise aiding them in all their actions. Hillebrandt [10] indeed sees in some passages the tendency to reduce Rudra to the rank of little more than a demon, but, while Rudra is a terrible god and is in some ways akin to the demons, the evidence adduced by Hillebrandt is not altogether in point. Rudra is to be addressed when a man is on a path, at cross-roads, crossing a river, at a mountain, a forest, a burial-ground and a stable, but the fact that he is so to be invoked is expressly explained by his omnipresence,[11] and we have here not so much a primitive idea as the extension to every sphere of activity of the great god Rudra, the sign of an advanced theistic view of the god rather than a degradation of his nature. More kinship to legends of demons is to be seen in such a legend as that of Indra becoming a horse's tail ; [12] the gods are able to change form at

1 PGS. i. 16. 24.
2 PGS . i. 12. 4.
3 PGS. ii. 6. 10.
4 HGS. i. 6. 5.
5 i. 28.
6 AB. ii. 7, 1.
7 TS. ii. 6. 6, 2 ; RV. x. 36. 4 ; ÇB. vii. 7. 1. 2 ; ApÇS. xi. 11. 6. Araru is a demon banned from the place of sacrifice, TS. i. 1. 9 ; MS. i. 1. 10 ; iv. 1. 10 ; VS. i. 26 ; TB. iii. 2. 9. 4 ; possibly in RV. x. 9. 9, 10.
8 PGS. iii. 7. 3.
9 PGS. i. 9. 5.
10 *Ved. Myth.* iii. 425.
11 PGS. iii. 15. 7 ff. ; HGS. i. 16. 8 ff. ; AGS. iv. 8. 40 ; MP. i. 13. 8 ; ApGS. ix. 3 ; Oldenberg, *Rel. des Veda*², pp. 220 ff. Arbman's objections (*Rudra*, pp. 222 ff.) are irrelevant.
12 Geldner, *Ved. Stud.* ii. 183 ; perhaps an ant, RV. i. 51. 9 ; Hillebrandt, *op. cit.* iii. 172, 173.

will, a fact of which Indra makes free use in his amourettes, but it is rarely that they adopt anything but a noble form such as the eagle form of Indra, but that god has a tendency to assume popular traits. Kubera, later the god of wealth, is a Rakṣas and lord of robbers and evil-doers in the Çatapatha Brāhmaṇa ;[1] in the Sūtras[2] he is invoked with Īçāna for the husband in the marriage ritual, and his hosts plague children. Comparison[3] with Greek Kabeiros and explanation as a mountain spirit of hiding propensities are most doubtful.

A certain interest attaches to the very late Nejameṣa, who appears apparently as banned in the ritual of the parting of the hair of the bride,[4] for he reappears in the form of Naigameṣa in the medical work of Suçruta, and as Nemesa in a Mathurā inscription.[5] It is dubious whether the name is found in the epic, though possibly the Naigameya there recorded may be an error for it.[6]

In the somewhat late Mānava Gṛhya Sūtra[7] we have a rite prescribed for one who suffers from possession by the Vināyakas, Çālakaṭaṅkaṭa, Kūṣmāṇḍarājaputra, Usmita and Devayajana, in which a strange variety of deities are invoked, Vimukha, Çyena, Baka, Yakṣa, Kalaha, Bhīru, Vināyaka, Kūṣmāṇḍarājaputra, Yajnāvikṣepin, Kulaṅgāpamārin, Yūpakeçin, Sūparakroḍin, Haimavata, Jambhaka, Virūpākṣa, Lohitākṣa, Vaiçravaṇa, Mahāsena, Mahādeva, Mahārāja. Mahādeva is doubtless Rudra, Mahāsena appears elsewhere[8] as a disease demon and is an epithet of Skanda, Vaiçravaṇa is Kubera. In Yājñavalkya[9] we find a single Vināyaka, who is here son of the goddess Ambikā, and appointed by Brahman and Rudra to be the overlord of the Gaṇas, troupes, perhaps akin to those assigned to Rudra's entourage in the Yajurveda.[10] Doubtless we have here something akin to the later Gaṇeça, who is not Vedic, but it is by no means certain that we are to interpret Vināyaka as denoting 'leader', instead of 'remover of obstacles',[11] or the epithet Vighneça, which later is found applied to Gaṇeça, as lord of Vighnas, conceived as destroyers. The term Yakṣa,[12] which occurs in this list, is far better known in the Buddhist form of Yakkha ; we find the term applied to a wondrous thing in the Jaiminīya Brāhmaṇa ;[13] the Ṛṣis seek to behold something of this kind, and Indra reveals to them the tortoise Akūpāra, of boundless dimension, who is clearly the cosmic tortoise who finds the earth in the ocean. The specification of the term to mean a species of spirit, usually associated with Kubera, is not found until the period of the Gṛhya Sūtras.

1 xiii. 4. 3, 10 ; cf. AV. viii. 10. 28.
2 ÇGS. i. 11. 7 ; HGS. ii. 1. 3. 7.
3 Hopkins, JAOS. xxxi. 55–70.
4 ÇGS. i. 22. 7 ; AGS. i. 14. 3.
5 Bühler, EI. ii. 316 ; Winternitz, JRAS. 1895, pp. 149 ff. ; Hillebrandt, *Ved. Myth.* iii. 424.
6 Hopkins, *Epic Myth.*, pp. 103, 227, 229.
7 ii. 14 ; Arbman, *Rudra* .pp. 57 f. 219 ff. *contra*, Winternitz, JRAS. 1898, p. 383.
8 PGS. i. 16. 24 is cited by Arbman, but wrongly. Skanda appears in BhGS. iii. 9 ; AV. Par. xx ; BG. Par. iv. 2.
9 i. 271 ff.
10 TS. iv. 5. 4.
11 Jacobi, ERE. ii. 807.
12 Boyer, JA. 1906, i. 393 ff. ; Oldenberg, RV. ii. ff. ; Hopkins, *Epic Myth.*, pp. 30 f.
13 iii. 203, 272.

CHAPTER 16

THE GODS AND THEIR WORSHIPPERS

As men fashion their concepts of their gods in accordance with their own attitude towards life, it is natural to find in the Rigveda the expression of the real religious spirit of the day. It must, however, be borne in mind in any estimate of that spirit that the sources are all priestly, and that, therefore, they express the views not so much of the ordinary man even of the higher ranks, and social distinctions certainly existed then, but of the priest himself, and of a priesthood which had already advanced a long way in the direction of the elaboration and definition of religion. This fact, however, while it explains much that is to be found in the thought of the Rigveda, and warns us against imputing that thought to a simple people living in immediate contact with nature and the birth of the gods, does not alter the impression which is unquestionably made by the Rigveda as a whole, and which is of a definite and intelligible character.

The Indians of the Rigveda, from even the comparatively scanty traces of their ordinary activities to be gathered from that collection, were essentially an active, energetic, warrior people, engaged indeed in struggles with the aborigines, and even among themselves, but in the main prosperous, and contented with their life. The tone of the great gods reflects, therefore, the character of the people, and in no case better than in that of Indra. Indra is the victorious warrior : he is also the jovial and human god : he is a great drinker, a mighty eater, and the poets do not scorn to tell how he drank over much and required skilled tendance as the result. He is hot-tempered, as befits a god who wars ever with demons : there are signs of a qnarrel with the gods, of interference with Sūrya, of an onslaught even on Uṣas, and, worst of all, of killing his father for the sake of the Soma. But the presence of such traits is only incidental and occasional : they cannot have formed any serious element in his character, save in so far as they gave rise to the feeling which is frankly expressed in one hymn,[1] that Indra is changeable, that he is inconstant in his friendships, that he makes the first last at pleasure, and that he is angry with the man who has wealth. We must be careful not to overestimate the force of such remarks : the wealthy against whom the god is wroth are the Paṇis, who withhold treasures from men and gods alike : we have nothing of Herodotos's doctrine of the jealousy of heaven. But it must be owned that Indra by these traits seems to have created misbelief, for we find here and there firm assertions in his divinity, which is proved when he

[1] RV. vi. 47. 15–17.

manifests his great deeds and which refutes the sayings of men who deny Indra's existence. Of no other god have we any such doubt expressed in the Rigveda.[1] In the main, however, Indra is a kind and generous friend to his votaries, and the Rigveda does not seem to know the legend which makes him seduce Ahalyā by assuming as a disguise the form of her husband, a performance more in accord with the ways of demons than of a great god.

The position of the other gods is essentially similar to that of Indra ; on the one hand, most of them are not so near to men in feeling and have less human life in their natures, but at the same time they are free from the less creditable aspects which belong to Indra. Agni is in special closeness to the worshipper, as he is the guest who dwells in the house, and, therefore, a very present friend, but his close relation to the element renders his personality less clear than that of Indra, and so places a difficulty in the way of the generation of deeper human relations. His parentage of men is hardly marked: he is rather the prototype, as Añgiras, of the priest, and the great god of the priests. The only exception to the general rule is Rudra, and in a minor degree the Maruts, his companions.[2] Rudra is emphatically a terrible god : the ritual exhibits this characteristic in the constant assimilation of his character to that of the dead and the demons, and in the prayers this fact is clearly shown by the efforts ever made to induce him to spare the worshipper, his wife, his children, his horses, his cattle, to keep his weapons afar from him, and to be merciful. The wrath of the god is evidently easily awakened whether by prayer wrongly offered or obtruded upon him when busy otherwise,[3] or merely spontaneously and without good cause : the complaint of Indra's inconstancy is quite different from the uneasy feeling of terror inspired in his votaries by Rudra : they had no doubt at all of his reality or his deadly powers. Of the other gods a hint or two of hostility is mentioned, but merely in the vaguest way, the gods themselves are once or twice—perhaps by assimilation to the Asuras—deemed hostile,[4] but in an overwhelming number of cases we hear of the gods as good and true and generous to their worshippers.

That the gods are kind to their worshippers is supplemented by the assertion that they do not deceive and are true, doubtless in the main an assertion that the gods send the blessings which they are asked to give, and for which offerings are bestowed on them. But it is an essential distinction between the religion of the Veda and many other religions, not merely Semitic, that there is no great stress laid on the moral quality of the gods, and that the sense of sin is only very feebly represented in the hymns : the moral aspect of the Rigveda is practically confined to the case of the gods Varuṇa, the Ādityas, and Aditi herself, and it is doubtless from these gods that here and there other gods assume the aspect of punishers and remitters of sin. Moreover, despite the stress which is laid on the position of these gods, the Rigveda itself, and in far

[1] RV. ii. 12. 5. ; viii. 103 ; Deussen, *Gesch. der Phil.* I. i. 96 ff.

[2] Bergaigne, *Rel. Véd.* iii. 154.

[3] RV. ii. 33. 4.

[4] The Avestan Daēvas are of course demons. Cf. AV. iii. 15. 5 ; TS. iii. 5. 4. 1.

greater degree the Atharvaveda, present us with a much simpler conception of sin, which assimilates it to a disease. Sin is something which sticks to a man, which confers a taint upon him as a disease does, and it is to be fought against in the same way as a disease : it may be banished by spells, water may wash it out, fire may purify it ; it has precisely the same remedies as a disease, and is as external as a disease itself. The sinner has no consciousness of any more sin than would be produced by a disease. The hieratic poetry of the Rigveda cannot be said to take normally this view of the case, but it is obviously in itself the more popular view, and the Atharvaveda here certainly reflects the feelings of those classes to whom the high gods, the doctrine of consciousness of sin, and the forgiveness of sin were far away.

The physical nature of sin accounts for the fact that it can be conferred by others without any act of human volition on the part of him whom it attacks ; the bird of Nirṛti bearing the infection can pass it upon men : [1] when the sin of the slaying of a Brahman falls on Indra he successively manages to pass it off on a series of other kinds of beings. The gods wipe sin off on Trita and he on men.[2] The victim at the sacrifice by its lowing or tearing the ground with its feet creates a sin which passes on to those around.[3] The wailing of the women at the house of the dead produces by itself a sin.[4] Sin is brought upon men by others, and even by the gods : [5] it is inherited from the father or other relative and made by one self.[6] But this process of transfer has an obvious advantage : even as man may be affected by sin without action of his own, so he can transfer sin or even a good deed [7] to others, and so get rid not merely of sins which have been passed on to him, but also of sins which he himself has committed. The absence of the element of consciousness explains also why it is possible for sins to be committed even in sleep.[8] There is no essential distinction when the sin is spoken of as a fetter : the fetters of death, the fetters of sickness, or the fetters of Nirṛti seem to convey no more meaning than the natural comparison of the constraint, which is put on man by sin in its physical aspect, with the fetters imposed by man for a civil crime, although the use of such metaphors must have aided the growth of the idea that the fetters are imposed by a god, as when the gods are besought not to catch men as in a net.[9]

There is clear proof that the feeling of sin in many cases did not exist : the poets freely confess to lies, to failure to keep promises, to treachery, to other forms of sin, and by magic means or by prayers to the gods, mingled with magic, seek to divest themselves of the sin, just as they seek in the same way to rid themselves of a disease : [10] the sense of guilt is still external, and

[1] AV. vii. 64.
[2] TS. ii. 5. 1. 2.
[3] TS. iii. 1. 4. 3.
[4] AV. xiv. 2. 59, 60.
[5] RV. ii. 28. 9 ; vi. 51. 7 ; vii. 52. 2 ; VS. iii. 48 ; viii. 13 ; ÇB. iv. 4. 5. 22 ; PB. i. 6. 10.
[6] RV. vii. 86. 5 ; AV. v. 30. 4 ; vi. 116. 3 ; x. 3. 8.
[7] RV. vii. 35. 4.
[8] RV. x. 164. 3 ; VS. viii. 13 ; xx. 16.
[9] RV. ii. 29. 5 ; cf. ii. 27. 16 ; AV. iv. 16. 6 ; viii. 8. 16.
[10] RV. i. 23. 22 ; x. 164. 3 ; AV. vi. 119 ; Oldenberg, *Rel. des Veda*[2], pp. 297 f.

suggests that we must connect it in thought with such things as the blood of the clansman in murder: it is in such instances that we may see the growth of the conception of the substance which as sin clings to a man, an idea which must have been aided by the conception that a disease is some such substance. The intervention of a god like Agni in such a case is merely to be compared with his intervention in the case of a disease: a deadly substance affects the man, and must be removed from him: it is not a case of searching of heart and forgiveness accorded to the contrite soul by heaven.

It is by no means certain exactly in what way the conception of the connexion of Varuṇa with sin sprang into such prominence, if we assume, as we must in the absence of evidence to the contrary, that the conception of sin as punished by Varuṇa is an Aryan one, and not a conception borrowed from a Semitic race. It is possible that the point of contact lay in the fact that the disease of dropsy by its accumulation of fluid suggested the action of the god who is always connected with the waters: there seems every reason to suppose that the connexion of the god and that disease is as early as anything else in this regard. If, therefore, the disease became associated with the action of the god, it may have been an easy step to evolve the view that the disease was a punishment for sin, for the idea of Varuṇa as the overseer of moral order may have been produced at a comparatively early date from the kindred conception that the order of the universe is particularly his care. This moral character of Varuṇa is expressed repeatedly in the most emphatic manner.[1] Mitra and he are barriers furnished with many fetters against falsehood, his fetters are cast threefold and sevenfold, snaring the man who tells lies, he is a dispeller, hater, and punisher of falsehood, and afflicts with disease those who are sinful. But, on the other hand, stress is laid also on the mercy of the god: he releases from sins committed by men and by their fathers also: the prayer of men who day by day trangress his ordinances, through thoughtlessness and through the sinful nature of man, is efficacious to secure forgiveness. The poet in one hymn [2] represents in an effective and interesting way the feeling of the sinner, who approaches the god in full consciousness that he or his fathers has sinned against him, but who urges as excuse lack of thought, passion, and other causes, wine, dice, anger, slumber, and begs for forgiveness and to be set free from the fetters in which he is bound. It is, of course, possible to exaggerate the moral character of this confession of sin: the poet is not a prophet, and he takes his position with a calm which is not expressive of any deep movement of repentance or consciousness of sin,[3] but the attitude is clearly moral; the punishment is admitted to be just, repentance is expressed, and the god is asked to forgive. In another hymn,[4] perhaps of the

[1] Varuṇa is essentially connected with Ṛta, whereas Indra with Satya; his great might is true, while his fierce nature is less in accord with Ṛta; Bergaigne, *Rel. Véd.* iii. 249; Oldenberg, GN. 1915, p. 175.

[2] RV. vii. 86. To assert that the sin here confessed is a ritual error is wholly without justification.

[3] The fact that the sin may be of one's ancestors or committed in sleep is significant.

[4] RV. vii. 88.

same authorship, we have a striking expression ; the poet reflects on his former companionship with the god, when Varuṇa and he sailed on a ship together in Varuṇa's heaven, and the god made him to be a seer ; if he has sinned against the god, still as his true friend he begs for forgiveness. In yet another [1] the sinner presents himself as tottering along, blown out like an inflated skin, athirst in the midst of the waters, and begs pardon for the sins he has committed whether from lack of thought or feebleness of will. Elsewhere the sinner admits violating day by day the laws of Varuṇa or of the gods.[2] Passages such as these, with admission of sin committed, must be put beside the emphatic assertion of the omniscience of Varuṇa which is found in a hymn of the Atharvaveda,[3] and which asserts that he is present everywhere ; when two men are together Varuṇa is present as third : he numbers the winkings of the eyes of men : if a man should flee far beyond the heavens, yet he would not be free from Varuṇa who has a thousand spies, and who knows all things. There should also be added the emphasis which is laid on the conception of Ṛta as moral and not merely a physical or a sacrificial law of order : when Yamī urges Yama [4] to marry her despite the guilt of incest which thus would arise, he replies that the action is contrary to Ṛta, which is thus conceived as a firm and abiding principle binding on man.

In the light of this exalted conception of Varuṇa which seems clearly normal in the Rigveda, and which of course corresponds with the majestic figure of Ahura in the Avesta, though far inferior to the conception, it is easy to understand the references which are occasionally made to the spirits of deceit [5] which serve him and execute his ordinances, and his deceit [6] from which Agni is asked to save the worshipper. In this connexion also is the Māyā, magic power, of Varuṇa spoken of. The view of Geldner [7] that Asura is thus reduced to something no better than the normal demon is erroneous : it rests on the mistaken view that the Māyā is something in itself bad, and that deceit is never justifiable. But the term Māyā has in itself no bad sense, and, though Varuṇa is an elevated figure, it must be recognized that the Vedic Indian saw nothing wrong in the use of deceit against the wicked : how else indeed would the deceitful be destroyed save by superior cunning ? It is just to recognize this limitation on Indian ethics, but not to exaggerate its nature or significance.

It must be admitted that the figure of Varuṇa does not increase in moral value in the course of the development of Vedic religion : in the fact of the failure of morality to develop itself as an important factor in the nature of the gods lies a deep distinction between Indian and other religions. Varuṇa is remembered as the god who has fetters and becomes in the Brāhmaṇas a

[1] RV. vii. 89.
[2] RV. i. 25. 1 ; x. 2. 4.
[3] AV. iv. 16.
[4] RV. x. 10. 4. Cf. vii. 104. 14, *anṛtadeva*, perhaps a false dicer ; TB. i. 7. 2. 6, *anṛta* is stealing from a sister, oppressing Brahmans, falsehood.
[5] RV. i. 25. 2 ; ii. 28. 7 ; ix. 73. 8 ; vii. 61. 5, give his various punishments of men.
[6] RV. ii. 27. 16 ; i. 128. 7.
[7] *Ved. Stud.* i. 142.

dread god, whose ritual in some measure is assimilated to that of the demons and the dead. After the performance of the bath, which ends the Agniṣṭoma sacrifice, the performer turns away and does not look back to escape from Varuṇa's notice,[1] and in the ceremony of that bath, when performed after the horse sacrifice, a man of a peculiar appearance is driven into the water and an offering made on his head, as being a representative of Varuṇa : [2] this form of the expulsion of evils, which is a common idea throughout the world, shows Varuṇa reduced to a somewhat humble level, and degraded from his Rigvedic eminence. In the Varuṇapraghāsas, the second of the four-month feasts, which is one concerning him in the main, the wife of the sacrificer is made to declare her lovers if any, and if she does so she is made formally free from guilt in respect of them, but here there is no trace of an exalted moral conception.[3]

Of the other gods Aditi and the Ādityas share with Mitra in the attributes of Varuṇa as a matter of course. The position is different with the rest : here and there an odd reference to forgiving sin and even to punishing sinners is of little or no consequence. In the case of Agni, however, these characteristics are more marked, as is natural in the god who is essentially the god of the house, and therefore a friend of men. Moreover, his position as the messenger between earth and heaven fits him for the role of acting as a go-between in propitiating the wrath of Varuṇa : as we have seen, he is even implored to avert the deceit of Varuṇa. With Indra the position is different : [4] it is true that he is asked to forgive sins and that he punishes the evil man, the liar, and the haughty, but these are merely characteristics which the most popular of gods must borrow from Varuṇa in a religion so fond of syncretism as that of the Rigveda, and the dependent position of Indra in this regard is sufficiently seen by the fact that he vindicates the ordinances of Mitra and Varuṇa,[5] not his own, and, when invoked with these gods, is asked for the material, not for the spiritual, blessings which they grant.

The ethical terminology of the Rigveda presents points of interest.[6] The term for cosmic order,[7] Ṛta, and its opposite, Anṛta, express also moral order as in the dialogue of Yama and Yamī ; Ṛta forbids and doubtless also commands positive action.[8] Ṛta is more than truth, Satya, nor can we say with Wundt [9] that Vedic India makes the good and the true identical, though truth is given an extraordinary high place, in its various senses of accuracy of statement, faithful performance of promises, and the assurance that what should

1 TS. vi. 6. 3. 5 ; MS. iv. 8. 5.

2 ApÇS. xiii. 19. 1 ff.

3 Hillebrandt, *Ved. Myth.* iii. 27. A somewhat cynical morality is indicated by the rites to encourage a wife's lovers in BhGS. ii. 28 ; ApGS. xxiii. 4, which is unsuccessfully referred to the levirate by the comm. on BhGS.

4 Bergaigne, *Rel. Véd.* iii. 200 ff.

5 RV. x. 89. 9.

6 Bergaigne, *Rel. Véd.* iii. 210 ff. ; Oldenberg, *Weltanschauung der Brāhmaṇatexte*, pp. 186 ff.

7 Oldenberg, GN. 1915, pp. 167 ff.; *contra*, Lüders, SBA. 1910, p. 931 ; Andreas and Wackernagel, GN. 1911, p. 28.

8 RV. x. 10. 4 ; iv. 23. 8.

9 *Ethik*[4], i. 24.

happen will happen, and that the order of things is as it ought to be. Law is denoted by Dharman,[1] which denotes that which supports and that which is supported ; it applies like Ṛta to all aspects of the world, to the sequence of events in nature, to the sacrifice and to man's life ; 'The gods by the sacrifice offered the sacrifice ; these were the first ordinances ', says the Puruṣa hymn ; it is according to Dharman that the sacrificial flame is enkindled, that the pious man duly propagates himself with offspring. Law is also expressed by Vrata,[2] a term which has been compared with *verbum* in Latin and word in English, and which in any case denotes often the command or law of a deity ; thus on Varuṇa the laws rest firmly as on a rock, and the gods make the abiding laws ; under the law of Indra are Varuṇa and the sun, the streams obey his laws ; before Parjanya's law the earth bows ; the pious man lives righteously according to the law. The term can be applied more widely ; [3] under the law of the king the rich man prospers ; the bridegroom brings the heart of the bride under his command. A development gives the term the sense of the rule of life or of ritual conduct which men observe, originally as commanded ; thus we hear of the Vrata of the carpenter, doctor, priest, or smith, or of the Brahmans who keep their year-long Vrata.[4] Sin, Āgas or Enas, as we have seen, is the lot of him who violates the Vratas of the gods.

The term for individual goods is, as in the Avesta, Vasu, which is used repeatedly of every conceivable sort of desired object. Çrī again denotes primarily what is beautiful, to the primitive taste, that is something possessing show and brilliance, but even in the Rigveda it tends to designate the pomp of the man of high position.[5] Pāpa [6] is the term for evil, for it is used of the man who commits incest, but it also applies to mere poverty ; the god is besought to be generous and not to abandon his worshipper to evil days, Pāpatva ; it is opposed to Bhadra in one of those contrasts which are regular in the Rigveda and later.

Despite the importance which legitimately attaches to it, the moral element in the Rigveda and the subsequent literature is of comparatively small extent, and the vast majority of the Vedic hymns are not concerned in the remotest degree with questions of morals. The chief requirement for man, in the opinion of the poets, is not that he should be good or be conscious of sin and attain forgiveness, but that he should have faith in the gods and pay them their honours due, nor should he fail in so doing to remember his obligation towards the priest, who alone can rightly perform the sacrifice for him and create the hymn of praise. The personification of Faith is a very essential thing in the eyes of the priest : [7] it is Faith which makes a man believe in the existence of such a god as Indra, and which makes him appre-

[1] RV. i. 164. 50 ; x. 90. 16 ; iii. 17. 1 ; vi. 70. 3.
[2] RV. ii. 28. 8 ; i. 36. 5 ; x. 65. 11 ; i. 101. 3 ; v. 83. 5 ; i. 136. 5.
[3] RV. x. 60. 4 ; PGS. i. 8. 8.
[4] ix. 112 ; vii. 103.
[5] Oldenberg, GN. 1918, pp. 35 ff.
[6] RV. x. 10. 12 ; iv. 5. 5 ; vii. 32. 18.
[7] RV. ii. 12. 5 ; i. 55. 1 ; vii. 32. 14 ; x. 151. 1 ; AV. vi. 133 ; VS. xix. 77 ; TB. ii. 8. 8 ; iii. 12. 3.

ciate the need of sacrifice to Indra and of generosity to the priests. Faith becomes a very real goddess in the Rigveda: she receives formal obligations and is exhalted by a priesthood, who had her to thank for their daily food. The priests soon realized that the patron must be induced to realize that he gained something from his offerings which must have gravely reduced his possessions: they promise the offerer long life for his gifts;[1] they assure him that what the god—and his priest—takes does not in any wise diminish his goods, an idea found in the latest as well as the earliest[2] literature, they promise immortality to the giver of gold, the sun to givers of horses.[3] No exaltation is too high for Faith: it is through her that Naciketas in the Kaṭha Upaniṣad insists on his father giving him to death, when his father offered a sacrifice of all he had, but yet did not propose to include his son in it. On the other hand a poet[4] makes clear the causal nexus of life in the sequence, Faith, Consecration for Sacrifice, the Sacrifice, the Sacrificial Fee: all that is lacking is the eternal life in the world to come, which is the share of the sacrificer. A technical term, Iṣṭāpūrta, denotes the merit won by offering and gifts to the priest a distant precursor of the later Karman: in the funeral hymn[5] the dead man is bidden to unite himself with the Fathers, with the fruit of his offerings and gifts; the gods are bidden to unite him with his Iṣṭāpūrta, when he has attained their abode,[6] and it is declared that the liberal giver[7] is he who gazes on the third step of Viṣṇu set in the sky: no more clear way of attaining heaven has often been offered to man. But it must be remembered that the man must be rich: the true sacrificer is he who gives all his wealth to the priest as the fee, or who at least gives, like Kaurama among the Ruçamas,[8] a hundred jewels, ten chaplets, three hundred horses, and ten thousand cattle. In return for this generosity the sacrificer, however, gets something, which in the eyes of the priest doubtless seemed worth more than even immortality, the glory of mention of his generosity in a Vedic hymn.

The later Vedic age[9] appreciated these praises of liberality, Dānastutis, and celebrations of the fame of men, Gāthā Nārāçaṅsī, at their true worth when they treated them as lies and placed the makers in the same rank as drunkards, but to the Vedic poet they doubtless shared the glory of his poetry. The poets of the Rigveda took themselves in all seriousness: they called themselves inspired, and believed in their high powers of workmanship: they repeatedly extol the value of their new and beautiful songs, which surpass those of others. To Indra they can say unashamed[10] 'We have wishes; you have gifts; here are we with our songs', and expect that the god will see that the exchange is fair. The same spirit is shown in the elaboration of the

1 AV. vii. 103. 1.
2 RV. vi. 28. 2.
3 AV. x. 107. 2.
4 AV. xv. 16.
5 RV. x. 14. 8.
6 TS. v. 7. 7. 1.
7 RV. i. 22. 20.
8 AV. xx. 127. But giving all is censured, PB. xvi. 5. 6; 6. 1; 9. 2; Hopkins, *Trans. Conn. Acad.* xv. 31.
9 Bloomfield, *Atharvaveda*, p. 100; *Rel. of Veda*, pp. 196 ff.
10 RV. viii. 21. 6.

poems themselves, in the efforts by bold imagery and even by elaborate metre to produce perfect works of art. The poem is compared to a well-wrought chariot, it is likened to winnowed grain, to ghee well purified. It became in itself a divinity as Dhī, 'holy devotion', Suṣṭuti, 'lovely praise', and Manīṣā, 'holy thought'. In its expression of admiration of the gods, it is the highest product of the worship of the priests, the most attractive outcome of their religious consciousness, relieving and giving value to a cult which is of overwhelming tedium and complication.

It must, however, be admitted that this pride of creation was unhappily united with the feeling of rivalry: the gods are not conceived as able to be present at every offering at one and the same moment: they are too like to man to have true omniscience and therefore the sacrificers may compete. It is natural enough to find this idea in the late texts, where we hear often of competing of sacrifices, and devices to undo the ill results of the mingling of sacrificial fires with one another, or the interference of one invocation with another. But it is somewhat of a shock to find that these views are expressed in the earliest hymns preserved to us, that the Vasiṣṭhas complacently plume themselves on having induced Indra to prefer their oblations of the Soma to those of Pāçadyumna Vāyata, though the latter had gone to the trouble of recalling the god from far away.[1] It is a lower and more vulgar thought which pictures Kutsa tying Indra [2] up to keep him beside him, and the god being induced by Luça to extricate himself from his shameful bondage, but the conception is the same, and it is an essential part of the Vedic conception of the deity.

[1] Bloomfield, *Rel. of Veda*, p. 186; RV. vii. 33. 2.

[2] PB. ix. 2. 22; for the alleged reference to this in RV. x. 38. 5, see below Part III, Chap. 18, § 2.

PART III. VEDIC RITUAL

CHAPTER 17

THE RITUAL IN THE RIGVEDA

It is unfortunately clear that the ritual as it is presented to us in the ritual Sūtras, in general and often very minute accord with the texts of the Saṁhitās of the Yajurveda and Sāmaveda, is not precisely that which is contemplated by the hymns of the Rigveda. The divergences which can be proved, even with the comparatively scanty material available, are such as to cause it to be necessary to recognize that in many cases, where there is nothing available to show difference, the ritual may yet have considerably altered between the period of the collection, and still more the composition of the hymns, and the collections of the Yajus formulae and the Sāmans. The result, of course, is only what must be expected : the ritual in the Sūtras shows alterations as compared with the texts on which it is based : the priests were restless personages, far from content with merely following out a traditional ritual. They were given to reflection on the ritual, and to discussions of its meaning as is proved to the hilt by the Brāhmaṇas, and as a result we must regard the whole of the Vedic period as one of steady modification in detail of the rite. That the modification was only in detail we have every reason to believe : it is proved for the period from the later Saṁhitās to the Sūtras, as we can see that the ritual presupposed by the former is very closely similar in all essentials to that laid down by the latter, while for the period of the Rigveda the many similarities between the expressions of the hymns and the actual practice of the later ritual is conclusive of an ordered development, free from any catastrophic change.

It has also to be remembered that there are recorded in the Rigveda hymns from many families, and that we must assume that there existed according to the divisions of these families variations in the ritual and in the terminology, helped doubtless by considerations of metre which evidently weighed a good deal with the poets. The Rigveda contains in some places almost a superabundance of technical terms,[2] the precise point of which we cannot always now determine. The number of priests engaged is proof of the already high complication of the ritual. We have the names Hotṛ, Adhvaryu, Āvayās, Agnimindha, Grāvagrābha, and Çaṅstṛ in one place, and Hotṛ, Potṛ, Neṣṭṛ, Agnīdh, Praçāstṛ, Adhvaryu, and Brahman in another. In other

[1] Cf. Oldenberg, GGA. 1907, pp. 221 ff. ; 1908, pp. 711 ff.

[2] Hillebrandt, *Rituallitteratur*, pp. 11–19.

passages we find Upavaktṛ, Udagrābha, Purohita, Sāmagas, Sāmanyas, and the two Çamitṛs. Of these the Udagrābha and Grāvagrābha disappear as such in the later ritual: their manual acts became doubtless of less moment, and were left to the assistants of the Adhvaryu: the Upavaktṛ or Praçāstṛ became the Maitrāvaruṇa, and his duty of giving to the Hotṛ the direction to recite his verses is expressly mentioned.[1] Moreover, we find the clear distinction already made between the recitations of the Hotṛs to which the words *uktha* and *çaṅs* apply and the songs of the Sāman singers which are distinguished by the use of the Gāyatrī and Pragātha metres, and by the frequent use of triads of verses for singing as strophes.[2] For the Adhvaryus there were no doubt prose formulae: the long sets of verses which the Yajurveda provides for them are never hinted at.

The hymns of the Hotṛs were evidently even at this period united into litanies, Ukthas, and in the litanies were inserted the formulae called Nivids, celebrating the gods who were to enjoy the offering; the term Puroruc, which later means merely a Nivid in a different place from the usual Nivid, is also mentioned: even the curious breaking up and transposing of a verse in recitation which is common later (*viharaṇa*) is mentioned, it seems, in jest.[3] The Nivids are not preserved for us in the Rigveda, but they are extant in a collection, and it was asserted by Haug[4] that they take us to an earlier stage in the offering than the Rigveda itself; this is not borne out by their form and contents; while the Nivids of the Rigveda must often have been similar to those preserved, the latter are elaborated and later in date.[5] The Sāman singers were already divided into the two classes of Udgātṛs and Prastotṛs at least: the Sāmans, or tunes, Bṛhat and Rathantara were known, perhaps also others like the Çākvara: as in the ritual, the Sāmans were sung to the verses used by the Hotṛs in some degree at least. The Çakvarī verses preserved only in the Sāmaveda were known. The technical terms are found in which the Adhvaryu in the ritual is asked to give the word for the recitation to begin,[6] and his response, and the frequent formulae *astu çrauṣaṭ*,[7] *vaṣaṭ*, and *svāhā*. But one class of priest which is found in the later ritual, the Brahman as overseer of the whole sacrifice, is not recognized in most, if not the whole, of the Rigveda; the Brahman mentioned there seems to be the priest later distinguished from the Brahman as Brāhmaṇācchaṅsin, and the Purohita of the king, who is mentioned in the Rigveda as securing rain by an offering,[8] probably was at this stage of the offering ready to perform the part of one of the priests, not to supervise the whole. At this time we may fairly say that the importance of the ceremony must have belonged to the

[1] RV. ix. 95, 5.

[2] Oldenberg, ZDMG. xxxviii. 439 ff.; cf. xlii. 246.

[3] RV. vi. 67. 10 as rendered by Ludwig, *Rigveda*, iii. 222.

[4] *Aitareya Brāhmaṇa*, i. 36 ff. For the text see Scheftelowitz *Die Apokryphen des Ṛgveda*, pp. 136–41.

[5] Oldenberg, *Religion des Veda*², p. 387, n. 2.

[6] *çaṅsāvādhvaryo* and *prati gṛṇīhi*, RV. iii. 53. 3.

[7] RV. i. 139.

[8] RV. x. 98.

Hotṛ, as the composer of the hymns, rather than to any other priest. The name Hotṛ, which is the Avestan Zaotar, carries us a step farther back in the ritual when the priest was called by the name he bore from his performing the actual offering,[1] but the Hotṛ, who first meant offerer, had by the time of the Rigveda left to the Adhvaryu the actual manual work of the sacrifice. With this complication of the sacrifice it well accords that it seems clear that the practice was well established for Vedic priests to wander here and there, giving their services for hire for the performance of offerings. The formal choice of the priest (*ṛtvig-varaṇa*) which is known from the later ritual is clearly alluded to in the Rigveda.

The nature of the sacrifice appears clearly from the number of priests mentioned: it was as dealt with in the Rigveda an elaborate procedure destined for the advantage of some rich patron, prince, or noble, or wealthy commoner: the term Vivasvant here and there seems given in honour to the mortal sacrificer, as the priests liken themselves to the gods in their activity. The Vedic ritual and the Rigveda alike know no temple service or abiding places of worship: the altar, Vedi, is made in the house of the offerer: before it is placed the fire which is said to sit upon it: the pressing stones are there, and there the bunch of grass, which is gathered in the early morning in the east, and to which the gods are invited to come and sit down. The two altars[2] of the later ritual are here reduced to one only: this is in accord with the obvious fact that in the later rite the duplication of altars is artificial. The fire was carefully kindled by friction, and then placed in three separate places within the altar ground: one only, the Gārhapatya, appears by name in the Rigveda, but Hillebrandt [3] has attempted to prove that the later Āhavanīya and Dakṣiṇa are to be found in the Vaiçvānara and Narāçaṅsa or Kravyavāhana, though not with convincing evidence. The taking of the fire from one fire altar to another as later on is referred to. Thrice a day was honour paid to the fire with sacrifice, wood, and hymns. Mention is made of the ladle, Sruc, and two Darvīs used in making the offerings to the gods, around which fire was borne, doubtless as a magic purificatory spell. Among the offerings appear milk, butter, grain, and cakes, and animal offerings of the goat, bull, cow, sheep, and the horse. The last offering must already have been performed with stately ceremony: the hymns devoted to it mention the hewing and ornamenting of the post, the goat slain to precede the steed on the way to its last abode, the golden coverlet put on the horse, the cooking of its flesh, and the division of the pieces to the eager priests.

In the case of the Soma sacrifice, which in the Rigveda is the most important of all, the parallelism to the later offering is marked. There are clearly three pressings of the Soma, morning, noon, and night, the first and

[1] From *hu*, 'pour'; Macdonell, *Vedic Grammar*, § 146. As early as Yāska (Nir. iv. 26; vii. 15) it was derived from *hve*, 'call,' as well as from *hu* (Aurṇavābha's view). Cf. AB. i. 2.

[2] Vedi and Uttaravedi, 'High Altar.'

[3] *Ved. Myth.* ii. 98 ff.

last possibly denoted by the later obsolete terminology Prapitva and Abhipitva.[1] The metres Gāyatrī, Triṣṭubh, and Jagatī are divided as later among the three pressings. The Ṛbhus have as later a place in the evening, Indra and the Maruts in the middle pressing: the morning pressing later seems to have been extended in effect. The Soma was pressed and mixed as later: the terminology here seems to have changed: apparently in the Rigveda it was mixed with water in the Koça, then placed in two similar bowls, the Camūs, and there mixed with milk and afterwards poured into Kalaças for its use at the rite; in the ritual texts the Koça is replaced by the Ādhavaniya or mixing vessel, one of the Camūs became assimilated to it in material, clay, and became the Pūtabhṛt, 'containing purified Soma,' the other was called the Droṇakalaça, 'wooden vessel.[2] Grahas in both early and late ritual were used for the offerings to the gods. Even the Pravargya ceremony of the heating of milk in a pot was known,[3] and such details as the offering of a cake to Agni Sviṣṭakṛt at the end of the rite.

Besides Soma, Surā and honey were used in offerings: in the later ritual the former is used in the Sautrāmaṇī and Vājapeya rites, of which the former seems to be known to the Rigveda, while the latter appears only in the Vājapeya.

The giving of gifts to the priest at the end of the rite was evidently fully appreciated and valued, to judge from the repeated references to the practice, and the glorification of the faith which induces the sacrificer to bestow largesse.

Moreover, there is no doubt that in the Rigveda we have sets of hymns intended for use at the sacrifice as well as material less intimately connected with the sacrifice. Proof beyond doubt of this is afforded by the occurrence of series of verses which are used later at the Praüga Çastra of the Agniṣṭoma, and which must have from the beginning had their place there.[4] The Āprī hymns for the fore-offerings of the animal sacrifice, preserved in the different books of the Rigveda, are an invaluable proof of the difference of family tradition, which is obscured in the ritual text-books which we have. Other cases are clearly proved: thus we seem to have in one hymn a collection of Anuvākyā and Yājyā verses for the offering to Agni and Soma of the goat which is an essential element in the Agniṣṭoma rite: [5] there is further a set of Anuvākyā verses for the cakes offered at each of the three pressings of the Soma sacrifice,[6] and for the offering of the pot of curd.[7] One hymn clearly was meant for use at the anointing of the sacrificial post,[8] others at the kindling of the fire.[9] Still more interesting is the fact that the later practice of having sets of three verses to open the Vaiçvadeva Çastra is clearly found already in

[1] Bloomfield, JAOS. xvi. 24 ff.; Oldenberg, SBE. xlvi. 183 ff.

[2] Oldenberg, ZDMG. lxii. 459–70; Macdonell and Keith, *Vedic Index*, ii. 513, 514.

[3] Garbe, ZDMG. xxxiv. 319 ff.

[4] RV. i. 2, 3, 23 &c.; Hillebrandt, *Ved. Myth.* i. 259.

[5] RV. i. 93.

[6] RV. iii. 28, 52.

[7] RV. x. 179.

[8] RV. iii. 8.

[9] RV. v. 28; iii. 27.

force.[1] The end verses of the litanies, the Parıdhānīyās, seem to be found in the Rigveda,[2] but the further suggestions of Bergaigne [3] as to the tradition of the different schools open up difficulties not yet fully solved, indeed insoluble.

The chief point in which the Rigveda gives little parallelism with the later ritual is the household ceremonies of all kinds. There are indeed traces of hymns made for such occasions as the ploughing,[4] the return of the cattle from the pasture,[5] their driving in and driving out,[6] but these are almost isolated. There are, however, hymns for marriage [7] and the funeral ritual,[8] and a few hymns dealing with magic rites, such as the removal of jaundice by the sun,[9] the prevention of miscarriage,[10] and the prognostication of misfortune.[11]

The imperfection of the record of the Rigveda renders it necessary in any account of the Vedic ritual to deal with the ritual, as it stands in the later Saṁhitās and the Brāhmaṇas, and as it is set out in full detail in the Sūtras, while using the Rigveda wherever possible to explain in how far the views of that collection agree with the ideas later prevalent. This fact exposes it to certain danger : it is perfectly true that much which is recorded later is clearly old, and is omitted in the Rigveda, mainly because that collection is only concerned with a limited portion of religious practice. On the other hand, religion is in the constant process of change, and things recorded first in the later texts may be new inventions.

1 RV. v. 82. 1–3, and 4–6.

2 Hillebrandt, GGA. 1889, p. 421.

3 *Recherches sur l'histoire de la liturgie védique* (Paris, 1888 and 1889). He takes viii. 6, 81, 82, as intended for the Atirātra, i. 92 for the Prātaranuvāka and so on. For other guesses see Hubert and Mauss, *Année sociol.* ii. 80, n. 2, 93, n. 7.

4 RV. iv. 57.

5 RV. vi. 28, according to AGS. ii. 10. 7.

6 RV. v. 112 ; x. 169.

7 RV. x. 85.

8 RV. x. 14–18.

9 RV. i. 50.

10 RV. v. 78. 7–9 ; KÇS. xxv. 10. 5.

11 RV. ii. 42 and 43.

CHAPTER 18

THE NATURE OF THE VEDIC SACRIFICE

§ 1. *The Sacrifice as a Gift*

As we have seen, the Vedic pantheon is essentially a body of great and powerful gods before whom the worshipper realizes to the full his comparative weakness and inability to exist satisfactorily without their constant aid. By the most simple logic he applies to the powers divine the same principle which he applies to other more powerful men, or which are applied to him by his inferiors. He seeks to propitiate them by the process of giving gifts.[1] Doubtless, beside this view of the relation of man to the gods, there existed the belief that he could do much for himself by the power of the magic art, which we need not doubt flourished as much then as in later India, and against demons of all kinds magic is freely employed, but the essential distinction of magic and religion is plainly to be seen in the whole of the Vedic religion. Often too in place of using magic, or still oftener in supplement of magic, the aid of the gods is employed in the battle with the demons. In the case of one of the higher gods alone is there any trace of other than a relation of friendship: the aim of the worshipper is to satiate Rudra and to avert his dangerous presence: this fact, which expresses itself in the ritual in many ways, makes a certain degree of difference between the case of Rudra and the other gods, though occasionally some of these, such as Varuṇa, show slight traces of a similar conception of their nature to that of Rudra.

The dead stand in a peculiar relation to man, since they deserve from him consideration and honour, but mingled with that conception is the fear of the quick for the dead. It is often asserted [2] that the mode of honouring the gods is a direct imitation of the mode of providing for the dead, but the assertion admits of no proof, and must stand or fall with the effort to demonstrate *a priori* that all sacrifice or worship of gods is secondary, and dependent on the cult of the dead. In the Vedic, as in the Greek ritual, the nature of the cult of the gods and that of the dead is markedly and in important measure different,[3] a fact which tells, as much as any such argument can tell, against the original identity of the two cults. This fact renders it at once desirable and

[1] This is recognized even by Feist (*Kultur der Indogermanen*, p. 351), though he inclines to trace all worship to the cult of the dead. Cf. Tylor, *Primitive Culture*, ii.[2] 372 ff., who shows the ease of developing the ideas of homage and renunciation from that of gift; Hopkins, *Origin of Religion*, chap. xi.

[2] Hirt, *Die Indogermanen*, pp. 514, 515; Eitrem, *Opferritus und Voropfer der Griechen und Römer* (1915).

[3] Stenzel, *Opferbräuche der Griechen*, pp. 127 ff.

convenient to treat of the cult of the dead together with Vedic eschatological conceptions in the next part of this work.

In the Rigveda and in the later period alike the cult of the gods is marked by the absence of any temple or house of the god, even of the simplest kind. The nearest approach to such a conception is perhaps the fires of the Sabhā and the Āvasatha which in the Sūtras are mentioned as to be kept up by kings;[1] but in this we have merely an occasional use, and the Vedic ritual has nothing similar to the tending of a perpetual fire by Vestal Virgins in the house of the king as at Rome.[2] There is no public cult, merely the carrying out of offerings for princes and other men wealthy enough to employ professional priests, and the performance of a much simpler cult by the householder himself. The essential form of the sacrifice is one which can be carried out under these circumstances, and it reduces itself to the invitation of the god to come to the place of offering, and to partake of the food and drink provided for him. The gifts of costly jewels or garments and of chariots or weapons or other accoutrements, are wanting in the ritual, partly no doubt from the absence of any place in which such jewels and other gifts might be kept, but more perhaps from the fact that the priests considered it in their own interest to secure that these things should be disposed of most wisely by bestowal upon them. In so highly developed a priestly atmosphere as that of the ritual it is at least reasonable to believe that gifts, which an earlier piety might have conveyed by fire to heaven, were converted to their own use by the vicegerents of the god on earth, who even in the Brāhmaṇas claim the title of god for themselves, while in the classical literature it is assumed by the king.

It was of course essential that the god invited should be received in a due place, and that any honours which were possible should be paid to him. Hence the hymns of praise, the sound of music, and the dance: even perhaps the theosophical riddles[3] with which at the great horse sacrifice the priests delighted one another, and it may well be the god, since gods were built by priests in their own image. But in addition to these features there was much more in the Vedic sacrifice, mimic combats, ribaldry, chariot racing, archery, dicing, and much else, which cannot be deemed save in quite a secondary way to have been thought to be part of the entertainment provided for the god. In the vast majority of these cases the nature of the ritual can be solved at once by the application of the concept sympathetic magic, and this is one of the most obvious and undeniable facts in the whole of the

[1] Above, Part II, Chap. 10, § 1.

[2] This fact very markedly distinguishes Vedic from Babylonian religion; the lack of temples assimilates it to Iranian religion, which, however, seems to have known fire altars of a somewhat permanent character; cf. Jackson, GIP. ii. 688, 701; Moulton, *Early Zoroastrianism*, pp. 52, 53. For the lack of temples, as opposed to sacred groves, in Germany, see Tacitus, *Germ.* 9; Helm, *Altgerm. Rel.* i. 235, 286 f.

[3] Bloomfield, JAOS. xv. 172; it has been suggested (Koegel, *Gesch. d. deutschen Lit.* I. i. 5, 64 ff.) that such riddles are Indo-European, but the best parallel from Teutonic sources is late (cf. Helm, *Altgerm. Rel.* i. 110 ff.).

Vedic sacrifice : it is from beginning to end full of magic elements,[1] which can as a rule be perfectly easily disentangled from the rest of the rite. In some cases it is impossible not to feel that the rite is merely magic dressed up with sacrifice, but in the majority of rites no such view is possible, and in many the magic element is wholly secondary.

The nature of the ordinary offering to the god is expressly stated to be an offering made to the god for the purpose of attracting his attention and good-will, so that, delighted himself, the god may reward in the appropriate way his worshipper. This is essentially the standpoint of the Rigveda where the sacrificer is promised wealth both temporal and in the world to come in return for his sacrifice, and his gifts to the priest, and where the gods are invoked to delight themselves with the offering and to reward their votaries.[2] The Brāhmaṇas bluntly state the doctrine of *do ut des* in so many words,[3] and Suçravas, we are told, was approached by Indra, who told him he was hungry and gladly took from him the cakes of the offering.[4] But the gods in the Rigveda are not less frank in their expression of feeling : they can sympathize with the poor man who can offer but little,[5] but they are bitterly indignant with the rich man who gives nothing. The whole formula is excellently expressed in the Sūktavāka formula uttered near the end of the sacrifice, where it is said,[6] 'The god hath accepted the offering ; he hath become strengthened ; he hath won greater might,' to which the sacrificer for whom the rite is performed replies, 'May I prosper in accordance with the prospering of the god.' It is, however, needless to multiply examples : this theory of the sacrifice and its result as an exchange of gifts, of strength for strength, is the fundamental fact of the whole Vedic religion.

Beside this form of offering in hope of favours to come very small traces can be found of the offering which expresses grateful thanks for favours paid. The two ideas are clearly closely connected and to a generous people the existence of the one might seem to bring with it essentially the existence of the other. But it is clear that as in Roman religion the traces of the thank-offering are scanty and, though the idea is known, it has a feeble existence. A Sūtra [7] prescribes such an offering for the case in which a man after falling ill recovers his health : the case is interesting for its simplicity : if a man falls ill after establishing the three offering fires, he should go away from his place of abode : the fires love the village and in their desire to return thither may

[1] Similarly in Babylon and less markedly in Greece ; Farnell, *Greece and Babylon*, pp. 176–8, 291 ff. The gift theory of sacrifice is accepted by Baudissin, ZDMG. lvii. 832 ff.; Westermarck, *Origin and Development of the Moral Ideas*, i. 623. It in part is akin to the dynamic theory as accepted by Warde Fowler, *Religious Experience of the Roman People*, p. 184, from Hubert and Mauss, *Mélanges d'histoire des religions*, pp. 55 ff. ; *Année sociol.* ii. 29 ff., for a criticism of which see below, § 4.

[2] RV. i. 54. 9 ; iii. 36. 3, 9 ; vii. 32. 6 ; x. 49. 1.

[3] TS. i. 8. 4. 1 ; cf. iii. 2. 9. 7 ; ÇB. i. 2. 5. 24 ; viii. 1. 2. 10.

[4] PB. xiv. 6. 8.

[5] Bergaigne, *Rel. Véd.* ii. 227.

[6] Hillebrandt, *Neu- und Vollmondsopfer*, p. 144.

[7] AGS. iv. 1. 1 ff.

heal him, in which case he should perform a Soma or an animal sacrifice. The offering of firstfruits,[1] however, is mainly if not entirely an offering to secure the safe eating of the new products,[2] an idea which is of world-wide extension. If a man has a son born to him [3] or attains a thousand cattle [4] he sacrifices, but merely to secure the health of one or the other; if he makes a vow and keeps it on the fulfilment of the occasion, as for instance if he says to a god, 'Slay him and I will offer to thee,' the keeping of the promise, which was not always done, is not a thank-offering.[5] If the dead have a feast made for them when there is a birth in the family or a wedding,[6] it is not according to the texts for thanks at their bringing about the good fortune: it may rather be that they are expected to share in the common joy, or that it is hoped to avert their envy of the good fortune of the house. The horse sacrifice [7] is indeed offered after the attainment of the position of a great prince, but the ritual shows that it concludes with a prayer for the welfare of the king and his people and the birth of a prince: it is in effect an offering to secure the maintenance of the success arrived at, a fact hinted clearly by the assertion of the Brāhmaṇas that it is fatal to a weak king to make such an offering.

§ 2. *The Sacrifice as a Spell*

In the theosophy of the Brāhmaṇas it is an accepted fact that the sacrifice has a magic power of its own, and that it brings about the effects at which it aims with absolute independence: the old idea of the working upon the good will of a deity has disappeared, and in the philosophy of the Pūrva Mīmāṅsā,[8] which is the logical outcome of the Brāhmaṇas, the idea of god is effectively disposed of. But the theosophy of the Brāhmaṇas is of no value as religion, and the question arises whether the Rigveda shows any real trace of the belief in the magic efficacy of the sacrifice. Much of the evidence which has been adduced by both Bergaigne [9] and Geldner [10] for the view that the priests claim to control the gods, to capture them in the net of the sacrifice, and make them do their bidding, is clearly without weight: the simple imagery of the poets cannot be pressed to mean more than it says. The later literature, which regards the priest as powerful to control the gods, openly says so,[11] and provides the believer with magic devices in order to bind hard the Ādityas until they

[1] Lindner, *Festgruss an Böhtlingk*, pp. 79 ff.

[2] ÇGS. iii. 8; Oldenberg, *Rel. des Veda*², pp. 310 ff.; Hubert and Mauss, *Année sociol.* ii. 96, 97; Lagrange, *Études sur les religions sémitiques* (1905).

[3] TS. ii. 2. 5. 3.

[4] TS. ii. 1. 5. 2.

[5] AV. vi. 111. 1; TS. vi. 4. 5. 6; AB. vii. 14. Vows of this kind play a very prominent part in Roman religion, but not in Vedic. Cf. Warde Fowler, *Religious Experience of the Roman People*, pp. 201–2; for Germany, Helm, *Altgerm. Rel.* i. 242 ff.

[6] Caland, *Altind. Ahnenkult*, pp. 37 ff.

[7] AB. viii. 21 ff.; Hillebrandt, *Festgruss an Böhtlingk*, pp. 40, 41; cf. Weber, *Ind. Stud.* x. 150.

[8] Gangānātha Jhā, *The Prābhākara School of Pūrva Mīmāṅsā*, pp. 87 ff.

[9] *Rel. Véd.* ii. 229 ff.; iii. 164.

[10] *Ved. Stud.* i. 139 ff.

[11] VS. xxxi. 21.

yield what is desired,[1] and Kutsa is said to tie Indra up in disgraceful fashion,[2] but nothing of that gross kind can certainly be found in the Rigveda. The most that can be adduced are a passage where Indra is spoken of as pursued by the priest with milk as hunters the wild beast,[3] a prayer that the mortal may be lord over Agni in his house,[4] and an assertion that honour, Namas, is above the gods themselves,[5] nothing more than occasional expressions of exaltation in the priestly power. Moreover, when the Vasiṣṭhas pride themselves on drawing Indra away from Pāçadyumna, they evidently assume that the god was free to choose, and preferred them to their rival.[6] But, while the idea of the power of the sacrifice over the gods is merely commencing to manifest itself, there is clear evidence that the belief in the greatness of the sacrifice was in process of steady development. It is seen in such declarations as that the sun was born through the result of the sacrifice of Atharvan,[7] and from the fact that the offerings of the Añgirases won the treasures of the Paṇis is deduced the doctrine that great might is that of the Soma-presser.[8] The greatness of the sacrifice is also brought out by the doctrine of the first sacrifice of the gods in which they offered up the giant Puruṣa:[9] from this sacrifice were born the hymn and the metre of the sacrifice: the idea of the production of sacrifice by sacrifice is precisely in the strain of shallow mysticism which is characteristic of the Vedic conceptions. That the human offering could produce results by itself is here and there, it would seem, recognized in the Rigveda, where the morning Agnihotra seems to have power to aid the sun to rise,[10] and more distinctly in a late hymn the bringing down of rain is treated as if it were the direct work of the Purohita Devāpi.[11]

It would, however, be a complete error to assume that the magic side of the sacrifice is the primitive one, and that the whole sacrifice is really a magic performance. The sacrifice might well have in it *ab initio* elements of magic, and certainly the Vedic sacrifices known to us have many, but the Brāhmaṇas enable us to see clearly that the priests were determined to find in them throughout a magical effect. To every point some special working is attributed, and it becomes possible to secure ruin or prosperity for the sacrificer by the mere manipulation of some detail of no importance. All this is clearly the work of a later constructive religious outlook, and what is most noteworthy is not that, here and there, the same spirit is to be found in the Rigveda, but that it should play so small a part in that collection. Nor can there be any doubt that, in the course of the fixing of the ritual, many details must have

[1] TS. ii. 3. 1. 5.

[2] PB. ix. 2. 22; JB. i. 228 (JAOS. xviii. 32). The view accepted by Hillebrandt (*Ved. Myth.* iii. 291) that RV. x. 38. 5 really means this is hardly credible. Cf. ZDMG. xl. 713; Oldenberg, *Ṛgveda-Noten*, ii. 243.

[3] RV. viii. 2. 6; cf. iii. 45. 1.

[4] RV. iv. 15. 5.

[5] RV. vi. 51. 8.

[6] RV. vii. 33. 2.

[7] RV. i. 83. 5.

[8] RV. i. 83. 4, 3.

[9] RV. x. 90. 6, 9.

[10] Bergaigne, *Rel. Véd.* i. 140; Hillebrandt, *Ved. Myth.* ii. 83.

[11] RV. x. 98.

been added or altered, simply for the purpose of introducing elements of magic potency: it is impossible not to see such influences effective in the drawing up of many of the details of the horse sacrifice,[1] which is reduced by the Vedic texts to a performance, which cannot possibly have ever been realized in practice, and in which the magic purpose of much of the machinery is plain and undeniable.[2]

A further question arises whether we can trace behind the Vedic sacrifice as a gift offering the older view that it is really not a gift at all, but an effort to secure the propagation of the life of the herds and of the world of vegetation by the periodic slaying from time to time of the spirit of vegetation, or in the case of animals of a representative of the species, in order to secure the freshness of the life of the vegetation and of the beasts of the earth. In this view, which is that of Sir J. Frazer,[3] the sacrifice in the long run is reduced purely and simply to a piece of magic: it represents a period before man ceases to believe himself lord of nature, and master of all that he desires, and, recognizing the futility of his high belief in humanity, turns to the conception of supernatural powers, whom he supplicates for the results, which he thought formerly to bring about by his own magic powers. The substantial element at the back of the theory is, of course, the considerable mass of facts adduced by Mannhardt, and before him by Grimm, which illustrate the widespread usage of the killing of the outworn corn spirit, perhaps with some idea of strengthening it, though of late a very formidable opponent to that theory [4] has appeared in the shape of the view that the thing which is destroyed is not the corn spirit at all, but the witches and wizards whose attacks on the crops are perpetual, an idea which is richly proved for India by the figures of the Rakṣases and their constant conjunction with sorcery. There are, however, features of the later religion of India such as the legend of Kṛṣṇa and Kaṅsa,[5] which point to the old vegetation ritual in which the contest between the spirits of winter and summer is revealed, and this conception has certain affinities with the theory of the killing of the corn spirit when outworn. In the Vedic ritual, however, it is extremely difficult to find any case in which this theory can be applied with much plausibility.

One instance has been adduced by Hillebrandt [6] which is of interest in itself. At the concluding bath of the horse sacrifice a sacrifice to Jumbaka is offered on the head of a man of repulsive appearance, who is driven into the

[1] Cf. Weber, *Rājasūya* (Berlin, 1893).

[2] Roman religion shows a similar tendency to degradation into magic, though this fact can be exaggerated; thus Warde Fowler (*Religious Experience of the Roman People*, Lect. iii) insists that the magic element in Roman religion was diminished by the priesthood.

[3] *The Golden Bough*[3] (London, 1911–14); see my criticism, JHS. xxxv. 281–4; Lang, *Magic and Religion* (1901); F. Legge, *Forerunners and Rivals of Christianity*, i. 91–7; A. B. Cook, *Zeus*, i. 13, 776.

[4] Westermarck's view based on his investigation among the Berbers; see *Golden Bough*[3], x. 328 ff.; xi. 1 ff.; below, § 4.

[5] Keith, JRAS. 1911, pp. 1108 ff.; 1912, pp. 413 ff.; 1916, pp. 335–49.

[6] *Ved. Myth.* iii. 28–33.

water, and the texts make it clear that Jumbaka is believed to be Varuṇa and that the appearance of the man is intended to correspond with that of Varuṇa. Now the man who plays the part in this rite is said to be an Ātreya, bought with a thousand cows, and it is further mentioned that the formulae used at the time of the oblation include 'To death hail! To the slaying of an embryo hail!' and it is therefore suggested by Hillebrandt that we have here the trace of the slaying of a man, a view which was also taken by Weber,[1] who thought that the man was drowned in the waters. Hillebrandt further connects the story with the legend [2] of the proposed killing of Çunaḥçepa, who was bought in the same way from his father to be offered in the place of the son of the king Hariçcandra who has offered to sacrifice his son to Varuṇa, and he concludes that there was a practice at one time of slaying the old king and substituting another, the slaughter taking place at the end of the horse sacrifice. The theory is ingenious, but it is clearly without any contact with fact. The story of Çunaḥçepa is one which has no allusion anywhere to the practice of slaying the old king: it is the son whom the father offers to kill, and connexion with the killing of the old king could only be arrived at by supposing that, in view of the existence of the custom in question, the old king took the precaution of seeing that no son to supersede him was forthcoming, which is really absurd. The case of the offering to Jumbaka is also clearly misunderstood: there is preserved for us in a Sūtra [3] an invaluable hint of the meaning in the statement that the guilt of the village outcasts is thus removed: the ceremony belongs to the numerous and important class of services for the expulsion of evil, and the ceremonial bath acts as a purificatory element rather than, as suggested,[4] as a piece of vegetation magic. The hideous appearance of the man is explained by the same fact, for the Pharmakoi [5] in the analogous rite in Greece, in whom have been seen by an amazing piece of ingenuity the prototypes of Adam and Eve, are also hideous, and the assumption that we have in the features of the man the imitation of the features of Varuṇa is an absurd idea, well worthy of the Brāhmaṇas. The payment is only natural: the priests were always well aware of the value of their services, and honesty must admit that they were fully entitled to expect high payment for the disagreeable duty of taking on themselves the burden of the sins of the village outcasts. The idea that the Ātreya priest was really once the old king thus vanishes into the limbo of practical impossibilities.

It is, however, more important to consider whether such an idea can be seen in the horse sacrifice itself, not in the bath ceremony which is a mere appendix. The essence of the horse sacrifice is the slaying of the steed, which is treated with great honour, gaily caparisoned, and is invited to eat the remains of the night oblations of grain which, if refused by the steed, are thrown into water,

[1] See Keith, JRAS. 1908, pp. 845–7.
[2] AB. vii. 13 ff.; ÇÇS. xv. 17 ff.
[3] ÇÇS. xvi. 18. 21 should probably be thus interpreted; Eggeling, SBE. xliv. p. xl. According to KÇS. xx. 8. 17, 18, outcasts by bathing in this bath are purified.
[4] Hillebrandt, *op. cit.* iii. 30, n. 1.
[5] Murray, *Greek Epic*[3], pp. 317 ff.; cf. Frazer, *The Scapegoat*, pp. 252 ff.

doubtless because their sanctity is too great to permit of their consumption by any one else. Nor is it possible to doubt that in the rite the horse is really the horse of the sun; the steed Dadhikrāvan, whom we have seen to be the steed of the sun, is said to be the sacrificial horse. It may, therefore, be suggested that by the slaying of the horse, which is solemnly performed, it was originally intended to perpetuate the race of horses, and that later on, when the horse was regarded as representing the sun, the rite became a sun spell. It is right to state the possibility of such a development: the probability is obviously practically negligible. The same remark applies to the other cases of the ritual: if for instance the goat is offered to Pūṣan as it often is, then, as we must admit that Pūṣan seems to have been once conceived as in goat form, it is possible that the original offering was simply that of a goat, in order to propagate the race of goats, or at a later period of a goat as the representative of the corn spirit; but in this case also we would have to admit that the whole theory had been entirely forgotten in Vedic times, where the offering was in no sense periodical, and when the goat form of Pūṣan was far from being vividly present to the worshippers, while the gift theory of sacrifice remains for this case the most simple and obvious explanation possible. The horse sacrifice presents more difficulties, but none that are helped by the theory of the corn spirit.[1]

§ 3. *The Removal of Sin by Sacrifice and Magic*

In the ritual of the sin offering the mixture of magic and sacrifice presents itself in the clearest way. The sin offering is only in essence a special form of the gift sacrifice: the gift is offered to avert the wrath of the god: it seeks to produce in him not the positive action of furthering the welfare of the suppliant as is normally the case, but the negative attitude of sparing the guilty man. In its rudest form the chain of ideas must be assumed to be that the food and drink will delight the god, and thus he will forget his anger: such a view is based on one of the most primitive instincts of mankind: the hungry man is unlikely to forgo his wrath, while the soothing effects of meat and drink on humanity, however just its anger, and moral its indignation, are notorious. Nor is there any doubt that simple sacrifices to avert the anger of the god, usually Varuṇa, were common: it is legitimate to suppose that the hymns of deprecation[2] of the anger of Varuṇa and of expressions of hope to be reconciled with him, which are found in the Rigveda, were accompanied by sacrifice: it would be very remarkable if this were not the case, but apart from that point the ritual is well aware of such offerings. Thus for the breach of an oath an offering is ordered to Agni Vaiçvānara,[3] who may safely be assumed to have been the god by whom in the special instance the oath was sworn, and who therefore must be appeased if he is not to execute vengeance for the breach of faith.

[1] Keith, *Taittirīya Saṁhitā*, i. pp. cxxxii–vii.
[2] e. g. RV. vii. 86. [3] TS. ii. 2. 6. 2

On the other hand, the element of magic enters very largely into the ceremony of the Varuṇapraghāsas,[1] the second of the four-month offerings. On the first day of the offering barley is roasted on the Dakṣiṇa fire, the one used for all ritual acts of an uncanny description: then a number of dishes of a porridge made from the barley are prepared, one for each member of the family with one over, apparently for the members yet unborn. The wife of the sacrificer is then asked by the priest what lovers she has; she must name them, or at least indicate the number by holding up as many stalks of grass as she has lovers, and by this action she purifies herself from her sins in this regard: otherwise, if she does not tell the truth, it will go badly for her connexions. She is then taken to the southern fire, in which she offers the plates with the words, 'Whatever sin we have committed in the village, in the forest, among men and in ourselves, that by sacrifice we remove here,' and further on an offering is made to Varuṇa, who is asked to spare the lives of his suppliants, and not to be wroth. The nature of the sacrifice is evidently in the main magical: the offering to Varuṇa and the consciousness of sin are there, but it may be legitimately be said that the essential part of the rite is the expulsion of sins by means of the magic rite, though due note must be taken that, as preserved to us, the other ethical element comes in. The burning of the dishes is of course essential, as they are laden with the sin: it may be compared with the purification by water of the scapegoat in the horse sacrifice, to which reference has been made above. In the course of the Soma sacrifice [2] the priests throw into the fire splinters of the wood of the sacrificial post, charging them with the removal of the sin wrought by the gods, the Fathers, man, and themselves. In the Sautrāmaṇī [3] offering a vessel filled with a special preparation is allowed to float away with the sins of those concerned. In the case in which a younger brother commits the crime of marrying before the elder,[4] the sins of both in the form of fetters are thrown into the foam of the water, and thus allowed to vanish. The washing of the mouth removes the sin of untruth for three years [5]—the mystic three or the unit one [6] are most common in these statements of time—and the evil brought by an ill-omened bird can be washed away and removed by the carrying round of fire.[7] In the same way are used plants,[8] the Apāmārga plant seems to owe its very name to its uses in such rites, amulets,[9] and spells.[10] On the other hand, the intervention of the gods is constantly mentioned: Agni Vaiçvānara, Agni Gārhapatya, Savitṛ, Pūṣan, the Maruts, Viçvakarman, the All-gods are invoked to remove the evil.[11] The evil in fact is treated precisely like a disease,

[1] ÇB. ii. 5. 2. 20. Hubert and Mauss (*Année sociol.* ii. 111, n. 3) compare the Levitical examination of the adulteress.

[2] Oldenberg, *Rel. des Veda*², p. 325.

[3] VS. xx. 14 ff.; KÇS. xix. 5. 13.

[4] AV. vi. 113. 2; Kauç. xlvi. 28.

[5] AV. x. 5. 22; Kauç. xlvi. 50.

[6] TS. vi. 6. 3. 1.

[7] AV. vii. 64; Kauç. xlvi. 47, 48.

[8] AV. viii. 7. 3; x. 1. 2.

[9] AV. x. 3. 8.

[10] AV. v. 30. 4.

[11] AV. vi. 119; vii. 64. 2; xii. 2. 11, 12; xiv. 2. 59 ff.; vii. 77. 3; ii. 25. 3; vi. 112. 3; 113. 2; 115, &c.

and is to be dealt with in just the same way. Moreover, as is natural, the concept of evil is of the widest possible kind : every sort of error in the sacrifice, every sort of out-of-the-way occurrence in the life of the home and the herds, such as the birth of twins, every sort of strange occurrence in ordinary nature, is made the cause for such an offering, and the Brāhmaṇas and still more the Sūtras pile up long lists of offerings under the rubric Prāyaçcitta,[1] a term which is not yet found in the Rigveda. The taste for such inventions is clearly one which grew with the development of the priestly system, and must from the constant number of such Prāyaçcittas, and the gifts to the priest which were enjoined as an essential part, have counted for much in the life of the priesthood. For religious purposes they are of little interest, since they consist in the main of offerings overlaid with magic practices of the most simple and obvious kind.

There is another set of practices connected with the removal of sin which present difficulties, and which are only recorded at the very end of the Vedic period, but the antiquity of which can hardly be seriously doubted. The Brahman student is under a duty of chastity : if he fails in this duty he is required to make an offering of an ass to the goddess Nirṛti : his portion of the victim is cut from the penis : and thereafter he goes about clad in the skin of the victim and begging for alms, duly proclaiming his sin to those from whom he begs.[2] The husband who sins against his wife wears also an ass's skin and begs, proclaiming that he has sinned against her.[3] The murderer carries the skull of the dead man, drinks out of it, wears an ass's skin or the skin of a dog, which indicates him as a murderer to all and sundry, and lives on alms, declaring to those from whom he begs the crime which he has committed.[4] There are here obviously many and varied elements of belief : the element of confession is clear in all these cases : the wickedness is made less by being declared, a doctrine which is of course prominently exhibited in the case of the Varuṇapraghāsas, at a much earlier date than the customs reported in the Sūtras. A second motive may be the warning of others of the nature of the being with whom they deal ; to a primitive people, believing in the physical transfer of evil, such a warning was a real necessity : this is parallel with the fact that the guilty generally are often ordered to remove from contact with the living.[5] The bearing about of the skull of the dead and drinking from it is attributed by Oldenberg [6] as possibly due to the belief that demons drink from the skulls of the dead, an idea which might of course be traced back to the reflection in belief of an actual custom : [7] as the custom and

[1] ApÇS. ix ; xiv. 16 ff. ; KÇS. xxv ; AÇS. iii. 10–14 ; vi. 6–10 ; ÇÇS. iii. 19–21 ; xiii. 2–12, &c.

[2] GDS. xxiii. 17 ; PGS. iii. 12. 8.

[3] ApDS. i. 10. 28. 19. For the use of the skin cf. Cook, *Zeus*, i. 422 ff.

[4] ApDS. i. 9. 24. 11 ; 10. 28. 21 ff. ; GDS. xxii. 4 ; BDS. ii. 1. 1. 3.

[5] ApDS. i. 9. 24. 13 ; 10. 28. 13 ; 10. 29. 1.

[6] *Rel. des Veda*², pp. 327, 328.

[7] HGS. ii. 1. 7. Cf. the use of Vṛtra's head as the *droṇakalaça* in the Soma sacrifice (TS. vi. 5. 9. 1), perhaps also that of Makha's head (RV. x. 171. 2 ; Oldenberg, *op. cit.*¹ p. 90).

the belief are reported to us both from the same late stage of the literature, there is no external evidence to aid in a decision. Oldenberg suggests also that it is the idea that the crime must be allowed to take the fullest control of the sinner, and in the observances in question expression is given to this rule. It is, however difficult to feel assured that this is a plausible explanation; it is required in reality only for the episode of the carrying of the skull, and this carrying seems in itself rather to be reminiscent of the carrying of such a skull, and the use of it for very different reasons, namely the keeping under one's own control of the spirit of the angry dead,[1] modified no doubt in later belief often merely to an added insult to the memory and spirit of the dead. It is possible that in the rite which is handed down to us what was originally a habit of head-hunters had been reduced to a punishment of murderers. But beyond speculation we cannot, it is clear, go.

The wearing of the skin of an ass or of a dog, which were both unclean animals [2]—that is to say, animals of a peculiar nature—cannot be regarded as explained by the theory of Oldenberg, even if it could be given credence to any extent. The case of the student is here the most interesting, as it involves a sacrifice, and has the most primitive appearance: the dog was clearly in some ways a peculiar beast: nothing but the utmost hunger would drive a man to eat a dog: [3] it is therefore quite possible that the wearing of the skin has no reference to any sacrifice, and the wearing of the ass-skin by the murderer may easily be due to the fact that the practice was customary in other cases. In that of the Brahmacārin the most obvious and simple explanation of the rite is that the virility of the ass [4] is its most marked feature, that the wearing of the skin and the eating of the special part assigned to the student were intended to replace the manhood expended improperly. The fact that the offering was made to Nirṛti then ceases to stand in special relation to the goddess, as connected with the ass: Nirṛti is the personification of dissolution: to her an offer might properly then be made in the circumstances, and, as often, we find the offering intermingled with the magic rite, as in the case of the offering to Varuṇa at the Varuṇapraghāsas.[5] The wearing of the skin might then easily degenerate into an intimation of the sinfulness of the wearer, as it certainly was recognized in this use in the

[1] The head-hunting and preservation of heads were characteristic of the Celts (MacCulloch, *Rel. of Anc. Celts*, pp. 240 ff.), Germans (Müllenhoff, *Deutsche Alt.*, iv. 145), and other Aryans (Brunnhofer, *Arische Urzeit*, pp. 322–4, 372).

[2] PB. xxi. 3. 5; ApDS. i. 3. 10. 17. The totemistic theory of tabooed animals may be applied both to the dog (as in the case of the dogs of Aktaion) and the ass (Marsyas as an ass) as has been done for Greece by Reinach, *Cultes, Mythes et Religions*, iii. 37; iv. 40–4. Similarly for the Celts, MacCulloch, *Rel. of Anc. Celts*, pp. 219 ff., without any convincing ground. Cf. Keith, JRAS. 1916, pp. 542 ff.

[3] Cf. Manu, x. 106; RV. iv. 18. 13 (a very obscure text).

[4] Cf. Reinach, *Cultes, Mythes et Religions*, iv. 29 ff.; Cook, *Zeus*, i. 626.

[5] That the ceremony there is really sacrifice pure and simple (Eitrem, *Opferritus und Voropfer der Griechen und Römer*, p. 136) is very improbable.

Sūtras, but that this idea is primitive is absurd. The case of the man who has abandoned his wife is probably the same: the magic power of the skin is to give him virility, and induce him to perform his duty which he has abandoned: it must be remembered that, as with most primitive peoples, and in the Roman Catholic faith of the present day, cohabitation with his wife is a man's bounden duty, an idea reflected in various Indian stories.

The only other explanation of the rite which may at first sight seem plausible is the idea that the ass is the representative of the man, in that the man instead of sacrificing himself to the angry deity offers a substitute. We might, if we accepted this view, rank with this case the instances of the representation of the members of the family by the dishes in the Varuṇapraghāsas, the offering of hair to the dead,[1] and the assertion of the Brāhmaṇas that the victim which is offered to Agni and Soma in the course of the Soma sacrifice is really offered as a ransom for oneself.[2] This theory, however, will not stand any close examination. The explanation [3] of the hair offering is open to the gravest objection: it seems rather a mere mode of bringing the living into the closest possible connexion with the dead, through the medium of part of himself, without any idea that he either should or would give himself as an offering. The case of the dishes is obviously a case of simple material transfer without any idea of offering of the members of the family, and the victim for Agni and Soma is only said to be a substitute in explanatory and speculative passages, and even there the view is evidently not always accepted: its true nature will be explained later. The explanation in the case of the ass sacrifice is also most improbable: it treats the sin which is evidently by no means a very serious one—the chastity of the Brahmans was evidently of a somewhat mild order of virtue—as if it were a deadly sin, a conception not at all a favourite one with the priests.

§ 4. *Communion and Sacrament in the Sacrifice*

While in the view of Sir J. Frazer the essence of early sacrifice is the magic art of perpetuating the life of the herds and of vegetation and even of man, the gift theory of sacrifice has also been declared [4] to be merely derivative, on the ground that it is really a faded remnant of the sacrifice in which the worshippers eat together of the flesh and blood of the deity, thus renewing and strengthening the bonds between themselves on the one hand and the god on the other. That such a form of sacrifice existed is beyond all doubt attested for the Semites, but not for the Babylonians, and there are traces of it in Greek

[1] Oldenberg, *Rel. des Veda*², p. 323, n. 1.

[2] TS. vi. 1. 11. 6; AB. ii. 9; KB. x. 3; ÇB. iii. 3. 4. 21; cf. xi. 7. 1. 3 (of the Paçubandha generally); Keith, *Taittirīya Saṁhitā*, i. p. cxiv.

[3] G. A. Wilken, *Rev. Col. Internat.* iii. 225 ff.; iv. 353 ff. For other views see Frazer, *The Magic Art*, i. 28 ff.; Gruppe, *Griech. Myth.*, pp. 913 ff.; Cook, *Zeus*, i. 23–5, 593. Cf. also Keith, JHS. xxxvi. 108; *contra*, Eitrem, *Opferritus und Voropfer der Griechen und Römer*, p. 387, n. 4.

[4] R. Smith, *Rel. of Semites*, p. 365; Reinach, *Cultes, Mythes et Religions*, i. 96; ii. 101.

and in other religions.[1] It is not necessary to insist, as does S. Reinach, that the origin of such an offering is totemistic : it is perfectly possible without any such system at the base to explain it : O. Gruppe [2] treats this form of sacrifice as the oldest and most primitive of all, the effort to obtain directly and most effectively a share in the divine power felt in the world. But it is one thing to believe in the existence of the sacrifice in this form, and to prove that it is the only type of sacrifice, and unless this can be done the gift form of sacrifice must continue to stand as an independent form. The objection that the gift theory must be later than the communion and sacrament form of sacrifice, because the conception of private property is necessary for the making of gifts, is not worth the consideration which has been sometimes shown to it. It is obvious that, apart from all other considerations, it has from the first been possible to offer to a god material things without any precise conception of ownership having been attained.

Now in the conception of the sacramental communion there are clearly present two elements which need not necessarily be combined. It is possible for the communion to appear by itself alone : the worshippers are imagined to eat and with them the deity eats, so that the deity and his worshippers have thus a common bond in the food which they consume : of this the Homeric sacrifice [3] clearly presents us with a good example, while another is given by the Latin festival on the Alban Mount.[4] In the second place, however, there may be more than this : the victim may be in some way divine : the most developed idea will be found when the victim is imagined as actually being an embodiment of the god for the time being, but it may be that the victim is merely more or less affected by the divine spirit from the fact that the god comes to the place of offering, and therefore that the divine spirit affects the victim and the place of offering.[5] Of the latter idea there is a clear hint in the Homeric ritual of sacrifice of an animal victim : the barley seems to have been laid on the altar, and then brought into contact with the victim to convey to the victim the divine spirit present in the altar, and this idea is confirmed by later evidence, such as the sacrifice at Athens known as the Bouphonia,[6] and

[1] Farnell, *Greece and Babylon*, pp. 241 ff. A good example of the common meal as a means of producing harmony is given in Kauç. xii. 8, 9. The same Sūtra (xiii. 6) prescribes a magic rite, in which portions of the members of some animals, lion, tiger, he-goat, ram, bull, a warrior and a Brahman student are to be eaten, to attain the possession of certain qualities ; there is, of course, no totemism in all this ; Henry, *La magie dans l'Inde antique*, pp. xxviii, 87, 95.

[2] Cf. Murray's theory (*Four Stages of Greek Religion*, p. 37), which holds that the victim is devoured not as divine, but merely to obtain its *mana*, the divinization arising later.

[3] Cf. Lang, *The World of Homer*, p. 129, with Murray, *Greek Epic*³, pp. 61 ff.

[4] Cf. Warde Fowler, *Roman Festivals*, pp. 95 ff.

[5] Cf. the worship paid to the offering implements by the Vedic Indian, to their *ollae* by the Arval Brethren (Warde Fowler, *Religious Experience of the Roman People*, pp. 436, 489), to the bells of their cattle and milk pails by the Todas (Rivers, *Todas*, p. 453).

[6] Cf. Keith, *Taittirīya Saṁhitā*, i. pp. cvi–viii ; Farnell, *Cults of the Greek States*, i. 56–8, 88–92 ; Hubert and Mauss, *Année sociol.* ii. 107 ff., 65, n. 3.

apparently the same idea is to be seen in the sprinkling of the *mola salsa* on the head of the victim in the Roman ritual and of melted butter in the Vedic rite.

Now in the Vedic ritual, as in the Roman, we find a considerable amount of evidence of the eating of the offering by the priests, after the god had partaken of it. The essential feature of the ordinary sacrifice is expressed in the solemn invocation of the Iḍā,[1] the sacrificial food derived from the cow, which is repeatedly conceived in cow form. She is invoked to come forward, and she is expressly called a cow, and, when the god has eaten, shares in her are consumed by the priests and by the sacrificer,[2] in so far as he is qualified by being a Brahman to partake of the food. The latter restriction is one which we can only prove for the later period of the Vedic ritual, but the position of the priest at the outset of the ritual is such as to render it most probable that the rule was always in full operation in the historical period. The same practice applied to all normal kinds of offering, the animal sacrifice and the Soma sacrifice included, though we find in the Aitareya Brāhmaṇa[3] that the king is excluded at the royal consecration from the use of Soma and given Surā instead. The same rule applies to the Gṛhya ritual : it is laid down that a man should eat nothing without making an offering of a portion of it, every meal when an animal is killed for a guest is, as in Homer, a sacrifice.[4] A Snātaka, or Brahman student, after he has taken the final bath concluding the studentship, is allowed to eat remains of food offered to the gods and to the Manes : in the latter permission, as in the rule that the wife, who wishes offspring, should eat a portion of the food offered to the Fathers,[5] we must doubtless see the idea of placing oneself in close touch with the Fathers. In an offering to Kṣetrapati,[6] in which the god is represented by a bull, the remains of the food are duly eaten by the relatives, and in another offering, the Madhuparka, the Rudras, Ādityas, and the All-gods are first fed, then the sacrificer, and then a Brahman : if there is no Brahman available, then the food may either be thrown into water, or the whole may be consumed by the sacrificer. The practice is interesting : it is clear that in the domestic ritual the rule that the only person who may eat the food is the Brahman is not in force : the sacrificer, who is the householder himself—and who may of course be himself a Brahman, but need not be—and his relatives have the first claim : after that

[1] TS. vii. 1. 6. 8; VS. iii. 27 ; ApCS. vi. 3. 8 ; AÇS. i. 7. 7 ; 8. 1 ; ÇÇS. i. 10. 1 ; TB. iii. 5. 8. 1 ; 13. 1 ; Hillebrandt, *Neu- und Vollmondsopfer*, pp. 124 ff. ; Hubert and Mauss, *Année sociol.* ii. 81, 82, who compare the Christian Mass.

[2] In Babylon the worshipper did not eat, though the priests might do so ; they, however, did not eat with the god; Farnell, *Greece and Babylon*, pp. 241, 242. For Rome see Warde Fowler, *Roman Ideas of Deity*, pp. 58, 59 ; *Religious Experience of the Roman People*, pp. 172 ff. The idea of communion was seriously restricted in the official religion as in Vedic religion. So also in Iran ; cf. Herodotos, i. 132, where the flesh is not (as stated by Jackson, GIP. ii. 702) eaten by the priests, but used by the sacrificer as he pleases.

[3] vii. 26 f.

[4] ÇGS. ii. 14. 23 ; ii. 15 ; iv. 5. 10, 11, 12.

[5] GGS. iv. 3. 27 ; cf. AÇS. ii. 7. 17.

[6] HGS. ii. 9 ; Keith, JRAS. 1907, pp. 939 ff.

the food which by its contact with the divinity is clearly specially valuable is either given to Brahmans, or disposed of in an effectual way. The ritual in many cases preserves express statements of the relation of the sacrificer to the sacrifice: if he does not eat a portion of it, he is excluding himself from it,[1] the Aitareya Brāhmaṇa says; but at the same time it is clear that it is rather a serious business: the hot milk in the Dadhigharma offering is expressly asked not to injure the partaker of it.[2] In some cases the idea of community resulting from the sacrifice seems clearly marked: thus the newly married couple, after their first entry into the common home, share food together from an offering made by the husband;[3] in the ceremony of the initiation of a pupil the teacher gives the pupil to eat of the offering which has just been made, saying, 'May Agni place wisdom in thee';[4] the sacrificer partakes of the offering of butter, which he and the priest have together touched before the sacrifice of Soma, and thus embodies in himself the idea of fidelity which was created by the touching;[5] the mother eats part of the food which is given with ceremonial rites to the infant as its first solid nutriment,[6] a practice in which Oldenberg[7] sees the idea of securing for her future children the strength given by the rite to the existing child, but which is far more simply explained as a mere ceremony of communion. Possibly here too may be added the case of the ass sacrifice of the Brahman student which has already been noted: it may be conceived that the victim is made efficacious for its special purpose by the bringing it near to the god by sacrifice.

The same efficacy of the sacrifice is to be seen in cases where the offering produces its result by contact,[8] not by ordinary eating. Thus in place of eating food together the husband and wife may rub each other's hearts with the offering,[9] and at the end of the three days of continence enjoined upon them the remains of the offerings are rubbed into the body of the bride.[10] Similarly, if on the way to their home the car breaks, an offering is made, and the remains rubbed on the mended part.[11] The horses which are to engage in the race in the Vājapeya sniff the offering in order to gain swiftness;[12] the cows are driven so as to snuff the fragrance of the offering made in the fire;[13] in the Soma sacrifice, the Vājapeya, the piling of the fire, and the Sautrāmaṇī alike occur cases in which the offering is used to rub the sacrificer to convey to him strength and healing.[14] At the animal sacrifice by touching the victim the

[1] AB. vii. 26. 2; cf. TA. v. 8. 12.

[2] VS. xxxviii. 16.

[3] GGS. ii. 3. 18; MB. i. 3. 8; doubtless the same idea as in the Roman *confarreatio*.

[4] HGS. i. 4. 9.

[5] Weber, *Ind. Stud.* x. 362. It must be taken that Warde Fowler (*Religious Experience of the Roman People*, p. 181) is wrong in holding that the flesh which was eaten by the priests had lost its holiness, though in the case of Iran Herodotos (i. 132) gives the same impression.

[6] GGS. i. 27. 11.

[7] *Rel. des Veda*,[2] p. 333, n. 3.

[8] Hubert and Mauss, *Année sociol.* ii. 76 ff.

[9] AGS. i. 8. 9.

[10] GGS. ii. 5. 6.

[11] GGS. ii. 4. 3.

[12] Weber, *Vājapeya*, pp. 28, 31.

[13] HGS. ii. 8. 10; cf. SVB. i. 8. 14; for man, KÇS. iv. 9. 11.

[14] AÇS. v. 19. 6; KÇS. xiv. 5. 24; xviii. 5. 9; xix. 4. 14; Weber, *Ind. Stud.* x. 351; xiii. 285.

sacrificer is brought into contact with the sacrifice,[1] and when, in the case of an offering to Rudra, the cakes are hung up on a tree, the sacrificer should touch them and win healing power.[2]

On the other hand, when the deities to whom the offerings are made are terrible, it is clearly natural that the offering should be regarded as not suitable for human consumption : in Greece the offerings to the dead and the chthonian divinities were not normally eaten. So in India, when rice cakes are offered to the Fathers, the sacrificer refrains from eating them : he merely smells them : [3] it is normally not right to partake of an offering to Rudra ; [4] if an offering is made for one who seeks thus to find death, at the consecration one should only smell, not taste : [5] in another case, the Dadhigharma, or offering of hot sour milk, the remains of the sacrifice may be eaten by priests who have undergone the consecration, but not by others who are less well fortified for the risk : [6] it is the native explanation,[7] and it is reasonable enough to hold that the mere smelling is a compromise between the necessity of partaking as normally and the danger of the action. The terrible character of the offering is further indicated by other usages : when an offering is made to the Rakṣases, to Rudra, to the Fathers, or the Asuras, or when an imprecation is made,[8] the sacrificer should touch water. When an offering is made to the Fathers,[9] in one case, the sacrificer looks north, whereas the quarter of the Fathers is the south ; when he offers to Rudra, he looks south, for Rudra's place is in the north, and the offerer is constantly bidden not to turn round after an offering to Rudra, which is explicable only by the view that the dread god is on the scene in bodily presence. We may here also include the theory, already mentioned, of some theologians that the victim to Agni and Soma at the Agniṣṭoma should not be eaten : it may have seemed to some that the presence of the gods Agni and Soma made the victim too dangerous to permit of close contact. But the general rule was that it should be eaten as is in one case expressly stated.

On the other hand, it was always possible to eat of even the offering to a dread god ; thus in the case of the offering of an animal to the god Rudra,[10] which is to be made in a part from which the village cannot be seen, we meet with the same phenomenon as has already been seen in two cases in which it is

[1] TS. vi. 3. 8. 1, 2 ; ÇB. iii. 8. 1 ; Hubert and Mauss, *Année sociol.* ii. 67, n. 1.

[2] ÇB. ii. 6. 2. 16.

[3] ÇB. xii. 5. 1. 12 ; ii. 4. 2. 24 ; 6. 1. 33 ; ApÇS. viii. 6. 3, 12 ; KÇS. iv. 1. 20 ; v. 9. 13.

[4] AGS. iv. 8. 31.

[5] KÇS. xxii. 6. 2.

[6] KÇS. x. 1. 26.

[7] TB. i. 3. 10. 7.

[8] ÇGS. i. 10. 9 ; KÇS. i. 10. 14.

[9] ÇB. xiv. 2. 2. 35, 38.

[10] AGS. iv. 8. 1 ff.; PGS. iii. 8. Hubert and Mauss (*Année sociol.* ii. 93) by combining with this account the very different one of HGS. ii. 8, 9 ; ApGS. xix. 13–xx. 19, conclude that the rite consists of bringing into the victim the divinity of Rudra and then banishing it from the village. But this is wholly illegitimate : the animal is not divine at all in AGS. or PGS., and is not banished in HGS. or ApGS. That the rite is known to the Rigveda is wholly unproved.

allowed to eat of an offering to the dead. It is expressly said that the sacrificer must not eat any part of the victim, that he must not let the wind of it blow upon him, that he must not take any part of it into the village, and that he must keep his folk away from the place of offering, all clear proofs of the presence of the god, but it is also stated that he may eat of it on an express injunction, and that then the eating will bring him great luck. It is an error to underestimate[1] the value of this evidence : it proves that the nature of the effect on the offering is to fill it with holy power, and that the eating of part of it conveys that holy power, which may be well worth having in some special cases,[2] though normally when Rudra is the god concerned men may not care to come too near to it. From this point of view also we can understand the true force of the fact that the blood of the victim was not partaken of by the priest and the sacrificer : in this Hillebrandt[3] has seen a ground of distinction between the Indian and the Semitic theory of sacrifice, in which the blood is precisely the essential thing, which the worshippers desire to share, as is seen in the horrid Arabian rite reported by Nilus in which the worshippers eat the victim uncooked and take care to save all the blood, while in the Vedic view the blood is impure and given to the Rakṣases.[4] It is not that the blood is impure : it is rather that it is particularly full of the divine power, doubtless as the seat of life of the animal, and the part into which the divine spirit can most easily enter, and thus is offered not to men but to spirits, often it is clear to the snakes[5] as the representatives of the earth spirit, an idea which explains also the Greek theory of purification by blood : the person purified thus by the use of blood places himself in communion with the goddess of the earth.[6]

It is true that, as has been pointed out by Oldenberg[7] and others, the theory of the sacrifice as a communion with the deity, whether by the direct rite of eating with him, or as a sacrament through eating a victim, which has become impregnated in some degree with the deity, is not recognized as such in the formulae of the ritual : we simply find nothing of the view that the worshippers are eating together with the god in order to renew their relationship. The solitary prescription above mentioned regarding the victim to Agni and Soma does not hint at this view at all : it merely refers to the theory which is several times expressed in the Brāhmaṇas that man is the

[1] Oldenberg, *Rel. des Veda*², p. 337, n. 1.

[2] As a sick man can eat the offering to the dead, and have swift death or recovery, AÇS. ii. 7. 17.

[3] *Thiere und Götter*, pp. 3, 4 ; Hopkins, JAOS. xvi. p. ccxxxix ; Oldenberg, *op. cit.*, p. 360.

[4] The official Roman religion seems to have made little use of the blood (Warde Fowler, *Religious Experience of the Roman People*, p. 180) though the popular ritual recognized feasting on it (*ibid.*, p. 196). Greek religion was different in this regard. Cf. Hubert and Mauss, *Année sociol.* ii. 79, n. 1.

[5] AGS. iv. 8. 28 ; Winternitz, *Sarpabali*, p. 41.

[6] Farnell, *Cults of the Greek States*, iv. 304 ; the use of blood for purification is hardly Roman ; in the Lupercalia it is borrowed from Greece (Deubner, *Archiv f. Religionswissenschaft*, xiii. 481 ff. ; *contra*, Cook, *Zeus*, i. 677).

[7] *Rel. des Veda*², p. 331, n. 2.

original victim,[1] and that other victims are substitutes. We might expect to find the theory recognized in the case of the Soma sacrifice, when Soma was identified with the moon, and the Brāhmaṇas [2] do tell us that Soma is killed when he is pressed for the Soma drink, and that what is drunk at the rite is the moon, but all this remains merely an expression of the fact that the moon decays and is supposed to be drunk up by the gods in heaven, and analogously by the gods on earth, the priests who have the knowledge of the mystery of the identity of the Soma plant and the moon. The conditions which might have developed a conception of the sacrifice as a communion of men both *inter se* and with the god, and as a sacrament through the feeding on a victim which is really an embodiment of the god, were present only in germ, and they do not seem to have generated the consciousness of the sacramental nature of the offering, although the effort to assimilate the victim to the god was always present and effective. The victim was preferably an animal which was a theriomorphic form of the god, bulls to Indra, goats to Pūṣan and to Agni, and so on; the sex was assimilated and the colour chosen with regard to the nature of the god.[3] None the less we must admit that, whatever the reason, the Indians of the Vedic period, like the Romans, differed radically and vitally from the Semites who practised the sacramental sacrifice in the fact [4] that, though the animal victim might be chosen for its close connexion with the deity and in the actual offering be filled with the divinity, they did not in their normal thought press this view to the conclusion that the offering really caused the death of the god. Further, though the Vedic Indian recognized that by eating the remains of the offering he was bringing himself into close communion with the divine power and that the victim was in some sense semi-divine, he did not feel that in the death of the victim there was perishing some person essentially of kin to him, and therefore to be lamented, as the performers of Greek sacrifices in several cases may have lamented the victim, or for whose death punishment was necessary, as suggested by the ritual of the Bouphonia. Even in animal sacrifice there is no trace of kinship with man, though we have the clearest evidence of the desire to deprecate the anger of the kin of the dead beast [5] and the recognition of the fact that the victim will have power to confer richness in cattle as acceptable to the gods,[6] and there is no trace in the ritual of disapproval of the slayer as suggested by Hubert and Mauss.[7]

It is difficult also to ascertain what element of ecstatic enjoyment of the sense of union with the deity entered into the sacrificial ritual.[8] The gods,

[1] ÇB. vi. 2. 1. 2 ff.; i. 2. 3. 6; MS. iii. 10. 2; AB. ii. 8; Lévi, *La doctrine du sacrifice*, pp. 133 ff.

[2] ÇB. iii. 3. 2. 6; Lévi, p. 170; Hubert and Mauss, *Année sociol.* ii. 129 ff.

[3] Hillebrandt, *Thiere und Götter*; Stengel, *Opferbräuche der Griechen*, pp. 187 ff.; Cook, *Zeus*, i. 634.

[4] Keith, JRAS. 1907, pp. 940 ff.

[5] Hubert and Mauss, *Année sociol.* ii. 68, n. 3.

[6] TS. iii. 1. 4, 5; MS. i. 2. 1.

[7] *Op. cit.* 68, n. 4. The interpretation of AB. ii. 7. 10 is quite clearly not a general attack on the slayer, whose epithet *apāpa* refers to ritual accuracy.

[8] *Die Anfänge der Yogapraxis im alten Indien*, pp. 116 ff.

we learn later, once appeared in bodily presence at the offering, but had ceased to do so, but this is not conclusive against the natural belief that the singers in their sacrifices believed themselves actually to behold the gods whom they invoked. We find prayers [1] for the eye of Agni to enable the worshipper to behold the demons and sorcerers, a plant has the power to make demons visible, the dicer sees the dancing Apsarases, and in the stress of battle we may safely assume that Indians who prayed to their gods had visions, as in medieval or modern days, in which they beheld the objects of their invocation lending them divine aid. Especially in the invocations of Indra, the Maruts, and the Açvins, all gods of especially concrete character, who are of present help in time of trouble, do we find indications which suggest that the priest believed that the gods would, if duly praised, reveal themselves to his longing vision.[2] Possibly too we may reckon here the prayers in the Āprī hymns which bid the divine doors open wide to admit the gods to the offering, and the conception of the path of the gods to the heaven may be due to this cause. The Fathers, we know, appeared to their worshippers, for we hear of Yātus who smuggle themselves in among them assuming their form.

The offering produces also another sense of communion, in the divine ecstasy produced by the Soma drink. The Vedic poets have not the gift of imaginative description of a Euripides, and we find but little expression of the state of mind produced by imbibing the powerful potion. Still it is clear that those who drink can say, ' We have found the light, we have become immortal,' and that they truly feel the joy they asserted, even if they cannot claim, like the partaker of the sacred rite at Eleusis, ' to have escaped evil and found what is better '. The classical expression of this ecstatic state is found in the hymn [3] which tradition, in all probability with justice, holds to be the expression of Indra's mind after he has drunk the Soma. The worlds are his plaything, he rises aloft in his joy, he speeds on the wings of the wind. Ecstasy, naturally enough, is specially the product of drinking the Soma, who is hailed as the kind friend and father, who grants length of days, for this boon is eagerly desired by the Vedic mystic, as it is by the later Yogin. But similar powers are ascribed by the Atharvaveda [4] to the remains of the sacrificial offering, full of the divine power, and to the porridge (*odana*),[5] which, eaten, gives the worshipper the feeling of attaining the heaven, and in the Agni worship there are fainter traces of the development of a more refined form of mystic speculative activity.

Another aspect of sacrifice which has some affinity to a spell and a sacrament is that emphasized by Hubert and Mauss [6] in their theory of the nature of sacrifice, based on the evidence in the main of the Old Testament and the

[1] RV. x. 87. 12 ; AV. iv. 20 ; vii. 109. 3.

[2] RV. iii. 52. 2 ; v. 30. 1 ; iv. 17. 16 ff. ; vi. 29. 3 ; 32 ; viii. 100 ; x. 48, 49, 124 (Indra) ; v. 53 (Maruts) ; i. 118, 119 (Açvins).

[3] RV. x. 119.

[4] xi. 7.

[5] iv. 34, 35 ; xi. 1. 25.

[6] *Année sociol.* ii. 29–138.

Vedic ritual. Their attention has been attracted by the fact that a sacrifice produces a definite effect in the performer and the means which he employs : he is filled with a sacred spirit as is the victim which he offers, a fact of which we have already seen instances, and which cannot be for a moment called in question. The Dīkṣā or preliminary consecration, and the concluding bath, which provides a means of removing from man in some degree the excessive sanctity with which he has become endued in the process of offering, are significant proofs of this aspect of sacrifice. The sacrifice, many as are the uses which can be made of it, has an essential unity in that it aims at the establishment of communication between the sacred and the profane world by means of a victim, that is, a thing which is destroyed in the course of the ceremony. As opposed to Robertson Smith, the authors lay stress on the fact that the victim acquires its sacred character in the rite, and does not possess it normally *ab extra*, a fact which makes it well adapted for the accomplishment of the most varied ends : the current which runs through it can pass to the sky from the earth or *vice versa* equally well. The motive of this desire to enter into relations with the powers above is simple enough : man sees in them the source of life, and is anxious to attain as close contact with them as possible. But immediate contact would be fatal, and would unfit man for secular life, as is indeed the case with priests of too great sanctity like the unfortunate Flamen Dialis [1] or the Emperor of Japan : therefore he interposes an intermediary, who at the same time serves as a substitute for the sacrificer himself. This victim must be dispatched to the other world : its soul is liberated by death, with its own permission, for it becomes by the sacrifice a powerful being which no man would seek to irritate, and its body thereafter may be destroyed, whether by being consumed entirely by fire as in the Hebrew holocaust, or by being eaten by the priest or the worshippers, or again its skin or other portion may merely be brought into close contact with the worshipper. Incidentally the sacrifice accomplishes much more than its mere immediate aim : if the victim offered by the consecrated man serves to secure him his close relationship with the gods, it also sends the spirit of the victim to strengthen and multiply the species. All sacrifice is essentially social : it involves negation by the individual, but it strengthens the divine which is the ideal representative of the social unit, and thus indirectly benefits the individual himself. A further development of sacrifice in its ideal form is the conception of the sacrifice of the god himself, when the intermediary disappears *in toto*.

Brilliant as is the presentation of this theory, it is difficult not to feel that it is open to the same objection as must be taken to the theory of religion presented by Durkheim [2] in his exposition of totemism as the earliest stage of religion. Religion with him also is essentially a social fact : the totem is the

Warde Fowler, *Religious Experience of the Roman People*, pp. 34 ff.

[2] *Elementary Forms of the Religious Life* (1915). Contrast C. C. J. Webb, *Group Theories of Religion* (1916).

material object in which the conception of the unity of the primitive social group materializes itself. In both theories we have a tendency to find in primitive religion conceptions of too great elaboration and difficulty. Durkheim himself, however, does not abandon the gift theory in practice: he regards the gift as essential: the gods created by the collective mind of the group are the protectors and guardians of the group, but at the same time they require the gifts of the individuals to secure their existence and power. It is clear that much of Hubert and Mauss's theory is borne out by facts, and the doctrine that in the sacrifice the victim becomes peculiarly holy is valuable and correct, accounting naturally as it does for many peculiarities of the sacrifice, and affording in all probability the best explanation of the origin and development of the doctrine of slaying a god. But the view that the sacrifice is primarily an offering to please the god seems to be borne out by every probability, and by the undoubted fact that the sacrifice was normally so understood throughout antiquity. In this regard it is impossible not to feel that the authors have allowed themselves to be influenced unduly by the theories of the Brāhmanas as to the nature of sacrifice, and have underestimated the purely speculative and learned character of these suggestions. The objection to the gift theory insisted upon by Jevons [1] which represents it as unworthy of the relation of god and man is open to the criticism that it sets too high a standard for the beginning of religion. Moreover, the gift theory of sacrifice has the advantage that it affords in conjunction with other simple conceptions a perfectly natural origin for the various forms of offering: the sacramental rite in its simplest form of eating with the god follows naturally from the primitive conception that a sharing the same food confers similarity of nature, assisted perhaps, as Jevons holds, by the joyous feast celebrated by the worshippers at the moment when they feel that by their offering they have deprecated the wrath of the god and secured his loving-kindness to themselves and their families. From this form of the sacramental meal, coupled with the principle of sanctity of the offering at the sacrifice, is easily deduced the view that the victim which is being offered is the god himself embodied for the time being in the victim: Jevons himself explains in a somewhat analogous way the conception of eating the god which found a place in the Mexican worship. But it would doubtless be a mistake to assume that the idea of the death of the god was always produced in this way only: we must take into account the life and death of nature and the harvest rites in which the spirit of the corn is assumed to die in the cutting of the corn, and to revive in the growth of the young corn in the spring, and in which the spirit of the corn, when the harvest is reaped, though outworn, is deemed to seek to avoid its doom by passing into some animal, bird, or man, and is killed in order that it may revive afresh in the spring. But this conception is not developed in Vedic ritual so far as it is recorded, nor has it any necessary connexion with sacrifice: moreover, it is at least probable that in many cases there has been confusion between the

[1] *Idea of God in Early Religions*, pp. 78 ff.

killing of evil spirits, wizards supposed to endanger the crop, and the slaying of corn spirits proper.[1] In Vedic religion at any rate the conception of grain as containing a spirit is hardly to be found: the one piece of evidence from the ceremony of the Varuṇapraghāsas [2] adduced by Hubert and Mauss [3] is far from being convincing.

Jevons [4] insists that all sacrifice involves essentially the idea of drawing near to the god and making an offering to secure his favour, a step adopted originally when the community felt that its god was alien from it through the misconduct of one of its members, and had to be propitiated by tokens of repentance. The offering brought need not be consumable; if it were, it might easily be eaten after acceptance by the worshippers in a festival of joy at the feeling of reunion with their god. At first offerings are only occasional, evoked by fear of the anger of the god, who, however, is recognized to be justly wrath and to be also merciful and willing to forgive his worshippers, but the habit of solemn feasting on these occasions is gradually adopted in respect of the harvest fruits, when, as in the case of the occasional offerings, the worshippers first sacrifice to the god, before they partake of the fruits of the earth. But, as the fruits are thus sacred, they come to be regarded as divine, and as divine they take the rank of deities, the spirits of vegetation, to whom he denies in their own right divine status. Sacrifice thus is from the first much more than a gift offering or covenant offering; it is also not a communion feast, though both the gift and the communion theory of sacrifice are natural ways of interpreting the rite, which are adopted by the worshippers. In his view the gift theory is essentially irreligious; from it no true religion could spring. This, however, appears a decidedly dubious assertion; it is by no means obvious that the presenting of gifts to a god in the hope of favour, without consciousness of sin or divine wrath, is not an essentially primitive form of sacrifice.

§ 5. *The Materials of the Sacrifice*

On the gift theory of sacrifice it is natural that man should offer what he delights to feed upon, and in point of fact this undoubtedly is the rule in the great majority of cases: the Vedic Indians practised agricultural as well as pastoral pursuits, and we find therefore that they offered to the gods, not only milk in its various forms, as curd or melted butter in several varieties, but also grain, barley and rice, which served to make different kinds of cakes, or were mixed with milk or curds to form variegated messes. These materials served to satisfy many needs, but the animal and the Soma offerings were of still greater consequence in the eyes of the priest, though they must have been numerically very few in comparison with the sacrifices of simple materials.

[1] Westermarck, *Ceremonies and Beliefs connected with Agriculture . . . in Morocco*, pp. 93 ff.; Keith, JRAS. 1916, p. 546.

[2] ApÇS. viii. 5. 42; vi. 1 ff., 10 ff.

[3] *Op. cit.*, p. 111, n. 5.

[4] *Idea of God in Early Religions*, pp. 60–107.

Libations of water, not of blood as in Greece, for the dead were evidently directly connected with the conception of the thirst of the Fathers. Wild products such as wheat or sesame were reserved for Rudra, sesame grains were peculiar to the dead, and a puerile desire to assimilate the offerings to the gods appears in the rules that for Night and Dawn an offering of milk from a black cow with a white calf was appropriate,[1] that for the dead should be used the milk of a cow which has lost its own and is bringing up a strange calf,[2] that black [3] rice is the proper offering to Nirṛti,[4] that cakes for Agni should be offered on eight, those for Indra on eleven, those for the Ādityas on twelve potsherds, because the metres connected with these deities have those numbers of syllables, and so on in unending detail.

The Brāhmaṇas [5] set forth a list of five victims among animals, man, the horse, oxen, sheep, and goats : in practice the last three are the common victims, and the goat is the most usual of all : wild animals, fish, birds, the pig, and the dog are excluded ; the last two were not eaten, the others rarely, but it is possible that in their case practical difficulties may explain their exclusion from use. At the horse sacrifice, it is true, enormous lists of offerings of all sorts of animals are enumerated : the rule is, however, admitted that the wild animals were to be set free, and it is absurd to suppose that the lists were ever seriously meant to be followed. On the other hand, the offering of the horse is contrary to the practice, for the eating of horse-flesh, though never in all likelihood unknown in India,[6] and though practised by many peoples in ancient, medieval, and modern times, seems rare in India. It may be considered [7] as serving either to make swift the god, who thus appropriates the swiftness of the animal offered, and through the god to strengthen the man, or as is less likely it may be held to be merely dictated by the desire directly to secure the offerer the strength of the steed, or again it may be due merely to the feeling that the highest beast is in place at a great offering : to this question we shall return again. In the case of the offering of an ass to Nirṛti the aim to secure the replacement of virility by the offerer is obvious, and reduces the offering to its real character, a magic rite dignified by the introduction of the goddess and the form of sacrifice. The offering of a fish-otter to Apāṁ Napāt [8] is possibly to be attributed to the same idea : the otter suggests and creates the desired water, but it may also fall under the general rule of assimilation of the victim to the nature of the deity.

1 VS. xvii. 70; so often in magic; Henry, *La magie dans l'Inde antique*, p. 52.

2 AB. vii. 2 ; ÇB. xii. 5. 1. 4 ; TS. i. 8. 5. 1, and often.

3 Red victims for the gods, black for the Fathers, are usual; Caland, *Todtengebräuche*, p. 173.

4 TS. i. 8. 9. 1 ; ÇB. v. 3. 1. 13.

5 Weber, *Ind. Stud.* x. 347. The Suovetaurilia of Roman religion have no precise parallel. In Greece we hear of triads of victims, the Trittoia, ram, bull, he-goat ; Stengel, *Opferbräuche*, pp. 195, 196.

6 Mahāvagga, vi. 23. 11. On this point cf. Reinach, *Cultes, Mythes et Religions*, iii. 124 ; von Schroeder (*Arische Religion*, ii. 374 ff.) believes that the eating of horseflesh and its offering to the sun are Indo-European.

7 Oldenberg, *Rel. des Veda*[1], p. 356.

8 Kauç. cxxvii

This practice of assimilation is obvious and natural: it is not indeed strictly logical that, because a god is said to be a bull, he should eat bulls, for the Vedic Indian never in any time known to us thought that Indra or any other god [1] was merely a bull, but the connexion of ideas by which, in choosing a special victim, the form of the god suggested the choice is plain and obvious, and agrees with the conception that by eating certain animals certain qualities are attained by men; by eating bulls the god strengthens his nature in its bull aspect. Hence we find that Indra receives bulls and buffaloes,[2] Pūṣan goats, Agni with his fire and smoke a goat with a black neck,[3] the Maruts a speckled cow or a speckled animal because of their speckled mother,[4] the ruddy Açvins a red goat,[5] the sun and Yama a white and a black goat respectively, Tvaṣṭṛ [6] a special kind of goat because it occurs in his myth, and so on. But we must not exaggerate the rule of agreement whether in character, sex, or colour. The Maruts sometimes have a barren cow or a ewe, Sarasvatī a he-goat, Mitra and Varuṇa a barren cow; [7] in other cases the colour depends on the object of the offering, not on the god, as when a black victim brings rain,[8] and a red victim is offered by a priest with red raiment to destroy a foe.[9] It is possible, of course, that cases where the sex of the victim does not agree may be explained [10] by changes in the ritual, which has altered the allocation of victims to different gods, but for this theory there is hardly any real ground, as the rule of correspondence in Indian as in Greek and Roman religion is merely an approximate rule, and of no more than empirical validity.

The victim has to be killed, so that it shall make no sound and so that there shall be no effusion of blood: it seems to have been usually strangled: the cruel method of killing recorded by Haug is not shown to have existed at any early period.[11] Stress is laid in the verse addressed to it on the fact that it is not really being killed. The omentum of the victim, a part rich in fat, is then extracted and offered up: thereafter the remaining parts are divided for offering, a rice cake is offered, portions of the remainder of the flesh are offered to the gods with formulae recalling the fact that the omentum has already been used, and the priest and other Brahmans eat the rest, keeping only the tail for the final part of the rite. The same division of the ceremony is observed in the animal offerings to the Fathers made at the Aṣṭakā offering, and the distinction must be very old.[12] The separate treatment of the omentum

[1] Cf. Rapson in Cook, *Zeus*, i. 718, and Cook's own doubtless correct view of the motive for the selection of bulls and rams in special as victims for Zeus (i. 634, 717, 718).

[2] Hillebrandt, *Ved. Myth.* i. 231.

[3] VS. xxiv. 1.

[4] KÇS. xiv. 2. 11; TS. ii. 1. 6. 2.

[5] ÇB. v. 5. 4. 1.

[6] KÇS. viii. 9. 1; RV. i. 161. 3 (*basta*).

[7] Weber, *Ind. Stud.* x. 340, 358, 398, 394.

[8] TS. ii. 1. 8. 5.

[9] KÇS. xxii. 3. 14, 15.

[10] Oldenberg, *Rel. des Veda*², p. 356.

[11] Schwab, *Altind. Thieropfer*, pp. 112 ff.; AB. ii. 6; TB. iii. 6. 11. 1 ff.

[12] AGS. ii. 4. 13, 14; cf. ApDS. i. 6. 18. 25. The omentum is the self of the victim (TS. vi. 3. 9. 5) and its sacrificial element (TS. iii. 1. 5. 2; ÇB. iii. 8. 2. 28; AB. ii. 13. 6).

is proved for the Iranians by Strabo,[1] who explains that the soul only of the victim was given to the gods, except that a small piece of the omentum was put in the fire, and a corresponding distinction is to be found in the directions of Leviticus [2] regarding the sin and other offerings. It certainly seems to have been an early idea that the burning of the omentum made a sweet smell for the god : the Zulus burn it while leaving the rest of the victim untouched, believing that the spirits come and partake of it without leaving any trace of their feast. In this may be seen some evidence of the process of the transfer of the use of fire to its later employment as the normal way of conveying the offering to the gods.[3] The blood, as we have seen, was left for the Rakṣases,[4] along with the excrements, &c., of the victim, with which may be compared the practice of offering to the same powers oddments of the offerings of grain-stuffs, perhaps merely to deprecate their interference by this cheap form of sacrifice; but it is possible, as we have seen, that the offering to the Rakṣases must be taken seriously as an offering to chthonian powers of the earth, as is suggested by the fact that the snakes are often conceived as receiving blood.

There is nothing here to interfere with the usual view that the sacrifice is essentially a gift offering, not a relic of totemism, or of the offering of a vegetation spirit or, earlier, of a spirit of animal life, in order to keep it ever young. No such explanation is at all requisite in order to explain the connexion of the gods with particular victims, nor to explain the silent death of the victim, from which the principal celebrants avert their heads, or the efforts to persuade it that it is not being killed, a device applied also to the tree which is being cut for the sacrificial post. The death of the victim is that of an animal with a soul which could be wroth, and also full of the divine spirit—sometimes so full, as in the case of the victim for Agni and Soma, that some would not eat of it—and it is a dreadful thing, therefore, to slay it, though necessary. Apart, however, from the place of offering, the animal is merely an ordinary animal, and therefore it is difficult to read into the sacrifice more than the theory of a gift, sometimes with magic qualities.[5]

The question of the human sacrifice is of importance, as in it we should expect to find, if anywhere, the clearest recognition of the nature of sacrifice. Here, however, the material is wholly inadequate to establish any result. In one case we have perfectly good proof that down to a comparatively late date [6]

[1] xv. 732 ; Vendidad, xviii. 70 ; Catullus, 89 ; cf. the special treatment of the *exta* in Roman worship ; Warde Fowler, *Religious Experiencc of the Roman People*, p. 181.

[2] iv and vii.

[3] Oldenberg, *op. cit.*[2], pp. 359 ff.

[4] TS. i. 3. 9. 2 ; ApÇS. vii. 18. 14 ; AB. ii. 7. 1, 10 ; AÇS. iii. 3. 1 ; so in the case of the blood in the cooking of the heart of the victim (KÇS. vi. 7. 13).

[5] Keith, *Taittirīya Saṁhitā*, i. pp. cv–cviii. For the averted heads of the priests cf. the *capite operto* of the Roman ritual (as opposed to the Greek), which may be a sign of separation from the profane world (cf. Reinach, *Cultes, Mythes et Religions*, i. 300 ff.), but which may be merely a more efficacious means of escaping recognition by the soul of the indignant victim, as in the case where the criminal is veiled before execution.

[6] ÇB. vi. 2. 1. 39 ff. ; vii. 5. 2. 1 ff. ; cf. P. Sartori, *Zeit. f. Ethn.* i. 32 ff.

in the building up of the great altar for the fire ritual, a construction of such elaboration that it was doubtless a rare feature in the ritual, it was customary to sacrifice five victims, including a man, to build their heads into the altar, and to throw their bodies into the water whence the clay for the making of fire-bricks was taken, in order to give it abiding strength. Here, however, we cannot ignore the obvious fact that under the fashion of a sacrifice, last performed on earth by Çyāparṇa Sāyakāyana, we have dressed up the old practice of giving a building strength by associating it with guardian spirits of the dead, a usage which has persisted in India down to the most recent times. The other cases in which human sacrifices have been seen are extremely doubtful.[1] The ritual texts, indeed, and some late Brāhmaṇa evidence agree in describing a Puruṣamedha, ' human sacrifice ', which follows but on a more gorgeous scale the horse sacrifice. We have no reason to believe that it was ever a primitive rite : the effort of Hillebrandt [2] to show that the passage in the funeral hymn in the Rigveda,[3] which has been supposed to apply to the widow of the dead man in the funeral service, really applies to the widow of the king, who is supposed, as in the horse sacrifice, to lie beside the victim, is a *tour de force*. If ever the sacrifice was performed, it must merely have been an isolated act, produced by the speculations of the priests. There is clear evidence that the sacrifice of the mythical Puruṣa was in some cases at least taken as the model of the supposed human sacrifice. Possibly here and there myth generated the ritual : there is no conceivable reason to believe in view of the evidence that the ritual generated the myth.

More worth consideration perhaps is the legend of Çunaḥçepa ; [4] in it Hariçcandra the king promises to sacrifice his son to Varuṇa, if the god will give him a son : but, when the child is attained, he defers the offering until he manages to obtain a Brahman Ajīgarta, who consents to sell his son Çunaḥçepa for a vicarious sacrifice, the king having been afflicted by Varuṇa with dropsy and thus recalled to the sense of his duty. When the father binds the son to the post and is about to slay him, the gods set him free in answer to his prayer and he is adopted by one of the priests present at the rite, Viçvāmitra, leaving his wicked father, while Varuṇa frees the king from his disease. The sacrifice was to have taken place at the royal consecration and the rule is laid down that at the consecration of the king the priest must tell the tale, and thus free the king from all sin and the fetters of Varuṇa. It has been suggested therefore, very naturally, by Weber [5] that we have here the trace of an old practice of human sacrifice at the rite which has been abolished, the tale instead showing how the practice was done away with. The story, as it is recorded, is obviously meaningless, as the king undertakes to slay the son which is sent to him, and the motive is as it stands therefore an absurd one.

[1] Keith, *op. cit.* i. pp. cxxxvii–cxl.
[2] ZDMG. xl. 708.
[3] x. 18. 8 ; Keith, JRAS. 1907, p. 226 ; Oldenberg, GGA. 1907, p. 218, n. 1.
[4] AB. vii. 13 ff. ; ÇÇS. xv. 17 ff. ; Roth, *Ind. Stud.* i. 457–64 ; Keith, HOS. xxv. 61 ff.
[5] *Rājasūya*, pp. 47 ff. ; Hillebrandt, *Ved. Myth.* iii. 32, n. 3.

The Brahman Ajīgarta fares very hardly at the hands of the narrator, and one motive in it is clearly the connexion of Çunaḥçepa with the family of Viçvāmitra. The most that can be deduced from it in favour of human sacrifice is that it is possibly a far-off and dim reminiscence of a possible offering of the son of a king in time of distress as a sin offering. Obviously such a story allows us to see in it other explanations, for instance that it is an echo of the slaying of the divine king or of his son in him—if so, a very distant and distorted echo, or that it is due to totemism. In view, however, of the lack of better evidence of any kind for totemism or slaying the divine king,[1] the piacular explanation may stand, if it is realized that the tradition is clearly so distorted that we do not know what it means. The conclusion is an important one: in later India there are not a few traces of human sacrifice, and offerings to Kālī have taken place within recent years: the aborigines had clearly no hesitation in following certain forms of worship which involved human sacrifice,[2] but the Brahmans remained, like the Roman priests, superior to this particularly unlovable peculiarity of the human mind.

The most important of all offerings in the eyes of the priest was certainly the Soma, as is proved by the fact that the Rigveda in the main is a collection based on the Soma sacrifice, though not exclusively devoted to it. The question of the origin and nature of the plant is insoluble: the efforts made to identify it have led to interesting investigations,[3] but to no sure result, and the only thing certain is that the plant, which has been used in modern India as the Soma plant, is one which would not be considered by modern tastes as at all pleasant in the form of pressed juice mixed with water. We are unable naturally to say what would seem pleasant to the Vedic Indian: we know that surfeit in the drink had disagreeable results. Curiously enough too we do not know whether the drink was really popular outside the circle of priests, who took it sacrificially: there is just enough evidence in the Rigveda [4] to suggest that it was a popular drink, though the normal civil drink is Surā. This beverage was made from a decoction of herbs of various sorts, and seems to have had characteristics which ally it to beer on the one hand and brandy

[1] Either in India or elsewhere, save piacularly; see Lang, *Magic and Religion* (London, 1901). In Çunaḥçepa's case we should have to admit the custom of sacrificing the son in place of the king (Frazer, *The Dying God*, pp. 160 ff.) and to hold that the king really wanted a son in order to save his own life, all of which is absurd.

[2] For human sacrifice in Greek and Semitic religion, see Farnell, *Greece and Babylon*, pp. 244–6; for the scanty evidence in Rome, Warde Fowler, *Religious Experience of the Roman People*, pp. 33, 320 ff.; Cichorius, *Röm. Stud.*, pp. 7 ff. for Germany, Helm, *Altgerm. Rel.* i. 293; for the Celts, Rhys, *Celtic Heathendom*, pp. 232 ff., 675.

[3] Max Müller, *Biographies of Words*, pp. 222 ff.; Hillebrandt, *Ved. Myth.* i. 12 ff.; Macdonell and Keith, *Vedic Index*, ii. 474 ff.; Brunnhofer, *Arische Urzeit*, pp. 297–301; Weber, SBA. 1894, p. 787; Pischel, *Ved. Stud.* ii. 217 ff.; Meyer (*Gesch. d. Alt.*[3] II. i. p. 903) holds that Bactria and the Western Himalaya was its original home and therefore the home of the Aryans (Indo-Iranians).

[4] RV. viii. 19. 8–10.

on the other : that it was intoxicating is proved by the ill repute in which it normally was held, and by its very limited use at the sacrifice, in the Sautrāmaṇī, where it figures in the rite by which excess in Soma drinking is cured, and at the Vājapeya, in both cases in rites which appear to owe their present form to priestly action. There is, however, enough evidence to indicate that the corresponding Avestan Hurā was used in the offering.

Oldenberg [1] is inclined to suggest that the plant was never very popular : that it really took the place of the old Indo-European mead,[2] and that therefore it was traditionally the subject of sacred use and appreciation without having any very real claim to pleasantness of character. It is possible that this was so, but it is not very natural, and it seems more reasonable to suppose that the mead of the older period was fully replaced by a really pleasant drink. The term Madhu, which is properly honey, is applied to it in the Rigveda, though not in the Avesta : the origin of the use is uncertain : it is especially connected in the mythology with the Açvins, and in point of fact it seems to have been originally offered to them in the Dadhigharma offering, though in the ritual as recorded the offering is practically confined to milk.[3] It is possible, therefore, that in point of fact honey as well as milk might be mixed with the Soma, though it is also true that the term ‘ honey ’ in the Veda is applied in the most promiscuous way as to the milk or butter of the cow, or to the waters of the rain. On the whole, however, we are hardly entitled to doubt that the drink was originally a really pleasant one : in the course of time the long distance from which the shoots had to be brought may easily have made it less attractive, as it certainly encouraged the use of various substitutes described in the ritual text-books.

There is no ground on which any totemist nature can be applied to the Soma sacrifice : [4] much as the Brahmans speculated on the question,[5] there is no real proof that the offering ever really lost its true character, that of the offering to a god, in the main Indra, of the intoxicating and exhilarating drink, and the share in the drink by the priest. The killing of king Soma in the pressing, the eating of the substance of the moon, were no doubt seen by the ingenuity of the Brahmans, but these are speculations, not Vedic religion.

In some cases it is true that we find alleged sacrifices of things which cannot be regarded as eatable or indeed of any use to the gods at all. In these cases the explanation is simple : a magic rite is dressed up as an offering : if a man seeks a hundred years, the normal term of life, and offers a hundred nails of

[1] *Rel. des Veda*², pp. 366 ff.

[2] Feist, *Kultur der Indogermanen*, pp. 257, 356. In Greece wine replaced, under the influence of the Thracian Dionysos cult, mead as a sacred drink. Wine and blood are closely connected in Greek and Roman ritual alike.

[3] Garbe, ZDMG. xxxiv. 319 ff. ; cf. Hillebrandt, *op. cit.* i. 238 ff. Henry (*L'Agniṣṭoma*, pp. 472 ff.) thinks that the Aryans took over the drink from the aborigines of Iran, whence its popular but yet not orthodox nature is derived. Cf. Moulton, *Early Zoroastrianism*, pp. 70 ff.

[4] Henry, *L'Agniṣṭoma*, pp. 470 ff. Keith, *Taittirīya Saṁhitā*, i. pp. cxix–cxxi.

[5] These speculations (Lévi, *La doctrine du sacrifice*, p. 169) have misled Hubert and Mauss, *Année sociol.* ii. 129 ff.

Khadira wood, he turns a magic rite into a sacrifice *pro forma*: [1] similarly, if he offers manure to produce plenteousness in cattle,[2] or gives the sacrificer the strength of a lion, wolf, and tiger by mixing in the oblation at the Sautrāmaṇī hairs of these animals.[3] Such cases are instructive as they show that the idea that the horse sacrifice might in itself merely be intended to secure to the sacrificer the strength and swiftness of the horse is by no means absurd or unreasonable, even if it is not quite a complete view of the rite.

§ 6. *Fire and Sacrifice*

The constant interrelation of magic and religion in the Vedic cult is seen in its most complete form in the position of the fire, which serves the double end of the mode in which the sacrifice is brought to the gods, and of the most effective agency for the banning of evil spirits. The Vedic hymns show clearly enough the enormous value of the fire for the driving away of the Rakṣases, and the ritual bears this out in the most marked manner. There is lighted a special fire, the Sūtikāgni, in place of the normal fire for the woman in child-birth: it is not used for any offering except for the fumigation of the newly born infant and the warming of dishes, but its object of driving off evil spirits is attested by the list of evil spirits who are banned in the ritual.[4] The hair-cutting of the child is likewise performed to the west of a fire, which is not used for any offering, though utensils of the rite are put around it.[5] The teacher initiates his pupil and girds on the sacred girdle, which marks his second birth, in the presence of a fire,[6] but in this case the making of an offering in it shows the tendency to mingle religion and magic: the recitation goes on in the presence of a fire. Such a fire is absolutely essential, when the passages recited are of special importance and therefore holiness.[7] The consecration of the offerer of Soma takes place before a fire; after a death, fire is used to drive away the evil powers, fire is used even in battle,[8] the third of the holy fires of the ritual seems to have been intended from the first to drive away evil spirits: the south is the region of the Fathers and of the demons [9] akin to them, and, when it is being used for offerings to the Fathers, a brand is taken out from it to drive away the evil spirits, which seek to have a share in the sacrifice.[10]

A further important function of the fire as used at the ritual is cathartic in a different way: at the end of the offering it is desirable to remove from possibility of human contact the apparatus of the sacrifice, which has been filled by its use at the sacrifice with a superhuman character and danger. The

1 GGS. iv. 8. 11, 12.
2 GGS. iv. 9. 13, 14.
3 Weber, *Ind. Stud.* x. 350.
4 HGS. ii. 3; cf. BhGS. i. 26.
5 ÇGS. i. 28.
6 ÇGS. ii. 7.
7 ÇGS. ii. 1. 28; PB. xxi. 2. 9.
8 Weber, *Ind. Stud.* xvii. 180. Brunnhofer (*Arische Urzeit*, pp. 356–61) finds Greek fire and some sort of powder in the Rigveda!
9 ÇB. iv. 6. 6. 1, as the region where the sun at the winter solstice seems to be about to die; Henry, *La magie dans l'Inde antique*, p. 162, n. 1.
10 KÇS. iv. 1. 9; VS. ii. 30.

strew of grass, which covers the altar, is burnt, and the same mode of disposal is applied to the Svāru or chip of wood, which is used for several mystical purposes at the animal offering, the ointment used for the anointing of the piler of the fire altar, the twig with which at the new and full moon offerings the calves are driven away from the cows which are to give the milk, the spits used at the animal sacrifice for holding the pieces of the victim : the idea animating these usages, and the parallel one of burying such dangerous objects, is illustrated very clearly [1] by the rule that the spit which has been used for the heart of the victim, the seat of life, must not be laid on the earth or water, but must be buried in secret, the burier turning away without looking back. A further kind of purification is the final bath at the end of the offering and the use of washing : the sense of cleansing and destroying is seen in the practice of letting things float away on water.

In addition to these uses the practice observed in the burning of the omentum in the first place for the deities, in order at least in part to convey a pleasant savour, must be reckoned as a function of the fire, and further there must be borne in mind the case where the fire itself was adored : the natural way of serving the fire was, and must have been, to offer the oblations directly in it, and thus to let the god taste in actual presence the gifts of his adorers.

These different uses of the fire suggest the process by which the practice of sacrifice among the Iranians came to be changed in the Vedic period. The evidence of Herodotos [2] we have no ground to doubt, and he is quite clear that the Persians used no fire : the victim was cut up, and the flesh laid down on grass, the Magos recited over it what he calls a Theogony, and after a short time the sacrificer took away the flesh and did what he liked with it. The grass on which the victim is laid is beyond possibility of doubt the strew, Barhis, of India : the Avestan name Baresman is undoubtedly cognate, though differently formed, and the Avesta used of it the expression *fra-star*, 'spread out', which is the Vedic *stṛ*. But in the Avesta, for reasons which we do not know, the strew became a bundle of grass tied together, which is used for various purposes.[3] In the Rigveda the strew is clearly often still thought of as the place to which the gods come to receive the offerings,[4] but the fire has its essential place within the altar, ready for the burning of the offerings. Hence we meet that constant confusion noted already in the conceptions of the functions of Agni : he is bidden on the one hand to carry the offerings to the god : in the other he is to invite them to come and to sit down on the strew

[1] ÇB. iii. 8. 5. 9 f.; ApÇS. viii. 23. 10; KÇS. vi. 8. 3; Oldenberg, *Rel. des Veda*², p. 346, n. 2.

[2] i. 132; Strabo, xv. 3. 13, 14, p. 732. For many parallels, see von Schroeder, *Arische Religion*, ii. 314 ff., 364 ff.; cf. Herodotos, iv. 60; for Germany, Mogk, *Germ. Myth.*, p. 165.

[3] Moulton (*Early Zoroastrianism*, pp. 68, 198, 408) holds that the old Iranian practice was perverted by the non-Iranian Magoi, but this theory is most doubtful; see Keith, JRAS. 1915, pp. 790–9.

[4] Ovid (*Fast.* vi. 307) recognizes this as the old Latin belief; Warde Fowler, *Religious Experience of the Roman People*, p. 193. Cf. Keith, JHS. xxxvi. 109.

to partake of the offerings: the two ideas are actually found in the same hymn.[1] The character of the strew is seen also in the rule that the gifts to the gods are first deposited on it, and that anything which falls upon it is not counted as wasted [2] and so unfit for offering. The exact form of the process of development by which the fire came to be treated as the normal mode of the offering to the deity is uncertain: the making of a sweet odour may have been adopted, even when the gods were still supposed to come to the strew, in order perhaps to call their attention to the performance of the offering, and to attract them there; the strew and perhaps even the remains of the offering were burnt as too full of holy power to be safe to keep, or sometimes even in the case of the offerings to eat; the fire has a strong power to drive off demons, or the fire was the actual god to whom the offering was made, all reasons from which the new use could arise. But it must be remembered that it never became the sole manner of offering: [3] the throwing of gifts to water deities in the waters is a natural and common use; the placing of food in pits for the dead is a very old and common usage; the offerings to Rudra and other demoniac figures may be placed in ant-heaps, a sort of natural entrance to the earth, or hung on trees, or even merely thrown in the air.[4]

The Vedic ritual, however, is long past the period when the use of fire originated: the Çrauta ritual demands not one but three fires, and the time when the three were the mere expansion of the one is far behind the Rigveda: we find already there a distinction between the ordinary fire and the three fires of the more elaborate ritual.[5] Each householder is bound by the ritual texts, if he be pious, to keep one fire and in it each day to perform the cult of the house: the rich, nobles and princes, and even men of lower status, who can afford it, maintain in the same way a set of three fires, and with them a number of priests who are essential to the carrying on of the cult. In both cases certain ceremonies may be performed, and indeed ought to be performed, the offering night and morning of the Agnihotra, the new and full moon sacrifices, and the difference in the two modes of performance is one only of elaboration. Many other kind of cereal and animal offerings are also available for performance in both ways, but the family rites proper, those deeply affecting private matters, are only allowed to be performed in the domestic fire, while on the other hand the Soma sacrifice cannot be performed without the whole of the three fires. The great sacrificer therefore has the three fires beside the domestic fire: the older position that on great occasions

[1] vii. 11. 5.

[2] TS. vi. 3. 8. 3.

[3] On the Bali type of offering see especially Arbman, *Rudra*, pp. 68 ff.; for Germany, see Helm, *Altgerm. Rel.* i. 244 f., 294. Throwing in the air is appropriate for celestial deities; thus the Mongolian milk offering to the sun is thus performed, Ratzel, *Völkerkunde*, i. 649.

[4] KÇS. i. 1. 16; ix. 3. 7; v. 10. 13, 18; HGS. ii. 9. 5. For the practice of hanging gifts to deities of fertility on trees, cf. Cook, *Zeus*, i. 533, 592; Helm, *Altgerm. Rel.* i. 244 f. Hubert and Mauss (*Année sociol.* ii. 75, 76) ascribe to offerings by precipitation the character of the expulsion of evil.

[5] Ludwig, *Rigveda*, iii. 355; Oldenberg, SBE. xxx. p. x, n. 1.

the domestic fire was divided into three is suggested quite irresistibly by the name of the one of the three fires, which occurs in the Rigveda, the Gārhapatya, which means clearly the fire of the householder, and must have derived its name from the domestic fire, but it had disappeared before the tradition begins. It is a natural conjecture that it was in the Soma ritual that the origin of the fires developed, but it is not capable of proof.[1] Nor is there any evidence at all that the three fires represent an amalgamation of different forms of fire worship.[2] The number suggests such a conclusion, but the mere fact of the number is of course not sufficient evidence and of other proof none is forthcoming.

Of the three fires the Gārhapatya alone was continually maintained: the other fires, the Āhavanīya and the Dakṣiṇa, were derived from it, and the leading forward of the fire is already referred to in the Rigveda, though it is not possible to prove that the process was identical with that applied in the ritual.[3] The central position of the Gārhapatya is also to be seen in its relation to the man who goes on a journey: he takes formal leave of it first and then of the Āhavanīya, on his return he as solemnly greets first the Āhavanīya, and then the Gārhapatya.[4] The Āhavanīya, with which Hillebrandt seeks to identify the Vaiçvānara of the Rigveda, is the fire for the offering, not that, as a Brāhmaṇa says, in which the cooking is done, but that in which the cooked food is made over to the gods: the Gārhapatya therefore serves to cook the food and to warm the dishes, an act which seems clearly both in its nature for which no practical purpose is seen, and through the assertion that thus the demons are destroyed, to have been a piece of magic.[5] But the relations of the two fires are not in practice so simple as this: there are cases in which the functions are inverted.[6] The third fire is the Dakṣiṇāgni, also called the Anvāhāryapacana because the sacrificial fee for the new and full moon sacrifices, which was called Anvāhārya, was cooked on it. This fire was probably in its origin, as shown by its place at the south, intended to drive away by its flames the evil spirits and the souls of the dead, but it was natural that it should serve also for offerings to such spirits, though in the case of the Fathers pits were also used. We are expressly told that the fire served to avert danger from the Fathers,[7] and in the rite of the royal consecration a brand is taken out of this fire, and used as the place for an offering to drive away evil spirits, and in the same rite another fire-brand is taken out and an offering made on it to Nirṛti.[8] The Dakṣiṇāgni is also used both at the monthly offerings to the

[1] Oldenberg, *Rel. des Veda*², p. 349, n. 3; Knauer, *Festgruss an Roth*, p. 64.

[2] Ludwig, *Rigveda*, iii. 356. Three is a sacred number, because of its being the first expression of plurality and indivisible, and the mere growth in elaboration may have produced the three; cf. Meyer, *Gesch. d. Alt.*³ II. i. p. 588.

[3] Hillebrandt, *Ved. Myth.* ii. 97 ff.

[4] ÇB. ii. 4. 1. 3.

[5] ÇB. i. 7. 3. 27; iii. 8. 1. 7; Weber, *Ind. Stud.* x. 327, n. 5.

[6] ÇB. i. 7. 3. 26 ff.; KÇS. i. 8. 34, 35, &c.

[7] ÇB. ii. 3. 2. 6; ÇÇS. ii. 14. 3; 15. 4.

[8] ÇB. v. 2. 4. 15; 3. 2.

Fathers, and at the annual offering connected with the Sākamedhas, the third of the four-month sacrifices of the Çrauta ritual.[1]

The rules for the steps to be taken to set up the three fires or the householder's single fire are many and minute, but of little general importance: it is precisely in minutiae that the genius of the Brahmans shows itself to its complete extent, but, as in the case of the Roman priesthood, without gain to religious conceptions. The two normal methods are the old-fashioned one of producing the fire from the fire sticks, a process which is of immemorial antiquity in India,[2] and the obtaining of the fire from the fire maintained by a great sacrificer or wealthy master of cattle, the chief kind of Vedic wealth: in the first case the fire is new and pure, in the second it bears with it the associations of ceremony or of wealth or both. In the case of the household fire it is often preferred to take it from the last fire tended by the householder as a Brahman student, thus doubtless preserving the continuity of his holiness, or in the alternative from the fire with which his marriage ceremonies were performed, and which therefore is a suitable fire for the continuance of the rites arising from his married state. But in the case of the four-month offerings, and the Soma sacrifice as at the animal offering, it is the practice to produce by friction a new fire and unite it with the Āhavanīya, in order doubtless to refresh it and make it strong. In this usage may be seen the remnant of an idea that the fire grows from time to time tired, and should annually be refreshed by being superseded by a new fire. The evidence for such a belief being really held in any strong way in the Vedic period is, however, very weak: Hillebrandt's [3] suggestions that once a year the fire was normally relit rests on combinations which are without any value. The chief occasion recognized by the ritual for the setting up of new fires was when it was found that the existing fires were not bringing good fortune to the offerer. For this occasion the rite of re-establishment, Punarādheya, was prescribed.

§ 7. *The Performers of the Sacrifice*

As we have seen, it is an essential part of the Vedic sacrifice that it is a sacrifice for an individual, the Yajamāna,[4] or sacrificer, who provides the means for the sacrifice, and above all the rich rewards for the priests. The king is naturally the chief of sacrificers, for him alone such sacrifices as the royal consecration could be offered, but there are others, members of the royal house, high officers and soldiers among the Kṣatriyas, rich merchants or

KÇS. iv. 1. 2; v. 8. 6.

[2] Frazer, *The Magic Art*, ii. 248; Cook (*Zeus*, i. 325 ff.) traces to this the Prometheus myth, comparing *pramantha* with Zeus Pramantheus of Thourioi, but this is not plausible; for Prometheus cf. Keith, JRAS, 1916, pp. 553 ff.

[3] *Ved. Myth.* ii. 77 ff.

[4] Oltramare, *Le rôle du Yajamāna dans le sacrifice brahmanique* (Louvain, 1903); Oldenberg, *Archiv f. Religionswissenschaft*, vii. 222–4, who very properly insists that the priest differs from the sacrificer mainly in the fact that by reason of his office he has less need of elaborate ritual preparation than the lay sacrificer. In the actual rite he is as much as the priest made divine.

agriculturists, and also, we should certainly add, rich Brahmans themselves. After making all allowances for exaggeration, the gifts to the Brahmans must often have resulted in the accumulation by a Brahman of great wealth which would pass on to his son, and which in view of the conceptions of the Brahmans could certainly not be better spent than in the performance of sacrifice. But even in the case of the king, the sacrifice is for the prosperity of the king, and only incidentally for the prosperity of the realm and people : the prayer of the royal consecration shows this, and still more markedly the prayer of the horse sacrifice, which in effect is the real purpose of that sacrifice, and not a thank-offering or mere celebration of the success of the king : the Adhvaryu prays,[1] 'In holiness may a Brahman be born, full of holy radiance. In the kingly power be born a prince, a hero, a bowman, piercing with shafts, a mighty warrior. May the cow be rich in milk, strong the draught ox, swift the steed, fruitful the woman, eloquent the youth. May a hero son be born to the sacrificer. May Parjanya grant rain at all time according to our desire. May the corn ripen'. The bulk of the people are not even mentioned, but their pursuits, agriculture and the care of cattle, are alluded to.

The position revealed by the ritual seems hardly to be natural : it would certainly be expected that there should be some recognition of the sacrifices of the tribe, and the scant traces of an Agni Sabhya and Āvasathya, which are adduced by Hillebrandt[2] as proving the existence of tribal sacrifices, are a poor substitute for the evidence which should be forthcoming. We cannot, however, doubt that the Vedic attitude to the clan is unnatural and is a sign of developed ritual, not of primitive relations. There is but one exception to the rule that the sacrifice is for an individual in the Sattras, 'sacrificial sessions', long sacrifices extending as much as and even over a year, in which the sacrificers are the whole body of Brahmans officiating, the performance of such sacrifices being only possible when all are Brahmans : in that case the rule is that the whole of the merit of the offering belongs to them all, while any evil done belongs to the one who does it. It is possible that we have the record here of an older period of family offerings,[3] but it is far from certain that this is so, and it is not clear whether the Rigveda[4] really knows of such rites : if not they must be priestly inventions, as in many respects they most certainly are, representing the imaginations of a priesthood, which desired nothing better than to spend its time in the technique of a curious and complicated ritual.

In so developed a condition of religious practice it is not surprising to find that the priests had already made themselves indispensable at the Çrauta offerings :[5] the householder might perform many of the domestic services himself, if he preferred to do so, and the poor man must have been in this position, but the Çrauta sacrifices demanded a priest or often several priests.

[1] VS. xxii. 22 ; TS. vii. 5. 18 ; KSAçv. v. 14 ; MS. iii. 12. 6.
[2] *Ved. Myth.* ii. 118–26.
[3] Oldenberg, *Rel. des Veda*², p. 371.
[4] vii. 33. 13.
[5] Cf. Hubert and Mauss, *Année sociol.* ii. 52, who give Hebrew and Greek parallels.

It is beyond doubt that in the time of the Rigveda the priesthood was normally hereditary: we have no material for a history of the growth of the special connexion of the families mentioned in the Rigveda such as the Viçvāmitras, Vasiṣṭhas, Atris, Bharadvājas, with the sacrifice: we may assume that at a period when the simpler relations of life prevailed, some family became associated with the ritual through the skill of one of its members or some possession of unusual powers, but that period lies far behind the Rigveda, especially if we believe as is quite possible that a priesthood arose in the Indo-European [1] period. But these families differ essentially in some respects from parallel institutions in other Indo-European lands, showing that the Indo-European idea of priesthood cannot have been highly developed. There is no trace among them of the characteristics of the sacred colleges of the Romans, like the Arval Brothers or the Salii, charged with the oversight of definite parts of the public sacrifices, for there were no public sacrifices. Nor again are they like the Greek families which had hereditary priesthoods, often recognized by the state as at Eleusis, for these again had definite gods or rites to care for, while the Vedic families in the main dealt with the same kinds of rites, the differences between families in the times of which we know being in detail rather than in general aspect. Doubtless the different families were originally marked out by much more serious differences in cult than those which we can verify: the whole process of the relation of the Rigveda and of the ritual suggests syncretism on a large basis, but the possibility of the development of the distinct priesthoods of Greece and Rome was in all probability hampered and finally prevented by the lack of the temple, and of the organization of public worship by the state. The state is a much more permanent instrument than any private men or kings could be: the Vedic kingship was, it is certain,[2] far from assured, by reason of foreign war and internal dissension, and the priests could not therefore gather as a standing priesthood around the royal house. Nor, to do them justice, do the priests seem to have desired to do so: the impression left by the Rigveda and the ritual alike is that priests were fond of wandering from place to place, performing rites for now this patron, and now that, a fact which probably explains how the innovations discovered from time to time by individuals had comparatively little chance of affecting seriously the main body of the ritual, which has come down to us in essentially the same shape, despite endless variation in unimportant minutiae. The radical changes, if any, perished with their inventors, or at best soon after.

[1] Hirt, *Die Indogermanen*, pp. 514 ff.; Carnoy, *Les Indo-Européens*, pp. 235 ff.; Feist, *Kultur der Indogermanen*, p. 355. Meyer (*Gesch. d. Alt.*[3] I. ii. pp. 870, 871, 916, 917) holds that the Indo-Europeans had probably already magicians, but no priesthood proper, which developed itself in Indo-Iranian times. *Inter alia* this theory rests on the false view that a magician is the first priest as held by Frazer, *The Magic Art*, i. 371 ff., 420 ff.; Henry, *La magie dans l'Inde antique*, pp. 34 ff.

[2] Macdonell and Keith, *Vedic Index*, ii. 210 ff.

One priest alone seems to have been definitely attached to the king, and less often to other rich persons of the warrior or the agricultural and trading classes, Kṣatriya or Vaiçya. This was the Purohita, *praepositus*, who was charged with the general control of the offerings to be performed in households, which were large enough to maintain a considerable body of priests, and to hire others for special rites. As a rule there can only have been one Purohita who probably acted as long as he and the king were alive and on good terms : we hear, however, of changes of Purohita, as that of Viçvāmitra for Vasiṣṭha, with the result of the effort of the rejected rival to overthrow the king by bringing a coalition of ten princes against him,[1] and there is no Vedic evidence to show that the later practice, which made the priesthood hereditary in the family of the priest prevailed, though one Purohita in some cases at least evidently served more than one prince in succession, or even according to the later texts one man might be Purohita of as many as three allied kings at once.[2] In this case, however, we may imagine that there were subordinate Purohitas also employed. The relation of king and Purohita was created by a very formal act in which the precise words of the wedding service were repeated,[3] and there is abundant evidence that the Purohita was in religion and civil affairs the *alter ego* of the king.[4] The law books [5] make him out to be the king's teacher in sacred and other learning, his councillor in the performance of all his duties, the dispenser of justice in the place of the king, and prone to interfere in royal successions: popular tales represent the evil Purohita as bringing to ruin the kingdom as the good preserves it, and the Rigveda [6] already makes the prosperity of the whole realm depend on him. It may be taken as certain that he performed all the domestic ritual of the king's household, with its many formulae and magic rites [7] to secure the success of the king's undertakings in war and peace, the correctness of his judgements, and the prosperity of his subjects : we see clearly from the Rigveda [8] that the Purohita was expected to be in the battle to secure victory, not by arms, but by the weapons of his magic power ; the Atharvaveda [9] preserves a battle spell used by a Purohita in fight, and the Rigveda [10] tells how the Purohita Devāpi won rain by a spell. The Brāhmaṇas represent the gods defeated by the Asuras as rushing to Bṛhaspati, who is the divine Purohita, and asking him to devise a new rite to overcome the Asuras, which he very properly at once does. Moreover, in the address to Agni when he is invoked as having aforetime favoured

[1] RV. vii. 18 and 33 ; Hopkins, JAOS. xv. 259 ff. ; Oldenberg, ZDMG. xlii. 205 ff. ; *Ṛgveda-Noten*, ii. 16–18 ; Macdonell and Keith, *Vedic Index*, ii. 275 ; Bloomfield, *Rig-Veda Repetitions*, pp. 646 f. See also JB. iii. 199–202 for the story of Kutsa and Upagu.

[2] Macdonell and Keith, *Vedic Index*, ii. 5–8.

[3] AB. viii. 27.

[4] AB. viii. 24 ; ÇB. iv. 1. 4. 5, 6.

[5] Cf. Hopkins, JAOS. xiii. 151 ff. ; Foy, *Die königliche Gewalt*.

[6] iv. 50. 8.

[7] Henry, *La magie dans l'Inde antique*, pp. 34, 38, 146 ff. ; Bloomfield, *Atharvaveda*, pp. 73–76 ; N. N. Law, *Ancient Indian Polity*, pp. 152 ff.

[8] vii. 18.

[9] iii. 19 ; Kauç. xiv. 22, 23.

[10] x. 98 ; cf. Oldenberg, ZDMG. li. 274 ; Macdonell and Keith, *Vedic Index*, i. 377 f.

the ancestor of the invoker, when a king is the sacrificer, the name of his Purohita's ancestor is used in place of his own : the Purohita must take part in offerings made to undo errors of the king in his capacity as criminal judge,[1] and in the sacrifice of the horse certain libations must be offered, according to some authorities, in the house of the Purohita.[2]

From the Purohita must be distinguished the ordinary offering priest, and his relation to them may be assumed to have been that suggested by his name : he was the superintendent who took the care of the offerings, and saw that they were duly carried out. But it is obvious that he might, as a Brahman and as competent *ex hypothesi* to supervise every rite, undertake some part himself, and we have every reason to think that he did so. In the case of Devāpi he was not only Purohita, but at the sacrifice performed by him as a rain spell he acted as the Hotṛ priest : similarly Agni is Purohita as well as Hotṛ priest,[3] and the two divine Hotṛs who are invoked in the Āprī litanies are also called the two Purohitas.[4] That this was the older rule, seems suggested by the fact that the Hotṛ was clearly in the time of the composition of the poetry of the Rigveda the really important priest, and that the Purohita would naturally take his office, as it was taken in some cases by the sacrificer himself.[5] With the growth of the ritual, however, and its increasing complication, a sure sign that the poetry was ceasing to be the main point of interest to the priest, it was only natural that the overseer of the sacrifice should become a priest different from the Hotṛ, namely the Brahman priest to whom in the ritual as opposed to the Rigveda the duty of caring for the sacrifice as a whole is assigned. Hence we find that the Brāhmaṇas assert that the Purohita is the Brahman priest, and that the Vasiṣṭhas as Purohitas and Brahmans are specially meritorious,[6] while the divine Purohita, Bṛhaspati, becomes the Brahman priest of the god in the technical sense of the term. But even then the Purohita seems not to have been tied down to any one function : he could, if he preferred, act as a Sāman singer.[7]

In the later literature after the Vedic period the figure of the Purohita retains in even increased force the importance which it has for the Veda. It is clear that in him we have the aggressive and active side of priestly interference in human affairs : the ordinary offering priest must be deemed in comparison to have been a technical priest, or scholar engaged in reflection, and the proud position asserted for priests generally never in fact was attained by them. The position of the Purohita therefore never essentially affected the priesthood as a whole, and it was made only possible by the existence when the practice developed of the hereditary priesthood and the belief that offerings required priestly intervention to be successful. The Purohita, therefore,[8] is not to be

[1] VDS. xix. 40.

[2] ÇB. xiii. 4. 4. 1. So at the Rājasūya (TS. i. 8. 9) the Brahman in whose house sacrifice is made is probably the Purohita.

[3] RV. i. 1. 1 ; ii. 3. 2 ; 11. 1 ; v. 11. 2, &c.

[4] RV. x. 66. 13 ; 70. 7.

[5] ApÇS. xii. 17. 2 ; GGS. i. 9. 9.

[6] AB. vii. 26 ; TS. iii. 5. 2. 1 ; Geldner, *Ved. Stud.* ii. 144 ff.

[7] PB. xiv. 6. 8.

[8] Oldenberg, *Rel. des Veda*², pp. 375 ff.

treated as more than an incidental factor in the growth of the caste system, and it must be remembered that in the time of the later literature the whole aspect of the priesthood was profoundly affected by the existence of temple worship with its apparatus of bodies of priests and the growth of traditional practices.

Of the ordinary priest we have, as we have seen, a good many details in the Rigveda : specially often do we hear of seven Hotṛs, who presumably must correspond to the seven Seers whom the Rigveda [1] also mentions. This list may be given by detail in one passage of the Rigveda where Agni is identified with the Hotṛ, the Potṛ, the Neṣṭṛ, the Agnīdh, the Praçāstṛ, the Adhvaryu, and the Brahman as well as with the householder himself. The same list, save for the Upavaktṛ, who seems to be identical in essence with the Praçāstṛ, appears as the list of priests to whom the Achāvāka, a later addition to the priesthood, addresses a request to be admitted to share the Soma.[2] Another list, given in connexion with the morning pressing of the Soma, is slightly different : it includes the Hotṛ, two Adhvaryus, two Praçāstṛs, Brahman, Potṛ, Neṣṭṛ, and Āgnīdhra.[3] The second Adhvaryu is evidently an addition : in the later period he is the Pratiprasthātṛ ; the second Praçāstṛ is similarly the Achāvāka in the later ritual. The list also agrees, in the main but not completely, with the list of priests, who have cups and altars in the Soma sacrifice.[4] The old list is comparable with the eight of the Avesta,[5] but the comparison is not in detail exact, and we may doubt whether we can safely assume more than a general similarity between the Indo-Iranian and the Vedic cult : the exact degree of the development of the separation of functions is not to be determined with certainty. The Hotṛ is clearly the Zaotar, the Agnīdh has the same duty as the Ātarevakhša, and the Potṛ as the Āsnatare, the washer of the Soma. But it is impossible to find the counterpart to the singers of the Vedic ritual.

The Hotṛ must from his name have been originally at once the performer of the offering and the speaker of any words which accompanied it, but the distinction between the two portions of the functions of the Hotṛ must have developed quite early, perhaps even before the close of the Indo-Iranian period. In the Vedic ritual text-books a fundamental distinction is drawn between two kinds of offerings, which are called Yajatayas and Juhotayas respectively : in the former there is but one speaker and actor, who is, however, called Adhvaryu, not Hotṛ, from the more important side of his functions ; in the latter there is, beside the Adhvaryu who performs the manual acts, the Hotṛ to recite. The extent of the function of the Hotṛ varies very greatly : in a large number of offerings the only verses which he has to repeat are the Puronuvākyā and the Yājyā. The first is a verse addressed to the god

Macdonell and Keith, *Vedic Index*, ii. 5 ff. ; N. N. Law, *Ancient Indian Polity*, pp. 38 ff.

[1] ii. 1. 2.

[2] KB. xxviii. 5 ; ÇÇS. vii. 6. 7 ; AÇS. v. 7. 3 ; KÇS. ix. 12. 11.

[3] KÇS. ix. 8. 8 ff.

[4] Weber, *Ind. Stud.* x. 366, 377.

[5] Henry, *L'Agniṣṭoma*, pp. 477 ff.

inviting him to be present at the offering to be made to him ; the latter is said just at the end when the Adhvaryu is about to throw the offering into the fire ; after it the Hotṛ says the word Vauṣaṭ, of doubtful sense and meaning,[1] and thereafter often a brief formula addressed to the god bidding him enjoy the offering, terminating with Vauṣaṭ again, the whole phrase forming the ' secondary Vaṣaṭ ' (*anu-vaṣaṭkāra*) which is constantly referred to in the sacrifice. The Yājyā verse is preceded by the word *ye yajāmahe*, and it is very possible that it is merely a development from it : but at least in the Rigveda there were series of such verses composed. The Puronuvākyās seem to have been later in development, though some may be seen in the Rigveda. In their place often are found longer recitations such as accompany the main offerings of the Soma : there is a peculiarity in the verses thus used which suggests that the ritual in its development still retained traces of its older form. In the hymns used are inserted Nivids, apparently also called Madas, which are invitations to the god with an enumeration of his titles to come and intoxicate himself with the Soma. These Nivids, as they are preserved to us, are of undoubtedly later composition than the hymns of the Rigveda, but it is perfectly reasonable to believe that in principle they represent the oldest form of the invitation to the gods.[2] We may conceive a time when the Nivid and the mere formula *ye yajāmahe* represented the whole of the words of the Hotṛ, but we have no clear ground on which to trace the precise development of the form of the ritual. The Adhvaryu in his turn has a certain number of formulae, normally in prose, to repeat as the several acts of the sacrifice proceed, in order to avert evil and invoke prosperity, but his main duty must have at first been, and even in the later ritual was, the management of the practical part of the offering, the preparation of the cakes and the straining and purifying of the Soma, the arranging of the many utensils, and the actual pouring of the offerings in the fire appropriate to each. In this work he had the constant aid of the Agnīdh, whose name denotes him as specially concerned with the kindling of the fire. This priest with the Adhvaryu, the Hotṛ, and the Brahman to oversee it all, managed many of the lesser offerings, and he was specially in these cases concerned with the keeping of fire burning, but naturally did much else beside. The position in which he stood to the Adhvaryu is neatly shown by the procedure, which was gone through before the Hotṛ said his Yājyā verse : he must be told to do so by the Adhvaryu, but before this takes place the Adhvaryu must address the Agnīdh with the words, ' Om : make him hear ', to which the Agnīdh replies solemnly, ' Be it so. Let him hear '. The episode is deliciously significant of the absurdities of the developed ritual.[3] The close union of the two priests is perhaps the explanation of the two Adhvaryus in the list of priests already mentioned, though in the later tradition the second was the Pratiprasthātṛ.

[1] Cf. Foy, ZDMG. l. 139 ; Wackernagel, *Altind. Gramm.* i. 41, 177 (for *vakṣat*, ' may he bear ').

[2] Cf. Oldenberg, *Rel. des Veda*², p. 387 ; ZDMG. xlii. 242 ff.

[3] Hillebrandt, *Neu- und Vollmondsopfer*, p. 94 ; *Rituallitteratur*, p. 99.

These priests sufficed for the new- and full-moon offerings, but for the animal offering the Hotṛ required an assistant, the priest called variously Upavaktṛ, Praçāstṛ, and Maitrāvaruṇa. The first two names indicate his chief activity in the ritual, the giving of directions, called Praiṣas,[1] to the priests, and this function he already exercised in respect of the Hotṛ as early as the Rigveda. The ritual prescribes that he should give to the Hotṛ his Praiṣa for the recitation of the Yājyā, standing before him on the right hand of the Hotṛ's seat, holding a staff, slightly bent forward. Moreover, at the animal sacrifice he shares the Hotṛ's duties, often, when there are verses to be recited, taking the one and the Hotṛ the other.[2] In the case of the Soma sacrifice he has recitations of his own to perform, in large measure directed to Mitra and Varuṇa, from whom therefore he borrows his third name as '(The priest) connected with Mitra and Varuṇa', and, as the root whence comes the name Praçāstṛ, 'orderer', is an appropriate term for the commands of these gods, the human priest may have borrowed this designation from the gods themselves, though this is rather conjectural.[3] What is much more certain is that the two divine Hotṛs, of whom we hear in the Rigveda, are the heavenly representatives of the Hotṛ and the Maitrāvaruṇa.

In the Soma sacrifice lie the functions of the Potṛ and the Neṣṭṛ, who are included in the Rigveda list. The Potṛ is in the actual ritual a mere shadow, of no consequence or importance, whose former importance may be judged from his name and his obvious connexion with Soma Pavamāna. The Neṣṭṛ is also in the later ritual a priest with but one function of any interest or importance. It occurs in the course of the Soma rite, when an offering is made to Agni with the wives of the gods. The Agnīdh, who in this case has to partake of the Soma, sits in the lap of the Neṣṭṛ, and thereafter the Neṣṭṛ summons the wife of the householder, who then performs with the Udgātṛ a rite which is a mimicry of cohabitation and whose nature as a fertility spell was as clearly recognized by the ritual texts as by us.[4] The suggestion [5] that the rite is a barbarous one, and that the Neṣṭṛ is an intrusion into the Vedic ritual from a non-Vedic source, is clearly an error, and ignores the fact that fertility magic is looked upon by primitive peoples with very different eyes from those of the present day.

The remaining priest in the list of seven is the Brahman. It is uncertain exactly who is meant by this term, but the greatest probability is clearly that it is the Brāhmaṇācchaṅsin of the later ritual, who is also addressed as Brahman and whose older name was clearly Brahman.[6] His duty in the later ritual is to be an assistant of the Hotṛ, and at the Soma sacrifice to recite a litany for Indra. The alternative view, that of Geldner,[7] takes him to be

[1] For a collection see Scheftelowitz, *Die Apokryphen des Ṛgveda*, pp. 142–55.

[2] Schwab, *Altind. Thieropfer*, p. 90.

[3] Oldenberg, *Rel. des Veda*², p. 391.

[4] TS. vi. 5. 8. 6 ; ÇB. iv. 4. 2. 18.

[5] Hillebrandt, *Ved. Myth.* i. 250, 261, n. 2.

[6] KÇS. ix. 8. 11.

[7] *Ved. Stud.* ii. 145 ff. For Henry's theory of the Brahman as the primitive magician whence develops the priest see below, Chap. 22, § 8.

in the Rigveda already the priest charged with the whole of the supervision of the ritual, and it is possible, though not certain, that already in the Rigveda[1] in the latest parts such a priest was known. In the later ritual his place is one of the highest importance : he is set off against all the other priests as equal in value to the whole of the rest of them : he says very little, and is mainly engaged in supervision seated in the place of the Brahman near the chief fire altar, by his silent meditation repairing every flaw in the sacrifice. The later nature of the office is also reflected in the tradition that the Vasiṣṭhas alone were the owners of a certain litany,[2] which has to be spoken by the Brahman at the offering : this points to the tradition of an invention in one family, which led in course of time to the gradual adoption of the use of such a priest by all the families.

In the list of seven there is no mention of the Hotṛ's counterparts, the Sāman singers, but they are elsewhere mentioned in the Rigveda, and the names of the Udgātṛ and Prastotṛ are mentioned,[3] so that the omission of the Pratihartṛ may be merely accidental. The songs of the Sāman singers are of a really primitive kind,[4] in that they are made up with all sorts of meaningless syllables interjected among the words, in order presumably to fit them to the music of the song : the comparison of the chant to the revival ceremonies of American negroes is too attractive to be disregarded. The chants fall into two classes, those addressed to Soma Pavamāna, which are the chants that they must first have been expected to sing : they differ in form markedly from the ordinary hymns of the Rigveda, and are also differentiated by their position in book ix. In addition to these, however, they chant songs for the ordinary gods, to whom the libations are offered at the three pressings of the Soma : the ritual demands a precise parallelism, each recitation of the Hotṛ being preceded by a chant, and the chant and recitation being closely allied by the use in the chant of sets of verses of the recitation. The arrangement is artificial and not early, as the inaccuracies in the ritual[5] prove, and the absurdity of the theory of correspondence is proved by the case of the songs to Soma Pavamāna which have no real connexion at all with the recitations of the Hotṛ, to which they are alleged to be a parallel.

The evidence clearly does not allow us to say whether the Sāman singers were, or were not, present in the earliest form of the Soma sacrifice : the absence of their names from the Avestan list and the list of the seven Hotṛs might be cited in support of such a view, but at the same time the argument could not be pressed : the songs might easily have been chanted by some other priest—as by the Potṛ—before the Sāman singers came into existence.

The later ritual requires only the Adhvaryu for the Agnihotra offering performed daily ; for the piling or establishing of the fire, Agnyādheya, four

[1] x. 141. 3.

[2] TS. iii. 5. 2. 1 ; Macdonell and Keith, *Vedic Index*, ii. 7.

[3] RV. viii. 81. 5.

[4] Cf. Bloomfield, VOJ. xvii. 156–164; JAOS. xxi. 50 ; Oldenberg, GGA. 1908, pp. 711 ff.

[5] Weber, *Ind. Stud.* x. 374, n. 3 ; 385, n. 1.

priests, Hotṛ, Adhvaryu, Āgnīdhra, and Brahman; for the four-month offerings also the Pratiprasthātṛ; and for the animal sacrifice the Maitrāvaruṇa and Çamitṛs as aiders of the Adhvaryu. For the Soma sacrifice it prescribes sixteen, who are arranged as Hotṛ, Maitrāvaruṇa, Achāvāka, and Grāvastut; Adhvaryu, Pratiprasthātṛ, Neṣṭṛ, and Unnetṛ; Udgātṛ, Prastotṛ, Pratihartṛ, and Subrahmaṇya; and Brahman, Brāhmaṇācchaṅsin, Potṛ, and Āgnīdhra. The whole arrangement [1] is, however, artificial and worthless: the three assistants of the Brahman and the Neṣṭṛ in practice are reckoned rather with the Hotṛ, and the aim at sets of four has spoiled the natural order. The Kauṣītakins curiously enough had seventeen priests, a view not approved by the other schools, which naturally saw no need for a priest who was merely to sit in the Sadas at the sacrifice,[2] a function clearly sufficiently provided for by the Brahman who had nothing else to do.

In this ritual we find the fully developed form of what is already known to the Rigveda, the choosing of the priests by the offerer, who must satisfy himself as to their capacities, if for no other reason than that, while he attains the fruit of the sacrifice, all the errors of the priests fall upon him, so that they can if they like ruin him at any moment by making deliberate blunders, as the Brāhmaṇas tell them how to do if they so wish. In their turn they are entitled to ask the sacrificer questions and to make sure that he is a proper person to sacrifice for, and that other priests have not already been engaged in the offering and left it unfinished by reason of disagreement with the sacrificer. The point is of interest, as illustrating how firmly organized the Brahmans were on the best trade-union models. The sacrificer must be of the three highest castes; exceptions are of the rarest character, and mainly concern the makers of chariots, Rathakāras, who seem to have occupied at quite an early date a peculiar position, not included in the third caste but still distinctly superior to the Çūdras, a fact which suggests that they were of inferior origin to the three castes, but by skill too important and useful to be neglected.[3]

The evidence, however, is somewhat confusing. We find in Āpastamba [4] a form of words prescribed at the new- and full-moon offering in the case of a Çūdra, where it seems that we are expected to see in the Çūdra either a Rathakāra or a Niṣāda, two special classes permitted a share in the sacrifice. A Çūdra appears also at the Pitṛmedha in the Çatapatha Brāhmaṇa,[5] and it is permitted to eat food from a carpenter (*takṣan*), who, of course, is closely allied to the Rathakāra. Āçvalāyana [6] permits the carpenter to establish the sacred fire, and Bharadvāja expressly says that some permit this to the fourth caste, while others do not.[7] The later theory [8] makes the Rathakāra to

[1] Weber, *Ind. Stud.* x. 143 ff.

[2] Generically as in TS. vi. 5. 1. 4 a group of priests bears the term Sadasya, but to them the Kauṣītakins added another.

[3] Macdonell and Keith, *Vedic Index*, ii. 203, 204. A classical example of disagreement between priests and sacrificer is recorded in AB. vii. 27; Macdonell and Keith, *Vedic Index*, i. 120.

[4] i. 19. 9.

[5] xiii. 8. 3. 11; MS. ii. 4. 1; KS. xii. 10.

[6] ii. 1. 13.

[7] See Caland's tr. of ApÇS., p. 136.

[8] BDS. i. 17. 6.

be the son of a Vaiçya by a Çūdra mother. On the other hand Āpastamba [1] expressly contemplates any of the first three classes including in its ranks Rathakāras, which certainly seems an artificial view, in view of the comparatively late period of that Sūtra. The Niṣādas who appear occasionally as permitted to have some concern in the sacrifice are reckoned by the ancient authority Aupamanyava as a fifth class, and they have some claim to be regarded as members of the pre-Aryan population who remained in a less dependent condition than the Çūdras, presumably retaining their own tribal organization under the suzerainty of Aryan princes.[2]

In the later ritual the chief duties of the sacrificer himself were of an inferior type: he had certain formulae to repeat, he might perform the manual throwing of the offering in the fire, and he had various restrictions to undergo: his wife was in the same position, but her part in the rite was rather smaller than her husband's: she was, however, clearly considered throughout to be concerned in the sacrifice, and a formal place is provided for her at the Soma sacrifice and still more clear is her participation in other offerings. The sacrificer had, however, the most important duty of dividing the sacrificial fees, or Dakṣiṇās, so called either from the literal fact that the gifts, usually of cows, were placed on the right side for the sacrificer to divide, or because the word Dakṣiṇā from its literal sense had come to mean acceptable.[3] This duty is prescribed in precise terms with regard to the several offerings, and there is often an obvious attempt to make the reward fit the service which has taken place in respect of the nature of the gifts given, e.g. a black beast for an offering for the dead. It must remain doubtful to what extent we may not see in the Dakṣiṇās the alteration of the older practice of offering the things given at the sacrifice: the priests determined to keep them, and converted the sacrifice into gifts to themselves.

Of the additional priests at the Soma sacrifice none have much importance or interest: the Subrahmaṇya was introduced because of a particular formula only,[4] with which has been compared the Bahrām Yašt of the Avesta, and the Achāvāka is of special interest only because he is so obviously an introduction when the ritual was well defined, as is practically admitted in the Brāhmaṇas and in the ritual itself.[5]

[1] v. 3. 19. Cf. Bühler, SBE. xiv. p. xxxviii.
[2] Yāska, Nir. iii. 8.
[3] Macdonell and Keith, *Vedic Index*, ii. 203, 204; Bloomfield, *Religion of the Veda*, pp. 71 ff.
[4] ÇB. iii. 3. 4. 18; AB. vi. 3; TB. iii. 8. 1. 2; ṢB. i. 1; KB. xxvii. 6; Oertel, JAOS. xviii. 34 ff.; Hillebrandt, *Ved. Myth.* iii. 209 ff., 298; Charpentier, *Kleine Beiträge zur indoiranischen Mythologie* (1911).
[5] KB. xxviii. 4–6; AB. vi. 14. 8.

CHAPTER 19

RITES ANCILLARY TO THE SACRIFICE

§ 1. *The Consecration*

THE Dīkṣā is a rite which has to be performed by the sacrificer and his wife before the Soma sacrifice.[1] It is carried out in a hut near the fire: the sacrificer bathes, has his hair cut, is anointed, puts on a fresh garment, is girded with the sacred cord, and sits down on a black antelope hide, in which there resides, in the view of the tradition, holy power. His head is covered, an antelope horn is tied to his garment, and it is prescribed that, when he suffers from itch, he is to use that only with which to scratch himself. He sits in this condition in silence until night comes, when he drinks cooked milk, which is the food appropriate for the consecration, and then keeps awake all the night, or goes to sleep after commending himself to Agni to preserve him from evil spirits. He is also enjoined to stammer when he speaks, and to keep the three last fingers closed into his hand. Some authorities insist that he is to remain in this condition, until he is reduced to skin and bone and until the black in his eyes disappears: he is to be pure for the sacrifice only when he is reduced to complete exhaustion. The loneliness, the silence, the lack of food, are not however the only elements in the prescription: the heat is also indicated by the provision regarding scratching, reference to the sweating of the performer is made, and it is said that water will spoil the consecration, Tapas; the last term clearly means the process of heating, which is also said to be affected by any breach of the rules imposed. This Tapas is one of the earliest conceptions of the Rigveda:[2] the power produced by it is great in the extreme, and it marks out seers like the Aṅgirases; through it a poet can behold the old creations of the Fathers, speech is born of Tapas, which procures dreams and which elevates man to the state that gods may enter in. If the king wrong a Brahman, then the Tapas of the Brahman is capable of ruining him. Indra was borne by Aṣṭakā by practising Tapas, by it also Indra won immortality. Prajāpati before creation practises Tapas to bring about the desired result of power to create; it is a significant case that once the stars come from him in this condition. Already in the Jaina litera-

[1] Lindner, *Die Dīkṣā* (Leipzig, 1878); Weber, *Ind. Stud.* x. 358 ff.; Oldenberg, GGA. 1917, pp. 328 ff.; *Rel. des Veda*², pp. 397 ff.; Hillebrandt, *Ved. Myth.* i. 482 ff.; iii. 355; Hubert and Mauss, *Année sociol.* ii. 53 ff.; Hauer, *Die Anfänge der Yogapraxis im alten Indien*, pp. 55 ff.; von Schroeder, *Arische Religion*, ii. 249 (assimilation of sun and heat, rain and water).

[2] viii. 59. 6; x. 136. 2; 154. 2, 4; 167. 1; 109. 4; AV. iii. 10. 12; xix. 56. 5 and often.

ture,[1] the common feature of modern Indian thought, the ascetic who presents himself to the heat of four fires and the sun, is found, and the idea of the connexion [2] of heat with creative power and ecstasy is clearly one of the most assured ideas of Indian thought.

The Dīkṣā has obvious affinities with the ceremonies, which all over the world have been used to spread that feeling of ecstasy which makes man akin to the divine, and of which the Bacchic rites of Greece present the most obvious and convincing classical parallel. The idea is found but rarely in the Rigveda but it is to be noted in one hymn of the tenth book,[3] in which is described the long-haired Muni, clad in dirty garments, who claims to speed along with the winds on the path of the Apsarases and the Gandharvas, to have entered into the winds leaving his body only for men to see, and who, it is clear, regards himself as quasi-divine for the moment. In that case there is no reference to Tapas, but the long unshorn hair and the dirty garments remind us of the plight of the unhappy sacrificer. At any rate it would be absurd to doubt for a moment that in this figure we have a case of the effort made to obtain religious exaltation, or that the attitude is similar to that of the medicine man of tribes in a lower stage of civilization. It is not, of course, in any sense irreligious or opposed to religious feeling : it is the same spirit as that of mysticism throughout all ages and among all peoples. The discomforts of the performance are merely intended to melt away the solid flesh, which retards the communion of the spirit with the divine. The wearing of the black antelope skin is a practice which is especially enjoined on the Brahman student, and it is natural to see in it some special connexion with the power to be derived from wearing such a skin. The sacrificer wears a pair of shoes of antelope hide.[4] The use of the horn of the antelope is parallel to its use for the pouring out of the mixture used for the anointing of the king.[5] The parts of the offering which fall down are offered to the Rakṣases under such a skin.[6] The actual intention is uncertain : the prohibition of the use of the hand to scratch is paralleled in many lands, especially in initiation ceremonies, and it is clearly due to the fact that the body is full of the divine essence, and that therefore contact with the hand is undesirable : a non-conducting material should be interposed. But the choice of a black skin also suggests that the idea of making the wearer invisible to the demons may have something to do with the use. The idea that the antelope is divine as a representative of any god cannot be proved or even made probable for this rite, and similarly there is no trace of totemism to be seen in regard to the antelope in Vedic literature.

[1] Bhagavatī, ii. 1. 65.

[2] Cook (*Zeus*, i. 28) suggests that Herakleitos's doctrine of heat as the world principle is connected with Zeus as the burning sky or aether.

[3] RV. x. 136 ; Oldenberg, *Rel. des Veda*², pp. 404, 406 ; otherwise, Bloomfield, JAOS. xv. 157 ff. Cf. Hubert and Mauss, *Année sociol.* ii. 100 ; below, Chap. 22, § 9.

[4] TS. v. 4. 4. 4.

[5] ÇB. v. 4. 2. 4. For the use of the horn generally cf. Evans, JHS. 1901, pp. 135 ff. ; Cook, *Zeus*, i. 506 ff.

[6] Hillebrandt, *Neu- und Vollmondsopfer*, p. 171.

Probably enough there is here religious conservatism : the antelope hide is the natural garment of the early Vedic Indian, and the one worn by the student who is in a special condition of religious communion with the divine : these motives may go far to explain the use.

There is, however, another element in the rite, which is emphasized by the Brāhmaṇas, but denied as primitive by Oldenberg. It is that the performance is a new birth, that the performer is reduced to the condition of an embryo, and the use of milk, the stammering speech, the clenched fist, are thus explained. There can be really no doubt that the ceremony was meant by the Brahmans to convey and to have this effect, and the result of the consecration in the case of one who was not a Brahman, was to convert him into a Brahman, not of course permanently, but for the time being. The Rigveda [1] is one place seems perfectly clearly to allude to the rite as making the performers born, that is newly born again,[2] and while we may, if we like, say that the older idea was merely that of the production of religious ecstasy, still we have no right to deny that the rite was as early as the period of the Rigveda carefully remodelled so as to suit the idea intended to be seen in it by the Brahmans. An explanation of the stammering speech is offered by Oldenberg as indicating the moment when the ecstasy seizes on the offerer, but, though this may be paralleled with the broken utterances of the priestess of Delphi and elsewhere, the other interpretation deserves preference.[3]

A very different theory of the whole rite is suggested by Hillebrandt,[4] who relies on the derivation of the word from *dah*, ' burn ', in place of that from *daç*, ' serve a god ', or perhaps *dakṣ*—preferred by Oldenberg. He therefore thinks that the Dīkṣā was a voluntary death by fire, the desire to burn oneself to attain the heaven of Viṣṇu, and adverts to the suicide by fire of Kalanos of Takṣaçilā, which is recorded by the Greek writers. He admits, of course, that this is not the purpose of the rite as known to us, in which the offerer had no intention at all of departing from life, but undertook the offering in the hope *inter alia* of prolonging his days, and multiplying his possessions in this world, but he points out that Brāhmaṇa texts [5] lay down that the victim for Agni and Soma, which is offered after the Dīkṣā, is not to be eaten, and that it is a buying off of one's self, which he interprets to mean that the ceremony of offering this victim was ingeniously intended to redeem the man from death. The stammering speech of the consecrated man he explains in another way, from the offering of enemies to the gods, the stammering being the view taken of their strange and unintelligible speech. The evidence for this view is, however, clearly of the weakest kind : there is no trace of the practice of

[1] RV. vii. 33. 13 ; cf. AB. i. 3. 22, &c. Cf. also RV. i. 164. 36 ff. ; Hauer (*op. cit.*, pp. 68 ff.) interprets the frog hymn (vii. 103) as alluding to the Dīkṣā, and finds in x. 106. 5 ff. specimens of the stammering speech of the consecrated.

[2] From another view-point consecration is a death, JUB. iii. 9. 4 ; 10. 6.

[3] Keith, *Taittirīya Saṁhitā*, i. pp. cxiii–cxv.

[4] *Ved. Myth.* i. 482 ; iii. 354 ff. ; (Kl. Ausg.), p. 138.

[5] MS. iii. 7, 8 ; AB. ii. 3. 11 ; KB. x. 3 ; TS. vi. 1. 11. 6.

voluntary religious suicide in the age of the Vedas: the pessimism which leads to this suicide is not, in historic times, known in the Veda, and the idea that as later [1] captured enemies were sacrificed to the gods is without any evidence for the Vedic age. The sanctity of the victim to the two gods is much more probably to be explained by the excess of divinity embodied in it, in view of the greatness of the two gods to whom it is dedicated, both of whom must be deemed to appropriate it for their own, and it must be remembered that the explanation of the offering being a redemption is merely a priestly speculation, not finally held valid by the Taittirīya Saṁhitā.

§ 2. *The Avabhṛtha*

As the Dīkṣā is the beginning of the Soma sacrifice, so the end of it and also of many other offerings is the Avabhṛtha, or 'concluding bath'.[2] The word is found already in the Rigveda,[3] and undoubtedly in the original sense, and the practice must therefore be assumed to have existed from the earliest period of the Vedic religion. The meaning of it is clear: it is the carrying down to the waters of the various things which are to be disposed of after the offering is over. The ceremony at the end of the Soma sacrifice is simple: the skins of antelope hide and the girdles, which the sacrificer and his wife have been wearing throughout the rite, are taken off, and cast into the water along with the utensils which have come into contact with the Soma and with the pressed shoots of the Soma plant. Then the two go into the water and rub the backs of each other: then they come out from the water, and thereupon put on fresh garments. The performance is made into a sacrifice by the fact that offerings are made and verses addressed to Varuṇa, claiming him as the possessor of many healing powers, imploring him to drive away hate, and to pardon sin. The bath itself is addressed as the cause of the removal of sin. But these forms are obviously mere cloaks for the fact that the washing is the chief thing, and that it concerns itself with the removal of the mysterious potency, which has clung since the Dīkṣā to the sacrificer and his wife, rendering them unfit for normal human life. That this was realized by the priest is clearly proved by the language used of the rite: [4] the waters are distinctly said to remove the consecration and the Tapas, and it is stated that the sacrificer takes the consecration with him into the bath. The meaning is illustrated by the parallel procedure in the case of the undertaking of a vow of study by a Brahman. He then assumes a girdle, an antelope skin, and a staff, and at the end of the vow all these things are solemnly laid aside, and he takes a bath.[5]

[1] So King Jarāsandha in the epic; Eggeling, SBE. xliv. p. xxxvi, n. 1. For German parallels, see Dio Cassius, liv. 20; Tacitus, *Ann.* xiii. 57; Helm, *Altgerm. Rel.* i. 293.

[2] Oldenberg, *Rel. des Veda*², pp. 407–10; ApÇS. viii. 7. 12 ff.; xiii. 19 ff.; KÇS. vi. 10. 1; x. 8. 16 ff.; Hubert and Mauss (*Année sociol.* ii. 86 ff.) give Hebrew and Greek parallels and compare the concluding service of the Mass.

[3] viii. 93. 23.

[4] MS. iii. 6. 2; ApÇS. xiii. 21. 3.

[5] HGS. i. 7. 8; 9. 8–10.

The nature of the bath is further elucidated by the fact that through the performance of ablutions in it the waters become charged with magic potency and power: thus at the end of the bath at the horse sacrifice, those who go in, though evil doers, are released from all their sins.[1] The bath too serves as the mode of driving out evil in a curious rite, which is recorded of the same sacrifice:[2] a man is driven into the water up to his mouth, and on his head offerings are made to Jumbaka, to death, and to the slaying of an embryo: the man is of an ugly appearance, and is said in the Çatapatha Brāhmaṇa to be the symbol of Varuṇa. It is clear from the notice of a Sūtra that the real meaning of the ceremony, which ends with the man being driven away, is that he is a scapegoat, who bears with him the sins of the community, but who is also purified from them in some measure by the driving into the water. The offering on his head may well be derived from the mere mode of transferring[3] the sin by touching him on such a part as the head, or merely be based on the fact that an offering to Varuṇa was an essential part of the rite for the priest, and that the obvious place to make it was in the man who had the sins of the people upon him. That a human sacrifice is meant, as was imagined by Weber,[4] who thought that the potency of the bath to remit sin was due to this, is obviously wrong: there is no trace in any of the texts of the death of the man, who is on the contrary clearly driven away[5] as an essential part of the rite.

§ 3. *Taboos*

While the bath has the power of removing what is attached to a man's person, and thus is often used before undertaking a rite, as before the Dīkṣā itself by the sacrificer, by bridegroom and bride before marriage, and by a woman after the spell to produce offspring has been performed for her,[6] it is also necessary to avoid its use to prevent the removal of the holy power, which has been attained by some means or other. The theory would therefore demand that, after the initiation of the Brahman student, he should not take a bath until the final bath, so as to preserve his undoubted condition of holiness to the end, as the sacrificer can do in the case of the sacrifice, but obvious practical considerations rendered it impossible to carry that out in the times recorded for us. Though the more recent ascetics in India often never wash at all, and the seclusion of girls from ordinary life before and during puberty is practised for long periods in some lands, the use of the bath was not normally in the slightest degree forbidden to the Vedic student.[7] But we hear

[1] Above, Part III, Chap. 18, § 2; KÇS. xx. 8. 17, 18.

[2] ÇB. xiii. 3. 6. 5; TB. iii. 9. 15.

[3] So in the ancient Hebrew rite of consecrating a thing the touching by the people was the essential element; Wellhausen, *Archiv f. Religionswissenschaft*, vii. 33–39.

[4] See Eggeling, SBE. xliv. p. xl.

[5] ÇÇS. xvi. 18. 20; the expulsion was not in all likelihood permanent, though Eggeling thinks he may have been expected to live an anchorite's life. But he had been bought to perform the rite for 1,000 cows: so, if he went away, he would probably not trouble about asceticism.

[6] KÇS. vii. 2. 15, &c.

[7] BDS. i. 2. 3. 39; GDS. ii. 8, &c.

of cases where the theory was worked out: in the case [1] of the period of a year connected with the ceremony of cutting the beard of the youth, which is introduced by a ceremony comparable to the initiation to studentship and during which the carrying of a girdle, the living on alms, and so on are prescribed as for a student, washing, combing the hair, cleaning the teeth, and washing the feet are forbidden. In the case of the four-month ceremonies,[2] it is a rule of perfection, at least, that the performer should not bathe until the final bath. The sense is clear, and throws light on the famous reference in the Aitareya Brāhmaṇa [3] to the dirty condition of the ascetic, which is also echoed in the hymn of the Rigveda [4] regarding the inspired Muni.

The case of the hair is analogous to, and closely connected with, that of the washing or refraining from washing the body. The Vedic domestic ritual lays stress on the cutting of the child's hair once in early childhood, and then later for the youth when he has grown up: the hair is carefully cut, and after that was arranged in the characteristic manner in which the family wore its hair, this being a marked sign of differentiation among the Vedic families and one already recorded to us in the Rigveda; the beard of the youth was also shorn.[5] The aim of the performance is expressly stated in the formulae accompanying it to be the production of long life, and the giving of health and purity, and obviously it served also to mark the family connexion of the child or youth. That in the ceremony there was any idea of an offering whether to gods, or to demons, or to the Fathers [6] is not indicated by anything in the ritual texts nor in the formulae used, and, if any such idea was ever present, it was not felt in Vedic times. There is indeed no obvious reason for distinguishing the action in these cases from the action in the cases of sacrifices. The sacrificer before the new- and full-moon offerings has his hair cut, except the family knot, and his beard shaven, and even his nails pared: so the sacrificer in the case of the Dīkṣā, and at the four-monthly offerings, and the motive expressed in these cases is the removal of the dead skin to make the body pure.[7] The same principle of shaving was observed by the living after the death of a member of the family,[8] at the same time as the putting on of new garments, the renewal of the domestic fire, and the washing of their bodies. The same performances were applied as in all lands to the dead: [9] perhaps we can say nothing more than that the feeling of impurity from contact with the dead was very strong, and required to be removed as vehemently as possible.

On the other hand, as in the case of abstaining from washing, so we have

[1] GGS. iii. 1. 10 ff.

[2] KÇS. v. 2. 21.

[3] AB. vii. 13.

[4] x. 136.

[5] AGS. i. 17. 12, 16; 18. 5; GDS. xx. 5. For Greek parallels see Cook, *Zeus*, i. 23–5, 93. For peculiarities of arrangement of hair as characteristic of tribes and families cf. Ridgeway, *Anthropological Essays presented to E. B. Tylor*, p. 305; Hillebrandt, *Ritualliteratur*, pp. 7, 8. For the soul in the hair, see Hopkins, *Origin of Religion*, pp. 116 ff.

[6] Oldenberg, *Rel. des Veda*[1], p. 426.

[7] ÇB. iii. 1. 2. 1; MS. iii. 6. 2.

[8] AGS. iv. 6. 4.

[9] AGS. iv. 1. 16; AV. xix. 32. 2.

instances in which the hair must not be cut at all. The newly wedded bride on the fourth day, before the consummation of the marriage is permitted, must be rubbed with an ointment from the remains of oblations up to the nails and the hair.[1] The ascetic of the Rigveda wears long hair; the description of the attributes of asceticism in the Aitareya Brāhmaṇa include dirt, long hair, a girdle, and an antelope skin. In the period of a year before the shaving of the beard referred to above the hair may not be cut. In the royal consecration the sacrifice is followed by period of a year in which the consecrated may rub but not wash himself, shorten, but not cut off the hair.[2] The reason for the usage is given with perfect distinctness by the Brāhmaṇa: the anointing has put the strength of the waters of anointing into his hair, and he would destroy the virtue thus engendered, if he cut off the hair. The same principle is applied to the animals of the sacrifice: the steed for the horse sacrifice must not, for the year in which it wanders free before its death, be allowed to bathe in water, and the manes of the horses in the realm should not be cut for a year after the royal consecration.[3] Naturally the end of the period of allowing the hair to grow is marked by a formal act of shaving: this is the case with the man consecrated by the Dīkṣā, with the king at the end of the year of consecration; at the Samāvartana ceremony, which ends the period of studentship, the hair, the beard, the hair on the body, and the nails are all carefully cut.[4]

In a considerable number of cases we find that at certain times the intending sacrificer must abstain from sexual intercourse, must fast, or feed on certain specified foods alone, must sleep on the ground, and so on. The man who intends to establish the sacred fire must for the night before the performance lie awake in silence:[5] thus he is said to secure purity and Tapas for his approach to the gods next day. For the day before the new- and full-moon sacrifices the sacrificer must be careful not to eat meat or have sexual intercourse; at evening he may eat wild plants and fruits, but nothing of what he is to offer next day; he must sleep on the ground with his wife for the night, and some even demand that the pair shall spend it in telling stories.[6]

When the student is performing his period of studentship,[7] he is forbidden intercourse, and a high bed: when he has been admitted to study[8] by the solemn offering, he must stand silent for the rest of the day, and eat no salted food for the day. When he comes to a specially sacred part of his work of

1 GGS. ii. 5. 6.
2 LÇS. ix. 2. 18, 21; ÇB. v. 5. 3. 1; KÇS. xv. 8. 28.
3 KÇS. xx. 2. 12, 13; LÇS. ix. 2. 26. In Persia we have an obscure record (Herodotos, ix. 110) of an annual hair washing (?) by the King, with which Strabo's (xv. 69) remark as to a similar Indian practice has been compared, and far-reaching conclusions as to Persian influence on Candragupta's court drawn but with little cogency; cf. Keith, JRAS. 1916, pp. 138–43.
4 ApÇS. xiii. 23. 16; ÇGS. iii. 1. 2.
5 ApÇS. v. 8. 1 ff.
6 Hillebrandt, *Neu- und Vollmondsopfer*, pp. 3, 6, 14.
7 GGS. iii. i. 17 ff.
8 GGS. ii. 10. 45 ff.

learning, then he must shut his eyes, and in silence for a day and a night or three days eat nothing, the shutting of the eyes being no doubt in order not to be blinded by the excessive majesty of the work, which he has studied. Before he imparts such important knowledge to his pupil, the teacher himself for a day and a night must practise chastity, and eat no flesh.[1] In the offering of the Çabalīhoma it is provided that the offerer must lie on the ground for twelve nights, speak as little as possible, observe chastity, and take only sweet milk.[2] The fasts are deemed by the Brāhmaṇas to be the essence of Tapas,[3] or again the fasting before an offering is deemed courtesy to the gods, just as one does not eat before one's guests.[4] The former motive is very probably a real one : the use of hunger to produce states of ecstasy is well attested, but other reasons are possible : the motive of refraining from eating flesh is doubtless connected with the spirit, which is in the dead animal, and which may be dangerous, especially to a man undertaking a solemn rite. The refraining from salt, which is even extended by some authorities to cover the offering of any salted food to the gods, is a strange taboo which is very well known in many parts of the earth, and which in some way seems to stand in connexion with fertility : Oldenberg [5] suggests that if it is not an inheritance from a time which knew no salt, as is very possible, the unfruitfulness of salt ground and of sea water suggested its evil character, but of that we have no adequate proof, and in point of fact salt passes in some measure as a sign of prosperity,[6] through its use for animals to lick. Other motives may be the danger of evil spirits entering the man who eats, seeing that at a festival such spirits will be present in large numbers ; the desire to secure that there will be enough food for the gods—which is paralleled by the Vedic politeness theory ; or the desire not to interfere with the full benefit to be obtained by the holy food, which is not expressed in any Vedic passage, but with which may be compared fasts ordered after consuming forbidden food until all trace of it has disappeared.[7] In the case of sexual intercourse probably the same idea is at work as in the case of the loss of seed generally : the horse for the horse sacrifice is kept away from mares as well as from the water, and the motive appears clearly enough in the ritual and the formulae : [8] it is undesirable in this case as in the case of the Brahman student and the consecrated man to lose any strength whatever. Even laughter [9] is regarded as loss of strength : the consecrated man must put his hand before his mouth to prevent the loss of his laughter, which is compared with light on the strength of the Rigveda,[10] by which laughter and lightning are already closely connected.

In addition to these taboos there are others of more curious character.

[1] GGS. iii. 2. 37 ; ÇGS. ii. 11. 6.
[2] Weber, *Ind. Stud.* v. 440 ff.
[3] ÇB. ix. 5. 1. 6.
[4] ÇB. i. 1. 1. 8 ; ii. 1. 4. 1, 2.
[5] *Rel. des Veda*[2], p. 414, n. 1.
[6] ÇB. v. 2. 1. 16.
[7] ApDS. i. 9. 27. 3 ; GDS. xxiii. 23.
[8] ÇB. xiii. 3. 8. 1 ; TB. iii. 9. 17. 4 ; TA. i. 30 ; ii. 18 ; KÇS. xxv. 11. 21 ; AGS. iii. 6. 8 ; Vait. xii. 9.
[9] TA. v. 1. 4 ; contrast TS. vi. 1. 3. 8.
[10] Oldenberg, *op. cit.*, p. 429. For the lucky sneeze (*āṣkāra*), see PB. viii. 1. 1 ; 2. 2.

When the ground is ploughed for a fire altar, there are sowed upon it seeds of every kind except one, and of that the sacrificer never tastes again in his life.[1] If a man use a goat or Kuça grass as a fetish of the fire, then he must not eat either the goat or sit on Kuça grass ; [2] if a man takes his fire from the house of a wealthy man, he may not again eat in his house ; [3] at the Vājapeya the sacrificer is anointed, or deluged, with various libations, in preparing which all kinds of food are mixed with water, one only being excepted of which he never eats again.[4] The builder of the fire altar in bird form must not again eat a bird in his life,[5] and the same rule is laid down for the learner of the Jyeṣṭha Sāman.[6] To see here traces of totemism is of course possible, but like all possibilities, which have no evidence to raise them into probabilities, not a very helpful mode of procedure. The case of the altar is clearly due to its bird form : the bird is invested with the holiness of Agni, and must not be eaten by a man who is closely connected with Agni, as is the builder of the fire altar. The borrowing of the same taboo by the learner of the Jyeṣṭha Sāman must not mislead us : once a taboo starts, others easily follow. The idea that the taboos represent an agreement with spirits to abstain from one food, in return for being allowed to use others, is one which has no support of any kind in the Vedic religion.[7]

The silence taboo may be variously explained : possibly it may denote the desire to avoid the attacks of evil spirits who may enter the open mouth : retirement into solitude which is further recommended may denote the same feeling, and the sleeping on the ground is interpreted by Oldenberg as a device for avoiding the attacks of such spirits, who will be misled by the change of couch. So also, he thinks, one of the causes of the abstinence from intercourse is the avoidance of attack by the demons whom such conduct deceives. It is possible, however, that in the case of sleeping on the ground another motive was at work, the desire to obtain the power which belongs to the earth spirit : we are reminded of the priests of Zeus at Dodona who slept on the ground.[8]

The fear of the spirits is of course an undoubted motive in the case of the constant taboo of anything connected with death. The teacher who desires to instruct his pupil in the secret texts which cannot be recited in the village must not see blood, a cemetery, nor certain beasts, which are said to be shaped like a corpse.[9] The pupil himself is to avoid the sight of a place of burning bodies or the bearers of such bodies ; he should not look into a well, nor climb a tree : [10] the first of these rules reminds us that the spirits dwell in the depths of the earth, that it is dangerous to see one's own reflection in the water, and the second may refer to the part played by the tree as giving the coffin or covering for the body or ashes of the dead. Again the Snātaka may

[1] ÇB. vii. 2. 4. 14 ; cf. GGS. iii. 2. 58.
[2] KÇS. xxv. 4. 4 ff.
[3] ApÇS. v. 14. 2.
[4] ÇB. v. 2. 2. 4 ; Weber, *Vājapeya*, p. 36.
[5] ÇB. x. 1. 4. 13.
[6] GGS. iii. 2. 57.
[7] Oldenberg, *Rel. des Veda*[1], p. 416.
[8] Kretschmer, *Gesch. d. griech. Spr.*, p. 87.
[9] ÇGS. ii. 12. 10 ; vi. 1. 4, 5.
[10] ÇGS. iv. 12. 27 ff.

not sit directly on the bare earth, which may be thus explained or by the fear of his losing his holiness by contact with earth.[1] He may not go by evening to another village or by any but the main road, probably lest he meet evil spirits.[2] There are also innumerable other taboos, connected not only with death but with lying-in women, and women in their courses, who are regarded as specially full of danger by many peoples, an idea which is often to be traced to the blood taboo.[3] Of special frequence is the occurrence of taboo against the use of vessels of clay : the consecrated man must not use such a vessel for his milk food, the butter used at the Tānūnaptra service must not be covered by such a vessel, the learner of the Jyeṣṭha Sāman must not eat or drink from such an utensil, the milk for the new-moon offering must not be covered in this way, and so on.[4] The vessel used when certain secret texts are recited must be of metal.[5] In these cases the Brāhmaṇas show clearly that the sense of the connexion of the earth with the dead was the cause of the objection.

On the other hand there are instances in which the aim of man is precisely the opposite from that seen in the working of taboos : he desired to come into the closest possible relations with the object which he desires to provide. Thus in the case of the Çakvarī verses which are already alluded to in the Rigveda the rules for the conduct of the pupil who desires to study the verses are of a peculiar nature. He is required to follow certain rules for a period of from twelve years to a year—in fixing lengths of courses the Brahmans are always accommodating—which include the duty of touching water thrice daily, wearing black garments, eating black food, exposing himself uncovered to the rain : he must not cross flowing water nor save in case of the greatest need go on a ship, because the strength of the Çakvarī rests in the waters. At the end, when he has learned to sing the verses, he must plunge his hands in water in which vegetables are placed.[6] The whole performance has only one possible meaning : it is a Brahmanized version of a rain spell. Moreover, the ordinary student is encouraged to expose himself to the rain : [7] the holy youth is not to shrink from the holy element. The same sort of observance in the case of the sun is laid down for students of the Sāmaveda : [8] they are not to cover themselves from the sun with more than a single garment, and not to allow anything save trees to get between them and the sun. The performer of the Pravargya [9] ceremony is forbidden to cover himself in the sun, or to defile it by performing before it any of the acts of nature : [10] at

[1] ÇGS. iv. 12. 21.

[2] GGS. iii. 5. 32.

[3] Reinach, *Cultes, Mythes et Religions*, i. 162 ff. ; Frazer, *Taboo*, pp. 145 ff. This work contains examples of all the kinds of Vedic taboos.

[4] KÇS. vii. 4. 33 ; viii. 2. 1 ; GGS. iii. 2. 60, 61, &c.

[5] GGS. iii. 2. 35 ; PGS. i. 3. 5.

[6] PB. xii. 13. 14 ; TS. ii. 2. 8. 5 ; GGS. iii. 2.

[7] PGS. ii. 7. 11 ; GGS. iii. 5. 11. Cf. Usener, *Archiv f. Religionswissenschaft*, vii. 285.

[8] GGS. iii. 1. 31 ff.

[9] ÇB. xiv. 1. 1. 33.

[10] Cf. the rule for the Brahman student, ÇB. xiv. 1. 2. 33 ; AV. xiii. 1. 56 (with Lanman's note) ; Hes. *op.* 725 ; Brunnhofer, *Arische Urzeit*, pp. 324, 325.

night he must make a light, and eat by it, thus creating for himself a presentment of the sun. The performer of the second form of consecration at the Soma offering takes nothing save hot milk in the effort to make complete the state of heat which the performer of the first consecration aimed at.[1]

It is of interest to mention in conclusion the conjecture put forward by Weber [2] that the word taboo as *tābuva* was actually found in the Atharvaveda;[3] it is clear that such a suggestion could not possibly be made good, and the idea has been rejected with almost entire unanimity by scholars.[4]

§ 4. *The Forms of Prayer*

The Rigveda shows quite clearly that the conception of prayer for aid to a god without the performance of any sacrifice was quite natural and intelligible. The heroes of its narratives of the deeds of the Açvins in special seem to have been specially eager in their prayers for the aid they desired. But the priests were, from the earliest period of the later Saṁhitās and probably earlier, ready to find the exact formulae with which the deity should be addressed in every stage of trouble, and, what was still more important, to lay down the nature of the necessary offering. Hence we find even in the Taittirīya Saṁhitā [5] an elaborate account of the different offerings to be made to the gods for a vast variety of cases of special desires: the verses used by the priests for the Anuvākyās and Yājyās are taken from the Rigveda, many however in a very far from natural way, showing that the only interest of the composers of these lists of offerings was to find some verse, which by connexion of sound or sense might be thought appropriate. On the other hand the ritual still here and there allows the offering of prayers which were not immediately dictated by the necessity of accompanying libations: thus in the Agniṣṭoma the morning litany, the Prātaranuvāka with its address to Agni, to the Dawn, and to the Açvins is independent of any actual libations. In the domestic [6] ritual the rule is laid down that the student is to perform the devotion to the twilight, both night and morning in the wood: after the twilight is over, he has to repeat the three sacred words Bhūḥ, Bhuvaḥ, and Svar, and the Sāvitrī verse: the sacred words denote, the first earth, the third heaven, but the intermediate expression has no obvious relation to the intermediate space, save in so far as it may be a compound, as suggested by Oldenberg,[7] of the two elements of the first and third words. In another form of ritual the prayer is connected not with a libation, but with a ceremonial reverence to the fire, the

[1] Weber, *Ind. Stud.* x. 363.

[2] SBA. 1896, pp. 681 ff., 873 ff. (with remarks of Jacobi, E. Kuhn, and Bendall); cf. *Ind. Stud.* xviii. 215; Bloomfield, *Atharvaveda*, p. 61.

[3] v. 13. 10. For other strange terms in this hymn, cf. Tilak, *Bhandarkar Comm. Vol.*, pp. 27 ff. See also App. G.

[4] Hillebrandt, *Rituallitteratur*, p. 171. *Contra*, Hauer, *Die Anfänge der Yogapraxis im alten Indien*, p. 63.

[5] ii. 1. 1 ff. There is a considerable similarity in many of the magic rites of the Kauçika Sūtra as is pointed out by Caland (*Altindisches Zauberritual*, p. viii).

[6] ÇGS. ii. 9.

[7] *Rel. des Veda*², p. 431, n. 4.

Upasthāna, where by the mention of his devotion to the fire the votary intends, in the naïve conception of the Brāhmaṇas, to call the attention of the god to the fact of his existence and doubtless also of his needs.[1]

In the main the rule is observed that the prayers, which celebrate the actions of the gods and invoke their aid, are in verse, while the prose is restricted to the formulae, which accompany each act of the sacrifice and in special each offering as it is made. But there are here and there prose prayers spoken by the Adhvaryu, as at the new- and full-moon offering and at the horse sacrifice. But, whatever the type of the prayer, the result is the same: the priest prays that the sacrificer—who may of course be himself—shall have long life, riches, especially in cattle and horses, in chariots and gold, sons in abundance, freedom from disease, success over his enemy, and prosperity in general; he also prays that his enemies may be brought to ruin.[2] It is undeniable that the prayers are nearly always for material objects, and that the occasional expressions of desire for spiritual goods are in the extreme exceptional: here and there we find admissions of sin and desire to be at friendship with the gods, especially Varuṇa, but that there is much ethical content in the hymns generally it would be absurd to assert. The real object of the hymn is to please the god by the references to his past deeds and his power, and thus induce him to manifest again the strength of his right arm for the benefit of his servants. The hymns often remind the god of their ancestral connexion, and in the pride of their production and of the value which the gods must attach to them are extremely naïve. It is wholly impossible to doubt that, if the Adhvaryu really thought that the acts of the sacrifice and the actual offerings were what mattered, his view was not in the least shared by the Hotṛ, who was of opinion that his perfectly constructed hymns would give the god the greatest possible amount of pleasure. It is a question of interest, but one which cannot be answered, how it came about that this love of poetry died out, after it must have flourished for some centuries. The Brāhmaṇa period is clearly a time when the priests are content in the main to use the traditional poetry, and, if they composed, to base their compositions very closely on the traditional models. The pride of the Vedic poets in their own powers is perfectly evidenced, when they claim that their hymns strengthen Indra for the slaying of Vṛtra or that through the prayers the steeds are yoked to the chariot of the god. Here as everywhere the tendency of the sacrifice to pass into magic is illustrated: the prayer which is really essentially free from magic is at last turned by the pride of its composers into nothing but a spell.

[1] ÇB. ii. 3. 4. 7.

[2] The theory that the spell precedes prayer, which is widely held (Meyer, *Gesch. d. Alt.*[3] I. ii. pp. 870, 871; Usener, *Archiv f. Religionswissenschaft*, vii. 15 ff.; Feist, *Kultur der Indogermanen*, pp. 349 ff.; cf. Farnell, *Evolution of Religion*, pp. 163 ff.), stands or falls with the view that magic precedes religion. On the view here taken that they are independent, prayer is not originally a spell; cf. Bloomfield, *Religion of the Veda*, pp. 205 ff.; Jevons, *Idea of God*, pp. 108 ff.; Heiler, *Das Gebet* (1921).

The Brāhmaṇas and the ritual [1] give advice to the priest how to make use of the service for ends not openly expressed. If the ritual contain in a liturgy the word 'possessing heroic sons', he has but to think of the wife of the sacrificer, and he will bring it about that she has a strong son: the word 'embryo' if thought on will bring her fertility. But, on the other hand, the power can be used for evil as effectively: if the priest but think of the enemy whom he hates, when he takes up the pressing stone in his hand, he can overthrow the enemy: the pressing stone thus becomes a weapon to slay him.[2] Of these puerilities the Brāhmaṇas are never tired,[3] and this attitude of mind must be accepted as a fundamental fact of their mental outlook.

[1] ÇB. iii. 9. 4. 17; ÇÇS. iv. 8. 4. 3; v. 9. 19; 14. 12, &c. The highest pitch of absurdity is perhaps reached in the narrative how by the error in placing an accent a foe of Indra ruined himself and not Indra; Keith, *Taittirīya Saṁhitā*, i. p. 185; TS. ii. 5. 2. 1; ÇB. i. 6. 3. 10.

[2] ÇB. iii. 9. 4. 17; cf. PB. ii. 13. 2; vi. 5. 18; 6. 2; MS. i. 4. 12; 6. 3; ii. 5. 8; iii. 1. 9, &c.; AB. iii. 3. 2 ff.; 6. 1 ff.

[3] TS. vi. 4. 4. 3 (device to secure women's love); MS. iv. 5. 7; ÇB. i. 4. 3. 11 ff.